The Palgrave Handbook of Global Rehabilitation in Criminal Justice

"A remarkably comprehensive overview – including strengths and weaknesses – of the concept of penal rehabilitation and the way it remains an aspiration for much of the corrections field."
—John Pratt, *Emeritus Professor of Criminology, Victoria University of Wellington, New Zealand*

"From Fiji to Finland, Uruguay to the USA, this fascinating collection of authors and essays provides the most comprehensive and up-to-date portrait of the state of rehabilitation around the world today. Although not uncritical of these efforts, these chapters give hope that efforts to promote reparation and reintegration will continue to grow and adapt in the face of a global penal culture characterised by punitiveness and risk aversion."
—Shadd Maruna, *Professor of Criminology, Queen's University Belfast, UK and President of the American Society of Criminology*

"This Handbook represents a comprehensive collection of rehabilitation measures adopted by various countries in supporting people in contact with the law. The various chapters provide country specific description of the criminal justice system with focus on rehabilitation mechanisms, progression, and challenges. This unique collection will be of great value to those in academia and for practitioners who are exploring ways to promote desistance."
—Razwana Begum, *Associate Professor, School of Humanities and Behaviour Sciences, Singapore University of Social Sciences*

"This is an incredibly important edited work that unpacks what is referred to as 'rehabilitation', mostly in a manner that is common-sensical. Drawing on country experiences from the global south and the global north, and across epochs in time, what is demonstrated is the complexity of reintegrating, humanising, and prevention. The editors state in the introduction that the book is not intended to be comparative. Yet with the vary many country cases covered in the book, one cannot but make very incisive comparisons, not necessarily between countries, but rather between inter-connected policy, public opinion, and thought trends. While the global north might appear to be leaders is humanising penal systems, this book brings to the fore the importance of indigenous and first people systems of governing 'deviance' and 'crime'. This book is a must read to all interested in rehabilitation, penal policy, restorative justice, and knowledge transfer in criminal justice."
—Monique Marks, *Head of Urban Futures Centre at the Durban University of Technology and Co-Director of Bellhaven Harm Reduction Centre, South Africa*

"Most criminal justice systems around the world include rehabilitation as one of their aims. This fascinating, wide-ranging and deeply scholarly collection describes how rehabilitation is understood and practised in more than thirty jurisdictions in seven continents, doing full justice to the particular social and political contexts of each. Criminologists and criminal justice practitioners will find this a unique and valuable resource, and a persuasive invitation to think more widely and imaginatively about what rehabilitation can achieve."

—Peter Raynor, *Professor of Criminology, Criminology, Sociology and Social Policy, School of Social Sciences, Swansea University, UK*

Maurice Vanstone · Philip Priestley
Editors

The Palgrave Handbook of Global Rehabilitation in Criminal Justice

palgrave
macmillan

Editors
Maurice Vanstone ⓘ
Criminology, School of Law
Swansea University
Swansea, UK

Philip Priestley
Wells, UK

ISBN 978-3-031-14374-8   ISBN 978-3-031-14375-5 (eBook)
https://doi.org/10.1007/978-3-031-14375-5

© The Editor(s) (if applicable) and The Author(s), under exclusive license to Springer Nature Switzerland AG 2022

This work is subject to copyright. All rights are solely and exclusively licensed by the Publisher, whether the whole or part of the material is concerned, specifically the rights of translation, reprinting, reuse of illustrations, recitation, broadcasting, reproduction on microfilms or in any other physical way, and transmission or information storage and retrieval, electronic adaptation, computer software, or by similar or dissimilar methodology now known or hereafter developed.

The use of general descriptive names, registered names, trademarks, service marks, etc. in this publication does not imply, even in the absence of a specific statement, that such names are exempt from the relevant protective laws and regulations and therefore free for general use.

The publisher, the authors, and the editors are safe to assume that the advice and information in this book are believed to be true and accurate at the date of publication. Neither the publisher nor the authors or the editors give a warranty, expressed or implied, with respect to the material contained herein or for any errors or omissions that may have been made. The publisher remains neutral with regard to jurisdictional claims in published maps and institutional affiliations.

Cover illustration: © Fanatic Studio/Gary Waters/Alamy Stock Photo

This Palgrave Macmillan imprint is published by the registered company Springer Nature Switzerland AG
The registered company address is: Gewerbestrasse 11, 6330 Cham, Switzerland

Dedicated to the memory of
Saskia Jones and Jack Merritt
Champions of rehabilitation

Acknowledgements

Firstly, we would like to thank all our contributors who with their commitment and hard work have made this volume possible. Some were able to help in the process of identifying appropriate people in their part of the world who might join us in the project. Of course, some people that we contacted were unable to contribute but invariably suggested alternatives and we thank them for that. In addition, particular thanks are due to Dr. Bankole Cole, Reader in Criminology and Human Rights at the Helena Kennedy Centre for International Justice, Sheffield Hallam University for his help in identifying contributors from Africa, Carolina Aurora Villagra Pincheira, University of Chile for her help with those from South America, and Professor Bill Hebenton, Research Associate of Manchester University's Centre for Chinese Studies not only for his participation but also for his help with those from Asia. In this regard, we are also grateful to Dr. Leon Moosavi, Director of the University of Liverpool in Singapore. Finally, our thanks are due to Josie Taylor, Commissioning Editor at Palgrave MacMillan for her encouragement in the early stages of our planning of the book, and Sarah Hills, Saranya Siva and Liviyaasree for their guidance during its production.

Contents

Prospect 1
Maurice Vanstone and Philip Priestley

**Law, Economic Crisis, and Diversity: An Overview
of Rehabilitation in Argentina** 17
María Jimena Monsalve

**Rehabilitation and Beyond in Settler Colonial Australia:
Current and Future Directions in Policy and Practice** 33
Sophie Russell, James Beaufils, and Chris Cunneen

**Exploring Expectations and Realities of Rehabilitation
in the Canadian Context** 53
Katharina Maier and Rosemary Ricciardelli

**History and Transformations of the Model of Rehabilitation
in the Criminal Justice System in Chile** 71
Carolina Aurora Villagra Pincheira

Rehabilitation in a Risk Society: 'The Case of China' 89
Enshen Li

Penitentiary System in Colombia 107
José Ignacio Ruiz-Pérez

Rehabilitation Practices in the Adult Criminal Justice System
in England and Wales 127
John Deering and Martina Y. Feilzer

Blending Culture, Religion, and the *Yellow Ribbon Program*:
Rehabilitation in Fiji 145
John Whitehead and Lennon Chang

Rehabilitative Aims and Values in Finnish (and Nordic)
Criminal Justice 161
Tapio Lappi-Seppälä

France: Executive Managerialism, Frantic Law Reform,
but Desistance Culture 181
Martine Herzog-Evans

Rehabilitation in Ghana: Assessing Prison Conditions
and Effectiveness of Interventions for Incarcerated Adults 201
Kofi E. Boakye, Thomas D. Akoensi, and Frank D. Baffour

Approaches to Rehabilitation in Hong Kong 219
Wing Hong Chui

From Need-Based to Control-Based Rehabilitation: The
Hungarian Case 237
Klára Kerezsi and Judit Szabó

A Critical Commentary on Rehabilitation of Offenders
in India 257
Debarati Halder

Beyond the Treatment Paradigm: Expanding the Rehabilitative
Imagination in Ireland 271
Deirdre Healy

Serving a Sentence in Italy: Old and New Challenges 289
Luisa Ravagnani and Carlo Alberto Romano

Community-Based Rehabilitation in Japan: Some Unique
Characteristics of the Japanese System and Recent
Developments 307
Kei Someda

Criminal Rehabilitation in Kenya: Opportunities and Pitfalls 325
Karatu Kiemo

Framing and Reframing the Rehabilitation in Criminal Justice in Latvia   339
Anvars Zavackis and Janis Nicmanis

Criminal Justice Rehabilitation in Macao, China   359
Donna Soi Wan Leong and Jianhong Liu

The Legal Flaws and Material Implementation Gaps of Mexico's Rehabilitation Paradigm   377
Corina Giacomello

Rehabilitation Within the Criminal-Legal System in Missouri   395
Kelli E. Canada and Scott O'Kelley

Resocialisation and Reintegration in the Netherlands: Political Narrative Versus Reality   413
Sonja Meijer and Elanie Rodermond

Rehabilitation, Restoration and Reintegration in Aotearoa New Zealand   429
Alice Mills and Robert Webb

An Overview of Rehabilitation Mechanisms in Nigeria's Criminal Justice System   449
Emmanuel C. Onyeozili and Bonaventure Chigozie Uzoh

Penal Welfarism and Rehabilitation in Norway: Ambitions, Strengths and Challenges   467
John Todd-Kvam

Rehabilitation in Romania—The First 100 Years   485
Ioan Durnescu, Andrada Istrate, and Iuliana Carbunaru

Rehabilitation of Offenders in the Scottish Criminal Justice System   505
Liz Gilchrist and Amy Johnson

Offender Rehabilitation Approaches in South Africa: An Evidence-Based Analysis   525
Shanta Balgobind Singh and Patrick Bashizi Bashige Murhula

Rehabilitation in Spain: Between Legal Intentions and Institutional Limitations   541
Ester Blay

Criminal Justice Rehabilitation in Sweden: Towards
an Integrative Model — 559
Martin Lardén

Rehabilitation in Taiwan — 577
Susyan Jou, Shang-Kai Shen, and Bill Hebenton

Rehabilitation and the Adult Correctional Population in Texas — 597
Anita Kalunta-Crumpton

Key Practices in Thai Prisons: Rehabilitation — 619
Nathee Chitsawang and Pimporn Netrabukkana

Probation and the Prevention of Recidivism in Tunisia: Still
Uncertain Beginnings — 639
Philippe Pottier

The Unfinished Symphony: Progress and Setbacks Towards
a Rehabilitation Policy in Uruguay — 651
Ana Vigna and Ana Juanche

Reentry and Reintegration in Virginia, U.S. — 667
Danielle S. Rudes, Benjamin J. Mackey, and Madeline McPherson

Retrospect: Looking Back—Looking Forward — 687
Philip Priestley and Maurice Vanstone

Index — 701

Notes on Contributors

Akoensi Thomas D. is Senior Lecturer in Criminology and Criminal Justice at the School of Social Policy, Sociology and Social Research, University of Kent, UK. His research interests are in the fields of penology, legitimacy and criminal justice, comparative criminology, and organizational behaviour.

Baffour Frank D. is Lecturer in the Faculty of Arts, Design, and Architecture at the University of New South Wales, Australia. He holds a Ph.D. in criminal justice social work. He received prestigious awards such as the James Cook University Excellence Doctoral Research Thesis Medal and passed his Ph.D. thesis with cum laude (rated within the top 5% of Ph.D. candidates worldwide). His work has been published in high-impact peer-reviewed journals such as the *Journal of Interpersonal Violence* and *Victims and Offenders*.

Beaufils James is a Research Fellow and Ph.D. candidate at the Jumbunna Institute of Indigenous Education and Research and the Faculty of Law University of Technology Sydney. He has researched in the fields of child protection, youth justice, and education in Australia and the UK. His doctoral thesis explores the experiences of Aboriginal people in New South Wales Out-of-Home-Care system. James was previously a parole officer, educator, and social worker. Now working closely with Aboriginal children's organizations, his work engages with the meaning and implementation of child development and well-being with respect to child protection.

Blay Ester is currently a reader in Criminology at the University of Girona (Spain). She has a Ph.D. in Law and has conducted research on community sanctions and measures, sentencing and courts, often with a comparative perspective. She regularly presents her research in European criminological fora and publishes both in English and Spanish. She teaches at undergraduate and post-graduate level on penology and related subjects.

Boakye Kofi E. is Senior Lecturer in Criminology at Anglia Ruskin University, and affiliated fellow at Institute of Criminology, University of Cambridge where he completed his M.Phil. and Ph.D. He is also a Senior Fellow at the Centre for Suicide and Violence Research at University of Ghana. He was a Betty Behrens Fellow at Clare Hall, University of Cambridge, and a visiting professor at Cornell Law School. He is a former Gates Cambridge Scholar, and currently serves on the Equality, Diversity and Widening Participation Taskforce of the Gates Cambridge Trust. His work has appeared in *Child Abuse & Neglect, Law & Social Inquiry, Journal Interpersonal Violence, Policing and Society.*

Canada Kelli E., Ph.D., LCSW is Associate Professor at the University of Missouri—Columbia, School of Social Work. She worked more than 15 years in social work in direct services and administration. Dr. Canada's research focuses on interventions for people with mental illnesses who become involved in the criminal justice system. She examines interventions throughout the criminal justice system including pre-arrest, alternative sentencing, community supervision, and within institutions. She also examines the policies and practices impacting overall health and quality of life.

Carbunaru Iuliana is currently probation inspector in the National Probation Directorate within the Romanian Ministry of Justice ensuring the development and implementation of the international projects and promoting the probation system at the international level. Starting with 2017 she is Board member of the Confederation of European Probation (CEP). As an employee of the probation service for the past 21 years Ms. Cărbunaru has served as probation counsellor, probation inspector, and director of probation service. She holds a B.A. in Social Work, a M.A. in Community Justice Administration and she is currently doing her Ph.D. at Bucharest University on penal policy transfers in Europe.

Chang Lennon is Senior Lecturer in Criminology in the School of Social Sciences at Monash University. He was awarded his Ph.D. by the Australian National University in November 2010. He is co-coordinator of the Asia Pacific Forum for Restorative Justice. He is also a co-founder and vice-chairman of the Asia Pacific Association of Technology and Society. He authored 'Cybercrime in the Greater China Region: Regulatory Responses and Crime Prevention' (Edward Elgar, 2012). He is particularly interested in the regulation and governance of cyberspace in the Asia-Pacific region. His professional interest in Asia continues and he is currently researching internet vigilantism in the Indo-pacific region. He was also undertaking research into cybercrime and cyber-deviance in this region.

Chitsawang Nathee is currently the Advisor at Thailand Institute of Justice (TIJ). After graduating L.L.B. from Chulalongkorn University and M.S. in Criminology from Florida State University under the Royal Thai Government sponsorship, he began his long career with Thailand's Department of Corrections and also started a part-time job as a visiting lecturer and researcher in many universities. He has been recognized as an experienced expert in Thai criminology, penology, and correctional spheres, both professional and academic aspects. Dr. Nathee held various positions in criminal justice system agencies, including the Director General of Department of Corrections and the Director General of Department of Probation. Following his retirement, Dr. Nathee was awarded a Ph.D. in Public Administration from Ramkamhaeng University in 2012.

Chui Wing Hong, Ph.D. is Professor in the Department of Social and Behavioural Sciences at City University of Hong Kong. Prior to his academic career, he was a youth social worker who worked with street kids and juvenile offenders in Hong Kong. He has continued to seek to build a better world through his varied contributions at work—outreach social work, youth studies, criminology, criminal justice, and published works. Some of his publications include *Responding to Youth Crime in Hong Kong* (with Michael Adorjan, 2014, Routledge), *Understanding Criminal Justice in Hong Kong* (with T. Wing Lo, 2017, Routledge), and *The Hong Kong Legal System* (with Stefan Lo and Kevin Cheng, 2020, Cambridge University Press).

Cunneen Chris is Professor of Criminology at Jumbunna Institute for Indigenous Education and Research, University of Technology Sydney, and has a national and international reputation as a leading criminologist specializing in Indigenous people and the law, juvenile justice, restorative justice, policing, prison issues, and human rights. Chris has participated with a number of Australian Royal Commissions and Inquiries (including the Stolen Generations Inquiry, the Royal Commission into Aboriginal Deaths in Custody, and the National Inquiry into Racist Violence), and with the federal Australian Human Rights Commission. Before his current appointment Chris has held teaching and research positions with a number of Australian universities.

Deering John now retired, was Associate Professor of Criminology and Criminal Justice at the University of South Wales where he was awarded his Ph.D. His research interests include probation, youth justice, and the criminal justice system in England and Wales. He is Co-Deputy Director of the Welsh Centre for Crime and Social Justice. He previously worked for the Probation Service.

Durnescu Ioan is Professor at the University of Bucharest, Faculty of Sociology and Social Work. He teaches and conducts research in the area of probation, prison, and deradicalization fields. His special interest is comparative probation, staff skills, and re-entry. He is one of the editors of the Probation in Europe collection available on the CEP website at: https://www.cep-probation.org/knowledgebases/probation-in-europe/ Ioan Durnescu is currently co-editor of the European Journal of Probation, a journal published by the University of Bucharest in partnership with SAGE Publishing, and co-chair of the RAN Rehabilitation Working Group. His recent book—Core Correctional Skills. The Training Kit—can be found at: www.corecorrectional.eu.

Feilzer Martina Y. is Professor of Criminology and Criminal Justice at Bangor University. She is the Bangor Co-Director of the Wales Institute of Social and Economic Research and Data and Co-Deputy Director of the Welsh Centre for Crime and Social Justice. Her research interests lie in policing and probation, the legitimacy of criminal justice institutions, transitional justice, and mixed methods research.

Giacomello Corina is Professor at the Institute of Judicial Studies of the University of Chiapas, Mexico, and international consultant on gender and criminal justice, drug policy, prison system, and children's rights. Among her latest publications lie 'The gendered impacts of drug policies on women. Case studied from Mexico' (Graduate Institute Geneva, 2020); *Childhood that matters. The impact of drug policy on children with incarcerated parents in Latin America and the Caribbean* (Church World Service, 2019) and *Children in Prison with their mothers. A comparative judicial perspective* (Mexico's National Supreme Court of Justice, 2018).

Gilchrist Liz is Professor of Psychological Therapies at the University of Edinburgh and an HCPC Registered Forensic Psychologist. Prof Gilchrist holds a Scottish Government appointment as Chair of the Scottish Advisory

Panel for Offender Rehabilitation and is a senior member of the Division of Forensic Psychology-Scotland committee. A leader in the forensic psychology and criminology field, Professor Gilchrist served 8 years on the Parole Board for England and Wales and 6 years on the Parole Board for Scotland; she works independently as a consultant forensic psychologist and has published extensively on the assessment, planning, and evaluation of rehabilitative interventions. An expert on risk assessment tools for domestic abuse, sexual offending, and violent offending; she was a member of the Research Advisory Group for the Risk Management Authority and has worked internationally as an advisor on implementation and review of offending behaviour programmes and interventions for the Council of Europe in Turkey, Georgia, Bulgaria, and Armenia, with IVAT in San Diego USA and for the Department of Corrections in New Zealand.

Halder Debarati is Professor of Law at Parul University, Gujarat, India. She was awarded her Ph.D. in Law at NLSIU, Bangalore. She had been a practitioner in law before joining academia. She is deeply interested in Cyber Law, Victimology, and Therapeutic Jurisprudence. Debarati is also a pro-bono Cybercrime victim counsellor, and she specializes in cybercrimes against women. She was the first in India to propose a law to penalize Revenge Porn. She is a doting mom and pet parent.

Healy Deirdre is Director of the UCD Institute of Criminology and Criminal Justice and Associate Professor in the UCD Sutherland School of Law. She completed her Ph.D. at the UCD Institute of Criminology in 2006. Her teaching and research interests include desistance from crime, community sanctions, white-collar crime, criminological theory, and victimization. Her work has been published in prestigious international journals, including Theoretical Criminology and Justice Quarterly. Her books include: the Routledge Handbook of Irish Criminology (with Claire Hamilton, Yvonne Daly and Michelle Butler; Routledge, 2015); The Dynamics of Desistance: Charting Pathways through Change (Willan, 2010); and Rape and Justice in Ireland (with Conor Hanly and Stacey Scriver; Liffey Press, 2009).

Hebenton Bill is Professor in the Department of Criminology at the University of Manchester, UK and Research Associate of the Manchester China Institute. His research in the UK has been primarily on the management of sexual offenders, sentencing and the 'smoke and mirrors' of English criminal justice. In recent years, he has published widely on Greater China and co-edited the *Routledge Handbook of Chinese Criminology*. He is a past President of the Association of Chinese Criminology and Criminal Justice in the United States (2018–2020), and with Professors Susyan Jou and Lennon Chang, is a co-editor of the current flagship book series '*Palgrave Advances in Criminology and Criminal Justice in Asia*' published by Palgrave Macmillan.

Herzog-Evans Martine (aka Herzog-Evans) is Professor of criminal law and criminology, and teaches law and criminology at Reims University, France. Dr. Evans also develops offender treatment programmes for the third sector and regularly trains Criminal Justice practitioners. Her majors are legitimacy of justice, sentences, courts, probation, prisons, and re-entry. She has published extensively (see http://herzog-evans.com). Her latest publication as co-editor with Massil Benbouriche is Evidence-Based Work with Violent Extremists. France as a case example, with Lexington Books, 2019. She is currently working on an EBP probation treaty with French publisher Dalloz and on two co-edited books, respectively, with Springer (with Stephen Morewitz—Terrorism case studies) and Routledge (with Dr. Jerome Thomas—Prisoners' vote).

Istrate Andrada studied sociology at the University of Bucharest and EHESS, Paris, and sociology and social anthropology at Central European University in Budapest. Her previous work investigates the recent history of financial fraud in post-socialist Romania. She was involved in several research projects dealing with marginality and precarity: prisoners and former prisoners; people with disabilities; women and men living off social welfare; gamblers and addicts; immigrants and subsistence farmers. Currently, she is involved in research on crime and delinquency in contemporary Romania, focusing on how re-entry policies (or lack thereof) determine ex-prisoners' trajectories.

Johnson Amy leads the Criminology programmes at the University of Worcester and is a researcher at the University of Edinburgh. Amy enjoys researching offending behaviour and exploring how the criminal justice system is designed to support individuals identified as having challenges with their behaviours and those who have a lower intellectual ability. Amy has an interest in the development of behaviour change interventions and evidence-based practice, particularly within the community and criminal justice settings. More recently, Amy has been working with local prisons to consider integrating rehabilitative programmes designed to reduce substance use and domestic abuse.

Jou Susyan is Distinguished Professor of Criminology and was the founding director of the School of Criminology at National Taipei University, Taiwan. She has been General-Secretary (2009–2012) and Vice Chair (2013–2015) of the Asian Criminological Society. Her research interests have focused on comparative punishment, white-collar crime, juvenile justice and the development of the subject area of criminology in Taiwan and China. She co-edited the influential *Handbook of Asian Criminology* (Springer) and is joint editor of the book series 'Palgrave Advances in Criminology and Criminal Justice in Asia' (Palgrave Macmillan).

Juanche Ana is Doctor in Latin American Studies (National Autonomous University of Mexico) and a Master's in Human Rights (Pontifical Catholic University of Peru). For 20 years she has been working and researching in the field of human rights and prisons. She has been a consultant for various agencies of the United Nations, the European Union, and other international cooperation agencies. Between 2016 and 2020 she was Technical Assistant and Manager and Director of the National Rehabilitation Institute Uruguay.

Kalunta-Crumpton Anita, Ph.D. is Professor of Administration of Justice at Texas Southern University, USA. She received a Ph.D. in criminal justice from Brunel University London, United Kingdom. She is the author of *Race and Drug Trials: The Social Construction of Guilt and Innocence* (1999), *Drugs, Victims and Race: The Politics of Drug Control* (2006), and editor (with Biko Agozino) of *Pan-African Issues in Crime and Justice* (2004). She is also the editor of *Race, Crime and Criminal Justice: International Perspectives* (2010), *Race, Ethnicity, Crime and Criminal Justice in the Americas* (2012), *Pan-African Issues in Drugs and Drug Control: An International Perspective* (2015), and *Violence Against Women: Global Perspectives* (2019). Kalunta-Crumpton's work has also appeared in a wide range of peer-reviewed academic journals, including the *British Journal of Criminology, Criminology and Criminal Justice*.

Kerezsi Klára is Emerita Professor of Criminology, Doctor of the Hungarian Academy of Sciences. She is the Founding Mother and former Head of the Doctoral School of Police Sciences at the University of Public Service between 2015 and 2021. Before retiring, she has been a Senior Adviser at the National Institute of Criminology, with 40 years of research experience in criminology, policing, and social work. Her research interests include minorities and criminal justice, critical policing, crime control, restorative justice, penal institutions, punishment, and rehabilitation practices. In 1996 she was engaged in elaborating the first national crime prevention concept, and she also elaborated on the idea of the reform of the Hungarian probation service. Between 2011 to 2016, she was an Honorary Senior Research Fellow at the University of Kent, School of Social Policy. She has published more than 240 books, articles, and studies in more languages in the above fields. Her works also appeared in different international journals and publications. She was one of the editors of 'The Routledge Handbook on European

Criminology' and acted as a member of the Scientific Board of the ISC between 2006 and 2012. She is the vice president of the Hungarian Society of Criminology.

Kiemo Karatu is Sociology Lecturer and Researcher at the University of Nairobi, Kenya. He has deep interest in criminology with some of the specialization areas being theories of crime; criminal law; and law, society and public policy; gender-based violence and violence against women; drug use and control; organized criminal groups, suicide and penology. He also has deep interest in social psychiatry. Some of the recent publications are on the topics of violence against women and the feasibility of an early warning system, drugs and drugs control, alcohol-related deaths and illnesses, gender-based violence, organized criminal groups, and international elderly suicide. Kiemo is well skilled in application of statistical and qualitative methods of research and in comparative international studies. His future focus is particularly on international applied criminology and criminal justice.

Lappi-Seppälä Tapio is Professor of criminal law and criminology and the director of the Institute of Criminology and Legal Policy at the University of Helsinki. He holds a long career first as a senior adviser in the Ministry of Justice, then as the director of National Research Institute of Legal Policy. He has taken actively part in criminal justice policy planning in several committees, both nationally and internationally. In 2015 he was awarded by the American Society of Criminology's Sellin-Glueck award for his comparative research and in 2019 by the European Society of Criminology's award in recognition of his lifetime contribution to European criminology. His publications cover numerous titles (around 300) in several languages in criminal law, criminology, and penal policy.

Lardén Martin is head of client treatment and education in the Swedish Prison and Probation Service. He is a clinical psychologist and researcher in the field of criminal rehabilitation with more than 25 years' experience in criminal justice rehabilitation. From 1996 he worked as a clinical psychologist in the National Board of Institutional Care. A large part of his work consisted of research and development. His research has focussed on risk factors and treatment of serious offending behaviour. International cooperation with countries like Canada, England, Norway and Finland among others, has been an important part of his work.

Leong Donna Soi Wan earned her Master's degree in Social Sciences in Criminology from the University of Macau in 2018. She has since then worked in the Institute for the Study of Commercial Gaming at the University of Macau. Her research is on occupational and gambling-related crimes and deviances in casinos, Macao gambling-related issues, and government consultancy projects. Donna's research interests include occupational crimes, victimization, corrections, social statistics, as well as Macao-related and gambling-related issues. She is currently a Vice president of the Macau Society of Criminology.

Li Enshen is Senior Lecturer at the TC Beirne School of Law, The University of Queensland. He researches in the areas of comparative criminal justice, theoretical criminology, socio-legal studies of punishment with a special focus on Chinese criminal justice system. His work has been published extensively in the leading law and criminology journals, including British Journal of Criminology, Law and Social Inquiry, Social & Legal Studies, and Columbia Journal of Asian Law. Prior to entering academia, he practised as a criminal defence lawyer in Shanghai, China.

Liu Jianhong is Distinguished Professor in the Faculty of Law at the University of Macau. He earned his Ph.D. from the State University of New York at Albany in 1993. His primary research interests are crime and justice in Asia, comparative criminology, and criminal justice theory, and empirical legal studies. Prof Liu has published more than 170 academic publications. He is the winner of the 2016 'Freda Adler Distinguished Scholar Award' of the American Society of Criminology, and the winner of the 2018 'Gerhard O.W. Mueller Award for Distinguished Contributions to International Criminal Justice', Academy of Criminal Justice Sciences, USA. He is the Founding and Honorary President of the Asian Criminological Society and elected President of the Scientific Commission of the International Society for Criminology. He is the Editor in Chief of the Asian Journal of Criminology, and Editor of the Springer Series on Asian Criminology and Criminal Justice Research.

Mackey Benjamin J., M.A. is a Graduate Research Assistant at the Center for Advancing Correctional Excellence (ACE!) and a doctoral student in the Department of Criminology, Law and Society at George Mason University. He received his B.S. and M.A. in Criminology, Law and Society from George Mason University. Benjamin's scholarship centres on the sociology of punishment, with a particular focus on community-based forms of penality in the U.S. and beyond. Some of his current research explores the effect of the COVID-19 pandemic on community-based systems of care and control in the DC-Maryland-Virginia area. In addition to his academic experience, Benjamin has experience in the field of re-entry, where he worked to address the needs of individuals who are currently or formerly incarcerated.

Maier Katharina is Assistant Professor in the Department of Sociology and Anthropology at the University of Guelph (Canada). She holds a Ph.D. from the Centre for Criminology & Sociolegal Studies at the University of Toronto. Her research focuses on issues pertaining to punishment, community supervision, prisoner re-entry, drugs, crisis, and the intersection between criminal justice and public health responses to social problems. She has also a special interest in global and comparative criminology. Her work has been funded by the Social Sciences and Humanities Research Council of Canada and other funding sources. Dr. Maier's work has appeared in Punishment & Society, Theoretical Criminology, Probation Journal, and Criminology & Criminal Justice, among other outlets.

McPherson Madeline, M.S. is a doctoral student and Graduate Research Assistant with both the Center for Evidence-Based Crime Policy (CEBCP) and the Early Justice Strategies (EJS) Lab in the Department of Criminology, Law & Society at George Mason University. She received her dual B.A. in Sociology and Psychology at Duquesne University and M.S. in Justice, Law, & Criminology at American University. Madeline is a former justice practitioner having worked in policy and legislative affairs for the Pennsylvania Department of Corrections and the International Association of Chiefs of Police. Her research interests focus on the integration of mercy and redemption in institutional policy and criminal justice administration.

Meijer Sonja is an endowed professor of Penitentiary Law at Radboud University Nijmegen. She is also a university lecturer in Criminal Law and Procedure at the VU University Amsterdam. She is also a councillor at the Dutch Council for the Administration of Criminal Justice and Youth Protection. Her expertise is penitentiary law and, in particular, the legal position of detainees. Her main research focus is on rehabilitation, resocialization, and reintegration of former offenders, life imprisonment, criminal justice policy, and comparative criminal law. She is the co-editor of a book on legal consequences of criminal conviction (Meijer, S., Annison, H., and O'Loughlin, A., *Fundamental Rights and Legal Consequences of Criminal Conviction*, Oxford: Hart Publishing 2019).

Mills Alice is Senior Lecturer in Criminology at the University of Auckland. She has extensive experience of research in criminal justice, including mental health in prisons, the role of community and voluntary organizations in criminal justice, specialist courts, and prisoner reintegration. She is currently leading a study examining the links between stable housing and recidivism among those who have left prison, funded by the Royal Society of New Zealand Marsden Fund.

Monsalve María Jimena is Judge of the of 5th National Penal Enforcement Court, in Buenos Aires, Argentina. She was born in Buenos Aires in 1972. She has worked in different federal and national courts for over 30 years. She is President of the Argentine Association of Penal Enforcement Justice, Vice President of the Argentine Association of Therapeutic Jurisprudence, and the General Pro Secretary of the National Justice Judges Association. She is also a member of the International Women Judges Association and the Argentine Women Judges Association. She graduated from the University of Buenos Aires with a law degree and has a post-graduate degree as a Specialist in Criminal Law and Criminal Sciences. María Jimena is a teacher at several universities and directs a post-graduate course, 'Diplomacy in Penal Enforcement', at the University of Mendoza. She is the author of several pieces she has written about the 'National Penal Enforcement Law', from Argentina and México and several articles about alternatives to incarceration, Therapeutic Jurisprudence (TJ), Restorative Justice, Mental Health in prisons, vulnerable groups, gender, and diversity. She also co-directs 'Interdisciplinary Overviews of Penal Enforcement'. She collaborates with OEA-CICAD's Gender Program for Penal Justice. Furthermore, she rules in her court the 'Programme of Therapeutic Jurisprudence-TTD for drug abusers who committed crimes'. She has given numerous presentations and lectures at different universities and public institutions.

Murhula Patrick Bashizi Bashige, D.Phil. (Criminology and Forensic Studies) is a Postdoctoral Researcher, Department of Law, Walter Sisulu University. He is particularly interested in research relating to Criminal Justice, Restorative Justice, Gender-Based Violence, Forensic Criminology, Human Trafficking, and African Criminology. Dr. Murhula has published numerous articles in national and international journals, book chapters, and other scholarly works.

Netrabukkana Pimporn presently works at Thailand's Department of Corrections as the Director of Strategy and Planning Division. In 2003, she won the Royal Thai Government scholarship to pursue M.A. in Criminology and Sociology, and Ph.D. in Sociology from University of Essex (UK), after finishing B.A. in Political Science at Chulalongkorn University. For 15 years of work experience at the department, she has obtained important positions, i.e. senior staff officer to the Director General and Director of Foreign Affairs Sub-division. As a part-time lecturer, she teaches criminology and penology to different groups: newly recruited and junior prison staff at Correctional Staff Training Institute; undergraduate students at Faculty of Law, Rattana

Bundit University; students at Judge Advocate General's School and Provost Marshal's School.

Nicmanis Janis started his work in criminal justice field in 2008 as probation officer at State Probation Service (SPS). From 2013 to 2017 he was involved in project management field both at SPS and Prison Administration of Latvia. Currently he is a SPS Head Assistant of the Performance Analysis and Development Department. Janis received Theology and Science of Religion Master's degree at the University of Latvia. Among his academic and professional interests is the historical development of the idea of justice and its application in modern legal systems. Jannie is also interested and actively involved in volunteering on behalf of people with a criminal sentence history.

O'Kelley Scott, LPC is a licensed professional counsellor who has worked in the behavioural health field for 20 years. He worked in community mental health and has now been in correctional mental health since 2011. In 2014, he became the director of the department's institutional mental health services and in 2020 the department's comprehensive behavioural health services. He has been involved with corrections-based CIT since 2013 and is currently active in Missouri CIT Council and the department's CIT Steering Committee.

Onyeozili Emmanuel C. is a tenured full Professor of Criminology and Criminal Justice at the University of Maryland Eastern Shore, and a Carnegie Scholar (2017, 2018, and 2020). He holds a B.A. degree in History from University of Ibadan; an M.A. in Criminal Justice Administration from Clarke-Atlanta University; and a Ph.D. in Criminology from Florida State University. He has published extensively both locally and internationally, and his most recent publications are: 'Gunboat Criminology in the History of People of African descent' in 'The Routledge Handbook on Africana Criminologies, (2020) eds', and 'Community Policing in Nigeria (2021), eds'. He serves as the Managing Editor of the African Journal of Criminology and Justice Studies (AJCJS), with membership in several professional associations.

Pottier Philippe works as an international consultant on penitentiary and probation issues for Expertise France, particularly in North and West Africa. Born in 1952, a graduate in anthropology and criminology, Philippe Pottier was director of the National School of Prison Administration (ENAP), which trains all French prison and probation officers. He has directed several penitentiary services for integration and probation (SPIP), held the positions of teacher-researcher at ENAP and inspector of the penitentiary services. Former assistant to the Deputy Director of Persons Placed in the Hands of Justice at the Directorate of Prison Administration, he had then worked on the drafting of the penitentiary bill and the renovation of the intervention methods of the SPIPs, work which he continued at ENAP by encouraging the introduction into French probation of structured assessments, the RNR model and Core Correctional Practices. He chaired the French Association of Criminology (AFC) of which he is currently vice president.

Priestley Philip has worked in probation and prisons and is author of *Victorian Prison Lives* (1985). He was a founder member of *Radical Alternatives to Prison,* and helped set up the first-day reporting centre in the UK; campaigned for victims of crime to get a better deal; directed thirty broadcast films for UK television, including *Video Letters* (BBC 2 1991); *Prix Europa* award, Berlin; trained CJ staff in Scandinavia to deliver CBT-based offending behaviour programmes; co-author with Maurice Vanstone of three books about rehabilitation in criminal justice.

Ravagnani Luisa is Researcher in Criminology and Penitentiary Criminology and Professor of Criminology of Terrorism and International Crimes at the University of Law, Brescia—Italy. She was an Expert Judge at the Surveillance Court of Brescia from 2005 to 2015 and she renounced to this position to serve as prisoners' Ombudsman of the city of Brescia. She is a member of the International Society of Criminology, of the European Society of Criminology, and member of the scientific committee of the Italian Society of Criminology and RAN (Radicalisation Awareness Network) expert since May 2020. She has an extensive experience of the extra-European prison systems, developing international projects in this field and strengthening collaboration with universities and public institutions. She is author of more than 80 publications in the mentioned fields. She is volunteer in prison, authorized by the Italian Ministry of justice since 1996 and vice president of the Ngo Carcere e Territorio which works for the social rehabilitation of offenders in prison and probation.

Ricciardelli Rosemary is Professor of Sociology and Criminology, the Coordinator for Criminology, and Co-Coordinator for Police Studies at Memorial University of Newfoundland. She is the Vice Chair of the Academic, Researcher, and Clinical Network Advisory Committee (ARC NAC) for the Canadian Institute for Public Safety Research and Treatment (CIPSRT). Beyond being elected to the Royal Society of Canada, she has additional affiliations and appointments at Ontario Shores Centre for Mental Health and Toronto Rehabilitation Institute. She was awarded her Ph.D. in sociology by McMaster University in 2009. She has published over 150 journal articles, 40 chapters, and over 300 presentations and invited talks, all in a range of academic journals including the British Journal of Criminology, Punishment & Society, Sex Roles, and Theoretical Criminology. She has authored four edited collections and five monographs. Her research interests include gender, and experiences and issues within different facets of the criminal justice system. Her current research looks at prisons, desistance from crime, and the mental health and lived experiences of prisoners, prison officers, and police officers. Her sources of active research funding include Correctional Services Canada, the Social Sciences and Humanities Research Council of Canada, the Union of Canadian Correctional Officers (UCCO-SACC-CSN), the Union of Safety and Justice Employees (USJE), and the Canadian Institute of Health Research (CIHR).

Rodermond Elanie is Assistant Professor at the Criminal Law and Criminology department, Faculty of Law, and Researcher at the Netherlands Institute for the Study of Crime and Law Enforcement. Her research focuses on the life-course, criminal career, and re-entry experiences of offenders, most notably extremist and women offenders.

Romano Carlo Alberto is Associate Professor of Criminology, Penitentiary Criminology, and Criminology of terrorism and of International Crimes at the Department of Law, University of Brescia, Italy. He also teaches in numerous Master's and specialization courses that deal with prison, probation, and restorative justice, organized by national universities and public agencies. Since 2013, he has been appointed advisor for security and prevention of crimes by the mayor of the city of Brescia, inside the ad hoc special committee. Since November 2017, he has been appointed as delegate of the Dean for the social responsibility of the University. He is author of more than 100 publications on the mentioned themes. He is a member of the management committee of the Italian Society of Criminology. Since 2004, he is President of the Ngo Carcere e Territorio which works for the social rehabilitation of offenders in prison and probation.

Rudes Danielle S., Ph.D. is a Professor of Criminal Justice & Criminology at Sam Houston University and the Deputy Director of the Center for Advancing Correctional Excellence (ACE!) within the Schar School of Policy & Government at George Mason University. She received her Ph.D. from the University of California, Irvine. Dr. Rudes is an expert qualitative researcher whose methods include ethnographic observation, interviews, and focus groups with over 20 years of experience working with U.S. corrections agencies at the federal, state, and local county levels including prisons, jails, probation/parole agencies, and problem-solving courts. She is recognized for her work examining how social control organizations and their middle management and street-level workers understand, negotiate, and at times, resist change.

Ruiz-Pérez José Ignacio is a psychology (Ph.D.) and Criminologist (M.Sc.) and Associate Professor of legal and social psychology at the Universidad Nacional de Colombia, in Bogotá. He is founder and coordinator of the Psychology and Law Laboratory and since 2020 is director of the Center for Orientation of Victims of Road Accidents, of the Bogota District Mobility Secretariat. His academic interests are penitentiary treatment programmes, psychosocial processes regarding fear of crime and collective efficacy (community resilience, citizenship culture, democracy social representations), assessment in forensic psychology, pathological gambling, and psychology in road traffic safety. He has written around 100 publications (mostly articles, several book chapters and editor of four books) on these fields. He was forensic psychologist for trials in Colombia.

Russell Sophie is the Research Associate for the Rethinking Community Sanctions Project at the Faculty of Law, University of New South Wales. Prior to this position, Sophie worked at the Sydney Institute of Criminology and in research, policy, and advocacy in the community sector. She is involved in a voluntary capacity with the Women's Justice Network and as a Director on the Board of Glebe House, a residential therapeutic community for men with complex needs. Sophie is currently undertaking a Ph.D. in the Faculty of Law, University of Technology Sydney on the experience of adults leaving prison in NSW and the role of family relationships in supporting desistance from crime.

Shen Shang-Kai is the Section Chief of Probation and Parole at Taiwan's Hsinchu District Prosecutors' office. He graduated in Psychology, and has a Master's degree in Criminology. He is responsible for criminal offenders under probation and parole orders, and specializes in sexual offenders' community supervision, treatment and electronic monitoring programmes, as well as drug-addicted offenders' community treatment programs.

Singh Shanta Balgobind is Full Professor in the programme of Criminology and Forensic Studies at the University of KwaZulu-Natal. Research areas are diverse and include Crime and Criminality, Migration, Religious Tolerance, The Criminal Justice System, Correctional Theory and Practise; Human Rights, Women and Health Issues; Youth; The Indian Diaspora in the 21st Century, Indigenous Knowledge Systems and Higher Education; qualifications: B.A. (UNISA); B.A. Honours—Cum laude (UNISA); Master of Arts—M.A. (UNISA); DLitt et Phil (UNISA); University Post-Graduate Diploma in Higher Education with Distinction (UKZN).

Someda Kei is Professor in the Faculty of Law at the Surugadai University (Japan). He is the former Deputy Director in the Department of Research at the Research and Training Institute Ministry of Justice, a Professor at the United Nations Asia and Far East Institute (UNAFEI) and the Chief Probation Officer at several probation offices. His research and study mainly focus upon community supervision and support of justice-involved persons, substance abuse and behavioural addiction, restorative justice, prevention of recidivism, crime victimization survey, and international comparative study on community supervision. Although his major backgrounds are criminal justice policy and criminology, he also is a certified social worker and has especially interested in a multidisciplinary approach among agencies in criminal and juvenile justice, social welfare, public health and medicine, education, housing for prevention of crime and promotion of reintegration. Dr. Someda's work has appeared in UNAFEI publications, research publications of the Ministry of Justice, Legal Medicine (Elsevier), a publication of International Centre for the Prevention of Crime, and so forth.

Szabó Judit is Senior Research Fellow at the Division of Criminal Law Sciences at the National Institute of Criminology in Budapest. She received an M.A. in psychology, a J.D. in law, and a Ph.D. in legal sciences from Eötvös Loránd University in Budapest. Prior to becoming a junior research fellow she spent a few years working as a psychologist and then was employed by the Hungarian News Agency. She also worked as a lecturer in criminology at Eötvös Loránd University and now occasionally gives lectures at local universities. At the National Institute of Criminology she takes part both in legal and in criminological projects. Her Ph.D. dissertation was based on research conducted in Hungarian correctional institutions and probation services on the prevention of reoffending and on desistance from crime. Her main research interests include crime prevention, sexual offending, and themes on the intersection of criminal law and psychology.

Todd-Kvam John is Postdoctoral Researcher at the Norwegian Centre for Addiction Research. He has published research in *The British Journal of Criminology, Punishment & Society* and *Criminology and Criminal Justice* on topics like bordered penal populism, debt and desistance in Norway and Norwegian probation. In addition to desistance and penality, John has researched populism and Euroscepticism. He has previously worked in a number of civil service policy roles in Belfast and London.

Uzoh Bonaventure Chigozie holds a Bachelor of Science (B.Sc.) degree in sociology/Anthropology from the University of Nigeria, Nsukka, a Master of Science (M.Sc.) degree in Sociology of Development from the University of Port Harcourt, and a Doctor of Philosophy (Ph.D.) degree in Industrial and Labour Relations from Nnamdi Azikiwe University (UNIZIK), Awka, Nigeria. He is currently Senior Lecturer in the Department of Sociology/Anthropology, Nnamdi Azikiwe University, Awka. He is also a resource person at the School of General Studies, UNIZIK Business School and Centre for Migration Studies. He has served/serves in many Departmental, Faculty, and University Committees. He has published extensively in both international and local journals.

Vanstone Maurice worked in the probation service for 27 years and currently is Emeritus Professor of Criminology and Criminal Justice at Swansea University. His research and publications are focused mainly on the effectiveness of community sentences and the international history of probation. He is the author of *Supervising Offenders in the Community: A History of Probation Theory and Practice* (2004 and 2007) and co-editor (with Philip Priestley) of *Offenders or Citizens? Readings in Rehabilitation* (2010) and *Probation and Politics. Academic Reflections from Former Practitioners* (2016).

Vigna Ana is Associate Professor at the School of Social Sciences, University of the Republic. She is a Doctor in Sociology (University of the Republic) and has worked in several research projects dealing with rehabilitation, desistance, recidivism, gender and crime, prison policies, and punishment. She has been a consultant for multiple national and international agencies on topics such as prison reform, prison Ombudsman, gender in criminal justice System, and gender-based violence.

Villagra Pincheira Carolina Aurora is Doctor of Philosophy and Master of Sciences in Criminology, University of Leicester, England. Psychologist, University of Chile. Over 15 years dedicated to the study of penal reform in Latin America, female criminality, desistance from crime, and design and evaluation of rehabilitation programmes, she has participated in several studies and consultancies in criminal reform matters in Chile and other Latin American countries. She has a decade of formal experience as a lecturer. Currently she works as a part-time academic of legal psychology at the Department of Psychology of the University of Chile, and as a specialized consultant in criminal justice. She presided over the Chilean Association of Therapeutic Jurisprudence for the 2018–2021 period.

Webb Robert is Senior Lecturer in Criminology at the University of Auckland. His research and teaching interests include criminal justice policies and Māori, youth justice, Indigenous criminology, and Māori ethics and organ donation. He is currently part of a research project examining Māori and Samoan experiences of the youth justice systems in NZ, Australia, and the USA.

Whitehead John is Lecturer in Criminology at the Australian College of Applied Psychology (ACAP). He was awarded his Ph.D. by Monash University. His work engages with the need for legal pluralism across Pacific Island countries, restorative and customary justice as a response to sexual violence, and cyber-deviance. His research has further highlighted the importance of Indigenous methodological and theoretical frameworks, and the need for located scholarship across the Global South.

Zavackis Anvars is Leading Researcher at the State Probation Service of Latvia. He began his career in the justice system in 2004, participating in the development of policies and practices of the State Probation Service related to risk assessment and management, presentence reports and community supervision of probation clients. In 2009, he became a researcher and later a leading researcher in the Service. Anvars received his education at the University of Latvia, first in psychology and later in sociology. In 2014, he received a doctoral degree (Ph.D.) in sociology defending his doctoral dissertation on the risk assessment of probation clients. In addition to working in the probation service, Anvars is a lecturer at the University of Latvia, giving lectures to social workers and sociology students.

List of Figures

Penitentiary System in Colombia

Fig. 1	Penitentiary system into criminal justice system (*Source* Own elaboration)	108
Fig. 2	Injuries suffered in prison by other inmates or guards (*Sources* Taken from the 2017 Prisons Report)	114

Rehabilitative Aims and Values in Finnish (and Nordic) Criminal Justice

Fig. 1	Prison population rates in Denmark, Finland, Norway, Sweden and England & Wales 1960–2020	163
Fig. 2	The share of prisoners in open prisons 2000–2020 (% of all prisoners including remand)	172
Fig. 3	Entries to prison, community service and electronic monitoring/pop 1991–2020	176

Framing and Reframing the Rehabilitation in Criminal Justice in Latvia

Fig. 1	Dynamics of Conditional Sentencing (supervision) and Community Sanction (community work) in Latvia in 2010–2016 (percentage of total penalties imposed) (*Source* Data from the Court Information System of Latvia used in author's previously published paper. Zavackis, A., & Ņikišins, J. [2016]. Piespiedu darbu un nosacītas notiesāšanas piemērošana un izpilde [Application and enforcement of community sanction and conditional sentencing]. Rīga: Valsts probācijas dienests https://www.vpd.gov.lv/lv/media/301/download)	352

Penal Welfarism and Rehabilitation in Norway: Ambitions, Strengths and Challenges

Fig. 1	Punishment that makes a difference	476

Rehabilitation in Romania—The First 100 Years

Fig. 1.	The number of people incarcerated and on probation are valid for the end of each year (December 31). Romania 1 (*Source* National Directorate of Probation and National Administration of Penitentiaries)	494

Rehabilitation in Taiwan

Fig. 1	Re-offending percentages for inmates and parolees in Taiwan, 1993–2019 (*Source* Authors)	588
Fig. 2	Percentage completion rates for harm reduction and community social labour orders, Taiwan, 2011–2021 (*Source* Authors)	589

Key Practices in Thai Prisons: Rehabilitation

Fig. 1	Prison and punishment timeline in Thailand (*Source* Netrabukkana, 2012)	622
Fig. 2	Number of Prison Population, 1995–2021 (*Source* Centre of Prisoner Statistics, Planning Division, DOC)	624

List of Tables

Rehabilitation and Beyond in Settler Colonial Australia: Current and Future Directions in Policy and Practice

Table 1	Age standardised rate of imprisonment (per 100,000 adult population) in Australian states and territories by Indigenous status, 2021 (ABS, 2021a)	36
Table 2	Rate of imprisonment and community-based orders (per 100,000 adult population) in Australian states and territories, 2021 (ABS, 2021a, 2021b)	37

Rehabilitation in a Risk Society: 'The Case of China'

Table 1	A Typical Daily Timetable of the Chinese Prison	96

Penitentiary System in Colombia

Table 1	Types of penitentiary facilities and associated programs	110
Table 2	Inmates' perceptions on corruption in jails	116
Table 3	Some study programs and job training in the Colombian penitentiary system	119
Table 4	Risk factors for suicide in prison: clinical, penitentiary, family and stressor events	120

Rehabilitative Aims and Values in Finnish (and Nordic) Criminal Justice

Table 1	Imprisonment, community service and electronic monitoring in a statistical comparison. Enforcement statistics 2020	175

Approaches to Rehabilitation in Hong Kong

Table 1	Average daily number of persons in custody by category and gender	227
Table 2	Five values of CSD staff members	228
Table 3	Success rates of reintegration programmes within the supervision period	230
Table 4	Recidivism rate of local rehabilitated offenders between 2014 and 2018	231

From Need-Based to Control-Based Rehabilitation: The Hungarian Case

Table 1	Pillars of reintegration process	241
Table 2	Regimes in Hungarian penitentiary institutions	242

Criminal Rehabilitation in Kenya: Opportunities and Pitfalls

Table 1	Incarceration rate (per 100,000) and prisoners' characteristics in comparison with other East African countries and global ranking (in parentheses)	329

Criminal Justice Rehabilitation in Macao, China

Table 1	Recidivism of Macao Residents who Convicted Incarceration Sentence, 2015–2018	369
Table 2	Recidivism of Macao Residents who Convicted Non-custodial Sentence, 2015–2018	369

The Legal Flaws and Material Implementation Gaps of Mexico's Rehabilitation Paradigm

Table 1	Prison Population 2011–2021	382

Offender Rehabilitation Approaches in South Africa: An Evidence-Based Analysis

Table 1	DCS offender rehabilitation path	530
Table 2	DCS Matric results 2016–2021	536

Rehabilitation in Taiwan

Table 1	Probation offices, caseload numbers and level in 2021	581
Table 2	Fiscal budgets for the probation and protection services of the MOJ in Taiwan: 2013–2022	582

Rehabilitation and the Adult Correctional Population in Texas

Table 1	Rehabilitation programs and services in community supervision	603
Table 2	Prison-based rehabilitation and reentry programs and services	605
Table 3	Parole division: Specialized programs and services	608
Table 4	Number of parole referrals and number of unsuccessful referrals by services in FY2020	609

Key Practices in Thai Prisons: Rehabilitation

Table 1	Recidivism Rates, 2013–2018	625

Prospect

Maurice Vanstone and Philip Priestley

Grounded in curiosity about how rehabilitation is practiced internationally within diverse criminal justice and penal systems, cultures, and political contexts, this book sets out to identify common features of criminal justice in a variety of countries, while scrutinising their differences and gauging the degree to which the concept of rehabilitation is faring in the face of ever increasing populist and punitive criminal justice policies. As several contributions demonstrate, populist responses to the social problem of crime are not exclusive to countries ruled by authoritarian and doctrinaire governments. It is hoped, therefore, that by providing a counter-narrative focused positively on rehabilitation, the book might reinforce the point that 'law' itself also has the capacity to constrain rulers, and that 'order' in the form of social peace is universally approved as a civic asset.

Our intentions are one thing, but of equal importance is some clarification about what this book does not purport to be. It does not claim to be a comparative study because each contribution is presented in its own right and there is no permeative and connecting commentary. Our retrospect reflects on

M. Vanstone (✉)
Criminology, School of Social Sciences, Swansea University, Swansea, UK
e-mail: m.t.vanstone@swansea.ac.uk

P. Priestley
Peace Close, West Horrington, England

commonalities and differences but the onus is on the reader to apply what Hamai et al. (1995: 23–24) describe as 'a comparative imagination'; and as they suggest, this requires readers, first to position themselves 'as part of a large, variegated enterprise relevant to one's own activities' and second, to assume 'a sense of underlying collegiality and mutual interest, but then to use this sense as a basis for exploring points of difference as well as similarity'.

Although the contributors were asked to take a broad view of rehabilitative work, we acknowledge that probation has been a cornerstone of efforts to assist the rehabilitation of people who have offended, and therefore it would be remiss, in an introduction to a collection of international criminal justice stories, not to pay respect to previous reflections on probation across the world. In one, Timasheff (1941, 1943) introduced readers to probation systems in the USA, Britain and the Commonwealth, Europe and, briefly, Latin America, Asia, and Africa; and in another at the end of the century, Koichi Hamai et al. (1995) examined criminal justice provision in Australia, Canada, England and Wales, Hungary, Israel, Japan, Papua New Guinea, the Philippines, Scotland and Sweden. In the introduction to the latter work, the authors claimed it was the first world-wide study of probation but strangely made no reference to Timasheff's earlier work. While it is important to acknowledge the contribution made by Hamai and his colleagues to an understanding of probation in its international forms and the reaffirmation of its importance, as indicated above this book lays emphasis on rehabilitation more generally and presents a more comprehensive examination of attempts to restore people who are dealt with by the criminal courts to citizenship and constructive lives within their communities.

The forthcoming Chapters will throw light not only on how geographically distinct jurisdictions define rehabilitation and accord its varying levels of priority, but also on the potential of rehabilitation to be a moral counterweight to the rising tide of populism and punitiveness referred to above. In broad terms, the three models of rehabilitation critically examined are positive change in individuals, reintegration into the community, and removal of criminal records, all three of which are associated with the restoration of citizenship. We asked the contributors to bear in mind McNeill's (2012) four forms of rehabilitation, namely, personal, judicial or legal, moral and social in order to determine how common, or otherwise, they are to contemporary criminal justice systems.

Rehabilitation

As has been implied by the earlier reference to populism, the current and ubiquitous emphasis on punishment and retribution places rehabilitation in a perilous position in many criminal justice systems. It survives in political discourse and intent in as much as there continues to be a recognition that helping people to resolve offence-related problems has a part to play in reducing crime and protecting communities, but the punitive narrative often dominates. Any defence of the notion of rehabilitation, however, needs to pay heed to the complexity of the concept arising as it does from contested issues surrounding individual identity, the numerous and varied causal theories and the intricacies of the process of personal change.

Rehabilitation in its many manifestations has been the subject of criticism. These include, Wootton's (1959) disparaging observations on the uncritical belief of social workers in the unproven effectiveness of the application of psychoanalytical theory and their adherence to a magical medical model; Reid and Epstein's (1972) equating that belief with eighteenth-century bloodletting; C. S. Lewis's (1949) critique of a humanitarian theory that fosters unfettered treatment by experts and erodes human rights; and Bean's (1976) assessment of a social pathology model that in his view ignored the broader social context of offending, equated social disease with physical disease and expertly determined what was normal and what was good for people.

Embedded in the casework of many probation officers in the 1950s and 1960s in England and Wales the treatment model had a dubious and unevaluated theoretical base that accorded unrestrained power to what was in effect pseudo-expertise. More recently Carlen (2012: 99) has argued that '*rehabilitationism's* fundamental flaw has always been inherent in its individualism, routine targeting of poorer lawbreakers and irrelevance to corporate, political or other white-collar criminals'. In a reiteration of the point that rehabilitation's treatment model focused on individual psychological theories like psychoanalysis and cognitive-behaviouralism, Hollin (2001) also suggests that these theories and their association with determinism and pathology sit uneasily within criminal justice systems premised on notions of free will and individual responsibility.

Defining rehabilitation is problematical too. Bean (1976) argues that the definition is either too wide or too narrow with a lack of precision in key words such as diagnosis and therapy, is based on a simplistic notion of reform, and fails to differentiate treatment and training, and reform and rehabilitation. Further weight is given to Bean's argument by the number of models recently identified by several academics (Carlen, 2012; Crow, 2001; Farrall 2002; Maruna, 2001; McNeill, 2012; Raynor & Robinson, 2005). They include an embellished version of the individual-focussed model mentioned above, now aimed at modifying behaviour and invariably based on psychological, psychiatric or psychoanalytical theories about how to effect positive change in individuals in terms of the way they feel, think and behave. In more positive vein the model has recently been associated more with the recognition of the damaging effects of prison and deemed as a vehicle for the reintegration of the individual into the community. Other less dominant models include, the judicially based cleaning of the slate or deletion of criminal records after punishment drawing to some degree on the positive effects of de-labelling; the social welfare approach aimed at changing the social environment through, for example, resolving financial or employment problems and stemming from the recognition of the State's obligation to address basic needs; the psycho-social model in which attempts are made both to change individuals and their social environment; and a corrections approach that combines populist justice and or therapeutic jurisprudence.

Recently, in a move away from psychologically inspired approaches some commentators have fashioned a reimagined rehabilitation. Carlen (2012: 100) puts forward the idea of a 'two-dimensional reparative social justice' that applies to rich (including corporations who should face appropriate penalties) and poor lawbreakers alike and considers the degree of harm caused and the capacity to repay. It would encompass regeneration of communities, community or neighbourhood-based education (as opposed to indoctrination) in citizenship and citizen rights, and active involvement in the process of change with the caveat that, in the case of violent lawbreakers, public protection would prevail. In this way, Carlen argues that rehabilitation becomes reparative justice with increased equality generally and before the law. In earlier work focussed on women, Carlen (2002) put forward the idea of *gendered justice* and questioned whether it is appropriate to address the particular problems of women, be they material, social or psychological, within a psychological and legal model that positions economic problems and abuse alongside mental disorder and moral deficiency. In a more recent treatise, Burke et al. (2019) have put the case for a reimagining of rehabilitation that incorporates the personal model concerned with personal problem-solving, but offers equal status to the judicial and legal model with its emphasis on the restoration of citizenship, the moral that takes account of victims and the harms caused to communities, and the social that responds to the criminogenic needs of individuals, strives for empowerment and embraces collaborative relationships in pursuit of change. As these contributions show, reimagined rehabilitation, therefore, is not a static concept but a dynamic, adaptive one and this book reflects that reality.

Structure and Content of the Book

In order to represent rehabilitation as a global feature of criminal justice we settled on the continents (excluding Antarctica for obvious reasons) Asia, Africa, Australia, Europe, North America, Oceania and South America, and searched for representatives from component countries. Among the criteria for Chapter selection were knowledge of the mechanisms of criminal justice and the rehabilitation of people subject to them; specialised understanding of rehabilitation methods; a record of research and publications in relevant areas; insider understanding of the cultures and societies within which criminal justice operates; and a sensitivity to the experience of minority populations and women. With this latter criterion in mind we were determined to have a balance in terms of gender and ethnicity.

The process of identifying contributors was not entirely smooth, but it has produced an interesting combination of the well-known and lesser known, of well-established experts and those in the early stages of their careers, a variety of experience within the field of criminal justice, and the diversity that we were hoping to achieve. Some of the contributors we approached were known to us because of their distinguished records of research and publications; however, one of our aims in producing this book was to identify lesser known (at least to us) people who might have a valuable contribution to make from countries that have received far less attention hitherto in criminological literature. In this endeavour we were helped by Dr. Bankole Cole, Reader in Criminology and Human Rights at the Helena Kennedy Centre for International Justice, Sheffield Hallam University in identifying contributors from Africa, Carolina Aurora Villagra Pincheira, University of Chile with those from South America, and Dr. Leon Moosavi, Senior Lecturer in the Department of Sociology, Social Policy and Criminology at the University of Liverpool and Bill Hebenton, Director of the Undergraduate Criminology Program and a Research Associate of the University's Centre for Chinese Studies at the University of Manchester with those from Asia. Their specific knowledge filled some of the gaps in ours. For our part, however, we began by scanning key criminological and international publications for potential contributors and when we had made our choices, sent a request letter firstly, explaining that the book *would* cover probation but have a broader scope that would include parole, prison regimes, reparation, and reconciliation and secondly, outlining a suggested structure for the Chapters.

Through this process we brought together contributors drawn from the disciplines of sociology, criminology, psychology and law that together, we believe, present a genuinely representative, and in terms of gender and ethnicity, a truly diverse global cohort. The country and State-based settings reflect the populations they serve as well as important features of criminal justice in action such as the specific community-based and custodial provisions made for male and female defendants, juveniles and sentenced individuals, and the different ways in which they are dealt with by type of offence, previous history and criminogenic needs. Our contributors reflect on the work they and others have undertaken in different places with different people and include details that root the political, organisational and historical aspects of rehabilitation in the realities of lived experience. Many were not writing in their first language, and we have been impressed by the way they dealt with this. It has resulted in some challenging translation issues but also colloquialisms that add character to the Chapters. We hope the reader finds them as interesting as we do. As far as organisation is concerned, we wished to avoid creating the appearance of a hierarchy of importance and relevance so have simply presented the countries in alphabetical order.

Against the background of constant economic crisis in Argentina and the Criminal Popular Punitive Movement that has increased poverty-related crime and imprisonment in old, underfunded buildings, María Jimenez Monsalve, a Judge of the 5th National Penal Enforcement Court in Buenos Aires, casts a legal eye over the evolution of rehabilitation in Argentina. She includes the response to diversity and the rights of women, LGBTQ+ groups and vulnerable people. Sophie Russell, James Beaufils and Chris Cuneen begin their examination of rehabilitation in criminal punishment settings across the State, territory and federal jurisdictions in Australia with a stark reminder of how colonisation and stolen land has led to the over-criminalisation of First Nations People (their preferred term for the Indigenous population). They home in on New South Wales that has the highest prison population and people on community sentences than any other State as a means of arguing for a more transformative vision of rehabilitation in the country as a whole, a vision that includes as an exemplar, the concept of Healing programmes. In Canada, Katharina Maier and Rosemary Ricciardelli explore the meaning and practice of lived reality of rehabilitation through their research in which they interviewed parole officers and ex-prisoners to produce a reflection on clarity of purpose, accountability, public safety and productivity in relation to (in an intriguing echo of the spirit of Spain's *rooms of respect* below) 'healing lodges' and half-way houses and parole supervision. In their examination of how these, and rehabilitation generally, fit into Canadian penalty they lay bare the structural disadvantages and barriers in relation to gender, race and indigenous populations and how they impact negatively on those ex-prisoners' ability to take advantage of rehabilitation, and follow that with conclusions about the required policy changes.

Carolina Aurora Villagra Pincheira begins her Chapter with a reminder that Chile's penal system began in the mid-nineteenth century with the first penitentiary in Santiago based on Bentham's Panoptican and then, in what will become a repeated refrain in the book, charts the tensions between the increased use of imprisonment and the post-military dictatorship legal reforms entrenching rehabilitation as the main aim of a penal system characterised by private prisons, a new system of alternatives to custody, and a parole system all designed to foster rehabilitation. Enshen Li weaves some fascinating insights about rehabilitation into China's revolutionary history. He explains how the hybrid penal system that incorporates rehabilitation alongside punishment and discipline emerged from Mao's idea of revolutionary justice characterised as it was by rehabilitative responses to minor offending and suppression and harsh sentencing for those designated as class enemies, and how after Mao's death crime was separated from the political struggle. He cautions that while there have been moves to modernise approaches to criminal justice and an expansion of rehabilitation through laws that endorse community-based orders the prime objectives of China's rehabilitation programme are risk assessment and social control. Accordingly, its aptly named *Combining Leniency with Severity* (Bangjiao) penal policy integrates rehabilitation with harsh punishment.

Based on laws reviews, statistics, official reports and academic articles on treatment programmes and an historical review of the evolution of prisons in Columbia, José Ignacio Ruiz-Pérez's account of the primary features of Columbia's penitentiary system and the pivotal role of Sentence Enforcement and Security Measures Judges reveals a disregard for human rights in prison, overcrowding and prison violence. He describes treatment programmes for men and women (including the intriguing Preservation of Life Programme) that are adversely affected by the scarcity of human and economic resources. In reflecting on approaches to rehabilitation in England and Wales, John Deering and Martina Y. Feilzer reveal how a diverse range of rehabilitation practices, delivered by statutory, private and third sector organisations, occur at various stages of the criminal justice system and the extent they are linked to different theoretical conceptions of rehabilitation. They set their Chapter not only within an historical context but also against a background of tension between a utilitarian approach with its emphasis on personal responsibility and a desistance focus on people's social capital, plus the recovery from the scars of privatisation. With echoes of the issues raised in Sophie Russell, James Beaufils and Chris Cuneen's Chapter John Whitehead and Lennon Yao-Chang explain how the Europeanisation of the iTaukei customary justice system of bulubulu (mediation between victim and offender, which often included reparations) has created particular difficulties for the prisoners and their families from smaller islands in the Fijian archipelago. While many rehabilitation programmes, such as the Yellow Ribbon Programme, are attuned to Indigenous culture, they argue for a more integrative design that focuses on other cultures and religions and caters for the LGBTIQ+ populations.

While setting his account of rehabilitation in Finland in the context of some other Nordic countries Tapio Lappi-Seppälä recounts the story of ideological transformations and legislative and policy changes over the last few decades in Finland that have resulted in the codification and total reform of community sanctions and a long-term reduction of imprisonment. He stresses the significance of Finland joining the Council of Europe and pinpoints open prisons as a defining feature of Finnish penality and Nordic exceptionalism. (This Chapter should be read in conjunction with the Norway and Sweden Chapters). In her critique of what she calls France's schizophrenic penal policies, Martine Herzog-Evans asserts they are caught between punitive stances and a concern about human rights. She describes how commitments to the notion of desistance and restoration of citizenship through the expunging of criminal records have been undermined by the merger of probation and prison (prisonbation), a form of McDonaldisation, and limited resources. Hope, in her view, lies with desistance-friendly practitioners and a population less punitive than assumed by politicians. Kofi Boakye, Thomas Akoensi and Frank Baffour's historical reflections provide a salutary reminder that Ghanian traditions of rehabilitation and reintegration were effectively eschewed by colonisation. In the pre-colonial Ashanti State there were no prisons and crime was viewed as a harm to the community to be ameliorated by a collective commitment to restoring the transgressor's place in the community. The prison, they inform us, was imported from Europe to Ghana in the mid-nineteenth century and remains the dominant conduit of rehabilitative practices, the probation service being weak and ineffective.

Rehabilitation in Hong Kong, largely modelled on the English system, has held steady and in Wing Hong Chui's Chapter he elucidates how. Remarkably, despite the return of sovereignty to China in July 1997 and an increasingly populist and punitive criminal justice culture, rehabilitation survives because of positive evidence of its success and ensuing popular support. From that standpoint he looks back over the history of non-custodial and custodial sentencing, casts a critical eye over the theories behind rehabilitation and evidence of their effectiveness and ruminates on its future. Klára Kerezsi and Judit Szabó tell the story of how the Hungarian idea that the main goal of imprisonment is reducing recidivism emerged from the positivist criminology of the nineteenth century and how after World War11 Stalinian criminal justice policy re-instated punishment as the tool of State politics. As we see from their account, a professional probation service evolved out of the 1978 Penal Code underpinned by a socialist model of rehabilitation grounded in education rather than treatment. However, the greater modern emphasis on reintegration and resocialisation with programmes such as the Prison for the City and Storybook Mums is jeopardised by concerns about security. Debarati Halder begins her examination of the Indian Penal Code with reference to the symbolic influence of the redemptions of the notorious thief, Maharshi Valmikt (who wrote the Ramayana Hindu epic) and the ruthlessly cruel Emperor Ashokari on pre-colonial history of India's correctional administration. She then breaks down the process by which it has been amended to fit in with the needs of adults and juveniles in modern India. With a different twist, Deirdre Healy takes a look back at a dark history of coercive reform in post-independence Ireland facilitated by Catholic Church organisations like the Magdalene Laundries, reform schools, and psychiatric Hospitals. She highlights how the changes in the 1960s and 1970s, driven by individual champions, led to a distinct form of pastoral penalty and how these progressive ideals were mixed with traditions that, for instance, did not always benefit women. In bringing us up to the present, she points to an emerging reimagined rehabilitation manifested in the role of the voluntary sector, social enterprise schemes and restorative justice initiatives such as Circles of Support and Accountability.

As Luisa Ravagnani explains, voluntary work has been a prominent feature of community supervision in Italy. In a brief analysis of the history of the Italian correctional system and the current legislative framework about the enforcement of the sentence and its underpinning fundamental principles, she draws attention to problems in Italy common to other countries that impede the effectiveness of rehabilitative effort, but adds the additional problems that relate to the omission of rehabilitative aims from the constitution and the over-reliance of the goodwill of probation officers and prison staff. She makes a strong case for a move to a restorative justice model. In an optimistic vein, Kei Someda introduces us to the more liberal approach to rehabilitation of Japan. As he notes, Japan was introducing volunteer-based rehabilitation as early as the late nineteenth century at the time of the international origins of probation and the use of volunteers increased in the years after World War 11. He brings us up to date with an introduction to the Offenders Rehabilitation Act 2007 that broadened probationary and parole conditions and paved the way for evidence-based treatment programmes and other important changes. However, what is distinct, innovative and influential about Japan's approach, no doubt derivative of its criminal justice history, is its use of *Hogishi* or Volunteer Probation officers and its Yellow Feather crime prevention campaign. The recurring theme of how colonisation has impacted negatively on indigenous populations is a feature of Karatu Kiemo's Chapter on Kenya. He introduces us to the 2010 Kenyan constitution and how it emerged in what he describes as a transitory society in which colonial-era crimes included in British Criminal Law such as vagrancy and trespass had put the indigenous population at greater risk of punishment. It heralded a shift from punishment to rehabilitation programmes and humane treatment characterised by more bail remands and prison visits. He adds fascinating detail about the particular plight of women enduring the tension between the threat to them while in prison and the dangers in the community.

At a time when Russia is waging war in Europe, Anvars Zavackis and Janis Nicmanis' account of how Latvia's criminal justice system has emerged from its experience as a republic in the former Soviet Union has a particular resonance. They describe how a country that in the last 200 years has experienced several invasions and endured the mass repression and harsh penal policies of the communist era, has drawn on the experience of other countries to shape modern forward-looking penal policies that have placed rehabilitation at its heart. In their Chapter, Jianhong Lui and Donna Soi Wan delineate how the Macau Penal Code ensures that sentencing, while having the notion of punishment at its core, is oriented towards rehabilitation and how responsibilities are divided between the Department of Social Rehabilitation whose focus is on non-custodial sentences, and the Social Reintegration Committee and Correctional Services Bureau whose collective responsibility is the reintegration of ex-prisoners. As the authors make clear, government policy is positive in intent, as is evidenced by the self-discovery workshops run in prisons; nevertheless they conclude that there is a dearth of effectiveness research with the result that knowledge about the impact or otherwise of that policy is limited. Since 2008, the criminal justice system in Mexico has changed from an inquisitorial to an adversarial model that itself has triggered changes to the design and implementation of alternatives to incarceration, increased national oversight, new models of practice and a new approach to imprisonment and rehabilitation. In this Chapter Corina

Giacomello introduces an interesting case study of a female drug user released on licence with an electronic tag to exemplify how traditional mindsets and the lack of an integrated approach perpetuate the criminalisation and stigmatisation of the poor and lead to the reproduction rather than the reduction of punishment. In Missouri there appears to be a more stable situation and a declining prison population. Kelli Canada and Scott O'Kelley remind us that the incarceration rate in the USA is the highest in the world with a continuing over-representation of Black, Native American and Latinx people, but add that its criminal justice system is one of the largest mental health service providers. Against this background, they use rehabilitation programmes in Missouri to illustrate how people are diverted or engaged as they progress through the system, and they do this using the five points of the Sequential Intercept Model. While the current criminal justice policy in the Netherlands pays increasing attention to rehabilitation, Sonja Meijer and Elanie Rodermond begin their Chapter with a glance back at the discipline of the 'spinning houses' of the seventeenth century and move on to describe the system of promotion and demotion to either the plus or basic programmes in Dutch prisons. They expose the limited interpretation given to the principle of rehabilitation in the Netherlands and how more emphasis is placed on an approach to reintegration using among other methods, mentors. While this is driven by a desistence model, they argue that it is undermined by the credence given to individual self-reliance.

Alice Mills and Robert Webb point to the paradox that Aotearoa New Zealand is reputed to be the home of restorative justice approaches but has a punitive criminal justice system that impacts disproportionately on the Māori who are overrepresented in prisons, community sentences and recidivism rates. The authors look critically at attempts to make rehabilitative processes more culturally appropriate for Māori through the adoption of tikanga (cultural) Māori practices such as Te Hikoitanga, a corrections-based reintegration unit, but conclude that the recent trend towards self-responsibilisation, 'risk' management and individual change-focused rehabilitation has led to the neglect of other approaches to rehabilitation such as strengths-based and Good Lives models. Beginning with Durkheim's famous dictum that crime is normal, Emmanuel Onyeozili and Bonaventure Chigozie Uzoh describe the failure of the Nigerian Criminal Justice System to deal with what they term an existential crime problem, and how colonisation led to the replacing of informal houses of detention like the Ogboni House of the Yoruba people with formal prisons. While they argue that the shift from punishment to reformation and rehabilitation has been undermined by corruption, inadequate support systems and lack of financial backing, they point to glimmers of hope in the form of the Nigerian Corrections Service Act of 2019 and the first custodial centres for women. John Todd-Kvam's broad sweep of Norwegian penality and rehabilitation provides the historical and contemporary context for mechanisms of rehabilitation and reintegration. With a nod towards what he describes as the dark side of Scandinavian exceptionalism with its poor remand conditions and treatment of immigrants, and harsh drug sentencing, he explores the thinking behind the rehabilitative efforts of the Norwegian Correctional Service. The Chapter gives a clear picture of how the theoretical and evidential bases of practice have shifted away from treatment and how the interventionist zeal of the State has become less oppressive and more informed by the two ethical and pragmatic rationales of rehabilitation. Like other contributions it looks ahead to some of the main challenges facing those attempting to promote rehabilitation and reintegration.

Ioan Durnescu, Andrada Istrate and Iuliana Carbunaru devote their critical attention to pre- and post-communist Romania, revealing how the reclassification of 'offenders' to citizens by the Penal Code of 1938 was later transposed into the communist regime's aim of producing 'docile people' of use to the State. They set out the process of probation's introduction after the fall of communism and the creation in the 2000s of 13 programmes based on cognitive-behaviouralism, social learning theory and desistance. Of particular interest is the reference to the use of a therapeutic community with women prisoners and a mentoring programme for Roma. Liz Gilchrist and Amy Johnson set their Chapter on Scotland against the background of the 2019 Growing Up survey that confirmed the continuing prevalence of adverse childhood experiences emanating from the poverty and deprivation that has a long history in Scotland. In an explanation of the differences in the Scottish criminal justice system compared to the rest of the United Kingdom they highlight how a community justice and social welfare approach, particularly with women and children, influences Scotland's approach to general practice and projects such as the Caledonian Programme. Shanta Balgobind Singh and Patrick Bashizi Bashigi Murhula introduce us to Department of Correctional Services' Batho Pele (people first) policy and the constitutionally mandated rehabilitation programmes in South Africa that are based on a needs-based care approach need and the targeting of problems associated with offending (criminogenic needs), but that are undermined by a limited level of political commitment. In addition, drawing on their interviews with prisoners, academics, and correctional centre personnel, they provide a critique of rehabilitation approaches and the reasons for their failure.

Although the principles of rehabilitation have been enshrined in post-Franco Spain's constitution and since the 1990s diversion from custody has been attempted through cognitive-behavioural programmes, Ester Blay tells a familiar story of a general hardening of penal policies, women and minorities having less access to programmes, and scarce research with mixed results. Although, following the death of Franco the language of law and order became less manifest, the criminal justice system became progressively more punitive. In contrast, however, in prison rehabilitation has manifested itself in the intriguing concept of drug-free *rooms of respect* in which inmates enjoy a greater level of autonomy provided they agree to abide by a stricter set of rules. Perhaps, a longer tradition of welfare systems and rehabilitation has been the characteristic of Sweden's criminal justice system but there too in the last three years rehabilitative programmes, influenced by 1990s *What Works* and incorporating the now well-established principles and showing some promising research results, have faced critical challenges in terms of access and quality as well as pressures for a more punitive response driven in part by the increase in gun homicides since 2005. As Martin Lardén tells the reader, prison and probation is a combined service that in the future needs to focus on better integration of rehabilitative interventions and effective transfer to the community. Susyan Jou, Shang-Kai Shen and Bill Hebenton introduce us to Taiwan's approach to rehabilitation with reference to four key developments, namely, the Juvenile Delinquency and Justice Act of 1962 that introduced a juvenile probation and parole service; the extension to adults by the Security Measures Execution Act of 1980; the provision of a voluntary re-entry service to people attempting to lead offence-free lives by the Taiwan After-care Association; and the post-2000 governmental purchased rehabilitation services that include family and victim support projects. In a critical account, they argue that the approach to rehabilitation in Taiwan is formal and legalistic and identify the critical tensions that flow from this.

Anita Kalunta Crumpton explains that in Texas, which is nearer the USA template of high incarceration rates, in recent years there has been an ideological and practical shift to rehabilitation with its intensive supervision programme involving such therapeutic interventions as Reality Therapy. Her Chapter provides an overview of the complicated context of rehabilitation in Texas and critiques the success or otherwise of the crime control strategies. Nathee Chitsawang and Pimporn Netrabukkana illuminate the early Western influence on Thailand's rehabilitation policies and the heavy reliance on imprisonment combined with vocational training. Familiar problems of overcrowding and the high percentage of prisoners both male and female with drug problems have dominated and stimulated a strong emphasis on rehabilitative programmes, such as the Therapeutic Community Programme that includes among other things, music therapy. They describe how approaches to rehabilitation and in particular the application of the United Nations Rules for the Treatment of Women Prisoners and Non-custodial Measures for Women Offenders, known as 'the Bangkok Rules', are hindered by overcrowding and limited resources. Philippe Pottier traces the history of the changes in Tunisia's Penal Code from the nineteenth century to post-independence in 1956 and the period since the 2011 revolution. The Chapter contains an interesting account of how against a backdrop of a high prison population and poor conditions, the freedom of expression that followed the 2011 revolution pushed the government towards rehabilitation and prevention of recidivism. This is brought vividly to life by the story of the first experimental probation office in Souse that came into being after the 2011 fire in Monastir prison that led to 70 deaths. The positivity of the story is, however, tempered by current uncertainty surrounding the suspension of parliament in 2021. Economic and social problems are a feature of Ana Vigna and Ana Juanche's exposition of how Uruguay at the beginning of the twenty-first century has the highest level of incarceration in South America and how, in 2009, the United Nations Rapporteur on Torture, Manfred Nowak ranked Uruguayan prisons among the worst in the world, despite the Frente Amplio (progressive party) being in power. Although the government has undertaken a process of prison reform and introduced Reasoning and Rehabilitation influenced programmes such as the Pro-Social Thought Programme and the Theatre with Masks for 18–24-year-olds, they identify the structural challenges it faces. Finally, within the context of Governor's claim, with little research evidence, that Virginia has the lowest reconviction rate (22.4%) of 45 States, Danielle Rudes, Benjamin Mackey and Madeline McPherson present the stark regional differences between the wealthy north and the poor west where confederate flags still fly. While there is a steadily increasing prison population, they point out that a large and robust community corrections system that includes, for example, a Cognitive Process Therapy programme for female survivors of sexual assault, gives cause for optimism.

References

Bean, P. (1976). *Rehabilitation and deviance*. Routledge and Kegan Paul.
Burke, L., Collett, S., & McNeill, F. (2019). *Reimagining rehabilitation: Beyond the individual*. Routledge.

Carlen, P. (2002). Women's imprisonment: Cross-national lessons. In P. Carlen (Ed.), *Women and punishment. The struggle for justice.* Willan Publishing.

Carlen, P. (2012). Against rehabilitation: For reparative justice. In K. M. Carrington, E. Ball, O'Brien & J. Tauri (Eds.), *Crime, justice and social democracy: International perspective.* Palgrave Macmillan.

Crow, I. (2001). *The treatment and rehabilitation of offenders.* Sage Publications.

Farrall, S. (2002). *Rethinking what works with offenders.* Willan.

Hamai, K., Villé, H. R., Hough, M., & Zvekic, U. (1995). *Probation round the world: A comparative study.* Routledge.

Hollin, C. (2001). Rehabilitation. In E. McLaughlin & J. Muncie (Eds.), *The sage dictionary of criminology.* Sage Publications Ltd.

Lewis, C. S. (1949). The humanitarian theory of punishment, *20th Century: An Australian Quarterly Review, 3*(3), 5–12.

Maruna, S. (2001). *Making good: How ex-convicts reform and rebuild their lives.* American Psychological Association.

McNeill, F. (2012). Four forms of offender rehabilitation: Towards an interdisciplinary perspective. *Legal and Criminological Psychology, 17*(1), 18–36.

Raynor, P., & Robinson, G. (2005). *Rehabilitation, crime and justice.* Palgrave Macmillan.

Reid, W. J., & Epstein, L. (1972). *Task-centred casework.* Columbia University Press.

Timasheff, N. S. (1941). *One hundred years of probation 1841*–1941, *Part One: Probation in the United States, England and the commonwealth of nations.* Fordham University Press.

Timasheff, N. S. (1943). *One hundred years of probation 1841–1941, Part Two: Probation in Continental Europe, Latin America, Asia, and Africa.* Fordham University Press.

Wootton, B. (1959). *Social science and pathology.* George Allen & Unwin.

Law, Economic Crisis, and Diversity: An Overview of Rehabilitation in Argentina

María Jimena Monsalve

The Broad Constitutional Context

The 1853 Argentine Constitution proclaims in section 18 that prisons are for rehabilitation not for punishment and, therefore, the pro homine principle should rule the sanction; however, there is some way to go before this is achieved. The later Argentine National Criminal Code[1] enacted in 1921, has undergone many changes over the years, but the original text includes parole (sections 13, 14, 15, 16, and 17), conditional sentence (sections 26, 27, 28), and incorporates a restorative justice approach to criminal conflict (sections 29, 30, 31, and 32). It is section 76 bis that provides the conditional suspension of the process. Through section 27 the court can attach the conditional sentence to one or more requirements, including community service, medical treatments, and supervision, among others; and section 10 incorporates house arrest and specifies vulnerable groups such as mothers and their children, the disabled, adults over 70 years, the terminally ill, and people with illnesses that cannot be adequately treated in prison. Even though the code applies to the whole country, section 5 ensures that the 24 provinces have autonomy.[2] Accordingly, the criminal process has a federal code[3] that allows each province to make its own decisions about how to deal with crimes that

---

M. J. Monsalve (✉)
5th National Penal Enforcement Court, Buenos Aires, Argentina
e-mail: Jimenamonsalve12@gmail.com

are not federal. Moreover, procedural codes determine rules for the courts and give what are called the Penal Enforce Judges their authority: only two provinces do not have Penal Enforce Judges. These judges work on alternative measures, control prison conditions, and make decisions about early release. Most courts have been recently established and have a vast number of cases to attend to, social claims against them to deal with, and insufficient resources. The system originated with a commitment that its processes, and their legality would be monitored under the auspices of international Human Rights documents (dating from 1955 to 2015), one of which is the Mandela Rules.[4] Furthermore, most courts pay heed to the United Nations' Tokyo Rules, section 8,[5] and since 1994 article 75, paragraph 22 of the National Constitution has included international treaties that, like the Magna Carta, have enshrined fundamental rights (Beiras, 2008).

The Law and Rehabilitation

Since 1996, the National Law for Penal Enforcement[6] has incorporated several options for rehabilitation based on early release, semi-detention regimes, nightly or daily prison, and domiciliary prison, but there seems to be no scope for community-based rehabilitation. The purpose of sentencing proposed by this law is underpinned by the rehabilitative principle of social integration, not punishment. Although the language of the law fits with that principle, the truth is that the original letter of the law and its legislative foundations had a broader axis related to inter-discipline and prison treatment (Baratta, 2004). Thus, the law spells out the steps to follow in all areas related to life in prison, regulating work, education, relationships, and criminological aspects, including the steps to follow in the post-release stage.

Prisons in Argentina are commonly located in ancient buildings and in some jurisdictions the budget is not enough to maintain a minimum standard of conditions for prisoners. Moreover, the imprisonment rate is due to a phenomenon called the Criminal Popular Punitive Movement (Sozzo, 2019), which proposes to react to crime only with imprisonment strategies and no responsible analysis about crime or the need for reforms. Political interests, not based on research or statistics, exploit people's insecurities in order to introduce more strict laws.

The Federal Penitentiary Service (SPF) is the institution of the National State in charge of the management and administration of penitentiary establishments and the execution of criminological programmes aimed at reducing recidivism, discouraging crime, and contributing to public security. The treatment programmes aim to ensure that persons deprived of their liberty acquire behaviour guidelines and tools for reintegrating into society. The administration of human resources is committed to ensuring that prison staff integrate a humanistic, scientific, and efficient approach that leads to research on sentencing, and collaboration with academic institutions linked to the study of the theory of punishment. The SPF depends on the Sub Secretary for Relations with the Judiciary and Penitentiary Affairs of the Ministry of Justice and Human Rights. That role has its origins in the 1933 No. 11,833 law on the prison organization and penalty regime updated by Organic Law No. 20,416, the Law of Execution of the Deprivation of Liberty Sentence No. 24,660, and complementary regulations.[7] Most Argentine provinces have their penitentiary services with their own internal organisation unless they sign agreements with the federal government to use their federal prisons.

The conditions for granting early release and alternative measures are of the utmost importance in the law (except for parole) and are regulated by section 13 of the Penal Code. Some articles from the original text of Law 24,660 were removed or modified to limit the access (to early release) of people who have committed certain crimes considered too serious by the legislator. At the end of 2004, through Law 25,948 section 56, new articles were introduced that excluded temporary releases or semi-freedom, assisted freedom and the discontinuous prison regime or semi-detention for people convicted of homicide, sexual crimes, and coercive deprivation of liberty that result in the death of the victim, homicide committed in the course of a robbery, and kidnapping and demanding a ransom for the safety of the victim. Section 14 of the Criminal Code excludes people who had committed the same crimes listed above from conditional release. Subsequently, in 2009, Law 26,472 approved the use of house arrest for vulnerable group such as adults over 70 years of age, people with disabilities, pregnant women, or ill people whose imprisonment would violate their human rights. In addition, this section takes account of the welfare of the children of those sentenced and endeavours to ensure that innocent third parties are not indirectly punished.

In 2011, the Federal Law of Education introduced a positive reform in the form a prison educational system aimed at contributing to a more effective rehabilitation scheme. It allowed people who achieved academic qualifications to discount up to 20 months of their sentence by access to progressive institutions. There are two paths in this scheme: firstly, through the educational achievements that correspond to the primary and compulsory formal education that govern all citizens in primary and secondary school; and secondly, through professional training courses validated by institutions that teach them and certify the hours and content of learning. This depends, of course, on the educational programmes being in force in each province where the prisons are located (Herrera, 2011). This scheme includes university education as an option. It is worth remembering that in 1987 in the Argentine Republic, within the scope of the Federal Penitentiary Service,[8] the first university—the Devoted University Center (CUD), dependent on the University of Buenos Aires (UBA)—began to function inside a prison, teaching law, sociology, psychology, and economic sciences. Subsequently, university centres were extended to other prisons in the country, and agreements were reached with other universities (Parchuk, 2015).[9] For example, UBA XXII is a programme of the University of Buenos Aires, dependent on the Secretary of Academic Affairs, which teaches undergraduate courses and face-to-face courses (extension activities) in the Federal Penitentiary Service establishments. Its purpose is to guarantee access to curricular and extracurricular university training for people unable to travel to the university. Its approach to study is unique and distinguishes it from the rest of the university's proposals. The possibility of distance education has been gradually incorporated and intensified during the last two years of the Covid 19 pandemic.

Although it did not receive a favourable reception in the Federal Penitentiary System, another significant advance that occurred during the pandemic was the authorisation of the use of mobile phones in prison services of some provinces. It was thought that communication with the outside could not always be ensured by other means, such as videoconferencing and landline telephone communications. Moreover, in the provincial systems, especially in the province of Buenos Aires, overcrowding and massive incarceration made it impossible to ensure the right to effective communication with the family group.[10] Although the authorisation to use mobile phones emerged as necessary to facilitate family contact for prisoners during the isolation caused by Covid 19, approval also allowed access to distance education. This created the opportunity for inmates to access the same quality of education available to any student in the pandemic.

The 2017 Reform and Its Consequences

In 2017, Law 27,375 was passed, and it toughened the legal requirements for access to early release in any of its forms, while at the same time insisted on adherence to the formula, incorporated in 2004. This excluded people from the regimes of semi-liberty, temporary releases, parole, assisted freedom, and intermittent prison not only if they had been convicted of the crimes referred to above but also, human trafficking; financing of terrorism or any other crime that has been committed with the purpose of terrorising the population or forcing national public authorities or foreign governments or agents of an international organization to carry out an act or to refrain from doing so; and certain crimes related to narcotics, such as commercialization, transportation, and some forms of smuggling. This reform had several adverse effects. The first and most serious was to generate a loss of coherence in the text of the law as far as it states progressiveness as a fundamental principle of prison treatment and rehabilitation. It stipulates that people go through various stages or periods to obtain access to more beneficial regimes with fewer restrictions, and by limiting access for some people through assumption rather than fact undermines the very principles proclaimed by the law.

This has generated not only a lack of motivation in prisoners to take an interest in the activities and treatment programmes that once allowed them to leave prison earlier or access progressively more open regimes, but it has also produced overcrowding since a direct consequence of this rule has been the extension of the period people spend in prison. It has also entailed additional litigation, as jurisprudential evidence shows the existence of two interpretations that coexist, one that declares the unconstitutionality of the norm and another that says it is valid. This has only served the purpose of generating, for prisoners, greater inequality before the law, and it should be noted that this reform was not carried out based on empirical evidence that would allow these restrictions to be justified responsibly, rather it was produced for political reasons and emanated from a poor debate in the National Congress.

The Results of the Economic Crisis

Over the last few decades, Argentina has been suffering a constant economic crisis, impacting on the social situation. Crime is directly affected by poverty in the country. The incarceration rate was 94 over 100,000 in 1999, increased to 224 in 2019 and decreased to 209 in 2020. However, if detentions in non-penitentiary places (like police stations and other security forces places to put people in detention) are added the rate was 243 in 2019 and 235 in 2020. The reduction in 2020 is only due to the pandemic restrictions and the National System of Statistics of Penal Enforcement 2021 (SNEEP) is likely to report a further rise. Sadly, there are several problems with statistics. Since 2002, SNEEP[11] has provided statistics about prisons. The last official numbers from SNEEP are from 2020 so they do not account for the fact that because of the restrictions imposed during the pandemic crime and rates of incarceration fell but once the restrictions were lifted in 2021 both increased. There are 32 federal penitentiary institutions in Argentina, with establishments located throughout the country. There are also 286 prisons organised under provincial or police prison systems at the local level; 64 prisons and half the country's prisoners (42,791) are concentrated in the province of Buenos Aires and, therefore, prisons are located under different legal and political powers. It has not been easy to collect comparable data for the entire country because they do not have the same analysis parameters or the necessary scientific rigour. The first national prison census was carried out in 1906 and until the creation of SNEEP in 2002 data collection was partial.

The SNEEP survey of 2020 showed that between 2017 and 2018 the rate of incarceration increased by 155% and revealed a profile of prisoners similar to that of prison populations in many countries throughout the world in so far as the majority (96%) were single males from urban areas, were aged between 24 and 34 years with limited educational and professional qualifications (for details readers can refer to full report described in note 11). Only 4% were women, and just 0.1% were transgender (the number of women in prison in Argentina is significantly lower than the 10% figures reported by other countries in the region). Over 50% were receiving treatment for the control or prevention of drug abuse and a significant number had mental health-related problems. Just over a third were serving sentences of between 3 and 6 years, and a small percentage were serving sentences of more than 18 years or life. Attempts to rehabilitate prisoners were hindered by the fact that only a minority took up opportunities for job training or educational programmes, and the vast majority did not have access to, or agree to, schemes designed to assist the process of release and reintegration into their community. Against that, a considerable majority had regular contact with family and friends through prison visits and nearly three quarters maintained exemplary behaviour records.

Other SNEEP data illustrates some of the severe problems experienced by people deprived of liberty. For example, the prison population was made up of a total of 106,559 people housed in both prison and police establishments. Of this group, 11,615 were housed in police establishments or police stations, spaces that do not offer people any possibility of prison treatment or rehabilitation (a situation that also causes difficulty in data collection). Others were detained in buildings belonging to security forces, others were under house arrest, and adolescents in places specially prepared for them. When those on remand eventually appeared before the court just under a half were found not guilty. Similar problems are evident in post-prison policies. The federal system is poorly equipped to deal with the network required to apply alternative measures in response to offending, but each province deals with the design of this network aimed at people who commit common crimes in its territory. In addition to a scarcity of resources both at the national and local level and an absence of state responsibility to reinforce these networks, there is also no possibility of a homogeneous collection of data, which makes it impossible to know precisely how many people are being monitored or supervised throughout the country.

Diversity and the Law

Argentina has a strong tradition of developing laws and practices related to diversity and this includes LGBTQ+ groups, and vulnerable people. Gender policies, which continue to evolve, began with the efforts of feminist groups that created several opportunities for the legislature and non-governmental organisations to contribute to gender equality. Vulnerable groups are protected by provisions in the constitution and in 2018 the Argentine Chamber of Deputies gave their approval to Micaela's Law.[12] This law established mandatory training on gender and violence against women for all people who work in public office, at all levels and hierarchies in the Executive, Legislative and Judicial branches of the Nation, and made the National Institute of Women responsible for certifying the training implemented by each body. Thus, the federal and provincial penitentiary services, and the members of the armed and security forces, who depend on the local or national Executive power, as well as all the members of the Judicial Power (including the magistrates who control preventive prisons and sentences) are included in this legal obligation of training. This training and awareness-raising process is currently underway for all members of staff who make up the penitentiary services, both federal and provincial combined, and these developments have had an impact on judicial decisions, prison conditions, promoted gender-respectful measures for vulnerable groups, and reduced the number of mothers and LGBTI people in prison with their children. It is interesting to note that since 2020 the categories of the gender definitions have expanded to include, for example, trans women and men, and transvestites. Moreover, since 2016, trans people have been accepted in the Federal Penitentiary Service.

Argentina is going through a process of broad recognition of human rights, especially of vulnerable groups. The promotion of the gender perspective as the axis of public policy aims to protect these groups and, in this way, promote understanding of the principles of equality and non-discrimination. Although there is an arduous road ahead to achieve a consistent approach throughout the country, general access to their human rights has been formalised in law, and in turn this has not only given visibility to these problems, but also obligated everyone, including public officials, to adhere, without prejudice, to truly transformative policies. In particular, the Law for the Comprehensive Protection of Women, the Gender Identity Law, the Same-Sex Marriage Law, Micaela Law, and the Promotion of Access to Formal Employment for Transvestites, Transsexuals and Transgender Persons or Diana Sacayán-Lohana Berkins Law have traced a path of demand and interpretation that challenges inveterate norms without a gender perspective, such as the Criminal Code, the Federal Procedural Codes (both the version of the 1992 National Criminal Procedural Code and the still partially valid 2014 Federal Criminal Procedure Code), the Provincial Criminal Procedure Codes, the National Law of Criminal Enforcement, and provincial laws, all of which hinder progress. In addition to these impediments the internal regulations that govern the lives of prisoners have not been updated in line with these laws.[13]

On the positive side, it must be acknowledged that different public organisations, such as the National Institute against Discrimination (INADI),[14] have adopted, disseminated, and demanded compliance with these principles, and run programmes and activities related to the subject in prisons. At the same time, there has been a sustained growth in the presence of Non-Governmental Organizations (NGOs) dedicated primarily to the subject and to the vigorous defence of women's rights. In brief, links have been established between governmental and non-governmental organisations and federal and provincial prison services to raise awareness on the matter, offer activities, training for prison staff, and design treatment programmes aimed explicitly at cases of gender violence, femicide, and crimes against sexual integrity. A clear example is the programmes developed by the Federal Penitentiary Service that, through the psycho-socio-health and interdisciplinary approach, focuses on such crimes. The results of these programmes are contained in the quarterly reports issued by the disciplinary councils.

There is still room for improvement. Sentencing does not fully take account of the LGBTI group even though Law 24,660 has been reformed and modified. The public generally and the legislators specifically have yet to fully adjust to the gender and diversity perspective, and retrograde norms of a punitive nature have undermined the progressive intent of the laws. As a consequence, there are several situations when the rights of LGBTI people are violated as they enter the penal system, primarily when they encounter members of the security forces who have not had the necessary training and when they enter police stations and other detention spaces that do not have areas suitable for receiving LGBTI people. Indeed, these places have not even been modified to meet the needs of women so the chances of a response to the needs of LGBTI groups are distant.

Rehabilitation and Restorative Justice

Given that the majority of people who arrive in prison have throughout their lives been victims of violence, have not completed their education, have not accessed either formal or informal jobs, have problems related to drug and or alcohol abuse, have come from so-called 'popular neighbourhoods' with poor living conditions, and have difficulty of access to essential public services and even to a good diet, the necessity of rehabilitation programmes with some focus on the restitution of rights is axiomatic. In addition, such programmes need to focus on problems related to the personal circumstances of most prisoners. A study drawing on the perceptions of a representative sample of 1200 people imprisoned in federal prisons and the province of Buenos Aires showed that nearly 80% live in a criminal environment without a family or close relationships (CELIV, 2020). Imprisonment provides the State with the first opportunity to engage with these problems and help people access specific networks of support or social assistance rather than merely impose sanctions.

Unfortunately, when prisoners are released the general public, media, and a large part of the authorities are more concerned about the need for control rather than social integration. Concern about reoffending supersedes acceptance of the need for the generation of networks that allow people to strengthen family and social ties, acquire the skills to access education and formal employment in a free environment, and above all, free themselves from the stigma of being an ex-prisoner. According to Constitutional Law, Conventional System Law, and Criminal Law in Argentina, inclusion and rehabilitation are supposed to be elementary items related to penal sanctions. Even though many social assistance programmes may exist, they are not specifically for people who have offended: Public Health and Public Education help, but it is almost impossible to access formal work or a place to lives. According to the Criminal Code, a person's criminal record remains for ten years thus perpetuating stigma and labelling.

A recent initiative related to dealing with internal conflicts in prisons has been the approval of the protocol, developed for the Penal Unit No.

15 of Batán, Buenos Aires province, based on the principles of Restorative Justice as a basic tool for the resolution of conflicts. This is novel in the Argentine regulations. Based on restorative justice theory it deals with the victim-perpetrator relationship to ensure that the perpetrator identifies and recognises the damage inflicted and develops empathy in order to repair the pain caused. It was first applied in August 2019 and on June 25, 2020, prison staff and detainees were able, using digital media to explain the public and people involved in the imposition and execution of sentence with total clarity and simplicity that conflict had decreased more than considerably since implementing an approach in which victim and perpetrator cooperated in the diagnosis of problems. This process of good practice, opening the doors of the prison and normalising those involved, created the opportunity of a dialogue of understanding and the construction of solutions according to the actual needs of prisoners (Monsalve, 2020).

In contrast, the system in Argentina has several difficulties related to the control and assistance of people serving suspended sentences and the supervision of people on parole. The problem stems initially from the fact that human and economic resources are inadequate. Earlier, the work was undertaken in every province by private institutions with the support of some public funding. Then in 2015 national and federal jurisdiction was created by the Control and Assistance Direction of Criminal Enforcement (Dirección de Control y Asistencia de Ejecución Penal). Sadly, this is a prime example of what does not work. The law determined that 180 agents should be involved but the Federal Supreme Court created only half that number, so as the Directorate for Control and Assistance in Criminal Enforcement disclosed in its latest management report, in 2012 13,160 people were dealt with by 90 agents (Barreyro, 2022).

Historically, the approach to the social integration of people in conflict with the criminal law was undertaken by 'patronages of the liberated', some of which still exist. Many of them were civil society organisations that receive contributions from public organisations such as prison services. These models gradually became obsolete as the prison population grew and financing aid agreements were curtailed. One of the most traditional and historical was the Patronage of Liberated and Released Prisoners of the Autonomous City of Buenos Aires that Dr. Jorge H. Frías created in 1918 from his position as judge of the Chamber of Criminal and Correctional Appeals. A private institution, it proposed the readaptation of ex-prisoners to society by assisting their families while they were in prison and providing them with work and means of subsistence upon release. These schemes were based on the tradition of the Catholic Church of conducting charitable activities for the neediest groups. Frías always expressed great concern for the children of prisoners, always maintaining that because they had lost their freedom, they should not lose their rights to the aid of the religion (Nuñez, 2007).

Although since the enactment of Law 27,080 on January 27, 2015, the Frías patronage ceased to exist and became a public institution dependent on the Nation's Judicial Power (the Directorate of Control and Assistance of Criminal Enforcement), the relationship with the Catholic Church continues to offer alternatives through the 'Hogares de Cristo' network, whose purpose is to achieve social integration in general but also provide help to people who have passed through the penal system. They include programmes linked to [15] The Secretariat of Comprehensive Policies on Drugs of the Argentine Nation, (SEDRONAR) the body in charge of coordinating public policies focused on the prevention, care, assistance, and supervision of people with problematic substance use throughout the national territory. It offers housing in spaces conceived as halfway houses for people who need support and treatment for a time. The experience was born from the initiative of a group of priests who worked in widespread neighbourhoods. Today, they have built up a strong network of social assistance and rehabilitation, with the help of other public institutions.[16]

At the federal level, there are two public offices dedicated to the social integration of people who have passed through the penal system: the Directorate for Control and Assistance in Criminal Enforcement, which is dependent on the National Judiciary; and the National Directorate of Social Rehabilitation,[17] which in turn is dependent on the Ministry of Justice and Human Rights of the Nation (belonging to the Executive Power of the Nation). Both organisations have interdisciplinary teams that include psychologists and social workers, as well as lawyers. Although they have common objectives, the National Directorate for Social Rehabilitation has more scope to make agreements about employment even with private companies: moreover, it has a specific office—a subsidiary of the National Registry of Persons—to provide documentation to anyone who needs it. Despite limited financial resources both organisations have the capacity to be helpful, especially in emergencies.

Conclusion: Future Possibilities

A fundamental problem in the way of rehabilitation and reintegration into the community is the length of time a person's offending remains on their criminal record. As indicated previously, the Penal Code, section 51, determines that the conviction record remains in force for ten years after the prison sentence or suspended sentence and five years after the expiration of a fine and disqualification. This has the effect of entrenching stigmatisation, decreasing the individual's chances of gaining employment, and ultimately prolonging recidivism. Its constitutionality is challengeable on the grounds that it violates the principle of culpability, undermines the proportionality of punishment, and exposes the individual to being punished and sentenced again for the same offence. It has been viewed by some commentators as cruel, inhuman, and degrading (Bergalli, 1980; Zaffaroni, 2020; Zaffaroni et al., 2002).

Cooperatives represent an exciting and interesting means of dealing with this problem in so far as they increase the chances of individuals accessing a livelihood by bringing people with criminal records together within a cooperative model. They conduct organised activities and productive projects that allow such individuals to have an income, and in this way, Cooperatives constitute a significant source of work and personal development. Currently, people with criminal records are prohibited, by section 64 of the Cooperatives Law, from serving on the board of a cooperative, and there is a growing recognition that this inhibits rehabilitation. Congress, therefore, has been asked to approve the modification of this law. In 2019, the XIV National Meeting of Criminal Enforcement Justice organised by the Argentine Association of Criminal Enforcement Justice (held at the National University of Mar del Plata in the Province of Buenos Aires) issued the following statement:

> The reform of section 64 of the Law of Cooperatives that admits that people can integrate the Board of Directors of those with criminal records, is compatible with the provisions of section 18 of the National Constitution and the conventionality block integrated by section 75, paragraph 22, to ensure the broad right to work and social integration. In this way, it directly impacts the reduction of relapse in crime. It ensures the rights of the families of these people, especially minor sons and daughters who depend absolutely on the income of their parents to exist.

It is encouraging that in the prisons, various organisations have stimulated artistic expression through the development of music, painting, and writing workshops. In addition, committed volunteers, in collaboration with civil society organisations, have enhanced educational opportunities with the creation of libraries and literary workshops in spaces dedicated to reading and the exchange of ideas and knowledge. In the community, the social aid network promoted by the Ministry of Social Development allows access, without restriction, to all its programmes for people who have come into conflict with criminal law. However, many people do not become users of these programmes, because either they are unaware, lack the necessary documentation or simply believe that they are not allowed access. It is important, therefore, that networks are strengthened through the involvement of social workers who are better placed to support pre-release and early release programmes.

Improvements in research are needed too. Even though some public and private universities produce evidence, empirical studies on rehabilitation are thin on the ground. Some studies have focused on the social, working, or educational background of groups that commit crime, and others on the impact of imprisonment on vulnerable groups. However, researchers need to focus, for example, on the effectiveness of alternative measures, the effect of incarceration on prisoners and their families, and the cost of incarceration compared to community measures. All these positive developments are in jeopardy from a proposed Criminal Code project sent to Congress in 2019 intended to increase severe restrictions and sanctions. Fortunately, it has not yet been approved.

Notes

1. Law 11, 179 (1921) Penal Code of the Argentine Nation.
2. National Constitution of the Argentine Republic (1953–1994).
3. Law 23,984 (1991) Code of Criminal Procedure of the Nation. Official Gazette of the Argentine Republic No. 27.215.
4. The United Nations Estándar Minimum Rules for the Treatment of Prisoners (The Nelson Mandela Rules) (1955–2015) United Nations. United Nations Office on Drugs and Crime.
5. United Nations Standard Minimum Rules for Non-Custodial Measures, The Tokyo Rules (1990) United Nations. United Nations Office on Drugs and Crime.
6. Law 24,660 (1996) National Law of Criminal Execution, Official Gazette of the Argentine Republic No. 28436.
7. For more information about Servicio Penitenciario Federal https://www.argentina.gob.ar/spf/acerca-de-nosotros/mision-y-objetivos.
8. Agreement between the University of Buenos Aires and the Federal Penitentiary Service, Resolution 63/86, University of Buenos Aires. Brief history of CUSAM, https://www.unsam.edu.ar/cusam/historia.asp.
9. For more information about UBA XXII program consult https://www.uba.ar/academicos/contenidos.php?id=88.
10. Protocol for the use of cell phones by inmates of the Bonaerense Penitentiary Service, Penitentiary Service of the Province of Buenos Aires (2020).
11. System of Statistics on Execution of the Penal SNEEP 2020 (2020) National Directorate of Criminal Policy in Matters of Justice and Criminal Legislation.

Undersecretary of Criminal Policy. Secretary of Human Rights. Ministry of Justice and Human Rights of the Nation.
12. Named after Micaela Garcia who was murdered in 2017.
13. Law 26.485 Law on comprehensive protection to prevent, punish and eradicate violence against women in the areas in which they develop their interpersonal relationships' (2009) Official Gazette of the Argentine Republic No. 21,632.

    Law 26.743 Gender Identity Law (2012) Official Gazette of the Argentine Republic No. 32,404.

    Law 26,618 Civil Code. Modification. Civil Marriage Law (2010) Official Gazette of the Argentine Republic No. 31,949.

    Law 27,499, Micaela Law of Mandatory Training in the subject of Gender and violence against women (2018) Official Gazette of the Argentine Republic No. 34,031.

    Law 27,636, 'Law on the promotion of access to formal employment' Diana Sacayan—Lohana Berkins' (2021) Official Gazette of the Argentine Republic No. 34,697.
14. For more information about INADI consult https://www.argentina.gob.ar/inadi.
15. For more information about SEDRONAR consult https://www.argentina.gob.ar/jefatura/sedronar.
16. For more information about 'Hogares de Cristo' consult https://hogardecristo.org.ar/.
17. For more information consult https://www.argentina.gob.ar/justicia/politicacriminal/readaptacion.

References

Baratta, A. (2004). *Criminología crítica y crítica del derecho penal. Introduccion a la sociologia juridico-penal.* Siglo Veintuno Editores.

Barreyro, V. (2022). *Informe Periódico de Gestión de la DCAEP. Dirección de Control y Asistencia a la Ejecución Penal.* Federal Chamber of Criminal Cassation.

Beiras, R. I. (2008). La cuestión de la prisión. Port Editors.

Bergalli, R. (1980). *La recaída en el crimen: formas de reaccionar contra él: la perspectiva histórico-criminal en la República Argentina y su análisis según el enfoque etiquetado-Enfoque.* The Santor.

Centre of Latin American Studies about Insecurity and Violence (CELIV). (2020). *Presos en Argentina: un análisis comparativo en perspectiva temporal 2013–2019.* Universidad Nacional de Tres Febrero.

Herrera, P. F. V. (2011). Formación para el trabajo en contextos de confinamiento. Ministry of Education of the Nation.

Monsalve, M. J. (2020). Pequeños grandes cambios. Revista Asociación Pensamiento Penal.

Núñez, J. (2007). De Félix a Jorge H. Frías: catolicismo social, beneficencia y Estado en la Argentina. *I Jornadas Nacionales de Historia Social*, *30*, 31 de mayo y 1 de junio de 2007, La Falda, Córdoba.

Parchuk, J. P. (2015). La Universidad en Prisión: Teoría, Debates, Acciones. Redes de extension (pp. 18–36). University of Buenos Aires.

Sozzo, M. (2019). Populismo punitivo, proyecto normalizador y "prisión depósito" en Argentina, Jura Gentium, available at https://www.juragentium.org/topics/latina/es/sozzo/htm

Zaffaroni, E. R. (2020). Directrices de Derecho Penal. Ediar (pp. 290–293).

Zaffaroni, R. Alagia, A., & Slokar, A. W. (2002). Parte General de Derecho Penal. Segunda edición. Ediar.

Rehabilitation and Beyond in Settler Colonial Australia: Current and Future Directions in Policy and Practice

Sophie Russell, James Beaufils, and Chris Cunneen

As other Chapters in this edited collection have pointed to, and as scholars in the field of criminal legal punishment have previously noted (Burke et al., 2019), the concept of rehabilitation and its practice is both complex and contested—*what* is counted as rehabilitation, *where* it takes place, and *who* is subject to it—are all important questions with potentially different answers depending on who is asked. Providing an account of rehabilitation becomes distinctly more complicated in a federal nation such as Australia—with its states and territories responsible for administering the criminal legal system over an expansive continent. Nevertheless, the interrogation of rehabilitation is an important one—not least when we consider recent shifts in the Australian criminal legal system.

S. Russell (✉) · J. Beaufils
University of New South Wales, Sydney, NSW, Australia
e-mail: sophie.russell@uts.edu.au

J. Beaufils
e-mail: James.Beaufils@uts.edu.au

C. Cunneen
Jumbunna Institute for Indigenous Education and Research, University of Technology Sydney, Sydney, NSW, Australia
e-mail: Cunneen@uts.edu.au

© The Author(s), under exclusive license to Springer Nature Switzerland AG 2022
M. Vanstone and P. Priestley (eds.), *The Palgrave Handbook of Global Rehabilitation in Criminal Justice*, https://doi.org/10.1007/978-3-031-14375-5_3

Over the decade to 2021 the number of people in prison across Australia has increased by 48%, from 29,107 to 42,970 (Australian Bureau of Statistics [ABS], 2021a). First Nations people,[1] women, and those with complex disadvantages have been most affected—the number of First Nations people increased by 70% and the number of women by 62%. Alongside this, we have seen the number of people imprisoned on remand more than double and a 30% increase of people in prison with known prior imprisonment (ABS, 2021a). In some states—such as New South Wales (NSW), the Australian jurisdiction which is the focus of this Chapter—we have seen an explosion in the numbers of people under community sanctions, increasing 75% over the last 3 years (ABS, 2021b). At the same time, there has been enormous prison infrastructure expansion (NSW Government, 2019), and significant investment into rehabilitative strategies intended to reduce reoffending (Elliot, 2016).

NSW has the largest population of any Australian state or territory, as well as the largest number of people—including non-Indigenous and First Nations people—in prison and under community supervision (ABS, 2021b). Throughout this Chapter, we centre our analysis of rehabilitation within the context of settler colonialism in Australia, drawing on empirical findings from recent exploratory research into the experiences of First Nations people on parole in NSW[2] (Beaufils et al., 2021).

In Australia, the criminal legal system is managed at a state or territory level. Each of the six states and two territories operates their own sentencing regimes, as well as custodial (youth and adult prisons) and community (probation and parole) 'correctional' services.[3] Most funding for non-government organisations (NGOs) that support people under community supervision also comes from respective state government agencies, with some NGOs funded through the federal government or philanthropic grants. While there are particularly marked differences across each of the Australian jurisdictions—such as rates of community-based orders and imprisonment and the provision of rehabilitative programmes and services—there are also notable similarities, such as the high rates of imprisonment of marginalised groups, including First Nations people (ABS, 2021a).

Settler Colonialism and the Criminal Legal System in Australia

Between 1787 and 1868, approximately 160,000 British convicts were transported to the continent now known as Australia. The 'global phenomenon' of the forced migration of convicts, along with indentured workers and slaves, involved all leading colonial powers. Through transportation, nation states expanded their 'spheres of influence' by securing economic, political, and military advantage, and seizing resources and land (Cunneen et al., 2013: 21–22). In Australia convictism in particular was central to the establishment of a settler colonial state. While the British claimed sovereignty over the sacred lands, the lands were not, as declared, Terra Nullius; 'land belonging to no one'. The lands were—and continue to be—the social and cultural place of First Nations peoples who have lived here for over 65,000 years prior to the arrival of European convicts and settlers.

The invasion by the British and the colonial project involved the massacre of First Nations peoples, the brutal dispossession of land, the denial of traditional law, language, and cultural practice, enforcement of Eurocentric norms and values, the forced removal of First Nations children, and the subjugation of First Nations peoples through various forms of enforcement and imprisonment. From the end of the nineteenth century, First Nations peoples were confined in reserves and missions under 'protection' legislation, which, despite its name, was essentially 'a penal mode of administration and control utilising the institutions of criminal justice and punishment based on the deprivation of liberty' as all aspects of the lives of First Nations peoples were regulated and controlled (Cunneen et al., 2013: 29). Colonial policies also impacted the development of the penal system for non-Indigenous people. The demand for labour in the colony saw the introduction of the 'ticket of leave' scheme—a form of conditional release for convicts, which formed the original basis for the contemporary parole system in Australia. While the ideology of rehabilitation has always been present in community supervision, extraneous economic, political, and social factors have continuously impacted on policy (Figgis, 1998; Simpson, 1999; ATSISJC, 2011).

We take this context of colonisation and stolen land as the starting point for our discussion of rehabilitation in the context of the Australian criminal legal system. In settler colonial states such as Australia, the enduring legacy of colonisation and invasion is evidenced by extraordinarily high rates of surveillance, policing, and over-criminalisation of First Nations people across all levels of the criminal legal and child 'welfare' systems (Behrendt et al., 2019). First Nations adults make up around 3% of the national population, but constitute 30% of those in prison, making them 14 times more likely to be in prison than those who are non-Indigenous (ABS, 2021a).[4] The range of structural and systemic disadvantages experienced by First Nations people make contact with the criminal legal system more likely—including structural poverty, ill-health, higher levels of disability and mental illness, and significant levels of institutional intergenerational trauma as a result of government policies and intervention (Anthony et al., 2020). The 1991 Royal Commission into Aboriginal Deaths in Custody (Johnstone, 1991) found that the dispossession of land and resultant economic marginalisation of First Nations communities has contributed significantly to disproportionate rates of imprisonment and contact with the criminal legal system. The Australian Law Reform Commission (ALRC, 2017) described this over-representation as a persistent and national problem, highlighting the high levels of systemic discrimination and the consequent social and economic disadvantage experienced by First Nations people as a result of colonisation.

While First Nations people are over-represented in criminal legal systems across Australia, imprisonment rates are not monolithic and differ from jurisdiction to jurisdiction. As Table 1 shows, the general rate of imprisonment is lowest in the Australian Capital Territory (ACT) at 113 per 100,000 and highest in the Northern Territory (NT) at 971 per 100,000. The rate of imprisonment for First Nations people is lowest in Tasmania (Tas) at 776 per 100,000 and highest in Western Australia (WA) at 3,449 per 100,000 (ABS, 2021a).

The rate of people serving community-based orders[5] also differs across these jurisdictions. It is the lowest in Victoria (Vic), at 168 per 100,000 and highest in the NT at 616 per 100,000. In most states and territories, the rate of community sanctions is considerably higher than the rate of imprisonment (see Table 2). It is therefore common in Australia that a larger number of people appearing before courts are sentenced to lesser penalties such as community sanctions, as opposed to harsher penalties, such as imprisonment—thus emphasising the principle of imprisonment as a sanction of last resort.

Table 1 Age standardised rate of imprisonment (per 100,000 adult population) in Australian states and territories by Indigenous status, 2021 (ABS, 2021a)

	NSW	vic	Qld	SA	WA	Tas	NT	ACT	Aus
Indigenous	1906	1816	2144	2531	3449	776	2557	1642	2223
Non-Indigenous	165	128	185	197	216	148	195	84	164
Total persons	206	139	248	221	326	149	971	113	214
Ratio	12	14	12	13	16	5	13	20	14

Table 2 Rate of imprisonment and community-based orders (per 100,000 adult population) in Australian states and territories, 2021 (ABS, 2021a, 2021b)

	NSW	vic	Qld	SA	WA	Tas	NT	ACT	Aus
Rate of imprisonment	206	139	248	221	326	149	971	113	214
Rate of community-based orders	556	168	486	379	280	491	616	285	395

Sources Australian Bureau of Statistics (2021a) Prisoners in Australia, 2021. Canberra: Australian Bureau of Statistics
Australian Bureau of Statistics (2021b) Corrective Services, Australia, September Quarter 2021. Canberra: Australian Bureau of Statistics

However, it is important to point out that the 'frontier states' in Australia of WA and the NT (which were the last to be colonised) and the relative size of the First Nations population impact on the rates of imprisonment and community sanctions. In the NT, which has the largest proportional First Nations population of any Australian jurisdiction (31%),[6] imprisonment rates are the highest in Australia and significantly higher than rates of community-based orders (see Table 2). We can see that when a penalty is imposed in this jurisdiction, imprisonment is favoured over a community-based order. Nearly 90% of people imprisoned in the NT are First Nations.

Over recent years, there has been growing recognition that criminal legal systems—and particularly prisons—are disproportionately filled with people who have multiple and complex support needs, including mental health diagnoses, cognitive impairment, substance dependency, experiences of homelessness, and backgrounds of disadvantage, and that these needs manifest in a way which is both intersecting and compounding (Baldry, 2014, 2017; Butler et al., 2011; McCarthy et al., 2016; Sharma, 2018). Disability in particular is intimately linked with the prison system—both from the disabling effects of imprisonment to the pervasiveness of people with disability within prisons (Ben-Moshe, 2020). First Nations people in particular experience high rates of mental health disorders, cognitive impairment, and other health concerns, yet have significantly lower rates of access to appropriate health and disability support (Baldry et al., 2015; JH & FMHN, 2017; Sharma, 2018). Women are particularly vulnerable: 43% of First Nations women (v 31% non-Indigenous) and 23% of First Nations men (v 24% non-Indigenous) reported having a disability and 12% of First Nations women (v 12% non-Indigenous) and 23% of First Nations men (v 17% non-Indigenous) reported receiving a mental health diagnosis while in custody (JH & MHN, 2017: 20, 28). Alongside this, First Nations people with disability are likely to have experienced earlier and more significant contact with the criminal legal system and to experience higher levels of disadvantage (Baldry et al., 2015), and are more likely to face difficulties with parole related to difficulties in understanding or comprehending parole conditions and complying with the terms (ALRC, 2017; Grunseit et al., 2008). At the same time, in many parts of Australia we see a shortage of culturally safe and appropriate, and adequately funded and evaluated First Nations community-controlled and specific services, particularly for those living in regional, rural, and remote areas and who require specialist support (ALRC, 2017).

The multiple and intersecting forms of disadvantage experienced by those under penal supervision bring to bear questions of the very concept of 'rehabilitation'. As others have pointed out, the prefix 're' symbolises a return to a previous condition (Robinson & Crow, 2009), yet for many of those enmeshed in the system, the emphasis should not be on returning to a diminished state but instead be focused on healing, building, and creating life anew.

The Law and Policy Context of Rehabilitation in NSW

Rehabilitation is one of the key purposes of sentencing set out in legislation across Australian jurisdictions and, at least theoretically, forms a component of the sentence for those serving orders in the community and in prison. Depending on the specific order, people under supervision may be required to engage in supervision by Community Corrections, attend specific government-run programmes, and/or engage with various external agencies, such as those focused on addressing substance dependency, or providing mental health and disability-related support.

The pre-eminent model of rehabilitation in many Anglophone nations, including Australia—and particularly within NSW—is Risk-Needs-Responsivity (RNR), developed by Canadian psychologists Andrews and Bonta (1994). The Risk principle determines *who* should be treated for intervention (only those considered to be at the highest risk of reoffending); the Need principle provides *what* should be targeted ('criminogenic needs' related to offending behaviour); and the Responsivity principle refers to *how* these interventions are to occur (typically through cognitive behavioural therapy). In this way, rehabilitation becomes tightly *linked* to risk and the broader project of reducing reoffending (as defined by criminogenic need). The Corrective Services NSW Officer Handbook for example makes this point explicitly, stating that 'Community Corrections is not responsible for providing welfare or therapeutic services unless they are directly related to risk of offending' (Corrective Services NSW, 2015: 11).

The NSW Reducing Reoffending Strategy 2016–2020 included a significant investment into 'correctional' rehabilitation, predominantly focused on short-term interventions based on criminogenic needs frameworks and underpinned by RNR. Part of this included an expansion of its various CBT programmes under the EQUIPS umbrella (Explore, Question, Understand, Investigate, Practice, Succeed) and the introduction of the Practice Guide for Intervention (PGI) to structure community-based supervision in accordance with RNR principles. Supervision is predominantly focused on behaviour change, with correctional agencies stating that 'the most significant role that Community Corrections can play in reducing the impact of crime is in changing offending behaviour' (Corrective Services NSW, 2015: 24). As a result, the welfare needs of people under supervision are referred to external agencies—who may or may not be able to meet these basic needs (such as secure, stable accommodation).

The RNR model and its use in NSW (and other jurisdictions) tell us very little about exactly how the welfare needs of people may or may not affect their interaction with the criminal legal system. Moreover, it operates as a very narrow form of *personal* rehabilitation, as Burke and colleagues note (2019)—limited to addressing cognitive skills. In our research with First Nations people on parole in NSW, interviewees pointed to a range of systemic, structural, and social factors which they identified as driving their interaction with the criminal legal system and as hindering their efforts at desistance. Examples included a lack of housing, limited access to drug and alcohol support services, inadequate transport in regional or rural areas, and the difficulties of managing mental illness and disability alongside limited access to necessary pharmacotherapies. A lack of employment opportunities, systemic failings at the point of release from prison, and at times a complete absence of throughcare were other factors highlighted repeatedly by interview respondents. These needs superseded requirements for discrete programmes or interventions focused primarily on 'offending behaviours' (see ALRC, 2017: 299). Libby, a Bundjalung woman on parole who we spoke with, described feeling:

> It's like they set you up for failure. It's a set up for failure all together getting out of gaol. They wanted me to do a course in [town] 20 minutes away by car, knowing that I have a baby… he was only a couple months old at the time. Knowing that I've got a young child. Wanting me to come up here to [town], no transportation of my own, public transport. And it's hard, you know. Get

up, make sure the child's right. You've got to make sure you have someone to watch the child to do the programmes. And I told them, and they were notified that I didn't have the resources at the time. (Libby, Parolee)

Our research, alongside others (Baldry & McCausland, 2009; Day et al., 2019; Tubex et al., 2020) indicates that a thorough exit plan from prison is essential. Throughcare, a form of comprehensive and holistic case management from prison to the community, is recognised as a best practice approach to the operationalisation of reintegration and rehabilitation. All Australian jurisdictions have a policy commitment to throughcare, however the gap with practice can be a chasm. For several First Nations parolees in our research, such as Joe, Niah, and Richard below, throughcare was incompetent and almost non-existent:

I was just let out on the street. I had to try and find a way back here. They didn't give me any directions or any plan on what I should do. I tried to get on a bus and then work out how to get from the bus to train station and all that with a phone that doesn't work anymore, because of how long I've been locked up… I didn't know where I was going. I knew where I had to go, I didn't know how to get there. So that was my first problem. [I had] just my gate money, that I'd stored up from not spending in buy-up, about $60 or something… and the Opal [public transport] card. I had to sign in by two o'clock at parole that first day. They [prison] didn't even give me medication that I was meant to get – six days of medication. I didn't get that. They did help with three days accommodation. And then I had to just go through the stress of trying to sort more accommodation out… Initially I guess your biggest stress was a roof over my head. (Joe, Parolee)

It's a bit scary when you first get out because they don't sort of give you anything on the way out, you know? They don't offer anything. You just get out and just land on your feet or not… I think there should be more in place. They make out like there's all these pre-release programmes and shit, but there's not. I sat in gaol for 12 months and then got out and that's it. I think one person came to see me. There's no plan put in place. (Niah, Parolee)

We interviewed Richard, a young Wiradjuri man, seven days after being released from a regional prison over 200 kms from the parole office where he needed to report. He stated,

It's just stressful when I got out. I lost everything when I went to gaol. I got out with not even socks and jocks. Like I've got no ID and Corrective Services give me a release certificate with the wrong date of birth, and the wrong spelling of my name. So I can't access none of my bank accounts. I can't do nothing. I've got out with no ID, no birth certificate. (Richard, Parolee)

Research from Australia indicates that throughcare models are likely to be more successful for First Nations people if they are culturally competent, strengths-based, incorporate family members, and are led by Aboriginal community-controlled organisations (ALRC, 2017; Day et al., 2019; Willis & Moore, 2008). One concern regarding throughcare in NSW is that people in prison are often transferred to prisons across the state and released to locations far away from their home communities, as was the case for Richard noted above. This separation from community and Country can have the effect of hindering family support (Day et al., 2019), feeling dislocated, and be another imposed obstacle to desistance.

Correctional agencies in NSW maintain that the group programmes and supervision structure they deliver have been developed 'to ensure that programs are available to all offenders irrespective of their culture, language, motivation, or whether they accepted responsibility for their offending. By design, this core suite of programmes should be suitable and available to all moderate to high risk offenders' (Grant et al., 2017: 169–170). However, in our interviews with Community Corrections Officers (CCO)[7] and Aboriginal Community Support Officers (ACSOs), there were comments about the cultural relevance and suitability of rehabilitative approaches that are grounded in RNR. One CCO, Sally, commented on the suitability of some exercises used in supervision:

> I find that cravings one's a pain in the butt… "Managing cravings". I just think that just doesn't fit well. I think there should be a little bit more that's relating to their thoughts and feelings on things. Like what they personally think about instead of trying to direct them to this is how they should think… There's others [PGI exercises] that I wouldn't even touch with them because they are Aboriginal. It's some of the relationship ones… the pro-social ones. It talks about someone who hasn't been in trouble before and why can't you…? Do you know anyone like that? Some of these kids don't know anyone that hasn't been in trouble before and that might be their role model. And they might have been in trouble before and they still might have a little infringement against them now but they're not bad people. But that model actually just talks about you have to be a pro-social person that's squeaky clean… I just struggle with that one very much… Because the best role model could be Uncle Joe that's at home and pulls them into line and whatever else. But Uncle Joe could still smoke a cone or do whatever, but he still has his moral compass right… And

that [worksheet] doesn't cater for that… But just the whole word, pro-social, antisocial just doesn't sit… If they're reading it or they can see it, and you're trying to ask the questions of it, they go, 'Oh, this is crap, Miss'. (Sally, CCO)

Western rehabilitation and reintegration frameworks are based on risk management and focused on addressing individualised 'criminogenic needs' may ignore core, underlying issues and complexities related to involvement with the criminal legal system. For example, for First Nations people, the grief and intergenerational trauma associated with historical and ongoing colonial processes related to stolen land, environmental destruction, the removal of babies and children, and over-policing of First Nations families and communities, may all have the effect of driving substance dependency. 'Criminogenic needs' frameworks place significant emphasis on individual choice, even in circumstances where freedom for First Nations people may be significantly constrained by both historical injustices from colonisation and by contemporary systemic discrimination, police surveillance, and criminalisation.

A related problem concerns the focus on risk and the use of risk assessment tools such as the Level of Service Inventory-Revised (LSI-R) for determining needs and levels of supervision. The validity of these tools for diverse populations, including First Nations people and women, have been questioned both in Australia and internationally (Cunneen & Tauri, 2016: 158–160). The legacy of colonisation and contemporary discrimination means that First Nations people are likely to score higher on the LSI-R and be deemed 'high risk' according to this assessment (Hsu et al., 2010). These scores can lead to more stringent conditions, reporting and monitoring for those undergoing community sanctions as well as requirements to undertake certain programmes, which may in turn lead to higher rates of breach and non-compliance. CCOs we interviewed spoke of the need to move beyond conceptualisations of risk when supervising First Nations people:

> Try not to make it all about just focussing on the risks/needs. But actually have real, meaningful conversations, that are meaningful to them, about their community. About where they fit in, about who their family is, how they view themselves… Focus on things outside the fact that, "okay, you're an offender, this is the offence you committed and what we're going to do about that". Look at some of the other things and find the foundation of who that person is. (Camilla, CCO, regional area)

Future Directions in Rehabilitation Policy and Practice: Abolitionism and First Nations Justice Approaches

Burke and colleagues (2019) have developed a more interdisciplinary conceptualisation of rehabilitation in order to move beyond some of the common 'paradigm conflicts' (McNeill, 2012) between competing models of rehabilitation. They argue in favour of departing from a central focus on any one form of rehabilitation, such as personal (i.e., psychological) and to recognise its other forms—judicial/legal, moral, and social—which are equally important to processes of desistance (Burke et al., 2019). These various personal, social, judicial/legal, and moral forms of rehabilitation have particular specificity in the context of First Nations people being caught in a non-Indigenous justice system, where for example personal/social formations are deeply affected by kinship and community relations and systemic racial discrimination which prevents access to a range of social goods. If judicial or legal rehabilitation refers to processes or practices which work to restore the civil or human rights of people under penal control, then the profound disregard of First Nations law, and confronting the ongoing levels of police violence against First Nations people must be at the forefront of rehabilitation, as well as the existing legal barriers that diminish the opportunity for rehabilitation for all people leaving prison. If moral rehabilitation has a focus on repairing the harm caused through moral redress to victims and communities then it would need to include legal processes that are suitable for First Nations people such as the development of First Nations sentencing courts and procedures.

These four forms of rehabilitation might achieve social, rather than criminal justice. However, in the context of settler colonialism in Australia, the need for approaches to rehabilitation for First Nations people must be grounded in First Nations justice approaches and healing practices, which are underpinned by self-determination. In looking towards the future directions in rehabilitation policy and practice in Australia, here we explore the contribution that Indigenous studies and abolitionist perspectives have for the future of rehabilitation. Both perspectives challenge the efficacy of contemporary approaches to punishment and demand a reconsideration of the role of civil society as well as broader questions of political legitimacy. First, we turn our attention to healing as an Indigenous justice approach and practice framework for rethinking rehabilitation.

Healing is an integral part of Indigenous justice approaches, and diverse healing approaches have developed in settler colonial states focusing on different areas—including the Stolen Generations, residential schools, family violence, and substance dependency (Cunneen & Tauri, 2016: 128–131). In Australia, there are various healing programmes based on Indigenous ways of knowing (McKendrick et al., 2017). In the context of the criminal punishment system, individual rehabilitation and risk/need paradigms have the effect of marginalising First Nations standpoints and epistemologies in the design and delivery of rehabilitative interventions. The imposition of Eurocentric values and beliefs is reflected in the institutional dominance of these approaches and the focus on CBT-based interventions within custodial and community settings undermines First Nations approaches to health, healing, and wellbeing (Cunneen & Rowe, 2014; Tauri & Porou, 2014).

In contrast to dominant models of rehabilitation grounded in risk/need, First Nations approaches to healing are not just an individual practice focused on reducing offending as an individual phenomenon but are about working with families and seeing treatment as a *community* objective (Atkinson, 2013; Cunneen, 2002). The Aboriginal and Torres Strait Islander Social Justice Commissioner (ATSISJC) has previously stated that:

> Indigenous concepts of healing are based on addressing the relationship between the spiritual, emotional and physical in a holistic manner. An essential element of Indigenous healing is recognising the interconnections between, and effects of, violence, social and economic disadvantage, racism and dispossession from land and culture on Indigenous peoples, families and communities. (ATSISJC, 2004: 57)

In this way, healing is grounded in the recognition of the significant and ongoing harms of colonisation to First Nations individuals, families, and communities. As Black and colleagues (2019) point to mainstream therapeutic approaches such as counselling may be insufficient for First Nations people, as they may 'not have the appropriate frameworks or the cultural safety for addressing the unique experiences of multiple traumas, disconnection, loss and grief for Aboriginal peoples' (2019: 1060). Within First Nations healing approaches there is a greater focus on community-controlled interventions that are strengths-based, holistic, and underpinned by self-determination. Critical Indigenous and non-Indigenous scholars have alerted us to the importance of looking at First Nations-owned and led strategies that occur *outside* state interventions or 'justice' agencies (Anthony et al., 2020).

The UN Declaration on the Rights of Indigenous Peoples recognises that First Nations people have the collective right to self-determination. Put simply the right to self-determination is the right to make decisions. At a community or regional level, it includes the right to exercise control over decision-making, community priorities, how communities operate, and processes for resolving disputes (ATSISJC, 2011: 109–110). The recognition that self-determination is a process rather than a single act has important implications: it requires that there are *ongoing* processes that facilitate self-determination, and these may change over time. The right to make decisions might include First Nations controlled and operated criminal legal processes, but it might also involve collective decisions to participate in non-Indigenous processes where First Nations people negotiate processes and outcomes.

We argue for a more transformative vision of rehabilitation in Australia. One that moves the processes away from 'correctional' penal apparatuses and returns them to the community. Such an approach is consistent with both penal abolitionism and First Nations demands for self-determination. It is an approach that is grounded in 'collective practices of safety, accountability, and healing, untethered from the existing criminal legal system' (Davis et al., 2022: 5). There is such transformative work happening across Australia. Often, this is grassroots, community-developed and led, and in some cases led by community sector organisations who have people with lived experience embedded throughout the organisation—importantly in executive positions, driving the strategic direction of the organisation.[8] First Nations community owned, led, managed, and designed services and programmes to address the needs of First Nations communities and redefine needs for their community which is in direct contrast to the dominant government universalist approaches of one-size-fits all—largely embodied in the CBT/risk-based approaches. Moreover, in contrast to government and 'justice' departments, First Nations community-controlled organisations are accountable to their communities, helping to build legitimacy. A result of Australia's history and treatment of First Nations people is a distrust of government services, and our research in NSW found that there are few First Nations operational staff in community corrections and even less in middle or senior management levels. Our research points to the benefits that could flow from shifting decision-making from government 'correctional' agencies back to the community by involving First Nations organisations and communities in processes related to supervision. We found that while ACSOs may assist in developing supervisory relationships and act as a conduit between CCOs, First Nations individuals, families, and communities, they are directly employed by the system and bounded by its institutional structure and therefore have limited autonomy.

In Western Australia there is a legislative base for local First Nations communities providing court-ordered supervision of adults and young people. Legislation allows for the use of contractual arrangements between

WA Corrective Services and First Nations communities for the local provision of community supervision. However, there has been no evaluation of the extent to which the provision is used or of the outcomes. First Nations legal services in Queensland have argued for the establishment of a community authority to assist with the reintegration of First Nations people on parole back into the community through working with specific communities and supporting reintegration (ATSILS Qld, 2016: 36). Moving beyond individual rehabilitation, First Nations-led justice reinvestment projects in Australia provide an example of a whole community approach to the problem of entrenched criminal legal system involvement. Distinct from the US model, justice reinvestment in Australia takes a more radical approach as First Nations community-led and underpinned by self-determination (Brown et al., 2016: 130–138, 240–241).

There are also good examples of non-Indigenous NGOs providing holistic, community-based outreach and throughcare support to people leaving prison, such as the Community Restorative Centre (CRC) where its alcohol and other drugs, transition and reintegration programmes have led to a dramatic reduction in criminal system contact (Sotiri et al., 2021). In our research, we noted the importance of both systemic and structural factors driving criminal legal system contact and the relational factors supporting desistance, in particular the necessity of building rapport and genuine relationships grounded in patience, trust, honesty, and respect (Beaufils et al., 2021). An evaluation of CRC's programme similarly noted:

> incarceration disadvantage is itself located in the context of a lifetime of other kinds of disadvantage; that meeting basic welfare, housing, health and support needs is fundamental to building a life outside the prison system, and that the way in which support is provided (flexible, outreach, relational, long term) and the manner in which people who have experienced incarceration and disadvantage are treated by workers (respectful, non-judgmental, compassionate, consistent) is a fundamental factor in achieving change in a range of areas, including breaking cycles of recidivism and alcohol and other drug use. (Sotiri et al., 2021: 4)

Conclusion

Decades of Australian research, government inquiries, reports, and commissions have confirmed that the vast majority of those under penal supervision come from backgrounds of complex disadvantage (ALRC, 2017). Macro policies and structural forces—such as poverty and marginalisation—drive cycles of contact with the criminal legal system. There remain a range of institutional barriers to reintegration and rehabilitation in NSW—particularly for First Nations people—including a shortage of adequately funded, culturally led First Nations community-controlled services. Across Australia, but particularly in NSW, we are seeing increasing investment into narrow conceptualisations of 'correctional rehabilitation' which are focused on individual choice and narrative without adequate acknowledgement or understanding of the ways in which choice may be constrained by historical injustices. Our research points to the need for a more transformative and collective vision of rehabilitation in Australia—one that shifts decision-making from penal apparatuses to the community and is grounded in both penal abolitionism and First Nations demands for self-determination.

Notes

1. Throughout this Chapter, a number of different terms are used to refer to First Nations people, including 'Aboriginal', 'Aboriginal and Torres Strait Islander', and 'Indigenous', depending on the context and protocols of government and non-government organisations that may be referenced. We have chosen primarily to use the term First Nations, as it is becoming increasingly preferable in Australia. We acknowledge that any broad term is imperfect as it fails to reflect the diversity of the more than 250 nations—each with their own culture, customs, and language—and over 800 dialects spoken across the continent. We specifically refer to a person's identification with an Aboriginal nation where appropriate.
2. As part of this research, we interviewed 19 First Nations people with experience on parole—13 who were at different stages of their parole order and 6 who were returned to prison following parole revocation. This cohort included 8 women and 11 men. We also interviewed 4 Aboriginal Client Services Officers in urban and regional areas and 9 Community Corrections Officers who supervise First Nations people on parole in urban and regional locations throughout NSW. Ethics approval was granted by the UTS Ethics Committee and Corrective Services NSW.
3. Throughout this chapter we use the government term 'community corrections' and 'correctional services' to refer to punishment and supervision which takes place in the community and the agencies which are responsible for administering these systems. However, we acknowledge the problematic nature of this language, in that many of those who are criminalised need not be corrected but require equality and equity in opportunity and access to resources and capital.

4. The age-standardised imprisonment rate of Aboriginal and Torres Strait Islander people is 2223 per 100,000. For non-Indigenous people it is 164 per 100,0000 (ABS, 2021a).
5. The data drawn on in Table 2 is from the ABS (2021b) which defines types of community-based orders to include: restricted movement; fine options; community service; parole; bail; sentenced probation; and post-sentence supervision.
6. The estimated Indigenous population is 4% in NSW; 1% in Vic; 4% in Qld; 3% in SA; 4% in WA; 6% in Tas; and 2% in the ACT (AIHW, 2021).
7. In NSW, the term Community Corrections Officers to refer to Officers who supervise people under community-based orders, sometimes referred to as a Probation/Parole Officer in other jurisdictions.
8. See, for example, Aboriginal community-controlled organisation Deadly Connections (https://deadlyconnections.org.au/) and women's specific service Sisters Inside (https://www.sistersinside.com.au/).

References

Aboriginal and Torres Strait Islander Social Justice Commissioner. (2004). *Social justice report 2004*. Human Rights and Equal Opportunity Commission.

Aboriginal and Torres Strait Islander Social Justice Commissioner. (2011). *Social justice report 2011*. Australian Human Rights Commission.

Andrews, D. A., & Bonta, J. (1994). *The psychology of criminal conduct* (1st ed.). Anderson Publishing.

Anthony, T., Sentance, G., & Bartels, L. (2020). Transcending colonial legacies: From criminal justice to Indigenous women's healing. In L. George (Ed.), *Neo-colonial injustice and the mass imprisonment of Indigenous women*. Palgrave Macmillan.

Atkinson, J. (2013). *Trauma-informed services and trauma-specific care for Indigenous Australian children*. Australian Government.

ATSILS Qld. (2016). *Submission on the review of the Queensland parole boards*. ATSILS Qld.

Australian Bureau of Statistics. (2021a). *Prisoners in Australia, 2021a*. Australian Bureau of Statistics.

Australian Bureau of Statistics. (2021b). *Corrective services, Australia, september quarter 2021b*. Australian Bureau of Statistics.

Australian Institute of Health and Welfare. (2021). *Australia's Health 2020*. Australian Institute of Health and Welfare.

Australian Law Reform Commission. (2017). *Pathways to justice—An inquiry into the incarceration rate of aboriginal and torres strait Islander peoples: Final report*. Australian Law Reform Commission.

Baldry, E. (2014). Complex needs and the justice system. In C. Chamberlain, & C. Robinson (Eds.), *Homelessness in Australia: An introduction*. UNSW Press.

Baldry, E. (2017). People with multiple and complex support needs, disadvantage and criminal justice systems: 40 years after the sackville report. In A. Durbach, B. Edgeworth, & V. Sentas. (Eds.), *Law and poverty in Australia 40 years after the poverty commission*. The Federation Press.

Baldry, E., & McCausland, R. (2009). Mother seeking safe home: Aboriginal women post-release. *Current Issues in Criminal Justice, 21*(2), 288–301.

Baldry, E., McCausland, R., Dowse, L., McEntyre, E., & University of New South Wales. (2015). *A predictable and preventable path: Aboriginal people with mental and cognitive disabilities in the criminal justice system*. UNSW Australia.

Beaufils, J., Cunneen, C., & Russell, S. (2021). *Exploratory research into post-release community integration and supervision: The experiences of aboriginal people with post-release supervision and reintegration in NSW*. Corrective Services NSW and Jumbunna Institute for Indigenous Education and Research, UTS.

Behrendt, L., Cunneen, C., Libesman, T., & Watson, N. (2019). *Aboriginal and torres strait Islander legal relations* (2nd ed.). Oxford University Press.

Ben-Moshe, L. (2020). *Decarcerating disability: Deinstitutionalization and prison abolition*. University of Minnesota Press.

Black, C., Frederico, M., & Bamblett, M. (2019). Healing through connection: An aboriginal community designed, developed and delivered cultural healing program for aboriginal survivors of institutional child sexual abuse. *The British Journal of Social Work, 49*(4), 1059–1080.

Brown, D., Cunneen, C., Schwartz, M., Stubbs, J., & Young, C. (2016). *Justice reinvestment: Winding back imprisonment*. Palgrave Macmillan.

Burke, L., Collett, S., & McNeill, F. (2019). *Reimagining rehabilitation: Beyond the individual* (1st ed.). Routledge.

Butler, T., Indig, D., Allnutt, S., & Mamoon, H. (2011). Co-occurring mental illness and substance use disorder among Australian prisoners: Comorbidity among Australian prisoners. *Drug and Alcohol Review, 30*(2), 188–194.

Corrective Services NSW. (2015). *Community corrections officer handbook*. Corrective Services NSW.

Cunneen, C. (2002). *NSW aboriginal justice plan: Discussion paper*. Aboriginal Justice Advisory Council.

Cunneen, C., Baldry, E., Brown, D., Brown, M., Schwartz, M., & Steel, A. (2013). *Penal culture and hyperincarceration: The revival of the prison*. Routledge.

Cunneen, C., & Rowe, S. (2014). Changing narratives-colonised peoples, criminology and social work. *International Journal for Crime, Justice and Social Democracy, 3*(1), 49–67.

Cunneen, C., & Tauri, J. (2016). *Indigenous criminology*. Policy Press, hsu.

Davis, A.Y., Dent, G., Meiners, E. R., & Richie, B. (2022). *Abolition. Feminism. Now.* Penguin.

Day, A., Geia, L., & Tamatea, A. (2019). *Toward effective throughcare approaches for Indigenous people leaving prison in Australia and New Zealand*. Indigenous Justice Clearinghouse.

Elliot, D. (2016). *$237m investment in reducing reoffending*. Available at: https://www.justice.nsw.gov.au:443/Pages/media-news/media-releases/2016/$237m-investment-in-reducing-reoffending.aspx (Accessed: 25 September 2019).

Figgis, H. (1998). *Probation: An overview*. NSW Parliamentary Library Research Service.

Grant, L., Martin, A. M., Ware, J., & Hainsworth, J. (2017). Enhancing the quality of programs and supervision to reduce reoffending in New South Wales. *Advancing Corrections Journal, 3*, 167–182.

Grunseit, A., Forrell, S., & McCarron, E. (2008). *Taking justice into custody: The legal needs of prisoners*. Law and Justice Foundation.

Hsu, C.-I., Caputi, P., & Byrne, M. K. (2010). Level of service inventory–revised: Assessing the risk and need characteristics of Australian Indigenous offenders. *Psychiatry, Psychology and Law, 17*(3), 355–367.

Johnstone, E. (1991). *Royal commission into aboriginal deaths in custody*. Australian Government Publishing Service.

Justice Health and Forensic Mental Health Network. (2017). *Network patient health survey—Aboriginal People's Health Report 2015*. Justice Health and Forensic Mental Health Network.

McCarthy, J., Chaplin, E., Underwood, L., Forrester, A., Hayward, H., Sabet, J., Young, S., Asherson, P., Mills, R., & Murphy, D. (2016). Characteristics of prisoners with neurodevelopmental disorders and difficulties. *Journal of Intellectual Disability Research, 60*(3), 201–206.

McKendrick, J., Brooks, R., Hudson, J., Thorpe, M., & Bennett, P. (2017). *Aboriginal and torres Strait Islander healing programs: A literature review*. The Healing Foundation.

McNeill, F. (2012). Four forms of offender rehabilitation: Towards an interdisciplinary perspective. *Legal and Criminological Psychology, 17*(1), 18–36.

NSW Government. (2019). *Safer, purpose-built prison to open under expansion program., NSW Government*. Available at: https://www.nsw.gov.au/news-and-events/news/safer-purpose-built-prison-to-open-under-expansion-program/ (Accessed: 30 March 2020).

Robinson, G., & Crow, I. (2009). *Offender rehabilitation: Theory, research and practice*. Sage.

Sharma, K. (2018). *I needed help, instead I was punished: Abuse and neglect of prisoners with disabilities in Australia*. Human Rights Watch.

Simpson, R. (1999). *Parole: An overview*. NSW Parliamentary Library Research Service.

Sotiri, M., McCausland, R., Reeve, R., Phelan, L., & Byrnes, T. (2021). *They're there to support you and help you, they're not there to judge you breaking the cycle of incarceration, drug use and release: Evaluation of the community restorative centre's AOD and reintegration programs*. CRC, UNSW and NSW Government.

Tauri, J. M., & Porou, N. (2014). Criminal justice as a colonial project in contemporary settler colonialism. *African Journal of Criminology and Justice Studies: AJCJS, 8*(1), 20–37.

Tubex, H., Rynne, J., & Blagg, H. (2020). Throughcare needs of Indigenous people leaving prison in Western Australia and the Northern Territory. *Trends and Issues in Crime and Criminal Justice*, (585).

Willis, M., & Moore, J.-P. (2008). *Reintegration of Indigenous prisoners*. Australian Institute of Criminology, Research and Public Policy Series.

Exploring Expectations and Realities of Rehabilitation in the Canadian Context

Katharina Maier and Rosemary Ricciardelli

Riddling notions of rehabilitation are inherently contradictory challenges tied to what one is rehabilitating to, tensions between past and present selves, pressures to conform to normative expectations of what it means to be rehabilitated, and desires to desist and/or embrace various behavioural practices and ways of thinking about diverse aspects in life (Maier, 2021). To this end, on both a conceptual and practical level, defining and making sense of what rehabilitation is and how it is practised within a particular penal context is not easy (Ward & Maruna, 2007). This may especially be true for Canada, a penal field described by Canadian-based researchers Goodman and Dawn (2016: 808) as 'complex, variegated, full of struggle and conflict and, of course, distinctly Canadian'. It is the struggle between Canadian penal progressiveness and benevolence on the one hand, and punitiveness

---

K. Maier (✉)
Department of Sociology and Anthropology,
University of Winnipeg, Winnipeg, MB, Canada
e-mail: k.maier@uwinnipeg.ca

R. Ricciardelli
Fisheries and Marine Institute at Memorial University of Newfoundland,
St. John's, Newfoundland and Labrador, Canada
e-mail: rose.ricciardelli@mi.mun.ca; rricciardell@mun.ca

on the other that creates complexity and conflict when examining rehabilitative ideas and practices within the Canadian context. Moreover, rehabilitation is made more complicated in Canada by its diverse population needs, the vast geographic space, and the diverse access to support experienced by those living across such spaces, as well as different logics and ideologies that inform understanding of rehabilitative practices during a person's incarceration and post-release.

To unpack what it looks like in any national context, rehabilitation requires an agreed upon definition or at least a conceptual starting point, a reality that is difficult to confirm in any penal context. In Canada, rehabilitation is largely engrained into prevailing systems of risk assessment, specifically the Risk-Need-Responsivity (RNR) model (Andrews & Bonta, 2010; Andrews et al., 1990). As the name suggests, the RNR model is rooted in the three core principles of *risk* (i.e., the notion that a person's risk is predictable and should be treated); *need* (i.e., that systems should respond to people's criminogenic needs); and *responsivity* (which refers to the ways treatment should be delivered). We are neither suggesting such risk-informed models are effective nor that they create sound definitions of rehabilitation, as the literature is laced with criticism directed at the RNR model and other forms of risk assessment (see Hannah-Moffat, 1999; Grieger & Hosser, 2014; Ward et al., 2012). As a starting point, however, we do note Canada is largely reliant on the RNR model and that it informs many official practices across correctional jurisdictions.

Moving beyond the RNR model, the goal of this chapter is to provide an overview of Canada's penal system with a focus on the nature and use of rehabilitative logics and programmes both in prison and upon people's release from prison into the community. We begin with a brief overview of the macro-developments in Canadian penality as a background to provide a more in-depth account of rehabilitation after incarceration. Here, we pay particular attention to two specific issues: the role of community-based supports in prisoner reintegration, and the role of gender in informing correctional and rehabilitative programming. We also provide insight into available correctional programmes, specifically correctional healing lodges. We point to further avenues of research in the realm of corrections and rehabilitation in Canada.

Corrections and Rehabilitation in Canada—An Overview

In Canada, individuals sentenced by the court to a prison term of at least two years serve time in federal penitentiaries operated by the Correctional Service Canada (CSC), whereas those with a prison sentence of less than two years (e.g., a maximum sentence of two years less one day), remanded into custody, or serving intermittent sentences are held in provincial/territorial correctional centres. The latter are the responsibility of the respective ten provinces and three territories' ministries/departments of justice, public safety, and/or solicitor generals. Both the re-entry process and the specific reintegrative programmes and supports look quite different for these groups of incarcerated individuals (see further below). The Canadian correctional systems are 14 in total, each operating independently but always interconnected. Each has personalized programming, policies, and practices and thus consistency across jurisdictions is subject to the functioning, practices, and available supports in each system.

Criminalized individuals in Canada are disproportionately drawn from poor and racialized communities with little opportunity for upward mobility (Bucerius et al., 2020), and given structural constraints, criminalized individuals, as research has shown, often return to these same communities post-release (Leverentz, 2010). Ex-prisoners' lived experiences of social marginalisation and resulting vulnerabilities (e.g., unstable housing, lack of food and employment) are often compounded by the disruptions and harms of imprisonment (see e.g., Western, 2018), creating a range of short and long-term challenges individuals must navigate as they transition from prison to community living (Durnescu, 2018). While those exiting the Canadian federal prison system typically have access to temporary housing and other basic supports, these supports are usually tied to increased supervision: for example, federal ex-prisoners may be required to reside at a community-based residential facility (i.e., a halfway house) following their release from prison. Although a requirement of their conditional release, which means that non-compliance can lead to penal and legal consequences (at worst, re-imprisonment), it means that federal ex-prisoners are provided with at least some material supports, structures, and in some cases temporary housing. In contrast, those released from provincial or territorial custody often leave the prison gates with little more than a bus ticket.

Rehabilitation and reintegrative supports should be an essential facet of a person's confinement and their release and re-entry, accordingly CSC 'prioritizes correctional programs as a means of reducing recidivism rates and increasing the safety of Canadian communities' (CSC, 2021a). However, in a Canadian context, what this looks like in practice is rather unclear as comparatively few researchers have studied the Canadian federal parole system (but see Norman & Ricciardelli, 2022a, 2022b), and even fewer researchers have studied the provincial release context. Thus, there remains comparatively little knowledge, literature, and research—both theoretical and applied—on the topic of prisoner re-entry and release in Canada.

Canadian Penality in a Global Context

People's experiences of imprisonment, rehabilitation, and prisoner re-entry are shaped by larger penal and social structures. As such, an overview of how Canadian penality, and how it compares to other jurisdictions, is essential for understanding practices and experiences of rehabilitation in prison and beyond. Canada has been described as a carceral outlier in the context of global penal trends. Its fairly stable and moderate rate of imprisonment, currently lying at 127 per 100,000 residents (Malakieh, 2020), has distinguished it from other Western countries, the United States in particular, that have seen much clearer upward trends in the use of incarceration and other penal measures for most of the past 60 years (see Garland, 2001; Tonry, 2004).

Scholars have argued that Canada was mostly able to avoid a 'punitive turn' at a time when other countries (the United States and England and Wales in particular) experienced notable shifts towards a more punitive culture that heavily relied on the use of imprisonment (see Meyer & O'Malley, 2005). More than 15 years ago, Doob and Webster (2006) attributed Canada's stable imprisonment rate to a combination of 'protective factors' (historical, cultural, and structural) and the absence of 'risk factors' that have made other countries more susceptible to punitive influences. Regarding the lack of 'risk factors', they highlight Canada's variegated sentencing goals and point out that Canada, compared to other countries, 'has never experienced a crisis of principles in sentencing whereby disillusionment with one predominant objective leads to the wholesale adoption of another' (Doob & Webster: 339). Rehabilitation and restoration have held strong as guiding sentencing principles alongside the more punitive approaches of deterrence, denunciation, and incapacitation. Moreover, a lack of appetite for, and/or reluctance to adopt a 'tough-on-crime' approach among politicians, legal actors, media, and the general public has been a notable difference between Canada and the United States in terms of policymakers, who in Canada, as the authors point out, have traditionally called for restraint in the use of prison time (see also Webster & Doob, 2015).

Canada's penal system, thus, has traditionally been noted for its stable imprisonment rate, penal restraint, use of rehabilitation, as well as a commitment to the provision of diverse supports for criminalized populations (Brodeur, 2007; Doob & Webster, 2006). Another point of deviation from the United States, Doob and Webster (2006) also note is that Canada has at least attempted to curb the imprisonment of racialized groups, including Black and Indigenous people, for instance through legislative attempts that codify that 'all available sanctions, other than imprisonment, that are reasonable in the circumstances and consistent with the harm done to victims or to the community should be considered for all offenders, with particular attention to the circumstances of Aboriginal offenders' (sec. 718.2 e, Criminal Code of Canada) (but see below).

About 10 years after Doob and Webster published their analysis of Canadian penality, they revisited their initial claims in light of notable shifts in Canadian politics towards a more punitive agenda (Doob & Webster, 2016; Webster & Doob, 2015). Various Canadian-based scholars have analysed changes to Canadian penal policy under former Prime Minister Stephen Harper of the Conservative Party, noting a trend towards an increasingly punitive and regulatory approach to crime and criminalized people (Hermer & Mosher, 2002; Moore & Hannah-Moffat, 2005; Munn & Bruckert, 2013; Webster & Doob, 2015). Evidence of this more punitive approach to crime has included the increase of existing and imposition of new mandatory minimum penalties (e.g., for trafficking, sex crimes), various limitations that were placed on judges' ability to impose conditional sentences, and a broader shift in penal culture and ideology. Changes were also made to existing laws and policies that directly impacted people's chances of early release. For example, the process of accelerated parole review for most of those convicted of property and other non-violent offences and serving their first federal sentence, introduced in 1992 to ensure their cases were reviewed by the Parole Board of Canada (PBC) in advance so that they would be granted parole as soon as possible without the need of a formal parole, was abolished. In addition, various restrictions were made to the pardon process (referred to since as 'record suspension'). The process of obtaining a record suspension became more cumbersome. Criminalized individuals had to wait longer before they could apply for record suspension, certain groups of criminalized people were excluded from the ability to apply for record suspension, and application fees were raised.

However, these legislative reforms, as Doob and Webster also noted, did not resulted in any discernible changes to Canada's incarceration rates (Doob & Webster, 2016; Webster & Doob, 2015). In fact, the national incarceration rate has been in decline for the past four years, though several provinces have seen an increase in their respective imprisonment rates (Malakieh, 2020). Despite not seeing the kind of upward trend witnessed by the United States and other countries, these legislative reforms are reflective of changes in penal ideology and values. Webster and Doob (2015) argue there was a notable ideological shift towards a tough-on-crime approach. For example, restrictive changes to 'record suspensions' are significant in 'othering' criminalized populations, making it harder for them to remove the label of criminality (Doob & Webster, 2016). Such measures, thus, signify shifts in penal ideology, in addition to increasing barriers for people to re-enter the community after a period of incarceration.

To summarize, penality in Canada can be described more restrictive in scale and scope, compared to other countries, specifically the United States, yet a more restrictive penal system should not be conflated with a 'rehabilitative' penal system. As we have outlined above, punishment in Canada has also undergone notable policy changes over the years that have changed the nature of punishment and rehabilitation. In this context, it is also worth commenting, at least briefly, on other, arguably more rehabilitative forms of punishment in Canada (see also Robinson, 2016). Probation, defined as a community-based sentence imposed by the court, continues to be the most common sanction with a rate of 294 adults per 100,000 population (Malakieh, 2020); it is also the most common sanction for youth who transgress the law. Probation and other community-based sentences (e.g., fines) are an important aspect of the Canadian penal system; yet, they have received comparatively little empirical attention. Further research should focus on experiences of probation and other community-based sentences (but see Sylvestre et al., 2019). In the next section, we provide further insight into a select number of current issues in Canadian correctional services, focusing on both punishment and rehabilitation in prison and beyond incarceration at people's release.

Imprisonment and Rehabilitation

Before providing insight into specific prison programmes and measures, it is worth highlighting the profile of the Canadian prison population in terms of gender and race, as we return to issues around gender and rehabilitation below.

Males account for 85% of adult admissions to provincial/territorial prisons, and 93% of the federal prison population. Younger adult males, aged 20 to 39 years, are over-represented in prison admissions (Malakieh, 2020). Indigenous adults are vastly over-represented in Canadian prisons. While they represent 4.5% of the general population, they composed 31% of admissions to provincial/territorial prisons, and 29% of admissions to federal custody. In the Western provinces, Canada's Prairie region (Manitoba, Saskatchewan, Alberta), Indigenous peoples make up around 75% of admissions to custody. While the number of women behind bars is fairly small, Indigenous women are disproportionately represented, and are the fastest growing prison population group (OCI, 2021). In fact, in the last ten years, the Indigenous prison population has increased by approximately 18%, while the non-Indigenous prison population has decreased by roughly 28% at the same time (see OCI, 2021).

Existing research has examined various facets of prison life in Canada. Ricciardelli (2014), based on interviews with former prisoners, examined the lived experiences of prison culture, risk, violence, and masculinities in federal prisons (see also Maier & Ricciardelli, 2019; Ricciardelli et al., 2015). Other scholars have unpacked issues around drug use in prison (e.g., Bucerius & Haggerty, 2019); food (Ifeonu et al., 2022); youth and incarceration (e.g., Adorjan & Ricciardelli, 2018); and how prison can act as a 'temporary refuge' for people who experience social marginalization on the streets (see Bucerius et al., 2020). Other scholars have examined more specifically the nature, operations, and effects of certain rehabilitative programming, such as prison farms (e.g., Goodman & Dawn, 2016); prison gardens (Timler et al., 2019); and correctional healing lodges.

Healing lodges are correctional institutions that provide access to Indigenous-specific programming and services. Healing lodges were designed to address the over-representation of Indigenous peoples behind bars, and to recognize and remedy the failure of 'traditional' prisons and prison programming for Indigenous female prisoners in particular. CSC (2021b) defines healing lodges as:

[…] environments designed specifically for Indigenous offenders. They offer culturally appropriate services and programs to offenders in a way that incorporates Indigenous values, traditions and beliefs.

There are currently four CSC-operated healing lodges across Canada, in addition to another six that are operated by Indigenous community and partner organizations. Healing lodges only take prisoners who are classified as 'minimum risk' and, on an individual basis, 'medium risk'. Healing lodges were officially designed and conceived of as a progressive and responsive correctional and rehabilitative measure, focused on creating a safe space for Indigenous prisoners, an understanding of Indigenous history, culture, and teachings, and correctional practice based on teaching and learning (Combs, 2018). They have been described as a 'penal practice coded as a benevolent enterprise' (Carrier, 2022: 2). Scholars however have pointed out that despite their benevolent, progressive, and caring intensions, healing lodges remain carceral spaces 'available to prisoners desiring to follow what CSC constructs as a traditional healing path' (Carrier, 2022: 6). Further, scholars have voiced concern regarding access to healing lodges given that Indigenous persons are more likely than non-Indigenous people to be classified at higher security levels; as a result, many prisoners may not even be eligible for a healing lodge, despite official attentions to strengthen access to these correctional programmes (Combs, 2018).

Rehabilitation Post-Prison: The Role of Government

Prisoner re-entry, traditionally defined as 'the process of leaving prison and returning to free society' (Visher & Travis, 2003: 89), is tied to a range of personal, psychological, and socio-economic challenges: those include, as noted, finding and retaining employment, re-connecting with family and friends, securing care for physical and mental health needs, and meeting parole or other supervision (e.g., probation) conditions (Durnescu, 2011; Harding et al., 2019; Solomon, 2006; Werth, 2018; Western, 2018). The stigma attached to having a criminal record, in addition to ex-prisoners' generally limited economic resources, pre- and post-prison (e.g., limited formal education and skills; little economic capital) make employment one of the hardest barriers to reintegration into the community (O'Brien, 2001; Pager, 2003; Western, 2018; Wheelock et al., 2011). If ex-prisoners manage to re-enter the labour market, they are typically limited to low-paying, unstable work rather than gainful employment, resulting in chronic economic insecurity and a constant need for survival (Sugie, 2018). To secure material needs, help from family and other social networks is frequently sought, in addition to public benefits and other services, including those offered by non-profit organizations (Western, 2018) that may provide some short-term assistance, especially during the early stages of release (see also Durnescu, 2018).

Post-prison supervision plays an essential role in prisoner reintegration and is framed by the Canadian government as an important step in the pursuit of public safety. According to the Parole Board of Canada (PBC), the goal of post-prison supervision is to 'contribute to public safety by helping offender re-integrate into society as law-abiding citizens through a gradual, controlled, and supported release with conditions' (PBC, 2011). Individuals released from federal prison remain under the supervision of a community parole officer (when in federal prison, prisoners are on the caseloads of an institutional parole officers) and subject to a number of release conditions (e.g., curfews, treatment, residency requirements, geographic boundaries). Violations of these conditions can carry punitive consequences, including re-imprisonment. According to CSC, the goal of release conditions is to ensure the 'gradual release' from prison to the community, 'helping them [ex-prisoners] adjust to life beyond institutional walls'. Community supervision is defined by CSC as consisting of 'three interrelated activities—supervision, programming and community involvement'.

Three forms of conditional release exist in Canada for federal prisoners. First, individuals are usually eligible for full parole after serving one-third of their sentence in custody, or seven years (whichever is less). These people can establish their own residency in the community but remain under the supervision of a community parole officer and must abide by their conditions of release. Second, day parole six months prior to their full parole eligibility date. Day parolees are permitted to spend their day in the community (i.e., for purposes of work, training, and/or programming), but must return nightly to a supervised residence, most often a halfway house or community correctional centre (CCC). Finally, statutory release which is a release by law, meaning incarcerated individuals are almost always released after serving two-thirds of their sentence unless there is a substantial risk of serious reoffending, as decided by the PBC. Though statutory release is a release by law, it is still considered a form of conditional release and as a result, these individuals too, have conditions attached to their release, are supervised by a parole officer, and are subject to the same revocation regime as parolees. Former prisoners on conditional release remain under penal supervision until their warrant expiry date (i.e., the end of their sentence).

Parole approval rates in Canada are relatively high. According to official statistics, 79% of applications for day parole are approved; the parole grant rate for federal full parole is 40% (Government of Canada, 2019). Prisoners whose applications for parole are denied are usually released on their *statutory release* date, i.e., after serving two-thirds of their prison sentence. Statutory release is a release by law; as such, individuals are invariably released after serving two-thirds of their sentence unless there is a substantial risk of serious reoffending, as decided by the PBC. All ex-prisoners on conditional release are subject to supervision by a parole officer until their *warrant expiry date* (i.e., the date their criminal sentence officially ends, as imposed by the court at the time of sentencing). It is worth noting that the majority of federal ex-prisoners on conditional release successfully complete their day and full parole, at a rate of 92.2 and 90.5%, respectively (Government of Canada, 2019).[1] Among the population of federal releasees, those on statutory release have the lowest rate of successful completion at a rate of 67.1% (Government of Canada, 2019). Breach of conditions is the main reason for reincarceration for all federal ex-prisoners regardless of their particular status (i.e., day parole, full parole, conditional release).

As is indicated here, parole is more difficult to be awarded; it is earned for good behaviour and requires dedication and a commitment from prisoners who seek to demonstrate their interest in ceasing to engage in antisocial or criminal acts early in their sentence. Statutory release, as previously noted, is awarded (not earned); it serves as a safeguard in society because it ensures that releasees pass time in the community under the supervision of the CSC. Thus, the criteria for being deemed eligible for release after serving two-thirds of a sentence is neither as delicate nor as ingrained in prisoner lifestyles as that tied to being paroled. In either case, the PBC decides on the timing and nature of conditional release and the CSC is responsible for carrying out the actual supervision regime.

Post-Prison Supports and the Role of Community

In addition to support and supervision provided through parole and the correctional system, Canada boasts an extensive network of non-governmental organizations that provides support to criminalized populations post-prison; yet our understanding of the role of these organizations in the context of rehabilitation continues to be rather limited. Here again, we urge further research on the differential role these organizations may play in particular for provincial versus federal prisoners.

Given the multitude of state and non-state actors that shape people's re-entry pathways, recent scholarship, mostly based in the United States, has expanded our understanding of prisoner re-entry by highlighting its organizational dimensions (Mijs, 2016; Miller, 2014; Prior, 2020). The focus of the work has been on providing theoretical and empirical insight into the role and work of prisoner re-entry organizations (conceptualized as organizational 'hybrids') situated at the nexus of punishment and welfare, and their impact in the lives of former prisoners (Mijs, 2016). More specifically, the work explores how these organizations work to reconstitute ex-prisoners' selves and ways of thinking about the past, present, and future, often through programmes that teach soft skills and normative ways of being. For example, Halushka (2016), in his ethnographic study of a 'Workforce Development Program' run by a re-entry organization in a northeastern U.S. city, demonstrates how ex-prisoner clients received lessons in what Halushka calls 'work wisdom' that involved teaching participants a number of soft skills and cultural scripts that were believed to help clients establish contact with employers. As Halushka (2016: 86) explains, 'lessons of work wisdom were meant to offer clients a short-term solution to this problem by providing former prisoners with the dramaturgical resources to perform the role of a rehabilitated and respectable citizen during interactions with employers'. What Halushka (2016) describes here is perhaps best encompassed by Miller's (2014: 317) conceptualization of prisoner re-entry as 'a "people changing institution" that seeks to transform former prisoners into "productive citizens" through programmes that locate the inner life as the primary site of social policy intervention' (see also Miller, 2021). Other scholars have documented the 'overarching security culture' (Prior, 2020: 391) of prisoner re-entry organizations (In Prior's research, a government-run re-entry programme), and the disciplinary gaze ex-prisoners experience as part of their involvement with these organizations.

Expanding on this line of research by primarily U.S. scholars, we call on Canadian researchers to expand work on how the 'organisational dynamics' of prisoner re-entry play out in Canada (but see Maier, 2021). This line of work is particularly important in the context of the ongoing impacts of the COVID-19 pandemic. Indeed, emerging research points to the central role of community-based, non-governmental organizations for criminalized populations during the COVID-19 pandemic. Casey et al. (2021), drawing on surveys, letters, and interviews with justice-involved people (prisoners, supervisees) and a small number of staff at community-run organizations in Scotland (referred to here as the 'third sector'), examine how pandemic restrictions and related changes have shaped the 'pains' and 'gains' of re-entry and penal supervision (Hayes, 2015). Returning from 'lockdown imprisonment' to 'lockdown communities', their participants experienced the 'pains' of continued isolation and exclusion despite having regained some of their mobility and freedoms—'the weight and depth of lockdown imprisonment travelled into the community with them' (Casey et al., 2021: 8). Recognizing these challenges, the authors explain how 'community groups and grassroot organisations responded by taking on new and demanding roles during the pandemic, working intensively and creatively to fill the gaps in support left by the statutory sector' (8). In the Canadian context, Ricciardelli et al. (2021: 24) suggest a greater need for correctional services to 'strengthen partnerships with community-based organisations and other community actors' to ensure rehabilitative services and support systems are in place when people return from prison. Such concrete calls to action necessitate an understanding of how a variety of organizations active in marginalized neighbourhoods see their role and have responded to COVID-19, with the goal of considering what these organizations may offer in terms of supporting ex-prisoners in building a resilient post-pandemic infrastructure of re-entry services and supports.

Gender and Rehabilitation

The transition from prison living to community re-entry is challenging, a source of anxiety and even distress for many who experience incarceration indifferent to their gender identity (Martin, 2018). For all prisoners, rehabilitation is thought to include institutional correctional programming, however participation in programming is rooted in diverse motivations. For some, interest falls in the desire to change, to desist from crime, and for personal growth; however, the spectrum is vast with many reporting motivations that are largely oriented towards acquiring parole and presenting as being ready for their future release. In speaking to formerly incarcerated men, Ricciardelli (2014) learned that many did not feel the programmes had value, at least while inside the prison. Some spoke of learning of how to manage their anger and practising skills that had no possibility of being implemented while inside prisons. Other discussed the trials and tribulations that could follow if they were to be outed by attending a programme designed for individuals convicted of sex offences. Yet, others still felt they learned in programming, and many wanted more. Instrumental here, was a desire to learn skills that could translate into employment opportunities. Particularly desired was employment that started inside prison and continued once released, but such programmes, to our knowledge, do not yet exist. Programming for incarcerated persons varies by gender of identification of the participant.[2] There are programmes oriented to men and to women. Programmes for women include those focus on family reunification, which is slightly less apparent for programming for men. Overall, one could easily argue that the prisoner code of conduct—the need to present a stoic and solid—may create disengagement and impression management among men who are in programming, and this may not be as much the case for incarcerated women.

At re-entry, additional challenges do exist that are gendered. Durnescu (2019), in his study of released men from Romania, spoke of the shock of release and pains tied to isolation and lack of social connection on the outside, something we also have learned about in the Canadian context. While Turnbull and Hannah-Moffat (2009: 532) write that in Canada 'parole boards constitute the female parolee as a fractured subject consisting of various 'risk/need factors' to which parole conditions are applied'. Women are thought to be governed by their re-entry conditions, a form of risk governance, as they experience the varying pains of release that are constituted by a slew of challenges that collectively are invisible forms of continued punishment (Travis & Petersilia, 2001). Their pains of release are compounded by the fact that the skills and actions required to survive release may counter those involved in surviving incarceration (Caputo-Levine, 2015). Moreover, in a study of the criminal records of women released from federal prisons, McKendy and Ricciardelli (2021: online) found that 'women, particularly those who had been incarcerated for extended periods of time, described to their POs feeling overwhelmed by the social changes that accompany the transition from the institutional to community settings' and that '[w]omen describe experiencing sensory overload as they adjusted to the various sounds and sights of the outside world'. Thus, perhaps impeding rehabilitation is the overlooked areas of the shock of release (Durnescu, 2019) that women (just like formerly incarcerated men) experience. The pressures on criminalized mothers to return, as part of their rehabilitation, to their mothering role is also rather gendered in systems of parole in so far as mothering and family reunification are prioritized among women and only an afterthought for men. The process of rehabilitation during re-entry, therefore, may be different for women and men. As for the parole experiences of transgendered or non-binary formerly incarcerated individuals in Canada, there is a gap in research that needs to be filled.

Conclusion

This chapter provided an overview of rehabilitation in the Canadian penal system with a focus on re-entry supports and structures and research on gender and rehabilitation. Compared to the United States relatively little research has been conducted on rehabilitation post-prison in the Canadian context. As such, we call on criminologists and others to continue to provide and expand empirical studies on how rehabilitation is practised, understood, and experienced in different realms. In particular, we urge scholars to turn the focus to the rehabilitation experiences of provincial prisoners who have little access to correctional post-prison supports. Community-based organizations and supports may be the first point of contact after release for this group of ex-prisoners, and the first (and sometimes only) source of formal support and help in the struggle to re-build their lives and survive. Studying in further depth the work of these organisations, as well as the experiences of the ex-prisoners with whom they engage will tell us much about the conditions of low-income communities and, therefore, the needs and struggles of ex-prisoners and other criminalized populations disproportionately drawn from those communities. Moreover, we call on researchers to expand work on how gender shapes re-entry and rehabilitative experiences.

Notes

1. Day parole and full parole are considered successful if they were completed without a return to prison for a breach of conditions or for a new offence (Public Safety Canada, 2016).
2. Specialized programming also exists in prisons and upon release for Indigenous prisoners/parolees. We refrain from a discussion of such programming given our focus in this section is on gender. However, we do note that, in the current Canadian context, incarceration rates of Indigenous individuals, particularly women, are at an all-time high and efforts are needed to fully understand the release experiences and rehabilitation experiences of self-identifying Indigenous individuals.

References

Adorjan, M., & Ricciardelli, R. (2018). The last bastion of rehabilitation: Contextualizing youth correctionalism in Canada. *Prison Journal, 98*(6), 655–677.

Andrews, D. A., & Bonta, J. (2010). *The psychology of criminal conduct* (4th ed.). Anderson.

Andrews, D. A., Bonta, J., & Hoge, R. D. (1990). Classification for effective rehabilitation: Rediscovering psychology. *Criminal Justice and Behavior, 17*(1), 19–52.

Brodeur, J. P. (2007). Comparative penology in perspective. *Crime and Justice, 36*(1), 49–91.

Bucerius, S., & Haggerty, K. D. (2019). Fentanyl behind bars: The implications of synthetic opiates for prisoners and correctional officers. *International Journal of Drug Policy, 71*, 133–138.

Bucerius, S., Haggerty, K. D., & Dunford, D. T. (2020). Prison as temporary refuge: Amplifying the voices of women detained in prison. *British Journal of Criminology, 61*(2), 519–537.

Caputo-Levine, D. D. (2015). *Removing the yard face: The impact of the carceral Habitus on reentry and reintegration.* State University of New York at Stony Brook.

Carrier, N. (2022). Monstrosity, correctional healing, and the limits of penal abolitionism. *Crime, Media, Culture* (pp. 1–19) First published April 1, 2022.

Casey, R., McNeill, F., Barkas, B., Cornish, N., Gormley, C., & Schinkel, M. (2021). Pervasive punishment in a pandemic. *Probation Journal, 68*(4), 476–492. https://doi.org/10.1177/02645505211050871

Combs, L. (2018). Healing ourselves: Interrogation the underutilization of Sections 81 and 84 of the corrections and conditional release act. *Manitoba Law Journal*, 163–189.

Correctional Service Canada. (2021a). *Correctional programs.* Available at: https://www.csc-scc.gc.ca/002/002-0001-en.shtml. Last accessed: May 20, 2022.

Correctional Services Canada. (2021b). Indigenous healing lodges. Available at: https://www.csc-scc.gc.ca/002/003/002003-2000-en.shtml. Last accessed: June 8, 2022.

Doob, A. N., & Webster, C. M. (2006). Countering punitiveness: Understanding stability in Canada's imprisonment rate. *Law and Society Review, 40*(2), 325–367.

Doob, A. N., & Webster, C. M. (2016). Weathering the storm? Testing the long-standing Canadian sentencing policy in the twenty-first century. *Crime and Justice, 45*(1), 359–418.

Durnescu, I. (2011). Pains of probation: Effective practice and human rights. *International Journal of Offender Therapy and Comparative Criminology, 55*(4), 530–545.

Durnescu, I. (2018). The five stages of prisoner reentry: Toward a process theory. *International Journal of Offender Therapy and Comparative Criminology, 62*(8), 2195–2215.

Durnescu, I. (2019). Pains of reentry revisited. *International Journal of Offender Therapy and Comparative Criminology, 63*(8), 1482–1498.

Garland, D. (2001). *The culture of control: Crime and social order in contemporary society.* University of Chicago Press.

Goodman, P., & Dawn, M. (2016). Prisoners, cows and abattoirs: The closing of Canada's prison farms as a political penal drama. *British Journal of Criminology, 56*(4), 793–812.

Government of Canada. (2019). Statistics: Parole, pardons and clemency. Available at: https://www.canada.ca/en/parole-board/corporate/publications-and-forms/statistics-parole-pardons-and-clemency.html. Last accessed: June 13, 2022.

Grieger, L., & Hosser, D. (2014). Which risk factors are really predictive?: An analysis of Andrews and Bonta's central eight risk factors for recidivism in German youth correctional facility inmates. *Criminal Justice and Behavior, 41*(5), 613–634.

Halushka, J. (2016). Work wisdom: Teaching former prisoners how to negotiate workplace interactions and perform a rehabilitated self. *Ethnography, 17*(1), 72–91.

Hannah-Moffat, K. (1999). Moral agent or actuarial subject: Risk and Canadian women's imprisonment. *Theoretical Criminology, 3*(1) 71–94.

Harding, D. J., Morenoff, J. D., & Wyse, J. J. (2019). On the outside. In *On the outside*. University of Chicago Press.

Hayes, D. (2015). The impact of supervision on the pains of community penalties in England and Wales: An exploratory study. *European Journal of Probation, 7*(2), 85–102.

Hermer, J., & Mosher, J. (2002). *Disorderly people: Law and the politics of exclusion in Ontario*. Fernwood Publishing.

Leverentz, A. (2010). People, places, and things: How female ex-prisoners negotiate their neighborhood context. *Journal of Contemporary Ethnography, 39*(6), 646–681.

Ifeonu, C., Haggerty, K., & Bucerius, S. (2022). Calories, commerce, and culture: The multiple valuations of food in prison. *Punishment and Society*. First published May 2, 2022.

Maier, K. (2021). Mobilizing prisoner reentry research: Halfway houses and the spatial temporal dynamics of prison release. *Theoretical Criminology, 25*(4), 601–618.

Malakieh, J. (2020). *Adult and youth correctional statistics in Canada, 2018/2019*. Statistics Canada. Available at: https://www150.statcan.gc.ca/n1/pub/85-002-x/2020001/article/00016-eng.htm. Last accessed: April 27, 2022.

Maier, K., & Ricciardelli, R. (2019). The prisoner's dilemma: How male prisoners experience and respond to penal threat while incarcerated. *Punishment and Society, 21*(2), 231–250.

Martin, L. (2018). Free but still walking the yard: Prisonization and the problems of reentry. *Journal of Contemporary Ethnography, 47*(5), 671–694.

McKendy, L., & Ricciardelli, R. (2021). The pains of release: Federally-sentenced women's experiences on parole. *European Journal of Probation, 13*(1), 1–20.

Meyer, J., & O'Malley, P. (2005). Missing the punitive turn? Canadian criminal justice, 'balance', and penal modernism. In K. Pratt, D. Brown, M. Brown, S. Hallsworth, & W. Morrison (Eds.), *The new punitiveness—Trends, theories, perspectives* (pp. 201–215). Willan Publishing.

Mijs, J. J. B. (2016). The missing organizational dimension of prisoner reentry: An ethnography of the road to reentry at a nonprofit service provider. *Sociological Forum, 31*(2), 291–309.

Miller, R. J. (2014). Devolving the carceral state: Race, prisoner reentry, and the micro-politics of urban poverty management. *Punishment and Society, 16*(3), 305–335.

Moore, D., & Hannah-Moffat, K. (2005). The liberal veil: Revisiting Canadian penality. In K. Pratt, D. Brown, M. Brown, S. Hallsworth, & W. Morrison

(Eds.), *The new punitiveness—Trends, theories, perspectives* (pp. 85–100). Willan Publishing.

Munn, M., & Bruckert, C. (2013). *On the outside: From lengthy imprisonment to lasting freedom.* University of British Columbia Press.

Norman, M., & Ricciardelli, R. (2022a). Operational and organizational stressors in community correctional work: Insights from probation and parole officers in Ontario. *Canada. Probation Journal, 69*(1), 86–106.

Norman, M., & Ricciardelli, R. (2022b). It's pure chaos every day: COVID-19 and the work of Canadian federal institutional parole officers. *European Journal of Probation, 14*(1), 1–20.

O'Brien, P. (2001). Just like baking a cake: Women describe the necessary ingredients for successful reentry after incarceration. *Families in Society, 82*(3), 287–295.

Office of the Correctional Investigator. (2021). Proportion of Indigenous women in federal custody nears 50%: Correctional investigator issue statement. Available at: https://www.oci-bec.gc.ca/cnt/comm/press/press20211217-eng.aspx. Last accessed: June 8, 2022.

Pager, D. (2003). The mark of a criminal record. *American Journal of Sociology, 108*(5), 937–975. http://search.proquest.com.ezproxy.library.yorku.ca/docview/64017048/abstract/13C54E7465DA79E004/92?accountid=15182

Prior, F. B. (2020). Security culture: Surveillance and responsibilization in a prisoner reentry organization. *Journal of Contemporary Ethnography, 49*(3), 390–413.

Ricciardelli, R. (2014). *Surviving incarceration: Inside Canadian prisons.* Wilfrid Laurier University Press.

Ricciardelli, R., & McKendy, L. (2021). A qualitative analysis of parole suspensions among women on parole. *Canadian Journal of Criminology and Criminal Justice, 63*(1), 89–105.

Ricciardelli, R., Bucerius, S., Tetrault, J., Crewe, B., & Pyrooz, D. (2021). *Correctional services during and beyond COVID-19.* RSC Policy Briefing. Available at: https://rsc-src.ca/sites/default/files/images/Corrections%20PB_EN.pdf

Ricciardelli, R., Maier, K., & Hannah-Moffat, K. (2015). Strategic masculinities: Vulnerabilities, risk and the production of prison masculinities. *Theoretical Criminology, 19*(4), 491–513.

Robinson, G. (2016). The cinderella complex: Punishment, society and community sanctions. *Punishment and Society, 18*(1), 95–112.

Solomon, A. L. (2006). Understanding the challenges of prisoner reentry: Research findings from the Urban Institute's prisoner reentry portfolio.

Sugie, N. F. (2018). Work as foraging: A smartphone study of job search and employment after prison. *American Journal of Sociology, 123*(5), 1453–1491.

Sylvestre, M.-E., Blomley, N., & Bellot, C. (2019). *Red zones: Criminal law and the territorial governance of marginalized people.* Cambridge University Press.

Timler, K., Brown, H., & Varcoe, C. (2019). Growing connection beyond prison walls: How a prison garden fosters rehabilitation and healing for incarcerated men. *Journal of Offender Rehabilitation, 58*(5), 444–463.

Tonry, M. (2004). *Thinking about crime: Sense and sensibility in American penal culture.* Oxford University Press.

Travis, J., & Petersilia, J. (2001). Reentry reconsidered: A new look at an old question. *Crime & Delinquency, 47*(3), 291–313.

Turnbull, S., & Hannah-Moffat, K. (2009). Under these conditions: Gender, parole and the governance of reintegration. *British Journal of Criminology, 49*(4), 532–551.

Visher, C. A., & Travis, J. (2003). Transitions from prison to community: Understanding individual pathways. *Annual Review of Sociology, 29*, 89–113.

Ward, T., & Maruna, S. (2007). *Rehabilitation: Beyond the risk assessment paradigm.* Routledge.

Ward, T., Yates, P. M., & Willis, G. M. (2012). The good lives model and the risk need responsivity model: A critical response to Andrews, Bonta, and Wormith (2011). *Criminal Justice and Behavior, 39*(1), 94–110.

Webster, C., & Doob, A. (2015). US punitiveness 'Canadian style'? Cultural values and Canadian punishment policy. *Punishment and Society, 17*(3), 299–321.

Werth, R. (2018). Frederic G Reamer, *On the Parole Board: Reflections on Crime, Punishment, Redemption and Justice.*

Western, B. (2018). *Homeward: Life in the year after prison.* Russell Sage Foundation.

Wheelock, D., Uggen, C., & Hlavka, H. (2011). Employment restrictions for individuals with felon status and racial inequality in the labor market. *Global perspectives on re-entry*, 278.

History and Transformations of the Model of Rehabilitation in the Criminal Justice System in Chile

Carolina Aurora Villagra Pincheira

A Brief Historical and Contextual Background to the Arrival of the Rehabilitative Ideal in the Chilean Criminal Justice System

With just over a century of formal existence, the Chilean penal system is quite new. In 1843, a decree was promulgated to build the first Penitentiary of Santiago, which was based on the idea of Bentham's panopticon and thought to be a model for all prisons in the country. It was not until 1911 that the General Directorate of Prisons was created, and the first regulation was issued for all prisons. However, the penal system has a longer history that dates from the colonial centuries when public executions, the use of torture and acts of public humiliation were frequent. During the decades that followed independence,[1] those practices remained in force, and the use of itinerant prisons became a popular custom. In 1874, the enactment of the Penal Code introduced liberal legislation that replaced the colonial laws and modernised the judicial system. By the end of the nineteenth century

---

C. A. Villagra Pincheira (✉)
Department of Psychology, University of Chile, Santiago, Chile
e-mail: cavillagra@uchile.cl

and inspired by prison models of the United States and Europe, the Chilean prison system started introducing new practices such as the imposition of a common discipline and the obligation to work inside prisons so prisoners could become honest citizens and hard workers (Memoria Chilena, 2021). In this way, the prison system slowly began to address rehabilitation goals, under a correctional rationality close to the prevailing positivism of the time.

During the twentieth century, Chile had an inquisitorial justice system inherited from Spain during the early days of the colonisation. It was mostly a written system in which the judiciary was in full charge of the functions of investigation, prosecution, and judgement, and the resolution of the cases could last for years, and even longer as most cases were appealed (Blanco et al., 2004). By the end of the century, in the context of the return to democracy after the military dictatorships that ruled most of these countries between the late 1960s and 1980s, most Latin American countries started processes of reform oriented to the modernised criminal legislations to meet the standards set out in international treaties and to reflect the principles of the Rule of Law (Riego & Duce, 2008). The Criminal Procedure Reform (CPR), started in 2000 and fully implemented in 2005, is the most significant transformation in Chilean justice history, introducing an oral procedure, separating the functions of investigation, prosecution, and judgement, and creating institutions ad hoc. In its early years, studies claimed that the CPR improved the overall standards of efficacy of the criminal justice system (Ministerio Público de Chile & Vera Institute, 2004), though, other studies suggested that improvement in the efficiency of prosecution, along with a penal structure that promoted the use of imprisonment over community sanctions, resulted in an exponential increase in the number of people sent to prison (Alvarez et al., 2007; Consejo de Reforma, 2009; Salinero, 2012). However, recent studies have disputed the idea that the upsurge in prison population is a result of the CPR, advocating that this sustained upward trend originated in the 1990s, which in any case confirms the punitive historical trend of the country (Arriagada et al., 2021).

In fact, already in the twenty-first century, the prison population has grown from 33,000 to 52,000 between 2000 and 2009, reaching the highest imprisonment rate in South America at 323 inmates per 100,000 inhabitants[2] (Walmsley, 2011), and generating serious problems of overcrowding, impoverishment of the quality life, high reoffending rates, and high public spending on maintaining prison infrastructure. In response, in 2002 the Government launched the 'prison modernisation process' inspired by foreign models of privatisation that proposed the building of ten new prisons to resolve the overcrowding situation and to contribute to the rehabilitation of prisoners

(Dammert & Díaz, 2005a). The Chilean model resulted in a mixed system in which both the State and the private companies participate within the regulatory framework of the Concessions Law, whereby the concessionaire (grant holder) is responsible for the design, financing, construction, and maintenance of infrastructure, as well as the provision of services such as social reintegration, health, food, laundry, cleaning, and pest control, among others. Gendarmería, for its part, continued to oversee security and guarding (BID, 2013). The first concession prison was built in 2005 and there are currently eight concession prisons in force that house about 40% of the country's prison population (Gendarmería, 2020).

As the Inter American Commission of Human Rights and the Supreme Court reported in 2009, despite the increase in prison capacity the situation in both traditional and concession prisons was critical in terms of overcrowding, living conditions, and lack of policies to support rehabilitation (UDP, 2010). The critical prison situation reached a fatal point in December 2010 when 81 inmates died and several others were left severely wounded in the fire at San Miguel prison, the worst tragedy in Chilean prison history (UDP, 2011). This disaster prompted several initiatives to relieve pressure on the prison system through the enactment of the law 20.603 in 2013,[3] which modified the alternative measures and established a new system of community sentences. This was a crucial reform that placed the rehabilitative ideal in the community and brought with it updated knowledge about intervention and specialised supervision. Since then the imprisonment rate has fallen, currently standing at 215 (Prison Studies, 2022), and community sentencing has been on the rise, comprising 55% of sentenced population and contributing to the reduction in the use of imprisonment as the main penal sanction.

As far as rehabilitation approaches are concerned, the Risk, Need and Responsibility model (RNR) was officially introduced in a prison programme in 2007, which later expanded to a broader sample of prisons, setting new standards for intervention, based on empirical criminological evidence. From then on, the RNR model expanded to the open system in 2013 and the post-penitentiary system in 2015. Gendarmería, the public institution in charge of executing sentences, carries out its intervention work based on the model which, although unevenly, has been implemented throughout the penitentiary system. The RNR model has been assessed as appropriate for guiding intervention strategies in Chile; however, State evaluations quantify the overall performance results of the penitentiary system as low (DIPRES, 2019).

The Concept of Rehabilitation[4] Within the Chilean Normative Structure

Unlike some countries that enshrine the right to social reintegration in their Political Constitution, Chile does not do so, nor does it have a specific law that regulates the control of criminal execution, nor a judicial body specialising in this matter (EUROsocial, 2014). Likewise, the national regulation does not explicitly establish rehabilitation or reintegration as aims of punishment; notwithstanding that, treaties and conventions ratified by Chile imply that the criminal justice system and national regulation should be oriented towards the achievement of special preventive purposes (Ramírez & Sánchez, 2021).

The Secretary of State in the Ministry of Justice and Human Rights[5] is responsible for formulating policies and plans for prison treatment and rehabilitation of the convicted population, as well as the evaluation of the results of these policies, plans, and programmes (DFL3, 2016). Gendarmería de Chile, is a public institution, created in 1921 and dependent on the Ministry of Justice and Human Rights, whose purpose, as stated in Art. 1 of its Organic Law, is to 'care, monitor and contribute to the social reintegration of persons who, by resolution of competent authorities, were detained or deprived of liberty and fulfil the other functions indicated by law' (Ministerio de Justicia, 1979). Gendarmería is organised into three systems: the closed system, which deals with people who are deprived of their liberty by order of the competent courts, either in pre-trial detention, serving a sentence of imprisonment or serving a coercion measure; the open system, which deals with people who are serving community sentences, and the post-penitentiary system, mostly concerned with people who have already served their sentence, that expunges their criminal records.

The purpose of prison activity is governed by the rules established in the Decree Law 518 of Regulations for Penitentiary Establishments (Ministerio de Justicia, 1998), which declares in its article 1 that the prison:

> will have as its primary purpose the care, custody, and assistance of detainees, subject to preventive detention and sentenced, as well as the educational action necessary for the social reintegration of those sentenced to custodial or community sentences.

Therefore, while rehabilitation and social reintegration are not recognised at the constitutional or higher-level laws, they are part of the Chilean penal normative structure. However, this normative fragility has had implications for intervention. The fact that the regulation does not provide clear conceptual definitions of rehabilitation or social reintegration, and that these expressions are used as synonyms, has allowed numerous and diverse practices to be classified as rehabilitative in correctional practice. With this, the necessary strength and theoretical precision that must underpin the specialised intervention is lost. It affects the operationalisation of the terms, and consequently, limits the possibilities of having shared indicators that allow the monitoring and evaluation of the impact of the interventions, comparison of results, longitudinal monitoring, among other public policy actions that facilitate assessment of the efficacy of interventions and establish short and long-term goals.

The Penal Population and a State of Fragile Stability

A key component of rehabilitation and social reintegration is knowledge of the characteristics and criminogenic needs of the penal population. The adult penal population includes all those deprived of liberty, serving community sentences, and attending the post-penitentiary system. In April 2022, the adult penal population comprised 121,922 people, of which 46,647 were in prison, 57,700 serving community sentences, and 17,597 in the post-penitentiary system (Gendarmería, 2022a). In 2020, in the 85 penitentiary units throughout the country, the crime for which most men entered prison was robbery (44%) and drug-related crimes in the case of women (40%) and the most common sentence length 5–10 years (37%). The most represented age group, 25–34, accounted for 40% of the total number of people in custody. 6.8% of the total prison population were foreigners. Regarding ethnic groups, 6% declared to belong to an ethnic group, of which 58% identified themselves as Mapuche, 21% Aymara, and 14% Quechua (Gendarmería, 2020). In the open system 44% were serving conditional remission, 37% probation, 11% partial imprisonment, and 7% community service (Gendarmería, 2020).

In terms of gender, the female population accounts for 7.5% of those in prison, 13% of those serving community sentences, and 11% of those in the post-penitentiary system. While the general average of Mapuche, is 33% (15,359 people by April 2022), when disaggregated by gender, data shows that 32% of males deprived of liberty are in pre-trial detention, while in the case of females that rises to 45% (Gendarmería, 2022a, b, c). This is a critical gender issue, as the disproportionate portion of women in pre-trial detention means that almost half of all women in custody are not yet convicted of a crime. It is well known that the abuse of pre-trial detention contributes to prison overcrowding, placing detainees in a vulnerable position for abuse and torture and can inflict persistent mental and physical damage on people who go through it. Studies have shown that the impact of pre-trial detention can be more severe for women than men, even for short periods, affecting different areas of life that include their children (UNODC, 2014). In terms of rehabilitation, this population can receive basic support but are formally excluded from the model of social reintegration of Gendarmería, which is intended for convicted people only; as a consequence, a considerable number of women in prison are left unattended.

The prison regime is guided by the progressive principle, this is, that people in custody should be granted growing levels of freedom to guarantee a safety return to the community. This principle is closely related to rehabilitation and social reintegration (Eurosocial, 2014). Permissions and early release mechanisms are key to compliance with the progressive principle and the Chilean regulation considers both. The Prison Regulations in the art. 96 sets out the four types of furlough[6] to which inmates are entitled to apply once several requirements are fulfilled. While in the regulations these permissions are described as rehabilitative actions, in practice the proportion of prisoners granted furloughs has decreased in the last two decades from 51% of the prison population in 1995 to 1.3% in 2011 and a similar number in 2020, figures that are extremely low (Gendarmería, 2022a, b, c; Villagra & Droppelmann, 2015). Studies have suggested that a more risk-averse approach to judicial decision-making and the lack of use of technical criteria by practitioners in charge of the final decision are contributing factors to this decrease (FPC-CESC, 2012). A comparable situation has been observed with parole (the only early release mechanisms contemplated in the Chilean regulation), granted to a fraction of the prison population (Villagra & Droppelmann, 2015).

As has been described, although the statistics show that the system of alternative sentences to prison is being used, the prison system still faces some critical problems with its population. A high percentage of its population is in preventive detention—A situation that especially affects women—and the length of the sentences is quite high. Although the regulations state that the principle of progressivity should be followed, in practice extremely limited use is made of permission and parole mechanisms. Accordingly, the incarcerated population remains rather static, and at least a third cannot access specialised intervention because they are in the category of defendants.

The Model of Rehabilitation and Social Reintegration Delivered by Gendarmería

Until well into the 2000s, intervention work with the prison population was based on a psychosocial model, a generic name with poorly defined theoretical guidelines. The first milestone in the incorporation of criminological evidence into interventions in prison occurred in 2007 with the launch of the 'Programme of Social Reintegration' designed and implemented by a Secretary of State in the Home Office in one of the most complex prisons in the country, Colina 2. This was an offender-focused intervention which followed the principles of the RNR model, was delivered by trained staff, and focused on high-risk individuals. This was undoubtedly a brave initiative in a public context of disbelief in correctional rehabilitation and in a time of expansion of tough criminal policies that set the criminological standards of specialised interventions that would later permeate the entire penitentiary system.

The Executive affirms that during the last two decades, efforts have been made to introduce criminological-based strategies for supporting rehabilitation and social reintegration into Gendarmería's work guidelines, striving to consolidate a model capable of reducing criminal recidivism and promoting the integration of people into society after serving a custodial or community sentence (Ministerio de Justicia y Derechos Humanos, 2018). The current model of intervention based on the RNR approach, targets convicted people who have been assessed as high and very high risk of reoffending, focuses on variables that influence the recurrence of offending behaviour, namely, dynamic risk factors related to attitudes, pro-criminal cognitions, violent behaviour patterns, antisocial peer associations, addictions, and poor development of prosocial work and training competences (Gendarmería, 2022c).

The model guides the delivery of the intervention in the three systems, and is executed in four phases: *Initial evaluation*, in which risk assessments are carried out through the 'Inventory for Case/Intervention Management (IGI)', a tool that is an adaptation of the 'Level of Service Case Management Inventory' (LS/CMI) by Andrews et al. (2004); *Individual Intervention Plan*, which is prepared jointly by a professional and the user based on the results of the initial evaluation; *Intervention*, which will address the needs detected in the evaluation phase and consigned in the plan. The intervention modalities include one-to-one and group sessions, training courses, school remediation, and referrals to public or private institutions, among others. The intervention can include attendance to specific programmes, depending on what has been indicated on the Individual Intervention Plan; and *Exit phase*, when a new risk assessment is carried out for everyone who had an initial risk assessment and completed their individual intervention plan, to evaluate the intervention progress (Gendarmería, 2022b).

How the Model Works in the Three Systems, Closed, Open, and Post-Penitentiary

Within this framework of phases, each system organises its own supply of interventions and programmes:

- In the closed system, intervention is organised around the Programme of social reintegration for people in custody, which includes both services for social integration (such as work and education) and psychosocial criminological intervention. Specific programmes in the closed system include treatment for problematic alcohol and/or drug use, an intervention for individuals convicted of sex offences, an education and work centre, and care for pregnant women and women with nursing children.
- In the open system, Law 20.603 (Ministerio de Justicia, 2013) that introduced a new scheme of community sentences[7] in December 2013 was a milestone in terms of specialised intervention. This law modified the previous scheme of alternative measures regulated in the Law 18.216 of 1983 that had three sanctions: conditional remission of the sentence, night detention, and probation. The main problem with the alternative measures was that judges considered them too 'soft' and were not perceived as real punishment. Probation, meanwhile, was the measure with the greatest special preventive content as it included treatment addressed to change criminal behaviour supervised by a probation officer; however, its imposition was limited by the catalogue of crimes to which it was applicable (Salinero & Morales, 2019). Therefore, for offences where the sentence could be an alternative measure or imprisonment, the judges tended to deem the latter more effective as a punishment, thus contributing to the prison crisis and years of political and academic debate. The broader catalogue of sanctions introduced in 2013 included conditional remission, partial imprisonment, expulsion of foreigners, provision of services for the benefit of the community, and a strengthened form of probation and an intense probation, both based on updated criminological evidence related effective supervision and provided by qualified officers. These forms of probation were explicitly included to fulfil the social reintegration of

the sentenced person (Ministerio de Justicia, 2012). Specialised intervention in the open system can include attendance to specific programmes such as work intermediation or psychosocial criminological intervention. This reform also introduced a completely new control mechanism for domestic violence and some sexual crimes in the form of telematic monitoring, applicable to those sentenced to partial imprisonment and intensive probation.

- In the post-penitentiary system, since 2015 RNR principles have been included in the post-prison support programme and a work reinsertion programme.

The last State budget evaluation of the performance of the rehabilitation and reintegration programmes in the three systems, reported that the intervention model based on an adequate theoretical framework had raised the standards of criminological intervention. However, they also identified several areas that needed improvement, such as the design of the programmes, case management, network management and identification of public spending, information and monitoring systems, and implementation of budgets (DIPRES, 2018, 2019). Overall, the performance results show low levels of achievement for the closed and post-penitentiary systems, and medium for the open systems. These results might be related to factors such as the lack of systematised data that impede assessments of results or impact, the low budget allocated for reintegration work[8,9] and the reduced coverage of the model,[10] all factors in which the closed and post-penitentiary systems score lower than the open one.

The situation of prisons merits more attention. Successive reports on human rights carried out by academic institutions during the last two decades have consistently reported serious problems that have not substantially improved despite the reforms and the inclusion of the concession system. The last study of prison conditions reported persistent problems related to overcrowding, poor living conditions, and situations that threaten the personal integrity of prisoners, and that challenge compliance with international human rights standards in prison matters (INDH, 2021). Of course, this is relevant for rehabilitation and social reintegration in Chilean prisons because in order to start processes of personal change that can lead to desistence from offending people need to have decent standards of living and to be treated with respect and dignity.

The Concession System of Prisons

Any analysis of the prison situation must include the concession (private) system, which, although it has only eight out of a total of 85 prisons nationwide, houses about 40 per cent of the total incarcerated population in the country (Gendarmería, 2020). As mentioned earlier, the crisis of the Chilean prison system in the late 1990s and early 2000s, made it urgent to improve the capacity and quality of care of the entire system; however, the State did not have a budget for prison infrastructure. Privatisation appeared as an attractive alternative, as it was thought it would encourage a more efficient management of penal facilities, improve living conditions and access to services and programmes, and reduce the costs of prison maintenance. However, total privatisation would exclude a State that has the non-delegable legal obligation to restrict certain rights of individuals and to care for those in vulnerable situations (Martínez & Espinoza, 2009). Accordingly, the Chilean government opted for a system of public–private partnership, an alternative model to total privatisation where the State maintained its various functions (Dammert, 2006).

This project required a strong initial investment of around 280 million dollars for the construction, equipping, and maintenance of ten new medium and high security prisons with space for approximately 16,000 new places (Dammert & Díaz, 2005b). The implementation of the prison modernisation process was not at all expeditious, largely due to the rigidity of a Concessions Law that is quite incompatible with the dynamic nature of the prison world. In 2002, the construction of ten prisons of medium to high complexity was meant to take ten years, however, this deadline was never met. The first concession prison was opened in 2005, two prison buildings were abandoned in the process of construction, and, by 2022, eight prisons are operational rather than the promised ten.

The prison modernisation process had a strong rehabilitative aspiration based on the idea that private management would offer more efficient strategies to reduce recidivism, compared with the State-run prisons. The Deputy Minister of Justice of the time declared that the main aim of this process was 'to advance to a more efficient system, capable of granting guarantees to citizens, reconciled with a real rehabilitation effort for a significant percentage of the prison population, and always safeguarding the international standards of respect for fundamental rights' (Arellano, 2003 in BID, 2013: 32). Indeed, during the first years of operation, it was the private company's obligation to include a model of intervention in their bid for the contract. The one chosen was the prosocial skills model developed by Vicente Garrido, which includes a set of techniques designed to improve, among other things, social skills, critical reasoning, moral education, and problem solving (BID, 2013). Years later, the role of the State in matters of theoretical models and their implementation took more prominence. Currently, the rehabilitation plans are regulated in the Annual Plan for Social Reintegration (PARS for its acronym in Spanish), a document containing the technical guidelines indicated by the Gendarmería, including the RNR model strategies used in the traditional prisons. Before being put into operation in the concession prisons these plans must go through an annual review and approval of the Ministry of Justice.

Almost two decades after the implementation of the prison modernisation process, there are no comprehensive evaluations of the performance and results of the concession prisons in the three areas in which they were expected to introduce substantive improvements: infrastructure, living conditions; provision of services, and rehabilitation. Early studies on concession prisons' performance are not encouraging). showed that rather than being less costly as expected, the daily cost per person in concession prisons was more than three times the cost of the traditional prisons.[11] Moreover, the overall living conditions did not show a substantial improvement (indeed, there was a worsening in the living and work conditions for prison officers); and among other worrying results, there was an alarming rise in the number of suicides (UDP, 2007). In 2013, Fundación Paz Ciudadana and the Interamerican Bank of Development conducted the most comprehensive empirical study to date comparing the efficacy in reducing recidivism of the concession system with the traditional system.[12] The results showed that the levels of recidivism did not present any statistically significant differences associated with the type of prison: nor was it possible to distinguish inmates who served time in a traditional prison from those who had served their sentence in a concession prison (BID, 2013). In fact, Gendarmería, in its study of the recidivism of individuals who left prison in 2010, found a statistically significant differences in the rate of recidivism between both types of prisons, 41.1% for concession prisons compared to 38.2 for State-run prisons (Gendarmería, 2013).

As far as rehabilitative aspiration is concerned, studies have shown that one of the main problems of the concession prisons relates to the access, supply, and quality of the rehabilitation programmes. On one hand, the theoretical model of intervention does not match the needs and characteristics of the Chilean prison population (BID, 2013), and on the other, there is a statistically significant difference in access to social reintegration programmes in so far as concession prisons have less compared to traditional prisons (Sanhueza & Pérez, 2017). Although the results of both studies are preliminary and cannot be generalised, they still show some worrying trends in the approach to rehabilitation in the concession prisons, which replicates and perpetuates some of the historic and entrenched problems of the prison systems in matters of rehabilitation and social integration, namely inadequacy, lack of access, lack of focalisation, and low coverage.

Future Directions in Policy and Practice

In the last two decades, there have been numerous efforts to improve prison conditions, the performance of prison management, and the real chances of reintegration of convicted persons in Chile. This is evident in numerous legal initiatives, improvement of specialised intervention practices, institutional strengthening actions, execution of studies, and countless proposals presented at various levels of political, academic, and public discussion. This same enthusiasm collides with the political pressures that call for tougher sentences and the short-term punitive State response. In other words, there have been clear intentions to strengthen the rehabilitation approach; however, it is still inorganic, fragmented, and weak in terms of its theoretical and applied foundations. Among the numerous and varied milestones of the last two decades in the adult penal system, this Chapter highlighted the inclusion of private companies in the prison system through the concession model in 2002, and the modification of the alternative punishment system towards a system of sanctions in the community in 2013. In so doing, it left out numerous and valuable initiatives developed in recent years, some of them with a strong transformative potential. These include the creation of the National Youth Social Reintegration Service that promises to be a substantive collaboration with juvenile justice and rehabilitation approaches emerging from the latest developments in criminology. Important as those initiatives are, the Chapter has concentrated on the adult justice milestones because, from their inception, they had a declared interest in strengthening the value of reintegration as a public project, and they had strong public backing that allowed, among other things, the inclusion of specialised work teams and improvement of facilities.

Studies have shown that Law 20,603, which is largely a response to the deteriorated state of the prison estate introduced a new system of community sanctions, has led to some decongestion of the prison system through judges making use of those sanctions. However, without a direct focus on the prison system that alone cannot achieve a change in the punitive rationality or resolve the numerous problems, including overcrowding, which persist. It is important to note that in public performance evaluations, the open system has been showing a good management capacity for specialised intervention. That includes the RNR model, but it was only with the introduction of Law 20,603 that it became entrenched in prison management and progressively permeated the closed and post-penitentiary systems. Studies of the concession prisons have been less positive, showing that they have not brought about substantial improvement in terms of quality of life, access to rehabilitation programmes, or a decrease in recidivism.

The fact that two reforms of this scope have not been capable of transforming the prison system into one focused on rehabilitation and social reintegration, has to do with the fact that sustained efforts are required with long-term objectives at the normative, theoretical, practical, and financial levels. As mentioned above, rehabilitation as an aim of punishment is referred to by various regulatory bodies, but it is not embedded in the Constitution or in any prominent law, such as a law for the execution of sentences. This normative recognition is fundamental to an adequate public discussion about the need for the State to budget appropriately for medium and long-term objectives. Currently, less than 10 per cent of the funds granted annually to the Gendarmería are dedicated to the achievement of its rehabilitation ideal, thus demonstrating not only the enormous gap between the legal design and practical application but also the need for a review of public policy.

Undoubtedly, rehabilitation being recognised legally and financially does not end the problems. A discussion about the real meaning of the term rehabilitation and its associated concepts is required not only because it is desired by academics but, not with an academic desire but because such a discussion goes to the heart of what a society expects for its citizens, the meaning of punishment, and even the forms of coexistence within communities. Currently, rehabilitation achievements are measured through compliance with indicators, which is a limited way of understanding rehabilitation and social reintegration. Any State effort in this area should embrace a broader and more complex concept of rehabilitation, in line with the evidence of empirical research.

Theoretical discussion has strong implications for practice. Once society's understanding of rehabilitation and social reintegration is identified, there must necessarily be a discussion about the ways in which the State and other relevant actors, such as the community and the private sector, can collaborate in their achievement. At the State level, specifically Gendarmería, this theoretical-practical discussion must review the application modality of the

RNR model, evaluate its strengths and the areas that require development, and incorporate new criminological evidence that can enhance and improve the efficacy of desistance-focused and gender-sensitive interventions. Moreover, it should reflect on the four forms of rehabilitation—personal, moral, social, and legal—put forward by Burke et al. (2018), and their implications for the achievement of significant and sustained social change.

Notes

1. The independence of Chile took place in the period from 18 September 1810, date of installation of the First Government Board, until the establishment of the first National Congress, on 4 July 1811.
2. Chile's population in 2011 was 17,233,584 (Banco Mundial, 2022).
3. The origin of this reform can be found in a message from the Executive power in 2008 (Salinero & Morales, 2019).
4. In the Spanish language in general and in Latin America in particular, the word 'rehabilitation' is used interchangeably with others such as reintegration, social integration, resocialisation, meaning different things for different countries (Villagra, 2008). The most accurate translation to the meaning given to the term 'rehabilitation' in Chile would be 'social reintegration'.
5. Organic Law art. 2. The art. 1, defines that this Ministry is responsible of relating the Executive with the Judicial Branch, fostering and promoting human rights, and executing the actions that the law and the President of the Republic entrust to it.
6. These are the sporadic, Sunday, weekend, and daily permissions.
7. Sentences served in the community have over a century of history in the Chilean regulation, first regarded as suspension formulas, then as alternative measures and later and currently, substitute penalties, having been named according to the spirit of the political and criminological debates of each moment (Salinero & Morales, 2019).
8. Gendarmería has a military approach, therefore, it is organised around the functions of custody and security, which consume around 55% of the total budget, followed by 28 % dedicated to the delivery of basis services, and only 8% allocated for rehabilitation and social reintegration (Ramírez & Sánchez, 2021).
9. According to information reported by Gendarmería, the model of intervention the intervention model covers around 25% of the user population of the closed and open systems, and around 6% of the users of the post-penitentiary system (Gendarmería, 2018 in Ramírez & Sánchez, 2021).
10. US$35 versus US$11 (Dammert & Díaz, 2005a, 2005b: 5).

11. This study is the most comprehensive, although its sample is reduced to group 1: Alto Hospicio, La Serena, and Rancagua. At that time, there were 7 concession prisons in operation: Concepción in group 2, and Santiago I, Valdivia, Puerto Montt in group 3.

References

Alvarez, P., Herrera, R., & Marangunic, A. (2007). Impacto de la Reforma Procesal Penal en la población penal carcelaria del país. *Revista De Estudios Criminológicos y Penitenciarios De Gendarmeria De Chile, 11*, 117–133.

Andrews, D. A., Bonta, J. L., & Wormith, S. J. (2004). *LS/CMI: The level of service/case management inventory*. Multi-Health System.

Arriagada, I., Farías, J., & Walker, A. (2021). Evolución de la Población Penal en Chile desde 1991 a 2007: Aproximación empírica a los efectos de la reforma procesal penal. *Política Criminal, 16*(31), 62–82.

Banco Interamericano de Desarrollo, BID. (2013). Evaluación del sistema concesionado versus el sistema tradicional en la reducción de la reincidencia delictual. Banco Interamericano de Desarrollo, Fundación Paz Ciudadana. p. cm. (IDB Technical note; 558).

Banco Mundial. (2022). *Datos. Población total, Chile*. Available at https://datos.bancomundial.org/indicator/SP.POP.TOTL?locations=CL

Biblioteca del Congreso Nacional (n.d.) Historia política de Chile. Período 1810–1811. Available in https://www.bcn.cl/historiapolitica/hitos_periodo/detalle_periodo.html?per=1810-1811

Blanco, R., Hutt, R., & Rojas, H. (2004). Reform to the criminal justice system in Chile: Evaluation and challenges. *Loyola University Chicago International Law Review, 1*(2), 253–269.

Burke, L., Collett, S., & McNeill, F. (2018). *Reimagining rehabilitation: Beyond the individual* (1st ed.). Routledge.

Consejo de Reforma Penitenciaria. (2009). *Recomendaciones para una Nueva Política Penitenciaria*. Documento de trabajo no publicado.

Dammert, L. (2006). *El sistema penitenciario en Chile: desafíos para el nuevo modelo público-privado*. Paper prepared to be delivered at the 2006 Meeting of the Latin American Studies Association. San Juan, Puerto Rico. March 15–18, 2006.

Dammert, L., & Díaz, J. (2005a). *Cárceles privadas en Chile. ¿Modelo de gestión penitenciaria o inversión inmobiliaria?* FLACSO Chile.

Dammert, L., & Díaz, J. (2005b). *El costo de encarcelar*. FLACSO Chile.

DFL 3. (2016). *Fija el texto refundido, coordinado y sistematizado de la Ley Orgánica del Ministerio de Justicia y Derechos Humanos*. Biblioteca del Congreso Nacional. Available at http://bcn.cl/2qvrp

Dirección de Presupuestos, DIPRES. (2018). Informe final, evaluación programas gubernamentales. Programa intervención y/o control de la población penada sujeta a la Ley N° 18.216, Gendarmería de Chile, Ministerio de Justicia y Derechos Humanos. Available at https://www.dipres.gob.cl/597/articles-177351_informe_final.pdf

Dirección de Presupuestos, DIPRES. (2019). Informe final, evaluación programas gubernamentales. Programas de rehabilitación y reinserción social, Gendarmería de Chile, Ministerio de Justicia y Derechos humanos. Available at https://www.dipres.gob.cl/597/articles-189326_informe_final.pdf

Eurosocial. (2014). Ejecución de la pena privativa de libertad: una mirada comparada. Documento de trabajo N°17. Serie Guías y Manuales del Área Justicia. Madrid, 2014.

Fundación Paz Ciudadana—Centro de Estudios en Seguridad Ciudadana de la Universidad de Chile, FPC-CESC. (2012). Estudio de evaluación del programa de fortalecimiento de los consejos técnicos y seguimiento de los beneficiarios con salida controlada al medio libre. Estudio comisionado por el Ministerio de Justicia.

Gendarmería de Chile. (2013). La reincidencia: un desafío para la gestión del sistema penitenciario chileno y las políticas públicas. *Estudio de reincidencia de individuos egresados el año 2010.* Subdirección técnica.

Gendarmería de Chile. (2020). *Compendio estadístico 2020.* Subdirección de Reinserción Social.

Gendarmería de Chile. (2022a). *Estadística general penitenciaria.* Available at https://www.gendarmeria.gob.cl/est_general.html

Gendarmería de Chile. (2022b). *Modelo de intervención.* Available at https://www.gendarmeria.gob.cl/modelo_intervencion.html

Gendarmería de Chile. (2022c). *Orientaciones técnicas 2022c.* Subdirección de Reinserción Social.

Instituto Nacional de Derechos Humanos, INDH. (2021). *Quinto Estudio de Condiciones Carcelarias en Chile, 2019.* Diagnóstico del cumplimiento de los estándares internacionales de derechos humanos en privación de libertad. INDH Chile.

Martínez, F., & Espinoza, O. (2009). Cárceles concesionadas en Chile, ¿el camino a la privatización? *en Debates Penitenciarios, 9*: 3–16. Available at https://www.cesc.uchile.cl/publicaciones/debates_penitenciarios_09.pdf

Memoria Chilena. (2021). *Formación del sistema carcelario en Chile (1800–1911).* Available at http://www.memoriachilena.gob.cl/602/w3-article-628.html

Ministerio de Justicia. (1979). *Decreto ley 2859. Fija Ley orgánica de Gendarmería de Chile.* Biblioteca del Congreso Nacional. Available at http://bcn.cl/309wg

Ministerio de Justicia. (1998). *Decreto 518. Aprueba Reglamento de establecimientos penitenciarios.* Biblioteca del Congreso Nacional. Available at http://bcn.cl/2nle9

Ministerio de Justicia. (2012). *Material de capacitación nueva Ley 18.216. Análisis de las modificaciones introducidas por la Ley 20.603.* División de Reinserción Social.

Ministerio de Justicia. (2013). *Ley N° 20.603 que modifica la Ley N° 18.216, que establece medidas alternativas a las penas privativas o restrictivas de libertad.* Biblioteca del Congreso Nacional. Available at http://bcn.cl/2kcru

Ministerio de Justicia y Derechos Humanos. (2018). *Política Pública de Reinserción Social 2017*. Available at https://www.reinsercionsocial.gob.cl/media/2018/02/Pol%C3%ADticas_Públicas_Reinserción_Social_2ed2017.pdf

Ministerio Público de Chile y Vera Institute of Justice. (2004). *Analizando la Reforma a la Justicia Criminal en Chile: un Estudio Empírico entre el Nuevo y el Antiguo Sistema Penal*. Vera Institute of Justice.

Prison Studies. (2022). *World prison brief data of Chile*. Available at https://www.prisonstudies.org/country/chile

Ramírez, M. A., & Sánchez, M. (2021). Ejecución panel y sistema penitenciario en Chile en Sistemas penitenciarios y ejecución penal en Latinoamérica. Una mirada regional y opciones de abordaje. Centro de Estudios de Justicia de las Américas.

Riego, C., & Duce, M. (2008). *Prisión Preventiva y Reforma Procesal Penal en América Latina, Evaluación y Perspectivas*. Centro de Estudio de Justicia de las Américas.

Salinero, S. (2012). ¿Por qué aumenta la Población Penal en Chile? Un Estudio Criminológico Longitudinal. *Lus Et Praxis, 18*(1), 113–150.

Salinero, S., & Morales, A. M. (2019). Las penas alternativas a la cárcel en Chile. Un análisis desde su evolución histórica. *Revista De Derecho (valparaíso), 52*, 255–292.

Sanhueza, G., & Pérez, F. (2017). Cárceles concesionadas en Chile: evidencia empírica y perspectivas futuras a 10 años de su creación. *Política Criminal, 12*(24), 1066–1084.

United Nations Office on Drugs and Crime, UNODC. (2014). Handbook on women and imprisonment. *Criminal justice handbook series* (2nd ed.).

Universidad Diego Portales, UDP. (2007). *Condiciones carcelarias y derechos humanos, en Informe Anual sobre Derechos Humanos en Chile* (pp. 17–59). Salesianos Impresiones.

Universidad Diego Portales, UDP. (2010). *Informe Anual sobre Derechos Humanos en Chile*. Salesianos Impresiones.

Universidad Diego Portales, UDP. (2011). *Informe Anual sobre Derechos Humanos en Chile*. Salesianos Impresiones.

Villagra, C. (2008). *Hacia una política postpenitenciaria en Chile*. Ril Editores.

Villagra, C., & Droppelmann, C. (2015). The law, practice, and experience of conditional freedom, In Chile: No man's land'. In R. Armstrong & D. Ioan (Eds.), *Parole and beyond: International experiences of life after prison*. Palgrave Studies in Prison and Penology.

Walmsley, R. (2011). *World prison population list* (9th ed.). International Centre for Prison Studies.

Rehabilitation in a Risk Society: 'The Case of China'

Enshen Li

A Historical Snapshot of Rehabilitation in China

Since the founding of the People's Republic of China (China), rehabilitation has always been an integral part of the country's penal discourse and practice. Driven by the Confucian canon that 'every person is capable of being reformed' (Fyfield, 1982: 64), rehabilitation has been relied upon by the Chinese authorities for decades to inform the treatment of wrongdoers in conjunction with punishment. This rehabilitative orientation tends to be all-encompassing and penetrative, in the sense of not only the traditional forms of sanction such as prison confinement, but also with more recent innovative types of punishment such as community corrections. It is generally assumed that the principles of rehabilitation and corrections are equally, if not more, important than the principles of censure and retribution in converting wrongdoers into 'useful and law-binding citizens' of society (Cao & Cullen, 2001; Wu & Vander Beken, 2018). Compared to the latter, the former is believed to be predicated on a raft of thought/behaviour-reforming approaches, for example, education, labour, academic, and vocational training.

The rehabilitative ideal of punishment first manifested itself in revolutionary China during Mao Zedong's reign (1949–1976). In Maoist China,

E. Li (✉)
School of Law, The University of Queensland, St Lucia, QLD, Australia
e-mail: e.li@law.uq.edu.au

an 'antagonistic contradiction' dichotomy was hoisted by this first leadership of the Communist Party ('the Party'), creating a conflicting class society—one class of the masses and the other of political foes deemed criminals (Leng & Chiu, 1985). Conceived as the 'class enemy' of the people, political criminals were the target of the state's dictatorial movement and thereby handled with repression, coercion, and harsh punishment. Even so, apart from those sentenced to the death penalty, most political criminals were also sent to reform through labour (Laogai) institutions to receive re-education and ideological indoctrination (Mühlhahn, 2009). Contrarily, Mao advocated the use of administrative coercive measures for the day-to-day management of people in 'non-antagonistic contradictions'. In the name of re-socialising 'bad elements' from disturbers of social order to self-supporting persons, the Re-education Through Labour (RTL) system was devised to detain and educate adults engaged in public nuisance, prostitution, drug abuse, and the like (Biddulph, 2007). Meanwhile, established work-and-study schools were broadly based on restorative justice principles that include an arrangement between administrative agencies and guardians to place children involved in a broad range of delinquent offenses referred to as 'unhealthy behaviours' in specialised schools (Li & Su, 2020). The primary aim of work-and-study schools is to promote the correction of minors' misbehaviours and their acceptance of responsibility.

This criminal-administrative dual systems model has continued to prevail in the State's correctional framework following Mao's death. During the economic reform era where Deng Xiaoping and his successor Jiang Zemin took power (1978–2003), the conception of crime was no longer associated with political struggle. Instead, crime was more closely linked to the Party's evolving priorities of maintaining economic development and social order (Curran, 1998). In this context, harsh law enforcement and punishment characterised by the 'Strike Hard' campaigns were regularly carried out at the national and local level in response to a spike in crime that marketisation brought in its wake (Trevaskes, 2007); and yet, prisoners were continuously subjected to Laogai for the purpose of 'correcting their attitudes' and making them productive citizens (Zhou, 1991). In doing so, they were mandated to engage in productive labour while participating in education and vocational training. In the meantime, more administrative measures were created to target low-level perpetrations alongside RTL. This initiative conducted by police includes Public Order Detention, Drug Compulsory Detoxification, Detention for Education (for sex workers), and Minor Reformatory Camps (for juvenile delinquents), among others. In rhetoric, the administrative coercive measures rest on correction and reformation of delinquents while keeping them in custody (Li, 2012). In parallel with the Laojiao system, administrative penalties are exclusively imposed by the police, and the power to implement associated rehabilitation programming is similarly in the hands of the police (Biddulph, 2007). However, the rehabilitation of those who breach the law does not stop at the level of coercive measures. In the 1980s, a programme called 'Bangjiao' was created to provide assistance and guidance to residents who have committed petty offenses or have been released from prison. By regularly conducting interventions for individuals at risk of recidivism, Bangjiao employs social forces and familial connections to facilitate the reintegration of delinquents or ex-prisoners back into the community (Zhang et al., 1996).

Just as the rehabilitative ideal was brought down in the 1970s across many Western jurisdictions, rehabilitation did not occupy a central position in China's campaign-style justice. This trend, however, has been slightly reversed over the past two decades since the Hu Jintao administration (2003–2013) began to promote a penal policy called 'Combining Leniency and Severity'. The dominant tenor of this policy refers to a bifurcated system of punishment; namely the imposition of harsh penalties on a small minority of extremely serious crimes while encouraging the application of a relatively more lenient sentence for a majority of crimes with minimal social impact or mitigating circumstances (Trevaskes, 2010). Fundamentally, the state's endorsement of 'Combining Leniency and Severity' is to reconstruct harmonious and stable social relations which were once imperilled by a blatant reliance upon a 'Strike Hard' approach to combating crime. Evidence shows the new penal policy has produced an effect of tempering the overall penal punitiveness (Li, 2018). More remarkably, it revitalised rehabilitation as a salient aim of punishment which applies correctional treatment to wrongdoers so that they are capable of returning to society. In the criminal penal system, this is particularly demonstrated by the induction of community corrections in 2003—a programme aimed primarily at transforming less serious criminals from 'rule-breakers' to 'rule-observers' by means of neighbourhood-based education, assistance, and social support (Jiang et al., 2016). Within the administrative penal system, on the other hand, police-dominated sanctions have remained widely employed, although their implementation is becoming increasingly community-oriented. A case in point is the emergence of the community-based drug treatment as a prerequisite to compulsory drug treatment in 2008. Though, holistically, this new arrangement is a product of the gradual decline in prominence of administrative coercive measures (Biddulph et al., 2017)—typically illustrated by the successive abolition of RTL and Detention for Education in 2013 and 2019.

The corollary of these legal reforms is that delinquents who were previously placed under administrative penalties are channelled into either community with social services or the criminal correctional system with coercive rehabilitation programmes.

Rehabilitation has become more diversified during the latest government of Xi Jinping (2013–present). With overcriminalisation becoming an overriding theme of justice administration in the past decade (He, 2015), rehabilitation is visibly growing in a range of pre-sentence stages, albeit with discursive controversies and practical intricacies. In the criminal justice system, for example, criminal reconciliation has been introduced to allow the victims and the accused to 'reconcile' (*Hejie*) and then finalise the criminal cases by way of financial compensation and forgiveness. The underlying tenet of this programme is to not merely penalise wrongdoers, but to also restore the harmonious relationship between the victim and the accused, which aims to protects the victim's interests and remould the wrongdoer (Jiang, 2016). Reconciliation or restoration is similarly reflected in the recent reform of juvenile justice to deal with minors caught in the criminal process (Zhang & Xia, 2021). In particular, procuratorates are encouraged to hold off prosecuting minors who are suspected of committing specified offences under Chapter 4 (infringement upon citizens' personal and democratic rights), Chapter 5 (perpetrations against property), and chapter 6 (obstruction of administration of social order) of the Chinese Criminal Law (CL). This conditional non-prosecution entails, like most correctional programmes, the attendance at rehabilitation programmes for dependency/addiction, psychological counselling, and other proper treatments, as well as the providing of service of public interests to communities and charity organisations (Jiang, 2016).

The Status Quo of Rehabilitation—The Legal and Operational Contexts

A genealogical review of how rehabilitation has developed over time helps to identify two notable features of rehabilitation in China. First, rehabilitation is closely intertwined with punishment in both Laojiao and the community-based programmes. Second, while rehabilitation remains unexplained in law, it is linked to education, training, labour work, and social assistance in hopes to 'eradicate criminal mind and behavioural vice'. This section aims to tease out these characteristics within the legal and operational framework of rehabilitation in the Chinese justice system. In doing so, one specific purpose is to unravel any new functionality and manifestation of the current rehabilitative initiatives in the context of China's changing penal culture in the recent decades.

Since the promulgation of the first Criminal Law in 1979, China has classified illegal conduct into two categories, namely criminality and petty offences (equivalent to misdemeanours in some common law countries). While criminal conduct is dealt with by the criminal justice system, petty offences are handled by the police-dominated administrative justice system (CL, Article 13). While this binary categorisation has generated a two-tiered rehabilitation structure, both models share great affinities in terms of their coalescence with punishment and association with an eclectic mix of education, production, and re-socialisation.

Regulated by the Chinese Prison Law (PL), adults convicted of criminal offences and sentenced to imprisonment are sent to prison (Laogai). According to Article 3 of the PL, a prison ought to 'implement the principle of combining punishment with reform and combining education with labour, in order to transform them into law-abiding citizens'. In addition, Article Four provides that a prison 'should, in accordance with the needs of reforming prisoners, organise prisoners to engage in productive labour and conduct ideological, cultural, and technical education among prisoners'. Markedly, the PL requires the post-sentence re-socialisation to be part of ex-convicts' rehabilitation. According to Article 37, the local government should 'assist a person released after serving sentence in settling down'. To a great extent, this requirement needs 'state organs, public organisations, units of armed forces, enterprises, institutions, personage of various circles and family members or relatives of prisoners to assist prisons in performing well in his or her education and reform'—a legal justification for Bangjiao. Similarly, the rules of rehabilitation are set out in the Management Regulation on Minor Reformatory Centres (the Regulation) that deals with young delinquents. Section three of the Regulation states that minor reformatory centres should 'implement the principle of combining punishment with correction with the primary goal of reforming individuals'. It is required that these centres focus on 'educating', 'rehabilitating (Ganhua)', 'rescuing' minors, and 'turning them into law-binding citizens with reasonable levels of knowledge and skills' (the Regulation, Section 3). More specifically, Section Four states the management of minor reformatory centres should be 'premised on education, with differing levels of educational programmes in alignment with one's psychological, mental and behavioural traits' as enumerated in Chapter 4 of the Regulation with various educational programmes. More importantly, the labour assignment of minors needs to focus on studying and learning new skills (the Regulation, Section 4). Of course, while the national statutes set the tone for rehabilitation, numerous local regulations have been adopted to provide guidance on how to perform on-the-ground correctional activities in light of different cultural dynamics of local prisons and minor reformatory centres.

Rehabilitation is not always bound up with institutional confinement. Over the past twenty years, the increasing use of community corrections has enabled a large cohort of less serious individuals to serve a sentence in the community. As stipulated in the Community Corrections Law (CCL) enacted in 2020,[1] this neighbourhood-based penal measure has a dual purpose of punishment and rehabilitation with a focus on public surveillance, probation, parole (granted to serve sentence outside prison). Community corrections are clearly aimed at managing and supervising convicts with a high level of education and support in the community (the *CCL*, Article 3). This needs to be done, as per Article 4, through 'employing categorical management and individualised corrections for the targeted elimination of factors that might lead individuals to commit new crimes, helping them to become law-abiding citizens'.

At the other end of the spectrum, though, the rehabilitation of individuals committing petty offences is scattered across a raft of administrative laws and rules. With the RTL and Detention for Education being annulled, the existing administrative coercive measures are Public Order Detention and Compulsory Drug Detoxification. Primarily, the Administrative Punishment Law (APL) puts forth the underlying tenet for administrative penalties—'in enforcing administrative penalties and rectifying violations of law, the combination of penalty and education shall be adhered to, and citizens, legal persons or other organisations shall be educated to consciously abide by law' (the APL, Article 6). Then, the Public Order Management Punishments Law (POMPL) which regulates Public Order Detention requires that police comply with the principle of combining punishment and education while handling public order cases (the POMPL, Article 5). By the same token, with respect to Compulsory Drug Treatment, the Anti-Drug Law (ADL) emphasises treatment and production as the fundamental pillars of rehabilitation. Article 44 of the ADL states that 'the compulsory isolation centres for drug rehabilitation shall manage the persons receiving treatment of drug addiction by dividing them into different groups according to their sex, age, health condition, etc.' In addition to providing psychological treatment and physical rehabilitation training, Compulsory Drug Treatment centres are expected to 'organise the persons receiving such treatment to engage in the necessary production or other work and train them in vocational skills' (the ADL, Article 43).

Clearly, the Chinese laws characterise rehabilitation as a salient discourse of the penal system. Though equally important as punishment, rehabilitation is legally required to include education, labour work, and vocational and skill training. So, how does the practice of rehabilitation live up to those official rationales? Statistics have showed that the Chinese prison population in 2017 was around 1.7 million, which is believed to be second to the US (World Prison Brief, 2018). Notably, this number excluded pre-trial detainees and those held in administrative detention. Furthermore, the annual work report released by the Supreme People's Procuratorate in 2020 indicated that there were 1,818,808 people prosecuted in 2019 (The Supreme People's Procuratorate, 2021). Given the nearly 100% conviction rates at any time in China (Li, 2014), almost all individuals charged have been sentenced to imprisonment or received other forms of punishment. Together with 9,624,881 public order cases reportedly handled by the police in 2019 (Lu, 2022), the total figure of individuals caught in the country's penal system has remained steady during the past few years. Against this backdrop, a timely question is raised as to whether rehabilitation operates in the way it is intended by the law. While it is unrealistic to provide an exhaustive assessment of all rehabilitative programmes in force, the scrutiny below will focus on prison and community corrections to illustrate the on-the-ground implementation of rehabilitation and the gulf between practice and principle, if any.

Prisons or Laogai camps in China are managed by the Ministry of Justice. It is widely documented that punishment, education, and production are at the forefront of prison corrections, as mandated by the Prison Law. While punishment attached to prison refers to the deprivation of freedom and disciplinary measures used in the institution, education of prisoners generally involves activities aimed at reforming thoughts, teaching academic subjects, and training occupational skills. Among these activities, thought reform is believed to form the cornerstone of prison corrections (Smith, 2012). Though variations may exist, thought reform typically includes political education to allow inmates to understand the narratives of Chinese polity; legal education to increase inmates' awareness of law; and morality education to help inmates acquire virtues or moral habits that will lead them to live good lives and simultaneously, be productive (Shaw, 2010). Zhao et al. (2019), in their latest study on the participation of inmates in educational programmes, discover that the overall participation rate is about 97% in the four selected prisons in Zhejiang. It is consistent with the findings of other prison research that point to nearly 100% participation across the country (Wang, 2019). In addition, this empirical study highlights inmate participation as subject to a variety of push and pull factors, of which prison calls are deemed the most pertinent (Zhao et al., 2019).

No less important than education, production serves as 'a secondary goal but a primary activity' of prison rehabilitation (Shaw, 1998: 192). On a daily basis, prisoners are required to undertake a fixed amount of productive labour in addition to the attendance of educational programmes (Liu et al., 2020). As shown in the prison timetable below,[2] production takes up a large quantity of time for inmates' monotonous daily routines. In the eyes of prison authorities, labour work is conducive to rehabilitation in several respects. First, productive physical work is thought to help inmates get rid of their criminogenic habits. This appears to resonate with the Chinese traditional belief that one's mind can be exercised by labour. Second, production complements education in the sense that prison staff are able to use labour to reflect upon education and maximise the effects of education through actual practice. This explains, as indicated in Table 1, the juxtaposition of labour work and education at the same time slot. Third, the production serves as an opportunity for inmates to learn work skills and make vocational preparations for re-entry into society.

Despite these considerations, research reveals that the ideal of rehabilitation is, in practice, undermined by the prison's overt preoccupation with punishment and control. In other words, while programmes of rehabilitation are in use in prison, they are more often than not in the shadow of

Table 1 A Typical Daily Timetable of the Chinese Prison

6:00 a.m.–6:30 a.m.	Wake-up
6:30 a.m.–7:00 a.m.	Roll-call, muster, breakfast
7:00 a.m.–10:00 a.m.	Prisoners to work or study
10:00 a.m.–10:20 a.m.	Break
10:20 a.m.–12:00 p.m.	Prisoners to work or study
12:00 p.m.–13:30 p.m.	Roll-call, muster, lunch
13:30 p.m.–15:30 p.m.	Prisoners return to work or study
15:30 p.m.–15:50 p.m.	Break
15:50 p.m.–17:30 p.m.	Prisoners to work or study
17:30 p.m.–18:00 p.m.	Roll-call, muster, dinner
18:00 p.m.–20:30 p.m.	Spare time, meetings
20:30 p.m.–10:30 a.m.	Watching TV
10:30 p.m.	Lights out, sleeping

Source Wang, C. (2019), The Empirical Study of the Correctional Model and Effectiveness of Chinese Prisons—Based on 163 Correctional Cases collected from the Chinese Legal Service Website (我国监狱罪犯矫治模式及效能问题实证研究——以163例12348中国法网监狱矫治个案为例分析), *Policing Study (警学研究)*, 6, 31–58

the authorities' concerns over discipline, security, and order maintenance of prison. In their account of the evolution of China's prisons, for example, Wu and Vander Beken (2018) point out that rehabilitation and punishment are paradoxical goals. While the prison is more devoted to 'shaming and repression for order maintenance' (Wu & Vander Beken, 2018: 716), educative and rehabilitative values of imprisonment are paid less, if not minimal, attention. In particular, to maintain a tight control, paternalistic approaches to prison corrections have become the norm in the treatment of inmates. Then, the corollary is that there is 'an inherent risk of abuse and inhumane or degrading treatment' (Wu & Vander Beken, 2018: 714). As a result, inmates' rights are not fully recognised, hence leading to a departure of reformative incarceration as promised by the PL.

This is particularly demonstrated by the fact that each prison in China has adopted a Performance Credit System as its main managerial tool, which measures the performance of inmates based on a series of numerical ratings on their mundane behaviours (Liu and Chui, 2018a, 2018b; Liu et al., 2020). By giving the prison the sole authority to quantify inmates' performance and determines punishments and awards, it yields a power of control and discipline. In line with Michel Foucault's (1977) theory of disciplinary power, this system encourages compliant behaviours of inmates, and more importantly, regulates them in all respects of their prison life. In Zhang's study of female prisoners in Province X, it is found that the score is divided into three categories: labour, order maintenance, and educational assessment (Zhang, 2022). In every month, the prison officers in each district gauge each prisoner's basic points, and then decide whether the points are to be increased or deducted on the basis of each inmate's behaviours. In another study drawing on interviews with same respondents, Zhang (2020a, 2020b) sees the use of the Performance Credit System as evidence that the prison management in China is weighted heavily towards the maintenance of long-term order and security in prison. By employing such actuarial technique, rehabilitation is left in the cold and most inmates are found to seek good scores as their end goal—'the incentive becomes the goal itself' (Zhang, 2020a, 2020b: 677). As the findings suggest, this nevertheless seems to be a win–win situation for prisons and prisoners—while the prison preserves prison order and safety by controlling the prisoners' conduct via a scoring system, the prisoners are motivated for good behaviours in an attempt to obtain benefits, for example, the commutation of sentence or parole.

More evidence has consistently alluded to the pattern that Chinese prisons focus more on control than rehabilitation (Lambert et al., 2018). However, the correctional mode of incarcerated wrongdoers does not epitomise a full picture of rehabilitation in the Chinese penal system. With community-based sentencing options becoming increasingly popular during the last decades, it is also important to explore rehabilitation in the out-of-prison context to understand its resemblances and divergences to prison corrections. This leads to important questions such as to what extent convicts are rehabilitated while serving the sentence in the community? Does rehabilitation in community penalties play an equal or more visible role in changing convicts into law-binding citizens? What are the agencies that carry out rehabilitation in the community and what kind of working mechanism shapes such implementation? To answer these questions, the following discussion will centre on community corrections to sketch out its practical traits of rehabilitation and correction.

Analogous to Western versions, Chinese community corrections target those convicted of criminal offences typically punishable by less than three years of imprisonment (Jiang et al., 2014). Introduced in 2003, community corrections have rapidly become a prime alternative to short-term imprisonment. As of 2019, approximately 4.78 million people have been placed under community corrections (Zhang, 2020a, 2020b). Also, about 4.11 million people completed their sentences and were released back to society in 2019 (Zhang, 2020a, 2020b). At a practical level, the local judicial office is responsible for carrying community correction orders. This agency was established by the local Bureau of Community Corrections Management (some regions have a different name) and is accountable to the police, courts, and justice bureaus. The management sets the standard of practice for community corrections according to local legal and regulatory requirements. In a run-of-the-mill situation, the power to administer a community correction order is held by the local governments and delegated to community corrections offices, which particularly authorises social workers (Li, 2015). In Shanghai, for example, social workers are not laypeople recruited from local neighbourhoods, but external contractors employed by the government; Shanghai has adopted a unique 'government-purchase model' by contracting out services with the Community Service Provider—a form of outsourcing (Li, 2017). Together with local residential committees and volunteers, social workers are the frontline staff enforcing community corrections programmes outside the prison.

The official policy of community corrections is advertised as a conduit through which convicts are allowed to retain their social ties with their families and friends who can support their treatment and to develop necessary living and professional skills (Jiang et al., 2014). Over time, different models have emerged due to regional divergences of bureaucracy, economy, and culture, creating models like the 'Beijing', 'Shanghai', and 'Zhejiang' system (Yang, 2017). For example, one distinctive feature of the community corrections programme in Beijing is their focus on addressing criminogenic needs with correctional activities. Specifically, six educational and correctional programmes are employed in the Beijing neighbourhoods—namely, criminal identity education, repentance education, law and order education, thought and social cognition education, psychological health education, and employment and social welfare education (Jiang et al., 2014). Each individual is mandated to receive education under these six programmes. In particular, the first three are aimed at transforming anti-social personality patterns and attitudes. Then, thought and social cognition education and psychological health education are designed to promote the individual's moral values and sense of social and familial ethics. Prisoners are placed in designated halfway houses (e.g. Sunshine community corrections centre) and expected to establish a 'correct perception' of his or her role in family, society, and work, which carries a strong social responsibility (Yang, 2017).

While it is evident that rehabilitation serves as an integral part of community corrections, empirical evidence suggests a more discernible pattern of practice—risk control—in both developed and developing regions. Resembling the prison management on several fronts, community corrections manifest themselves in an essential praxis of a stringent regulatory, supervisory, and reporting system. Particularly as many local models deploy a risk evaluation mechanism based on the numerical ratings of risk variables to determine the dangerousness of those under a community correction order (Yuan, 2019a, 2019b). This mechanism is enforced for several reasons. The first being that a risk-oriented approach at a macro level for community corrections helps to control 'potential threats' posed by people who offend the community. Unlike a prison sentence, community corrections integrate individuals into the public without any separation, which China's Government finds to be a menace to public safety. On the other hand, at a micro level, risk management of individuals under community corrections can reduce recidivism. If educational and correctional measures are soft behaviour-changing techniques, supervision, and control are tougher measures to realise the incapacitation of individuals in preventing their repeat crimes.

In Beijing, for example, Yang (2017) notes that people in community corrections are ranked in groups from A, B to C, depending on their perceived risk to society and re-socialisation. With A being the highest level of risk and C being the lowest, this risk classification corresponds with a managerial hierarchy of 'intensive supervision', 'normal supervision', and 'minimum supervision', in which social workers play a leading practical role

(Yang, 2017). Having conducted interviews with community corrections officials in Shanghai, one of my studies (Li, 2017) illustrates that community corrections are predominantly considered intensive correctional supervision premised on ideas of control, surveillance, and education. To serve the purposes of management and supervision, measures such as approvals for travel and changing residences, spot visits, daily reporting, and electronic monitoring have formed an effective social security network to restrict the individuals' mobility in the community. The political pursuit of social stability in recent decades has arguably driven the practice of this measure to be more managerial by means of classifying and regulating risks of convicts, in an attempt to control the dangerousness they may present (Li, 2017). Static factors such as an individual's age, gender, number, and type of convictions are relied upon to make predictions about one's risk of recidivism. Depending on the risk classification per individual, different measures are imposed to specifically supervise and control the concerned person during his or her time in the neighbourhood.

Likewise, evaluating risk tendency plays a crucial role in determining the individual's eligibility of going back to society (Li, 2017). To qualify for being released, they are required to submit a written report detailing their physical and psychological status after serving the sentences in the community. Based on their self-assessment and the appraisal reports on their risk profiles from police, social workers, and communities, then the Justice Bureaus will advise the courts to make the final decision as to whether a community correction order ought to be discharged or expanded. These practices under community corrections share an affinity with selective incapacitation adopted in many Western penal systems (Feeley & Jonathan, 1992). While high-risk people are more restrictively grounded and subject to more reporting obligations, medium- and low-risk people receive less surveillance and supervision with more flexible reporting duty (Li, 2017). This is a managerial approach to imposing control on 'more dangerous' individuals by either limiting their mobility or requesting them to report on their whereabouts—a way to achieve incapacitation of the risky population.

Of course, risk assessment tools are not uniformly used nationwide. Even in Shanghai social workers are reportedly reluctant to take them on at times (Yuan, 2019a, 2019b). But risk evaluation and governance as the underlying rationales of community corrections have significantly shaped the way in which this non-custodial punishment is enforced. In the latest study on Chinese community corrections, Jiang and Liu (2022) seek to understand the local variations of this penal measure. Their findings submit that risk control and minimisation have become a paramount driver of community correction practices on a large scale, as articulated by one of the interviewed social workers (Jiang & Liu, 2022: 18):

> …We tried to design individualized programs for them to quickly return to the community. But correctional officials think they (offenders) are incorrigible and constantly mention intensive supervision is appropriate for certainty and minimal risk.

Overall, the mixed approach of strict supervision, risk control, and rehabilitation suggests that community corrections are not too different from imprisonment in practice, except for the fact this punishment is still non-custodial and precludes harsh measures that are usually part of custodial sentences. It also appears that the coexistence of punitive, managerial, and rehabilitative norms in the penal practices is a coherent phenomenon across almost all other punishments, even in the administrative nature. For instance, the Compulsory Drug Detoxification programme includes rigorous supervision, labour work, and rehabilitative interventions which amount to a trifecta approach in dealing with drug abusers (Liu & Chui, 2018a, 2018b). Typically, drug addicts are subject to a process known as 'dynamic management' (Dongtai Kongzhi), which operates at the behest of all police forces to ensure the compliance of drug addicts with onerous conditions attached to forced detoxification (Yuan, 2019a, 2019b). Akin to imprisonment and community corrections, the authorities are paying too much heed to control discipline and management. Inevitably, thus, it has weakened the programme's ability to adequately address the drug-dependence problem and prevent addicts to relapse with their drug addiction.

Discursive Underpinnings and Future Directions

As Ashworth and Zedner (2014) aptly claim, rehabilitation and risk management are not mutually exclusive. Both penal ideals share and pursue a common objective of reducing crime. Although rehabilitation has long been the defining feature of punishment in China, risk management is emerging as a dominant rationale and overshadows rehabilitation which leaves a strong imprint within the present correctional system. As discussed above, rehabilitative and educative programmes are still at play in most penal forms, but state resources are gradually moving towards risk identification and control in a manner that education and correction have been de-prioritised as a secondary consideration.

Against this background, it begs the question as to how rehabilitation can reconcile with the ideal of risk management. If a traditional form of rehabilitation entails education, production, and training, then how these activities are likely to be melded with a risk-control network of regulating wrongdoers determines where the future of rehabilitation lies. At this juncture, notably, rehabilitative programmes and risk governance efforts are operationally disconnected. They espouse different measures, processes, and outcome evaluations. This mismatch is not surprising because although rehabilitation and risk control seek to achieve the same ends, they cling to distinct values and principles. Specifically, rehabilitation tends to fix the problem of perpetrations *ex-post*, whereas risk control strives to prevent perpetrations as an *ex-ante* measure. But what really distinguishes rehabilitation from risk control, at least on the premise, is the extent to which authorities prioritise the re-socialisation of wrongdoers. In both criminal and administrative penalties, wrongdoers are forced to take on education, labour work, and vocational training. Although such undertaking is coercive, it is not uncommon that effort is made by authorities to respond to the conditions of individuals more or less and to mobilise social forces for better rehabilitative effects. By contrast, risk categorisation and regulation focus disproportionately on the level of individual dangerousness (Li, 2020). As many preventive initiatives are cloaked with draconian law enforcement measures, particularly in the form of liberty deprivation, they cannot be separated from the concerns hanging over the scarcity of safeguards and humanitarianism available to persons in compulsory and intrusive measures (Harcourt, 2012). Risk-driven management in both criminal punishment and administrative detention has yet to afford the individual a real chance of reintegration and supportive social networks.

That being said, for rehabilitation to achieve its intended goal, its fusion with risk control is not only inevitable but imperative. On this note, a borrowable model perhaps is the Risk-Need-Responsivity (RNR) model which has been widely used to assess and rehabilitate wrongdoers in Canada and around the world. First formalised in 1990 (Andrews et al., 1990), the RNR model has been designed and reinforced within a general personality and cognitive social learning theory of criminal conduct (Andrews & Bonta, 2006). With an explicit aim of combining rehabilitative interventions with risk identification, the RNR model is grounded on three principles: (1) *the risk principle*—deviant behaviours can be reliably predicted and treatment should vary according to the different level of risk; (2) *the need principle*—criminogenic needs are the decisive factors in the design and delivery of treatment; and (3) the *responsivity principle*—the treatment that responds to the wrongdoer's risk and need should be provided (Andrews et al., 1990). In a nutshell, the key to the success of the RNR model is the authorities' ability to differentiate wrongdoers in terms of their criminal risks and criminogenic needs, based on evidence-informed techniques and instruments, and to subsequently assist them with becoming more prosocial after applying tailored correctional programmes.[3]

However, one of the greatest challenges facing the legal and penal system in China is the gap between the ideal and practice in reality (Li, 2018). As discussed above, correctional narratives prescribed in law are not always put into action. So, if the RNR offers a possible solution to the plight of rehabilitation, efforts should not stop at the legislative and policy level. Rather, attention should be paid to how to make it work in correctional agencies with a diverse workforce in terms of education, production, and control are predicated on many things. Not only does it require a paradigm shift that accommodates conflicting sentencing purposes and management practices, but it needs investment of resources conducive to selecting and training of staff in effective assessment and correctional techniques. After all, the RNR model being an effective means of rehabilitation in China and is best practised by professionals and specialists with knowledge and experience in law, criminology, sociology, psychology, and the like to construct a clinically driven mechanism that informs a harmonious enforcement of rehabilitation and risk control.

Notes

1. Prior to the Community Corrections Law, community corrections were regulated by administrative directives such as the *Notice on Implementing Experimental Work of Community Corrections* and the *Measure for Implementing Community Corrections*.
2. The daily routine of prisoners varies slightly in different prisons.
3. It is noted that the RNR model is deemed imperfect as human behaviour is far too complex for risk assessment instruments and treatment programmes. The difficulty of translating theory into practice is a common criticism of the RNR model. For example, see Ward et al. (2007).

References

Andrews, D. A., & Bonta, J. (2006). *The psychology of criminal conduct* (4th edn.). LexisNexis.

Andrews, D. A., Bonta, J., & Hoge, R. D. (1990). Classification for effective rehabilitation: Rediscovering psychology. *Criminal Justice and Behavior, 17*(1), 19–52.

Ashworth, A., & Zedner, L. (2014). *Preventive justice*. Oxford University Press.

Biddulph, S. (2007). *Legal reform and administrative detention powers in China*. Cambridge University Press.

Biddulph, S., Nesossi, E., Sapio, F., & Trevaskes, S. (2017). Detention and its reforms in the PRC. *China Law and Society Review, 2*(1), 1–62.

Cao, L., & Cullen, F. (2001). Thinking about crime and control: A comparative study of Chinese and western ideology. *International Criminal Justice Review, 11*(1), 58–81.

Curran, D. (1998). Economic reform, the floating population, the crime in the transformation. *Journal of Contemporary Criminal Justice, 13*(3), 262–280.

Feeley, M., & Jonathan, S. (1992). The new penology: Notes on the emerging strategy of corrections and its implications. *Criminology, 30*(4), 449–474.

Foucault, M. (1977). *Discipline and punish: The birth of the prison*. Vintage Books.

Fyfield, J. (1982). *Re-educating Chinese anti-communists*. Routledge.

Harcourt, B. (2012). Punitive preventive justice: A critique. In A. Ashworth, L. Zedner, & P Tomlin (Eds.), *Prevention and the limits of the criminal law*. Oxford University Press.

He, R. (2015). The critical analysis of the jurisprudence of overcriminalisation in social governance (社会治理过度刑法化的法哲学批判). *Peking University Law Journal (中外法学), 2*, 523–547.

Jiang, J. (2016). *Criminal reconciliation in contemporary China: An empirical and analytical enquiry*. Edward Elgar Publishing.

Jiang, J., & Liu, J. (2022). Penal welfare or penal sovereignty? A political sociology of recent formalization of Chinese community corrections. *Punishment and Society, 24*(4), 501–528.

Jiang, S. H., Xiang, D. P., Chen, Q., Huang, C. X., Yang, S. Y., Zhang, D. W., & Zhao, A. (2014). Community corrections in china: Development and challenges. *The Prison Journal, 94*(1), 75–96.

Jiang, S., Jin, X., Xiang, D., Goodlin-Fahncke, W., Yang, S., Xu, N., & Zhang, D. (2016). Punitive and rehabilitative orientations toward offenders among community corrections officers in China. *The Prison Journal, 96*(6), 771–792.

Lambert, E., Liu, J., & Jiang, S. (2018). An exploratory study of organizational justice and work attitudes among Chinese prison staff. *The Prison Journal, 98*(3), 314–333.

Leng, S., & Chiu, H. (1985). *Criminal justice in post-Mao China: Analysis and documents*. State University of New York Press.

Li, E. (2012). Between reality and idea: Is the socialization of chinese administrative offenders realizable? *Asian-Pacific Law and Policy Journal, 13*(2), 164–209.

Li, E. (2015). Chinas community corrections: An actuarial model of punishment. *Crime, Law and Social Change, 64*(1), 1–22.

Li, E. (2017). The rhetoric and practice of community corrections in China. *Asian Journal of Criminology, 12*(2), 1–20.

Li, E. (2018). *Punishment in contemporary China: Its evolution, development and change*. Routledge.

Li, E. (2020). In the name of prevention? Policing social dangerousness through arrest in China. *Social and Legal Studies, 30*(4), 581–604.

Li, L. (2014). High rates of prosecution and conviction in China: The use of passive coping strategies. *International Journal of Law, Crime and Justice, 42*(3), 271–285.

Li, E., & Su, M. (2020). From punishment to control: Assessing juvenile diversion in China. *Law and Social Inquiry, 45*(2), 372–397.

Liu, L., & Chui, W. H. (2018a). Chinese culture and its influence on female prisoner behavior in the prisoner–guard relationship. *Journal of Criminology, 51*(1), 117–134.

Liu, L., & Chui, W.H. (2018b). Rehabilitation policy for dug addicted offenders in China: Current trends, patterns, and practice implications. *Asia Pacific Journal of Social Work and Development, 28*(3), 192–204.

Liu, L., Chui, W. H., & Hu, Y. (2020). Make sense of self in prison work: Stigma, agency, and temporality in a Chinese women's prison, Asian. *Journal of Criminology, 15*(2), 123–139.

Lu, J. (2022). The strategy for crime control in the era of misdemeanours (轻罪时代的犯罪治理方略). *Politics and Law (政治与法律), 1*, 51–66.

Mühlhahn, K. (2009). *Criminal justice in China*. Harvard University Press.

Shaw, V. (1998). Productive labour and thought reform in Chinese corrections: A historical and comparative analysis. *The Prison Journal, 78*(2), 186–211.

Shaw, V. (2010). Corrections and punishment in China: Information and analysis. *Journal of Contemporary Criminal Justice, 26*(1), 53–71.

Smith, A. (2012). *Thought reform and Chinas dangerous classes: Reeducation, resistance, and the people*. Rowman and Littlefield Publishers.

The Supreme People's Procuratorate. (2021). *The Annual Work Report*, viewed on 10 November 2021. https://www.spp.gov.cn/spp/gzbg/202103/t20210315_512731.shtml

Trevaskes, S. (2007). Severe and swift justice in China. *British Journal of Criminology, 47*(1), 23–41.

Trevaskes, S. (2010). The shifting sands of punishment in China in the era of harmonious society. *Law and Policy, 32*(3), 332–361.

Wang, C. (2019). The empirical study of the correctional model and effectiveness of Chinese prisons – Based on 163 correctional cases collected from the Chinese legal service website (我国监狱罪犯矫治模式及效能问题实证研究——以163例12348中国法网监狱矫治个案为例分析). *Policing Study (警学研究), 6*, 31–58.

Ward, T., Melser, J., & Yates, P. (2007). Reconstructing the risk–need–responsivity model: A theoretical elaboration and evaluation. *Aggression and Violent Behavior, 12*(2), 208–228.

World Prison Brief. (2018). The prison population in China, viewed on 17 November 2021. https://www.prisonstudies.org/country/china

Wu, W., & Vander Beken, T. (2018). Understanding criminal punishment and prison in China. *The Prison Journal, 98*(6), 700–721.

Yang, X. (2017). Community corrections programs in China: New forms of informal punishments? *Asian-Pacific Law and Policy Journal, 19*(1), 49–109.

Yuan, X. (2019a). Risk, risk assessment, and community corrections in China. *International Journal of Offender Therapy and Comparative Criminology, 63*(14), 2466–2482.

Yuan, X. (2019b). Controlling illicit drug users in China: From incarceration to community? *Journal of Criminology, 52*(4), 483–498.

Zhang, A. (2020a). Chinese practice of foucault's disciplinary power and its effects on the rehabilitation of female prisoners in China. *British Journal of Criminology, 60*(3), 662–680.

Zhang, A. (2022). The failure of *Ganhua* education: Revisiting relational-cultural theory in Chinas female prisons. *Woman and Criminal Justice*. https://doi.org/10.1080/08974454.2022.2040694

Zhang, J. (2020b). The legislative connotations of community corrections law and its difficulty for implementation (社区矫正法)的立法意义与执法难点). *Chinese Criminology Review (犯罪研究), 4*, 6–17.

Zhang, Y., & Xia, Y. (2021). Can restorative justice reduce incarceration? A story from China. *Justice Quarterly, 38*(7), 1471–1491.

Zhang, L., Zhou, D., Messner, S., Liska, A., Krohn, M., Liu, J., & Lu, Z. (1996). Crime prevention in a communitarian society: *Bang-jiao* and *Tiao-jie* in the peoples community corrections in China: Development and challenges. *Justice Quarterly, 13*(2), 199–222.

Zhao, Y., Fessner, S., Liu, J., & Jin, C. (2019). Prisons as schools: Inmate's participation in vocational and academic programs in Chinese prisons. *International Journal of Offender Therapy and Comparative Criminology, 63*(15–16), 2713–2740.

Zhou, J. (1991). The Chinese correctional system and Its development. *International Journal of Comparative and Applied Criminal Justice, 15*(1–2), 15–32.

Penitentiary System in Colombia

José Ignacio Ruiz-Pérez

It must be specified that the chapter refers to penitentiary institutions administered by the Colombian national government, by means of the Ministry of Justice and the National Penitentiary and Prison Institute (INPEC for its acronym in Spanish). There are about 15 penitentiary institutions administered by municipal or departmental governments in Colombia. The administration of these facilities must comply with national laws, but they can develop their own prison policies (for example, specific treatment programmes), and there is currently no repository of information in Colombia that brings together the practices, problems, and statistics of these prisons.

In that context, the penitentiary system can be considered a part of the criminal justice system within which persons are sent to prison (pretrial detention or conviction) as seen in Fig. 1. Pivotal to this are Sentence Enforcement and Security Measures Judges (JEPMS, for its acronym in Spanish) who are in charge of monitoring detention conditions and penalty compliance. For example, the psychosocial team in a penitentiary facility may recommend that a person proceeds to the probation phase, but it is

---

J. I. Ruiz-Pérez (✉)
Department of Psychology, Universidad Nacional de Colombia, Carrera 30 #45-03, Edificio 212, oficina 230, Bogotá, Colombia 111321
e-mail: jiruizp@unal.edu.co

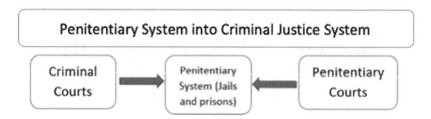

Fig. 1 Penitentiary system into criminal justice system (*Source* Own elaboration)

a JEPMS who makes the decision. In addition, these judges ensure that a person is released immediately at the end of its sentence (the initial length of the sentence minus discounts for participating in work or study activities). Finally, the reader should understand that penitentiary facilities in Colombia are public institutions, since at the time of writing there are no private prisons, even though from time to time the social and media debate arises about the privatization of said establishments.

Recent History of the Colombian Penitentiary and Prison System

Expressions of civil and criminal law in Colombia can be traced back to some Indigenous communities with greater social structure before the conquest and colonisation of Colombian territory by Spain in the fifteenth century (National Penitentiary and Prison Institute, S/F, in Spanish). However, in this text we will focus, for practical reasons and space limitations, on the most recent period since 1991, when the current Political Constitution of Colombia came into force and brought important criminal and penitentiary legal innovations. (Those readers interested in the period prior to 1991 should consult authors such as Mercado et al. [2014].)

The Constitution of Colombia, which came into force in 1991 (Congreso República de Colombia, 1991) was followed by the approval of a series of penitentiary regulations that would configure the current penitentiary and prison system in Colombia[1] and the following significant milestones:

- In 1992, the National Penitentiary and Prison Institute (INPEC) was created by Decree 2160 (Ministerio de Justicia y del Derecho de Colombia, 1992). This is the state institution for the administration of penitentiaries, prisons, and women's detention facilities. This administration refers to the aspects of security, application of conviction sentences and registration of

deductions from the time of sentence to be served, if the convicted person participates in work, study, or teaching activities.
- In 1993, by means of Decree 1242, penitentiary and prison facilities were grouped into six geographical-administrative areas (each one called Regional) (Ministerio de Justicia y del Derecho de Colombia, 1993), and Law 65 of 1993, which is the penitentiary code, was approved. This is an essential law because it establishes a progressive phases system, from isolation in a cell or maximum security to parole, in addition to an initial phase when the person arrives at the facility. In this initial phase, the behaviour of the inmate is observed, and a resocialisation activities plan (penitentiary treatment) is proposed to the individual, who is classified in one of the following phases. In addition, Law 65 of 1993 established the types of criminal facilities, defines prison treatment, establishes prison benefits, and indicates which disciplines must be part of the teams that evaluate convicted persons and apply penitentiary programmes. These prison benefits consist of mechanisms for the person deprived of liberty to gradually resume contact with society, and range from the possibility of being released from prison for a few days (permit up to 72 h) to being able to live outside the prison if they have shown good behaviour inside, there have been no escapes during a permit, if there are non-criminal social ties abroad or a work or study activity is going to be carried out. The Law 65 of 1993 (Congreso República de Colombia, 1993) was updated by Law 1709 of 2014.
- Comprehensive Care activities and Treatment activities, which are regulated by Resolution 7302 of 2005, differ (Ministerio del Interior y de Justicia de Colombia, 2005). Comprehensive Care activities are related to the promotion of education and health and are offered to the population in preventive custody (defendants) because they are sheltered by the principle of presumption of innocence, whereas Penitentiary Treatment is offered to convicted persons and, among other things, consists of a set of educational, job training, psychosocial, health, and spiritual activities aimed at treating the behavioural causes of crime and reducing the risk of recidivism. This set of ideas is articulated in Table 1.
- Finally, the Judgment T-921 of the Constitutional Court of Colombia (2013a) recognises the right of members of Indigenous communities originating from the territories of present-day Colombia, to be judged by authorities of their Indigenous communities (Indigenous Jurisdiction). In the event of conviction, they have the right to a form of punishment proper to the community as long as a series of principles are respected, such as: the penalty must have a resocialising purpose and not be merely punitive;

Table 1 Types of penitentiary facilities and associated programs

	Preventive custody population (Defendants)	Convicted population
Type of men's facilities	Prisons	Penitentiaries
Types of women's facilities	Women's prisons: criminal facilities only for women	
	Detention facilities for women in criminal facilities for men	
Activities and Programs	Comprehensive Care	Penitentiary Treatment

Source Own elaboration

it must respect the principles of the Constitution, such as the right to life and dignity, and keep in mind the best interests of children.

The application of the indigenous jurisdiction rather than the conventional criminal and penitentiary legislation to a crime does not depend only on the person accused of the crime self-categorising as 'Indigenous' but must meet another condition, that its vision of the world is clearly determined by their belonging to an Aboriginal population. Thus, among other conditions, it must be demonstrated that they communicate in an Indigenous language, with little or no command of the Spanish language, and that they have not signed any employment contracts written in Spanish. Despite this, there may be people of Indigenous origin in conventional criminal facilities, but Judgment T-921 of 2013 indicates that even in these cases, the penitentiary system must respect indigenous identity; therefore, people of Indigenous origin will be gathered in the same prison yard or pavilion and be segregated from contact with the non-Indigenous prison population.

Colombian Penitentiary System Structure

INPEC managed 138 criminal facilities in 2014 (Mercado et al., 2014), although by 2021 132 establishments were reported (Rojas-Castañeda, 2020), a reduction that may be due to the closure of several small premises. According to Mercado et al. (2014), the following types and numbers of criminal facilities can be differentiated in Colombia, most of which are provided for, in Law 65 of 1993:

- Penitentiaries: for convicted inmates: 10
- Prisons: for pretrial detention inmates without conviction: 19

- Agricultural Colony: for inmates from rural environments: 1
- High and Medium Security Penitentiary Facilities and Prisons: 4
- High and Medium Security Penitentiary Facilities: 2
- Detention facilities for women: 12
- Penitentiary and Prison Facilities (EPC): 89
- Special Detention Centers: detention centers for police or army members: 2.

In general, both the central and regional INPEC offices, as well as each facility, have a hierarchical structure with a Directorate at the highest level and the distribution of prison employees in four sections, namely, an administrative area, for the administrative management of the facilities, a legal area, for legal matters of the population deprived of their liberty, a surveillance and security area, assigned to the protection of the facilities, custody of the inmate population and maintenance of obedience to formal norms of the centre, and a care and treatment area, in charge of the design and application of penitentiary care and treatment programmes.

Penitentiary facilities in Colombia can be classified into four types, depending on the time of their construction and the type of architectural design. The type of design, in turn, will significantly condition the possibility of carrying out or not, penitentiary treatment activities and cultural activities. They are:

- First-generation facilities constructed before the 1990s that are generally small facilities with little space to carry out treatment activities.
- Second-generation facilities built in Colombia from mid-1990s to 2009. These are large facilities, with many security measures on the perimeters. They were financed by the United States Bureau of Prisons and were intended to be fortified places for the custody of drug cartel bosses. For example, the 'Cómbita Maximum Security Facility' was built on a plain, with several external security circles, to detect and prevent drug-trafficking bosses from being rescued by their gangs. These facilities respond to the model of the Supermax prisons in the United States (Ruiz-Pérez, 2017).
- Third-generation facilities in Colombia are called 'Penitentiary and Prison Complexes' and were built between 2010 and 2011. These are large facilities, with different buildings with several floors. They can include bedrooms and lounges and bring together buildings for both male and female inmates. The prison environment is harsher than the others: These prisons are vertical buildings, there is a lack of exposure to natural lights,

all activities (for instance, bedrooms, medical resources, treatment activities) are into the same building, and visual access to landscapes outside the prison is very scarce. Also, frequently, these prisons are a long way from urban centres.
- Fourth-generation facilities were designed in 2014 in order to increase the number of places or rooms and reduce overcrowding in other facilities. They present a modular distribution of spaces with each module having its own kitchen space and bedrooms for eight or ten people who are expected to coexist prosocially. Outside the modules, in addition to conventional educational spaces there are areas for learning crafts and for studying, with environmental designs that, on the one hand, try to facilitate visual contact with the outside landscape. In other words, without subordinating the security dimension, the design of these facilities is intended to have the inmates feel that they are in a normalised and even pleasant environment, with a perspective reminiscent of the Good Lives Model (Willis et al., 2013). It is, however, important to highlight that while criminal facilities operating in 2022 in Colombia correspond to one of the four previous types, first-generation facilities are still operating despite their relative age.

Structural and Functional Problems of the Penitentiary System in Colombia: Human Rights Compliance

The quality of penitentiary services in a country can be defined by evaluating the degree of compliance with the basic services that States must offer to the incarcerated population. In this context, a series of violations of basic Human Rights are discernible in Columbia criminal prison facilities. These violations have been studied and denounced by civil Non-Government Organisations (NGOs, in Martínez-Castrillón, 2021) and by the Ombudsman and are reflected in Judgment T-388 of 2013 of the Constitutional Court of Colombia, entitled The Unconstitutional State of Affairs of the Penitentiary and Prison System (Constitutional Court of Colombia, 2013b). The title responds to the fact that the Colombian penitentiary and prison system in general[2] often fails to adequately cover basic constitutional rights. For this reason, Judgment T-388 of 2013 obliges the Colombian State, through the Ministry of Justice, to build a system of human rights non-compliance indicators and to prepare an annual report about the prisons and penitentiaries of the country. Combining official statistics and the results of the 2017 Prison

Report,[3] it is possible to identify a series of issues in which there is a frequent violation of human rights.

It is possible to differentiate between food services schedule and the perceived quality of food. According to the 2017 Prison Report, breakfast and lunch are provided at times similar to society habits, but dinner, in 96% of the facilities, is served very early, between 3 and 4 in the afternoon before a period of socialising from 7 to 9 in the evening. Dinner distribution is subject to security issues so that after this meal the inmates must return to their cells until the next morning. The report found that in 98% of the facilities inmates, unless they went 12 h without food. Moreover, measured by the Food Insecurity Scale of the Food and Agriculture Organisation of the United Nations (FAO) the report found there to be severe problems with the quantity, quality, or variety of food. In addition, 33% of the inmates interviewed in ten facilities indicated that they did not have access to water during the day due to damage to the water connection and distribution facilities.

Violence can be defined and measured in several ways. In 2002, a survey was carried out in five criminal facilities in the capital of Colombia (Ruiz & Páez, 2002) in which it was found that 58% of inmates and 42% of prison officials had been robbed or knew about robberies in the facilities, and 52% of the inmates and 48% of officers knew of cases of homicide within their criminal facility. Likewise, among the inmates, direct or indirect experiences of being victims of extortion (71%), beatings (61%), or threats (48.6%) were frequent. It is important to remember that indirect experience—witnessing an event or hearing others talk about a traumatic event that happened to others can also lead to post-traumatic stress (Finklestein et al., 2015). Report found that more than 30% of inmates had been attacked by other inmates and that between 8% and 45% had been attacked by custody and surveillance officials (see Fig. 2).

In Colombia, prisons overcrowding began to occur in the mid-1990s due to the increase in detainees from the fight against drug cartels and armed guerrilla organisations ('guerrillas') and paramilitaries (Ruiz, 2004). For recent years, Rojas-Castañeda (2020) reports an overcrowding rate of 54.9%, with 80,150 beds in INPEC facilities for a prison population of 124,188. However, Acosta-Argote (2021) reports a global overcrowding rate of 20%, and the 2017 Prison Report reports overcrowding rates in a sample of 10 prisons, between 1.2 and 390%, which is why there are wide differences in this problem between facilities and even between yards of the same facility. Overcrowding rates are lower in high-security yards, and in those intended for those convicted of white-collar crimes, foreigners, or elderly or physically disabled inmates.

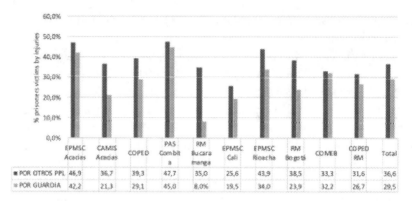

Fig. 2 Injuries suffered in prison by other inmates or guards (*Sources* Taken from the 2017 Prisons Report)

Law 65 of 1993 created the Evaluation and Treatment Councils (CET for its acronym in Spanish) in charge of the desing, application, and evaluation of penitentiary treatment programmes. According to this law, CETs must be composed of a professional psychologist, a social worker, an occupational therapist, a lawyer plus a member of the security staff and the director of the centre or his representative. Agreement 011 of 1995 insists on this composition, but practically none of the 132 establishments in the country meet this requirement due to lack of personnel. This is shown in the 2017 Prison Report, in which the rates of members of the CET, combining all areas, and the inmate population of each facility range between 0.001 and 0.01, that is to say, one CET member per 100 to 1000 inmates. This often entails extraordinary difficulties in carrying out on time the first psychosocial and criminological evaluation that the penitentiary law establishes for every person who enters prison, as well as in carrying out periodic evaluations.

Only two of the 132 criminal facilities in the country have a pavilion for the care of people with serious mental health problems, and none of them deal with cases involving women. During 2020, the INPEC tried to contract prevention and promotion of mental health services with third parties, but the calls were declared void because private companies that provide health services do not see it as a profitable operation to attend these calls because the population is highly within those 132 facilities (Presidency of the Republic, 2020). Meanwhile, the 2017 Prison Report includes a statement on mental and physical health care by the InterAmerican Commission on Human Rights in Colombia, in relation to the lack of health professionals and the low quality of care provided:

...the poor health care received by most of the population deprived of liberty is one of the main problems and challenges, since various civil society organisations denounce that those penitentiaries are characterised by insufficient medical personnel, inadequate medicines supply, and lack of necessary elements to provide quality care. In relation to psychiatric care, the Commission has received allegations that the treatment is limited to the daily supply of medication without patient rehabilitation, psychiatric care does not meet treatment needs of most pathologies, the time intended for the assessment and monitoring of people with mental disabilities is insufficient, being 5 to 8 minutes of consultation; mental illness is made invisible; and the staff is not trained to deal with psychotic crises. (2017 Prison Report: 78)

Interestingly, the author of this chapter visited and verified experiences of therapeutic communities for the treatment of drug addiction and care for nursing mothers. In the therapeutic communities the activities are sometimes carried out by personnel with training in psychology and postgraduate studies in addiction to psychoactive substances. However, the activities are not usually systematised or based on scientific evidence of their role in avoiding relapses in consumption; in contrast, at times military forms of discipline such as training exercises in the mornings, or group punishments in the form of group physical exercises, for example, push-ups. On the other hand, this author has visited some care facilities for nursing mothers and those with small children. The spaces are built even outside the walls, have an adequate environmental design, and all kitchen and bedroom elements, as well as recreational activities for these mothers and their children are taken care of by university or technical qualified personnel.

Colombia appears in successive indicators of International Transparency as far from the position of countries with greater transparency (La República, 2022), and this also seems to be reflected in its penitentiary system, expressed in facts such as the celebration of unauthorised parties with alcoholic beverages consumption, escape of inmates with the collaboration of guards, entry of weapons, cell phones and other prohibited objects, and extortion of companies that supply food to the inmate population (Editorial Staff EL Tiempo, 2022). The 2017 Prisons Report found that the most frequent corrupt behaviours that generate disciplinary investigations of prison officials are introducing prohibited items, requesting or receiving money, improper use of money or public resources, documents falsification and irregularities in administrative contracting. The inmates' perceptions of corruption in jails extracted from the survey applied to the inmate population in the preparation of the 2017 Prison Report are presented in Table 2.

Table 2 Inmates' perceptions on corruption in jails

Questions related to Corruption indicators	% affirmative responses
In the last year, have you had access to any prohibited item brought in by INPEC officials (for example, cell phones, liquor, drugs)?	11.4
Have you ever had to pay INPEC officials for any procedure within the facility?	12.2
Have you offered to pay an INPEC official to carry out or speed up a process within the facility? (For example, yard change, work assignment, phase classification, certificates)	9.6
Do INPEC officials enter prohibited items for PPL?	16.8

Source Own elaboration based on the 2017 Prisons Report

Social Support Network

Prisons do not exist outside of their social context and the Colombian penitentiary system is no exception. In order to fulfil its mission of resocialising persons deprived of liberty, it has resorted to establishing alliances with different sectors of the economic and the educational life of the country. The nature of these alliances will also depend on the socioeconomic fabric of each region of the country, and the geographical location of each criminal facility. Thus, a facility located outside the city in a rural area that has cultivation areas may, for example, offer training in agriculture or livestock activities. Some of these social and economic actors that establish agreements or alliances with the penitentiary system are:

- Universities: These higher education centres provide students in their final years of careers such as psychology, social work, law, and occupational therapy. They support penitentiary treatment activities, clinical support, and legal assistance to male and female inmates.
- National Learning Service (SENA for its acronym in Spanish): this public institution has offices in many cities of the country and provides training in technical careers from hospitality to metallurgy, for example. It frequently develops training cycles in many penitentiary facilities, granting degree titles equivalent to those assigned in the extramural training venues. Possibly it is the institution with presence and collaboration in most criminal facilities.
- Churches: Catholic Church, evangelical churches and others such as the Jehovah's Witnesses have a presence in many facilities in the country, and their activities are connected with the spiritual dimension of people. Inmate participation in religious activities is voluntary, and such activities

have been shown to promote a more positive emotional climate in prisons (Ruiz, 2007).
- Companies: public and private business organisations establish agreements with specific criminal facilities to take charge of manufacturing products such as for example, bread, uniforms, and handicrafts. Inmates who manage to access these jobs in prison not only receive deduction days from their sentence in this way, but also a salary, although lower than what would correspond to the same work activity in the free environment.
- Other organisations: members of Alcoholics Anonymous, cultural or artistic foundations are usually allowed to carry out sporadic or periodic activities with one or another subgroup of the prison population.

Evaluation Processes

Three moments can be distinguished in the Colombian penitentiary system in terms of multidisciplinary evaluation strategies on the prison population. Before 2009, the psychological, social work, educational, and legal evaluation, among other areas, were carried out through ad-hoc interview formats. The structured interview was, therefore, the main and almost only tool of the different professionals who dealt with the assessment of people arriving to the INPEC penitentiary and prison facilities. An evaluation by disciplines was conceived, including the evaluation of a possible addiction to alcohol or drugs. In the psychology area, any kind of specific tests such as some version of the MMPI, 16-PF, or WAIS was rarely used because criminal facilities did not have these tests and the evaluation professionals had to obtain them on their own. As a result, psychological evaluation was unspecialised, in addition to the fact that most psychologists did not have postgraduate training.

In 2009, an evaluation strategy called 'Instrument for the Comprehensive Assessment of Convicts' was designed (in Spanish Instrumento para la Valoración Integral de Condenados IVIC 1.0) (Mónoga et al., 2009). This instrument is made up of 180 questions to be answered by the imprisoned person. These questions are grouped in blocks, according to the discipline from which they were formulated: anthropology, legal and criminology, pedagogy, psychology, health, prison security, occupational therapy, and social work. There are some limitations to this instrument: firstly, the questions were prepared by areas of knowledge, with some items that were similar and could correspond to more than one discipline; and secondly, the IVIC 1.0 measures risk for each disciplinary area. This being the case, the third period in terms of evaluation strategies for the inmate population corresponds from

2017 to the present time (2022). Because some limitations were found in IVIC 1.0 (for instance, it is not always clear to which risk it refers, and the absence of evidence about recidivism predictive validity) a new assessment tool was created: IVIC 2.0 (National Penitentiary and Prison Institute, 2017). The passage from IVIC 1.0 to 2.0 was due to different circumstances, including its relative length and, more precisely, to the participation of many areas of knowledge and the lack of a specific risk prediction model. So, the IVIC 2.0 has an increased risk accuracy, includes fewer items or factors, and is based on current theoretical models such as Risk, Needs and Responsiveness (RNR) (Bonta & Andrews, 2017) and the Good Lives Model (Willis et al., 2013). It consists of nine main dimensions, distributed among the three axes of the main model, which is:

- Risk: Violent behaviour (for example, injury to people) and Criminal career (for example, criminal career or parasitic lifestyle).
- Criminogenic needs: Dynamic variables (for example, personal antisocial relationships, or consumption of psychoactive substances) and static variables (for example, school processes or past family).
- Antisocial personality traits: for example, impulsiveness, hostility, antisocial cognition, among others.

IVIC 2.0 too may have a number of limitations. Firstly, no study was conducted on the predictive value of the IVIC 1.0 in relation to the risk of recidivism: in other words, there are no studies to date on the relationships between the scores in each dimension of the IVIC 1.0 and 2.0 and the return to prison of those who were evaluated with any of these tools and whether or not they have returned to prison. Secondly, even though the IVIC 2.0 is anchored in more recent recidivism models, the observation of the dimensions and subdimensions seems to consider constructs such as antisocial personality and psychopathy but with unclear criterion, for example, parasitic lifestyle as a component of psychopathy (Hare, 2010) and it does not appear in the antisocial personality dimension but rather in the Criminal career axis. Moreover, by focusing on violent behaviour, it can underestimate the risk of recidivism of white-collar criminals, related to corruption, fraud, money laundering which often affect tens and even thousands of victims. On the other hand, in 2020 new procedures were introduced for labour skills and attitudes assessment of convicted inmate population. For this purpose, a psychometric test was designed and validated (Consultancy Universidad Nacional de Colombia, 2020).

Penitentiary Programmes

These programmes bring together any formal or non-formal education activity (secondary, technical, or university levels) aimed at inmate population literacy or the carrying out of some type of work in prison. These jobs are usually paid, although with wages lower than the labour market of the outside society. Regarding teaching, this is the programme in which an inmate self develops training activities for other inmates. Participation in JST activities allows the person deprived of liberty to receive discounts on their sentence, approximately one day discount for two days of any JST. According to the prisons report, coverage of these activities is greater than 82%, although the figure may be lower because the same person can simultaneously carry out two or more JST activities in order to achieve a greater discount, and these cases are not detectable in the available statistics. Some of the most frequent programmes in the Colombian penitentiary environment, both for study and work, are presented in Table 3.

Globally, suicide rates in prison are higher than in the general population (Fazel et al., 2017). Although in Colombia there are no reports or studies that compare suicide rates in prison with the general population, these events are the object of attention and concern for the penitentiary system, since each suicide is a human drama and a failure of the State to protect the human rights of persons deprived of their liberty. In one study, it was found that in a sample of 60 people deprived of liberty who had exhibited some indication of suicide (thoughts, attempts, and completed acts), 76.5% had made a suicide attempt, the risk factors being the initial stage of imprisonment and a younger age. The most frequent instrument for the suicide attempt was a sharp weapon (66.5%), followed by hanging (18.3%). In addition, successful cases were more frequent in men and unsuccessful attempts more frequent in women, but there were very similar levels between genders in terms of thoughts of suicide (Larrotta et al., 2014). In another, Calderón-Velandia (2014) found, in a sample of 120 inmates, that the risk factors for suicide in

Table 3 Some study programs and job training in the Colombian penitentiary system

Study Programs	Work programs
• Primary education • Secondary education • Technical studies • University studies	• Crafts • Leather goods • Agriculture and Livestock • Kitchen • Carpentry • Artistic paint

Source Own elaboration

Table 4 Risk factors for suicide in prison: clinical, penitentiary, family and stressor events

Clinical	Health problems
	Alcohol and/or drug use
Penitentiary	Previous incarcerations
	Having suffered threats or bullying in prison
Family	Physical and/or emotional abuse suffered in the family
	Suicide of a family member or close person
Stressors	Recent breakup with partner
	Death of a loved one

Source Own elaboration based on Calderón-Velandia (2014)

prison are multiple and correspond to both clinical and penitentiary, family, and recent stressor dimensions (see Table 4).

Considering this framework, the Preservation of Life Programme aims to promote, through group intervention, coping strategies for the proper management of internal and external stressors that can be experienced during the confinement period. Therapeutic spaces are promoted so that people deprived of liberty can talk about the issues and experiences that concern them, activities that favour experiences of well-being and quality of life are facilitated, guidelines are established so that criminal facilities detect those inmates who can exhibit emotional vulnerability, and self-support groups that will act as leaders in each yard, are formed in prisons, identifying possible partners in risk scenarios (Ariza & Zafra, 2020).

According to several studies, about 23% of the inmate population shows some relationship between their crime and drugs: whether it is a crime committed under the influence of a drug or to obtain resources to pay for drugs[4] (Ruiz, 2006). Faced with this reality, INPEC has promoted actions to prevent relapse into drug use: among these actions are informative workshops on the harmful effects of drug use, conformation of mutual support groups and endorsement of initiatives by some penitentiary professionals to create Therapeutic Communities in the areas of some facilities. As indicated above, theoretical assumptions behind community experiences are varied, since most of the current therapeutic communities in criminal facilities in Colombia were born from the initiatives of some prison officials, so there is no common institutional conceptual model. Recently (2019, 2020) INPEC has financed external evaluation of these programmes, although studies are still needed on the predictive validity of this programme in relation to the risk of recidivism or relapse in drug use when the person leaves prison.

The Comprehensive Responsibility with Life Programme (in Spanish, Responsabilidad Integral con la Vida, RIV) consists of structured sessions to address clinical self-deception, which is frequently present in people with drug abuse (Sirvent & Moral, 2016) and in Colombia, it has been associated with crimes such as homicide, fraud and drug micro-trafficking (Consultancy Universidad Nacional de Colombia, 2011). The programme is based on the concept of self-deception and an intensive intervention of two sessions per week run by specialised psychology professionals with clinical experience who take participants through pre-contemplative and contemplative phases (Consultancy Universidad Nacional de Colombia, 2013a). The Comprehensive Responsibility with Life Programme had a significant pre-post effect in its initial phase or pilot test, it is implemented in several criminal facilities by psychology students, not by skilled professional psychologists.

The Life Chain Programme (LCP, in Spanish, Programa Cadena de Vida, CV) has an intensity of one session per week, it is directed to any person deprived of liberty, although it is expected that it will be of interest to people convicted for homicide (Consultancy Universidad Nacional de Colombia, 2013b). It is framed within the concepts of salutogenesis and Sense of Coherence (Antonovski's, in Lindström & Eriksson, 2006). According to the salutogenesis view, efforts should be focused on health's origins rather than to look for the causes of disease. On the other hand, Sense of Coherence (SoC) is the way people view their life and a coping capacity with life stressors. SoC components are comprehensibility, manageability, and meaningfulness, and it is found that a high SoC has a positive influence on health. LCP is intended to generate reflection on concepts such as life and death, and teach skills for life maintenance and rescue, such as cardiopulmonary resuscitation. The piloting of this programme found an increased sense of coherence and a more positive perception of life in the post phase compared to the pre phase.

The Education and Life Quality Programme (in Spanish, Programa Integral de Educación y Calidad de Vida) is inspired by some principles of closed therapeutic communities, and specifically by the experiences of the Educational Therapeutic Units of Spain (UTE, for its acronym in Spanish). It is a voluntary prison programme that takes place in an entire yard (Rodríguez-Diaz et al., 2011). The yard or pavilion constitutes a coexistence unit in which the tasks are distributed among its residents, based on principles of co-responsibility and development of prosocial attitudes and behaviours, among other psychosocial and collective efficacy principles (Consultancy Universidad Nacional de Colombia, 2013c). The disadvantage of this programme is that it requires having a yard exclusively dedicated to implementing the community of coexistence, and this faces difficulties due to overcrowding in many criminal facilities in the country.

The Social Adaptation Intervention Programme is aimed at intervening with people convicted of sexual crimes and was the first of its kind in Colombian prisons. It is based on a cognitive behavioural perspective that includes relapse prevention. It must be applied by postgraduate psychology professionals with knowledge of, and experience with the inmate population and sexual behaviour (Consultancy Universidad Nacional de Colombia, 2013d). Unfortunately, it is usually applied by undergraduate psychology students in internships, and it is often partially applied because the duration of the programme is adjusted to the period that the student must complete the internship.

Directed towards inmates who have little time left to serve their sentence, the Preparation for Freedom programme aims to work on their expectations and fears; for example, fear of reuniting with family, expectations of being rejected when looking for a job or returning to the neighbourhood. It also seeks to work on the development of soft skills for attending job interviews, preparation of resume, among others, in order to support the inmate's process of returning to life in freedom (Consultancy Universidad Nacional de Colombia, 2013e). This programme is related to the ultimate goal of the custodial sentence in Colombia: resocialisation, understood to be a life in freedom with a purpose and respect for other citizens, according to Law 65 of 1993. It is offered in criminal facilities and must connect with the post-penitentiary services determined in the same law. These post-penitentiary services are external to the facilities, and have little history in the country, in 2019 taking place in only two cities in Colombia. In parallel and for years, some NGOs have offered shelter or guidance services to ex-inmates. However, these experiences are not systematised since they emerged from the initiative of some people. To date, most of these programmes have been, or are going to be, subject to evaluation processes of their effectiveness, impact, and theoretical content, in an important effort by the Colombian penitentiary and prison system to improve its intervention processes based on to objective indicators.

Notes

1. In the Spanish language and for the Colombian penitentiary legislation, a difference is made between *Prisons*, as places of confinement for people who are in the criminal investigation phase and have not yet been convicted (*Defendants*) and *Penitentiaries*, or facilities for people who have been convicted to a custodial sentence (*Convicted*).
2. With logical differences and variations between facilities. Here we will refer to general trends, finding good practices in one or another subject in different facilities. On the other hand, Colombia lacks a compilation of human rights compliance indicators in district and departmental prisons.

3. Includes official statistics review and results of a survey to 1410 people deprived of liberty, from 10 criminal facilities in the country, covering all regions of the country. Indicators for district and departmental prisons are not included in these Report (Consultoría Universidad Nacional de Colombia, 2017).
4. Apart are the crimes of macro and micro-trafficking. The latter is committed in a greater proportion by women with low educational and socioeconomic levels.

References

Acosta-Argote, C. (2021). *El hacinamiento en las cárceles colombianas es de 20% a marzo según datos del INPEC* [Overcrowding in Colombian prisons is of 20% as of March according to INPEC data] https://www.asuntoslegales.com.co/actualidad/el-hacinamiento-en-las-carceles-colombianas-es-de-20-a-marzo-segun-cifras-del-inpec-3133024

Ariza, C. F., & Zafra, A. P. (2020). *Transformando ideas en un medio cerrado.* [Transforming ideas into a prison environment] Bogotá: INPEC.

Bonta, J., & Andrews, D. (2017). *The psychology of criminal conduct*. Routledge.

Calderón-Velandia, J. E. (2014). *Factores de riesgo y de protección asociados a conducta suicida: Estudio en una muestra de población penitenciaria Colombiana-* [Risk and protective factors associated with suicidal behaviour: Study in a sample of colombian prison population] Bogotá: Universidad Nacional de Colombia.

Congreso República de Colombia. (1991). *Constitución Política de Colombia.* [Political Constitution of Colombia]. Secretaria Senado. http://www.secretariasenado.gov.co/senado/basedoc/constitucion_politica_1991.html

Congreso República de Colombia. (1993). *Ley 65 de 1993.* Código Penitenciario y Carcelario. [Law 65 of 1993: Penitentiary and prison code] Secretaria Senado. http://www.secretariasenado.gov.co/senado/basedoc/ley_0065_1993.html

Consultancy Universidad Nacional de Colombia. (2011). *Detección de Necesidades de Tratamiento en la Población reclusa colombiana en establecimientos del INPEC.* [Detection of Treatment Needs in the Colombian Prison Population in INPEC facilities]. Bogotá: Universidad Nacional de Colombia-Instituto Nacional Penitenciario y Carcelario.

Consultancy Universidad Nacional de Colombia. (2013a). *Programa Responsabilidad Integral con la Vida.* [Comprehensive Responsibility with Life Programme] Bogotá: Universidad Nacional de Colombia-Instituto Nacional Penitenciario y Carcelario.

Consultancy Universidad Nacional de Colombia. (2013b). *Programa Cadena de Vida.* [Life Chain Programme] Bogotá: Universidad Nacional de Colombia-Instituto Nacional Penitenciario y Carcelario.

Consultancy Universidad Nacional de Colombia. (2013c). *Programa de Educación y Calidad de Vida.* [Education and Life Quality Programme] Bogotá: Universidad Nacional de Colombia-Instituto Nacional Penitenciario y Carcelario.

Consultancy Universidad Nacional de Colombia. (2013d). *Programa de Intervención Para la Adaptación Social (PIPAS)* [Social Adaptation Intervention Programme] Bogotá: Universidad Nacional de Colombia-Instituto Nacional Penitenciario y Carcelario.

Consultancy Universidad Nacional de Colombia. (2013e). *Programa de Preparación para la Libertad (en español, Programmea de Preparación para la Libertad, PL)* [Preparation for Freedom Programme] Bogotá: Universidad Nacional de Colombia-Instituto Nacional Penitenciario y Carcelario.

Consultancy Universidad Nacional de Colombia. (2017). *2017 Prisons Report.* Universidad Nacional de Colombia and Justice Department.

Consultancy Universidad Nacional de Colombia (2020). Diseño y validación de un test para evaluar actitudes y actitudes laborales para población reclusa en establecimientos de reclusión de orden nacional [Desing and validation of a work skills and attitudes test for convicted inmate population]. Bogotá: Universidad Nacional de Colombia-Instituto Nacional Penitenciario y Carcelario.

Constitutional Court of Colombia. (2013a). Sentencia T-921/13 (Jorge Ignacio Pretelt Chalhub, M.P.). [Judgment T-921 of 2013a, from Constitutional Court: on human rights in Colombian prisons]. https://www.corteconstitucional.gov.co/relatoria/2013a/t-921-13.htm

Constitutional Court of Colombia (2013b). Sentencia T-388/13 (María Victoria Calle Correa, M.P.). [Judgment T-388 of 2013b, from Constitutional Court: on human rights in Colombian prisons]. https://www.corteconstitucional.gov.co/relatoria/2013b/t-388-13.htm

Editorial Staff El Tiempo. (2022). *El INPEC, acorralado por la corrupción y los escándalos.* [INPEC, cornered by corruption and scandals]. https://www.eltiempo.com/justicia/investigacion/inpec-carlos-mattos-aida-merlano-y-otros-escandalos-en-carceles-655401

Fazel, S., Ramesh, T., & Hawton, K. (2017). Suicide in prisons: An international study of prevalence and contributory factors. *The Lancet Psychiatry, 4*(12), 946–952.

Finklestein, M., Stein, E., Greene, T., Bronstein, I., & Solomon, Z. (2015). Post-traumatic stress disorder and vicarious trauma in mental health professionals. *Health and Social Work, 40*(2), 25–31.

Hare, R. (2010). *Handbook of PCL-R.* TEA.

La República. (2022). *Colombia se vuelve a rajar en corrupción según índice de Transparencia Internacional.* [Colombia cracks again in corruption according to Transparency International index]. https://www.larepublica.co/globoeconomia/colombia-se-vuelve-a-rajar-en-corrupcion-segun-indice-de-transparencia-internacional-3291811

Larrotta, C. R., Luzardo B. M., Vargas C. S., & Rangel N. K. (2014). Características del comportamiento suicida en cárceles de Colombia [Characteristics of suicidal behaviour in Colombia prisons]. *Revista Criminalidad, 56*(1), 83–95.

Lindström, B., & Eriksson, M. (2006). Contextualizing salutogenesis and Antonovsky in public health development. *Health Promotion International, 21*(3), 238–244.

Martínez-Castrillón, S. D. (2021). Estado de Cosas Institucional (ECI), unidad de la jurisdicción, y acceso a la justicia de las personas privadas de libertad en Colombia. [Unconstitutional State of Affairs, unity of jurisdiction and access to justice of the people deprived of liberty in Colombia]. Medellín: Universidad Eafit.

Mercado, C., Arango, G. A., & Segura, S. M. (2014). *Cien años de construcción de un sistema carcelario y penitenciario en Colombia.* [One hundred years of building a prison and penitentiary system in Colombia] Bogotá: Instituto Nacional Penitenciario y Carcelario de Colombia.

Ministerio del Interior y de Justicia de Colombia. (2005). Resolución 7302 de 2005 por medio de la cual se revocan las Resoluciones 4105 del 25 de septiembre de 1997 y número 5694 del 9 de diciembre de 1998 y se expiden pautas para la atención integral y el Tratamiento Penitenciario. [Resolution 7302 of 2005: Differentiation between Care Activities and Treatment Activities]. Bogotá D.C.: Ministerio del Interior y de Justicia de Colombia. https://scj.gov.co/sites/default/files/marco-legal/RESOLUCIÓN_7302_DE_2005_.pdf

Ministerio de Justicia y del Derecho de Colombia. (1993). Decreto 1242 de 1993 por medio del cual se aprueba el Acuerdo número 001 del 25 de mayo de 1993 del Consejo Directivo del Instituto Nacional Penitenciario y Carcelario - INPEC. [Decree 1242 of 1993: Division of prisons in six national regions]. Ministerio de Justicia y del Derecho de Colombia. https://www.suin-juriscol.gov.co/viewDocument.asp?id=1736976

Ministerio de Justicia y del Derecho de Colombia. (1992). Decreto 2160 de 1992 por medio del cual se se fusiona la Dirección General de Prisiones del Ministerio de Justicia con el Fondo Rotatorio del Ministerio de Justicia.. [Decree 2160 of 1992: The creation of the National Penitentiary and Prison Institute]. Ministerio de Justicia y del Derecho de Colombia. http://www.secretariasenado.gov.co/senado/basedoc/decreto_1170_1999.html

Mónoga, N. E., Carrillo, D. A., Flórez, D. E., Mantilla, A., Porras, C. A., & Gómez-Quesada, Z. (2009). *Instrumento para la Valoración Integral de Condenados IVIC 1.0.* [Instrument for the Comprehensive Assessment of Convicts – IVIC 1.0] Bogotá: Universidad Pontificia Bolivariana – Instituto Nacional Penitenciario y Carcelario.

National Penitentiary and Prison Institute. (S/F.). *Reseña histórica documental.* [Historical documentary review]. Recovered from https://www.inpec.gov.co/web/guest/institucion/resena-historica-documental, March 12, 2022

National Penitentiary and Prison Institute. (2017). *Instrumento para la Valoración Integral de Condenados IVIC 2.0.* [Instrument for the Comprehensive Assessment of Convicts IVIC 2.0] Bogotá: Universidad Industrial de Santander – Instituto Nacional Penitenciario y Carcelario.

Presidency of the Republic. (2020). *Octavo informe semestral del estado de cosas inconstitucional en el sistema penitenciario y carcelario.* [Eighth semi-annual report on the unconstitutional state of affairs in the penitentiary and prison system]. Gobierno de Colombia.

Rodríguez-Diaz, F. J., Alvarez-Fresno, E., García-Zapico, F., Longoria-González, B., & Moriega-Carro, M. I. (2011). *El sistema penitenciario: un análisis desde el ayer para el mañana.* [The prison system: an analysis from yesterday to tomorrow], in E. García (Ed) Psicopatología forense: comportamiento humano y tribunales de justicia [Forensic psychopathology: human behavior and courts of law] Bogotá: Manual Moderno.

Rojas-Castañeda, D. (2020). *El hacinamiento en las cárceles colombianas sobrepasa 54,9% según estadísticas del INPEC.* [Overcrowding in Colombian prisons exceeds 54.9% according to INPEC statistics]. https://www.asuntoslegales.com.co/actualidad/el-hacinamiento-en-las-carceles-colombianas-sobrepasa-549-segun-estadisticas-del-inpec-2982618

Ruiz, J.I. (2004). Un modelo sociocultural del encarcelamiento: afectividad, factores psicosociales y cultura [A sociocultural model of jail punishment: affectivity, psychosocial factors and culture]. San Sebastián: Basque Country University (Doctoral thesis).

Ruiz, J. I. (2006). *Relaciones crimen-droga en Colombia: un estudio a partir de una muestra de internos en establecimientos del INPEC.* VI Congreso Iberoamericano De Psicología Jurídica. [Crime-drug relations in Colombia: a study based on a sample of inmates in INPEC establishments] Bogotá, November 24–26, 2006.

Ruiz, J. I. (2007). Emotional climate in organizations: Applications in Latin American Prisons. *Journal of Social Issues, 63*(2), 289–306.

Ruiz, J.I. & Páez, D. (2002). Comparación de factores psicosociales y estrés post-traumático en internos y empleados de cinco centros penitenciarios: Un estudio exploratorio [Comparison on psychosocial factors and post-traumatic stress into offenders and officers from five prisons: An exploratory study]. *Anuario de Psicología Jurídica, 12*(1), 69–85.

Ruiz-Pérez, J. I. (2017). Marco histórico y análisis funcional del establecimiento penitenciario de alta seguridad de Cómbita. [Historical framework and functional analysis of the high-security penitentiary establishment of Cómbita] *Notas Criminológicas,* 3, 9–26.

Sirvent, C., & Moral, M. (2016). *Evaluación del autoengaño. Validación del inventario IAM-40.* [Evaluation of self-deception. IAM-40 Inventory Validation] Oviedo: University of Oviedo.

Willis, G. M., Prescott, D. S., & Yates, P. M. (2013). The Good Lives Model (GLM) in theory and practice. *Journal of Sexual Abuse in Australia and New Zealand., 5*(1), 3–9.

Rehabilitation Practices in the Adult Criminal Justice System in England and Wales

John Deering and Martina Y. Feilzer

A Short Introductory History of Rehabilitation Mechanisms

Rehabilitation in probation emerged as a one-to-one engagement between a volunteer 'practitioner' and a defendant within the Police Courts in England and Wales in the mid-late nineteenth century, whereby the former sought to offer advice and support to the latter as an alternative to a sentence. Such voluntary services to courts in England and Wales focused on the 'needs' of the individual, ensuring that courts had a constructive alternative to sentencing that aimed to prevent reoffending and, in this way, might be seen as the basis of 'traditional probation practice'.

The Probation Service itself was not formally constituted until the 1907 Probation of Offenders Act. The Act famously declared that the role of the probation officer was to 'advise, assist and befriend' those under its supervision (Whitehead & Statham, 2006). For most of the next 50 years or so,

J. Deering (✉)
University of South Wales, Cardiff, UK
e-mail: johndeering@btinternet.com

M. Y. Feilzer
Bangor University, Bangor, UK
e-mail: m.feilzer@bangor.ac.uk

practice was unregulated, grounded in social work practice, but not based upon particular theoretical approaches. Instead, it involved an eclectic range of interventions utilised as a result of the interests and preferences of practitioners, all delivered by locally based probation services (Deering & Feilzer, 2019; Vanstone, 2004). However, from the 1950s, some doubts emerged about the efficacy and effectiveness of probation interventions in terms of reducing reoffending rates. For example, studies in North America and England and Wales (Folkard et al., 1976; Martinson, 1974) concluded that it was difficult to identify consistent positive outcomes for probation and Martinson famously concluded that *Nothing Works*. Unusually for academic research, these studies had a significant impact upon government policy. Their timing was important, as they coincided with a general political and perhaps societal shift in attitudes towards crime and offending at the start of what has been referred to 'late modernity', a period said to have seen the emergence of more punitive attitudes within government and across some but by no means all 'western' criminal justice systems (Garland, 2001; Pratt et al., 2005). At this time, the government of the day reviewed its aims and objectives for the probation service in England and Wales (Home Office, 1984) and in the 1980s, at least in the eyes of government, probation officially became an alternative to custody, managing higher risk individuals than had been the case previously (Deering & Feilzer, 2019; Raynor & Vanstone, 2002).

The 1991 Criminal Justice Act saw further radical changes to the service's official aims and identity and the idea of rehabilitation began to take on a revised meaning in the following decade. Under the Act, the probation order became a sentence of the court and new National Standards limited practitioner discretion in important ways, emphasising compliance and accountability to the court, rather than a commitment to rehabilitation (Home Office, 1992). Officially, probation supervision became punishment in the community, but in an apparent reinforcement of the Service's role, it also came centre stage in the criminal justice system with an enhanced role supervising individuals who might otherwise have received custodial sentences. Along with the emerging importance of the assessment and management of risk, this period saw government positioning probation as primarily a law enforcement and public protection agency (Deering & Feilzer, 2019; Kemshall, 2003).

Despite these changes, traditional rehabilitation practices remained central to much practitioner behaviour, and it seems likely that practitioners continued to join the service to pursue this goal (Annison et al., 2008; Deering, 2011; Williams, 1995). Moreover, rehabilitation did begin to re-assume more importance through the 1990s, employing cognitive behaviourist interventions that had emerged from academic study in Canada in the 1980s. This empirically based movement, which became known as 'What Works' stood in direct challenge to the 'Nothing Works' era and paradigm. 'What Works' proponents argued that such an approach could reduce recidivism by teaching participants in a group setting a range of cognitive and social skills (Ross & Fabiano 1985). Whilst not adopted by government initially, the interest of a number of individual probation services in England and Wales did bring it to government's attention and, following the election of the Labour government in 1997, the Home Office launched the Effective Practice Initiative (Home Office, 1998) which led to cognitive-behavioural 'accredited programmes' becoming the primary focus of rehabilitation in the early 2000s, along with elements of what has been called the 'new' rehabilitation. Clearly, this did not constitute a return to 'traditional' rehabilitation, delivered one-to-one by a probation officer using full discretion, but saw groups undertaking cognitive behaviourist programmes within a probation order that focused upon risk assessment and management alongside compliance and enforcement (Vanstone, 2004).

Whilst seemingly an endorsement of a form of rehabilitation, in some ways, the 'What Works' movement was controversial, being criticised by some as a 'one size fits all' approach that emphasised the 'fixing of the individual', rather than the need to address wider structural inequalities that were seen by critics as at the core of offending (Gorman, 2001; Merrington & Stanley, 2000). Nevertheless, the government became firmly wedded to this approach and, during the 2000s, accredited programmes based on cognitive behaviourism were significantly expanded. However, by the end of the decade, this approach had begun to run into problems related to programme completions and outcomes which suggested limited effectiveness.

To add further complexity, the government began to develop radical plans for probation governance, for a future based on possible marketisation and privatisation that came to be realised under the Coalition government's Transforming Rehabilitation (TR) agenda (Deering & Feilzer, 2015). These changes to probation structures and governance are outlined below together with a wider discussion of how specific forms of rehabilitation practices started to permeate various stages of the adult criminal justice system.

Theoretical Underpinnings to Models of Rehabilitation

As outlined above, for most of its history, rehabilitation in England and Wales was an eclectic mix of practices based upon various theoretical frameworks. However, after decades of a range of psychology-based 'therapeutic' approaches being employed, by the 1970s and 'Nothing Works', the government began to consider probation's role to be one of providing cheaper and more efficient alternatives to custody. Later via the 1991 Criminal Justice Act, the government created a new role for probation of law enforcement and 'punishment in the community', an idea that has remained as the underlying theoretical justification for probation, at least in the eyes of successive governments, which have been wedded to a continuing punitive, retributive criminal justice system. Additionally, perhaps in part due to philosophical uncertainty and inconsistency, since the 1990s, this has been overlaid to some extent by theories of public protection (themselves underpinned by risk theories) and the 'new rehabilitation' (Vanstone, 2004).

Theories for risk and public protection began to emerge in earnest in the 1990s, based on the idea that it was becoming increasingly possible to successfully predict the future behaviour of individuals, based on their assessed risk (Kemshall, 2003). This risk was made up of two components, namely the risk of reoffending (i.e. the likelihood of an individual committing an offence) and the risk of harm (i.e. the impact of this offence upon any victim). This utilised risk assessment instruments, which had evolved to make use of both 'clinical' personal knowledge of an individual and 'objective' actuarial knowledge of their past behaviour. In England and Wales, this was operationalised by the Offender Assessment System (OASys, later e-OASys) which categorised individuals according to their potential risk of reoffending and harm. This then became the basis of all supervisory practice (including rehabilitation) with more intensive supervision being afforded to those of the highest risk of harm—the practice of resources following risk (Deering, 2011; Home Office, 2002).

Thus, whilst the main focus for supervision in the 1990s and into the 2000s was risk management, at the same time practice encompassed 'What Works' principles and the new rehabilitation. Theoretically, this approach also incorporated the Risk/Needs/Responsivity (RNR) model (Andrews & Bonta, 2003) under which intervention is delivered in proportion to the risk of reoffending and aims to focus on criminogenic (rather than generalised welfare) needs, with the overall aim of reducing reoffending. This model has remained dominant ever since, although the use of accredited programmes and supervision itself has declined quite sharply in the last decade, accelerated by the changes brought in under TR (Deering & Feilzer, 2017).

Successive governments have also influenced the practice of rehabilitation via legislation and policy. Since 2013, all Community Orders are required to have a punitive element within them and, with the 2014 Offender Rehabilitation Act (which facilitated TR), there is no longer a requirement for generic supervision within a Community Order, with the Rehabilitation Activity Requirement (RAR) doing no more than identifying a specific period for some form of intervention to take place. Furthermore, after the majority of the lower risk of harm caseload transferred to the marketised Community Rehabilitation Companies (CRCs) in 2015, a significant amount of community supervision was until 2021 somewhat hidden from view, although a number of reports by the Probation Inspectorate raised significant concerns about its quality (Her Majesty's Inspectorate of Probation, 2016). Thus, it is not easy to identify clearly how rehabilitation has actually been practiced over the last five to six years prior to the reunification of the probation service within the public sector in June 2021 (HMPPS, 2021).

Moreover, cracks had begun to appear within the dominance of cognitive behavioural-based rehabilitation, due to the emergence of theories of desistance. Although not primarily concerned with practice, desistance theories have had some impact over the past decade in terms of casting doubt upon the usefulness of probation interventions, as reported by ex-offenders (Farrell, 2002). Rather than pointing to particular interventions as being useful in their desistance, desisters have identified the creation and use of a good supportive relationship as the most useful element within supervision (Rex, 1999). As a result, some theorists have turned their attention to a role for desistance in supervision and argue for an approach that uses assessment to consider the supports and barriers to individual desistance, rather than as a basis for some treatment-based intervention (Weaver & McNeill, 2010). In this way, the role of the practitioner is to act as motivational counsellors, educators for human capital and advocates for social capital (Deering & Evans, 2021), and others (McNeill et al., 2012) argue that practitioners should work to assist the individual to make personal changes and to help in negotiating social barriers.

Thus, supervision should be recast from the assessment of past risks by the expert practitioner that are then fixed by rehabilitative programmes, towards a more positive, forward-looking approach, which includes the co-identification of strengths and the encouragement of pro-social bonds and motivation. Whilst desistance has become influential theoretically, its impact upon practice is far from clear and indeed there are still significant questions about how desistance and traditional rehabilitation can co-exist or converge in the future. With the launch of the new National Probation Service (NPS) in 2021, both approaches are claimed to be part of an intended future, but the Target Operating Model document fails to discuss such a development at a sufficiently theoretical level (HMPPS, 2021) given their apparently very different approaches to supervision.

Theoretically, attempts have been made to address the tension between principles of rehabilitation practice and desistance. For example, McNeill (2018) sets out four forms of rehabilitation and their relationship with correctional practice as well as desistance. The four forms of rehabilitation are: personal rehabilitation; social rehabilitation; judicial rehabilitation; and moral and political rehabilitation. Rehabilitation services including probation have focused most on personal rehabilitation and equipping individuals with the skills, motivations, and identity to stop offending. Judicial rehabilitation is the 'post'-sentencing stage once a punishment has been served, whereas moral and political rehabilitation is relational and moves the discussion from the relationship between the citizen and the state to one of relationships with civil society and other citizens. Where wider society is exclusionary towards those who committed a crime, this can cause problems for the agencies supporting such individuals in the rehabilitation process. Finally, social rehabilitation is about an individual's social position and identity and how the process of change is supported by those around them. These four forms of rehabilitation are interdependent, and the desistance of an individual is impacted by the scaffold of these rehabilitative processes (McNeill, 2018). The role of rehabilitation and that of a probation practitioner is to provide a collaborative relationship with a focus on the lack of social capital that can hinder the desistance process (Vanstone, 2021: 168).

Current Mechanisms and Their Policy and Political Context

It is clear that rehabilitation has been interpreted in different ways and rehabilitation practice has changed over time. For example, Robinson (2008: 430) highlights utilitarian, managerial, and expressive meanings of rehabilitation. The primary focus of the utilitarian approach is the reduction of offending behaviour, and this has been firmly adopted in governmental discourses, including those used in promoting TR. In highlighting tailored 'rehabilitative work with an emphasis on responding to *the broader life management issues* that often lead offenders back to crime' (Ministry of Justice, 2013: 6, emphasis added), the focus is on individual flaws and shortcomings, including anti-social attitudes, poor thinking skills, drug and/or alcohol misuse, homelessness, unemployment, and so on. In this way, it emphasises personal responsibility to respond positively to support offered to address individual flaws and ignores structural causes of offending.

At the beginning of 2022, this form of rehabilitation has become mainstream and such language and provision can be found at various stages of the criminal justice system. At the pre-court stage, several police forces have introduced diversion and deferred prosecution schemes for low to medium-level offences committed by adults—the Durham Checkpoint scheme introduced in 2015 has received most attention in that respect. The scheme offers individuals arrested for low-level crimes a chance to participate in a tailored four months' programme responding to individual needs (Weir et al., 2021). Some of the deferred prosecutions use set 'scripted' programmes, whereas others are based on individual risk assessments and are tailored to need. Whilst Weir et al. (2021) frame the scheme in terms of deterrence and desistance theory, a number of concepts are taken from the principles of utilitarian rehabilitation and 'What Works', namely addressing criminogenic needs, pro-social modelling, and the use of behaviour change techniques.

Similar rehabilitation principles are used in the National Liaison and Diversion Services operated by the NHS, which aim to identify and offer support to individuals with mental health needs and other vulnerabilities in contact with the criminal justice system (Disley et al., 2021). The services aimed to 'reduce offending by addressing the unmet needs of offenders through appropriate assessment and referral' in the main to drug/substance abuse and health services including psychological therapies (Disley et al., 2021: x).

Such systematic pre-court rehabilitation provision is relatively new, at least in the case of adult criminal justice provision. Longer established, as explained above, is rehabilitation provided as part of court sentences or as condition for a deferred or suspended sentence. For adults serving sentences in the community, rehabilitation is now offered through the NPS, thus reversing the six-year experiment of administering rehabilitation through privatised CRCs for low level and low and medium risk of harm individuals and through the NPS for those assessed as high risk of harm. The 2014 TR reforms led to a privatisation of around 70% of probation provision and were introduced against a backdrop of significant professional, practitioner, and academic resistance (Deering & Feilzer, 2015). TR proved to be disastrous in professional and organisational terms (see below), such that from June 2021, the new, reunified NPS has taken on responsibility for the whole probation caseload, although some small-scale involvement of third and private sector organisations remains (HMPPS, 2021). The structural upheaval of the past six years has left a probation profession needing to recover from the deep scars inflicted by TR, as a result of an exodus of experienced staff, high caseloads, tensions between staff in both areas of probation provision, an erosion of trust in senior management, and seemingly a crisis of self-legitimacy (Deering & Feilzer, 2017).

A lot has been said about the changes to probation values and the recasting of probation officers as 'offender managers' with a responsibility for assessing and monitoring risk in the late 1990s and early 2000s. The values of probation were seen to be under threat by the time the TR reforms were enacted but the unashamed marketisation and part-privatisation signalled a radical new phase in probation and rehabilitation history, and some commentators suggested it marked the 'death of probation' (Kirton & Guillaume, 2019: 937–940). The TR reforms saw a reduction in time spent in individual supervision across both CRCs and NPS, an increase in caseloads across the organisations, and a stifling of innovation—additionally, they were seen as an assault on practitioner professionalism (Kirton & Guillaume, 2019: 940–942). Some of the concerns expressed about the rushed and poorly conceived and planned implementation of the TR reforms seemed to be borne out by the 2019 report by the HM Probation Inspector. He judged 80% of CRCs to be 'inadequate' in terms of probation supervision, noted a significant reduction (56%) in individuals on accredited programmes, a significant loss of confidence in probation by Magistrates (38%), and significant financial losses (almost £300 million) forecast by the CRCs, in stark contrast to the profits initially predicted (HMIP, 2019: 4).

In addition to the TR changes, COVID-19 has had a significant impact on how rehabilitation services have been provided over the last two years. In its latest inspection report, HMIP (2022) stated that, in 2021, for the CRCs, almost 75% of contacts had been carried out via telephone, and outdoor unpaid work activities and group-based offending behaviour programmes had stopped. As a result, targets on almost all rehabilitation activities as part of sentences had been missed. Thus, the newly unified probation service faces a significant challenge in rebuilding rehabilitation services both from the wreckage of the previous structural reforms and the damaging impact of the pandemic on the lives of those under probation supervision and the probation professionals and mechanisms meant to support them.

Finally, rehabilitation is meant to be a core component of custodial sentences and much of the TR reforms were designed to embed rehabilitative practices into sentence management during custodial sentences and after release. Indeed, 'through the gate' resettlement services were expected to prepare those serving custodial sentences better for life after prison and offer opportunities for rehabilitation whilst in custody and beyond. Services were specifically designed to help with accommodation, finance and to support education, training, and employment and resettlement plans were meant to be set up at the beginning of a custodial sentence and reviewed 12 weeks prior to release. These services were supposed to remove barriers to reintegration for those released from prison and with that help reduce reoffending and provide public protection. However, HMIP's (2017) report found continued difficulties with the service, as insufficiently responsive to individual needs, with poor integration with prison systems and little evidence of an impact on reoffending rates (HMIP, 2017: 42). Subsequently, a new enhanced 'through the gate' service was established and an initial evaluation published in 2020 suggested some improvement on the previous arrangements (Fahy & Eginsoy, 2020).

Official prison policy is committed to offer those serving custodial sentences opportunities to engage in education, training and employment, offender management programmes, and wider rehabilitation provision. For some sentences, engagement in such a programme is a condition for parole applications. In research asking those serving sentences to reflect on access to rehabilitation in prison, Bullock and Bunce (2020) found a sense of cynicism and scepticism about the extent to which prisons offered opportunities for rehabilitation. Offender management programmes have been administered with limited success in the prison system driven by a fundamental mismatch of the institutional structures and adversarial cultures with the values of a genuinely rehabilitative approach (Bullock & Bunce, 2020: 115). The conclusion was that prisons failed to take institutional responsibility for rehabilitation and developing a rehabilitative culture and in turn, those attending offender management programmes would do so by complying superficially rather than engaging in the process of fundamental behaviour change (Bullock & Bunce, 2020: 122).

It could of course be regarded as a success that today, rehabilitation is part of the rhetoric of virtually all stages of the criminal justice system, however, it is important to recognise the limited and confused way in which rehabilitation is presented and implemented. Considering the various theoretical forms of rehabilitation outlined above, it could be argued that what is regarded as rehabilitative practice in criminal justice is conceptually inconsistent and narrow and instrumental in focus.

Rehabilitation and Diversity

Understanding the experiences of Black and minority ethnic adults in the criminal justice system has been a longstanding focus for research on policing, sentencing practices, and prisons. In the context of rehabilitation, concern about overrepresentation of minority ethnic adults in the criminal justice system led to the introduction of requirements to record ethnicity and improved monitoring of presentence reports (PSRs) (Hudson & Bramhall, 2005: 722). Hudson and Bramhall (2005) point to the paucity of research sensitive to ethnicity in risk assessments and PSRs and their research suggest that PSRs on minority ethnic male individuals were generally 'thinner' in content, using more distancing language and presented weaker, less clear, and negative recommendations than those for white males (Hudson & Bramhall, 2005: 727). In terms of assessments of risk, Asian males appeared lower risk than white males on static risk factors, and there were clear differences in dynamic risk assessments and the way that assessments were supported by evidence and discussions between white and Asian individuals. Hudson and Bramhall (2005: 735) also noted significant differences in the discourse of family background and concluded that OASys risk assessments 'reinforce entrenched stereotypes' about Asian males. Such differences are particularly important as the courts are known to place significant weight on PSR recommendations (although, the use of full PSRs has declined significantly over the last decade) and thus these are a way in which discrimination can creep into sentencing and rehabilitation practice.

In addition to the role of ethnicity influencing risk assessments and with that possibly sentencing outcomes, the reliance on 'one size fits all' offender management programmes and services have been highlighted as problematic by the Lammy Review (2017: 57). Reoffending rates vary between ethnic groups and gender and rehabilitation services need to be responsive to particular cultural and religious contexts and provide tailored support to offer the individuals involved a chance of success. There are questions whether probation services can deliver such culturally aware services or whether more effective use should be made of small third sector organisations in this area of work (Lammy, 2017: 59; Robertson & Wainwright, 2020: 8). Beyond identifying specific support needs for distinct groups of adults in the criminal justice system, little is known about the role of ethnicity in the desistance process. Whilst there is recognition that some ethnic groups suffer multiple forms of structural disadvantage and that most suffer from experiences of racism, how these experiences impact on desistance processes and could be addressed is less evident. Robertson and Wainwright (2020: 11) identify a clear gap in existing rehabilitation services linked to the dominant approach of offering generic programmes and services regardless of individual needs and preferences. Considerations of improving rehabilitation for minority ethnic women and men in the adult criminal justice systems need to include intersectionality and the relational aspects of rehabilitation and the influences of 'social structures and cultural conditions' (McNeil, 2018: 18).

Research Findings and Effectiveness

In the aftermath of the Second World War and the building of the welfare state, and in common with other areas of public life and social sciences more generally, there was perhaps some over-optimism about probation interventions and only relatively later did 'evidence-based practice' become important (Raynor, 2020), the assumption being that probation was 'a good thing' and trying to rehabilitate individuals was a morally good pursuit. As a result, for most of probation's history, there was little interest in conducting evaluative studies of probation practice, either within government or the service itself (Knott, 2004).

Nevertheless, as mentioned above, doubts did begin to emerge and in the 1970s (Martinson, 1974) asserted that 'Nothing Works'. However, as part of 'What Works', through the 1980s and 1990s, researchers were conducting empirical studies based upon cognitive-behavioural intervention with individuals whose offending was regarded as 'persistent' and devised evaluative methods that looked for patterns and effective elements of interventions (Ross & Fabiano, 1985). This was closely related to the RNR model which argued that the level of intensity of any intervention should be in proportion to the individual's risk of reoffending (not harm), that it should focus on criminogenic needs and be delivered via methods appropriate to supervisees' learning styles and culture (Andrews & Bonta, 2003, 2010). The argument made was that much persistent, low level, offending was the result of under-socialisation, as opposed to the deliberate, rational acts carried out by 'bad' people. Such under-socialisation had resulted in individuals with certain cognitive 'deficits' that were linked to a lack of social, inter-personal and other skills. Importantly, these were skills that could be learned and that once acquired could result in more pro-social behaviour. Moreover, such an intervention could be best delivered via cognitive-behavioural skills training group work, run by suitably trained practitioners (T3 Associates, 2000). In England and Wales, these theories and practices became increasingly influential through the 1990s, however, initially, this growth was driven by a small number of probation services, rather than government, for example, the use of the Straight Thinking on Probation Programme (STOP) used in Mid-Glamorgan Probation Service in the 1990s, which was fully evaluated using not only reconviction data but also qualitative data from staff and group members and observations of practice (Raynor & Vanstone, 1994).

Nonetheless, the New Labour government elected in 1997 did develop an interest in evidence-based practice and the Home Office came to promote the widespread use of such 'accredited programmes' via the Effective Practice Initiative (Home Office, 1998) and the Crime Reduction Programme 1999–2002. Unfortunately, in a rush to get large numbers of individuals through these programmes which had perhaps become to be seen as something of a panacea, other vital elements such as the need to target the 'right' people for programmes and the importance of continuing to address wider social issues outside group work sessions were forgotten. As a result, overall results were disappointing with group failures and pressure to achieve results from government, in terms of reconviction and 'value for money' said to have resulted in poor planning and implementation, and an over-reliance on one method of intervention (Raynor, 2020: 1160). Assessing this initiative eventually led to lessons about how not to implement programmes rather than the effectiveness of a particular approach (Maguire, 2004; Robinson & Crow, 2009).

Despite these disappointments, cognitive-behaviourist approaches have remained core to probation supervision, although the period of TR so disrupted practice that its trajectory has been unclear in recent years. Accredited 'offender management' programmes have continued as a core part of rehabilitation provision, see Regional Reducing Reoffending Plans 2021–24, and are recognised as an important part of a range of balanced rehabilitation services:

> … group programmes, if properly designed, targeted and delivered, and supported where necessary by appropriate individual supervision, can make a useful contribution to the effectiveness of probation services.
>
> Raynor (2020: 1160)

Alongside the programmes and interventions, the use of appropriate skills both within a supervisory process and in group work is vital to their potential effectiveness (Chadwick et al., 2015). Various studies suggest effectiveness depends upon both elements—an effective programme/intervention delivered by skilled practitioners—see work on Pro-Social Modelling (Trotter, 1999), Core Correctional Practices (Dowden & Andrews, 2004), the STICS study in Canada (Bonta et al., 2011) and the Jersey Reconviction Study (Raynor et al., 2014) with some of the studies showing significant reductions in reoffending rates. Other work added that effective rehabilitation depends on a suitable organisational structure and good management in enabling good practice to flourish (Rex & Hosking, 2013).

Future Directions in Policy and Practice

There are several aspects to the likely future of rehabilitation practices. The language of a utilitarian view of rehabilitation and risk dominates criminal justice and seems to be securely embedded in criminal justice practice. In policy terms, the distinction between different forms of rehabilitation and desistance has become less pronounced, allowing for a blurring of concepts and potentially a theory-free space of effective practice. Moreover, the rise and fall of TR has resulted in the future of rehabilitation practices as part of the probation landscape in England and Wales being unpredictable at present. However, as part of the changes that have reunified the service within the new NPS, the government has acknowledged the considerable damage done by TR to staff morale and staffing levels and to the confidence of the courts in the services provided. The new, reunified public sector NPS came into existence on 26 June 2021 and whilst the future directions in policy and practice is as yet unknown, the Target Operating Model for the new service (HMPPS, 2021) does indicate a new direction of travel. The document signals a shift of emphasis from the language of punishment in the community and offender management, discussing the importance of developing a good professional relationship between practitioner and individual service user to promote rehabilitation and desistance. It reflects on the need to use more positive, non-labelling language and in terms of theoretical underpinnings, the RNR model is regarded as the prime mode of intervention, alongside the promotion of desistance.

There is insufficient discussion about how a desistance-based approach might be operationalised in terms of policy and practice, nor indeed any discussion of how some of these ideas might challenge traditional modes of rehabilitation practice, including approaches to compliance, intervention, and assessment. However, discussion of the importance of the professional relationship is in evidence with an outline of what this means in terms of professional skills and practices, including, for example, Core Correctional Practices, the use of cognitive-behavioural-based accredited programmes and Pro-Social Modelling (HMPPS, 2021: Annex A). Thus, overall rehabilitation is promoted within what are now long-standing theories based within the overarching RNR model.

With regards to the purposes of supervision, the emphasis is on a more utilitarian model rehabilitation, which should involve an appropriate balance between referral to specialist and universal services alongside individual supervision promoting 'appropriate rehabilitative interventions and reinforcing progress and new ways of thinking and behaving to support behavioural change' (HMPPS, 2021: 88).

However, the status of supervision under a Community Order is not raised or explored, something of an omission perhaps, particularly as it has been argued that 'probation supervision' died under the terms of the Offender Rehabilitation Act (2014) when both the supervision and activity requirements were removed from the Community Order, to be replaced by the Rehabilitation Activity Requirement (RAR), which allows for activities aimed at rehabilitation taking place over a 'maximum number of days' (Robinson & Dominey, 2019). The RAR is seen as having a negative impact upon levels and quality of supervision during the period and Robinson and Dominey (2019) argue that 'proper' supervision needs to be reintroduced via a revived Supervision Requirement.

The NPS is at a point at which it could choose to base its future practice within a paradigm of evidence-based rehabilitation infused with more recent ideas of desistance. Indeed, the Ministry of Justice held a Research in Probation event in March 2022 setting out its research agenda and focus on effective practice. There is a renewed emphasis on gaining evidence on 'What Works' but also on research understanding ethnicity and diversity, risk management and all aspects of rehabilitation practice, from individual needs to supervision and offender management programmes. The re-engagement between the Ministry of Justice and the academic research community does signal a shift in attitude and we can only hope it builds into a critical evidence-based and theoretically informed framework for rehabilitation practices across the criminal justice system.

References

Andrews, D. A., & Bonta, J. (2003). *The psychology of criminal conduct*. Cicinnati, OH: Anderson.

Andrews, D.A. & Bonta J. (2010). *The psychology of criminal conduct* (5th ed.). New Providence, NJ: LexisNexis Matthew Bender.

Annison, J., Eadie, T., & Knight, C. (2008). People first: Probation officer perspectives on probation work, *Probation Journal*, 55(3), 259–272.

Bonta, J., Bourgon, G., Rugge, T., Scott, T., Yessine, A., Gutierrez, L., & LI, J. (2011). An experimental demonstration of training probation officers in evidence-based community supervision. *Criminal Justice and Behavior*, 38(11), 1127–1148.

Bullock, K., & Bunce, A. (2020). "The prison don't talk to you about getting out of prison": On why prisons in England and Wales fail to rehabilitate prisoners. *Criminology and Criminal Justice*, 20(1), 111–127.

Chadwick, N., Dewolf, A., & Serin, R. (2015). Effectively training community supervision officers: A meta-analytic review of the impact on offender outcome. *Criminal Justice and Behaviour*, 42(10).

Deering, J. (2011). *Probation practice and the new penology: Practitioner reflections*. Ashgate.

Deering, J., & Evans, J. (2021). Lost in Translation or a work in progress? Developing desistance-informed youth justice practice in the welsh context. *British Journal of Social Work*, 51(8), 3172–3189.

Deering, J., & Feilzer, M. Y. (2015). *Transforming rehabilitation: Is privatisation the end of the probation ideal?* Policy Press.

Deering, J., & Feilzer, M. Y. (2017). Questions of legitimacy in probation practice after Transforming Rehabilitation. *Howard Journal of Criminal Justice*, 56(2), 158–175.

Deering, J., & Feilzer, M. Y. (2019). Hollowing out probation? The roots of transforming rehabilitation. *Probation Journal*, 66(1), 8–24.

Disley, E., Gkousis, E., Hulme, S., Morley, K., Pollard, J., Saunders, C.,Sussex, J., & Sutherland, A. (2021), *Outcome Evaluation of the National Model for Liaison and Diversion*. Rand. https://www.rand.org/pubs/research_reports/RRA1271-1.html

Dowden, C., & Andrews, D. (2004). The importance of staff practice in delivering effective correctional treatment: A meta analysis. *International Journal of Offender Therapy and Comparative Criminology*, 48(2), 203–214.

Fahy, K., & Eginsoy, A. (2020), *A process evaluation of the Enhanced Through the Gate Specification*. Ministry of Justice. https://assets.publishing.service.gov.uk/government/uploads/system/uploads/attachment_data/file/923222/evaluation-of-the-enhanced-through-the-gate-specification.pdf

Farrell, S. (2002), *Rethinking what works with offenders*. Willan.

Folkard, M., Smith, D. E., & Smith, D. D. (1976). *IMPACT. Intensive matched probation and after-care treatment*. HMSO.

Garland, D. (2001). *The culture of control*. Oxford University Press.

Gorman, K. (2001). Cognitive behaviourism and the holy grail. *Probation Journal, 48*(1), 3–9.

HMIP. (2017). An inspection of through the gate resettlement services for prisoners serving 12 months or more. Joint inspection by HM inspectorate of probation and HM inspectorate of prisons. https://www.justiceinspectorates.gov.uk/cjji/wp-content/uploads/sites/2/2017/06/Through-the-Gate-phase-2.-report.pdf

HMIP. (2019, March). Report of the Chief Inspector of Probation. https://www.justiceinspectorates.gov.uk/hmiprobation/wp-content/uploads/sites/5/2019/03/HMI-Probation-Chief-Inspectors-Report.pdf

HMIP. (2022). 2021 annual report: Inspection of probation services. https://www.justiceinspectorates.gov.uk/hmiprobation/wp-content/uploads/sites/5/2022/03/FINAL-Probation-Annual-Report-2021.pdf

Her Majesty's Inspectorate of Probation. (2016). *Transforming rehabilitation. Early implementation 5*. Home Office.

HMPPS. (2021). *Target operating model for the probation service*. Home Office.

Home Office. (1984). *Statement of national objectives and priorities*. Home Office.

Home Office. (1992). *National standards for the supervision of offenders in the community*. Home Office.

Home Office. (1998). *Effective practice initiative: Probation circular 35/98*. Home Office.

Home Office. (2002). *Offender assessment system: OASys*. Home Office.

Hudson, B., & Bramhall, G. (2005). Assessing the "other". Constructions of "Asianness" in risk assessments by probation officers. *British Journal of Criminology, 45*(5), 721–740.

Kemshall, H. (2003). *Understanding risk in criminal justice*. Open University Press.

Kirton, G., & Gillaume, C. (2019). When Welfare Professionals encounter restructuring and privatisation: The inside story of the probation service of England and Wales. *Work, Employment and Society, 33*(6), 929–947.

Knott, C. (2004). Evidence-based practice in the National Probation Service. In D. Burnett & C. Roberts (Eds.), *What works in probation and youth justice: developing evidence-based practice*. Willan.

Lammy, D. 2017. The Lammy Review. Gov.uk. Available online: https://www.gov.uk/government/publications/lammy-review-final-report (accessed on 24 July 2018).

Lammy Review. (2017), *An independent review into the treatment of, and outcomes for, Black, Asian and Minority Ethnic individuals in the Criminal Justice System*. https://assets.publishing.service.gov.uk/government/uploads/system/uploads/attachment_data/file/643001/lammy-review-final-report.pdf

Maguire, M. (2004). The crime reduction programme in England and Wales: Reflections on the vision and the reality. *Criminal Justice, 4*(3), 213–237.

Martinson, R. (1974). What works? Questions and answers about prison reform. *The Public Interest, 35*, 22–54.

McNeill, F. (2018). Rehabilitation corrections and society. *Advancing Corrections Journal, 5*, 10–20.

McNeill, F., Farrell, S., Lightowler, C., & Maruna, S. (2012). Re-examining evidence-based practice in community corrections: Beyond a "confined view" of what works. *Justice Research and Policy, 14*(1), 35–60.

Merrington, S., & Stanley, S. (2000). Doubts about the What Works Initiative. *Probation Journal, 47*(4), 272–275.

Ministry of Justice. (2013). Transforming rehabilitation: A strategy for reform, May, Ministry of Justice.

Pratt, J., Brown, D., Brown, M., Hallsworth, S., & Morrison, W. (2005). *The New Punitiveness: Trends, Theories, Perspectives.* Cullompton, Willan.

Raynor, P. (2020). Probation evidence, research and policy. In P. Ugwudike, H. Graham, F. McNeill, P. Raynor, F. Taxman, & C. Trotter (Eds.), *Rehabilitative work in criminal justice.* Routledge.

Raynor, P., Ugwudike, P., & Vanstone, M. (2014). The impact of skills in probation work: A reconviction study. *Criminology and Criminal Justice, 14*(2), 235–249.

Raynor, P., & Vanstone, M. (1994). *Straight thinking on probation: Third interim evaluation report.* Mid Glamorgan Probation Service.

Raynor, P., & Vanstone, M. (2002). *Understanding community penalties: Probation, policy and social change.* Open University Press.

Rex, S. (1999). Desistance from offending: Experiences of probation. *Howard Journal of Criminal Justice, 38*(4), 366–383.

Rex, S., & Hosking, N. (2013). A collaborative approach to developing probation practice: Skills for effective engagement, development and supervision (SEEDS). *Probation Journal, 60*(3), 332–338.

Robertson, L., & Wainwright, J. P. (2020). Black boys' and Young Men's experiences with Criminal Justice and desistance in England and Wales: A literature review. *Genealogy, 4*(2), 50.

Robinson, G. (2008). Late-modern rehabilitation: The evolution of a penal strategy, *Punishment and Society, 10*(4), 429–445.

Robinson, G., & Crow, I. (2009). *Offender rehabilitation: Theory, research and practice* Sage.

Robinson, G., & Dominey, J. (2019). Probation reform, the RAR and the forgotten ingredient of supervision. *Probation Journal, 66*(4), 451–455.

Ross, R., & Fabiano, E. (1985). *Time to Think: A cognitive model of delinquency prevention and rehabilitation.* Institute of Social Sciences and Arts.

T3 Associates. (2000). *Reasoning and rehabilitation revised: A handbook for teaching cognitive skills.* T3 Associates.

Trotter, C. (1999). *Working with involuntary clients.* Sage.

Vanstone, M. (2004). *Supervising offenders in the community: A history of probation theory and practice.* Ashgate.

Vanstone, M. (2021). Give them the money: An illustrative history of forms of reimagined rehabilitation in probation practice in England and Wales. *Howard Journal of Crime and Justice, 60*(2), 167–184.

Weaver, B., & McNeill, F. (2010). Travelling hopefully: desistance theory and probation practice. In J. Brayford, F. Cowe, & J. Deering (Eds.), *What else works? Creative work with offenders*. Willan.

Weir, K., Routledge, G., & Kilili, S. (2021). Checkpoint: An innovative programme to navigate people away from the cycle of reoffending: Implementation phase evaluation. *Policing, 15*(1), 508–527.

Whitehead, P., & Statham, R. (2006). *The History of Probation. Politics, power and cultural change 1876–2005*. Shaw and Sons.

Williams, B. (1995). *Probation values*. Venture Press.

Blending Culture, Religion, and the *Yellow Ribbon Program*: Rehabilitation in Fiji

John Whitehead and Lennon Chang

Rehabilitation, a concept familiar to most western societies, is relatively new to Fiji (Fiji Corrections Service, n.d.a). In 2006, the Corrections Services Act (2006) placed rehabilitation at the centre of Fiji's correctional aims, and the past 18 years have seen significant growth and change in their rehabilitative praxis. Upskilling has become a central aspect of the Fijian incarceral experience (see Fiji Corrections Service, n.d.a), the Yellow Ribbon Project has been implemented to reintroduce inmates into the community (see Vuiyasawa, 2009), and diverse populations have emerged under Fiji Corrections Service's care (see Fiji Corrections Service, 2019). However, such changes have also created significant challenges for the Fiji Corrections Service, who have attempted to embed Indigenous iTaukei[1] culture at the centre of their rehabilitative praxis. While these changes create a suitable and effective

---

J. Whitehead (✉)
Australian College of Applied Psychology (ACAP), Melton South, VIC, Australia
e-mail: jwhitehead@liv.asn.au

L. Chang
Monash University, Brunswick East, VIC, Australia
e-mail: lennon.chang@monash.edu

J. Whitehead
Law Institute of Victoria, Melbourne, Australia

environment for some inmates, their generalised use on the entire incarceral population is problematic. Fiji Corrections Service's current approach to other diverse populations has led to segregation (see Buadromo, 1982), stereotyping, and stigmatisation. Moreover, the elements of Fijian culture that are central to Fijian rehabilitative efforts create victimisation (see Lees et al., n.d.; also, Whitehead, 2019), and traditional actors who were historically central to customary iTaukei reintegration praxis have been forgotten.

The incarcerable experience in Fiji currently excludes powerful cultural mechanisms of reintegration that would benefit inmates and the wider community. For example, despite a significant iTaukei focus, current rehabilitative efforts lack the core process and principles of bulubulu.[2] Moreover, there is a significant need to shift current the Fiji Corrections Service's rehabilitative efforts away from the Christian iTaukei majority and better recognise the other diverse populations under the Fiji Corrections Service's care. However, these efforts require a complete redesign of the current procedures and practices of Fiji Corrections Service, the integration of customary and restorative justice mechanisms, and embedding vanua, or connectivity to the land, family, and village (see Newland, 2016), into its core principles of rehabilitation.

Customary Justice in Fiji

The iTaukei practice of bulubulu is a reconciliation ceremony and the historic customary response to many offences in Fiji (Adinkrah, 1995; Merry, 2006; Newland, 2016; see Cretton, 2005; also Jolly, 2005). Bulubulu's customary reconciliation ceremonies are used to heal the vanua of a village (Newland, 2016), mediate the diverse power relationships in hierarchical iTaukei society, and acknowledge the importance of each villager to the wellbeing of the community. The ceremony requires the offending party to approach the victim as an act of contrition and compensation in the form of a tabua (a whale's tooth, and culturally important symbol of purity; see Abramson, 1995; also, Arno, 1976), and would be overseen or mediated by the chief. Like many forms of customary justice, concerns surrounding bulubulu centre on inmates escaping meaningful punishment or a custodial sentence (see Hickson, 1975; also Merry, 2006), particularly in cases of gendered violence (see Whitehead, 2019). However, despite concerns surrounding the ceremony, it has a firm rehabilitative aim. Bulubulu not only creates peace in the community by settling disputes and reintegrating a deviant individual

(Merry, 2006), but operates alongside community shame and tovo vakaturuga (conduct modelled by the chief or ratu; Hickson, 1975; see Newland, 2016) to modify behaviour.

This form of customary justice is so fundamental to the iTaukei experience that it has played a central role in Fijian politics and is used as a tool for apology and reconciliation following the 1987 and 2000 coups (Braithwaite, 2014; Cretton, 2005; see Whitehead & Roffee, 2016). Moreover, despite the introduction of a contemporary and westernised criminal justice system in Fiji, bulubulu remains firmly entrenched in many outlying areas that lack access to justice (Whitehead, 2019), contemporary scholars continue to debate its use in cases of gendered violence (Merry, 2004; Whitehead, 2019); and its use has been debated by international panels such as the Committee on the Elimination of Discrimination against Women (CEDAW; Merry, 2006). However, this ceremony is not utilised by Fiji Correction's Service. Instead, the core principles of bulubulu, have deconstructed and amalgamated with other rehabilitative and reintegrative programmes, with problematic results. Nonetheless, when framed appropriately and operating alongside the western criminal justice system, bulubulu can operate as a rehabilitative and reintegrative tool for iTaukei inmates, and potentially other groups who feel a strong connection to the iTaukei vanua.

Demographics and Diversity: New Challenges for the Fiji Corrections Service

Increased diversity has become a challenge for the Fiji Corrections Service. Like many countries, Fiji is experiencing a growth in prison populations. Rates of incarcerated inmates have steadily increased from 1,987 in the 2016–2017 period, to 2337 in 2017–2018 (Fiji Corrections Service, 2019), and 2,439 as of 2019[3] (Fiji Corrections Service, n.d.b). Most of these inmates are members of the island nation's largest demographics, with statistics from 2017 to 2018 suggesting iTaukei detainees represent 79% of the incarceral population and Indo-Fijians 17% (Fiji Corrections Service, 2019).[4] Other populations are classified as European (0.5%), Chinese (0.27%), and Other (2.5%) (Fiji Corrections Service, 2019), and these groups are likely to grow as Fiji invites further immigration, tourism, and trade. This increased diversity, alongside an increase in female inmates (see Fiji Corrections Service, n.d.b), creates concerns surrounding longstanding overcrowding issues and the rehabilitative needs of this culturally diverse population (See Nand, 2021; also, The Fijian Government, 2012).

Many countries are currently engaged in a wider debate on how to integrate and support LGBTIQ+ inmates. This often creates unique challenges for the correctional institution, including questions surrounding access to appropriate clothing, the use of preferred names and pronouns, and access to various medical needs (see Roffee & Whitehead, 2019 for a discussion of this in an Australian context). The only literature surrounding LGBTIQ+ inmates in Fijian prisons suggests that historically they were segregated from the wider prison population to prevent sexual violence (Buadromo, 1982). It is unknown if such segregation still occurs, but this policy can exacerbate risk factors for incarceration, lead to further social isolation, and as detailed below, significantly hamper rehabilitative praxis. The rehabilitative praxis of Fijian correctional centres remains relatively under-researched.[5] The only information on this is provided by Fiji Corrections Service (n.d.b), and a handful of researchers who have gained access to inmates incarcerated in these centres (See Whitehead, 2019). Despite such limited research, poor rehabilitative design is embedded within the Fiji Corrections Service's praxis (see Adinkrah, 1995; also, Whitehead, 2019), and significant changes to rehabilitation programmes are needed to better support inmates under their care. Moreover, there is limited evidence that the needs of culturally and gender diverse prisons are accounted for.

The Intake Process

The Fiji Corrections Service has segmented the intake process into a daily routine that will be experienced by all inmates: Day one, medical assessment and receipt of prison kits[6]; day two, family visit; and day three, psychological assessment and sentence planning[7] (Fiji Corrections Service, n.d.c). In particular, the family visit provides an interesting context for rehabilitation, as this pulls upon those close to the inmate to contextualise criminogenic risk factors in their environment (Fiji Corrections Service, n.d.c). Such an approach ties heavily to the wider iTaukei ideal of vanua and creates a space for the community to assist the rehabilitative process from its onset. However, such a programme assumes the inmate and their family are communicating, ostracises those individuals without close family, and excludes other important community actors.[8] Moreover, there is limited knowledge of the psychological assessment process used by the Fiji Corrections Service and if this aligns to the widely used Risks, Needs, Responsivity model.[9] As a result, it is unknown if this assessment successfully charts the criminogenic risk factors and rehabilitative needs of inmates. Instead, a significant weight is placed upon the pastoral care of inmates through spiritual counselling and militarised drills (Fiji Corrections Service, 2016, n.d.c; Whitehead, 2019).

The Fijian Incarcerable Experience

From the outset of their incarceration, inmates are required to engage in a basic foot drill (Fiji Corrections Service, n.d.c: 9) designed to instil self-discipline. However, this approach constructs a militarised ideal within the Fiji Corrections Service, further facilitated by the military titles used by staff.[10] An additional concern surrounds those inmates who may not be able to complete these drills. While medical grounds can be used to exclude individuals from foot drills (Fiji Corrections Service, 2016, n.d.c), the Fiji Corrections Service provides no details about the alternative programmes offered to inmates unable to engage in this physical activity. As a result, and despite the problematic ideals represented by these drills, a core element of Fijian rehabilitative praxis is not accessible to many inmates. Gender also plays a leading role in rehabilitative praxis. Innovative justice paradigms, such as restorative justice, are only offered to female sexual offence inmates (Fiji Corrections Service, n.d.c) and are conducted by the Pacific Centre for Peacebuilding (PCP), an organisation with a problematic record of victim coercion during restorative ceremonies (Whitehead, 2019). The limited information available on the PCP suggests this organisation targets restorative programmes towards 'women, youth, sexual gender minorities, vulnerable and minority groups' (PCP, 2021). However, doing so limits access to restorative justice for inmates outside of these groups, and while the organisation notes an overt focus on the LGBTIQ+ community, this has yet to be integrated into the rehabilitative programmes of the Fiji Corrections Service.

Such a gender divide continues throughout the design of Fijian rehabilitative programmes, with two programmes (named Female Offender Programme and Female and Male Recidivists Programme) offered to female inmates.[11] Both of these programmes are exceptionally general, focusing on criminogenic risk factors such as substance abuse, and have a significant amount of overlap between them (Fiji Corrections Service, n.d.c). Female inmates are also not segregated through offence type or sentence length (Fiji Corrections Service, n.d.c), creating a space where they could be victimised by other inmates or develop new deviant ideals from others. Moreover, programmes that target recidivists are overseen by the same staff members in the same institution (Fiji Corrections Service, n.d.c). Such repetition is unlikely to have any rehabilitative benefit.

For male inmates, short-term rehabilitative praxis includes domestic violence and general offence programmes, the latter incorporating a variety of offences and addressing these through male cognitive skills, alcohol and substance use, and anger management courses. Long termer rehabilitation programmes include violent offences, sex offence, and anger management programmes (Fiji Corrections Service, n.d.c). These are described as '[t]herapeutic interventions that addresses the emotional and cognitive aspects of the individual to ensure a sustainable element of therapeutic, emotional and cognitive change' (Fiji Corrections Service, n.d.c: 28), and in the case of sexual violence inmates the programme appears to have a basis in Gestalt therapy (Fiji Corrections Service, n.d.c). However, the wider therapeutic processes and practices of this approach are not detailed in any official Fiji Corrections Service documentation, and it is unknown if psychological therapy is offered to all inmates. As a result, it is difficult to analyse the suitability of these models, although Whitehead (2019) does note that sexual violence inmates maintain problematic patriarchal and victim-blaming belief structures, suggesting a limited therapeutic impact. Moreover, and as noted in previous sections, Fiji Corrections Service does not appear to have any programmes tailored to LGBTIQ+ inmates, which may be due to the highly religious nature of Fijian society and consequently its rehabilitative praxis.

Spirituality is deeply entrenched within Fijian rehabilitation models, and forms a core element of all rehabilitative praxis regardless of offence type, sentence length, or gender (Fiji Corrections Service, n.d.c).[12] The Fiji Corrections Service (2016: 11–12) states that the purpose of this spiritual counselling is to create a holistic response to offending, integrating 'body, mind and spirit [to] depict the wholeness of an individual' and better integrate culture into the rehabilitative praxis. Despite the predominance of Methodism throughout Fiji, the spiritual counselling programme is not limited to Christian inmates. Non-Christians are allowed access to their own denominational leaders, and spiritual wellbeing is framed through multiple diverse lenses (Fiji Corrections Service, 2016). However, there is little evidence of the impact of this spiritual counselling, and a lack of other religious leaders on Fiji Corrections Services staff frames the organisation as predominantly Christian. This creates a space for victimisation of those inmates from diverse religious backgrounds, and frames 'Moral Development Education' (Fiji Corrections Service, 2016: 13) through stereotypes. For example, the 'Muslim' programme lacks details on its practice and facilitator, while the 'Yoga' programme is facilitated by 'Hindu' (Fiji Corrections Service, 2016: 13). Moreover, no rehabilitation policy or documentation makes note of atheist or agnostic inmates, suggesting a lack of programmes targeting these groups, and such a heavy Christian focus could stigmatise and discriminate against LGBTIQ+ inmates. A lack of diversity further impacts the Fiji Corrections Service upskilling programme, designed to provide inmates with valuable skills upon release.

Upskilling and the Yellow Ribbon Project

A core element of Fiji Corrections Service rehabilitative praxis is the upskilling programme for medium and long-term inmates. Again, separated by gender and at the end stage of the rehabilitation framework, inmates are trained in various vocations to improve their employment opportunities, foster peer support between inmates, and provide financial support to the Fiji Corrections Service through the sale of any created products (Fiji Corrections Service, n.d.c). For men, most of these programmes reflect the needs of the Fijian economy and focus on agriculture and woodworking, although others such as refrigeration and air-conditioning, plumbing, automotive engineering, and welding and fabrication create a space for further tertiary study (Fiji Corrections Service, n.d.c). A further programme, open to those inmates who have some education history, allows for enrolment in the Montfort Boys Town vocational training institution (Fiji Corrections Service, n.d.c), an early release study programme that teaches similar trades to those listed above (Montfort Boys' Town, 2019). The diversity of these programmes is beneficial to inmates, as Fiji contains a blend of urban and rural environments, and inmates can be specifically equipped for skills needed in their community (Fiji Corrections Service, 2016). However, their segregation by gender is problematic.

Upskilling programmes offered to female inmates are heavily gendered and reinforce stereotypes of the suitable employment for this group. They include body massage, flower arrangement, skin care and stage make-up, and horticulture (for a full list of the programmes, see Fiji Corrections Service, n.d.c). While these may provide an opportunity to some inmates, none of the programmes offered focus on subsistence, a significant concern for those female inmates who will return to their rural homes. Of further concern is the patriarchal ideals of women represented by these programmes, and the lack of any opportunities for further tertiary education. It is crucial that the Fiji Corrections Service creates parity between male and female educational offerings, allow greater recognition of LGBTIQ+ inmates, and provide all inmates equal opportunities post release. Moreover, these vocational outcomes should be embedded within the Yellow Ribbon Project to better facilitate reintroduction of the inmate to their community.

Alongside the aforementioned restorative justice rehabilitation component, the Fiji Corrections Service has implemented the Yellow Ribbon Project (Vuiyasawa, 2009; also, Whitehead, 2019). Based upon a programme developed in Singapore of the same name (Fiji Corrections Service, 2013; Vuiyasawa, 2009), the Yellow Ribbon Project was deployed to reduce recidivism and improve reintegration (see Lees et al., n.d.). The Yellow Ribbon Project provides inmates with opportunities to interact with the public by selling their crops, crafts, or clothes, and taking part in community events such as parades (Vuiyasawa, 2009). At the completion of the programme, an inmate is taken back to their community, which has been educated about the purpose of the Yellow Ribbon Project, where facilitators assist them to reintegrate into the community and a welcome feast is held.

The Yellow Ribbon Project has been considered a success due to a drop in first-time offending recidivism (see Whitehead, 2019), although criticisms have been levelled at the programme. For example, Vuiyasawa (2009) notes that the Yellow Ribbon Project was initiated without consulting the affected communities and is perceived as a means of reducing the sentences of individuals connected to the military or government. Furthermore, certain aspects of the programme such as spiritual empowerment (Fiji Corrections Service, 2013; see Vuiyasawa, 2009) and religious counselling are not clearly defined, and questions remain as to the associated procedures used by this programme (see Whitehead, 2019). This focus on religious counselling can also position the programme as exclusionary, mirroring the problematic spiritual focus of other rehabilitative programs developed by the Fiji Corrections Service. Fiji Corrections Service has further styled the project's welcome feast celebration after bulubulu to repair village relationships. Lees et al. (n.d.: 9–10) describe this as:

> [A ceremony] that welcome[s] the return of an offender to his community. At the end of various culturally informed practices, which included an apology and the offering of kava to the community, a large feast is held. Though helpful to the offender to feel reintegrated, these ceremonies may have a traumatic or otherwise negative impact on the victim.

Echoing the above quote, non-government organisations (NGOs) argue that a welcome celebration held for inmates when returning to the community is inappropriate for gendered violence offences, that the programme has little focus upon the victim, and has led to a decrease in the reporting of offences against women (see Whitehead, 2019). For example, Whitehead (2019: 150) interviewed a Women's Rights NGO worker who stated:

> Yes, so what happened … [I was] concerned because these, they said that, you know, after rehabilitation, you know, incorporating them back into the community, and getting them to lead a normal life. Now I went to a community education program, and after facilitating a training. After three day[s], a few of the women approached me and said, 'You know, these offenders when they come in the community, they are treated like heroes, they get a hero's welcome'. You know, the whole village is there, there's a function and they're brought in. So, they say, 'We're standing in the back and we're thinking he is not back from a war, he's from jail', you know. So, what happens is I guess, I mean this my perception is that the other offenders realise that it is not a serious issue. You can go to jail, do what the hell you want to, go to jail, come back and be welcomed as a hero. So, you know, I mean it, it defeats the whole purpose.

As noted above, the Yellow Ribbon Project frames reintroductions through its welcome feast as inmate-centric despite correctional officers being instructed to consider the victim during this process (Lees et al., n.d.; see Whitehead, 2019); A further concern is that the programme is focused on iTaukei culture and traditions, and as a result could be exclusionary to Indo-Fijian or other inmates and communities. However, by basing the ceremony on cultural practices that are included in contemporary restorative conferences, such as an apology, the Fiji Corrections Service has created the groundwork to integrate the community into rehabilitative praxis, albeit through an inappropriate focus on iTaukei customary justice.

Embedding Community into Effective Rehabilitation

Community corrections efforts by the Fiji Corrections Service are limited. Whitehead (2019) notes that these programmes often do not engage with community. Instead, inmates are often required to work within criminal justice environments such as police stations (Whitehead, 2019). A key concern with such an approach is that it fails to reduce community stigmatisation of the inmate as they are not actively working in the community and alongside its members. However, an unexpected benefit of such an approach is to foster cooperation between inmate and criminal justice system and reduce the hostility between these actors. Nonetheless, the exclusion of community from the Fiji Correctional Service's rehabilitative praxis has further impacts, particularly for inmates from iTaukei backgrounds. Important actors such as iTaukei traditional leaders, who traditionally mediated disputes, are excluded from contemporary Fijian community corrections. As a result, attempts to embed the customary principle of tovo vakaturuga are not present, which creates a further separation of the inmate from their vanua. It is vital that the Fiji Corrections Service begin to integrate customary actors into their community corrections praxis. Through these actor's knowledge of inmates, their support structures, and the criminogenic risk factors within the community, traditional leaders would provide culturally appropriate supervision and support reintegration (see Whitehead, 2019). There is further space to use community corrections to improve infrastructure in Fiji.

There is a space to utilise community corrections in Fiji to improve rural infrastructure and create important community institutions. Such programmes could develop vital infrastructure needed by the community and embed the support of vanua into community corrections praxis. This approach was echoed by participants in Whitehead's (2019) study, who noted:

> I wish we have those programs, taking back those victims [offenders in context of statement, researcher mistake while transcribing notes] to serve the community. To dig drains, build a church.

Moreover, and despite the previous criticisms of rehabilitative exclusion through religion, the significance of religion to the iTaukei experience suggests the use of community corrections to construct buildings of worship would reduce the stigmatisation of inmates. Such community corrections praxis could also be used to support the current Yellow Ribbon Project and expand the skills taught by the Fiji Corrections Service upskilling programme.

Conclusion: An Inappropriate Cultural Focus and the Need for Change

Wider social and structural issues have significantly impacted the rehabilitative praxis used by the Fiji Corrections Service. It has resulted in LGBTIQ+ inmate segregation, stereotypical rehabilitation and upskilling programmes, and the exclusion of important community actors. Moreover, attempts to integrate customary justice processes such as bulubulu into the operation of contemporary reintroduction programmes have isolated Indo-Fijians and victims. There is also a significant need for more research into the Fijian incarceral experience. Nonetheless, and despite such limited research, the authors can state that a key concern with current rehabilitation programmes is Fiji Corrections Service's attempts to base these upon iTaukei culture.

While this praxis does address the cultural needs of iTaukei inmates, and early family visits begin to embed the process of vanua into the rehabilitative process, the Fijian correctional population is becoming increasingly diverse. As a result, there is a significant need for the Fiji Corrections Service to design and deploy rehabilitative programmes that focus on other cultures and religions and detail their therapeutic and psychological praxis. The needs of the LGBTIQ+ populations should further be a priority for Fiji Corrections Service. Segregation of these individuals impacts rehabilitation, creates further stigmatisation, and is in violation of their human rights. However, the reintegration of these inmates is more challenging. Christianity and its associated stigmas could still ostracise LGBTIQ+ individuals in various Fijian communities, and lead to isolation and recidivism. While various NGOs are working to support the Fijian LGBTIQ+ community, including the PCP (2021), such societal change will take time. However, there is the space for the Fiji Corrections Service to deconstruct gender barriers through the removal of stereotypical upskilling programmes. The current gendered approach of these programs does not assist women who live in rural areas, or those who would like to engage in employment outside of their expected social role.

There is the space to construct a rehabilitative and restorative approach in Fiji, but this approach needs to pull upon local culture. The use of international programmes, even when localised, fails to fully integrate important customary practices such as bulubulu. Instead, the ceremony has been deconstructed, and the elements that are utilised by the Yellow Ribbon Project create further victimisation. Moreover, the Yellow Ribbon Project can be framed as a politicised initiative that does not mediate customary power imbalances (see Vuiyasawa, 2009), does not create harmony in the village, and does not fulfil the purpose of bulubulu. Instead, it creates an inmate-centric process that excludes victims (see Lees et al., n.d.), could be argued to celebrate offending, and usurps the authority of traditional leaders. Moreover, Yellow Ribbon Project's overt focus on iTaukei tradition is problematic for Indo-Fijian inmates and other minorities within Fiji's increasingly diverse incarceral space. Instead, the Yellow Ribbon Project should integrate a dynamic recognition of an inmate's religion, background, and culture, and use this as a basis for reintegration. Alternatively, and as noted by Whitehead (2019), a culturally neutral restorative praxis would create a space where these programmes could be used regardless of the inmate's background and reintegrate them into a range of different communities. However, such an approach would impact the significant power of cultural rehabilitation and reintegration. As a result, and while resource intensive, a dynamic cultural reintegration programme would be an ideal solution.

This does not suggest the bulubulu and customary justice is not a powerful tool for reconciliation and rehabilitation in Fiji, and there is the space for iTaukei inmates to engage in this practice. Despite the debates surrounding bulubulu (see Merry, 2004; also, Whitehead, 2019) there is the space to use the original structure of this ceremony alongside the traditional criminal justice system to settle disputes and reintegrate the inmate. However, this pluralist approach should only be utilised when both the victim and inmate wish to proceed through customary justice, or where a non-iTaukei inmate wishes to use this to reconcile in a culturally appropriate manner.

The above focus on culture could further extend into community corrections. As noted above, there is the space for iTaukei traditional leaders to be embedded within community corrections praxis. These powerful individuals would supervise the inmate, alongside reinforcing appropriate behaviour through tovo vakaturuga. However, the authors note this suggestion has an inappropriate focus on iTaukei culture and excludes inmates from diverse backgrounds (Whitehead, 2019). Instead, and recognising that there are important actors in all Fijian communities, leaders from these diverse spaces could be integrated to create culturally specific and target community supervision programmes. Such an approach would further allow community corrections to expand beyond administrative roles within the criminal justice system, and instead, focus on vital infrastructure projects that would improve rural communities.

Rehabilitation is a relatively new focus of Fiji Corrections Service (see Fiji Corrections Service, n.d.a), and as discussed throughout this chapter this is apparent in their rehabilitative praxis. This has resulted in a hybridisation of customary and international reintegration programmes that are poorly researched and designed. A key challenge for Fiji corrections will be growing diversity within their incarceral centres, and a need to design programmes beyond the Christian iTaukei majority. However, these can still embed culture, important community actors, and the needs of diverse genders, but require a firm recognition of such challenges and local research to identify the needs of inmates across Fijian prisons.

Notes

1. Translates to "owner", which speaks to traditional ownership of the land. However, by Pauwels (2015: 192) notes '*itaukei ni qele*, or 'original occupant of the land' could be better expressed as 'responsible for the land'.
2. *iTaukei* Customary justice.
3. Statistics include convicted, remand, civil and detainee inmates.
4. More recent reports have removed a breakdown of inmates by ethnicity.
5. Fijian Rehabilitative Praxis is so under-researched that only two definitive sources for this this, Fiji Corrections Service *Semper Restituens* (n.d.c) and Whitehead (2019). As a result, these are the two citations that will be used for the majority of this section.
6. No information is provided on the contents of these kits.
7. Sentence planning further segregates inmates based upon offence category and recidivism history.
8. For example, the Victorian *Koori Court* pulls upon the testimony of traditional leaders to contextualise the inmate's behaviour and any criminogenic environment that may be present.
9. A common rehabilitation model used globally. Lester et al. (2020: 830), note 'Many in the field acknowledge the risk-need-responsivity (RNR) model as one of the most widely accepted approaches to [rehabilitative assessment and] treatment'.
10. A key socio-cultural underpinning to *iTaukei* culture, and therefore correctional praxis, is militarism. These ideals have been reinforced through the 'coup' culture that afflicted this small island nature and led to militaristic governance of many social institution. The Fijian language is also highly militarised, creating a wider social construction of authority that pervades education, sport, and political discourse (Teaiwa, 2005).
11. Italicised to represent the name of the various programmes (see Fiji Corrections Service, n.d.c). These names may appear informal, such as in the case of the *sex offence* programme, however their use is to ensure clarity by speaking directly to the Fiji Corrections Service rehabilitative praxis.
12. Christianity is firmly embedded within Fijian Indigenous identities and influences the wider social processes, including masculinity and militarism (see Presterudstuen, 2016).

References

Abramson, A. (1995). Beyond the Samoan controversy in anthropology: A history of sexuality in the eastern interior of Fiji. In P. Caplan (Ed.), *The cultural construction of sexuality*. Reprint, Routledge.

Adinkrah, M. (1995). *Crime, deviance and delinquency in Fiji*. Fiji Council of Social Services (FCOSS).

Arno, A. (1976). Ritual of reconciliation and village conflict management in Fiji. *Oceania, 47*(1), 49–65.

Braithwaite, J. (2014). Traditional justice. In J. J. Llewellyn & D. Philpott (Eds.), *Restorative justice, reconciliation, and peacebuilding* (pp. 214–239). Oxford University Press.

Buadromo, C. (1982). Fiji. In W. Clifford, J. Sandry, & B. Looms (Eds.), *The management of corrections in Asia and the Pacific,* Australian Institute of Criminology.

Cretton, V. (2005). Traditional Fijian apology as a political strategy. *Oceania, 75*(4), 403–417.

Fiji Corrections Service. (n.d.a). Strategic plan 2017–2020. http://www.corrections.gov.fj/wp-content/uploads/2017/05/FCS-2017-2020-STRATEGIC-PLAN.pdf. Accessed 31 March 2022.

Fiji Corrections Service. (n.d.b). FCS-2018–2019-ANNUAL-REPORT. http://www.corrections.gov.fj/wp-content/uploads/2021/11/FCS-2018-2019-ANNUAL-REPORT.pdf. Accessed 31 March 2022.

Fiji Corrections Service. (n.d.c). Rehabilitation Policy Semper Restituens. http://www.corrections.gov.fj/wp-content/uploads/2019/06/NEW-REHABILITATION-POLICY-2019.pdf. Accessed 31 March 2022.

Fiji Corrections Service. (2013). Fiji corrections services focuses on Offenders' Rehab. In S. Wai Wah (Ed.), *APCCA: Newsletter of the Asian and Pacific Conference of Correctional Administration* (pp. 19–23). APCCA.

Fiji Corrections Service. (2016). *Rehabilitation Policy-Four Streams-2016*. http://www.corrections.gov.fj/wpcontent/uploads/2017/05/FCS-REHABILITATION-POLICY.pdf. Accessed March 31 2022.

Fiji Corrections Service. (2019). *Fiji corrections service annual report*. http://www.corrections.gov.fj/wp-content/uploads/2021/11/FCS-2017-2018-ANNUAL-REPORT.pdf. Accessed 31 March 2022.

Hickson, L. (1975). *The Isoro: Social and psychological factors of dispute settlement and punishment avoidance in Fiji*. PhD Thesis, Harvard University, United States of America.

Jolly, M. (2005). Epilogue: Multicultural relations in Fiji—Between despair and hope. *Oceania, 75*(4), 418–430.

Lees, S., Lenisaurua, V., Baleinakorodawa, O., & Murdock, J. (n.d.). *Restorative justice in Fiji*. http://www.asia-pacific.undp.org/content/dam/rbap/docs/Research%20%26%20Publications/CPR/PC_RestorativeJustice.pdf. Accessed 31 March 2022.

Lester, M. E., Batastini, A. B., Davis, R., & Bourgon, G. (2020). Is risk-need-responsivity enough? Examining differences in treatment response among male incarcerated persons. *Criminal Justice and Behavior, 47*(7), 829–847.

Merry, S. E. (2004). *Tensions between global law and local social justice: CEDAW and the problem of rape in Fiji*. Available at: www.brandeis.edu/ethics/pdfs/internationaljustice/otheractivities/JAC_Merry.pdf. Accessed 31 March 2022.

Merry, S. E. (2006). *Human rights and gender violence: Translating international law into local justice*. The University of Chicago Press.

Montfort Boys' Town. (2019). *Our programs*. https://montfortfiji.org/our-programs/. Accessed 31 March 2022.

Nand, P. (2021). *Corrections centres in Fiji overcrowded by 12% – Panapasa*. https://www.fijivillage.com/news/Corrections-Centres-in-Fiji-overcrowded-by-12---Panapasa-548rfx/. Accessed 31 March 2022.

Newland, L. (2016). Villages, violence, and atonement in Fiji. In A. Biersack, M. Jolly, & M. Macintyre (Eds.), *Gender violence and human rights: Seeking justice in Fiji, Papua New Guinea and Vanuatu* (pp. 47–80). The Australian National University Press.

Pacific Centre for Peacebuilding [PCP]. (2021). *Pacific centre for peacebuilding*. https://appap.group.uq.edu.au/pacific-centre-peacebuilding. Accessed 31 March 2022.

Pauwels, S. (2015). Chiefdoms and chieftancies in Fiji, Yesterday and Today. *Journal De La Société Des Océanistes, 141*, 189–198.

Presterudstuen, G. H. (2016). Performing Masculinity Through Christian Devotion. *Interventions, 18*(1), 107–126.

Roffee, J. A., & Whitehead, J. (2019). *Literature review: LGBTIQ identifying young people and Youth Justice, Vulnerabilities, Challenges, and Opportunities*. Swinburne University of Technology.

Teaiwa, T. K. (2005). Articulated cultures: Militarism and masculinities in Fiji during the mid 1990s. *Fijian Studies: A Journal of Contemporary Fiji, 3*(2), 201–222.

The Fijian Government. (2012). New development to address prison overcrowding. https://www.fiji.gov.fj/Media-Centre/News/NEW-EDEVELOPMENT-TO-ADDRESS-PRISON-OVERCROWDING. Accessed 31 March 2022.

Vuiyasawa, L. (2009). Rehabilitating offenders? The yellow ribbon campaign in Fiji. *Journal of South Pacific Law, 13*(1), 19–23.

Whitehead, J. (2019). *Restorative justice in the South Pacific: Responding to sexual violence in Fiji*. PhD thesis, Monash University, Australia.

Whitehead, J., & Roffee, J. (2016). Child sexual abuse in Fiji: Authority, risk factors and responses. *Current Issues in Criminal Justice, 27*(3), 323–334.

Legislation

Corrections Services Act 2006 (Fiji) (No. 2, 2006).

Rehabilitative Aims and Values in Finnish (and Nordic) Criminal Justice

Tapio Lappi-Seppälä

From Treatment to 'Humane Neoclassicism'

Treatment ideology prevailed in the Nordics from the 1930/40s till late 1960s. Its position was strongest in the more affluent Sweden and Denmark, and weakest in Finland, which was recovering from the hardships of the first half of the twentieth century (including a bloody civil war, two wars against Russia, and one against Germany). The heritage of penal welfarism includes differentiated sanctions for distinct groups, the introduction of psychiatric treatment and psychologist services in prisons, and the adoption of conditional sentences and community supervision—all reforms that improved the position and conditions of those sentenced. But this period also introduced indeterminate sentences, the risks of abuse of power, and an overreliance in all kinds of institutions—all features that came to be criticised in the 1960s.

Trust in the rehabilitative potential of criminal justice started to erode in the Nordic countries in the 1960s. Extensive use of confinement and compulsory treatment in healthcare, child welfare, and prisons was criticised for being inhumane, arbitrary, and ineffective (for early critics, see Anttila, 2012). Critical findings on the modest effects of treatment influenced a shift in criminal justice policy priorities from custodial sanctions to

T. Lappi-Seppälä (✉)
University of Helsinki, Helsinki, Finland
e-mail: Tapio.lappi-seppala@helsinki.fi

community alternatives and open care measures. Prisoners' rights and the prison conditions became a target of political action in all these countries. The prison reforms that followed at the end of the 1960s and beginning of the 1970s improved the rights of the inmates, abolished humiliating disciplinary punishments, introduced prison leave, and expanded the system of open facilities. All countries either abolished or severely restricted the use of all indeterminate sentences in the 1970s. This concerned both preventive detention for dangerous recidivists and youth prisons. The progressive, main organising principle in enforcement was replaced by the principle of normality, the requirement that 'the conditions in prison should be set, to the extent this is possible, to correspond to the conditions in society in general' (Finnish Enforcement Decree, 1975: 3). Rehabilitative aspirations became less central but did not disappear altogether. Although conclusions and claims were less radical, it was accepted that imprisonment should not be used *because* of its rehabilitative potential, and that all forms of non-consensual treatment should be abolished: so, any prolonging of confinement on rehabilitative grounds was banned. Nevertheless, when imprisonment was used, time was to be given to reduce the risk of reoffending and to minimise the detrimental of prison life ('Negative individual prevention', Bondeson, 1989). However, initiatives to develop interventions or programmes that would have specific positive effects remained low.

At the ideological level, the justification and rational for punishment shifted from individual to general prevention. However, the traditional Nordic concept of general prevention differs from that of the English-speaking world. General prevention has been understood in Nordic criminal theory primarily as an indirect mechanism for the reinforcement of basic social norms through moral communication, rather than direct deterrent effects of punishment (Andenaes, 1974). Compliance with norms rests on norm internalisation and experienced legitimacy, not on fear. To achieve this effect criminal justice punishment should be able to convey a 'moral message' (a reproach), but the system should also be experienced as accepted and trusted (for discussion, see Lappi-Seppälä, 2019b: 219–220). The 'ideological vacuum' that followed the fall of the rehabilitative ideal was filled with a rights-based sanction ideology—'Humane Neoclassicism' (as the model of thinking was labelled in Finland). It combined forward-looking pragmatic considerations of indirect general prevention, the humanisation of the sanction system, and the requirements of proportionality, predictability, and equal application of the law. Policy conclusions were in several respects the opposite to those in many other countries. The decline of treatment ideology did not entail a general shift towards harsher penal regimes and

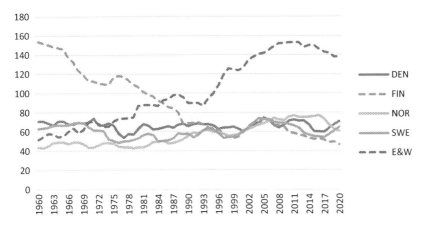

Fig. 1 Prison population rates in Denmark, Finland, Norway, Sweden and England & Wales 1960–2020

prison warehousing. For Denmark, Norway, and Sweden, the period from 1960s onwards represents a period of stable and low incarceration rates, also during a period of steep increase in crime. For Finland, this was the beginning of a long-term reduction of imprisonment from the level of around 150 prisoners/100,000 inhabitants to the general Nordic level of around sixty (Fig. 1).

New Trends—New Solutions

The principles that were laid down in the 1970s guided much of the reform work and enforcement practice until the early 1990s after which new trends started to emerge. In the course of the 1990s penal rehabilitation there was a revival of rehabilitation in prisons. New meta-analyses altered the picture of the effectiveness of rehabilitation. After all, treatment did seem to work under certain well-defined conditions. All Nordic countries also revised their prison enforcement practices from the mid-1990s onwards, guided by the Canadian-originated 'What works' movement (with which the Nordics also had good personal contacts). Reduction of reoffending was back on the agenda. The use of structured programmes increased, and so were investments in substance abuse programmes in prisons. Enforcement processes, as a whole, became more structured and planned.

As far as treatment orders and new community alternatives are concerned, even during the 'neoclassical period', the needs for alcohol and substance treatment in prisons had been acknowledged, (but not duly taken care of).

A worsening drug problem increased these pressures, and in 1988, Sweden adopted a new treatment-oriented alternative to imprisonment ('Contract care'). Different treatment-orders were incorporated in the Danish sanction system in the 1990s as part of a conditional sentence or as combinations with other sanctions for specific offence categories, such as drink driving, drug misuse, and sex offending (Kyvsgaard, 2001). Moreover, in 1995 Norway introduced a specific programme for drunk drivers to replace prison sentences ('promilleprogramme'). In addition, sanction systems were complemented with more widely targeted community alternatives; first by community service and then by electronic monitoring. Both alternatives were constructed as substitutes to imprisonment. Their advantages over prison were explained with reference to rehabilitative aims as well as practical cost-related arguments.

Similar changes took place in juvenile justice. Nordic youth justice is a complex system, searching for a balance between criminal justice and child welfare (for history see, Lappi-Seppälä, 2011). Each country has organised this co-operation in its own ways, but in all, child welfare bears the main responsibility. Moreover, in all countries, rehabilitative aims and the best interest of the child are uncontested overriding principles. However, in the 1990s criminal justice started to adopt a more active role by developing new alternatives designed specifically for juveniles. This also meant that rehabilitation gained more prominence in criminal justice. But disagreement also exists, whether this is the optimal way to pursue rehabilitative aims (and the best interest of the child), or whether it would be better to leave the matter in the hands of child welfare (see Lappi-Seppälä, 2016 and critical comments by Pettersson, 2017 and Storgaard, 2009).

The 1980s and 1990s saw the emergence of mediation and restorative justice as the mainstream criminal political ideologies were challenged by critical criminologists and the abolitionist movement; inspired by the writings of Nils Christie and Thomas Mathiesen in Norway and Louk Hulsman in the Netherlands. In the spirit of Christie's article 'Conflict as Property' (Christie, 1977), Norway started an experimentation in mediation in 1981 to return the 'stolen conflicts back to the community and the parties' and Finland followed in 1983. The movement expanded rapidly first in these two countries and later elsewhere in the Nordics. The annual number of mediated cases rose quickly to several thousands in both Norway and Finland. The 'official institutionalization' of mediation took place in the form of enactment of Mediation Acts. First in Norway in 1992, then in Finland and Sweden in 2006, and Denmark in 2010. Due to this institutionalisation, mediation may have been forced to compromise with some of its original abolitionist ideals. Having a specific law on mediation with legally defined roles and responsibilities for mediators may not have been what Christie, Hulsman and Mathiesen had in their minds in the 1970s. However, basic elements of informality, voluntariness, and community involvement remain the same. Today mediation is offering a widely used alternative way of resolving conflicts and it provides the victim and the individual who has offended against them a genuine possibility for communication. The annual number of referrals to mediation range around 10,000 in Finland, of which little over 7000 get started and 5000 end up to an agreement (which roughly equals the annual number of imposed prison sentence (see Lappi-Seppälä & Storgaard, 2015).

From 1990s onwards, growing international human rights movement and the establishment of the European Court of Human Rights (ECHR) and the European Committee for the Prevention of Torture (CPT) started to influence penal reforms. In Finland, reforms were further influenced by joining the Council of Europe in 1989, the ratification of the ECHR in 1989, and the constitutional reforms carried out in 1995 and 2000. Together, they opened the window of opportunity for the incorporation of human rights as part of fundamental rights in the constitution, and thereby exerted their influence on criminal legislation. The new constitution imposed stricter demands than before on legal regulation in all decisions that dealt with deprivation of liberty. It also obliged the legislator to define the rights and obligations of prisoners in greater detail than before. These requirements were noted in new prison law reform (Prison Act 2006). As stated in the Governmental Bill, the Act 'aims to bring the prison law in accordance with the requirements of the new constitution, to define the obligations of prison authorities in more detail, to increase legal safeguards and transparency in prison administration, to reorganise the imprisonment process to a more structured and planned process and increase investments in rehabilitative programmes and treatment work and thereby also to reduce recidivism' (Gov Prop, 262/2004). Constitutional principles also exerted their influences on other parts of the legislation, including the general part of the Criminal Code in 2004, and the codification of community sanctions under the same code in 2012 (see below).

Changes in organisational frameworks followed. The expansion of community alternatives changed gradually along with the work profile of probation service from social work towards sentence enforcement. Furthermore, defining rehabilitative action as part of punishment had organisational consequences. According to the new Constitution, functions that consist of 'substantial exercise of public power' such as enforcement of penalties, should be taken care of by state officials. This led subsequently to organisational changes in Finland. Probation work was removed from a semi-official

Probation Association to the Ministry of Justice and the Prison Service and Probation Service were united under the Criminal Sanctions Agency (CSA). Part of the earlier supportive and social work functions of the previous Probation Association were removed under a new Probation Foundation. Along with constitutional arguments, economic consideration played their part as well. One united organisation was cheaper to run than two separate ones. A further wish of the Government was that 'the role of community sanctions as part of the sanction system could be strengthened' (GovProp, 22/2009).

Normative Framework: Aims and Values in Finnish Sentencing and Enforcement

The classical question of 'The Aim of Punishment' receives different answers depending on whether criminalisation, sentencing, or enforcement are under consideration. Decisions on criminalisation are based on (politically decided) needs to protect important societal and individual interests, and the assumed theoretical mechanisms, in turn, rest on direct and indirect effects of general prevention. A definition of criminalisation based on rehabilitative needs would be bizarre. Sentencing is governed by a mixture of principles that combine both retributive and consequentialist (utilitarian) arguments. While all Nordic countries give the principle of proportionality the key organising role in sentencing, at the level of sentencing the extension of community sanctions has put rehabilitative arguments back on the table or more precisely, arguments that speak in favour of community alternatives and against the use of custodial sanctions. Sentencing provisions are built on the logic that the main function of the proportionality principle is to specify the upper limits of punishments. It is much less restrictive concerning punishments and less severe than the offence might, at a prima facie level, deserves. The question for the courts is, whether these rehabilitative and practical benefits are weighty enough to justify the replacement of a prison sentence by a community sanction.[1]

Enforcement principles are newly formulated in the 2006 Prison Act and the 2012 Act of the Enforcement of Community Sanctions. The reform of Prison Act (PA) can be characterised primarily as a *Rule of Law* reform. The CSA, in turn, builds much on the Council of Europe resolution on community sanctions and measures (Rec 1, 2010). Both laws define enforcement aims and principles in similar tones with emphasis on both rights-based and rehabilitative arguments. As condensed in the value statement of the Finnish Prison and Probation Service:

The central value of the CSA is the respect for human dignity and justness. We believe in the potential for individual change and growth. Commitment to the values in practice: Basic rights and liberties as well as human rights are protected; Treatment is humane, appropriate and equal; all activities are lawful and comply with justice and fairness; Enforcement is carried out so that it supports the sentenced persons' individual growth and development as well as their intention to lead a life without crime. (Criminal Sanctions Agency, 2020)

According to the Prison Act the aim of enforcement of imprisonment is 'to increase capacity for a crime-free lifestyle by promoting life-capacity and integration into society'—in other words social rehabilitation (PA 1:2). The aim of community sanctions is defined as 'to support the convicted person in promoting social coping and increase the capacity to live a crime-free life' (CSA 1:2 §). Provision on 'Social rehabilitation' (PA 10:5), further, states that 'Prisoners shall be provided with support in social rehabilitation, in maintenance of contacts with their close relatives and other close persons, and in attendance to matters relating to their accommodation, work, subsistence, social benefits and social services'.[2]

The term 'social coping' reflects a clear desistance orientation, pronounced explicitly in the preparatory works of Community Sanctions Act:

A more recent criminological study highlights that desistance and ceasing a criminal career is a more complex psychosocial process attached to the course of life than assumed. It is not straightforwardly causal in such a way that we can see that the exit has taken place at the point of time as a result of the combined effect of certain individual factors. ... It may take years to break away from the criminal lifestyle, its identity, and social networks, while the offender is constantly trying to build an identity that is in line with normal life. (GovProp, 215/2012)

The law also recognises realities and the limits of the rehabilitative powers of prison by a separate provision of harm minimisation. The code links the avoidance of harmful effects of prison life and maintaining health and social functionality in the same paragraph: 'The ability of a prisoner to maintain his health and functional ability shall be supported. The goal is to prevent any detriment resulting from the loss of liberty' (PA 1:3). Efforts in maintaining health include equal health care services for the prisoners (as compared to the rest of the population). Harms may be minimised by providing psychosocial support and treatment, but also by upholding prisoners' contacts with the outside world (prison leaves etc.).

The famous maxim of Alexander Paterson that people are sent to prison as punishment, not for punishment is enshrined in the Finnish Prison Act as, 'The content of imprisonment shall be loss or restriction of liberty' and not to impose extra hardship on prisoners due to reasons related to the 'aims of punishment' (PA 1:3.1): the loss of liberty, as such, is enough. This claim is underlined with the additional notion of *minimum intervention:* 'The enforcement of imprisonment may not restrict the rights or circumstances of a prisoner in any other manner than that provided in the law or necessary due to the punishment itself' (PA 1:3.1).

The Normality Principle can be conceived of as logical consequence of the same starting point: 'The conditions in a prison shall be arranged, to the extent possible, so that they correspond to the living conditions prevailing in society' (PA 1:3). In concrete terms, the principle calls for the abolition of certain practices followed in prison life only (for example, the use of prison clothes). It also affects the ways in which work, education, and training is arranged in prisons, and even the way prisons are built. However, the principle also expresses the normative demand that prisoners maintain their full rights as citizens and deserve to be treated with similar respect as any other member of the society (see also Engbo, 2017; Zyl van Smith & Snacken, 2009). For example, all Nordic countries have enshrined in law that prisoners have the same right to education as other citizens, not to mention the right to vote (on education see Nordic Prison Education, 2005).

In accordance with the unviability of human dignity, prisoners 'shall be treated fairly and with respect for their human dignity' and 'the authorities in charge of the enforcement of imprisonment shall ensure that, during the imprisonment, no person will unjustifiably violate the personal integrity of the prisoner' (FPL 1:3.2). Similarly concerning community sanctions: 'A person sentenced to community sanctions must be treated fairly and with respect for his or her human dignity' (CSA 1:4). The law further requires that 'authority must be used appropriately and impartially as in in a spirit of compromise' and maintained 'primarily through advice, requests and orders' (PA 1:6). Guidelines for sentence planning stress a positive instead of a fault-finding orientation as well as collaborative aspects. The point of the assessment, for example, is 'to support and help the prisoners forward. It is not only pointing out defects, but it must also show strengths…The aim is to reach a common view with the prisoners even if it would require long repeated discussions' (Guidelines for Assessment, 2010). Guidelines for enforcing electronic monitoring, in turn, stress the importance of discretion and sensitivity and the need to carry out the control elements in a manner that does not draw attention to the clients in their living environment (GovProp, 215/2012).

Programmes and Enforcement Practices

Prison and probation work consist of enforcement work (such as sentence planning, assessments, and guarding), client work, and programme work. Borders are not always clear. Work in more concrete terms may consist of debt and economic counselling, education and work activities, family work and work with volunteer supporters, courses on employment, creative activities and physical education as well as group activities to enhance life management skills. Post-release work in the community includes professional tutoring, housing support, service guidance and social work with intoxicant abusers, work with the clients' families, and with other meaningful people close to the client. Much of the work is also concentrated on practical issues, such as taking care of some basic tasks of everyday life, such as getting an ID card, bank account, travel card, a continuation of debt, and economic counselling.

Programmes can be divided according to aims and methods into motivational and impact (effectiveness) programmes. Motivation programmes aim to increase and maintain motivation to change and encourage participants to take further action on their life situation. They are usually short-term and implemented in either individual or group form. Impact programmes aim to influence the underlying thinking and behavioural patterns. They are intensive and long-lasting and aimed at clients with a medium to high risk of recidivism. As a rule, impact programmes are group-based and consciously utilise the group's experientiality and group dynamics. Depending on the targeted problem programmes can further be divided into (1) general programmes (such as 'Five Discussions on Change', see below), (2) offense-focused programmes for perpetrators of a specific crime (e.g. STOP programme for those convicted of sex offences) and (3) substance abuse rehabilitation programmes. Of these, substance abuse programmes have the longest history in Finnish prisons. An overwhelming majority of the prisoners have substance abuses problems. Investments in substance rehabilitation also increased during the 1990s. Current programmes are based either on cognitive behavioural therapy or community treatment. Despite increased supply of substance rehabilitation, supply of services and needs do not meet. According to a recent study, around 60% of released prisoners need substance abuse interventions. However, of these only one out of five actually received or participated in such treatment in prison (see Obstabaum, 2017).

The influence of What Works movement is visible in the adoption of accredited cognitive behavioural courses after the mid-1990s (including Cognitive Skills courses, programmes focused on sex offending, Anger Management, and Cognitive Self Change). From the 2000s onwards, programmes with a clearer desistance focus appeared, both in prison and community settings. These include, for example, 'Five Discussions on Change'—a general motivation programme implemented since 2006. The aim of the programme is to strengthen the client's internal motivation and promote decision-making in connection with possible change. The programme comprises of at least five discussions (plus the initial meeting). The discussions are based on a semi-structured manual and on the customer's own workbook. The creation of internal motivation is guided by four principles: (1) To strengthen a person's experience of the mismatch between the current and desired situation, (2) address resistance to change, (3) strengthen the customer's faith in his or her own ability to implement change, and (4) show empathy, especially through reflective listening (for description, see Tolonen, 2016).

Targeted programmes for younger inmates (below the age of 30) include the Work Out Project (WOP). Its primary objective lies in improving the social skills of the young inmates through systematic and target-orientated work, both during the prison term and after release. The plan covers both the prison term and the post-release phase. Work with inmates during the prison term focuses on holistic rehabilitation and the reinforcement of functional abilities. The goal is to support the client to find new contents for life and reinforce the experience of meaningful life.

Finnish legislation has adopted a broad view of rehabilitative aims and effects. Reducing reoffending may remain the ultimate goal, but the intermediate steps matter, as well. As formulated in the preparatory works of the Community Sanctions Act:

> Exiting crime is not a simple over-night change, but a long-term process in which the gradually strengthening components of individual capabilities and social resources have different roles in different times. Therefore, the effectiveness of rehabilitation work cannot be measured solely by short-term reoffending figures. The process may have already started, but the results are not yet visible in reconviction rates. Instead, they may appear in strengthened relationships and friendship networks, reduced substance use, increased motivation to study, increased admonition to working life, and so on. ... When considering the social impact of the various sanctions, it should be noted that the changes said are important, not only for future criminal behaviour, but also for other reasons of well-being. They are valuable in terms of the quality of life itself. (GovProp, 215/2014)

In relation to individual-level effects the legislation refers to *broader social effects* (broader 'social rehabilitation') and the possibility that organising community service work in volunteer and municipal originations, working together, and being in a daily contact with those convicted of a crime will also change the image of an 'offender' among the public (GovProp, 215/2014).

Measurements of reoffending effects of in prison programmes have produced partly positive but some weak results. Cognitive Skills courses seemed to reduce recidivism only marginally; programmes for those convicted of sex offences have produced stronger, but not statistically significant results (see Tyni, 2015). More favourable results have been obtained from motivation programmes directed towards substance rehabilitation. A follow-up of the 'Five Discussions on Change' provided positive results measured by changes in audit scores as well as by harms caused by drinking (see Tolonen, 2018). In general, there is more evidence of changes in motivation and thinking habits, but less of actual reoffending (as regards in prison programmes). For community alternatives, the situation looks somewhat different (see Endnote 6).

Open Prisons and the Normality Principle

Enforcement or the prison sentence starts with assessment, sentence planning, and placement in prison. Sentence plans are prepared for all prisoners to direct interventions and programmes and to create predictability to the process. A specific Risk and Need assessment is conducted for about 10% of prisoners. Also, release phases and post-release phases are guided by separate release and supervision plans. They will include information about the contact meetings, plans related to housing, work, education, studies, finances, programmes, and tasks. These preparations are made in co-operation with the Probation Service and the social service and employment authorities. This networking aims to ensure that the rehabilitation started in prison and continuing after release is the core part of the planned process. Still, aftercare forms the critical phase in the Finnish enforcement process. Many released prisoners lack proper housing. The housing services within the probation system were also weakened after the 'Unification of prison- and probation services' (see above). Enforcement takes place either in closed or open prison. No general security classification is in use, while some prisons have small security units for high-risk violent individuals.

The defining feature in Finnish—and Nordic—prisons lies in the concept of the open prison. Open prisons raised extensive international interest after World War II as a solution for the post-war overcrowding problems. The concept had also been tested extensively in Finland already before the war (also due to serious overcrowding in the country). Finland, Denmark, and Sweden enacted laws on open enforcement from different starting points, but eventually with comparable results. Arrangements that were first offered as practical and economical solutions for post-war overcrowding, developed in the course of time into a central device to realise the principle of normality in enforcement. Today, over 35% of all Finnish prisoners and almost half of prisoners serving a sentence are placed in open institutions. The rates are slightly lower in Denmark and Norway, and lower in Sweden and Iceland. Trends in the use of open prison since 2000 are visible in Fig. 2.

For many commentators, the open prison represents one of the key elements in the 'Nordic Penal Exceptionalism' and the more inclusive penal policies (see Pratt & Eriksson, 2013). Open prisons are in practice 'prisons without walls': the prisoner is obliged to stay in the prison area, but there are no guards or fences. Open prison may consist of a separate open ward in closed prison, or as a separate open prison. Placement in open prison can take place either directly from the start or after closed prison. Direct placement is applied usually for first timers with typically short sentences. The serving of longer sentences starts, as a rule, in closed prison, but the prisoner may later be transferred to open settings following the sentence plan. In 2020, there were 17 open prisons or open units in Finland, and around the same number of closed prisons. The size of open units varies between 13 and 120 with an average of 57 prisoners. Salaries paid for work are substantially higher in open prisons. All open institutions are drug free, and all inmates are required to make a controlled commitment not to use any intoxicants. A prisoner who

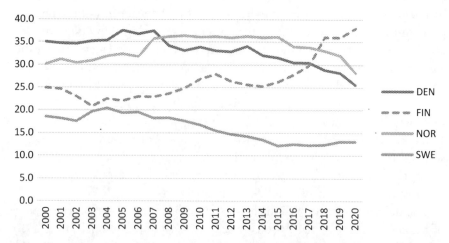

Fig. 2 The share of prisoners in open prisons 2000–2020 (% of all prisoners including remand)

does not comply with the rules of open prisons (i.e. who escapes, refuses to participate in activities or intoxicant abstinence controls) may be transferred to a closed prison.

Occasional reoffending studies from Sweden (Bondeson, 1974/1989; Pettersson, 2017) detected substantially higher prisonisation and reoffending rates after closed prisons in comparison to open regimes. A recent Finnish analysis found that open prisons' investment in promoting family contact seems to affect desistance optimism positively and provide useful means for reintegration. Open prisons seem to encourage prisoners actively to plan and prepare for their release, aiding them in job seeking, training, and education, and thereby seem to 'affect pre-release expectations positively, even if many social and structural challenges in reintegration prevail' (Villman, 2021). Nationwide 'quality-measurements' in Finnish prisons confirm higher satisfaction in open prisons regarding programme functionality, contacts with the outside world, respect, staff relations, health services, living conditions, general well-being, safety, or fairness. In short, open prisons seem to perform morally better [see Linderborg et al., 2015; similar results have been produced also in a Dutch survey (Eshter et al., 2021)]. Comparisons between open and closed enforcement in Norway and England and Wales confirm that open environments (contrary to some critics) provide a less painful environment with more freedom, less anxieties, and less frustration (Mjåland et al., 2021).

Open enforcement brings lesser prisonisation, lower costs and better prospects for social rehabilitation, and even lower reconviction rates. It provides more meaningful work and better salaries and work compensation for the inmates, a more relaxed atmosphere and better staff–inmate relations, better contacts with the outside world, all reducing the harmful and prisonisation effects resulting from the loss of liberty. In financial terms open prisons are cheaper to build and run. The price tag on open prison is about two-thirds of that compared to closed prison. But what matters most is to what extent enforcement practices meet the demands of decent and legitimate use of criminal law. In this respect, open enforcement, which express trust and confidence in the prisoner's own sense of responsibility, reflects a more civilised and enlightened view of 'offenders' as individuals capable of reform and capable of taking responsibility of their actions.

Prisons as a Last Resort: Community Service and Electronic Monitoring as Substitutes to Imprisonment

The introduction of new community alternatives took place under the flag of alternatives to prison. First proposals and plans of community service were drafted in the late 1970s, experimentations started in the 1980s, and nationwide practices followed in the 1990s. Community service was presented as a more constructive and less stigmatising alternative to imprisonment which would allow the individual to maintain his/her contacts with the outside world, and to create positive contacts with work life. Further arguments related to the need of developing functional 'intermediate' penalties, an additional step in the staircase of sanctions to slow down the move towards the most severe sanction, imprisonment. Occasionally, proponents stressed the symbolic reparative and restorative dimensions of a sanction which eventually would give the individual a concrete possibility to 'pay back' to society the damages and losses caused by the crime. Technically, community service is adopted either as an independent sanction (Finland and Norway), as a condition attached to conditional imprisonment (Denmark and Sweden) or as a form of enforcement of prison sentence (Iceland). Legislative solutions were guided by efforts to avoid of net-widening. Thus, in Finland, community service can be imposed for a consenting person and only as a 'commuted penalty' after he or she has first been sentenced to an unconditional prison sentence (of at most eight months (for technical details, see Lappi-Seppälä, 2019a, 2019b: 28–34).

First applications of electronic monitoring took place in Sweden in the mid-90s as a replacement of short prison sentence by the decisions of enforcement agencies. In the early 2000s, a 'Back-Door version' version was adapted in the form of EM-release. Other Nordic countries followed in the mid-2000s by adopting both Back-Door and Front-Door versions, albeit the technical details differ. As of today, all Nordic countries allow prison sentences below six months to be served under an electronically monitored supervision order, and all countries allow the possibility for pre-release on electronic monitoring at most six months before regular parole. In Denmark, Norway, Sweden, and Iceland, these decisions are taken by the prison administration. In Finland Front-Door EM is defined as a separate sanction ('Monitoring Sentence'), imposed by the courts (for details, see Andersen & Telle, 2022; Lappi-Seppälä, 2019a: 34–43).

Community service occupied a substantial role as an alternative to custody first in Finland during the early 1990s. Measured by court statistics the number of prison sentence fell in 1991–1995 from 11,000 to 6000 and the number of community service orders increased from zero to 4000. In Sweden, the application of community service increased from 500 in 1998 to 3000 in 1999, and the number of imposed prison sentences fell from 14,500 to 12,500. In Denmark, imposed community service orders increased in 1998–2001 from 850 to 3500, while the number of imposed prison sentences fell from 14,000 to 10,000. Current use of electronic monitoring is best analysed with enforcement data. Front-door and back-door options are used different extent in these countries, but the total volume of EM clients at any given day (stock statistics) roughly on the same level (but lowest in Sweden and highest in Norway, see Table 1).

Measured by the number of people placed under EM each year (flow statistics), differences are bigger. In Norway, the number of started EM supervision orders (65.3/pop) almost equals to that of started prison sentences (70.3/pop). In other countries, the number of people entering electronic monitoring equals 25–40% of the number of prisoners admitted annually to prisons. This implies substantial 'replacement-effect' for Front-Door EM, as was for community service.[3] This becomes visible in trend comparisons (see Fig. 3).

The increasing number of new community service and EM supervision orders is reflected in the concomitant declining numbers of entries to prisons (with the exception of Norway in early 2000). However, as shown in Fig. 1, the daily number of prisoners (stock) has remained more or less stable. Community alternatives decrease the number of entries and new prison sentences), but the overall number of prisoners serving a sentence is also affected by the length of impose sentences (and of course, in the number

Table 1 Imprisonment, community service and electronic monitoring in a statistical comparison. Enforcement statistics 2020

2020	Stock (daily average)/100,000 pop				Flow (entries during the year)/100,000 pop			
	In prison	In CSO	In EM	In prison + CSO + EM	To prison	To CSO	To EM	Tp prison + CSO + EM
Denmark	73.3	33.4	4.2	110.9	70.3	60.8	30.0	161.1
Finland	46.5	22.0	4.8	73.3	50.1	31.7	18.4	100.1
Iceland	41.7	53.3	4.4	99.4	43.9	69.8	11.3	125.0
Norway	56.2	18.8	6.7	81.6	70.3	30.4	65.3	165.9
Sweden	68.6	15.5	3.3	87.4	86.8	36.5	21.5	144.8

Source Compiled from Kristofferssen (2022)

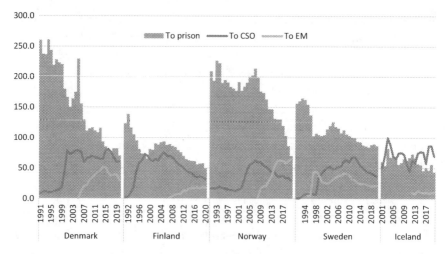

Fig. 3 Entries to prison, community service and electronic monitoring/pop 1991–2020

of offences). For these reasons, it is not possible to read out the clear 'netto-effect' of new community alternatives, without going to details in the other sentencing patterns.[4] But the evidence is clear enough to conclude that without new alternatives the annual number of persons sent to prison would be substantially higher than it is to today.

Reoffending rates for community service and electronic monitoring have been studied since the 1990s. Controlled reoffending analyses of community service from Denmark and Finland indicate around 10–15% decrease in reoffending rates (compared to prisons). Matched comparisons from Denmark, Sweden, and Norway display around 5–25% lower reconvictions rates in the EM group.[5]

The essential element in Nordic EM programmes is not the supervision technique, but the contents. Nordic EM includes an activity obligation. It can take the form of work, supportive social services, and programme work. Evaluation also reveals positive outcomes in terms of social and human effects, including positive contact to work life, better self-control over substance abuse, better preservation of family ties. A Danish study, based on comparisons with similar groups (before and after the law was passed) showed significant decreases (by 7%) in the social-welfare dependency rates after EM release compared to regular early release (Andersen & Andersen, 2014). The completion rates from upper secondary education were significantly higher (increase by 18%-points) among programme participants three years post release. Also, divorce rates were lower in the EM groups, a factor closely related to reoffending risk (Larsen, 2017).

Concluding Remarks

Penal policies in the Nordics echo the global mega-trends of the latter half of the twentieth century, however, shaped by local socio-economic and political conditions. Thus, trends with the same labels do not necessarily have the same contents, nor do they need to share the same value commitments. Retribution, Just Deserts, and Deterrence in the U.S. (or in the U.K.) have little—if anything—to do with General Prevention and Proportionate Sentencing in the Nordics. The 'Fall of the Rehabilitative Ideal' started in the Nordics around mid-1960s, as criticism of coercive care and due to the lack of legal safeguards, not due to 'Nothing Works'. The replacing ideology—humane neoclassicism–was most influential in Finland, where earlier individual preventive traditions had been weakest. Still, the values expressed through this ideology—legal safeguards, proportionality, predictability, and equality in the enforcement of the law—were shared across all Nordic countries. And so was the general policy priority to reduce the use of imprisonment through depenalisations, decriminalisation, diversion and by both new and traditional alternatives to imprisonment. While there have, since then, been shifts towards more punitive policies and increased risk-thinking, changes have been much more modest than in many other jurisdictions.

The revival of the rehabilitative ideal has not taken us back to the 60s and to the unrealistic hopes of treatment effectiveness and manipulative practices. Expectations are more realistic and to some extent in prison programmes manage to reduce reoffending, but this is no proof of prison's relative effectiveness. New rehabilitation does not justify imprisonment, but it does justify efforts to do something and more during the enforcement period. This was the point stressed already by the critics of treatment ideology in the 1960s.[6] Neither has new data cancelled the critical results of imprisonment. Rather, they confirm the conclusion that enforcement in community settings with focus on support and social rehabilitation, brings better results in terms of reoffending.

In addition, the concept of rehabilitation ('Individual Prevention') has undergone transformations in the direction already proposed by the early critics (see also Burke et al., 2019; McNeill 2012). Legal safeguards and normative constraints have retained their importance. In fact, international human rights movement (and constitutional reform in Finland) have lifted fundamental rights to the centre. In rehabilitation theory and practice, there is (should be) more respect for autonomy and agency. Rehabilitative aspirations have moved towards the social; from 'Cure' to 'Social Coping' and attention has been shifted from the 'end-result' to the process. This has also brought along a more nuanced view of effects. Even in the absence of direct reoffending results, one may find changes in factors associated with social marginalisation, employment, housing, social relations, substance abuse, and mental and physical health. These effects usually deal with factors which will—eventually—also affect crime and recidivism. But enhancing the dimensions of good and meaningful life is a valuable thing in itself—irrespective of direct crime prevention effects.

Notes

1. 'Asymmetric limitation of discretion' (see Törnudd, 1996 and for detail, see Lappi-Seppälä, 2019a, 2019b: 123–124).
2. Recent Anglophone discussion has expanded the concept of 'rehabilitation' by separating personal-, social-, legal-, and moral dimensions in rehabilitation (see Burke et al., 2019; McNeill, 2012). This also widens the discussion towards topics that have traditionally discussed in the Nordic criminal justice theory under slightly different labels. Social rehabilitation, as used in the Finnish law corresponds 'personal rehabilitation' in the conceptual framework of Burke et al. The dimensions of 'judicial/legal rehabilitation' ('processes or practices which work to restore the civil or human rights of people under penal control') are encompassed by the Human rights- and normative standards governing sentencing and enforcement. Dimensions related to 'moral rehabilitation' ('reparation, paying back, or making good') are part of the mediation project in the Nordics (and to some extent also community service). 'Social rehabilitation' in the form of 'informal social recognition and acceptance of the returning citizen' (Burke et al., 2019: 14) is hard to enhance through the means of criminal justice. However, the way the enforcement of community service has been arranged, seeks also to affect the views of the public about 'offenders as just regular members of the community' (see above).
3. There remains the theoretical possibility that courts have imposed more prison sentences anticipating that part of them would anyway be commuted to EM (or to CSO in Finland). Sentencing statistics, however, does not support this conclusion.
4. There is clear evidence of increased sentence severity in sexual and violent offenses in all Nordic countries (especially in Sweden and Norway). So, while the number of enforced prison sentences has declined, the length of sentences has increased.
5. For sources (see Andersen & Telle, 2022; Lappi-Seppälä, 2019a, 2019b: 43–47). Later analyses from Norway (Andersen & Telle, 2022) shows a 15% reduction in 1–2 year recidivism rates.

6. As formulated by Greve and Snare: '(t) there is probably not any recent criminologist who has coupled treatment options to the purpose of incarceration as such'. But as the authors also conclude '… it is remarkable that studies by and large no longer focus on prison culture, prisonisation etc., i.e. on the negative side of imprisonment' (Greve & Snare, 2009: 330).

References

Andenaes, J. (1974). *Punishment and deterrence*. University of Michigan Press.

Andersen, S., & Telle, K. (2022). Better out than in? The effect on recidivism of replacing incarceration with electronic monitoring in Norway. *European Journal of Criminology, 19*(1), 55–76.

Andersen, L., & Andersen, S. (2014). Effect of electronic monitoring on social welfare dependence. *Criminology and Public Policy, 13*, 349–379.

Anttila, I. (2012). *Conservative and radical crime policies in the Nordic Countries, in Nordic Criminology in fifty years*. Scandinavian Research Council for Criminology, University of Iceland.

Bondeson, U. (1989). *Prisoners in prison society*. Routledge.

Burke, L., Collett, S., & McNeill, F. (2019). *Reimagining rehabilitation. Beyond the individual*. Routledge.

Christie, N. (1977). Conflicts as property. *British Journal of Criminology., 17*(1), 1–15.

Engbo, H. J. (2017). Normalisation in Nordic Prisons – From a Prison Governor's Perspective. In P. S Smith & T. Ugelvik (Eds.), *Scandinavian penal history, culture and prison practice. Embraced by the welfare state?* Palgrave.

GovProp. (2004). *Government's proposal for the new prison law*, 262.

GovProp. (2009). *Government's proposal for reorganization of prison and probation services*, 22.

GovProp. (2014). *Government's proposal for the law on the enforcement of community sanctions*, 215.

Greve, V., & Snare, A. (2009). Ideologies and realities in Prison Law: Some trends. *Scandinavian Studies in Law, 54*, 305–332.

Kristofferssen, R. (2022). *Correctional statistics of Denmark, Finland, Iceland, Norway and Sweden 2016–2020*. University College of Norwegian Correctional Service.

Lappi-Seppälä, T. (2011). Nordic youth justice. In M. Tonry (Ed.), *Crime and justice in Scandinavia: A review of research* (Vol. 40). The University of Chicago Press.

Lappi-Seppälä, T. (2016). Nordic sentencing. In M. Tonry (Ed.), *Crime and justice in Scandinavia: A review of research* (Vol. 45). The University of Chicago Press.

Lappi-Seppälä, T. (2019a). Community sanctions as Substitutes to Imprisonment in the Nordic Countries. *Law and Contemporary Problems., 82*(1), 17–50.

Lappi-Seppälä, T. (2019b). Humane Neoclassicism: Proportionality and other values in nordic sentencing. In M. Tonry (Ed.), *Of One-eyed and Toothless Miscreants. Making the Punishment Fit the Crime?* Oxford University Press.

Lappi-Seppälä, T., & Storgaard, A. (2015). Nordic mediation – Comparing Denmark and Finland. *Neue Kriminalpolitic, 27*(2), 136–147.

Larsen, B. Ø. (2017). Educational outcomes after serving with electronic monitoring: Results from a natural experiment. *Quantitative Criminology, 33*(1), 157–178.

Linderbor, H., Blomster, P., Muiluvuori, M, L., Tyni, S., & Laurila, T. (2015). Yhtenäinen organisaatio – yhtenäinen laatu? Rise 2/2015.

McNeill, F. (2012). Four forms of 'offender' rehabilitation: Towards an interdisciplinary perspective. *Legal and Criminological Psychology., 17*(1), 18–36.

Mjåland, K., Laursen, J., Schliehe, A., & Larmour, S. (2021). Contrasts in freedom: Comparing the experiences of imprisonment in open and closed prisons in England and Wales and Norway. *European Journal of Criminology.* Online first. https://doi.org/10.1177/14773708211065905

Pettersson, T. (2017). *Young offenders and open custody.* Routledge.

Pratt, J., & Eriksson, A. (2013). *Contrasts in Punishment.* Routledge.

Storgaard, A. (2009). The youth sanction – A punishment in disguise. In I. P. Wahlgren (red.), *Scandinavian studies in law – Criminal law* (Bind 54, s. 381–386). The Stockholm University Law Faculty.

Tolonen, K. (2018). *Process and outcome of behaviour-interviewing-change (BIC) programme with clients in probation service.* University of Tampere.

Törnudd, P. (1996). *Facts, values and visions. Essays in criminology and crime policy* (p. 138). National Research Institute of Legal Policy.

Tyni, S. (2015). Vankeinhoidon vaikuttavuus. Rise 1/2015.

Villman, E. (2021). Work, support and solitude: Prisoners' desistance expectations and self-regulating strategies. *Journal of Offender Rehabilitation, 60*(2), 95–116.

Zyl van Smit, D., & Snacken, S. (2009). *Principles of European prison law and policy. Penology and human rights.* Oxford University Press.

France: Executive Managerialism, Frantic Law Reform, but Desistance Culture

Martine Herzog-Evans

Judges are very frustrated.... processing cases like a vegetable factory. Instead of cans of peas, you've got cases. You just move 'em, move 'em... I work for Mcjustice. (Berman, 2000, p. 80, quoting Chief Justice Kathleen Blatz)

When I learn that these women and men have managed to get up in the morning, that they got nearly on time at work, that they have actually done their community work, that they have taken on a path where they get an education to simply learn to read and write, then on such mornings I feel that I have been useful to society. (Le Böedec Maurel, 2022 – A French JAP)

Historical Mechanisms

The French legal system is the result of Roman law influences, Canon law, and customs. During the Middle Ages, criminal law was exceptionally brutal with a mix of torture as a regular procedural tool (Rocha-Harang, 2017) and extremely violent punishment (Carbasse & Vielfaure, 2014). Despite the religious concepts of repentance and redemption, rehabilitation was not on the cards.

M. Herzog-Evans (✉)
Reims University, Reims, France
e-mail: martine.evans@univ-reims.fr

Criminal procedure was not improved by something akin to the Magna Carta. It remained secretive and under the control of prosecutors who were the arm of an even more centralised and absolutist state. In 1670, the Colbert Ordinance regulated criminal procedure at a national level. The system it created was fully inquisitorial (Boulanger, 2000): totally in the hands of prosecutors, it left no possibility for the accused to have access to the charges or the file and defend him or herself. The 1789 French Revolution slightly improved substantive criminal law by proclaiming the principle of legality and that of non-retrospective punitive criminal law. It did not adopt any rehabilitative measures. During the nineteenth century, the main functions of sentences were to either eliminate the culprits, or, if they were still 'reformable' (*amendables*) to punish them in such a way that they would find their way back to God, through repentance, prayer, confinement, and silence (Merle, 1985). Here, the influence of Canon law is patent (Eckert, 2011), although it gradually became institutionalised through state criminal law (Fransen, 1986).

Napoleon Bonaparte exercised enormous influence on the French legal system inasmuch as he created the codification system. Criminal law rules were classified in the Criminal Code, the first of which was written in 1810 (Halpérin, 2003). This initiated the French obsession with the treatment of social phenomena by way of legal and, especially, penal norms.

It was during the Third Republic (1870–1940) that sentences began to diversify and include the possibility of redemption. In accordance with the now well-established idea that social problems are solved by legal reforms, Parliament adopted a legal approach as its very first step towards integrating the idea of rehabilitation into the Criminal Justice System (CJS). This took the form of diversification of community sentences and measures (CSM), a step which was achieved through 'sentence *individualisation*' as conceptualised by the jurist Saleilles (1898) and Senator Bérenger (Sanchez, 2005). At the time, individualisation meant, in very crude terms, treating people who had offended for the first time more generously and those who offended repeatedly more severely (Badinter, 1992). The first-timers were offered suspended sentences; recidivists were sent to prison unless their crimes were deemed more serious, in which case they were deported to French overseas territories, particularly to French Guiana, which often resulted in their deaths. For those more deserving, two new measures were enacted: conditional release (1885 Act) and a simple (without conditions) suspended sentence (1881 Act). The idea that children and adolescents were inherently amendable was introduced in the early twentieth century. Here, Senator Bérenger was influenced by French engineer Edouard Julhiet, who brought back the idea of a specialised juvenile judge (Perissol, 2015) and protective justice from the United States following a five-year stay in that country. This led to a 1912 Act which only adopted protective juvenile justice (Yvorel, 2015). Regarding adult probation, Jules Lamarque, head of office at the Ministry of Interior and a historian in his spare time, was the most influential person. In 1872, he created the *Société Générale pour la Patronage des libérés* (General Society for the Supervision of Released Offenders) which was to provide advice, supervision, and welfare assistance (Kaluszynski, 2016).

Both world wars dramatically slowed down any chance for CJS improvement (Frenkiel-Pelletier, 2021). However, after WWII, former resistance fighters and human rights reformers oversaw the Ministry of Justice (MoJ). This link with human rights maintained the prevalence of legal regulation of social problems. After so many atrocities, it brought the ideal of rehabilitation more clearly to the fore. This opened the door for the creation of state probation in 1946 (for CSM) and 1949 (for prison-based probation). The same year, there was experimentation with the implementation of sentences judge (*juge de l'application des peines* JAP) which was generalised in 1958. A similar hands-on judge, the *juge des enfants* (judge for children) was created in 1945. 1958 also saw the creation of a suspended sentence with probation.

It should be noted that the voluntary sector had been very active since the law of 1885 in the absence of state probation. After the war and to this day, this sector has actually been carrying out most of the rehabilitation work, social work, and treatment. The intervention of state probation bodies can be seen as the beginning of the state's takeover of the monitoring and treatment of delinquency (Fassin et al., 2013). This is not a coincidence: 1958 was also the year the new Fifth Republic Constitution was enacted, which still prevails today. This constitution is marked by a considerable strengthening of the powers of the executive.

The next turning point came in the first half of the 1970s after the social and student movements of 1968 that profoundly transformed society but ultimately led to a repressive backlash in 1978. Further diversification of CSMs took place with the introduction of semi-freedom, sentence suspension for social or medical reasons, and good time credit. Prison conditions slightly improved with, in particular, the right to an education and access to the press. A further step occurred in the early 1980s with the election of Francois Mitterrand and the appointment of his Minister of Justice Robert Badinter. Badinter abolished the death penalty and introduced contact visits and access to a television. In Parliament, he obtained a unanimous vote in 1983 in favour of community work. Sentence diversification continued in the

1990s with the introduction of Electronic Monitoring (EM). Thus, the diversification of CSMs was mainly conducted through sentence individualisation, which is the legal translation of rehabilitation.

The early 2000s marked the beginning of an excessive statute atomisation. Each time right-wing parties were elected, the law moved in a punitive direction; each time the left wing was in power, it slightly mitigated these effects. At the beginning of the 2000s, this was the object of unbridled political reform as well as extraordinarily complex sentence implementation, and it became an autonomous legal field (Herzog-Evans (2022a). A legal rehabilitation model is now firmly in place (Burke et al., 2019), incoherently sharing a Mikado like space with punitive policies. During Nicolas Sarkozy's 12 years in power, first as an interior Minister (2002–2007) and then as president (2007–2012), punitive penal policies were frantically enacted. Mr Sarkozy's reign saw the enactment of a dozen criminal Acts and twice as many decrees. His zero-tolerance policies led to the now classic combination of severe prison overcrowding and mass probation (McNeill 2020). From then on, CSM diversification has led to a widening of the net rather than to a rehabilitative goal, with EM occupying centre stage (Daems, 2020), both as a release measure and as a sentence.

Current Mechanisms and Their Policy and Political Contexts

From 2009 to 2019, French penal policies were somewhat schizophrenic. On the one hand, punitive stances became part of a common discourse at all levels of the political exchequer. On the other hand, political parties from the right, the centre, and the left were forced by the European Human Rights Court (EHRCt) (culminating in EHRCt, 2013) to reduce overcrowding and its enormous cost. In what has become a mad assembly line, the number of people processed through the CJS has consistently increased at the same time that multiple, intricate mechanisms are used to speed this pointless process up and push individuals towards the exit door. In such a context, rehabilitation is either not on the radar or not seriously funded or organised. Irrationally, what counts is whether cases are processed at speed (Ritzer, 2015).

The endless terrorist wave also tipped the scale towards punitive policies, and the COVID-19 pandemic increased state authoritarian control over criminal and other public issues. During the first lockdown in 2020, JAPs resorted to every available legal tool and released an impressive 10,000 prisoners (Herzog-Evans, 2022b). As of March 2020, other individuals have not been sent to prison because of the entry into force of a 2019 Act, which makes it difficult to pronounce short custodial sentences. However, the presidential election (April 2022) has given the majority of political parties, including that of president Macron, the opportunity to engage in hyper-punitive discourses, thereby encouraging prosecutors and courts to incarcerate even more criminals than before. Words like resocialisation or reinsertion, the French equivalent of rehabilitation, have completely disappeared from public discussion.

On 1 December 2021, there were 69,992 prisoners in French prisons compared to 62,980 one year before; this represents an 11.1% increase (French Ministry of Justice 2021). Regarding CSMs, France at this point has only published its 2020 statistics. On 31 December 2020, 177, 033 individuals were supervised by French probation services, not including the unknown number of people supervised by a third-sector agency in the context of pretrial probation or through a number of other CSMs. This is nonetheless a steep increase (resulting from the combination of COVID-19 and the 2019 Act) as compared to the total of 174,512 probationers on 31 December 2019. A suspended sentence with probation largely dominates the sentencing landscape with 122,196 measures in 2020 compared to 37,944 sentences of community work and 6,053 sentences of socio-judicial supervision for those convicted of sexual offences and others who are considered dangerous. Regarding release measures, there has been a widening of the net phenomenon within CSMs, with EM dominating (13,540 persons were sentenced to EM as of 1 February 2022 versus 710 on placement in the community and 1,653 on semi-freedom (French Ministry of Justice 2022). Other measures have been abandoned by the prison services and are not adequately funded. Thus, the JAP use them sparingly when there is either a need for more control (in which case, they opt for semi-freedom) or more rehabilitative work (in which case, they choose 'placement in the community' Herzog-Evans, 2014). In other words, while the law is becoming increasingly complex, it is also irrational and punitive, and only practitioners, in particular JAPs and the third sector, are keeping the focus on everyday rehabilitation.

This pragmatism and desistance orientation contrasts, and sometimes clashes, with growing state centralised and bureaucratic authoritarianism. Particularly since its anti-democratic 1958 Constitution (Rousseau, 2007), the state today is best characterised as a 'republican monarchy' (Duverger, 1974), and it was aptly described by François Mitterrand (1964) as a 'permanent coup d'état'. This constitution ignores the separation of powers by turning Parliament into a rubber stamp puppet and by considering that the judiciary is *not* a power. In particular, article 37 gives the executive considerable legislative power outside of Parliament, including the right to regulate prison and probation matters without democratic control. Even when a law is needed, it is the institution itself (here the prison and probation services) that drafts the provisions, which are then adopted in Parliament with little discussion. This allows direct power to be exercised over judges and courts since they are considered to be simple civil servants under the 1958 constitution who merely implement the law (Jeuland, 2018).

Through Kafkaesque bureaucracy (Suleiman, 2015) and through centralism, the prison and probation services additionally exercise very tight control over their own subordinates. Probation staff became part of this centralised system since they fully merged with the prison services in 1999. In 1993, the probation officers' (PO) corps was created. POs have been asked to leave the courts and to stop issuing pre-sentence reports (these were subcontracted to the third sector). Armies of middle managers were hired to ensure that POs would comply with the prison services' hierarchical discipline and culture. The term 'penitentiary' was added to the official name of the probation services and of POs themselves (Herzog-Evans, 2013). These new names also included the terms 'probation' and 'reinsertion' (rehabilitation). In the French language, the terms probation and reinsertion are considered to be the opposite sides of the coin that represents POS' dual role. Prison governor and probation chief of service positions were merged, making them interchangeable. The prison/probation merger has had a lasting effect on French probation culture, turning it into 'prisonbation' (Herzog-Evans, 2015). French probation services, the most powerful institution in the whole of the CJS, began to show signs of group narcissism. This is best illustrated by the delusion supported by some of their most prominent unions (e.g. SNEPAP/FSU, 2018) that probation represents a 'regalian' (regal—from *regis*, king) function. On the basis of a very inappropriate understanding of Weber's work (1919), this represents a claim that their jobs are quasi-sacred (as in the myth of the Sun King, Louis XIV). From the legal viewpoint, however, the concept of regal 'function' is non-existent. French administrative law does recognise a similar but less narcissistic concept called 'non-delegable public service mission'. These are missions that cannot be subcontracted to the third sector or the private sector. Very active constitutional law discussions occurred when the privatisation of French prisons was discussed in 1987 (Collectif, 1987). The conclusion was that only prison officers and governors held non-delegable missions, understood as those in which an authority has the power to hold someone prisoner or to make the decision to detain him/her, which exclusively means the missions exercised by prosecutors, judges, police officers, prison officers, and prison governors. Probation and rehabilitation are certainly not a nondelegable mission since these activities do not include depriving individuals of their freedom (Herzog-Evans, 2020).

Punitive Front Door but Releasing Back Door

President Nicolas Sarkozy led France towards both zero-tolerance policies and 'bifurcation'. Under zero-tolerance policies, even nanoparticular offences are now expected to receive a 'response'—the French MoJ proudly announced in 2015 that 91% of all cases received a 'response' (French Ministry of Justice, 2015). This has considerably increased the number of people that are processed by prosecutors. Prosecutors now deal single-handedly as both party and judge with more than 50% of all the crimes committed in France. Under the hierarchical authority of the MoJ, prosecutors obediently implement these new policies. Their enthusiasm has grown as they have within a few years become the 'kings of the courts', relegating judges to the rank of petty officials.

These policies have also led to 'bifurcation' (Bottoms, 1977, 1980; Pratt, 2002), which means that run-of-the-mill and low-risk individuals who are at one end of the spectrum are subjected to fast-track procedures with no particular purpose other than to issue some sort of response. In an ocean of useless sanctions, a minority of prosecutors nonetheless manage to develop short-term treatment programmes with the help of local third-sector agencies (Herzog-Evans, Couteron, and Vicentini 2021). At the other end of the spectrum, the Sarkozy era has persisted in making the CJS harsher on the dangerous, even though in practise, only the dangerous actually benefit from rehabilitative work (Herzog-Evans, 2016); conversely, the run-of-the-mill are unsupported (Herzog-Evans, 2017).

The sheer number of people now processed on the CJS assembly line (Danet, 2013) has, in turn, led to 'bad and fast' release procedures, characterised by a total lack of due process, resettlement preparation, or re-entry work. During the post-Sarkozy era, there has been remarkable policy convergence across all political parties. Four successive laws have tried to discreetly release as many prisoners as possible, using the senseless complexity of the French sentence implementation system: the Perben Act (2004), under the moderate right Jacques Chirac presidency; the Prison Act (2009) under the right-wing presidency of Nicolas Sarkozy; the Taubira Act (2014) under the left-wing presidency of Francois Hollande; and the '*Programmation* Act'

(2019) under Emmanuel Macron's centre. Other than microscopic differences, the three laws have done exactly the same. They have nonetheless predictably failed (Herzog-Evans, 2017) because they have not addressed the systemic issues at stake nor have they aligned with practitioners' professional culture, notably that of JAPs, that is, desistance and 'making CSMs work' (Herzog-Evans, 2014).

France has probably been the most appropriate receptacle for the McDonaldisation (Ritzer, 2015) movement denounced elsewhere (e.g. Robinson, 2019) because of its centralised, top–bottom institutional structure and total bureaucratic control. The main policy logic now is to process service users on the CJS assembly line; not to expect any particular outcome. For instance, the new flavour of the moment is 'internships' (initiated in 2002 [Gautron & Raphalen, 2013] and generalised in 2019 [Lavielle, 2020]), that is, 'treatment' (sic) programmes consisting of twelve hours spread across two days that are contracted out by prosecutors to third sector agencies. These internships are utilised for a motley crew of individuals that, on the one hand, represent complex cases, such as domestic violence perpetrators, authors of hate crime, and drug addicts whom the CJS expects to miraculously cure in 12 hours and, on the other hand, very low-risk individuals who should not have entered the CJS in the first place. Key to this pointless system is to 'do something' rather than to do 'the work' that needs to be done to solve socio-psychological–criminological issues and to let society (the health system, education, welfare, families, and the communities) deal with those for whom penal intervention does more damage than good.

Treatment Techniques: A Patchwork

The traditional methods used in French probation are called 'socio-educational' (*socio-éducatif*). *Socio-éducatif* is often confused with *social rehabilitation* (Burke et al., 2019) or social work, but it is in reality educational (De Robertis, 2018) and without any particular technique (Michel, 2013). To paraphrase the anglophone moto 'advise, assist and befriend', in France, it is mainly about advice, this, in the context of psychoanalytic talk support (De Robertis, 2018), while, at the same time, checking that there has been compliance with the judicial mandate (Dindo, 2011; Margaine, 2015). This is eons away from evidence-based practices (EBP) (Benbouriche et al., 2012; Vanderstukken & Benbouriche, 2014), which have recently been the subject of experimentation (Direction de l'Administration Pénitentiaire, 2018) but have rapidly been deemed irrelevant by the prison headquarters

(Dindo, 2020) in light of the punitive political discussion presiding over the (pre)electoral campaign, although they are nonetheless signs that, in practice, this movement still exists (Tschanz, 2021).

Currently, French POs comprise a patchwork of differential recruitment eras: social workers and pedagogues (*éducateurs*) recruited before the 1990s (Gras, 2008; Lhuilier, 2007); lawyers from the 1990s to the 2010s (de Larminat, 2012) and still very much today; since 2013, an icing sugar layer of criminology courses delivered in silos by the prison academy (Tschanz, 2021); and since 2010, a prisonbation culture following the aforementioned name change (Herzog-Evans, 2013). With these massive overhauls, the identity of POs has been and is still questioned and their practice is extremely diverse, ranging from registrars asking for documented proof of compliance (Margaine, 2015) to wannabe criminologists (Vanderstukken & Benbouriche, 2014), bureaucrats (Dubourg, 2015) and rapidly disappearing social workers (de Larminat, 2012). Nonetheless, even today, lawyers traditionally account for around 60% of French PO recruits (De Larminat, 2012; ENAP, 2019, 2021; Gras, 2008) and the law is still one of the five core components of their training, along with management, safety issues, registry, and criminology (Tschanz, 2021). Yet, the pandemic has offered a unique opportunity to uncover what remains of the heart and soul of probation when all else (supervision, welfare, treatment, and monitoring) disappears (Herzog-Evans & Sturgeon, 2022): 'rapport' and talk probation (Farrall, 2002).

Rehabilitation and Diversity

France's aforementioned hyper-centralisation has historically worked hand in hand with an existentialist terror of diversity and '*communautarism*'—a word which causes extremely negative reactions in France. France was built on the ashes of independent regions, with Parisian culture and language violently (Jung & Urvoas, 2012) replacing regional ones (Bistolfi, 2011). This makes the French population extremely ill-equipped to understand ethno-cultural diversity other than through the imperative of total assimilation (Guirous, 2021).

In recent years, the unique French concept of '*Laïcité*'—incorrectly translated to the softer word 'secularity'—which initially referred only to the separation of state and church has become a glutton Lambton worm, devouring everything (Scot, 2015) and turning into an anti-immigrant, anti-foreigner, anti-religious, anti-diversity, and anti-communities sweeping racist 'principle'

(Wolfreys, 2018). In a similar vein, in 2021, Mr Macron's government got a law through Parliament entitled 'Reinforcing the respect of the principles of the Republic' with the separatism red rag at its core. For example, it contained measures that made home-schooling illegal for fear it would prevent the state from exclusively shaping foreign children according to France's '*Laïcité*' and culture. This quasi-primal fear colours how France deals with diversity. For instance, France has repeatedly been hit by a series of murderous terrorist attacks, and it has classically oscillated between punitive knee-jerk reactions (Alix & Khan, 2021), Parisian centralism (with dedicated Parisian courts, atavistically deemed superior to provincial courts [Besnier & Weil, 2020]) and brainwashing re-education (Benslama, 2017; Beunas, 2019) focused on France's 'superior' values and *laïcité* principle. At a general level, French probation does not have any diversity policy. As an example, article 4 of the European Probation Rules (CM/Rec [2010]1) contains two principles, namely non-discrimination and responsive policies on diversity. A diversity policy has been purely and simply ignored by the French prison services even though their headquarters have distributed the European probation rules and used them to promote their probation guidelines (Direction de l'Administration Pénitentiaire, 2018). Adapting to cultural diversity would indeed be considered as dangerously giving in to separatism.

France also has no gendered policies whatsoever. As with foreigners who are required to become French, females who offend are treated 'like men'—or worse as we shall soon see. Traditional French feminism has corroborated this approach by being, in essence, collaborationist and negating the female experience, in particular as mothers (Badinter, 2001). A European Human Rights Court case, *Raffray Taddei v. France,* provides a sad illustration. A Corsican female prisoner had to be sent to the main continent because France has not found it necessary to build prisons for long sentences in Corsica. The situation for the Corsican women was particularly dire as there was only one such prison on the mainland, which was located in Rennes in the Northwest of France. It was, therefore, too expensive for her children to visit her. As a result, Ms. Raffray Taddei became severely anorexic, and France was sentenced by the EHRCt for not giving her appropriate treatment (EHRCt, 2010).

Theoretical Underpinnings to Models of Rehabilitation

The theoretical underpinning of the French model of rehabilitation is, unsurprisingly, laid down in the law. First, article 130-1 of the Criminal Code states that 'In order to ensure the protection of society, to prevent the commission of new offences and to restore social equilibrium, while respecting the interests of the victim, the functions of the sentences are: 1. To punish the offender; [and] 2. To promote his or her reformation, integration or reintegration'. Additionally, article 132-24 of the Criminal Code states that 'Sentences may be personalised in the manner provided for in this' code. In the past, in the absence of article 130-1, article 132-24 stated that sentences were pronounced on the basis of the severity of the offence and the culprit's personality. Article 130-1, created by the Taubira Act—under a left-wing government—has now made clear that one of the functions of a sentence is indeed to punish. Nonetheless, punishment is also balanced with a series of terms representing two forms of rehabilitation (Burke et al., 2019). Article 130-1 first refers to moral rehabilitation. The French term for reformation is amendment, which has an ancient religious connotation that includes repentance; that is *moral rehabilitation*. This is also new: this dated term has not been used in decades (Merle, 1985). Second, Article 130-1 refers to integration and reintegration, that is, *social rehabilitation*. These terms have two connotations: they first relate to the French concepts of resocialisation, which roughly relates to primary desistance (Maruna & Farrall, 2004) and the return to society via traditional hooks for change (education, employment, housing, family) as well as to the resocialisation effort expected from the individual (Herzog-Evans, 2022a). The second connotation relates to secondary (Maruna & Farrall, 2004) and tertiary desistance (McNeill, 2016); that is, identity change, recognition by others that the person has changed, a sense of belonging and full citizenship.

Similarly, the sentence's implementation phase, a fully developed legal field in France (Herzog-Evans, 2022a), has its own main introductory norm which is found in article 707 of the criminal procedure code. Since the Taubira Act, article 707 section II has stated that sentence implementation must also 'enable [the person] to act as a responsible person', which is similar to other guiding principles (integration and reintegration, society's interests, and the prevention of reoffending). This outdated language brings us back to nineteenth-century concepts like discipline and punish (Foucault, 1975) and to the *moral rehabilitation* imperative.

In contrast, France has a large array of very generous techniques to facilitate secondary and tertiary desistance and facilitate legal reintegration through the expunging of criminal records and the restoration of the full status of citizen (Herzog-Evans, 2011). So far, this has been, for the most part, untainted but for a law regarding sex offences which maintains the criminal records (bulletin number 1) that are only accessible to courts and reduces expungement opportunities (Herzog-Evans, 2022a). Nonetheless, recent punitive penal policies, an extreme lack of resources, McDonaldisation and prisonbation have led to a form of unsupportive probation in which probationers are expected to make most of the efforts themselves in order to deserve a modicum of support, as in 'help yourself and the state will support you a tiny bit'.

Research Findings and Effectiveness

Although change is slowly emerging, French language probation literature has not, for the most part, been made internationally available and is generally oblivious to international literature or theoretical models. The responsibility for this lies partly in an endemic lack of public service transparency and to the organisation of French universities where criminology and related sciences are embryonic. The Ministry of Justice has its own statisticians who have produced raw or quasi-raw data; for instance, counting how many people released with a CSM versus those maxing out on their prison sentences have reoffended (Tournier & Kensey, 2005). The executive has simplistically misinterpreted these unadjusted statistics as demonstrating the effectiveness of any type of early release measures, with or without re-entry work. This has legitimised the schizophrenic 'bad fast' release policies previously discussed. Without any statistical correction or matching, these quasi-raw data only show that JAP chose well those who would benefit from release measures.

French literature has not been able to measure whether other CJS rehabilitative work (e.g. prosecutor-led programmes or third sector supervision) produces positive outcomes. Qualitative and semi-ethnographic work has nonetheless been conducted recently. It has, inter alia, confirmed the top-down/closed shop nature of French probation (Bouagga, 2013), the identity crisis faced by POs as the compliance prisonbation and watered-down RNR (Vanderstukken & Benbouriche, 2014) has become prevalent (Larminat, 2012), in contrast with the identity certainty of yesteryear (Lhuilier, 2007). It has also shown the growing domineering stance of this prisonbation institution, particularly with regards to its interactions with JAPs (Herzog-Evans, 2014, 2017) and the third sector (Herzog-Evans, 2018).

Remember that the judicial mandate is set, for the most part, by JAPs. A triangular study conducted from 2009 to 2013 showed that JAPs have a strong desistance culture, understood in all its dimensions and including tertiary desistance. They do aspire to intrinsic motivation and change and are very favourable to CSMs (Herzog-Evans, 2014). More recently, the COVID-19 crisis has offered a window of opportunity into the absolute core of probation work according to French POs, that is, talk support (Herzog-Evans & Sturgeon, 2022).

Other than strongly suspecting that French probation is non-EBP (Vanderstukken & Benbouriche, 2014) in view of its programmes, although some limited progress is currently being made (Direction de l'Administration Pénitentiaire, 2018), it is impossible to know whether French rehabilitation works. However, the author is currently conducting a series of 'Black box of French probation' studies. The first one (Herzog-Evans, Berjot, and Keulen-de Vos, forthcoming) uses a revised version of the Jersey checklist (Raynor et al., 2009), notably augmented with RNR/CBT items, to code 78 PO/probationer audio-recorded interviews. To limit selection bias, we asked POs to select at least one probationer who was female, one who was driving under the influence, one resistant, one dangerous, and one who was 'ordinary' (simple to manage). Our results suggest that in line with their preferred activity, French POs are good in terms of their communication skills and are now quite at ease with motivational interviewing techniques in which they have been institutionally trained. Conversely, their pro-social modelling skills are lacking, and they struggle with complex cases. Surprisingly, we found that they were quite bad at guaranteeing privacy, but this can be explained by the prisonbation institution in which they operate. Unsurprisingly, their CBT techniques are virtually non-existent, leading back to the issue of their background and training. This can also be explained by the dominance of psychoanalysis in France.

The 78 audio files are currently being reused in conjunction with two other colleagues (Berjot et al., ongoing), this time with the use of an adapted TMIB-S (Tripartite Measure of Interpersonal Behaviors—Supervisor) tool. We want to know whether French POs are controlling or supportive within the self-determination theory framework (Ryan & Deci, 2017). Our data has just been coded and we cannot make firm conclusions at this stage. What does stand out statistically, though, is that French POs do not make much, if any, effort to help resistant probationers and female probationers. They also appear not to care about their needs. Why are French POs so indifferent, uncaring, and unsupportive of females? It could be a classic application of the 'bad girl' feminist theory (Chesney-Lind & Irwin, 2008), particularly in a country as patriarchal as France that is also in denial of its patriarchy (e.g. in CJ [Govard et al., 2016]; in families [Bessière & Gollac, 2020]). Another explanation could be France's *laïque* diversity-blind culture.

Conclusion: Future Directions in Policy and Practice

The candidates in the presidential elections of April 2022 promised more zero tolerance policies (Valérie Pécresse, right wing), 20,000 new prison cells (Macron, centre right; Pécresse as well as Marine Le Pen, far right) or youth prisons (Pécresse), mandatory minimum sentences (Pécresse), criminal legal majority at 16 (Pécresse), a true life sentence (Le Pen; Zemour, far right), virtually removing all good time credit (Zemour), doubling of police officers (Macron) and judges (Le Pen; Zemour) and an increase on cowboy style populist legislating, such as the facilitation of legitimate defence (Le Pen; Zemour; Midi Libre, 2022; Paris-Normandy, 2022). Totally absent from the candidates' propositions were rehabilitation or their French equivalent of (re)insertion or resocialisation. The left proposed less punitive reforms but stood no chance to even go past the second round. Indeed, Mr Macron predictably won the elections and became president. With the war in Ukraine, and pressing social and economic issues, Mr Macron has not had time to make public announcements regarding his future criminal policy. Nonetheless, in view of what he promised during his campaign, one can expect more authoritarian, executive dominance, legislating in this direction and more zero tolerance and thus more 'bifurcation', more policing, sentencing, and incarceration and more industrial McDonaldisation.

Yet, France is a very contrasted jurisdiction as front-line practitioners do aspire to existentialist meaning, particularly those who choose probation or judicial positions. These people have been able to create an oasis in the desert. Examples are hands-on desistance-friendly JAP, a very active and humane third sector, and an active minority of prosecutors who carry the baton of rehabilitation through rehabilitation programmes with the third sector. They sadly represent an exception to the rule.

References

Alix, J., & Khan, O. (2021). *Terrorisme et infraction politique*. Mare et Martin.
Badinter, E. (2001). *L'amour en plus*. Le livre de poche.
Badinter, R. (1992). *La prison républicaine (1871–1914)*. Fayard.
Benbouriche, M., Vantéjoux, A., Lebougault, M., & Hirschelmann, A. (2012). L'évaluation du risque de récidive en France: Expérience et attitudes des conseillers pénitentiaires d'insertion et de probation. *Revue Internationale De Criminologie Et De Police Technique Et Scientifique, 3*(12), 305–318.
Benslama, F. (2017). On radicalisation and its treatments. *Cités, 69*(1), 115–124.
Berjot, S., Herzog-Evans, M., & Huyghebaert-Zouaghi, T. (ongoing). French probation officers's controlling behaviour.
Berman, G. (2000). What is a traditional judge anyway? Problem-solving in the State Courts. *Judicature, 84*, 78–85.
Besnier, C., & Weil, S. (2020). *Les filières djihadistes en procès. Approche ethnographique des audiences criminelles et correctionnelles (2017–2019)*. Paris: Rapport Mission Droit et Justice.
Bessière, C., & Gollac, S. (2020). *Le genre du capital*. La Découverte.
Beunas, C. (2019). Du « radical » au « radicalisé »: Les usages médiatiques et politiques de la notion de « déradicalisation » en France (2014–2017). *Déviance Et Société, 43*, 3–39.
Bistolfi, R. (2011). Langues régionales: Il y a deux siècles, une mort programmée. *Confluences Méditerranée, 76*, 197–202.
Bottoms, A. E. (1977). Reflections on the renaissance of dangerousness. *Howard Journal of Crime and Justice, 16*(2), 70–96.
Bottoms, A. E. (1980). An introduction to 'the coming crisis'. In A. E. Bottoms & R. D. Preston (Eds.), *The coming penal crisis: A criminological and theological exploration* (pp. 1–24). Scottish Academic Press.
Bouagga, Y. (2013). *Humaniser la peine? Ethnographie du traitement pénal en maison d'arrêt*. Ph.D. dissertation, Ecole des Hautes Etudes en Sciences Sociales.
Boulanger, M. (2000). Justice et absolutisme: La Grande Ordonnance d'août 1670. *Revue D'histoire Moderne and Contemporaine, 47*(1), 7–36.
Burke, L., Collett, S., & McNeill, F. (2019). *Reimagining rehabilitation*. Routledge.
Carbasse, J.-M., & Vielfaure, P. (2014). *Histoire du droit pénal et de la justice criminelle*. Presses Universitaires de France.
Chesney-Lind, M., & Irwin, K. (2008). *Beyond bad girls: Gender, violence and hype*. Routledge.
Collectif. (1987). *Les prisons dites privées, une solution à la crise pénitentiaire? Actes du colloque Aix-en-Provence*, 23 and 24 janv. 1987. Paris: Economica.
Daems, T. (2020). *Electronic monitoring: Tagging offenders in a culture of surveillance*. Springer.
Danet, J. (Ed.). (2013). *La réponse pénale. Dix ans de traitement des délits*. Presses Universitaires de Rennes.

De Robertis, C. (2018). *Méthodologie de l'intervention en travail social.* Presses de l'EHESP, Nouvelle ed.

Dindo, S. (2011). *Sursis avec mise à l'épreuve: la peine méconnue. Une analyse des pratiques de probation en France,* Étude pour la Direction de l'administration pénitentiaire, bureau PMJ1, mai 2011.

Dindo, S. (2020). L'implantation de pratiques probantes en Franc : l'incertain déploiement du RPO1. *Cahiers De La Sécurité Et De La Justice, 48–49,* 139–148.

Direction de l'Administration Pénitentiaire (French prison services) (2018). *Référentiel des pratiques Opérationnelles (RPO1).* Ministère de la Justice.

Dubourg, E. (2015). *Les services pénitentiaires d'insertion et de probation. Fondements juridiques. Évolution. Évaluation et avenir,* PhD dissertation, University of Nantes.

Duverger, M. (1974). *La monarchie républicaine.* Robert Laffont.

Eckert, E. (2011). Peine judiciaire, pénitence et salut entre droit canonique et théologie (xiie s. – début du xiiie s.). *Revue De L'histoire Des Religions, 4,* 483–508.

ENAP. (2019). *Conseillers pénitentiaires d'insertion et de probation. 25ᵉ promotion.* Eléments de connaissances socio-démographiques. Département de la recherche.

ENAP. (2021). *Conseillers pénitentiaires d'insertion et de probation. 26ᵉ promotion.* Eléments de connaissances socio-démographiques. Département de la recherche.

Farrall, S. (2002). *Rethinking what works with offenders. Probation, social context and desistance from crime.* Willan.

Fassin, D., Bouagga, Y., Coutant, I., Eideliman, J.-S., Fernandez, F., Fischer, N., Kobelinsky, C., Makaremi, C., Mazouz, S., & Roux, S. (2013). Juger, réprimer, accompagner. Essai sur la morale: Essai sur la morale de l'Etat. Seuil.

Foucault, M. (1975). *Surveiller et punir: Naissance de la prison.* Gallimard.

Fransen, F. (1986). Écriture sainte et droit canonique. *Revista Española De Derecho Canonico, 43,* 7–22.

French Ministry of Justice. (2015). Une réponse pénale pour 91% des auteurs d'infractions. Retrieved March 2, 2022, from http://www.justice.gouv.fr/statistiques-10054/infostats-justice-10057/une-reponse-penale-pour-91-des-auteurs-dinfractions-28451.html

French Ministry of Justice. (2021). Statistique des établissements des personnes écrouées en France. Direction de l'Administration Pénitentiaire Bureau de la donnée (DAP/SDEX/EX3).

French Ministry of Justice. (2022). Statistiques des établissements des personnes écrouées en France. Direction de l'Administration Pénitentiaire Bureau de la donnée (DAP/SDEX/EX3).

Frenkiel-Pelletier, E. (2021). *Histoire de la probation durant la deuxième guerre mondiale, période d'exception, et sa refondation jusqu'aux années soixante-dix.* Ph.D. dissertation. Université de Reims.

Gautron, V., & Raphalen, P. (2013). Les stages: Une nouvelle forme de pénalité? *Déviance Et Société, 37*(1), 27–50.

Govard, C., Buyon, F., & Doyon, J. (2016). *Présumées coupables.* Iconoclaste.

Gras, L. (2008). *La socialisation professionnelle des conseillers d'insertion et de probation. Rapport intermédiaire*. ENAP.
Guirous, L. (2021). *Assimilation: En finir avec ce tabou français*. L'Observatoire.
Halpérin, J. (2003). L'histoire de la fabrication du code le code: Napoléon ? *Pouvoirs, 107*, 11–21.
Herzog-Evans, M. (2011). Judicial rehabilitation in France: Helping with the desisting process and acknowledging achieved desistance. *European Journal of Probation, 3*(1), 4–19.
Herzog-Evans, M. (2013). What's in a name: Penological and institutional connotations of probation officers' labelling in Europe. *Eurovista, 2*(3), 121–133.
Herzog-Evans, M. (2014). *French reentry courts and rehabilitation. Mister Jourdain of desistance*. L'Harmattan.
Herzog-Evans, M. (2015). France: Legal architecture, political posturing, 'prisonbation' and adieu social work. In G. Robinson & F. McNeill (Eds.), *Community punishment. European perspective* (pp. 51–71). Abingdon: Routledge.
Herzog-Evans, M. (2016). Legal constraints on the indeterminate control of 'Dangerous' sex offenders in the community: The French perspective. *Erasmus Law Journal, 2*, 67–82.
Herzog-Evans, M. (2017). *La libération sous contrainte dans le Nord-Est de la France*. Rapport Mission Droit et Justice.
Herzog-Evans, M. (2018). French probation and prisoner resettlement. Involuntary 'privatisation' and corporatism. In T. Daems & T. Vander Beken (Eds.), *Privatising punishment in Europe?* (pp. 104–123). Routledge.
Herzog-Evans, M. (2020). Probation française: comparaison analytique internationale et européenne. Cahiers de la Sécurité et de la Justice, 48–49. Retrieved March 2, 2022, from https://www.ihemi.fr/articles/probation-francaise-comparaison-analytique-internationale-et-europeenne
Herzog-Evans, M. (2022a). *Droit de l'exécution des peines* (6th ed.). Dalloz.
Herzog-Evans, M. (2022b). France. In Dünkel, F., Harrendorf, S., & van Zyl Smit, D. (Eds.), *The impact of Covid-19 on prison conditions and penal policy*. Routledge.
Herzog-Evans, M., Berjot, S., & Keulen-de Vos, M. (forthcoming). Exploring the black box of French community supervision. *European Journal of Probation*
Herzog-Evans, M., Couteron, F., and Vicentini, J.-Ph. (2021). *Les conditions scientifiques de l'efficacité des juridictions résolutives de problèmes pour la prise en charge des délinquants souffrant de toxicomanie : Enjeux et réponses*. Report to the Ecole Nationale de la Magistrature.
Herzog-Evans, M., & Sturgeon, J. (2022). French and Scottish probation during the first lockdown in search of the heart and soul of probation. *Probation Journal, 69*(2), 197–215.
Jeuland, E. (2018). *Towards a new court management? General report*. [Research Report] University Paris 1 – Panthéon Sorbonne.
Jung, A., & Urvoas, L.-J. (2012). *Langues et cultures régionales : En finir avec l'exception française*. Rapport pour la Fondation Jean Jaurès.

Kaluszynski, M. (2016). La prison (et sa réforme), un enjeu formateur pour l'État républicain en construction, *Criminocorpus* [Online]. Retrieved February 28, 2022, from 2https://journals.openedition.org/criminocorpus/3173

Larminat, X. (2012). *La probation en quête d'approbation. L'exécution des peines en milieu ouvert entre gestion des risques et gestion des flux,* Ph.D. dissertation, Cesdip-Université de Versailles-Saint Quentin.

Lavielle, B. (2020). Le juge correctionnel au bout de ses peines? *Actualité Juridique Pénal*, March, 150–163.

Le Böedec Maurel, B. (2022). *Jusqu'au bout de mes peines. Chronique d'un juge de l'application des peines.* Enrick Editions.

Lhuilier, D. (2007). *Changements et construction des identités professionnelles: les travailleurs sociaux pénitentiaires,* Rapport final, Psy Form, Paris.

Margaine, C. (2015). Etude des obligations applicables en milieu ouvert. Une analyse de la dimension coercitive de la probation. Rapport de Recherche. ENAP. Dossiers thématiques CIRAP.

Maruna, S., & Farrall, S. (2004). Desistance from crime: A theoretical reformulation. *Kolner Zeitschrift Fur Soziologie Und Sozialpsychologie, 43*, 171–194.

McNeill, F. (2016). Desistance and criminal justice in Scotland. In H. Croall, G. Mooney, & R. Munro (Eds.), *Crime, Justice and society in Scotland* (pp. 200–216). Routledge.

McNeill, F. (2020). *Pervasive punishment. Making sense of mass supervision.* Emerald Publishing Limited.

Merle, R. (1985). *La pénitence et la peine: Théologie, droit canonique, droit pénal.* CERF.

Michel, M. (2013). De l'éducation à l'accompagnement, quelles questions pour le travail social ? *Vie Sociales, 4*, 177–190.

Midi Libre (2022). DOSSIER SPECIAL. Sécurité et justice : ce que proposent les principaux candidats à l'élection présidentielle. Retrieved March 3, 2022, from https://www.midilibre.fr/2022/02/17/dossier-special-securite-et-justice-les-mesures-proposees-par-les-principaux-candidats-a-la-presidentielle-10116671.php

Mitterrand, F. (1964). *Le coup d'état permanent.* Plon.

Paris-Normandy. (2022). Présidentielle 2022. Cinq propositions de cinq candidats pour la sécurité et la justice. February 1st, 2022. Retrieved March 3, 2022 from https://www.paris-normandie.fr/id274724/article/2022-02-01/presidentielle-2022-5-propositions-pour-la-securite-et-la-justice

Perissol, G. (2015). *Juvenile Courts* américaines et tribunaux pour enfants français : les variations d'un modèle à travers la comparaison Paris/Boston (début XXe siècle – années 1950). *Revue d'Histoire de l'Enfance « irrégulière »* [Online]. Retrieved from https://journals.openedition.org/rhei/3819?lang=fr

Pratt, J. (2002). *Punishment and civilisation. Penal tolerance and intolerance in modern society.* Sage.

Raynor, P., Ugwudike, P., & Vanstone, M. (2009). *The Jersey supervision interview checklist, version 7C.* May, The Jersey Crime and Society Project.

Ritzer, G. (2015). *The McDonaldization of society* (8th ed.). Sage.

Robinson, G. (2019). Delivering McJustice? The probation factory at the Magistrates' court. *Criminology and Criminal Justice, 19*(5), 605–621.

Rocha-Harang, F. (2017). *La torture au Moyen-Age: Parlement de Paris, XIV-XV siècles*. Presses Universitaires de France.

Rousseau, D. (2007). *La Ve République se meurt, vive la démocratie*. Odile Jacob.

Ryan, R. M., & Deci, E. L. (2017). *Determination theory. Basic psychological needs in motivation, development, and wellness*. The Guilford Press.

Saleilles, R. (1898). *L'individualisation de la peine: étude de criminalité sociale*. F. Alcan.

Sanchez, J.-L. (2005). Les lois Bérenger (lois du 14 août 1885 et du 26 mars 1891). *Criminocorpus* [Online]. Retrieved February 28, 2022, from http://journals.opennedition.org/criminocorpus/132

Scot, J. (2015). Laïcité : Confusions, dérives et impostures. *La Pensée, 383*, 13–26.

SNEPAP/FSU. (2018). Audience à l'Elysée des garanties pour la filière insertion et probation à obtenir. Retrieved March 2, 2022, from https://snepap.fsu.fr/wp-content/uploads/sites/103/2018/10/audience-Elys%C3%A9e-01-10-2018.pdf

Suleiman, E. N. (2015). *Politics, power, and bureaucracy in France. The administrative elite*. Princeton University Press.

Tournier, P.-V., & Kensey, A. (2005). Sortants de prison : variabilité des risques de retour », *Cahiers de démographie pénitentiaire*. Prison Services, France.

Tschanz, A. (2021). La formation en criminologie des agents de probation français Quelle signification pour la réinsertion? *Criminologie, 54*(2), 143–167.

Vanderstukken, O., & Benbouriche, M. (2014). Principes de prévention de la récidive et principe de réalité en France: les programmes de prévention de la récidive à la lumière du modèle « Risque-Besoins-Réceptivité ». Ajpénal, 522–527.

Weber, M. (1919). *Politik als Beruf in Geistige Arbeit als Beruf. Vier Vorträge vor dem Freistudentischen Bund*. Zweiter Vortrag.

Wolfreys, J. (2018). *Republic of Islamophobia. The rise of respectable racism in France*. Hurst.

Yvorel, J. (2015). 1945–1988. Histoire de la justice des mineurs. *Les Cahiers Dynamiques, 2*(2), 21–32.

Cited Court cases

EHRCt, *Raffray Taddei v. France*, December the 21st 2010, applic. N° 36435/07.
EHRCt, *Canali v. France*, 25 April 2013, Applic. n°40119/09.

Rehabilitation in Ghana: Assessing Prison Conditions and Effectiveness of Interventions for Incarcerated Adults

Kofi E. Boakye, Thomas D. Akoensi, and Frank D. Baffour

The question of what to do with people who break the law has been a difficult one for scholars, policy makers and the public. A society's response to crime reflects fundamental belief in that society about the value of human life and the capacity of individuals to reform. In Ghana, and the African context, this value is most evident in the response of the traditional justice system to acts that transgress social norms (Abotchie, 1997; Rattray, 1929; Sarbah, 1968). The response to such infraction on social norms has largely been in the form of restoration and collective punishment that emphasise restitution for the harm caused by the individual (Abotchie, 1997; Appiahene-Gyamfi, 1989; Boakye & Akoensi, 2021). The colonial encounter, however, has significantly impacted the traditional notion and purpose of punishment in Ghana and Africa in ways that have persisted to date. Penal policy transfer is evident

K. E. Boakye (✉)
Anglia Ruskin University, Cambridge, UK
e-mail: keb47@cam.ac.uk

T. D. Akoensi
University of Kent, Kent, UK
e-mail: t.akoensi@kent.ac.uk

F. D. Baffour
University of New South Wales, Sydney, NSW, Australia
e-mail: f.baffour@unsw.edu.au

from how laws are conceived and enacted to how the system responds to persons who break the law, whether in the area of prison, community sanction or probation. In this chapter, we examine the response of the criminal justice system to adults who break the law with a particular focus on prisons and prison conditions. We contend that the current penal landscape in Ghana and Africa is heavily influenced by the peculiar history of penal policies inherited from the colonial period and the failure to embark on ambitious reforms based on traditional penal values underpinned by rehabilitation ideals and the research evidence about effective approaches to desistence, crime prevention and harm reduction. The chapter first examines rehabilitation as an ideal in the criminal justice system in Ghana. We then examine the colonial encounter and its influence on penal institutions and policies. We focus on prisons for two reasons. First, prisons offer important sites to assess the dominant form of punishment and the values underlying the penal system in Ghana, and second, there is a near absence of alternative forms of punishment beyond custodial sentences apart from cautions and fines for traffic offences and other minor infractions. The probation service is weak and ineffective. Whatever intervention programmes that exist for persons convicted of a crime are run in prisons. The chapter will assess the intervention programmes in prisons in Ghana and their effectiveness in transforming the lives of prisoners. We review current rehabilitations initiatives and their implications for the future of the penal landscape in Ghana. We conclude the chapter with suggestions about how rehabilitations can be reimagined to take into account social values and context dynamics to improve the lives of people who break the law.

Traditional Notions of Punishment and Rehabilitation

The traditional justice system in Ghana has at its core the principles of deterrence and restoration (Appiahene-Gyamfi, 1989; Boakye & Akoensi, 2021). Although these principles have hardly been properly articulated, they are evident in the ways in which the traditional system responded to individual breaches of social norms. Such breaches are thought to cause disequilibrium in social harmony, which must be quickly restored through restitution to avoid calamity for the entire society. For example, in writing about the traditional justice administration prior to colonialisation, Sarbah (1968: 30) observed in the *Fanti National Constitution* that:

Fines are paid for accidental homicide; such as carelessly wounding a person taking part in a chase. A person found guilty of criminal intercourse with a married woman is liable to pay to the injured husband a fine … In case of theft, the guilty offender is made to restore to the owner the stolen article or its value and to his ruler he pays a fine.

While extreme forms of sanctions existed in the traditional pre-colonial societies, including the death penalty for treasonable offences, these sanctions were rarely used. The majority of offences attracted fines or some form of restitution. Perhaps the most dreaded sanction in traditional societies was social ridicule. Rattray (1929: 372) noted this in the *Ashanti Law and Constitution*:

Even where we find supernatural or corporal sanctions in the form of punishments inflicted by the gods or by man, for breaches of tribal regulations, it appears probable that fear of ridicule was also ever present, and it is doubtful if even the worst of humanly inflicted punishments was more dreaded than this subtle weapon which came in laughing guise to rob a man of his own self-respect and the respect of his associates.

Rattray further observed that 'in the social world in which the Ashanti lived, there was not any escape for one who had incurred this penalty'. As can be seen, although varied forms of sanctions existed in traditional pre-colonial societies, it is evident that punishment in these societies was based largely on rehabilitation ideals that sought to reintegrate the individual back into society. Crime was considered harm not only to the individual but also to the community. Although the individual is primarily responsible for their actions, there is a measure of collective responsibility for the behaviour of individuals in traditional Ghanaian societies (Abotchie, 1997; Boakye, 2009; also see Clifford, 1964). As Rattray (1929: 374) observed 'The real power in all these sanctions lay in the fact that they were supposed to be operative not only against the individual, but, if the occasion demanded it, collectively'. Punishments were swift, even if at times capricious and disproportionate to the offence committed. They were also restorative with a strong focus on reintegration of the perpetrator back into the society and compensation of the victim for the harm suffered. Custodial sanctions such as prison was, therefore, non-existent in traditional societies until colonisation (Asare, 2021; Boakye & Akoensi, 2021).

Prisons and Rehabilitation

The 'pains of imprisonment' and the effects of this peculiar institution have been the subject of academic discourse and public interest (Cox & Abrams, 2021; Crewe, 2011; Liebling & Maruna, 2005; Martin, 2021; Sykes, 1958). At the core of the debate is the purpose of punishment and how those who break the law should be treated (Burke et al., 2019; Vanstone, 2019; Ward & Maruna, 2007). Beyond retribution, the prison system, since its inception in Europe in the sixteenth century, claims to have deterrence and rehabilitation as important goals. As this penal institution gained popularity in the mid-eighteenth century in Europe as the preferred punishment, its export to the colonies was inevitable. To further the aim of resource exploitation, it was necessary to control the native population and curb dissent. Following the abolition of slavery at the beginning of the nineteenth century, the slave dungeons were repurposed by the British empire to hold troublesome natives and captives of war (Seidman, 1969). In 1860, the promulgation of the Prisons Ordinance formally introduced the prison system in Ghana (Appiahene-Gyamfi, 1989; Seidman, 1969). It has seen little reform since this period and continues to reflect much of the ideals that underpinned its initial introduction (Asare, 2021). Seidman's (1969: 434) observation, a decade after Ghana's independence in 1957, best captures the state of the prison system in Ghana:

> The prison system is at the core of Ghana's penal organisation. It stands as a monument to colonial rule, as a memorial to confused goals, conflicting objectives, policies evolved and abandoned, and sometimes no policy at all. Today, it searches for its true role, if indeed there is any single role for it to play. It is caught between the urgings of a preventive policy, which recognises that preventative policy may work where cure cannot, the deterrent policy of the courts, whose judges remain convinced of the efficacy of punishment as a power in the hearts of men, and the rehabilitation ideal of the western world of which Ghana is a part.

The current statute of the Ghana Prisons Service (GPS) was enacted in 1972. The Prisons Service Act (NRCD 46, 1972) continues to define the primary responsibility of the prison service as to ensure the safe custody and welfare of incarcerated individuals. Rehabilitation of people in its care is considered a secondary goal dependent on the availability of resources and the capacity to undertake such a task (Prisons Service Act, 1972, [NRCD 46, 1972]). There are currently 44 prison facilities spread across the 16 regions of Ghana (GPS, 2020). All the facilities, except one, are for adults on remand or convicted and given a custodial sentence by the court. The GPS manages all prison facilities. Prison overcrowding remains a major challenge because of the limited facilities available. We return to prison conditions and the problem of overcrowding later in this chapter.

Ghana and several African countries have directed efforts at improving rehabilitation programmes since the recommendations of the Ouagadougou Declaration and Plan of Action on Accelerating Prisons and Penal Reforms in Africa [ODPAAPPR] in 2002. The declaration acknowledged the deficit in rehabilitation in prisons in Africa and charged state parties to make conscious efforts to improve it to meet international standards (ODPAAPPR, 2002). Robins (2009) reported that countries such as Zambia, Sierra Leone and Tanzania were making efforts to improve prison conditions and ensure effective rehabilitation, although they continue to be confronted with challenges in personnel and infrastructure. In 2015, the GPS launched a ten-year development plan which sought to achieve sustainable public safety through effective and constructive correctional programmes (GPS, 2015). To achieve part of this plan, the Prison Service launched an initiative called Project *Efiase* (Prison Project). The purpose of the project was to improve prison conditions, ensure effective rehabilitation and bridge the gap between the prison and the community through advocacy, fundraising and public–private partnership.

Rehabilitation Programmes in Prisons

Over the years, successive governments, and other stakeholders in Ghana and Africa, have made efforts to improve rehabilitation in prisons. Although skills development training and religious activities dominate rehabilitation programmes in the region post-independence, literacy and formal school programmes commenced in the early 2000s following the Ouagadougou and Kampala declarations. In Ghana, the introduction of the Free High School education policy in 2017 has had a positive impact on programmes in prisons through the provision of formal education and improving the literacy skills of persons in prison (Addai, 2020). Rehabilitation programmes in prison can be classified broadly under four themes. The first theme is vocational and technical skills training. This is the theme that dominates rehabilitation programmes in the prisons (Akoensi, 2014; Boakye & Akoensi, 2021; Seidman, 1969). Examples of vocational and skills training in the prisons include clothing and textiles, carpentry and joinery, ceramics, electronics, electricals, baking, plumbing, smock weaving, auto mechanics and electricals

(GPS, 2020). The second rehabilitation theme is literacy and basic education. The purpose of this correctional education is to ensure that incarcerated individuals at school-going age are provided with the opportunity to start or continue their academic journey while incarcerated (GPS, 2013). The need for functional literacy became important when it was revealed that most incarcerated persons in Ghana could not read or write (Addo, 2018). The third theme focusses on religious activities. There is a strong belief in the reformative power of religion in Ghana, although it is difficult to assess the evidential basis for this belief. Prison officers (prison chaplains and Imams) and external faith-based organisations (consisting of Christian organisations, Islamic organisations and other faith-based groups) provide religious programmes within prisons and the Religious Affairs Unit of the GPS regulates their activities. The continuous reliance on religious activities as a means of reforming incarcerated individuals in Ghana and other African countries calls for a thorough evaluation of its impact on the emotional, moral and psychological health of persons in custody, and effectiveness in reducing recidivism. For example, although the role of religion in the reformation of persons in custody has been documented in jurisdictions in and outside Africa (Connolly & Granfield, 2017; Ilechukwu & Ugwuozor, 2017; Morag & Teman, 2018), it is also possible that the impact of religion is mediated by other factors such as empathy which has been shown to reduce offending (Jolliffe & Farrington, 2021; Trivedi-Bateman & Crook, 2021). The fourth rehabilitation theme is programmes focussed on community transition. Baffour (2021: 1176) noted in his review of community transition programme in Ghana prisons that inmates who had three months or less left on their prison terms were made to perform unpaid services in the community under supervision. Such inmates are not on parole, neither are they discharged—they leave the prison to the community to perform the unpaid services under the supervision of prison officers and return before sunset. This programme which aims to promote interactions between persons in custody and the public, helps inmates to earn income, and mentally prepares them for release, ceases following their release from prison. There is a general lack of psychological services in prisons for inmates. Of the 44 prisons, only the Nsawam medium-security prison has counselling as a formal treatment regime. Prison officers usually engage in informal counselling of inmates on a variety of issues drawing on their life experiences and religious teachings (Akoensi, 2014). There is currently no evaluation of these programmes to assess their effectiveness.

Prison Rehabilitation Programmes: A Closer Look

In this section, we examine the priority of rehabilitation in Ghana prisons, the challenges confronting rehabilitation and the availability of research evidence on these rehabilitation programmes. As noted earlier in this chapter, the goal of the prison system in Ghana is primarily focussed on incapacitation and safekeeping of persons in custody, and the Prisons Service Act, 1972 [NRCD-46] considers rehabilitation as a 'third priority' (Baffour, 2019). Specifically, the Act stipulates that the main purpose of imprisonment is the provision of safe custody and welfare of persons in custody, and whenever practicable, their reformation and rehabilitation (NRCD-46, 1972). While safe custody includes incarcerated persons' adherence to the prison regime, securing prisons to avoid escapes and the maintenance of prison discipline, welfare provision involves the provision of adequate food, clothing and housing facilities, provision of recreational and health facilities. Thus, the measurement of success for the GPS is based on key performance indicators of safe custody and welfare provision. Also worth noting is the commissioning of the only maximum-security prison at Ankaful in 2011 which is still without the workshop infrastructure (phase 2) designated to provide essential vocational and educational skills. The lack of emphasis on rehabilitation in Ghana contrasts with countries that measure the success of imprisonment based on the rate of reentry into prisons and evaluation of the effectiveness of intervention programmes in prison (Martin, 2021; Petersilia, 2004; Raynor & Vanstone, 1996).

Following the Ouagadogou and Kampala declarations on prison conditions, some African countries such as Lesotho, South Africa and Zambia have made efforts to reform their prison system to meet the rehabilitation or correctional demands of persons in custody. Several of these countries have gone further to establish separate Ministries of correctional services to ensure the success of these initiatives (Kukupa & Mulenga, 2021; Mujuzi, 2015). In 2019, Nigeria passed the Nigerian Correctional Service Act [NCSA], aimed at transforming its prisons from punitive and safekeeping ideals to a correction-focussed service (NCSA, 2019). Since the Comprehensive Peace Agreement in 2003, Liberia has made efforts to restructure its prisons and measure the success of incarceration with rehabilitation and successful reentry (Ministry of Justice Liberia [MoJ, 2016]). In contrast, in Ghana, the 1972 Prison Act continues to guide a prison system that is based on punitive and warehousing motives and the demands of the time. The GPS is yet to meet current global standards and implement best practices in the treatment and management of persons in custody.

Baffour (2021) notes that the increasing rate of incarceration in Ghana presents challenges of effective rehabilitation in prisons and calls for a new policy and context-relevant intervention programmes targeted at reducing the prison population. The evidence currently available suggests that efforts by the GPS to improve effective community reentry and address recidivism have achieved little success (Dako-Gyeke & Baffour, 2016). This failure is partly due to the many challenges confronting the GPS one of which is overcrowding. Although the problem of overcrowding has marginally improved following the commissioning of the 2000 capacity Ankaful Maximum-Security prison, which increased Ghana's prison capacity to 9945 from 7945, the current overcrowding rate of 40% since 2016 to date is unacceptable (GPS, 2020). The overcrowding rate is also misleading considering that the Ankaful maximum prison which significantly increased the total prison capacity of Ghana to its current rate of 9945 is operating at 36.8% of its full capacity (CHRAJ, 2021) leaving one thousand unoccupied spaces because some people do not meet maximum-security prison criteria (i.e., long sentence and high profile). Thus far, overcrowding is heavily concentrated within central and local prisons, and among prisoners who have committed low-level crimes compared to maximum-security persons in custody who have committed serious offences. The practice of remanding people has compounded the problem of overcrowding. It is our hope the GPS will not be compelled to transfer persons in custody who do not fully meet the maximum prison threshold to Ankaful Maximum-security prison to partly address prison overcrowding. Such a move will undermine the limited rehabilitation efforts and must therefore be avoided. Prison overcrowding impacts effective rehabilitation with people serving short-prison terms denied the chance of vocational and technical training. Nkosi and Maweni's (2020) study in South Africa noted the emotional and psychological impact of prison overcrowding with direct consequences for rehabilitation. Baffour (2021) further observed that poor prison conditions and overcrowding create an unsupportive prison environment, which, in turn, negatively affects rehabilitation. Ibrahim et al. (2015) observed that Ghana's prison overcrowding further exacerbates mental health complications of inmates which are often left untreated. Overcrowding has also created conditions ideal for the smuggling and consumption of licit and illicit substances in Ghana's prisons which officers struggle to control because they are significantly outnumbered (Baffour, 2020). This is a major barrier to rehabilitation considering the negative impact of poor prison conditions on treatment programmes and recidivism (Schubert et al., 2011).

Assessing the current state of rehabilitation in prisons is important for two reasons; first, to make any efforts to improve rehabilitation in Ghana's prisons, it is imperative to have an accurate picture; and second, knowing the current state will help comparison of Ghana's situation with current best practices and the making of culturally appropriate suggestions for improvement where appropriate. We accomplish these two tasks by assessing the perspectives and experiences of various prison stakeholders in Ghana. The contributions of stakeholders to improving prison quality of life cannot be over emphasised. For example, in England and Wales, prison research, evaluations, monitoring and independent reports from organisations and bodies such as HM Inspectorate of Prisons Penal Reform Trust and the Howard Society, prison staff, Independent Management Boards of various prisons, the Parole Board and the Correctional Services Accredited Panel, have to an extent, contributed to upholding the human rights of persons in prison and improving prison conditions and rehabilitation programmes. We hope that an analysis of these various stakeholder perspectives including researchers, prison officers, persons in custody, prosecutors, NGOs and the Commission for Human Rights and Administrative Justice (CHRAJ) will shed some light on the current state of rehabilitation and the gap between rehabilitation aims and implementation.

Over the years, rehabilitation programmes in Ghana have focussed more on the impartation of physical skills and the provision of livelihood post-release at the expense of treatment programmes that target the behavioural, cognitive and emotional transformation of incarcerated individuals (Baffour, 2021; Boakye & Akoensi, 2021). Despite this situation, prison officers have expressed difficulties associated with achieving their goals of welfare and rehabilitation due to the lack of resources. For example, Akoensi (2014) noted the following remarks and observations by prison officers about rehabilitation:

The station does not have any tools and equipment, which would be used to train prisoners as part of their rehabilitation. This is stressful and frustrating. What then is our use as officers? (Male, Lance Corporal)

The conditions are poor. I will say that the job of a prison officer is to rehabilitate prisoners. You will agree that rehabilitation goes with certain ingredients that are virtually absent. This is frustrating. So, what the prison officer can do is to prevent escapes, curb certain behaviours that are prone to hurting others and not tearing the place apart. (Male, Sergeant)

Officers' observations illustrate their understanding and embracing of rehabilitation as integral to their role. Akoensi and Tankebe (2021) further observe that prison officers exhibit favourable attitudes towards the rehabilitation of persons in custody and that officers' relationship with those in custody, fair treatment received from superior officers and their perceptions of self-legitimacy (officers' recognition of their right to power) were important considerations that influenced their attitudes to rehabilitation. The lack of facilities and resources to support rehabilitation frustrates officers, and people in custody have expressed similar sentiments. Baffour's (2021, p. 1169) assessment of factors contributing to reentry in the male-only medium-security prison in Ghana reveals that those in custody are usually dismayed by the paucity of training facilities and how this undermined their motivation:

> During my first sentence I was introduced to many trades, and I decided to learn carpentry, but I couldn't learn because there were no tools for the training, and I don't want to bother myself at this time. (Male, person in custody)

Although persons in custody differed in their motivation to engage with rehabilitation provisions, such sentiments are quite common and tend to undermine their motivation. Obviously, this situation leaves individuals with limited opportunities and upon release, they rely on familial and social ties to assist with transition to community living. Following prison inspections, CHRAJ in its additional role as the prison's ombudsman, has over the years highlighted inadequate prison conditions and ineffective rehabilitation. An inspection in 2019 not only repeats previous observations but also provides a nuanced account of prison conditions and rehabilitation in some selected prisons including Ankaful maximum-security prison, Ho male and female prisons, Nsawam male and female prisons and the Tamale prison (CHRAJ, 2021). They observed that conditions in Ghana prisons, especially in relation to accommodation and feeding, fell short of the minimum requirements demanded by national, regional and international standards and that minimal effort was directed towards the reintegration of people released from the prisons. Young people were also held in these adult prisons in clear violation of the Nelson Mandela Rules that stipulate separation of juvenile and adult inmates (Boakye & Akoensi, 2021).

Even where training programmes exist, most inmates were not motivated to participate in these programmes due to their very long prison sentences, in some cases up to 160 years. What is common among all the prisons, however, is people in custody being allowed regular visits once a week from family members and friends as well as facilities for making phone calls although these varied significantly by prison. For example, at the Ho prisons, persons in custody had opportunities for internships and employment beyond the confines of the prison and they and their supervising prison officers earned wages. At the Nsawam prisons, while formal curriculum-based, vocational, technical training programmes were available, only 350 males out of a population of 3524 (3298 convicted persons and 226 on remand) were engaged in educational and vocational training. Overall, with the fragmented and limited state of rehabilitation programmes and facilities in Ghana's prisons, aspirations were rarely met as rehabilitation was available only to a handful of inmates (about 10% of the entire prison estate) and the opportunity of rehabilitation (and its outcomes) is determined by the particular prison where a person is serving their sentence. However, the fact that all the prisons allow regular prison visits (once every week for every prisoner) does at least create the potential to aid reformative attitudes among persons in custody. The role of family contact and support in facilitating desistance upon release from prison has been established in the criminological literature (Calverley, 2019).

Amnesty International (2012) also made similar observations about inadequate prison conditions undermining rehabilitation after visiting several prison establishments in Ghana. It noted that:

> The existing training options seen by Amnesty International, while welcome in themselves, seemed not adequate to equip prisoners for life after release, tended to have only basic and outdated equipment and were also relatively poorly attended by prisoners. A number of inmates expressed a need for training that was effective and meaningful. Prisoners who were not involved in training gave as a reason a lack of interest in the subjects being taught or a lack of energy due to the limited food they received. (Amnesty International, 2012: 31)

Andrews and Bonta (2010) suggest that effective rehabilitation programmes should focus on the 'criminogenic' needs of persons in custody. They argue that rehabilitation programmes must target specific needs such as substance use, strengthening social ties, antisocial cognition and associations, leisure and recreational activities and employment. Currently, prison rehabilitation programmes in Ghana are employment focussed without any informed careful assessment of the needs of persons in custody. For example, programmes such as drug-related treatment, sexual offense treatment programmes, counselling and other behavioural and cognitive treatments are limited and almost non-existent in most prisons. Moreover, there is no community-based reentry programme designed to ensure effective community reentry of persons who have completed their sentence (Dako-Gyeke & Baffour, 2016). Baffour (2021) argues that in its current form the prison-based community reentry programme administered by the GPS is used by most persons in custody to smuggle banned goods and prohibited substances into the prison. In France, a similar programme called 'permission', or Release on Temporary License (ROTL) in England and Wales, provides opportunities for those in custody to undertake important activities such as meeting their families, attending family functions and employment interviews, taking part in paid or unpaid work and visiting sick relations as part of the effort to prepare them for their release and reentry (Herzog-Evans, 2020; Prison Reform Trust, 2019). To this end, there is the need for the Ghana Prisons Service to review and refocus the reentry programme to advance successful community reentry and promote persons in custody's agency and confidence during reintegration. It will also be necessary to involve the families of persons in custody who often inherit the burden of supporting released persons in custody without appropriate guidance and knowledge.

Current Rehabilitation and Reform Initiatives

Currently, besides the trade training or the impartation of employable skills which is replete with a variety of issues, the diagnostic centre at Nsawam Medium Security Prison is the only programme providing some form of assessment and counselling services for adults in prison. This programme is, however, limited to those in the facility for their first offence and is unable to conduct follow-ups after transitioning into the prison or following release from prison. It is refreshing to learn that the GPS has recognised these impediments to rehabilitation and consequently has reached out to external organisations for assistance to remove them. This effort culminated in the establishment of the Ghana Prisons Reform Project (GPRP) in 2021. This 3-year collaborative project between the GPS, UNODC and US Embassy in Ghana, is funded by the US government with the UNODC as the implementing agent. The project which commenced in 2022 aims to improve prison conditions in relation to accommodation, health and basic services; and develop and implement a risk assessment tool to identify the risk and needs of individuals in custody. The programme further seeks to develop sustainable and effective rehabilitation programmes such as psychosocial support services and enhanced constructive activities for people in custody in some selected prisons (UNODC, 2022).

Overall, the GPRP is aimed at strengthening the GPS compliance with the Nelson Mandela Rules as well as helping the GPS develop a new legislative framework (Ghana Prisons Bill) that puts rehabilitation at the forefront of incarceration. Since the GPS is the originator of the project and actively pursued this package in line with the GPS 10-year strategic plan (2015–2025), the blueprint from international donor (US Embassy) and human right agencies (UNODC), it is hoped that the implementation of this project will benefit from local content. It is important that the project actively involves local experts with knowledge of Ghana's penal sector, prison culture and practices, and has an independent evaluative component to assess its benefits and effectiveness. The GPRP must assume a change from within strategy rather than change from without, where international penal organisations develop prison strategies characterised by a 'top-down didacticism [and] deny recognition to local practices, local people and local knowledge' and impose them on receiving agencies in the global south, which has often hindered reform projects from achieving intended objectives (Jefferson, 2008: 157; also see Boakye & Akoensi, 2021; Cohen, 1982). We also hope that the youth justice sector which is excluded from the current reform project will in the not-too-distant future receive similar priority through local content collaboration with international donors to put rehabilitation at its forefront (Boakye & Akoensi, 2021).

Conclusion

In this chapter, we examined punishment and rehabilitation initiatives in the penal system of Ghana. Our focus on rehabilitation in the prison system is informed by the overwhelming use of custody as punishment and the implicit belief in the deterrence and rehabilitative value of imprisonment and existing interventions for incarcerated persons. Our assessment of the history of prisons, the prison conditions in Ghana and the current intervention programmes for persons in prison challenges the basis for this belief about the deterrence and rehabilitative value of the penal regime. Prison conditions are characterised by overcrowding, neglect and a high degree of control that undermines the dignity of inmates and deny their fundamental rights as citizens (Burke et al., 2019). The problem is exacerbated by the lack of fundamental reforms of the penal system whether in relation to legislation, sentencing practices by the courts or interventions informed by context-relevant research and evidence. The consequence is the overwhelming use of custody and the emphasis the GPS places on discipline and control, with rehabilitation a secondary consideration. However, as Boendermaker et al. (2012: 264) noted 'interventions that focus on deterrence or discipline without aftercare or without therapeutic component, or on self-esteem, are not effective and can even produce negative results'.

As our review shows, the prison system largely survives on the generosity of key stakeholders including international donors and faith-based organisations, especially churches and mosques, who regularly donate food items and equipment to help improve prison conditions. Recently, the Church of Pentecost in Ghana, recognising the increased overcrowding in prisons, has entered an agreement with the Prison Service to build five open camp prisons and transfer their management to the GPS to ease prison overcrowding and improve prisoners' quality of life. In 2021 the church completed a 300-capacity prison facility with modern facilities and handed it over to the GPS as part of this agreement (Ghanaweb, 2021). Although this initiative may seem laudable, it overlooks the fundamental reason for prison overcrowding, which is a broken criminal justice system underpinned by punitive philosophy and laws. It is within this context that the passing of the non-custodial sentencing bill needs to be given the priority that it deserves.

Prison must always be the last resort as a remedy for crime. When deployed, it is important to reflect on its intended purpose. However, the ultimate question is whether prison by its very design can serve the purpose of deterrence or rehabilitation (Bottoms et al., 2004; Liebling & Maruna, 2005). That question about prisons as appropriate settings for effective rehabilitation has become increasingly relevant in western societies (Bottoms, 2022; Liebling, 2022; Maruna & Immarigeon, 2004). The question is more important in a context such as Ghana where prison is essentially an inherited penal institution with foundational ideals that do not necessarily reflect the traditional conception of punishment and rehabilitation.

These concerns also demand caution in our optimism about the effectiveness of intervention programmes in the prison context and call for attention and priority to be given to non-custodial sentencing options, especially for low-level crimes. Where it is considered necessary and appropriate to impose a custodial sentence this must be justified with evidence of the benefit of this option for the individual and society. An intervention programme based on context-relevant research and a robust post-released intervention plan is necessary for effective rehabilitation that promotes inclusion and restores full citizens to those who are found to break the law.

References

Abotchie, C. (1997). *Social control in traditional Southern Eweland of Ghana: Relevance for crime prevention.* Ghana Universities Press.

Addai, D. (2020). Learning behind bars: Motivations and challenges of learners in a correctional facility in Ghana. *International Journal of Education Research, 104*, 1–13. https://doi.org/10.1016/j.ijer.2020.101650

Addo, A. K. (2018). History of prison education in Ghana. In I. Biao (Ed.), *Strategic learning ideologies in prison education program* (pp. 178–196). https://doi.org/10.4018/978-1-5225-2909-5.ch008

Akoensi, T. D. (2014). *A tougher beat? The work, stress, and well-being of prison officers in Ghana.* University of Cambridge Press.

Akoensi, T. D., & Tankebe, J. (2021). Prison officer self-legitimacy and support for rehabilitation in Ghana. *Criminal Justice and Behavior, 47*(1), 22–38.

Amnesty International. (2012). *Prisoners are bottom of the Pile. The Human Rights of Inmates in Ghana.* http://www.amnesty.org/en/library/asset/AFR28/002/2012/en/d5616444-cfd1-482d-bcc5-2a338bb68456/afr280022012en.pdf

Andrews, D. A., and Bonta, J. (2010) (5th ed.) *The psychology of criminal conduct.* Oxford: Routledge.

Appiahene-Gyamfi, J. (1995). *Alternatives to imprisonment in Ghana: A focus on Ghana's criminal justice system.* Master of Arts Thesis, School of Criminology, Simon Fraser University, Burnaby, B.C. Canada.

Asare, A. A. (2021). Prisons as colonial relics: Anti-prison thought and Ghanaian history. In M. J. Coyle & D. Scott (Eds.), *The Routledge International Handbook of Penal Abolition.* Routledge.

Baffour, F. D. (2019). *Rehabilitation as a third priority in a twenty first century prison: Results from three prisons in Ghana* [Paper presentation]. Australian and New Zealand Society of Criminology (ANZSOC) conference 2019, Perth, Australia. https://anzsocconference.com.au/4368

Baffour, F. D. (2020). *Factors contributing to recidivism among inmates in selected Ghana prisons.* James Cook University. https://doi.org/10.25903/7gg4%2Dd857

Baffour, F. D. (2021). Recidivism: Exploring why inmates re-offend in a prison facility in Ghana. *Victims and Offenders, 16*(8), 1161–1181.

Boakye, K. E. (2009). Culture and nondisclosure of child sexual abuse (CSA) in Ghana: A theoretical and empirical exploration. *Law and Social Inquiry, 34*(4), 951–979.

Boakye, K. E., & Akoensi, T. A. (2021). Doing time: Young people and the rhetoric of juvenile justice in Ghana. In A. Cox & L. Abrams (Eds.), *Palgrave International Handbook of Youth Imprisonment.* Palgrave Macmillan.

Boendermaker, L., De Leonieke Boendermaker, Deković, M., & Asscher, J. J. (2012). Interventions. In L. Loeber, M. Hoeve, N. W. Slot, & P. H. Van Der Laan (Eds.), *Persisters and desisters in crime from adolescence into adulthood: Explanation, prevention and punishment.* Ashgate.

Bottoms, A. E. (2022). Criminology and 'positive morality.' In A. Liebling, J. Shapland, R. Sparks, & J. Tankebe (Eds.), *Crime, justice, and social order* (pp. 33–58). Oxford University Press.

Bottoms, A. E., Rex, S., & Robinson, G. (Eds.). (2004). *Alternative to prison: Options for an insecure society*. Willan.

Burke, L., Collett, S., & McNeill, F. (2019). *Reimagining rehabilitation: Beyond the individual*. Routledge.

Calverley, A. (2019). Exploring processes of desistance by ethnic status: The confluence of community, Familial and individual processes. In S. Farrall (Ed.), *The Architecture of Desistance* (pp. 75–95). Routledge.

Clifford, W. (1964). The African view of crime. *The British Journal of Criminology, 4*(5), 483–490.

Cohen, S. (1982). Western crime control models in the Third World: Benign or malignant? In S. Spizer & R. Simons (eds.), *Research in law, crime and social control* (Vol. 4, pp. 85–119). JAI Press.

Commission for Human Rights and Administrative Justice [CHRAJ]. (2021). *CHRAJ'S Monitoring Visits to Prisons: Protecting the Fundamental Human Rights of Persons Deprived of their Liberty in Ghana*. Accra.

Connolly, K., & Greenfield, R. (2017). Building recovery capital: The role of faith-based communities in the reintegration of formerly incarcerated drug offenders. *Journal of Drug Issues, 47*(3), 370–382.

Cox, A., & Abrams, L. (Eds.). (2021). *Palgrave international handbook of youth imprisonment*. Palgrave Macmillan.

Crewe, B. (2011). Depth, weight, tightness: Revisiting the pains of imprisonment. *Punishment and Society, 13*(5), 509–529.

Dako-Gyeke, M., & Baffour, F. D. (2016). We are like devils in their eyes: Perceptions and experiences of stigmatization and discrimination against recidivists in Ghana. *Journal of Offender Rehabilitation, 55*(4), 235–253.

Ghana Prisons Service. (2013). *Annual report 2013*. http://www.ghanaprisons.gov.gh/pdf/Annual%20Report%20Prisons%202013.pdf

Ghana Prisons Service. (2015). Ten-year strategic plan 2015b–2025. http://www.ghanaprisons.gov.gh/pdf/10%20years%20strategic%20Plan%20for%20Ghana%20Prisons.pdf

Ghana Prisons Service (2020). 2020 Annual Prisons Report. Unpublished report.

Ghanaweb News. (2021). *Church of Pentecost constructs ultra-modern 300-bed capacity prison at Ejura Nkwanta*. https://www.ghanaweb.com/GhanaHomePage/NewsArchive/Church-of-Pentecost-constructs-ultra-modern-300-bed-capacity-prison-at-Ejura-Nkwanta-1258867. Accessed 25 April 2022.

Herzog-Evans, M. (2020). French prison day leave and the rationale behind it: Resocialisation or prison management? *European Journal on Criminal Policy and Research, 26*, 247–264.

Ibrahim, A., Esena, R. K., Aikins, M., O'keefe, A. M., & Mckay, M. (2015). Assessment of mental health distress among prison inmate sin Ghana's correctional system: A cross-sectional study using the Kessler Psychological Distress Scale. *International Journal of Mental Health Systems, 9*(17), 1–6.

Ilechukwu, L. C., & Ugwuozor, F. O. (2017). Utilization of religious and philosophy education in uplifting the image of prison inmates and curtailing ex-prisoners' recidivism in Enugu prison yard in Nigeria. *SAGE Open*, 1–15. https://doi.org/10.1177/2158244017730109

Jefferson, A. (2008). Imaginary reform: Changing the postcolonial prison. In P. Carlen (Ed.), *Imaginary Penalities* (pp. 157–171). Willan Publishing.

Jolliffe, D., & Farrington, D. P. (2021). Empathy and reoffending in a UK probation sample. In D. Jolliffe & D. P. Farrington (Eds.), *Empathy versus offending, aggression and bullying: Advancing knowledge using the Basic Empathy scale* (pp. 89–100). Routledge.

Kukupa, P., & Mulenga, K. M. (2021). Does correctional education matter? Perspectives of prisoners at a male adult maximumsecurity prison in Zambia. *International Journal of Educational Research open, 2*, 1–9. https://doi.org/10.1016/j.ijendro.2021.100090

Liebling, A. (2022). Penal legitimacy, well-being, and trust: The role of empirical research in 'morally serious' work. In A. Liebling, J. Shapland, R. Sparks, & J. Tankebe (Eds.), *Crime, justice, and social order* (pp. 273–301). Oxford University Press.

Liebling, A., & Maruna, S. (Eds.). (2005). *The effects of imprisonment* Routledge.

Martin, L. (2021). *Halfway house: Prisoner reentry and the shadow of carceral care*. NYU Press.

Maruna, S., & Immarigeon, R. (2004). *After crime and punishment: Pathways to offender reintegration*. Willan.

Ministry of Justice, Liberia. (2016). *Bureau of justice and rehabilitation*. https://www.moj.gov.lr/bureaus/corrections/

Morag, M., & Teman, E. (2018). The "watchful eye of God": The role of religion in the rehabilitation and reentry of repentant Jewish prisoners. *International Journal of Offender Therapy and Comparative Criminology, 62*(7), 2103–2126.

Mujuzi, J. D. (2015). Human rights and the transfer of sentenced offenders within South Africa and how it could impact on the transfer of offenders from other countries to South Africa. *Journal of Third World Studies, 32*(1), 59–81.

NCSA. (2019). Nigerian Correctional Service Act. https://placng.org/i/wp-content/uploads/2019/12/Nigerian-Correctional-Service-Act-2019.pdf

Nkosi, N., & Maweni, V. (2020). The effects of overcrowding on the rehabilitation of offenders: A case study of a correctional center, Durban (Westville), KwaZulu Natal. *The Oriental Anthropologist, 20*(2), 332–346.

Ouagadougou Declaration and Plan of Action on Accelerating Prisons and Penal Reforms in Africa. (2002). https://www.achpr.org/legalinstruments/detail?id=42

Petersilia, J. (2004). What works in prison reentry? Reviewing and questioning the evidence. *Federal Probation, 68*(2), 4–8.

Prison Reform Trust. (2019). *Release on Temporary License (ROTL)*. London.

Prisons Service Act (NRCD). (1972). *National Redemption Council Decree (NRCD 46)*. https://lawsghana.com/pre_1992_legislation/NRC%20Decree/PRISONS%20SERVICE%20ACT%201972%20(NRCD%2046)/161

Rattray, R. S. (1929). *Ashanti law and constitution*. Clarendon Press.

Raynor, P., & Vanstone, M. (1996). Reasoning and rehabilitation in Britain: The results of the straight thinking on probation (STOP) programme. *International Journal of Offender Therapy and Comparative Criminology, 40*(4), 272–284.

Robins, S. (2009). *Improving Africa's prisons: Prison policy in Sierra Leone, Tanzania and Zambia*. Institute for Security Studies. https://www.files.ethz.ch/ins/112449/N09SEP09

Sarbah, J. M. (1968). *Fanti national constitution* (2nd ed.). Frank Cass and Co., Ltd.

Schubert, C. A., Mulvey, E. P., & Glasheen, C. (2011). Influence of mental health and substance use problems and criminogenic risk on outcomes in serious juvenile offenders. *Journal of American Academy of Child and Adolescent Psychiatry, 50*(9), 925–937. https://doi.org/10.1016/j.jaac.2011.06.006

Seidman, R. (1969). *Ghana prison system, historical perspective: African penal system*. Allan Miller.

Sykes, G. (1958). *The society of captives: A study of a maximum-security prison*. Princeton University Press.

Trivedi-Bateman, N., & Crook, E. L. (2021). The optimal application of empathy interventions to reduce antisocial behaviour and crime: A review of the literature. *Psychology, Crime & Law, 28*(8), 796–819. https://doi.org/10.1080/1068316X.2021.1962870

United Nations Organization for Drugs and Crime (UNODC). (2022). *Strengthening the compliance of the Ghana Prison Service with the United Nations Standard Minimum Rules for the Treatment of Prisoners (the Nelson Mandela Rules)*. Unpublished program summary.

Vanstone, M. (2019). Promoting inclusion and citizenship? Selective reflections on the recent history of the policy and practice of rehabilitation in England and Wales. In P. Ugwudike, H. Graham, F. McNeill, P. Raynor, F. S. Taxman, & C. Trotter (Eds.), *The Routledge Companion to Rehabilitative Work in Criminal Justice*. Routledge.

Ward, T., & Maruna, S. (2007). *Rehabilitation: Beyond the risk paradigm*. Routledge.

Approaches to Rehabilitation in Hong Kong

Wing Hong Chui

As societies contemplate changes in their criminal justice system to contain domestic crime rates, this chapter asks: Does rehabilitation have a role to play in a punitive society, which places great emphasis on 'being tough' on crime and passing down harsh punishments? Is rehabilitation a dying ideal? Being a concept and practice that varies across time, place and socio-cultural context, the value of rehabilitation in an era of stricter laws and rising crime rates needs to be reflected upon and discussed seriously. Owing to a lack of evidence that rehabilitation programmes reduce recidivism, since the 1970s, controversies about the rehabilitation ideal abounded in industrialised countries, such as England and Wales and North America, and industrialising former colonies, such as Hong Kong. As a former British colony, the criminal justice system, including legal and penal systems, in Hong Kong has been largely modelled after the system in England (Chui & Lo, 2017; Lo et al., 2020). While one might assume that the return of sovereignty to China in July 1997 called for a transition away from the rehabilitation ideal founded in England and Wales, contrarily, there is evidence that the practice of rehabilitation has remained stable and popular in the Hong Kong criminal justice system.

W. H. Chui (✉)
The Hong Kong Polytechnic University, Hung Hom, Hong Kong
e-mail: wing-hong.chui@polyu.edu.hk

This chapter aims to examine how various aspects of rehabilitation have been delivered in the Hong Kong criminal justice system. It is structured into four parts. Part I gives a brief account of why the rehabilitative ideal has been maintained in Hong Kong. Examples of rehabilitation mechanisms include the police diversion scheme for young people, non-custodial or community sentences and custodial penalties. In Parts II and III, the historical development and operation of the probation and the prison system are discussed. As both institutions provide service to major formal sentencing options and are firmly rooted on the rehabilitation ideal, they work towards assisting individuals with reintegrating into the community, while also aiming to prevent them from causing harm to the society. Where appropriate, official statistics and empirical research findings will be discussed to offer a comprehensive assessment of the effectiveness of rehabilitative practices. It is argued that the strong faith and commitment to maintaining rehabilitation in Hong Kong is based on strong public support for rehabilitation work as well as promising results derived from a variety of recidivism studies. The concluding part discusses future directions in rehabilitation practice and research in order to improve the quality and outcome of rehabilitation in Hong Kong.

Rehabilitation in the Hong Kong Criminal Justice System

At the outset, it should be emphasised that a consensus on the definition of rehabilitation is still lacking in the criminological literature and beyond (Crow, 2001; Forsberg & Douglas, 2020; Raynor & Robinson, 2009; Robinson & Crow, 2009; Wade & de Jong, 2000; Ward & Maruna, 2007). While acknowledging the fact that rehabilitation is a central goal of many criminal justice systems, conceptual clarity is very much needed. For instance, some use rehabilitation interchangeably with terms such as 'therapy', 'treatment', 'intervention', 'reform', 'punishment', 'harm reduction', 're-entry', 'reintegration', 'resettlement' and 'anti-recidivism' (Forsberg & Douglas, 2020; McNeill, 2014). A precise and concise definition that has been suggested by Cullen and Gilbert (1982) is that rehabilitation is defined as treatment aimed at reforming the miscreant and preventing future criminal behaviour (see pp. 48–50). It is very often conceptualised in behavioural terms such as desistance from crime, reduction of personal and social problems associated with offending behaviours and law-abidingness. Miller and Gaines (2018) suggested that the rehabilitation model is based on the premise that an individual's offending is related to various individual and social factors such as personality problems, poor schooling, unemployment, lack of adequate parental supervision, poverty and community disorganisation. It also follows that the removal of these factors will bring about his or her positive changes (Miller & Gaines, 2018). Furthermore, the model places great emphasis on the treatment, welfare and therapy of the individual in order to help him or her assume normal social roles.

It is worth briefly mentioning that in the 1970s doubts were cast on the effectiveness of rehabilitative treatment programmes in England and Wales, North America and other industrialised countries (Brody, 1976; Martinson, 1974). Hudson (1996: 29–30) summarises some of the criticisms of rehabilitative penalties:

> … some techniques used in the name of rehabilitation were grossly intrusive with respect to the moral integrity, personality and civil liberties of offenders. Behaviourist techniques such as aversion therapy, chemical reduction of aggression or libido, even psychosurgery, were used in the name of treatment—techniques which would be condemned as 'cruel and unusual' if they were acknowledged as punishment, but were more readily defended if they were supposedly for the offenders' own good. (Hudson, 1987; Kittrie, 1973; see also Chui, 2001: 278)

Despite this, based on various written reports and policy documents, Hong Kong criminal justice personnel and supporting institutions demonstrated considerable interest in the 'rehabilitation ideal' (Chui, 2017; Laidler, 2009; Lo, 2017; Vagg, 1991). As argued by Adorjan and Chui (2014, 2022), to make sense of Hong Kong's historical and contemporary commitment to rehabilitation, especially for the young, it is important to first understand Hong Kong's unique history. There is, in contrast to general global trends, still confidence in the rehabilitative efficacy of criminal justice responses to crime. Emphasis on the use of rehabilitative programmes, counselling services and social work interventions has been heavily placed by two major criminal justice organisations, including the Social Welfare Department (SWD) and the Correctional Services Department (CSD) of the Government of the Hong Kong Special Administrative Region. For instance, the SWD stresses the use of social work approaches in achieving rehabilitation (SWD, 2021a, 2021b), while the CSD has set up a new division to focus on rehabilitative services for persons in custody and those who are required to put on post-release supervision orders since 1998 (Audit Commission, 2015; Tam & Heng, 2008). Both probation officers and correctional officers may focus on offering help and assistance to people during their penalties or following their discharge from residential training or prison in order to address their family problems, unemployment, substance abuse issues and/or poor interpersonal skills. While acknowledging the varied approaches being used by these two government departments, their ultimate goals are to help transform those who offend into law-abiding citizens and contributing members to society, as well as to prevent them from causing further harm to society.

Robinson and Crow (2009) opined that rehabilitation can be relevant in a number of ways in the criminal justice system, including 'rehabilitation and diversion', 'rehabilitative punishment' and 'rehabilitation beyond punishment'. In Hong Kong, access to rehabilitative or treatment services during the pre-trial stage is made available to juveniles between the ages of 10 and below 18. Under the Police Superintendent's Discretion Scheme, subject to the discretion exercised by a police officer in the rank of Superintendent or above, a caution can be administered to the juveniles in lieu of laying a charge and initiating formal court prosecution. To be eligible for cautioning, juvenile and young suspects must confess voluntarily or unequivocally their criminal behaviour and the nature of the offence must be petty. Most importantly, the juveniles, who are usually before the court for the first-time or second-time, and their parents or guardians must agree to the cautioning. Under the Scheme, a juvenile is put on police supervision for a period of two years or until he or she reaches the age of 18, whichever is earlier (Hong Kong Police Force, 2022). Juveniles may either be directly supervised with the police officer or be referred to non-governmental organisations for rehabilitative help and social work treatment:

> Community Support Service Scheme (CSSS) aims at providing supporting services to children and youth cautioned under the Police Superintendent's Discretion Scheme, the arrested youth and their peers so as to assist them to be reintegrated into the community, eliminate their deviant and unlawful behaviour and to reduce their likelihood of law infringement. The service content includes individual and family counselling, therapeutic groups, skill training/educational groups, community services, crime prevention programmes … . (SWD, 2021c)

The inter-agency collaboration between the Hong Kong Police Force and the SWD is an illustrative example that demonstrates their commitment to rehabilitation through support and help, rather than punishment via formal prosecution and sentencing. A rehabilitative strategy that shapes at-risk young people and juveniles towards more pro-social behaviour during their formative stage is consequently particularly attractive (Chui, 2001, 2006). The next two parts of the chapter are concerned with the delivery of rehabilitation in the contexts of probation and prison.

Social Work Model of Probation

Undeniably, one of the key criminal justice actors involved in delivering rehabilitation is the probation officer. In many respects, the probation system in Hong Kong has been largely modelled from the one in England and Wales. However, a close examination of the two systems reveals that the aims and roles of the Probation Service are now very different from one another. For instance, the intended goal of probation is to provide individuals with supervision and social work counselling in Hong Kong (Chui, 2002, 2003). Rehabilitation has long been at the heart of the Probation Service throughout decades of its existence:

> The overall objective of services for offenders is to help them become law-abiding citizens and reintegrate into the community. This is achieved through both community-based and residential services, adopting social work approaches. It is hoped that through proper supervision, counselling, academic, vocational and social skills training, the offenders can be equipped with the necessary skills to deal with life demands. (Director of Social Welfare, 1997: 52)

> [Probation Service] provides statutory supervision and counselling service with utilisation of community resources to help probationers to reform, reintegrate into the society and become law-abiding citizens. (SWD, 2021d)

The specific objectives of the Probation Service are: (1) to make recommendation to the court on the suitability of a person to be put on probation order; (2) to implement the court's directives on statutory supervision, the treatment and rehabilitation of those put under probation order; (3) to assist probationers in making positive changes in their attitude and behaviour, and to become law-abiding citizens; (4) to enhance their life coping skills to avoid re-offending; (5) to strengthen their family support in the process of rehabilitation and (6) to utilise community resources to handle the needs of individuals referred by court and, where necessary, those of their family members (SWD, 2021d). Conversely, since the late 1990s, there have been drastic and 'radical' changes in the development of the Probation Service in England and Wales (Robinson, 2021; Tidmarsh, 2020). Probation is seen as one form of punishment to achieve crime reduction, crime prevention and public safety in England and Wales. According to the HM Prison and Probation Service (2021: 6), a simpler description of the Probation Service in England and Wales is now 'Assess, Protect and Change'.

Probation was introduced in Hong Kong on a formal statutory basis right from the beginning and was 'basically an import from overseas in colonial times' (Chan, 1996: 101, see also Lee, 2009) in the early twentieth century. Its inception was due to the belief that in giving the individual a chance to reform himself or herself the ethos of rehabilitation was still emphasised and valued. The use of social work approaches to rehabilitate people who have been offended was formally and explicitly spelt out in the *White Paper 1973* (Lee, 1973). On the one hand, during the probation period, the probationer is allowed to remain in the community for employment or schooling and can thus, from an economic point of view, be an asset to the society. On the other hand, the probationer is helped to stand on his or her own feet under the guidance of a probation officer, and this thus spares the government any expense involved in keeping him or her in custody (Lee, 1973; Mak, 1973). Chui (2017: 296–297) gives a brief account of the early development of probation:

> The first step towards putting the probation system into effect was the *Juvenile Offenders Ordinance* in 1933 under which juvenile offenders may be placed on probation at the direction of the court. The probation officers were attached to the Police Force until 1938 when the service was taken over by the Prisons Department. A further change took place in 1948 when the Probation Service was grouped under the Social Welfare Office established as a branch of the Secretariat for Chinese Affairs in post-war Hong Kong. The Probation Service was also upgraded to professional status upon the appointment in 1950 of the late Donald Peterson, a trained social worker from Australia, who headed the development of the Probation Section of the Social Welfare Office. … The final *Probation of Offenders Bill* was passed in 1956 which extended the probation system to adult offenders. (Chan, 1996; Huang, 1970; Lee, 1973; Mak, 1973)

In Hong Kong, the *Probation of Offenders Ordinance* (Cap. 298), as revised and amended, details the responsibilities and core tasks of probation officers, and how an individual should be supervised in legal terms. Section 9 of the said Ordinance sets out that the Chief Executive may by notification in the Gazette appoint a principal probation officer, and probation officers of either sex. Probation, as a formal community sentence, applies to those aged ten years old and up. Before making a probation order, the court shall consider carefully the circumstances leading to the offence, the seriousness of the offence, the attitude of the person towards his or her offending behaviour and the recommendation of the probation officer in the social inquiry report (or the pre-sentence report). A great variety of added conditions or requirements can be attached to the probation order, including: (1)

work and reside as directed; (2) abstain from dangerous drugs; (3) submit urine test; (4) any withdrawal drug treatment programmes as directed; (5) psychological treatment; (6) psychiatric treatment; (7) curfew order (usually between 11:00 p.m. and 6:00 a.m. of the following day); (8) progress report (that is attending the court usually at halfway through the sentence in order to demonstrate improvement in behaviour) and (9) attend group and rehabilitative programmes (cited in Chui, 2017). Probation officers usually recommend these additional conditions with reference to the needs and problems of probationers identified in the social inquiry report tendered to the court for final decision. The court shall explain to the individual in a language understood by him or her the effect of the order (including any additional conditions proposed to be attached). If they are under the age of 14, the court shall not make the order unless a willingness to comply with the order is expressed. According to Section 5 of the Ordinance, if at any time during the probation period it appears that a probationer has failed to comply with any of the requirements of the order or has committed another offence, he/she is liable to be brought back to the court for re-sentencing in the light of both new and old offences.

The Probation Service still preserves its social work identity, and a wide range of rehabilitative services provided by the authorities is mainly delivered through social work methods such as casework, groupwork and family intervention (Chan, 1996). All probation officers are required to have a degree in social work and be registered social workers in Hong Kong. They are employed in the position of Assistant Social Work Officers or Social Work Officers by the Government and will usually have a job rotation to other services within the SWD every two or three years. In order to supplement the generic social work knowledge and skills they have gained from their social work undergraduate training, new probation staff are offered induction training courses and regularly supervised by a senior probation supervisor. It is generally believed that a qualified social worker is equipped with professional knowledge, values and skills to establish a trusting relationship with probationers and to facilitate them to change their offending behaviours and promote a pro-social lifestyle. Probation officers retain considerable autonomy in designing treatment plans and methods of intervention. An empirical study with 115 adult probationers aged from 18 to 35 reported that the Probation Service placed emphasis on an individualised casework treatment approach to the probationer and the length of each interview ranged from 20 to 90 minute (Chui, 2003, 2004).

Apart from having regular individual face-to-face supervision meetings with probationers, probation officers may arrange home visits, family counselling and specialised treatment programmes felt necessary for successful rehabilitation. For instance, community-based drug treatment programmes will usually be arranged for drug-abusers and unemployed probationers will be referred to the voluntary sector to seek help with employment during their probation period. Where appropriate, probationers and their family members are referred to approved institutions run by the SWD or residential homes for children and youth with emotional or behavioural problems run by non-governmental organisations, related units or agencies for psychological treatment, welfare services and other services such as Volunteer Scheme for Probationers (SWD, 2021d).

Neither the doctrine of rehabilitation nor the social work model of probation is under public scrutiny and criticism in Hong Kong. This can be attributed to the fact that the Probation Service has achieved a high completion rate of probation orders. In the financial year 2020–2021, the total number of satisfactorily closed cases was 1094, whereas the total number of unsatisfactorily closed cases was only 113 (SWD, 2021e). Taking these official statistics at face value, around 10.3% of the cases closed are considered unsuccessful, thereby painting a rosy picture in terms of its overall effectiveness. Nevertheless, relying on official records to measure effectiveness of a penal sentence is not without problems. A number of re-offences may go undetected and unreported for various reasons. These statistics rely very much on the law enforcers' ability to detect crime and also their willingness to report the breach of the order to the court formally. Thus, the statistics are only a proxy of the effectiveness of the sentence, and empirical investigations on the effectiveness of probation are much needed in Hong Kong.

The Delivery of Rehabilitation in the Context of Prison

Another key criminal justice actor in delivering rehabilitation is the prison officer. In contrast to the Probation Service, a custodial sentence requires the individual to be locked up in the correctional institution. According to the sentencing tariff, prisons are suited to those who have committed serious offences or those who repeatedly offend who pose threats to community safety. CSD is a disciplinary force, administering a detention centre, drug addiction treatment centres, rehabilitation centres, training centres and minimum, medium and maximum security prisons for those aged 14 or above (Lo, 2017). In addition to these correctional institutions, halfway houses are offered to young and adult supervisees released under supervision of the Release Under Supervision Scheme, the Pre-release Employment Scheme and the Post-release Supervision of Prisoners Scheme for temporary shelter during their adjustment period after release (CSD, 2021a). Table 1 shows the average daily number of persons in custody (PIC) by category and gender. The official data show a decreasing number of people who are on remand and imprisoned from 2016 to 2020.

The vision of the CSD is to be an 'internationally acclaimed Correctional Service helping Hong Kong to be one of the safest cities in the world' (CSD, 2020a). The ways to achieve this aim are: to ensure a safe, humane and healthy custodial environment; to join hands with various stakeholders (such as volunteers, non-governmental organisations, business sectors and religious workers) to create opportunities for rehabilitation and to promote law-abiding and inclusive concepts through community education. Five values, including integrity, professionalism, humanity, discipline and perseverance, are upheld by all staff members of CSD (see Table 2). Prison officers see themselves as the 'rehabilitation facilitator' to bring about positive changes among the prisoners.

Table 1 Average daily number of persons in custody by category and gender

Category	2016 (No. of persons)	2017 (No. of persons)	2018 (No. of persons)	2019 (No. of persons)	2020 (No. of persons)
Sentenced persons					
Male	5421	5362	5030	4633	3919
Female	1453	1456	1382	1261	1020
Sub-total	6873	6818	6412	5894	4939
Persons on remand					
Male	1351	1419	1594	1548	1666
Female	322	292	296	295	296
Sub-total	1673	1711	1890	1843	1962
Overall[a]					
Male	6771	6781	6624	6181	5586
Female	1775	1748	1678	1556	1317
Total	8546	8529	8303	7737	6902

Source CSD (2021a: Table 1.1)
Notes There may be a slight discrepancy between the sum of individual items and the respective totals as shown in the above due to rounding
[a]Including detainees

Table 2 Five values of CSD staff members

- *Integrity*—We are accountable for our actions by upholding high ethical and moral standards, and have the honour of serving our society
- *Professionalism*—We strive for excellence in correctional practice and resource optimization, and take pride in our roles as society's guardian and rehabilitation facilitator
- *Humanity*—We respect the dignity of all people with [an] emphasis on fairness and empathy
- *Discipline*—We respect the rule of law with [an] emphasis on orderliness in the pursuit of harmony
- *Perseverance*—We are committed to serving our society, keeping constant vigilance and facing challenges with courage

Source CSD (2020a)

As mentioned earlier, since January 1998, the Correctional Services Department has set up a Rehabilitation Division, which is headed by an Assistant Commissioner, to oversee the rehabilitation of the individual and devise effective rehabilitative strategies. It comprises five major units or sections, including Rehabilitation Unit (Assessment and Supervision), Rehabilitation Unit (Welfare, Counselling and Supervision), Education Unit, Industries and Vocational Training Section and Psychological Services Section. The Rehabilitation Unit (Assessment and Supervision) is responsible for conducting the pre-sentence assessment for persons on remand, delivering rehabilitative programmes for inmates and providing a selected group of prisoners for statutory supervision upon their discharge. The Rehabilitation Unit (Welfare, Counselling and Supervision) offers welfare and counselling services to inmates and provides supportive services to those who are placed on post-release supervision orders. The Education Unit is responsible for delivering and co-ordinating half-day formal education classes for young PIC, and providing adult PIC with support to encourage their voluntary participation in self-studying. With the aim of enhancing their employability, the Industry and Vocational Training Section provides PIC with opportunities to acquire good work habits and contribute to society during incarceration. While the vocational training unit is available to prisoners under the age of 21, industrial employment is available for PIC to engage in work covering 13 trades such as garment making, leather products, sign making, metalwork, bookbinding and printing. About 6000 inmate workers are currently engaged in these types of industrial work every day and these products are then supplied to government departments and tax-supported bodies. Psychological services devise professional therapeutic programmes for PIC to improve their institutional adjustment and address their offending behaviours. A number of specialised initiatives, such as violence prevention programme and inmate-parent programme, have been developed by the Psychological Services Unit to improve the inmates' skills and knowledge instrumental to rehabilitation (CSD, 2021c). The creation of various learning and meaningful opportunities for PIC by collaborating closely with community stakeholders, such as social workers and their allied professionals from the non-governmental organisations, religious workers and volunteers is conducive to effective rehabilitation. This is referred to as 'creative rehabilitation' for PIC (CSD, 2021b).

The CSD has identified four important factors that contribute to successful rehabilitation in an inclusive society: (1) safe custody, (2) appropriate rehabilitative programmes, (3) the person's responsivity and determination to change and (4) community support (CSD, 2020b). In this respect, the Department is committed to look for strategies to improve the quality of the correctional services in relation to these four factors. The emphasis of the rehabilitative programmes may vary according to the type of institution. For example, Adorjan and Chui (2022) noted an emphasis on self-discipline and moral character in response to youth transgressive behaviour:

> ... the ethos and penal philosophy of welfare protectionism during this time was evident with the development of training centres for youth in Hong Kong, which were influenced by the British Borstal institutions during its penal-welfare era (Fox, 1998), and which were comparable to the Canadian training schools given their quasi-indeterminate sentences geared to holding youth in custody to enable character transformation (Chui, 1999, 2001; Jones & Vagg, 2007). The disciplinary welfare tariff was also applied through the youth detention centre, which was (and is) touted to instil rehabilitation through the application of 'short, sharp shock' sentences (Chui, 2005: 71), 'comparable to spending a short period in a military prison, which includes a combination of onerous physical labour, foot drills, physical education, vocational training, counselling, group therapy activities and recreation'. (Adorjan & Chui, 2014: 25) ... (p. 960)

Depending on the requirement imposed by the custodial sentence, the length of statutory supervision or post-release supervision varies from 12 months to 3 years. Young prisoners are subject to a period of statutory supervision by the two Rehabilitation Units. However, the provision of reintegration services is not available to all adult prisoners. The provision of reintegration or post-release supervision is to ensure continued care and support given to those who are released from the penal institution and who are released under various schemes, such as the Release Under Supervision

Scheme, Pre-release Supervision Scheme, Supervision After Release Scheme and Pre-release Employment Scheme (Lo, 2017). Regular face-to-face contact and home visit are arranged to ensure a gradual transition from the institution to the community. Table 3 shows the statistics on the success rates of different reintegration programmes within the supervision period.

The success rates are calculated based on whether the case complies with the conditions and requirements during the supervision period. As shown in Table 3, while most completed their orders satisfactorily under different post-release supervision schemes, slightly more than half of drug-related prisoners failed to comply with statutory supervision order. The Audit Commission (2015) put one recommendation:

> The CSD compiles success rates (measured by the percentages of the supervisees who have completed their statutory supervision periods without reconviction, and also without relapse to drug abuse in case of persons discharged from the Drug Addiction Treatment Centres) to monitor the effectiveness of its reintegration programme. Besides, it compiles recidivism rates (measured by percentages of re-admission of all local persons who have been under the CSD custody to correctional institutions within two years after discharge) to provide feedback for programme monitoring and evaluation. Audit noted that persons discharged from the Drug Addiction Treatment Centres had lower success rates and higher recidivism rates than those of discharged persons from other types of correctional institutions. The CSD needs to conduct a review of its rehabilitation services for persons detained in the Centres … . (p. viii)

Table 3 Success rates of reintegration programmes within the supervision period

Reintegration programmes	2016 (%)	2017 (%)	2018 (%)	2019 (%)	2020 (%)
Rehabilitation Centre Programme	95.5	94.2	96.1	100	100
Young Persons in Custody under Prison Programme	96.5	97.4	96.7	93.8	94.2
Detention Centre Programme	97.8	94.1	100	100	100
Training Centre Programme	74.2	77.8	79.2	76.9	77.8
Drug Addiction Treatment Centre Programme	50.6	53.4	51.6	56.6	57.6
Post-release Supervision Scheme	92.6	90	95.3	94.3	95.8
Supervision After Release Scheme	100	100	100	100	100
Pre-release Employment Scheme	100	100	100	100	100
Release Under Supervision Scheme	100	100	100	95.2	100
Conditional Release Scheme	100	N.A	100	100	100

Source Adapted from CSD (2021b: Table 2.4)
Note N.A. denotes Not applicable

Table 4 Recidivism rate[a] of local rehabilitated offenders between 2014 and 2018

	Year of discharge[b]				
	2014 (%)	2015 (%)	2016 (%)	2017 (%)	2018 (%)
Offenders aged below 21	12.6	11.9	10.2	9.8	10.2
Offenders aged 21 and over	27.2	28.3	25.7	25.8	23.1
All offenders	25.9	27.1	24.8	24.8	22.5

Source: CSD (2021b: Table 2.5)
[a]Recidivism rate is defined as the percentage of re-admissions of local rehabilitated offenders to the correctional institutions following conviction of new offences within two years after discharge. The local rehabilitated offenders refer to those persons who hold a Hong Kong Identity Card (but excluding imported labour, foreign domestic helpers and consulate staff) and are released after serving their sentence
[b]For a particular year, only the first discharge of a person in the year is included

Table 4 shows the recidivism rate of local rehabilitated people who hold a Hong Kong Identity Card. Recidivism rate is defined as the percentage of re-admissions of rehabilitated people to the correctional institutions following conviction of new offences within two years after discharge. The overall recidivism rate ranges from 22.5 to 27.1%.

The Future of Rehabilitation as a Prime Goal in Hong Kong

The primary aim of this chapter is to examine how the probation and prison systems in Hong play a significant role in delivering rehabilitation in Hong Kong. There is evidence that rehabilitation or reform has still been the prime goal in the Hong Kong criminal justice system, which was largely modelled from England and Wales. Rehabilitation—as a theory of sentencing, an objective of a criminal sentence, a means of therapeutic intervention, a process of personal transformation and an outcome of the penal sanctions—has been highlighted in various official documents and criminological literature. The strong faith and commitment to maintaining rehabilitation in Hong Kong is based on strong public support for rehabilitation work as well as promising results derived from official data (Laidler, 2009; Lo, 2017). In a telephone survey conducted by Chui et al. (2015), a random sample of 202 Chinese adults aged 18 and above were asked whether they believed rehabilitating individuals convicted of sexual offences was a waste of time. About 68.8% of the respondents disagreed that this was futile, with 22.5% neither agreeing nor disagreeing. This finding shows that public attitude towards rehabilitation is generally positive.

While rehabilitation has retained a significant role in the Hong Kong probation and prison system, the effectiveness of their rehabilitation programmes has not been fully investigated due to a lack of empirical research. Although it may be true that frontline practitioners have strong faith in the rehabilitative model of probation practice or prison work based on their practical experience, empirical evidence is required to develop 'evidence-based correctional practice'. Identifying what works and what does not work is important to developing an understanding of effective supervision. Otherwise, claims of the success of probation and prison are simply empty generalisations. Studying the effectiveness of criminal sentences is not an easy task. One of the first steps is to operationalise the goals of these sentences. In the context of Hong Kong, the rate of completion is primarily used as a measure of outcome to assess the success (or otherwise) of the sentences. It can be one of the indicators to examine the level of compliance, but we should not accept it uncritically. Other measures of outcome, such as self-reported offending, change of attitudes to offending and improvements in personal and social problems, should also be taken into consideration in future evaluation research. All this would help provide a more accurate picture regarding overall effectiveness. Based on the report compiled by the Audit Commission (2015), a proactive disclosure of the recidivism rates should be adopted:

> While the CSD regularly reported the success rates in its Controlling Officer's Reports, it only disclosed the recidivism rates upon request. As the reported success rates cover discharged persons subject to supervision (i.e. only accounting for 18% of all discharged persons in 2014), the CSD needs to consider proactive disclosure of the recidivism rates which have a wider coverage (i.e. all discharged persons except non-locals) … (p. ix)

On another note, actual probation practice in Hong Kong is still a 'black box' to the public because studies that investigate interactions between probation officers and probationers in reporting sessions are almost non-existent. This kind of study would inform practitioners and policymakers on how a probation sentence turns to a rehabilitative one. Another advantage of evaluation research is that it may help probation officers or social workers reflect on their own interventions, while at the same time proving whether one particular practice model works better than others.

On-going review and evaluation of the effectiveness of rehabilitative strategies is highly recommended to improve the quality of supervision and identify service gaps. For instance, the Audit Commission (2015) conducted a review of the provision of rehabilitative services with a view of identifying room for improvement. Several recommendations were made to CSD in order to improve the quality of counselling and psychological services, vocational training and industries and post-release supervision and community support. The Commission also recommended a thorough review of rehabilitative services for drug inmates and a proactive disclosure of the recidivism rates. All of these recommendations were well received by the Secretary for Justice and the Commissioner of Correctional Services, and appropriate measures have been adopted and implemented to address each of these recommendations. It is hoped that similar audit exercises will be conducted to review the overall rehabilitative strategies in Hong Kong, and that the public will consequently be better informed in both the processes and outcomes.

References

Adorjan, M., & Chui, W. H. (2014). *Responding to youth crime in Hong Kong: Penal elitism, legitimacy and citizenship*. Routledge.

Adorjan, M., & Chui, W. H. (2022). Penal paradigms of juvenile justice in Canada and Hong Kong. In E. Erez & P. Ibarra (Eds.), *The Oxford Encyclopedia of international criminology* (pp. 947–965). Oxford University Press.

Audit Commission. (2015). *Correctional services department*. Audit Commission. https://www.aud.gov.hk/pdf_e/e64ch08.pdf

Brody, S. R. (1976). *The effectiveness of sentencing*. Home Office.

Chan, W. T. (1996). Social work and services for offenders. In I. Chi & S. K. Cheung (Eds.), *Social work in Hong Kong* (pp. 98–111). Hong Kong Social Workers Association.

Chui, W. H. (1999). Residential treatment programs for young offenders in Hong Kong: A report. *International Journal of Offender Therapy and Comparative Criminology, 43*(3), 308–321.

Chui, W. H. (2001). Theoretical underpinnings of community-based sentences and custody for young offenders in Hong Kong. *Hong Kong Law Journal, 31*(2), 266–282.

Chui, W. H. (2002). The social work model of probation supervision for offenders in Hong Kong. *Probation Journal, 49*(4), 297–304.

Chui, W. H. (2003). Experiences of probation supervision in Hong Kong: Listening to the young adult probationers. *Journal of Criminal Justice, 31*(6), 567–577.

Chui, W. H. (2004). Adult offenders on probation in Hong Kong: An exploratory study. *British Journal of Social Work, 34*(3), 443–454.

Chui, W. H. (2005). Detention center in Hong Kong: A young offender's narrative. *Journal of Offender Rehabilitation, 41*(1), 67–84.

Chui, W. H. (2006). Avoiding early intrusion in the lives of children: The need for juvenile justice reform in Hong Kong. *Journal of Youth Studies, 9*(1), 119–128.

Chui, W. H. (2017). Probation and community service orders. In W. H. Chui & T. W. Lo (Eds.), *Understanding criminal justice in Hong Kong* (2nd ed., pp. 291–311). Routledge.

Chui, W. H., Cheng, K.K.-Y., & Ong, R.Y.-C. (2015). Attitudes of the Hong Kong Chinese public towards sex offending policies: The role of stereotypical views of sex offenders. *Punishment and Society, 17*(1), 94–113.

Chui, W. H., & Lo, T. W. (Eds.). (2017). *Understanding criminal justice in Hong Kong* (2nd ed.). Routledge.

Correctional Services Department. (2020a). *Vision, Mission and Values*. Correctional Services Department. https://www.csd.gov.hk/tc_chi/about/about_vmv/abt_vis.html

Correctional Services Department. (2020b). *4 critical success factors towards a safer and more inclusive society*. Correctional Services Department. https://www.csd.gov.hk/english/about/about_4factors/reh_over_4csf.html

Correctional Services Department. (2021a). *Half-way houses*. Correctional Services Department. https://www.csd.gov.hk/english/facility/facility_type/ins_ins_na.html

Correctional Services Department. (2021b). *Annual review 2020*. Correctional Services Department.

Correctional Services Department. (2021c). *Rehabilitation*. Correctional Services Department. https://www.csd.gov.hk/english/reh/reh_overview/reh_over.html

Crow, I. (2001). *The treatment and rehabilitation of offenders*. Sage.

Director of Social Welfare. (1997). *Departmental report*. Government Printer.

Fox, L. (1998). *The English Prison and Borstal Systems*. Routledge.

Frosberg, L., & Douglas, T. (2020). What is criminal rehabilitation? *Criminal Law and Philosophy, 16*, 103–126.

HM Prison & Probation Service. (2021). *The target operating model for probation service in England and Wales*. HM Prison & Probation Service.

Hong Kong Police Force. (2022). *What is police superintendent's discretion?* Hong Kong Police Force. https://www.police.gov.hk/ppp_en/13_faqs/faq_cri.html#:~:text=When%20a%20juvenile%2C%20from%2010,Superintendent's%20Discretion%20Scheme%20(PSDS)

Huang, T. P. (1970). A mini memoir of days gone by. *Hong Kong Probation, 1*(2), 2–9.

Hudson, B. A. (1996). *Understanding justice: An introduction to ideas, perspectives and controversies in modern penal theory*. Open University Press.

Jones, C., & Vagg, J. (2007). *Criminal justice in Hong Kong*. Routledge-Cavendish.

Laidler, K. J. (2009). Correctional services department. In M. S. Gaylord, D. Gittings, & H. Traver (Eds.), *Introduction to crime, law and justice in Hong Kong* (pp. 185–204). Hong Kong University Press.

Lee, S. M. (1973). The probation service in Hong Kong. *International Journal of Offender Therapy and Comparative Criminology, 17*(1), 90–94.

Lee, F. W.-L. (2009). Social welfare department. In M. S. Gaylord, D. Gittings, & H. Traver (Eds.), *Introduction to crime, law and justice in Hong Kong* (pp. 205–221). Hong Kong University Press.

Lo, S. H. C., Cheng, K. K. Y., & Chui, W. H. (2020). *The Hong Kong legal system* (2nd ed.). Cambridge University Press.

Lo, T. W. (2017). Prison and correctional services. In W. H. Chui & T. W. Lo (Eds.), *Understanding criminal justice in Hong Kong* (2nd ed., pp. 312–336). Routledge.

Mak, W. H. (1973). Reminiscence of the early probation work in Hong Kong. In O. D. S. Issue (Ed.), *Social welfare department* (pp. 7–9). Social Welfare Department.

Martinson, R. (1974). What works? Questions and answers about prison reform. *The Public Interest, 35*, 22–54.

McNeill, F. (2014). Punishment as rehabilitation. In G. Bruinsma & D. Weisburd (Eds.), *Encyclopaedia of criminology and criminal justice* (pp. 4195–4206). Springer.

Miller, R. L., & Gaines, L. K. (2018). *Criminal justice in action* (10th ed.). Cengage Learning.

Raynor, P., & Robinson, G. (2009). *Rehabilitation, crime and justice*. Palgrave Macmillan.

Robinson, G. (2021). Rehabilitating probation: Strategies for re-legitimation after policy failure. *The Howard Journal of Crime and Justice, 60*(2), 151–166.

Robinson, G., & Crow, I. (2009). *Offender rehabilitation: Theory, research and practice*. Sage.

Social Welfare Department. (2021a). *Community support service scheme*. Social Welfare Department. https://www.swd.gov.hk/en/index/site_pubsvc/page_young/sub_seryouthrisk/id_cssscheme/

Social Welfare Department. (2021b). *Services for offenders*. Social Welfare Department. https://www.swd.gov.hk/en/index/site_pubsvc/page_offdr/sub_introducti/

Social Welfare Department. (2021c). *Community support service scheme*. Social Welfare Department. https://www.swd.gov.hk/en/index/site_pubsvc/page_young/sub_seryouthrisk/id_cssscheme/

Social Welfare Department. (2021d). *Probation service*. Social Welfare Department. https://www.swd.gov.hk/en/index/site_pubsvc/page_offdr/sub_communityb/id_PO/

Social Welfare Department. (2021e). *Services for offenders: 2020–2021d annual service provision and statistics*. Social Welfare Department. https://www.swd.gov.hk/en/index/site_pubsvc/page_offdr/sub_offdrsps/

Tam, K. Y., & Heng, M. A. (2008). Rehabilitation for young offenders in Hong Kong correctional institutions. *The Journal of Correctional Education, 59*(1), 49–63.

Tidmarsh, M. (2020). The probation service in England and Wales: A decade of radical change or more of the same. *European Journal of Probation, 12*(2), 129–146.

Vagg, J. (1991). Corrections. In H. Traver & J. Vagg (Eds.), *Crime and justice in Hong Kong* (pp. 139–152). Oxford University Press.

Wade, D. T., & de Jong, B. A. (2000). Recent advances in rehabilitation. *British Medical Journal, 320*(7246), 1385–1388.
Ward, T., & Maruna, S. (2007). *Rehabilitation*. Routledge.

Legislations Cited

Juvenile Offender Ordinance (Cap. 266).
Probation of Offenders Bill 1956.
Probation of Offenders Ordinance (Cap. 298).

From Need-Based to Control-Based Rehabilitation: The Hungarian Case

Klára Kerezsi⊙ and Judit Szabó

A Short Introductory History of Rehabilitation Mechanisms

The notion of rehabilitation emerged in the Hungarian Criminal Justice system at the end of the nineteenth century under positivist criminal law and criminology. The new reformatory thoughts contributed to establishing individualisation and personality-based prevention in corrections, and the main goal of the deprivation of liberty became recidivism reduction (Pallo, 2020). As a shift away from proportionality, the Act I. of 1908 (First Criminal Novel) settled the institution of reformatory schools for juveniles with the primary goals being prevention, personality correction and moral change. The first criminal pedagogical theories emerged in this period, and methodological research also started to bloom (Lőrincz, 2006). The First Criminal Novel also established a separate criminal law for juveniles and incorporated probation supervision into the system of criminal law sanctions. Although the state probation supervision system was established in the 1910s, until the

K. Kerezsi (✉)
University of Public Service, Faculty of Law Enforcement, Budapest, Hungary
e-mail: kerezsi.klara@uni-nke.hu

J. Szabó
National Institute of Criminology, Budapest, Hungary

1940s, charities played a crucial role in the patronage of juveniles (Kerezsi, 2002). Helping persons released from prison gradually became a State task between the two world wars.

After World War 2, Stalinian criminal policy gained ground in the country resulting in a politically ideologically heavily determined era in law enforcement. Educational pedagogy was, at best, a slogan in this period (Lőrincz, 2006) and punishment served only as a tool of repression and an instrument of State politics. In the 1950s and 1960s, the aftercare was almost wholly abolished because party state leaders believed that full employment and work obligation alone ensured the social integration of convicts. The Criminal Code of 1961 first formulated the legal rules of probation supervision concerning juveniles, with the purpose of patronage being the increased educational effect and the facilitation of reintegration.

In the 1970s, the legislature began to think differently about rehabilitation. Prisoners released on parole or probation quickly got jobs in factories and were offered accommodation in workers' hostels. The system of professional probation was established in 1970, initially for juveniles and from 1975 for adults as well. The reorganisation of aftercare activity, a turning point in 1975, established the new service of professional probation officers as a part of the court system. Probation became a new criminal measure in the 1978 Penal Code, linking the activity of probation supervision to the formal system of criminal justice. The Penal Code defined the dual purpose of probation: (1.) to prevent the perpetrator from committing another crime and (2.) to assist resocialisation by creating favourable social conditions. The so-called resocialisation approach appeared in the Decree on Penal Enforcement (1979), a further step towards a scientifically grounded law enforcement practice. The Decree—instead of the unrealistic objective of re-education—considered prevention and integration into society the primary goal. The tool for this was thought to be 'pedagogical education'. As a result of the resocialisation approach, essential terms such as classification, differentiation and regime profile (regime characteristics and compatibility of a Hungarian prison) were established in Hungary.

According to the professional approach of the 1980s, 'the peculiarity of the Hungarian (usually socialist) version of treatment was that the formation of personality did not appear primarily as a therapeutic (i.e. psychological) task, but rather as a pedagogical [...] task' (Huszár, 1997: 67). Considering the reasonable possibilities of influence and the personality-damaging effects of the prison, a new concept of education was born and the change in attitude was most evident in accepting the principles of responsibility and self-esteem. After the regime change, employment opportunities disappeared and it became increasingly difficult to ensure the conditions for reintegration. Probation officers tried to supplement the meagre resources to support prisoners with institutional and professional collaborations in the changed situation.

At the start of the new millennium, an extensive development process in criminal justice and crime prevention began, including victim assistance and reparation justice. As part of the process, a new Criminal Procedure Act came into force in 2003, with a national crime prevention strategy and a law on victim protection. As part of the comprehensive penal policy reform, a unified Probation Service was established in 2003 under the supervision of the Ministry of Justice, with its activities extended to both juveniles and adults. The Legal Aid Service was established in 2004, and the Victim Support Service in 2005. The Ministry introduced mediation in criminal matters in 2007, and a new Penitentiary Code was enacted in 2013. In the last ten years, however, the organisation and the responsibilities of probation officers have changed. A Ministerial Decree ordered the risk analysis of probationers, and in August 2014, the execution of probation supervision tasks related to parole was transferred to the organisation of penitentiary administration.

Current Mechanisms and Their Policy, Political and Statistical Context

Rehabilitation in the correctional context in Hungary is a much less popular term than reintegration and resocialisation, perhaps because rehabilitation was discredited after the crisis of Western correctionalism (Nagy & Vig, 2018). Moreover, in the provisions of the Criminal Enforcement Code (Act CCXL of 2013), besides reintegration, the term (re)settlement is also used, while rehabilitation is only mentioned in its medical connotation and not in a social context.

Legal rehabilitation, so-called 'exemption' is regulated by the Hungarian Criminal Code. Upon exemption, the convicted person is 'relieved from the detrimental consequences attached by law to any prior conviction' and 'shall be deemed to have a clean criminal record, so he cannot be required to give an account of any conviction from which he has been exempted'. The general exemption method is decreed by the law after a specified period, but it can also be based on a court ruling or an act of clemency. The consequences of a conviction are determined not only by criminal law but also by sectoral laws, mainly in employment bans. These collateral consequences are linked to the punishment and may significantly hinder social reintegration, despite the institution of legal rehabilitation (Lukács & Víg, 2019).

The backbone of Hungarian legislation in prison-based rehabilitation is the new Penitentiary Code that entered into force in 2015. It moved towards a complex system of rehabilitation and reintegration that aims to build on the will and active cooperation of inmates involved in the process. The outmoded concept of 'correctional education' of the former regulations was replaced by 'reintegration'. Some conceptualise this move away from the previous paternalistic approach as a paradigm shift (Pallo, 2018). According to the Penitentiary Code, imprisonment enforces the adverse consequences outlined in the final judgement, facilitates reintegration into society and develops law-abiding behaviour. Reintegration programmes are all activities and programmes that aim to reduce the disadvantages resulting from the convicted person's former life circumstances and lifestyle and the development of their personality and social skills. During the enforcement of custodial punishment, the development of the convicted person's self-esteem, personality and sense of responsibility are to be ensured.

A new element of the system drawn up by the Penitentiary Code is the so-called risk analysis and management system. The risk assessment process starts at the time of admission to the prison and is based on applying a 'preventive measurement tool'. It is aimed at determining the risk of recidivism and other behaviours related to imprisonment, namely (a) prisoner escape and its attempt, (b) suicidal behaviour, (c) self-harm, (d) violent action or attempted violent action against any person, (e) leadership, organiser, executive role activity in the criminal and prisoner subculture and (f) abuse of psychoactive substances. The report on the risk assessment results contains the measured levels of risk for each behaviour and the medical, psychological, safety and reintegration tasks necessary for risk management. According to the principle of individualisation, the level of risk (low, medium, or high), respective regime rules to be applied for the individual and participation in employment, education and reintegration programmes shall be determined based on the risk analysis results. Among reintegration programmes the penitentiary system operates compulsory programmes (employment, participation in education under the age of 16, participation in a contracted programme), reward programmes (participation in a priority public education or sports programme) and optional programmes (self-help groups, school groups, professional circles) as well (Forgács, 2020).

Legal regulations outline several possibilities for contact with the outside world (see Table 1): In the recent few years, however, a strict policy was implemented in penitentiary institutions. In 2019 transparent plastic screens were installed in the visiting rooms of prisons, making physical contact of inmates with relatives practically impossible (Hungarian Helsinki Committee, 2020). Fixed tariff rates of phone calls are set at an extremely high rate, and the deposit for prison mobile phones also puts a heavy financial burden on inmates. Restrictions introduced due to the COVID-19 pandemic made contact with relatives and the outside world even more limited.

The goal of the Hungarian Prison Service is to maintain *full employment* in penitentiary institutions, only excluding those who are not able to work. Detainees are employed by industrial or agricultural prison companies, penitentiary institutions or public–private partnerships. A convicted person's employment is not considered an employment relationship but a special penitentiary relationship. Therefore, her or his time working during enforcement does not count towards the pension.

Access to *education* is essential in prisons (Ivanics, 2021; Miklósi & Juhász, 2019). Primary education provided by state and other schools that have a contractual relationship with the institution is available in most penitentiary institutions, and secondary education in many. Vocational training is mainly carried out within the frames of different projects. According to data from the Hungarian Prison Service (2020), in 2019/2020 the enrolment rate in primary education was 27%, secondary education 39.5%, vocational training 32.5% and in higher education, 0.76% among inmates. While enrolment

Table 1 Pillars of reintegration process

Traditional elements	New or partially new elements

(1.) Contacts (supporting family and social relationships)
(A.) Without leaving the institution
  (a.) Correspondence
  (b.) Telephone conversation
  (c.) Sending and receiving parcels
  (d.) Receiving a visitor
  (e.) Electronic communication (Skype)
(B.) Involving leaving the institution
  (a.) Reception of visitors outside the prison
  (b.) Absence and leisure
  (c.) Free weekend
	(4.) Exploration and optimisation of risk elements
	(A.) Primary risk analysis (admission)
	(B.) Periodic review risk analysis (every 6 months)
	(C.) Extraordinary risk classification

(2.) Improving labour market opportunities and maintaining physical and mental well-being	(5.) Strengthening of internal motivation
(3.) Education, vocational training, advanced studies	

Source The compilation was made by the authors

numbers for primary and higher education seem to have decreased in the last ten years, secondary and vocational training participation rates show a positive trend. In addition, prisons offer recreational, sports, cultural and religious activities to support the rehabilitation process. Special treatment programmes are also administered based on the risk analysis procedure results. Hungarian penitentiary institutions operate special regime units for inmates with special treatment needs (see Table 2). In these regime units, the order of enforcement and programmes and activities aimed at rehabilitation are adjusted to the specific needs of particular groups of people.

The most critical reintegration phases are the periods immediately before and after release. Release from prison can occur after completing the sentence and being placed in reintegration custody due to conditional release or based on an act of clemency. Before their expected release inmates receive help and support to ensure social and personal conditions conducive to successful re-entry. The length of this pre-release support period is regulated by law and depends on the length of sentence. Penitentiary probation officers are in charge of the preparation for release which is based on an individual care plan or reintegration programme and carried out with the cooperation of the reintegration officer. Help and assistance are given to inmates in several ways, such as obtaining official documents, preparing the social environment for their re-admittance, restoring family ties, organising programmes to support

Table 2 Regimes in Hungarian penitentiary institutions

REGIMES	
Statutory regimes	Regimes are established for practical purposes
Standard regime (detainees who do not require special treatment) • mild, general and strict regimes • lighter rules of execution (EVSZ) • transitional department • admission department • regimes for detainees	Regimes set up to organise the daily schedule of inmates • accommodate working and non-working prisoners separately
Special regimes (detainees with special treatment needs) • curative-therapeutic ward • long-term special regime (HSR) • drug prevention ward • psychosocial ward • low-risk at-risk group (ABE)	Regimes set up for particular groups of detainees considered locally important • non-violent unit • APAC group

Source Forgács. (2019). A fogva tartás és reintegráció fogalmi megközelítése, in Büntetés-végrehajtá reintegrációs ismeretek (Eds.) O. Czenczer and P. Ruzsonyi. Dialóg Campus Kiadó, Budapest, p. 43

social or vocational reintegration, and organising placements in a medical or social care institution.

If conditions specified by law are met, a prisoner sentenced to imprisonment for the first time for a non-violent crime against a person and serving a term of imprisonment not exceeding five years in prison may be placed in reintegration custody by the penitentiary judge based on a proposal from the institution. Reintegration custody means, in practice, the continuous supervision and control of individuals during the six months before release so that they cannot leave home, place of work or another designated place of residence. Sometimes they may be monitored with an electronic remote monitoring device. Although the period after release is of utmost importance it is the least supported part of the rehabilitation process in Hungary. Upon their request aftercare is offered for those released from penitentiary institutions for a maximum term of one year to enhance successful reintegration. According to law, support is given regarding employment and housing issues, continuing studies and medical and therapeutic care. Extra help in finding housing and employment is offered for those released after long-term imprisonment. The penitentiary probation officers provide aftercare with the contribution of local municipalities, employers, civil organisations, religious communities and other volunteers. In reality, aftercare is requested by people released from prison only rarely, and state-run services are minimal. The state relies heavily on NGOs, churches and other charitable organisations to reintegrate those offended, especially during the post-release period (Miklósi & Juhász, 2019). Recently a halfway programme was launched by Váltósáv Foundation and Hungarian Prison Service Headquarters, but services are only available in Budapest. Ex-prisoners face great difficulties on the job market too.

Conditional release or release on parole is a significant legal institution in the reintegration process. In Hungary, early release from prison is based on the discretionary decision of the penitentiary judge, if criteria regulated in law (e.g. that a certain proportion of the sentence has been served) are met. However, the Criminal Code stipulates that when life imprisonment is imposed, the sentencing judge can either exclude the possibility of conditional release or determine its earliest time (25 to 40 years). The person on conditional release may be placed under probation supervision. Supervision is mandatorily ordered for juveniles, recidivists and those released from life imprisonment.

Despite decreasing crime rates, between 2008 and 2016 Hungary's incarceration rate increased from 150 to 184 inmates per 100,000 inhabitants. This change was mainly due to a significant alteration in the length of prison sentences. While in 2010, 24% of the inmates had a sentence of more than five years, this ratio rose to 40% by 2019. Meanwhile, the average length of imprisonment has fallen since 2012 across Europe. After a few years of decrease, by the end of 2020, the imprisonment rate was 172 per 100,000 people. In contrast, a constant decrease can be observed in the rate of juveniles among inmates. In 2015 the rate of those under eighteen in the prison population was almost 2% (Hungarian Prison Service, 2020), but by the end of 2020, it had dropped to 1% (World Prison Brief). Until recently, overcrowding was a severe issue in Hungary with the highest average occupancy rate being 143% in 2014. Poor prison conditions cause suffering to the inmates, put a substantial financial burden on the country because of the compensation payments based on the European Court of Human Rights ruling and pose an extra obstacle to rehabilitation efforts. In response, the Hungarian Government financed capacity extension projects. New penitentiary facilities have been built in recent years, resulting in a notable decrease in the average occupancy rate to 96% by the end of 2020 (World Prison Brief). It is a significant achievement, although it leaves other issues, such as the variable occupancy rates and other physical conditions of detention, the problems of the compensation scheme and the suspension of compensations, unresolved (Hungarian Helsinki Committee, 2020). According to the latest data from the Hungarian Prison Service's website, at the end of June 2021, there were 3407 adults and 33 juveniles in preparation for release under the reintegration care of prison reintegration officers. Between January and June 2021, while only two adults received aftercare services after their release from prison, by the end of June 2021, penitentiary probation officers provided probation supervision to 1942 adults and 21 juveniles under conditional release.

The Hungarian Probation Service operates as a unit of government offices, separate from the penitentiary system, and enforces community sentences and controls individuals in the community. Its primary task is to carry out probation supervision ordered by the trial court, while other tasks include community service supervision and providing social inquiry and pre-sentence reports. According to the provisions of the Penal Code, probation supervision may be applied in addition to suspended imprisonment. In 2020, courts ordered probation supervision in 2838 cases, which is 5% of persons convicted that year (Legfőbb Ügyészség, 2021). Of those under probation supervision, 35% were juveniles. The Hungarian Probation Service caseloads gradually decreased after 2015. In 2019, it was 86,962, resulting in a 7% drop from the previous year's numbers (Igazságügyi Minisztérium, 2020). Nearly 24,409 probation supervision cases were in process, which shows an 8.1%

drop compared to 2018 and this is consistent with a trend that started in 2011. The number of juvenile preventive patronage cases (767) also decreased from the previous few years. Probation officers have the greatest caseloads regarding the task of community service supervision, which accounted for 42,146 cases in 2019.

Specific Programmes and Methods

The programmes in penitentiary institutions seek to promote effective reintegration, partly by using the tools of criminal pedagogy and partly by adapting the therapeutic and corrective methods of clinical psychology. Group activities can include targeted training that develops skills and abilities in a specific area, such as training on labour market reintegration, career guidance and job search techniques. Hungarian penitentiary institutions operate special regime units for those with special treatment needs, like the unit for prisoners serving long-term sentences, the medical-therapeutic unit, the psychosocial unit, the drug prevention unit, the low-security unit, the religious unit, the unit for elderly prisoners and the unit for people who have been convicted for the first time. Unique treatment programmes are also administered based on the risk analysis procedure results. Penitentiary institutions also offer recreational, sports, cultural and religious activities to support the rehabilitation process.

The new Prison Code introduced a social attachment programme in which a prisoner sentenced to up to one year in prison can participate at her or his request. The detainee is entitled to work at an external place of work and leave the institution for a maximum of ten days per month. The programme aims to help strengthen family ties and the social environment. The social attachment programme is promising, but there is little information on its effectiveness in practice, especially in light of the considerable workload of penitentiary probation officers and the high fluctuation rate (Juhász, 2017).

There are three basic types of programmes for the reduction of risky behaviours available in all Hungarian penitentiary institutions: assertiveness training, aggression reduction training and training for the prevention of drug use (Somogyvári, 2018). These programmes have elements based on cognitive behaviour therapy. The Hungarian Prison Service offers individual and group treatment programmes on an optional basis to prevent relapse for those who committed sexual offences (Somogyvári, 2022). A more complex, intense, and at least eight months long programme incorporating cognitive-behavioural elements specifically for those with victims under the age of eighteen is available in the Budapest Strict and Medium Regime Prison. In addition, among a range of options, there are bibliotherapy, literature and drama classes, art and creative classes, music classes and chess programmes. In particular, faith-based programmes and religious activities are exceptionally well promoted in penitentiary institutions. Libraries play their part in rehabilitation too and contribute to making the prison environment more humane.

Restorative justice programmes promoting moral rehabilitation and the taking of responsibility are also present in Hungary. Besides pilot programmes carried out in research projects (Barabás et al., 2011), different restorative programmes are operated by penitentiary institutions. Within the framework of the *'Prison for the city' programmes*, inmates do activities like cleaning, gardening and maintenance for the community outside the walls of prisons. There are tale-based programmes like 'Storybooks mums' faith-based restorative programmes like 'Zákeus' and creative rehabilitation programmes like the recently launched Picasso project. Restorative techniques are also used for handling conflicts in prisons. Reparative and restorative programmes and methods (e.g. family group conferencing) are part of probation service practice. Probation officers use other methods, for example, group sessions and training provide information on the job market, support in solving housing issues, developing personality and communication skills, promoting assertiveness and treating lifestyle problems. Some programmes and training are carried out in the two community day centres, helping individuals integrate into the community and the employment market after their release. These centres also provide conditions for the delivery of reparation programmes, the execution of special behaviour rules in the community and the achievement of the goals of relapse prevention and the protection of youth.

The European Union funds most programmes that target rehabilitation and the prevention of reoffending. Such projects were operated within the frames of the Social Renewal Operation Programme (TÁMOP, SROP in English) functioning between 2007 and 2013 as an operational programme of the New Hungary Development Plan. One such programme, TÁMOP 5.6.2, was launched between 2010 and 2012 to strengthen social cohesion through crime prevention and reintegration programmes. One of its sub-projects was a multi-phase model programme for the social and employment reintegration and the intensive aftercare of prisoners. The project offered information, skills training, vocational training, preparation for release and intensive aftercare for participants. TÁMOP 5.6.3, which terminated in October 2015, also targeted social and job-market reintegration of inmates, providing communication, aggression and conflict management, self-awareness and lifestyle training, vocational training, preparation for release and aftercare services. From 2014, the Human Resources Development Operational Programme (EFOP) provided the framework for reintegration projects. The most recent programme, EFOP 1.3.3. 'Reintegration of prisoners' was launched in 2016 and ended last year with the plan to involve 4600 inmates in reintegration programmes in order to support social and employment reintegration and the prevention of offending. The project supplemented the activity of the prison system, relying on the active role of the participants, individualised treatment and strong cooperation with communities, including organisations supporting employment. It also provided services for 1000 relatives of prisoners.

NGOs and charity organisations also offer programmes supporting the rehabilitation process (Miklósi & Juhász, 2019). The Váltósáv Foundation, for example, launched different projects and programmes and offered various services, such as competence development training, communication and self-awareness training and digital competency training. The Tévelygőkért Foundation established the penitentiary tale programme that has operated for years. Until recently, Prison radio of the Speak Out Association was also present in some institutions (Gosztonyi, 2018). Churches and religious organisations also take their share in establishing programmes in support of rehabilitation. Free practice of religion is ensured in all penitentiary institutions with the help of prison pastors from the four historical churches who provide services and organise religious activities.

Rehabilitation and Diversity

Certain groups of people with special needs in rehabilitation are well recognised in Hungarian academic literature and among professionals. Legal regulations and practices partly reflect this acknowledgement. These regulations, however, pertain to persons held in closed institutions, and some diversities are not addressed despite their relevance. Hungarian penitentiary institutions operate special regime units for inmates with special treatment needs. The enforcement and programmes and activities aimed at rehabilitation are adjusted to the specific needs of particular groups of people. Differentiation is a complex method affecting the whole process, and in terms of treatment, it can be divided into eight main categories: age, gender, degree of execution, legal nature of detention, health and mental status, people convicted for the first time, need for special treatment and educational attainment.

According to Section 122(j) of the Penitentiary Code, women, juveniles and persons with disabilities are entitled to special protection. Particular correctional institutions exist for juveniles and female-only prisons.

Hungary does not have a separate criminal justice system for juveniles. However, specific provisions on juveniles in criminal law, procedural law and criminal law enforcement consider their age-related characteristics. According to Hungarian criminal law, juveniles are minors who have turned twelve but have not yet reached eighteen, but in the penitentiary system, those between the age of fourteen and twenty-one are considered juveniles. The Criminal Code contains special regulations for juveniles. The duration limit for penalties is usually lower, penalties and measures involving the deprivation of liberty can only be imposed upon a juvenile if the aim of the sanctioned cannot otherwise be attained, and the spectrum of alternative sanctions is broader for this age group. Probationary supervision is obligatory for juveniles in case of a suspended sentence, conditional release, probation, compensational service and imprisonment suspension. A measure specifically for juveniles is placement in a reformatory institution, which may be ordered if the proper education of the juvenile (under twenty years of age) can only be provided in an institution. Most detained and not yet convicted juveniles who have offended are also held in these institutions.

In the case of juveniles, the Penitentiary Code also emphasises the reintegrative goal of punishment and contains special rules to be applied during the execution of penalties and measures. Essential tools for rehabilitation are two relatively new legal institutions, family consultation and family therapy aimed at strengthening family ties. Special reintegration programmes concerning juveniles can range from guided sports activities through anti-aggression training to various skill and ability development sessions, aimed at strengthening empathic and community competencies, increasing the chances of reintegration and resocialisation and supporting personality development. (Csemáné Váradi, 2019). The rate of females among prison inmates in 2019 was 7.5% and 5% among juveniles. According to recent research (Ács-Bíró, 2020), they are likely to have multiple special needs and vulnerabilities. Specific legal provisions pertain to imprisoned women's placement, sanitary needs and clothing. Legal regulations also guarantee a response to the unique needs of pregnant women and mothers with babies, and to that end a mother-and-child unit functions in the Bács-Kiskun County Remand Prison. Children can be co-placed with their imprisoned mother in the nursery unit until twelve months. Apart from this, no special rules apply to the rehabilitation of women, and the system lacks women-specific reintegration programmes, even though penitentiary institutions offer activities meant for women. Vig (2014) found that programmes and training offered to females usually concern vocations of low social prestige and reinforce traditional gender roles. A problematic infrastructural issue that hinders the reintegration of imprisoned people is being placed in remote penitentiary institutions far from their families, making family visits problematic. Since there are only a few penitentiary institutions or prison wings in the country specifically for women, they are particularly affected.

Although recording data on the ethnicity of inmates are not allowed in Hungary, research findings indicate that Roma people are overrepresented in penitentiary institutions compared to their rate in the general population (Vig, 2014). Among those serving their prison sentences, the proportion of Roma, even according to a minimum estimate, is more than six times (30%), realistically eight times (around 40%) higher than in the general population (Huszár, 1999). According to a recently published report, Roma people are subjected to discrimination in the Hungarian criminal justice system (Kazarján & Kirs, 2020). Despite the numbers in the prison population, no specific programmes tailored to the needs of Roma people exist in Hungarian penitentiary institutions, mainly for historical legal reasons (Nagy & Vig, 2018). Besides the fact that their particular needs in rehabilitation are not met, vocational training programmes provided by prisons are often not marketable, adding to Roma people's disadvantages in post-release reintegration (Vig, 2014).

Theoretical Underpinnings to Models of Rehabilitation

Historically, the forms and means of rehabilitation and interpretation have changed significantly. The question is how rehabilitation is perceived in Hungary. Is it a goal to be achieved independently, or a means to achieve another goal? In the history of the Hungarian prison system, the interpretation of rehabilitation has been intricately connected with the concept of education. It has had three major and significantly distinct stages (Forgács, 2020). The first interpretation of education broke away from the religious, moral interpretation and placed coercive education at the centre of the philosophy of the socialist-type penitentiary organisation. In the second stage, until the early 1970s, the concept of education was dominated by a criminal pedagogical interpretation. By the end of the decade, moving away from the previous narrower concept, it had become a collective term and included all the positive effects that could increase the chances of reintegration after release from prison. By the end of this development stage, the education paradigm witnessed a crisis because a considerable gap started to show between theory and practice. As a result of this, in the third stage, starting from the period of the change of regime, a notion of punishment and philosophically emptied education prevailed. This could explain why the Prison Act could so easily replace the vocabulary of education with reintegration—not caring much about the subtleties of content.

The Hungarian prison labour system has been thoughtfully redesigned in ten years. The idea of an autonomous prison system, the goal of full employment behind bars, and production efficiency have recently become guiding principles in the system. State-owned prison industry companies, which frequently struggled with financial and sustainability problems, have become economically prosperous businesses now. There is still growing pressure on expanding job opportunities within prison walls. Ivanics argues that the state is not only a crucial actor in setting up the political–economic context of prison labour but it also actively shapes the 'new market' for the products of prison labour, and on the lower scales it manages the ways in which different organisational logics are negotiated through organising prison labour' (Ivanics, 2022: 64).

Research Findings and Effectiveness

There is a growing body of research on rehabilitation, reintegration, re-entry and desistance from crime in Hungary, based on qualitative methodology. However, research on the effectiveness of rehabilitation programmes is almost wholly missing because conditions for follow-up studies are not adequate. In recent years considerable changes have taken place in institutional rehabilitation. However, the registration and accreditation of prison-based programmes are yet in their infancy. As Drexler and Sánta (2016) note, the Hungarian Prison Service is still developing a registry of reintegration programmes that is eligible for evaluation and statistical analysis. In Hungary, the question of effectiveness does not emerge in the context of the prevention of reoffending, but rather as an indicator of the effective functioning of the prison system as a whole. Despite this, Hungarian Prison Service carries out research and analyses to enhance the development of effective intervention strategies and management approaches (Somogyvári, 2019). The opportunities for the implementation of mediation and restorative justice practices in prison settings were researched within the frames of the MEREPS project (Windt, 2011).

The EU-funded projects were assessed after delivery (Belügyminisztérium, 2015a, 2015b). Assessments were based, though not exclusively, on qualitative methodology to explore the implementation process and evaluate the results and effects both among participants and staff. Besides favourable experiences, like the positive psychological effects of one-to-one meetings and different training, several obstacles to successful implementation were revealed. The projects seemed to have reproduced some of the dysfunctions of the penitentiary and aftercare system.

Research on conditions and obstacles to rehabilitation and reintegration, mainly in prison settings, is more extensive than research on specific programmes. Borbíró and Szabó (2012) researched prison-based tertiary prevention practice, exploring several shortcomings of the system that hinder the goal of rehabilitation and finding some promising programmes, attitudes and intentions for improvement. Several studies examining reintegration have found that both the staff interviewed, and the inmates see the preparation and aftercare phase for release as problematic (Albert & Bíró, 2015: 144; Borbíró & Szabó, 2012). Probation practice has also been investigated (Dávid, 2013; Kerezsi, 2006; Szabó, 2019).

According to research and experiences of professionals, tension between security and educational-treatment fields is a fundamental detention problem in the Hungarian penitentiary system. Research examining staff working in prison shows that the so-called 'treatment' staff are more characterised by a paternalistic attitude. In contrast, 'custody' staff (e.g. district supervisors) are characterised by an authoritarian attitude (Rózsa, 2015). Members of the security staff want to tighten control over the detainees, expecting that the activities of the inmates will be limited to the cell, whereas treatment professionals work to increase the time and frequency of out-of-cell detention programmes. The pedagogical influence has negligible effect on prisoners. Education staff are also dissatisfied because their actual role (administration, supervisory support activities) does not match the declared goals of personality development and support. Institutions think of prison educators as 'ossified fossils of the past' that have no function and are 'floating in the structure' and should be abolished (Módos, 2003). One of the main obstacles to social reintegration, according to staff members, is that prisoners cannot find a place to work, so not only education but also competitive education should be provided to enable the prisoner to enter the labour market. In connection with the programmes, a specific methodological renewal was considered necessary, which also meant an opening up to the civil sphere (Hegedűs & Ivaskevics, 2016).

Less empirical research has been carried out concerning community sanctions and the practice of probation officers (Dávid, 2013; Kerezsi & Kó, 2008; Szabó, 2019). These studies aimed to explore how the goals and tasks of the probation services are achieved and the obstacles that may hinder their fulfilment. In 2014, Szabó (2019) conducted qualitative research with probation officers and individuals under probation supervision, concentrating mainly on how this measure can foster desistance from crime and prevent reoffending. Characteristics of juveniles under probation supervision were also studied and analysed statistically (Dávid, 2013; Kerezsi & Kó, 2008). Forward steps were made recently in crime prevention for children and youth affected by criminalisation. Rubeus Association (2019) implemented model programmes in five locations for children and youth under probation supervision or preventive patronage, those at considerable risk of criminalisation, those in reformatory education and their parents.

Future Directions in Policy and Practice

The return of punitivism as the primary criminal policy can be described by highlighting how the penal systems expanded enormously in personnel, budget and work allocation and extensive prison construction programmes (Garland, 2001). The criminal justice policy in Hungary cannot be described as a 'return' because it has never faded; the governmental criminal policy is (and was) based on social control rather than social welfare. Welfarism has never become the essence of criminal policy in Hungary: help is permanently embedded in the control devices, and society seems to favour policing imprisonment and the execution of sentences to establish social order. The ordonationalist thought (Geva, 2018) combined with neoliberal punitive morality and racist nationalism (penal populism and penal nationalism) play a significant role in addressing social problems in post-transition countries (Haney, 2016). The populist criminal policy's primary purpose is to meet the public's expectations and thus gain political popularity. In recent years, Hungary has practised expulsion rather than integration and disrupting traditions of social inclusion. Mass incarceration fits nicely into the forms of social control exercised through the intense use of state punitive power.

Resocialisation is no longer based on work but on various philosophies of punishment. Political intentions and expectations are increasingly reaching the penitentiary system and the programmes within it. Borbíró and Szabó

(2012) consider the financial shortcomings of the penitentiary system, the heavy administrative burdens, the low number of psychological staff and the lack of method-specific training to be the biggest obstacles to the spread of rehabilitation practice. The Penitentiary Code replaces the term education with reintegration, and staff members directly dealing with detainees previously called educators are now named reintegration officers. In the concept of reintegration 'the special expertise related to detention is already being synthesised understandably. It means that the Hungarian penitentiary system pays lip service to rehabilitation as detention and security form the basis of treatment' (Kovács, 2019). There are spectacular new concepts, but their practical implementation is yet to come. For example, the Central Institute for Assessment and Methodology currently is only a department in the Hungarian Prison Service Headquarters. The extra financial resources led to an expansion of space, an essential factor in itself, but did not create the full conditions for rehabilitation. Practical experience indicates that the prison administration does not support prison research and that institutions are becoming increasingly closed. At the same time, official communication is becoming more optimistic, even though recidivism data do not confirm this view.

In recent years, the unfolding of a relatively slow but consistent process has taken place within the Hungarian Prison System, culminating in some erosion of the principles of openness and normalisation. Security considerations are placed before the goal of rehabilitation with the modernisation of information technology systems and security technology equipment in prisons becoming a priority and with the weakening contact with the outside world. COVID-19 measures introduced in Hungarian prisons in 2020 further exacerbated the problem. The pandemic situation indeed required strict changes, and some view the reactions of Hungarian Penitentiary System to the new challenge as adequate and effective (Forgács, 2021), but the duration and severity of restrictions raise questions. Restrictions in the pandemic period significantly altered opportunities for contact between inmates and their family members. These measures made correctional facilities even more closed and less transparent, fitting into the recently witnessed tendency (Kovács et al., 2021).

A community environment is indispensable to the success of rehabilitation, which, in the case of those imprisoned, can be assured mainly through the principle of openness. Without adequate conditions for realisation, even forward-looking and progressive legal institutions stay on paper. An overemphasis on norms of behaviour (such as the fulfilment of conditions and expectations) instead of enforcing a humanist perspective on human change and supporting the humanist theory of the probation officer's role results in more transgression and an inevitable failure of personal change.

References

Ács-Bíró, A. (2020). *Női fogvatartottak oktatás-nevelés szempontú egyéni és intézményi profiljának rendszerszintű vizsgálata az eredményes reintegráció érdekében*. PhD thesis. Pécsi Tudományegyetem, Pécs.

Albert, F., & Bíró, E. (2015). A sikeres reintegráció. In F. Albert (Ed.), *Életkeretek a börtönön innen és túl*. MTA Társadalomtudományi Kutatóközpont, Szociológiai Intézet.

Barabás, T., Fellegi, B., & Windt, Sz. (Eds). (2011). *Felelősségvállalás, kapcsolat és helyreállítás*. OKRI.

Belügyminisztérium. (Ed.). (2015a). 'Elítéltek többszakaszos, társadalmi és munkaerőpiaci reintegrációja és intenzív utógondozási modelljének kialakítása', 5.6.2-10/1-2010-0001 sz. TÁMOP projekt, https://tettprogram.hu/sites/default/files/uploads/Kutat%C3%A1s_562_1v%C3%A1lt.pdf?CSRF_TOKEN=16734fee4d0407a01ed07535cf434d8d8b6b68f2

Belügyminisztérium (Ed) (2015b). 'A fogvatartottak többszakaszos, társadalmi és munkaerő-piaci reintegrációja és az intenzív utógondozási modellje', 5.6.3-12/1-2012-0001 sz. TÁMOP projekt. https://bv.gov.hu/sites/default/files/A%20TEtt%20program%20megval%C3%B3s%C3%ADt%C3%A1s%C3%A1t%20%C3%A9rt%C3%A9kel%C5%91%20kutat%C3%A1s.pdf

Borbíró, A., & Szabó, J. (2012). Harmadlagos megelőzés a magyar büntetés-végrehajtási intézetekben a nemzetközi kutatások fényében. *Kriminológiai Tanulmányok, 49*, 158–192.

Csemáné Váradi, E. (2019). A gyermek- és fiatalkori kriminalitás. In Borbíró, A., Gönczöl, K., Kerezsi, K., & Lévay M. (Eds.), *Kriminológia* (pp. 631–665). Wolters Kluwer.

Dávid, L. (2013). *A hazai pártfogó felügyelet intézkedésének szerepe a fiatalkorúak bűnelkövetésének megelőzésében*. Ph.D. thesis. Pécsi Tudományegyetem, Pécs.

Drexler, B., & Sánta, L. (2016). Fogvatartotti programok értékelése és jóváhagyása az angol büntetés-végrehajtásban. *Börtönügyi Szemle, 35*(4), 107–118.

Forgács J. (2019). A fogva tartás és reintegráció fogalmi megközelítése. In O. Czenczer & P. Ruzsonyi (Eds.), *Büntetés-végrehajtá reintegrációs ismeretek* (p. 43). Dialóg Campus Kiadó ʊ Budapest.

Forgács, J. (2020). Prizonizáció és kapcsolattartás – A reintegráció gátló és segítő tényezői a büntetés-végrehajtásban. In A. T. Barabás (Ed.), *Alkalmazott kriminológia* (pp. 597–604). Dialóg Campus.

Forgács, J. (2021). Kapcsolattartás Járvány Idején. *Börtönügyi Szemle, 40*(1), 51–68.

Garland, D. (2001). *The culture of control: Crime and social order in contemporary society*. Oxford University Press.

Geva, D. (2018). On the Ordonationalist Political Party: The French National Front and Hungary's Fidesz. In J. Andersson, & O. Godechot (Eds.), *Destabilising orders*, MaxPo Discussion Paper 18/1. 49–56. http://sase.org/wp-content/uploads/2018/05/2-Geva-final.pdf

Gosztonyi, G. (2018). Prison radios: Communication on the periphery of a society. *Medialni Studia / Media Studies*, (1), 133–139.

Haney, L. (2016). Prisons of the past: Penal nationalism and the politics of punishment in Central Europe. *Punishment and Society, 18*(3), 346–368.

Hegedűs, J., & Ivaskevics, K. (2016). Büntetés-végrehajtásban dolgozók nézetei a reintegrációról. *Alkalmazott Pszichológia, 16*(4), 71–92.

Hungarian Helsinki Committee. (2020). *Overcrowding and prison conditions - An update on the Varga and Others v. Hungary cases*. https://helsinki.hu/wp-content/uploads/HHC_prison_conditions_august_2020.pdf. Accessed 1 February 2022.

Hungarian Prison Service. (2020). *Review of Hungarian Prison Statistics*. https://bv.gov.hu/sites/default/files/Review_of_Hungarian_Prison_Statistics_2020.pdf. Accessed 10 February 2022.

Huszár, L. (1997). Medikális modell. A treatment /nevelés történeti áttekintése. *Börtönügyi Szemle, 16*(3), 63–70.

Huszár, L. (1999). Roma Fogvatartottak a Büntetés-Végrehajtásban. *Belügyi Szemle, 47*(7–8), 124–133.

Igazságügyi Minisztérium. (2020). Áttekintés a Pártfogó Felügyelői Szolgálat 2019. évi feladatellátásáról. https://igazsagugyistatisztika.kormany.hu/download/c/c3/b2000/P%C3%A1rtfog%C3%B3k_2019_ev.pdf, accessed February 2022.

Ivanics, Zs. (2021). Kritikai pedagógia kísérletek lehetőségei és korlátai a büntetés-végrehajtásban. *Neveléstudomány, 2021*(1), 16–28.

Ivanics, Zs. (2022). Conceptual issues and theoretical considerations regarding the study of prison labour. *Belügyi Szemle, 70*(1. sp.i.), 53–68. https://doi.org/10.38146/BSZ.SPEC.2022.1.3

Juhász, F. (2017). A bűnismétlés megelőzéséhez kapcsolódó büntetés-végrehajtási pártfogó felügyelői szakmai feladatok. *Börtönügyi Szemle, 36*(3), 5–27.

Kazarján, A., & Kirs, E. (2020). *Discrimination against Roma people in the Hungarian criminal justice system*. Hungarian Helsinki Committee. https://helsinki.hu/wp-content/uploads/Discrimination_against_Roma_people_in_the_Hungarian_criminal_justice_system.pdf. Accessed 15 February 2022.

Kerezsi, K. (2006). *Kontroll vagy támogatás: az alternatív szankciók dilemmája*. Komplex Kiadó.

Kerezsi, K. (2002). A hazai pártfogó szolgálatok átalakítása. *Belügyi Szemle, 49*(2–3), 185–201.

Kerezsi, K., & Kó, J. (2008). A fiatalkorúak büntető igazságszolgáltatásának hatékonysága. *Kriminológiai Tanulmányok, 45*, 93–148.

Kovács, M. (2019). A foglalkoztatás és a szakmaképzés jelentősége a büntetés-végrehajtás reintegrációs feladataiban. *Börtönügyi Szemle, 38*(3), 19–34.

Kovács, P., Krámer, L., & Szegő, D. (2021). Kapcsolattartás a büntetés-végrehajtásban helyzetkép. FECSKE (Support Network for Detainees and their Families). https://www.fogvatartas.hu/wp-content/uploads/2021/05/kutatasi_jelentes_kapcsolattartas_210521_fin.pdf

Legfőbb Ügyészség. (2021). A büntetőbíróság előtti ügyészi tevékenység főbb adatai I. 2020. évi tevékenység. http://ugyeszseg.hu/wp-content/uploads/2022/01/lfi iga_65_3_2022_1-melleklet.pdf. Accessed 16 March 2022.

Lőrincz, J. (2006). A 'nevelés-gondolat' a XX. századi hazai börtönügyben – jogász szemmel. *Börtönügyi Szemle, 25*(3), 1–20.

Lukács, K., & Vig, D. (2019). The detrimental legal consequences of a conviction in Hungary. In S. Meijer, S. H. Annison, & A. O'Loughlin (Eds.), *Fundamental rights and legal consequences of criminal conviction* (pp. 107–128). Hart Publishing.

Miklósi, M., & Juhász, E. (2019). The role of education and NGOs in the reintegration of inmates in Hungary. *International Journal of Bias, Identity and Diversities in Education, 4*(1), 100–112.

Módos, T. (2003). A személyi állomány beállítódása a büntetés-végrehajtás rehabilitációs, nevelési feladataival kapcsolatban. *Börtönügyi Szemle, 22*(3), 55–72.

Nagy, A., & Vig, D. (2018). Prisoner resettlement in Hungary. In F. Dünkel, L. Pruin, I. A. Storgaard & J, Weber (Eds.), *Prisoner resettlement in Europe* (pp. 185–202). Routledge.

Pallo, J. (2018). Era of change in the Hungarian prison law. *Journal of Penal Law and Criminology, 6*(1), 55–71.

Pallo, J. (2020). The effects of the Trianon Peace Treaty on the development of corrections in Hungary. *Belügyi Szemle, Special Issue, 3*, 111–127.

Rózsa, S. (2015). A büntetés-végrehajtási intézetek személyi állományának kérdőíves vizsgálata. In A. Csóti (Edk.), *Körletmozaikok 2015. A büntetés-végrehajtási intézetek személyi állományának vizsgálata' című kutatás tanulmányai* (pp. 25–66). BVOP.

Rubeus Association. (2019). Bűnelkövetéssel érintett gyermekeket és szüleiket támogató modellprogramok a gyermekvédelemben. http://rubeus.hu/wp-content/uploads/2019/09/konyv_szulomkomp_BM2_final_201906.pdf. Accessed 5 March 2022.

Somogyvári, M. (2018). Kockázatelemzési Rendszerek a Büntetés-Végrehajtásban. *Börtönügyi Szemle, 37*(1), 69–86.

Somogyvári, M. (2019). Szervezeti Működést Támogató Kutatások. *Börtönügyi Szemle, 38*(3), 49–58.

Somogyvári, M. (2022). A szexuális bűnelkövetők karakterisztikája és kezelési lehetőségei büntetés-végrehajtási keretek között. *Belügyi Szemle, 70*(1), 99–117.

Szabó, J. (2019). *Speciális prevenció és dezisztencia.* OKRI.

Vig, D. (2014). Korlátlan fájdalom? A bebörtönzés kirekesztő hatásai a semlegesítésben és azon túl. Ph.D. thesis. Eötvös Loránd Tudományegyetem, Budapest.

Windt, Sz. (2011). A börtönmediáció lehetőségei a börtönszemélyzet, a fogvatartottak és a sértettek véleménye alapján. In T. Barabás, B. Fellegi, & Sz. Windt (Eds.), *Felelősségvállalás, kapcsolat és helyreállítás* (pp. 63–85). OKRI.

World Prison Brief. Hungary. https://www.prisonstudies.org/country/hungary. Accessed 15 February 2022.

A Critical Commentary on Rehabilitation of Offenders in India

Debarati Halder

Any reflection on rehabilitation in India necessarily begins with a glance back to mythology. The country has a rich history in Danda Niti (Penology) that is reflected in the epic Ramayana. The epic was created by Maharshi Valmiki who was born in a respectable Brahmin family but in his early life, ostensibly to make a living for himself and provide for his family, he turned to crime and became a notorious thief named Ratnakar. The mythological stories suggest that he wanted to rob the sage Narada. However, Narada asked him to go back to his family members and ask them if they were willing to share his sins. They declined and this caused him to reflect on his behaviour and the consequences for himself and others. Pained by these thoughts he asked Narada to direct him to the path of salvation and redemption. He was guided by divine commands to chant the name of Lord Rama (a god of Hinduism) (Sitaram, 2004). Consequently, he started meditating and chanting sacred words for many years, but despite his efforts, he could not pronounce the name Rama, instead chanted 'mara'. Directed by Narada he became so absorbed and occupied in the chanting of sacred words that he was covered by a huge anthill (Valmik in Sanskrit). Eventually, Lord Brahma

D. Halder (✉)
Parul Institute of Law, Vadodara, Gujarat, India
e-mail: debaratihalder@gmail.com

(another of the gods of Hinduism) heard his chanting, cleared the anthill from him, and renamed him Valmiki (the one who was covered by Valmik). Encouraged by Lord Brahma to continue the meditation and chanting of the sacred name of Lord Rama he emerged from his negative mindset and devoted his energy and intellectual powers to create the life story of Lord Rama which became the great epic Ramayana (Sitarem, 2004).[1] It is an epic ancient Indian example of the rehabilitation of a person who has led a life of crime, but it is not the only one.

Other ancient scripts (Veda, Manu Smriti, Artha Shashtra and other Smritis and Shrutis), written by sages who presented their ideas about the way societies should be governed and what rules of behaviour and norms they should have, indicated that a person who offends, unless guilty and convicted of heinous crimes (including crimes against the State), has a right to undergo correctional services and be rehabilitated and reintegrated into society (Bose and Silverman 1982). This legacy can also be seen in the case of Emperor Ashoka who in the great war of Kalinga killed several soldiers and innocent people including women and children and destroyed many villages (Long, 2004). His ruthless cruelty as a king and supreme commander of his army was symbolised in the historic blood flow in the Daya river (situated in the present Odhisha state of India) which turned the river red (Long, 2004). Like Maharshi Valmiki, Ashoka came to recognise the consequences of his deeds on society as a whole and transformed himself into an ambassador of peace conveying the message of Buddha, through his followers and his children to ancient Asian countries like Sri Lanka and Cambodia. The Danda Niti verses of Smritis and Artha Shashtra created the baseline of Indian Penology, and this was followed for a prolonged period up to the mediaeval ages when Muslim rulers invaded India and imposed their rules in different parts of the country. Mughals, particularly, formulated their own system for restitution of justice for criminal activities based on Sharia laws. But they did this without disturbing the customary Hindu laws governing marriages, successions, adoption and related issues and criminal behaviour arising out of the same unless it was a grave crime like serious bodily injury or major property damage (Dubey, 1951). Both Hindu and Islamic criminal laws recognised fines and imprisonment as forms of punishment. Moreover, they gave impetus to the concept of restitution of justice by returning or rebuilding property or paying for repairs: it included the paying of financial compensation for the death of a family member who would have provided financial and moral support. This system slowly enriched the concept of rehabilitation and empowerment of the victims.

From the middle of the nineteenth century onwards the colonial British rulers initiated the application of a uniform criminal law with the establishment of Indian Penal Code, Act Number 45 of 1860. This statute acknowledged five major types of offences including crimes against the State, public servants, government properties and public health (Chapters 6–13); against the person including threat to commit bodily harm or damage reputation (Chapters 16, 21, 22); offences against property including fraud (Chapters 17 and 18); against marriage and in marital relationships (Chapter 20) and against religion (Chapter 25). The Indian Penal Code also criminalised mental attitudes that would help in committing the crimes successfully (Chapters 5 and 23). However, the colonial rulers did not affect the existing *shashtric* understandings of criminal offences and penology but only those within the broader meaning of offences stated above. Along with the introduction of the uniform Penal Code, they introduced criminal procedural laws in 1861 which empowered police officers and magistrates to execute the provisions of Indian Penal Code. During a period stretching from the nineteenth century to the twentieth century, the criminal laws, including the procedural laws, were reformed, reframed and amended to suit the needs of the Indian socio-legal setup. This period also saw the rise of the concept of rehabilitation of those who committed offences and their victims, first from a colonial perspective and then, after Indian independence in 1947, from an Indian perspective.

This chapter aims to discuss the rehabilitation of individuals and the empowerment of their victims in India in the contemporary period. Post-independence India had become a signatory to an international covenant on civil and political rights that ensures the rights of the accused. As such, Indian criminal laws aim to provide proper correctional services to prevent an accused or a convicted person reoffending. While ensuring rights of the accused, the recent amendments in the Indian criminal procedural laws also guarantee that victim's rights and empowerment are properly balanced. In examining rehabilitation of adults and juveniles, this chapter argues that their rehabilitation (and that of victims) may not be possible in India unless there is first, a focus on positively changing the thinking and attitudes of those who have gone through correctional system and, second, a focus on helping communities accept the reintegration not only those individuals but also the victims of sexual crimes.

The Rehabilitation of Adults

As discussed in the above paragraph, Indian criminal laws are rapidly growing in consonance with notions of human rights and therapeutic approaches towards the perpetrators and victims of crime. However, practically this growth also brings with it several flaws and lacunae that have made human right activists and the judiciary think about the victim empowerment for the vulnerable, i.e. women, children, senior citizens, and socio-economically backward communities. Present Indian criminal laws and the correctional administration system place emphasis on socio-economic conditions related to the commission of crime rather than following the theory, established by the Positive school of criminology, that criminal behaviour may be genetic. Throughout India, the correctional administration system is, like many other jurisdictions, divided mainly into two segments: preventive custody of individuals and bail and monitoring by probation officers and the police. The latter is functional for less serious offences including those falling into the category of petty offences and less serious misdemeanours. In those cases, judicial discretion may be applied to adult men and women and juveniles appearing before the court for the first time whereby the judicial magistrate may put the individual under the monitoring of probation officers for a stipulated period (see below). In such cases, depending upon the gravity of the offences and the harm caused to the victim or victims, the judicial officer may also apply provisions for bail for the offender (Halder, 2014). It must also be noted that in cases of less serious offences when the case is registered with the police stations, the criminal procedure code also empowers the officer in charge of the police station to grant bail to the accused. In addition, the lower courts and the high courts in India are imposing certain community services as conditions of bail (see Agarwal, 2019). This is definitely a positive improvement in terms of reframing the mindset of those who commit crime to fit with an offence-free lifestyle especially in cases of less serious offences such as public nuisance, traffic rule violation cases, motor accident cases not amounting to serious to the victim and elder abuse.

Education and vocational training are important as rehabilitation mechanisms, but as indicated above, Indian prisons did not offer rehabilitative mechanism in the pre- and immediate post-independence period. Prisons were unhealthy and did not provide any mechanism for the inmates to lead a life of dignity. It was Justice Krishna Iyer who emphasised that Indian prisons should be therapeutic and for the inmates to undergo a correctional period rather than fester in unhealthy cells only to harbour more revenge and hatred against victims and the criminal justice system.[2] Over the years, the prison manual that governs the correctional administration in India was revamped to accommodate the views of Justice Iyer. So, accordingly, Section 360 of the Criminal Procedure Code, 1976 states that the court, after taking into account the character and personal history of a female or male under 21 years convicted of an offence punishable with a fine or imprisonment for a term of less than seven years (and not punishable by death or life imprisonment), and ensuring that she or he has a fixed place of abode and regular occupation, may make a probation order not more than three years during which the individual must keep the peace and be of good behaviour. The same section allows the court instead of sentencing to release an individual after 'due admonition', if there are no previous convictions and the current offence is only punishable with a fine or not more than two years' imprisonment. As with probation, age, character, antecedents or physical or mental condition must be considered, but for release after admonition either the offence should be of a trivial or there should be extenuating circumstances under which the offence was committed.

Moreover, in the early 1990s, Dr. Krian Bedi, then inspector general of police who was in charge of the administration of Tihar prison in Delhi, which is the biggest compound in south Asia, introduced meditation and specifically vipasanaa to the prison (Buddhist meditation) by (Taylor & Rynne, 2016). This has reportedly shown tremendous impact on the spiritual awakening and mental as well as physical well-being of the inmates which in turn may help them to lead a life with positive goals. The correctional administration system in India has developed specific rehabilitation programmes—tailored to age, maturity level and skills—for prisoners serving both short and long sentences. It has also determined that right to education of all inmates, especially children in conflict with law, must be achieved, and this includes access to higher education for adults (Taylor & Rynne, 2016). It is considered important that the criminal record of prisoners should not hinder social reintegration. Hence the Indian correctional administration system, in collaboration with Non-Government Organisations (NGOs) or other educational institutions, offers prison-based vocational training systems and skill-based certificate courses: these outside organisations endorse the certificates of learning (Taylor & Rynne, 2016). The courses include enhancing culinary skills, handicrafts manufacturing, carpentry and furniture making, welding, bookbinding, pen manufacturing, handloom-related work and computer training for mainstream markets (Taylor & Rynne, 2016). The author of this chapter in her legal capacity visited the central jail in Ahmedabad in Gujarat where prisoners were provided with facilities to sell their approved culinary products through the auspices of the prison authority directly to the customers.

While the present correctional administration provides the opportunity for rehabilitation and reintegration of the individuals into mainstream society, statutory provisions also have an important role, The Criminal Procedure Code (Cr.P.C) through S.360 empowers judicial magistrates to admonish and release males and females and juveniles appearing before the court for the first time as long as they have not been charged with offences for which sentences of over seven years or life or capital punishment are prescribed. The conditions for such release include surety and a bond, a fixed abode for the individual and their surer and strict behavioural restrictions to ensure that they do not breach the peace. However, such release on admonition is not an absolute release as the court may recall the individual to court if they have violated the terms of the bond. As a further contribution to rehabilitation and reintegration, India has the 1958 Probation of Offenders Act that provides statutory guidelines for the release of probationers with a condition of good behaviour. In fact, the Act expands the scope of S.360 of the Cr.P.C by enabling the court to release people on probation to be supervised and monitored by authorised probation officers.[3] Further, S.5 of the Act provides the court with discretionary power to direct the probationer to pay compensation and costs for damage and/or injury caused to victims caused by the offence(s).[4] This court-based, correctionally administered supervision and monitoring system is designed to assist the reintegration of the individual into society. Through the 1959 Prisons (Bombay furlough and parole) Rules, India also has a parole and furlough system for the release of prisoners who are not deemed dangerous to the security of the society as a whole.[5] Parole may be granted for specific social functions and duties such as attending to sick spouse or ailing parents, and performing duties for the weddings of children.[6] Finally, India also has an open prison system to facilitate rehabilitation and reintegration particularly facilitating re-entry into the employment market (Agarwal, 2019).

In conjunction with the above mentioned measures and resources, the correctional administration system has been revamped to ensure the rights of all individuals dealt with by the criminal justice system to exercise, good physical and mental health, free legal aid and bail. These rights apply equally to male, female and transgender people and people on trial and are intended to guarantee that the children of female inmates grow up in a positive environment without stigmatisation (Halder, 2019). As the recent release from custody of Indrani Mukherjee demonstrates, granting bail to prisoners who are awaiting trial is much within the discretionary power of the courts.

Indrani Mukherjee at one time was a socialite but she made her fortune in the showbusiness and entertainment industry as a Human Resources consultant and media executive in a company she had established with her ex-husband. In 2015 she was charged by the Mumbai police with the abduction and murder of her daughter, Sheena Bora (who had gone missing in 2012) and remanded in custody. As the news reports and the court case details suggest, Indrani Mukherjee was not happy with her daughter born from a previous relationship because she believed that she was in a relationship with the son of her present husband and his previous wife. Her bail applications were reused because it was the prosecution persuaded the court that if she was released there was a risk that she would attempt to influence the witnesses and destroy evidence. She spent the next six years in custody at a female prison in Mumbai. In May 2022 she applied successfully for bail. In making their decision, the judges in the Supreme Court took into account her prolonged stay in the jail and her good behaviour and cooperation with the correctional administration system. The case not only underlines the fact the high court may exercise powers of granting bail to defendants whose release may have been perceived by the lower courts as dangerous to society but also confirms that in India the concept of rehabilitation applies to both convicted people and those whose guilt has not been determined.[7]

At present, the Indian criminal justice administration and correctional administration systems do not have a digital monitoring system of people released from all the country's prisons on bail, admonishment, parole or furlough. However, there is a concern that the 2022 Criminal Procedure Identification Bill, which allows police officers to collect and retain sensitive personal information about the accused unless they are acquitted by the courts, may adversely affect reintegration into society and prevent a fair opportunity of rehabilitation.[8]

The Rehabilitation of Juveniles

In 1979, the Convention of Child Rights[9] was adopted by the General Assembly of the United Nations and it was made operational from 1990 onwards. While this international document lays down general principles of the rights of children and the responsibilities of the State to ensure fullest enjoyment of those rights, it did not specifically discuss the administration of juvenile justice for children in conflict with law. Since 1948, accused people have been covered by the Universal Declaration of Human Rights of 1948 and the international covenants on civil, political, socio-economic and cultural rights. They include the right to free legal aid, to a presumption of innocence until proved guilty, privacy and confidentiality and protection against torture in custody, and they apply equally to children in conflict with law. Before 1985, the United Nations Standard Minimum Rules for the Administration of Juvenile Justice (The Beijing Rules) came into effect, children had been subjected to punishment detrimental to their physical and mental wellbeing and overall development (Fox, 1969). The Beijing Rules, which under Rule under Rule 2© defines a juvenile 'offender' as 'a child or young person who is alleged to have committed or who has been found to have committed an offence'[10], were a holistic effort of nation-states and international stakeholders to bring uniformity to the administration of juvenile justice and the development of children irrespective of nationality, race, class, creed or language. They emphasise the need for a holistic development of children in conflict with law in a positive environment that does not traumatise them or cause them to lose the trust in the criminal justice system as happens with some adults. Moreover, the rules prioritise rehabilitation of children in their family environment over the prison environment.

India is a party to the 1990 Child Right Convention (CRC), and in 2015 adopted a Juvenile Justice Care and Protection of Children Act (JJCPCA) that is based on the Beijing Rules and adheres to the CRC. Researchers have shown that there may be several reasons for children to break the laws (Aultman & Welford, 1979). Children in conflict with law should not be brought into criminal liability even if their level of maturity is high because it may not only be detrimental to their physical and emotional health but may also hamper their overall development (Kalnins, 1971). On the negative side, the Beijing Rules skirt around the central idea of 'best interest of children', but the Juvenile Justice Care and Protection of Children Act has adopted the mandate of those rules for achieving the best interests of children generally and become a significant aspect of ensuring the rehabilitation of juveniles in conflict with the law specifically. Thus, juveniles who offend must be afforded proper care that should include legal and psychological counselling, and judicial and police intervention that are carried out in a child-friendly manner. Accordingly, the JJCPCA mandates that when a child in conflict with law is apprehended, criminal justice stakeholders must consider putting the said child in a monitoring system within the family rather than within custody (Brignal, 2002). The CCR as well as the Constitution of India through Articles 21 (right to life), 15, 39 (principles to be followed by the State) and 45 (free and compulsory education) also stipulate that holistic development and care in institutions must continue along the same lines as that provided by the family (Devarmani, 2017). In particular, Article 39 of the Constitution of India stipulates that State must follow certain principles and implement policies to ensure:

> that the citizens, men and women equally, have the right to an adequate means to livelihood;
> that the ownership and control of the material resources of the community are so distributed as best to subserve the common good;
> that the operation of the economic system does not result in the concentration of wealth and means of production to the common detriment;
> that there is equal pay for equal work for both men and women;
> that the health and strength of workers, men and women, and the tender age of children are not abused and that citizens are not forced by economic necessity to enter avocations unsuited to their age or strength and
> that children are given opportunities and facilities to develop in a healthy manner and in conditions of freedom and dignity and that childhood and youth are protected against exploitation and against moral and material abandonment.

Traditionally, a juvenile may be released on bail provided the parent or guardians of the child are not considered a security risk in relation to the juvenile's required presence in court, and they promise that their child will refrain from committing any criminal acts (Waite, 1929). However, in the light of Beijing Rules, the modern penological system does not advocate the refusing of bail to juveniles. In line with the aims and objectives of the Convention on Child Rights, the Beijing Rules and the JJCPCA support the reformation of children in conflict with law with the help of family and a child-friendly juvenile justice administration system.

Research has theorised various reasons for juvenile offending including, peer influences, lifestyle, violence within the home, socio-political unrest in the area in which the juvenile lives, the poor economic situation of the parents or guardian and the resulting deprivation, lack of adult monitoring and gender discrimination (Hildebrand, 1968; Hirschi, 1995; Rutter & Giller, 1983; Schlossman & Wallach, 1978). Age and maturity levels may affect the attitudes and feeling of juveniles too: after committing the offence they may feel triumphant, or they may experience trauma through guilt. Triumphalism, common with juveniles who have a history of offending, may result from feelings of self-gratification or revenge, or their actions being celebrated by friends (Khayambashi, 2015). On the other hand, guilt may arise when they come face to face with the victim for the first time and begin to understand the moral consequences of their actions (Paton et al., 2009). It is in consideration of all the above mentioned issues, that criminal justice and correctional administration systems in India have given special attention to the issues of investigation, prosecution, adjudication and disposition; and recognized the need for a specialized police force, trained judges, child-friendly court rooms and unique disposition methods that which will help the juvenile not only reform but also to reintegrate into society as a positive civil citizen.[11]

Even if all of this, backed by welfare laws, is in place the efforts to rehabilitate juveniles may fail if they do not get complete protection of privacy and confidentiality as they attempt to start a new life. It is important to note, therefore, that Chapter II of the JJCPCA in S.3 speaks about right to privacy in the following words:

> (xi) Principle of right to privacy and confidentiality: Every child shall have a right to protection of his privacy and confidentiality, by all means and throughout the judicial process.[12]

A detailed analysis of the above provision shows that a child whether in need of care and protection or whether in conflict with law is guaranteed the right to privacy throughout the judicial process. This includes their confidentiality, that of the doeket (court document), complete privacy of their home and family to ensure that they can lead stigma-free lives after the judicial process is over. The second provision about privacy in the JJCPCA is S.74 which prohibits the sharing of any information in any media about the juveniles who come before the courts.[13] This section adheres to parts two, three, four and five of the Beijing Rules which highlight the rights of the juvenile who come before the criminal courts, including right to privacy. It prohibits not only the media or any other third party but also the police from breaching the privacy of juveniles and revealing their identity. To further help juveniles to live a non-offending way of life, it that the rehabilitation process may include the provision of a completely new identity. The application of the Beijing Rules and the abovementioned provisions of the JJCPCA in this respect is best illustrated by the Nirbhaya gang rape case whereby the juvenile member was handed over to an NGO run special home for his rehabilitation and no information about him was shared.[14]

Conclusion: Future Challenges for Rehabilitation in India

Even though, since the ancient period, the traditional understanding of rehabilitation in India suggests that when a person has undergone a correctional process he or she has to be accepted as a changed person, in contemporary society this presents a considerable challenge. The ancient texts in India suggest that people can be changed provided they accept their guilt, offer an apology, undergo punishment to become a reformed person and above all change their attitudes and thinking (Bose et al., 1982). But seen from the modern perspectives of human counselling-based evaluation and technology-based evaluation of the mindset of individuals, it is extremely difficult to determine whether an individual has really changed or whether he or she still harbours deeply held thoughts of revenge against their victim. The latter may be more discernible in technology-based crimes, cases of intimate partner violence and property feuds where the perpetrator has been seen repeating the behaviour and causing harm even after undergoing rehabilitation sessions in prison or in the community. There is limited scope for prison authorities in India to prevent repeat victimisation especially in technology-based crime because unlike investigations into other kinds of crime, the non-cooperation of internet companies makes it difficult for the police to access data on the individual This lack of information has discouraged the general public from accepting people who have offended back into society, thus perpetuating stigmatisation and hindering chances of rehabilitation.

Statutorily and legally, India offers excellent rehabilitation opportunities for individuals and under trial prisoners. Presently, with the digitalisation of the criminal justice and correctional administration systems, the situation of serving and under trial prisoners, their access to and enjoyment of rights and their opportunities for rehabilitation have become more transparent.[15] However, knowledge about the effectiveness of these opportunities is limited if non-existent. It is clear, therefore, that more research is needed to enhance understanding of the contemporary situation of individuals and under trial prisoners who have been offered help to rehabilitate and reintegrate into society by official governmental programmes. Unless continuous and robust analysis and research are undertaken there will be no clarity about which rehabilitation programmes are effective and which are not. That lack of clarity will undermine the best intentions of practitioners and policymakers and, ultimately, may simply leave individuals with unchanged attitudes and behaviour, lacking the resources needed to change and therefore still socially excluded and likely to re-offend.

Notes

1. For more, see in Lobo Ashwin (2018). Know About The Great Sage Maharishi Valmiki – The Transformation Of A Robber Into Adikavi. Published in https://www.parentcircle.com/maharishi-valmiki-the-transformation-of-a-robber-into-adikavi/article. Accessed 12 March 2022.
2. Mohammad Giasuddin vs State Of Andhra Pradesh. 1977 AIR 1926, 1978 SCR (1) 153.
3. See in S.4 of The Probation of offenders Act, 1958.
4. S.5 of the probation of offenders Act states as follows:

   Power of court to require released offenders to pay compensation and costs.—(1) The court directing the release of an offender under Sect. 3 or Sect. 4, may, if it thinks fit, make at the same time a further order directing him to pay—(a) such compensation as the court thinks reasonable for loss or injury caused to any person by the commission of the offence; and (b) such costs of the proceedings as the court thinks reasonable. (2) The amount ordered to be paid under sub-Sect. (1) may be recovered as a fine in accordance with the provisions of Sects. 386 and 387 of the Code. (3) A civil court trying any suit, arising out of the same matter for which the offender is prosecuted, shall take into account any amount paid or recovered as compensation under sub-Sect. (1) in awarding damages.

5. For more understanding, see in the Prisons (Bombay furlough and parole) Rules, 1959. https://home.gujarat.gov.in/Upload/The_Prisons_Bombay_Furlough_and_Parole_Rules_1959_home_1_1_1.pdf.
6. Ibid.
7. See for more in https://www.livelaw.in/top-stories/supreme-court-grants-bail-to-indrani-mukerjea-in-sheena-bora-murder-case-199410. Accessed 21 March 2022.
8. See in Trivedi Diya (May 2022) Surveillance state: Parliament passes the Criminal Procedure (Identification) Bill. Published in https://frontline.thehindu.com/the-nation/surveillance-state-parliament-passes-the-criminal-procedure-identification-bill-2022/article38478336.ece on May 6, 2022. Accessed 7 May 2022.
9. See Convention on Rights of children, available @ https://www.ohchr.org/EN/ProfessionalInterest/Pages/CRC.aspx. Accessed 18 February 2021.
10. See in Rule 2© of the United Nations Standard Minimum Rules for the Administration of Juvenile.

    Justice ("The Beijing Rules") available @ https://www.ohchr.org/documents/professionalinterest/beijingrules.pdf. Accessed 18 February 2021.
11. For more See parts two and three of the Beijing Rule, 1985. These will be further discussed in the following portions.

12. See in S.3 of Juvenile Justice Care and Protection Act, 2015.
13. *S.74. of the JJ Act states as follows: (1) No report in any newspaper, magazine, news-sheet or audio-visual media or other forms of communication regarding any inquiry or investigation or judicial procedure, shall disclose the name, address or school or any other particular, which may lead to the identification of a child in conflict with law or a child in need of care and protection or a child victim or witness of a crime, involved in such matter, under any other law for the time being in force, nor shall the picture of any such child be published:*

    Provided that for reasons to be recorded in writing, the Board or Committee, as the case may be, holding the inquiry may permit such disclosure, if in its opinion such disclosure is in the best interest of the child.

    (2) The Police shall not disclose any record of the child for the purpose of character certificate or otherwise in cases where the case has been closed or disposed of.

    (3) Any person contravening the provisions of sub-Sect. (1) shall be punishable with imprisonment for a term which may extend to six months or fine which may extend to two lakh rupees or both.
14. For more, see Agency. 2015. Juvenile convict in Dec 16 gangrape case walks free; Nirbhaya's parents protest, get detained. Retrieved from https://www.dnaindia.com/india/report-juvenile-convict-in-dec-16-gangrape-case-walks-free-nirbhaya-s-parents-protest-get-detained-2157868 on 19.02.2021.
15. For more information, see https://eprisons.nic.in/Public/Home. Accessed 21 April 2022.

References

Agarwal, M. (2019). Beyond the prison bars: Contemplating community sentencing in India. *National University of Juridical Sciences Law Review, 12*(119), 120–143.

Aultman, M. G., & Wellford, C. F. (1979). Towards an integrated model of delinquency causation: An empirical analysis. *Sociology and Social Research, 63*(2), 316–327.

Bose, S., Varma, P., & Silverman, H. L. (1982). Philosophical significance of ancient Indian penology. *Journal of Indian Philosophy, 10*(1), 61–100.

Devarmani, N. (2017). Institutional treatment for juveniles in India. *International Journal of English Literature and Social Sciences, 2*(4), 10–14.

Dubey, T. P. (1951). Hindu penology or Hindu criminal jurisprudence and the need of its assimilation in the modern system of Penology in India. *Allahabad Law Journal, 49*, 29.

Fox, S. J. (1969). Juvenile justice reform: An historical perspective. *Stanford Law Review, 22*(6), 118–154.

Hirschi, T. (1995). Causes and prevention of juvenile delinquency. *Contemporary masters in criminology* (pp. 215–230). Springer.

Hildebrand, J. A. (1968). Reasons for runaways. *Crime and Delinquency, 14*(1), 42–48.

Halder, D. (2014). Women prisoners and their rights. In K. Jaishankar, T. Mukherjee, P. Bharadwaj, & M. Desai (Eds.), *Indian prisons: Towards reformation, rehabilitation and resocialization*. New Delhi: Atlantic Publishers.

Halder, D. (2019). Free legal aid for women and therapeutic jurisprudence: A critical examination of the Indian model. In N. Stobbs Nigel, L. Bartel, & M. Vols (Eds.), *Methodology and practice of therapeutic jurisprudence research*. Carolina Academy Press.

Kalnins, J. M. (1971). Right to bail for juveniles. *Chicago-Kent Law Review, 48*(1), 99–106.

Khayambashi, S. (2015). *The social and cultural alienation of first and second generation immigrant youths: Interrogating mainstream bullying discourse*. MA Thesis. University of Toronto.

Long, J. B. (2004). King Asoka's dharma-based program for social welfare: An ancient embodiment of "Humanistic Buddhism." *Hsi Lai Journal of Humanistic Buddhism (西來人間佛教學報), 5*, 301–311.

Paton, J., Crouch, W., & Camic, P. (2009). Young offenders' experiences of traumatic life events: A qualitative investigation. *Clinical Child Psychology and Psychiatry, 14*(1), 43–62.

Rutter, M., & Giller, H. (1983). *Juvenile delinquency: Trends and perspectives*. Penguin Books.

Schlossman, S., & Wallach, S. (1978). The crime of precocious sexuality: Female juvenile delinquency in the Progressive Era. *Harvard Educational Review, 48*(1), 65–94.

Sitaram, R. (2004). The Ramayana and world order: Past, present and future. *Nidan: International Journal for Indian Studies, 2004*(16), 21–31.

Taylor, A. J. W., & Rynne, J. (2016). Exemplary prisoner management. *Australian and New Zealand Journal of Criminology, 49*(4), 512–527.

Waite, J. B. (1929). Code of criminal procedure: The problem of bail. *American Bar Association Journal* 15. https://www.jstor.org/stable/pdf/25707573.pdf

Beyond the Treatment Paradigm: Expanding the Rehabilitative Imagination in Ireland

Deirdre Healy

Rehabilitation in Ireland has a long and chequered history, and its popularity has waxed and waned over time. Its origins can be traced to the court missionary system which was established before Ireland gained independence from Britain. Ireland also inherited a legal and criminal justice infrastructure from Britain that reflected penal welfare ideals (Rogan, 2012). However, penal welfarism was never fully embraced by post-Independence Ireland (Kilcommins et al., 2004). Instead, Catholic values played a central role in the evolution of rehabilitation philosophy, policy and practice, with the Church's influence enduring into the 1960s and beyond (Healy & Kennefick, 2019). Highlighting a darker chapter in the history of rehabilitation, criminal justice interventions coexisted within an extensive system of coercive confinement where marginalised and vulnerable groups were confined for the purposes of 'reform'. O'Donnell and O'Sullivan (2020) estimated that, during the first half of the twentieth century, approximately one percent of the Irish population was being held involuntarily in a variety of institutions including psychiatric facilities, Magdalene laundries, mother and baby homes, industrial and reformatory schools, county homes, an unusually high rate in

D. Healy (✉)
UCD Sutherland School of Law, University College Dublin,
Belfield, Dublin, Ireland
e-mail: deirdre.healy@ucd.ie

international terms. While some religious-run institutions claimed rehabilitative aims, the harsh conditions, degrading treatment and strict regimes were experienced as punitive by those confined there. To a large extent, these institutions existed to control female sexuality and punish gender infractions (Quinlan, 2016). In the community setting, voluntary organisations were empowered to deliver rehabilitative services by the Criminal Justice Administration Act 1914, which enabled societies involved in the provision of probation services to young people to apply to the Secretary of State for recognition and payment. This, in conjunction with a commitment to the Catholic principle of subsidiarity, which stated that governments should not assume control of activities that could be provided by non-state actors, limited state involvement in rehabilitation at this time (Healy, 2015; McNally, 2007). The ceding of control to the Church also resonated with conservative political thought, which viewed social problems as best addressed not by the state but by the family, community and church (Brangan, 2021; McNally, 2007).

Before the 1960s, the concept of rehabilitation seldom featured in prison-related discourse or policy (Rogan, 2012). In fact, there was very little reflection on the purposes of imprisonment at all. On the rare occasions when it was discussed, rehabilitation discourse was tinged with paternalistic and religious overtones, and was 'reminiscent of Victorian ideals of penality', surrounding 'saving', the regenerative power of work and moral reform' (Rogan, 2012: 11). Political inertia—due to the comparatively low imprisonment rate and the dominant role played by the Catholic Church in welfare service delivery and the containment of 'deviant' populations—meant that penal policy, prison regimes and rehabilitative opportunities changed little during this time (Behan & Baston-Gates, 2016). The 1960s and 1970s witnessed a sea change, however, with rehabilitation becoming a central organising principle in penal policy (Rogan, 2012). For instance, the Prison Act 1970 enshrined rehabilitation as an aim of the criminal justice system (Rogan, 2012). Professional rehabilitation workers such as probation officers and psychologists were also introduced to the prison system for the first time (Brangan, 2021). Progress was driven by individual champions, including senior civil servants and ministers for justice, who regarded rehabilitation as being at the cutting-edge of penal policymaking (Rogan, 2012).

The socio-economic climate also favoured the emergence of penal welfare ideals at this time; progressiveness was becoming fashionable; the country was experiencing a period of economic prosperity; and political ideologies were beginning to shift leftwards (Rogan, 2012; see also Garland, 2001). However, Brangan (2021) takes a different view, proposing that the era was characterised not by a commitment to penal welfarism but by a distinctly Irish form of penality, termed pastoral penality, a 'priestly form of power' comprising a blend of progressive ideals and traditional Catholic values (Brangan, 2021: 59). Pastoral penalty was characterised by a tolerance of crime and those who committed it, with criminality attributed to poverty rather than pathology and prisoners regarded as fully fledged members of society. Imprisonment was viewed as inherently harmful, so rehabilitation was designed not to 'treat' but to help people cope with the pains of imprisonment and maintain bonds with family and community. Proponents favoured individualised approaches and distrusted experts and scientific knowledge. While progressive in many ways, pastoral penalty did not extend to all; paramilitary prisoners were subject to a security-oriented prison and women—particularly those not conforming to gender norms—did not always benefit from the same level of compassion (Brangan, 2021).

The tide turned in the 1980s as rehabilitation came to be seen as an unaffordable luxury during a decade characterised by economic instability, rising crime rates and prison over-crowding (Rogan, 2012). Accordingly, any developments during this period should be viewed as pragmatic adaptations to challenging circumstances rather than attempts to advance the rehabilitation agenda (Brangan, 2021). A seminal report from the Committee of Inquiry into the Penal System was published in 1985 but had little impact on policy or practice due to a prevailing sense of crisis in the criminal justice system (Behan & Baston-Gates, 2016; Rogan, 2012). Of the four specialist services in prison (work, education, welfare and psychology), the Committee concluded that all were under-resourced, under-staffed and housed in inadequate premises. Recognising that institutional contexts can impact rehabilitative success, the authors observed that it was difficult for rehabilitation services to 'work' in prison environments characterised by outdated and austere Victorian architecture, limited space, unsanitary conditions, a culture of distrust and few opportunities for prisoners to exercise autonomy or express their authentic selves. In the community, the report advocated the provision of additional training opportunities and praised the workshops being run by the voluntary sector in partnership with the Probation and Welfare Service. This highlights the ongoing relationship between voluntary bodies and the state in the provision of rehabilitation support.

The criminal landscape was transformed again in the 1990s by rising rates of drug addiction and drug-related crime. Attitudes towards people who committed crime were also changing, and the tolerance of previous decades was replaced with a view of them as dangerous, chaotic and difficult to rehabilitate (Brangan, 2021). Political debate narrowed accordingly, with governments no longer endorsing rehabilitation and opposition politicians framing rehabilitative sentiments as being soft on crime (Rogan, 2012). In parallel, tensions emerged among senior civil servants at the fault line between the new law-and-order agenda and traditional philosophies (Brangan, 2021). The law-and-order agenda achieved precedence for a time at least and rehabilitation was reconfigured into a mechanism for reducing reoffending, representing a move away from its traditional goal of providing assistance to marginalised individuals (Rogan, 2012). Notwithstanding these shifts, some innovations were introduced during this period, including a treatment programme for prisoners convicted of sexual offences (Behan & Baston-Gates, 2016; Rogan, 2012). In the community context, an expert group highlighted the range of probation-funded initiatives in existence, including addiction treatment, hostel accommodation and therapeutic interventions in prison, the latter marking an extension beyond the traditional probation officer role of addressing routine welfare needs (Probation and Welfare Service, 1999). The community and voluntary sectors also continued to play a central role in policymaking during this period (Swirak, 2018).

By the 2000s, the economy was booming, facilitating increases in criminal justice expenditure which were used primarily to expand criminal justice infrastructure rather than enhance rehabilitative services (Rogan, 2013). Evidencing continuity in practice, a value-for-money study found that rehabilitative projects funded by the Probation Service continued to focus on traditional welfare needs like addiction, education and training, and counselling (Petrus, 2008). The authors also expressed concern about the absence of quantifiable objectives, performance measures, case tracking and evaluation in the sector, perhaps a legacy of the anti-scientific mindset associated with pastoral penality. Following the economic crash in 2008, efforts were made to increase the use of non-custodial options, but these were designed, not to facilitate rehabilitation, but to achieve cost savings via a reduction of the prison population during a time of austerity (Healy, 2015; Rogan, 2013). Policy and practice have begun to follow international trends in recent years, as evidenced by an increasing—but largely symbolic—emphasis on risk, responsibilisation and managerialism (Healy, 2012; 2015). Taken as a whole, this examination of the rehabilitation landscape through a historical lens reveals that Irish rehabilitation policy and practice is shaped primarily by expediency and pragmatism, supporting Rogan's (2012: 25) observation that severe 'deficits of imagination' existed with regards to policymaking in this area.

Policies, Programmes and Contexts

Mapping the exact contours of the contemporary rehabilitation landscape is difficult due to the diverse structures, philosophies, sites and methods of the services involved (Swirak, 2018). Most services are delivered on a small, localised basis and there is little in the way of an organised, state-led approach to rehabilitation (Fitzgerald O'Reilly, 2018). Services are delivered by a mix of charitable organisations, state agencies and ex-prisoner organisations but the voluntary sector continues to play a prominent role (Behan & Baston-Gates, 2016). Some voluntary organisations operate independently, but most are funded totally or in part by state agencies. For instance, 36% of the Probation Service's annual budget in 2020 was allocated to voluntary bodies delivering rehabilitative services to people involved with the criminal justice system (Probation Service, 2021). Support is available at all stages of the criminal justice process and some specialist services exist to support diverse populations (Swirak, 2018). Notably, rehabilitation providers still focus primarily on welfare needs such as employment, education, addiction, accommodation and family issues. Evaluations are scarce and mostly qualitative or small scale in nature, making it difficult to gauge the effectiveness of particular interventions. Due to space constraints, a full description of rehabilitative services in Ireland cannot be provided. Instead, two theoretical frameworks will be used to organise the discussion and reflect on current trends in rehabilitation. The first is Burke et al.'s (2019) four forms of rehabilitation, which elaborates an earlier model put forward by McNeill (2012, 2014). This is supplemented by Tomczak and Buck's (2019) four-part typology, which categorises the penal voluntary sector into *functionalist regulators* which aim to correct individual flaws, with the practitioner deciding what changes and supports are needed; *interpretivist regulators* which are client-centred and focus on helping people to fix their own flaws; *agents of radical change* which focus on raising awareness of social inequalities, thereby empowering people to campaign for social change; and *agents of social change*, which focus on changing social structures and redistributing resources. While the two frameworks do not directly map onto one another, they are complementary as will be shown. It should also be noted that the forms and categories referenced in these frameworks are ideal types and, in reality, organisational paradigms are best described as 'varied, fluid and hybrid' in nature (Tomczak & Buck, 2019: 914).

The most easily recognisable rehabilitative form is psychological rehabilitation, which is 'concerned with promoting positive individual-level change', usually through structured rehabilitative programmes (McNeill, 2012: 14).

People with convictions experience a range of difficulties, including financial problems (Central Statistics Office, 2020), substance misuse (Rooney, 2021), limited educational attainment (Cleere, 2021), poor employment histories (Fitzgerald O'Reilly, 2018) and mental health issues (Gulati et al., 2019). Given this, programmes addressing these needs can be beneficial and a wealth of research shows that such assistance can help to facilitate desistance. However, the rehabilitative potential of treatment programmes may be limited because, rather than addressing structural causes of crime, most programmes focus on the individual change process or on helping people to cope with the pains of punishment, thereby legitimising current penal and social arrangements and concealing social injustices (Tomczak & Buck, 2019). Cognitive behavioural programmes designed to address so-called cognitive distortions are a classic example of this type. Cognitive behavioural programmes are not commonplace in Ireland but have been used in relation to sex offending. The first dedicated treatment programme for people convicted of sex offences, the Sex Offender Intervention Programme, was launched by the Irish Prison Service in 1994, as the numbers of prisoners convicted of sexual offences began to rise (Behan & Baston-Gates, 2016; O'Reilly et al., 2010). This was a manualised programme which used cognitive behavioural principles to treat cognitive deficits and was delivered by prison psychologists and probation officers. O'Reilly et al.'s (2010) evaluation, based on a small sample, found that the programme was partially successful in addressing cognitive distortions, victim empathy, interpersonal skills and self-regulation. However, just 10–15% of those offered a place on the programme availed of this opportunity. The programme was replaced by the Building Better Lives programme in 2009, which uses a strengths-based approach to enhance motivation to change, help people to develop a better understanding of their offending behaviour and plan for the future, and provide practical supports to ease the transition from prison to the community. This programme has not yet been evaluated but participation rates remain low (Dail Debates 30 January 2019). There are parallels between psychological rehabilitation and the regulatory approaches described by Tomczak and Buck (2019), which are designed to address individual deficits and encourage people to comply with social norms. Such approaches may appear beneficent on the surface but typically downplay structural and systemic causes of crime, placing the blame instead on personal failings (see also Burke et al., 2019).

McNeill (2014) later expanded the concept of psychological rehabilitation to include all forms of personal rehabilitation. The broader definition encompassed 'any effort that seeks to somehow change, develop or restore the person; to develop new skills or abilities, to address and resolve personal limitations or problems' (Burke et al., 2019; McNeill, 2014). Personal rehabilitation may or may not involve formal intervention but in practice involves attempts to enhance hope, skills and personal strengths. Prison education is a good example of personal rehabilitation. In Ireland, prison education is provided in partnership between the Irish Prison Service and educational services including Educational Training Boards, Public Library Services and the Open University. Educational provision covers a range of areas from basic skills (e.g. literacy and numeracy) to university-level qualifications as well as vocational and personal development courses (e.g. arts and technology). Behan's (2014) research showed that prisoners engage with education for a variety of reasons but primarily to enhance skills and qualifications, to prepare for life after release, to escape the tedium of prison routines or to gain a degree of autonomy over their lives. Cleere (2021) found that those who participate in prison education experience greater levels of hope and agency as well as stronger social capital; for instance, education provided qualifications that could be used to gain employment as well as the knowledge and confidence to participate in civic society (e.g. through voting). In this way, prison education may have an indirect effect on desistance, fostering cognitive changes that act as stepping stones to the achievement of prosocial goals. However, there are numerous barriers to educational participation, both personal and systemic. Cleere (2021) found that non-participation was due to a sense of hopelessness about the future, issues around drug addiction and embarrassment due to literacy issues as well as systemic issues such as a lack of available courses, fears about safety and negative past experiences of education. Scholars have also expressed concern that prison education is being reframed as 'an instrument of rehabilitation and nothing more', fearing that this will shift its focus from personal development to the correction of personal failings (Cleere, 2021: 4). There are also questions as to whether efforts to facilitate personal development can be effective in austere and rigidly structured environments like prisons (Behan, 2014).

Legal rehabilitation, the second form, addresses 'questions of when, how and to what extent a criminal record and the formal stigma that it represents can ever be set aside, sealed or surpassed' and the person restored to full citizenship (McNeill 2012: 14). Rehabilitation programmes designed to change the individual (or help individuals change themselves) cannot 'work' unless the collateral consequences of punishment are addressed. Recognising that rehabilitative processes (and criminal justice processes in general) are shaped by wider structural contexts, Burke et al. (2019) argue that rehabilitation discourse and practice must be embedded within a broader social justice agenda. Tomczak and Buck (2019) offer an even more radical view, highlighting initiatives that aim to raise awareness of injustices perpetrated against people with convictions, empowering them to challenge and reform inequitable social arrangements. Drug treatment offers a useful lens through which to consider the political dimensions of rehabilitation in the Irish context. Collins (2019) notes that, while addiction is best viewed as a public health issue, government responses have centred on harm reduction and punitiveness (though the current strategy incorporates a public health dimension; see Department of Health, 2017). Exemplifying the punitive approach, the Criminal Justice Act 2007 (amending the Misuse of Drugs Act 1977) introduced a minimum sentence of ten years' imprisonment for people found guilty of possessing drugs with a value of €13,000 and above. With regards to harm reduction, methadone maintenance programmes have long been the treatment of choice. While these programmes have reduced drug-related crime, Harris and McElrath (2012) argue that the goal is social control rather than treatment. The emphasis on social control generates institutional stigma, evident for example in the language surrounding drug testing where it is common for tests to be described as 'clean' or 'dirty'. This in turn creates spoiled identities that equate addiction with criminality, irrespective of a person's recovery status. From a rehabilitation perspective, the social control agenda undermines trust between clients and service providers, diminishes client agency in the treatment process and creates barriers to reintegration as people cannot seek employment if required to attend methadone clinics regularly. This example illustrates the need for radical organisations of the kind described by Tomczak and Buck (2019) to campaign for social and criminal justice reform. Such organisations can contribute to system change by advocating for the rights of people with convictions, contributing to penal debates and scrutinising government actions (Swirak, 2018). Penal reform movements are rare in the Irish context and the Irish Penal Reform Trust is perhaps the highest profile advocacy organisation (Rogan, 2012). Like its British counterpart, the Trust works to promote system change with recent campaigns centred on spent convictions, mental health and the needs of ethnic minority groups (see www.iprt.ie).

In subsequent work, Burke et al. (2019) more fully articulated a specific sub-form of legal rehabilitation, namely judicial rehabilitation. They describe the ideal courtroom as a place where dialogue and communication between stakeholders in the rehabilitative process—namely victims, community representatives, criminal justice professionals and the person who committed the offence—can take place. With regards to the factors that should influence decision-making, they propose that courts consider structural as well as personal circumstances, alongside a person's rehabilitation prospects. Drug treatment courts are arguably well-placed to facilitate this kind of rehabilitation, but do not always live up to their potential. The Dublin Drug Treatment Court, established in 2001 to deal with adults who have pleaded guilty to non-violent drug offences, is a case in point. Participants progress through three phases—bronze, silver and gold—over a two-year period, during which time they must attend rehabilitation programmes, gradually reduce their drug use and report to the court on a regular basis. Butler's (2013) research highlighted several issues undermining the rehabilitative potential of the court (see also Collins, 2019). Despite a protracted planning process, the research documented significant implementation delays, ongoing friction between healthcare and criminal justice professionals, a lack of support from key stakeholders and a range of due process concerns (e.g. defence lawyers play a limited role in court processes). Stakeholders also felt that the new bureaucratic structures disrupted existing collaborative arrangements that had been working well, albeit on an informal basis. Participant numbers are low in international terms due to strict eligibility criteria and a lack of knowledge about the court among legal professionals and judges (Gavin & Kawałek, 2020). The goal of complete abstinence also appears unrealistic, given that just 14% of participants graduated from the court between 2001 and 2009, though some reduction in offending behaviour was evident (Department of Justice Equality and Law Reform, 2010). This highlights the need for discretionary and flexible court responses to non-compliance and setbacks in the desistance process (Burke et al., 2019). Notwithstanding low participation and success rates, the court has continued in operation due to its political and symbolic appeal (Butler, 2013).

Moral rehabilitation is the third form of rehabilitation and describes approaches that offer opportunities for people with convictions to repair the harm caused by their actions and earn redemption (Burke et al., 2019). This is only part of the story, however, as society must also make good on its debts, having failed to address the social injustices that contributed to the offending behaviour. As Burke et al. (2019: 14) put it, 'a person who has offended has to "pay back" [and] an unjust society that has permitted criminogenic social inequalities to go unaddressed [...] will have debts that it must settle'. Restorative justice interventions are a classic example of moral rehabilitation, with international research highlighting benefits for people with convictions, victims and communities (see e.g. Hansen & Umbreit, 2018). Within the Irish context, a range of restorative justice options are available to young people. Under An Garda Síochána's [Irish police service] Diversion Scheme, young people may be offered a restorative justice caution or the opportunity to participate in a restorative justice conference. In practice, the lines between these options are blurred, with some cautions resembling conferences and vice versa (O'Dwyer & Payne, 2016). Research is limited but O'Dwyer's unpublished research, conducted in 2004, documented high levels of victim participation, stakeholder satisfaction and compliance with outcome agreements, though approximately one-third of participants reoffended within 12 months (O'Dwyer & Payne, 2016). In spite of these benefits, the restorative justice mechanisms offered within this programme are under-used with referrals declining steadily in recent years (Marder, 2019). Young people can also participate in the Le Chéile Restorative Justice Project, launched in 2010 to provide restorative services such as conferencing, victim-offender mediation and reparation panels. Quigley et al.'s (2015) qualitative evaluation found that participants reported higher levels of victim empathy and stronger family relationships, felt well-supported and believed their voices had been heard. Their parents agreed, saying that they felt included and respected in the process and that their well-being and understanding of their children had improved as a result. Victims likewise described feeling heard and respected and experienced enhanced well-being following participation.

With respect to adults, restorative justice options are less readily available. The introduction of Circles of Support and Accountability represents perhaps one of the more interesting developments in recent years. The model, based on restorative justice principles, brings together an inner circle comprising a small group of trained volunteers, a core member (a person with convictions for sexual offences), and an outer circle comprising criminal justice professionals such as police and probation officers. The inner circle meets with the core member on a weekly basis to offer guidance and support, encourage the person to take responsibility for their behaviour, and participate in social activities like going to the cinema. An evaluation (Cresswell, 2020; PACE, n.d.) found that participants experienced a range of benefits including enhanced wellbeing, improved social skills, stronger relationships and greater involvement in community life. However, many experienced ongoing issues with employment, accommodation and social isolation due to the stigma attached to their offences, raising questions as to whether highly stigmatised groups can ever achieve full social integration and highlighting the close inter-connections between moral and social rehabilitation. The Probation Service is working to further embed restorative justice in its work, recently establishing the Restorative Justice and Victim Services Unit to support restorative justice activities. Plans are also underway to extend victim-offender mediation to serious offences including sexual violence (Probation

Service, 2021). Despite these developments, restorative justice provision in Ireland remains 'patchy' and under-developed (Marder, 2019: 61).

While restorative justice is overtly concerned with moral rehabilitation, other criminal justice mechanisms can also play a role. There is for instance growing awareness of the need to consider the moral quality of the institutional sites where rehabilitation takes place. Liebling (2011) concluded that moral quality in prisons is grounded in staff-officer interactions, with prisoners reporting a stronger sense of legitimacy when they are treated with respect, fairness, and dignity, have positive relationships with staff and feel safe in the prison environment. Within the Irish context, the limited research on prison life makes it difficult to judge the moral quality of prisons and their ability to foster moral rehabilitation. Existing research shows mixed results in this regard; for example, Garrihy's (2020) research on prison officer occupational cultures found that officers rely on social and communication skills to navigate interactions with prisoners, sometimes using discretion to assist prisoners. At the same time, officers also used a range of strategies to assert authority over prisoners and maintain order; for instance, threatening to move non-compliant prisoners to inferior cells.

Lastly, social rehabilitation is defined as 'the informal social recognition and acceptance of the returning citizen' and as such invokes concepts like social capital, community, citizenship and social justice (Burke et al., 2019: 14). The authors argue that the state has a duty to repair the harms caused by structural injustices, not only to help people with convictions but also to strengthen communities by enhancing collective efficacy and cohesion. To achieve this requires a whole system approach comprising collaborative, community-led approaches that are responsive to local needs and concerns and prioritise the common good over profit-making. Interestingly, rehabilitation services in Ireland already follow this template to some extent, given the prominence of local and charity-led organisations in the sector. However, Swirak (2018) highlights a range of concerns linked to increased state regulation and control of the voluntary sector which, in her view, signal a shift towards a marketisation and privatisation agenda. She argues that these changes create a power imbalance between the state and voluntary sector and could place pressure on voluntary bodies to dilute traditional welfarist or social justice goals to meet funding requirements. Voluntary organisations may also lose credibility with service users when they collaborate with state agencies; for instance, relationships can suffer when rehabilitative staff are required to monitor and report on compliance or share information with state agencies. It is possible too that growing state control of the voluntary sector will have a chilling effect on advocacy work, though lack of empirical research makes it hard to gauge the true impact of these changes in the Irish context.

Bearing these caveats in mind, there are a number of interesting initiatives designed to enhance community ties and build social capital among people with convictions. For instance, the Community Return Scheme, which was introduced by the Irish Prison Service and Probation Service in 2011, is an incentivised, structured, and reviewable early release scheme. The scheme is open to people serving sentences of one to eight years who have served at least half of their sentences, been assessed as low risk and engaged with prison services. Prisoners on the scheme are granted early release and must complete unpaid work in the community such as painting or gardening work. They also receive rehabilitative supports to address issues such as accommodation, addiction, and employment/training. An evaluation of the pilot scheme (Irish Prison Service/Probation Service, 2014) identified several benefits for participants including the addition of structure and routine to their days, the opportunity to gain vocational experience and transferrable skills, and the chance to improve their reputations in the community. Recidivism rates were low, though this is perhaps because suitable cases could be cherry-picked during the early stages of the scheme. However, many participants also experienced difficulties complying with the strict sign-on conditions, accessing welfare entitlements and covering the costs associated with travel to worksites.

Perhaps one of the most innovative examples of social rehabilitation is the Community Based Health and First Aid (CBHFA) programme, which was developed by the Red Cross and Red Crescent Societies to enhance community health and hygiene in developing countries. The programme was introduced to the prison system by the Irish Red Cross in 2009 and operates in partnership between the Irish Red Cross, Irish Prison Service, City of Dublin Vocational Education Committee and the Probation Service. As part of their training, 'special status' Irish Red Cross inmate volunteers identify health needs in their prison community and, in conjunction with healthcare staff and teachers, develop and implement projects to address these needs through peer-to-peer education. The volunteers played a particularly important role during the pandemic using their knowledge in the fields of health and hygiene to communicate information about COVID-19 to the prison community, support peers through a difficult and stressful time, and assist in the implementation of infection control measures (Orcutt, 2021). To date, over 1000 prisoners have participated in the programme and around half have graduated (Irish Red Cross, 2020). Recent quantitative studies found no differences in self-efficacy or self-esteem among CBHFA volunteers before and after programme participation but did show some improvement in measures of psychological well-being (Irish Red Cross, 2020). However, O'Sullivan et al.'s (2020) small-scale qualitative study showed that CBHFA participants were able to achieve acceptance and redemption through the enactment of prosocial roles and experienced a heightened sense of agency through taking action to improve the quality of prison life. The programme has also positively impacted the prison environment; for instance, official figures showed a 90% reduction in cutting incidents in one prison following the introduction of a Weapons Amnesty Project by volunteer inmates (Betts-Symonds, 2012). Because of this, O'Sullivan et al. (2020) described the CBHFA programme as an example of transformative rehabilitation, a form of rehabilitation that not only facilitates individual change but also transforms the structural barriers that impede personal change efforts. Despite its positive impact however, volunteers were aware that a criminal record would preclude volunteer work after release, highlighting the need to consider the intersection between legal and social rehabilitation in service provision.

People with convictions often find it difficult to achieve full social inclusion and restoration of rights and citizenship. Within regards to employment, Fitzgerald O'Reilly (2018) describes how such individuals are excluded from the labour market through a process that begins before criminal justice contact and continues after the sentence is completed. People with convictions typically have histories of low educational attainment, few qualifications and limited employment experience (see e.g. Central Statistics Office, 2020). Contact with the criminal justice system compounds these disadvantages by undermining self-confidence, disrupting employment and educational histories, and not properly preparing people for life after release. Post-release, people with convictions must contend with employer discrimination and legal barriers like the requirement to disclose criminal records in certain circumstances (see the Criminal Justice (Spent Convictions and Certain Disclosures) Act 2016). Despite recent improvements, Fitzgerald O'Reilly (2018) concludes that service provision in this area remains insufficient. The government is attempting to address these issues through innovative mechanisms like social enterprise, defined as 'a whole-systems approach to increasing employment options for people with past convictions that recognises their skills and capabilities, leading to active citizenship, safer communities, fewer victims and supporting desistance' (Cafferty, 2021: 99). While criminal justice agencies play a crucial role in social rehabilitation, the Department of Justice (2020) *Working to Change: Social Enterprise and Employment Strategy 2021–2023* acknowledges that social change can only be achieved through engagement with a wide range of stakeholders, including the public. With this in mind, the strategy adopts a multi-pronged approach to enhance pathways into mainstream employment (e.g. setting up an employer forum to identify ways to reduce barriers to employment), social enterprise employment (e.g. creating a funding stream for social enterprises); and entrepreneurship (e.g. implementing a new insurance scheme specifically for social enterprises) (Cafferty, 2021). Fifty social enterprises are currently offering employment or training opportunities to 100 people with convictions. While these initiatives have not yet been evaluated, their principles and practices are very much in accord with Burke et al.'s (2019) concept of social rehabilitation.

Conclusion

This chapter offered a critical reflection on the Irish rehabilitation landscape, using a historical lens to elucidate the philosophical, structural and political roots of contemporary policy and practice. Rehabilitation is a phenomenon with many faces, a broad and ambiguous concept that can be manipulated to serve multiple ideological positions. It is also ephemeral since the rationales underpinning rehabilitation are constantly evolving and adapting to retain relevance in a changing world (Behan & Baston-Gates, 2016; Robinson, 2008). Structurally, the Irish rehabilitation sector is populated mainly by local, charity-led services. While beneficial in many ways, these arrangements have given rise to a patchwork of services with little coordination, strategy or leadership. Politically, decisions around rehabilitation are guided more by pragmatism and expediency than ideology and, consequently, the vision underpinning rehabilitation has not been fully articulated.

The review also highlighted several risks facing the Irish rehabilitation sector. For instance, the growing emphasis on rehabilitation as a tool for reducing recidivism could supplant traditional goals of personal development and social inclusion; the failure to address structural, systemic and institutional barriers could undermine personal efforts to change; the lack of research and evaluation makes it hard to gauge the effectiveness of interventions; and the dearth of whole-system and whole-society approaches could lead to different parts of the system working at cross-purposes. Nevertheless, some promising initiatives have been introduced in recent years, most notably, social enterprise schemes designed to create pathways into employment for people with convictions. Further innovation will be needed as Irish society continues to develop and diversify. In recent years, there has been growing recognition that people in contact with the justice system are not a homogenous group and that tailored services are needed for cohorts such as women and ethnic minority groups including Travellers (an indigenous Irish minority). However, this work is at an embryonic stage. Other challenges include the lack of multi-modal services for people experiencing multiple issues simultaneously.

Overall, this chapter highlights the value of an expanded rehabilitative imagination encompassing the personal, legal, moral and social dimensions of change. Revisioning rehabilitation in this way could help to mitigate barriers to change and facilitate desistance, personal growth and social inclusion. While personal rehabilitation can help to enhance agency and human capital, moral rehabilitation creates space for redemption, reconciliation and reparation; both of which are known to play a central role in desistance. Additionally, social and legal rehabilitation can create a set of political, structural and institutional conditions that support rather than impede change. An expanded rehabilitative imagination encourages us to situate personal experiences within a wider social, cultural and-historical context (cf. Mills, 2000) and, in the case of rehabilitation, to understand change not just as an individual journey but as a collective project that requires all of society to play a part.

References

Behan, C. (2014). Learning to escape: Prison education, rehabilitation and the potential for transformation. *Journal of Prison Education and Reentry, 1*(1), 20–31.

Behan, C., & Baston-Gates, J. (2016). Prison education and rehabilitation: What works? In D. Healy, C. Hamilton, Y. Daly, Y., & M. Butler (Eds.), *Routledge Handbook of Irish Criminology* (pp. 356–376). Routledge.

Betts-Symonds, G. (2012). *Community based health and first aid in action in Irish prisons: Three-year evaluation.* Irish Red Cross.

Brangan, L. (2021). *The politics of punishment: A comparative study of imprisonment and political culture.* Routledge.

Burke, L., Collett, S., & McNeill, F. (2019). *Reimagining rehabilitation: Beyond the individual.* Routledge.

Butler, S. (2013). The symbolic politics of the Dublin drug court: The complexities of policy transfer. *Drugs: Education, Prevention and Policy, 20*(1), 5–1.

Cafferty, S. (2021). 'We cannot do this alone'–A co-designed, multi-departmental strategy to increase the employment prospects of people with criminal records. *Irish Probation Journal, 18*, 91–108.

Central Statistics Office. (2020). *Offenders 2016: Employment, education and other outcomes, 2016–2019*. https://www.cso.ie/en/releasesandpublications/fp/p-offo/offenders2016employmenteducationandotheroutcomes2016-2019/ (accessed 7 April 2020).

Cleere, G. (2021). *Prison education and desistance: Changing perspectives*. Routledge.

Collins, J. (2019). The Irish experience: Policy transfer from US Drug Courts. In J. Collins, W. Agnew-Pauley, & E. Sodcrholm (Eds.), *Rethinking drug courts: International experiences of a US policy export* (pp. 51–74). London Publishing Partnership.

Committee of Inquiry into the Penal System. (1985). *Report of the committee of inquiry into the penal system [Whitaker Report]*. Stationery Office.

Cresswell, C. (2020). 'Why would you choose to study sex offenders?': Assisted desistance and reintegration of perpetrators of sexual harm. *Irish Probation Journal, 17*, 63–86.

Department of Health. (2017). *Reducing harm, supporting recovery. A health-led response to drug and alcohol use in Ireland 2017–2025*. Department of Health.

Department of Justice. (2020). *Working to Change: Social enterprise and employment strategy 2021–2023*. Stationery Office.

Department of Justice Equality and Law Reform. (2010). *Review of the drug treatment court*. https://www.justice.ie/en/JELR/Pages/drug-treatment-court-review (accessed 7 April 2022).

Fitzgerald O'Reilly, M. (2018). *Uses and consequences of a criminal conviction: Going on the record of an offender*. Palgrave Macmillan.

Garland, D. (2001). *The culture of control: Crime and social order in contemporary society*. OUP.

Garrihy, J. (2020). "There are fourteen grey areas": 'Jailing', professionalism and legitimacy in prison officers' occupational cultures. *Irish Probation Journal, 17*, 128–167.

Gavin, P., & Kawałek, A. (2020). Viewing the Dublin drug treatment court through the lens of therapeutic jurisprudence. *International Journal for Court Administration, 11*(5), 1–15.

Gulati, G., Keating, N., O'Neill, A., Delaunois, I., Meagher, D., & Dunne, C. P. (2019). The prevalence of major mental illness, substance misuse and homelessness in Irish prisoners: Systematic review and meta-analyses. *Irish Journal of Psychological Medicine, 36*(1), 35–45.

Hansen, T., & Umbreit, M. (2018). State of knowledge: Four decades of victim-offender mediation research and practice: The evidence. *Conflict Resolution Quarterly, 36*(2), 99–113.

Harris, J., & McElrath, K. (2012). Methadone as social control: Institutionalized stigma and the prospect of recovery. *Qualitative Health Research, 22*(6), 810–824.

Healy, D. (2012). *The dynamics of desistance: Charting pathways through change*. Routledge.

Healy, D. (2015). The Evolution of Probation Supervision in the Republic of Ireland: Continuity, Challenge and Change. In G. Robinson & F. McNeill (Eds.), *Community punishment: European perspectives*. Routledge.

Healy, D., & Kennefick, L. (2019). Hidden voices: Practitioner perspectives on the early histories of probation in Ireland. *Criminology and Criminal Justice, 19*(3), 346–363.

Irish Prison Service/Probation Service. (2014). *Community return: A unique opportunity: A descriptive evaluation of the first twenty-six months (2011–2013)*. https://www.justice.ie/en/JELR/Pages/PB14000333 (accessed 7 April 2022).

Irish Red Cross. (2020). *Report on the dormant account funding 2018–20*. https://www.redcross.ie/wp-content/uploads/2021/01/Final-CBH-in-Justice-3-Year-Report-2018-2020.pdf (accessed 7 April 2022).

Kilcommins, S., O'Donnell, I., O'Sullivan, E., & Vaughan, B. (2004). *Crime, punishment and the search for order in Ireland*. Institute of Public Administration.

Liebling, A. (2011). Moral performance, inhuman and degrading treatment and prison pain. *Punishment and Society, 13*(5), 530–550.

Marder, I. (2019). Restorative justice as the new default in Irish criminal justice. *Irish Probation Journal, 16*, 60–82.

McNally, G. (2007). Probation in Ireland: A Brief history of the early years. *Irish Probation Journal, 4*, 5–24.

McNeill, F. (2012). Four forms of 'offender' rehabilitation: Towards an interdisciplinary perspective. *Legal and Criminological Psychology, 17*(1), 18–36.

McNeill, F. (2014). Punishment as rehabilitation. In G. Bruinsma & D. Weisburd (Eds.), *Encyclopedia of criminology and criminal justice* (pp. 4195–4206). Springer.

Mills, C. W. (2000). *The sociological imagination*. OUP.

O'Donnell, I., & O'Sullivan, E. (2020). 'Coercive confinement': An idea whose time has come? *INcarceration, 1*(1), 1–20.

O'Dwyer, K., & Payne, B. (2016). Restorative justice. In D. Healy, C. Hamilton, Y. Daly, & M. Butler (Eds.), *Routledge handbook of Irish criminology* (pp. 222–241). Routledge.

Orcutt, J. (2021). *Irish Red Cross (IRC): Community Based Health and First Aid (CBHFA) Prison Program: IRC Inmate Volunteers Response to COVID-19 in Irish Prisons*. https://www.redcross.ie/resources/?cat_id=8 (accessed 7 April 2022).

O'Reilly, G., Carr, A., Murphy, P., & Cotter, A. (2010). A controlled evaluation of a prison-based sexual offender intervention program. *Sexual Abuse, 22*(1), 95–111.

O'Sullivan, R., Hart, W., & Healy, D. (2020). Transformative rehabilitation: Exploring prisoners' experiences of the community based health and first aid programme in Ireland. *European Journal on Criminal Policy and Research, 26*(1), 63–81.

PACE. (n.d). *Assisted Desistance: An Evaluation of PACE Prevention Services for People with Convictions for Harmful Sexual Behaviour.* https://paceorganisation.ie/wp-content/uploads/pdf/ASSISTED%20DESISTANCE%20An%20Evaluation%20of%20PACE%20Prevention%20Services%20for%20people%20with%20convictions%20for%20harmful%20sexual%20behaviour.pdf (accessed 7 April 2022).

Petrus. (2008). Value for money and policy review report on projects funded by the probation service. https://www.justice.ie/en/JELR/Pages/PB08000394 (accessed 7 April 2022).

Probation and Welfare Service. (1999). *Final report of the expert group on the probation and welfare service.* Stationery Office.

Probation Service. (2021). *Annual report 2020.* Probation Service.

Quigley, M., Martynowicz, A., & Gardner, C. (2015). Building bridges: An independent evaluation of Le Cheile's restorative justice project. Research findings. *IRish Probation Journal, 12,* 241–257.

Quinlan, C. (2016). Women, imprisonment and social control. In D. Healy, D. C. Hamilton, Y. Daly, & M. Butler (Eds.), *Routledge Handbook of Irish Criminology* (pp. 500–522). Routledge.

Robinson, G. (2008). Late-modern rehabilitation: The evolution of a penal strategy. *Punishment and Society, 10*(4), 429–445.

Rogan, M. (2012). Rehabilitation, research, and reform: Prison policy in Ireland. *Irish Probation Journal, 9,* 6–32.

Rogan, M. (2013). The Irish penal system: Pragmatism, neglect and the effects of austerity. In V. Ruggiero, & M. Ryan, (Eds.), *Punishment in Europe: A Critical Anatomy of Penal Systems* (pp. 86–110). Palgrave Macmillan.

Rooney, L. (2021). Substance misuse and supervision: An examination of drug and alcohol misuse among probation service clients. *Irish Probation Journal, 18,* 137–158.

Swirak, K. (2018). Unmasking the "criminal justice voluntary sector" in the Republic of Ireland: Towards a research agenda. *Irish Probation Journal, 15,* 24–46.

Tomczak, P., & Buck, G. (2019). The penal voluntary sector: A hybrid sociology. *British Journal of Criminology, 59*(4), 898–918.

Serving a Sentence in Italy: Old and New Challenges

Luisa Ravagnani and Carlo Alberto Romano

When considering the rehabilitation of people who have committed a crime, it is important to note the lack of clarity of the very term rehabilitation in the literature, at both the national and supranational levels. Fergus McNeill (2014), in his attempt to define this, adopted the term 'tangle', that in the criminology literature spans both theory and practice. Sonja Meijer (2017) later pointed out that the concept of rehabilitation remains vague and is implemented differently in various European nations. In Italy, the term is not included among the fundamental principles in penal law: Article 27 of the Italian Constitution, which came into force in 1948, states in its third paragraph that 'sentences cannot consist of treatments that are contrary to the sense of humanity and must tend toward a re-education of the sentenced people'. The re-educational aim of the sentence thus became, for the first time in the national context, the principal aim of the sentence, relegating the ideas of retribution and deterrence to a secondary level. The term can be traced back to the scientific culture of the time when the Italian Constitution

---

L. Ravagnani (✉)
Dipartimento Di Giurisprudenza, Università Degli Studi Di Brescia,
Via san Faustino, Brescia, Italy
e-mail: luisa.ravagnani@unibs.it

C. A. Romano
University of Brescia, Brescia, Italy

was written, dominated by the pedagogic ethos. Nowadays the concepts re-socialization, rehabilitation and inclusion are preferred. Although not entirely interchangeable, in Italy these terms refer to the possibility of abandoning deviant behaviour.

The long history of the developmental pathway of this fundamental principle has not yet led to a concrete implementation of the concept, at least as regards the enforcement of prison sentences. The conditions of chronic overcrowding, lack of staff and inadequate institutions, have in practice prevented the period of detention from becoming a time of promoting change and a proper tool for assisting re-entry into society after the completion of the sentence. To deal with this partial failure, legislators have at various times introduced modifications of the norms, envisaging alternatives to prison sentences, such as probation. In recent years, new penal pathways, such as pre-trial probation, have been formulated and applied with positive results, starting in the Juvenile Courts. However, even today rehabilitation remains a target that depends too strongly on the goodwill of prison and probation officers rather than on well-structured good practices. Aware of the limits of the procedures currently applied, professionals are continually in search of applicative solutions that may most efficaciously achieve effective rehabilitation.

In this context, an important role has always been played by politics and public opinion. These tend to regard prison as a tool to be used to guarantee collective security rather than an opportunity for rehabilitation, not understanding that, often it perpetuates deviancy. Until a greater awareness of the need to contribute pathways encouraging desistance in an active and collective manner spreads more widely, the term rehabilitation runs the risk of remaining, for many more years, a concept that is full of shared general principles but is poorly carried out in practice.

A Brief Historical Outline of the Rehabilitation System in Italy

The historical evolution of the system of the enforcement of the sentences in Italy has been, ever since its first conception, characterized by a strong divide between the good intentions of the Constitution and the reality of their implementation. In the years after the Constitution became law, and, as we will see, still today (Manconi et al., 2015), the penitentiary system was very clearly different from the one envisaged in the Constitution itself. Penal institutes, whose structural conditions were 'shameful' (Corleone, 2015) have always been grossly overcrowded, a problem that was periodically but inefficaciously alleviated for a brief time by emergency measures like amnesty and pardons that temporarily brought the situation within slightly better limits. Moreover, the opportunity offered to spend the detention time fruitfully by practising work activities, was always extremely limited, and little more than lip service was ever paid to this option. Internal training opportunities were also minimal, and inmates spent 16–18 consecutive hours in their cells, in extremely distressing conditions.

Against this dark panorama offering no re-educational prospects in the form of probation, reduced sentences for good behaviour, or the granting of pardons (applicable only in rare cases by the Ministry of Justice), inmates had little to hope for, but also little to lose if they resorted, as they so often did, to violent behaviour inside the prison (Ricci & Salierno, 1971). This gave rise—in conjunction with the historical period in Italy from the 1960s characterized by high levels of violence—to a phase of riots inside penitentiaries in the attempt to draw attention to the huge gap between the principles of Article 27 of the Constitution and their complete non-application in the penitentiaries. There were some desultory attempts to humanize prisons, for instance, the fitting of a television per section to allow inmates to keep up to date with what was happening in the outside world, but the weak, under-resourced penitentiary administrations continued to use violence as the means to suppress the protests that sometimes developed into full uprisings. This recourse to violence during the most serious episodes that drove the inmates to decide to occupy the roofs of the prisons and shout out their protests to the world resulted in the death of some inmates and the wounding of others. In that out-of-control situation, there were numerous successful prison escapes.

The ongoing prison reform bill was finally presented in 1973 but modified in 1974, even before it became law, owing to the outbreak of more grave forms of violence that led to the introduction of restrictions of the proposed new alternative measures and penitentiary regime. Moreover, no provision was made in the law for increasing the human and economic resources in order to achieve the specified objectives. The Reform also introduced the figure of the *Surveillance Judge* and the *Surveillance Court* with a specific supervisory role in the enforcement of the sentences, but implementation of the latter was postponed, and it became operative only in 1974. Among all the innovative aspects dealt with in the new law, the introduction of licences for sentenced people was particularly important because it left the *Surveillance Judge* ample discretion in their application of discipline. However, the greatest novelty in the new norms was undoubtedly the introduction of the above-mentioned alternative measures to prison sentences and of the institution of early release which reduced the time spent in prison to 45 days every six months if the person maintained positive behaviour during the detention. However, the alternatives to imprisonment, as formulated in the new law, were soon revealed to be inadequate: they were too rigid, applicable to very few inmates and therefore only useful as a means of improving the difficult situation in the penitentiaries. Moreover, at the beginning of 1977 visiting permits were modified by a law that reduced them to the status of exceptional tools to be used only in the case of extremely serious family events. Between the 1970s and 1980s, in the tense climate induced by the internal terrorist actions that shocked the country, prison became a place where order was the most important priority, to be attained at whatever cost.

Maximum security prisons were created in these years for those prisoners considered to be most dangerous to society, while all others (except for those few fortunate individuals who were working or attending school) were kept in their cells all day except for the one hour spent in the outside courtyard. All this was clearly strongly at variance with the reform that had been passed shortly before. However, the show of force made in the penal institutions did not quell the ongoing disorders, riots and violence. It was not until the 1986 Legge Gozzini[1] came into force that a truly positive change occurred, and renewed attention was paid to the Constitutional principles in Article 27. Essentially, this law acted on two fronts: maximum security prisons and alternative measures, eliminating practically all the obstacles to the application of the latter to most inmates. This law played a fundamental role in reaffirming the principle of rehabilitation of each sentenced person, regardless of their offence. However, in the 1990s, following a strong revival of organized crime, the State responded with a heavy hand, introducing restrictions on access to alternative measures and to permits rewarded for good behaviour for those prisoners responsible for an extensive list of crimes considered particularly heinous. In addition, the extremely rigid detention system called the '41 bis' (from the number of the article in the penitentiary law that regulates it) was introduced, it being a permanent maximum security regimen for those who had taken part in organized crime activities.

In 1998, a new law[2] confirmed the pivotal role of the enforcement of the sentence outside of prison, and despite a few obstacles linked to specific situations as described above, the rehabilitation principle gained a new impetus and territorial probation measures started to be applied more widely. In the next years, many laws were passed that improved the applicability of the alternative measures for some specific categories of prison inmates (e.g. for people affected by AIDS, women with young children, and people aged over

70 years), in the hope of improving the application of individual treatment pathways aimed at effective rehabilitation. But it was not until the suspension of the sentence with probation for adults was introduced[3] that an increased number of people could benefit from external non-custodial treatment to degrees almost equalling those serving a prison sentence.

Currently, the area of alternative measures to prison is a major commitment of the *Surveillance Courts* and the probation offices. Data updated to 15 January 2022 indicate 31,183 alternative measures and 24,182 suspension of the sentences with probation in force throughout Italy (www.giustizia.it). Considering that in 1990 there were 6300, (www.giustizia.it), it is evident that this sector has grown enormously, confirming the utility of these rehabilitation tools in reducing recidivism. Nevertheless, the penitentiary system itself does not appear to have gained relief from these strong attempts to comply with the constitutional principles. In fact, the prison population has grown continually since 1990, generating such serious overcrowding that this situation has been a cause of condemnation of Italy by the European Court of Human Rights on more than one occasion (ECHR, 2013).

Rehabilitation Mechanisms: Context and Statistics

In Italian penitentiary law, the achievement of the rehabilitation purpose is directed towards both sectors, prison and probation, to which restorative justice in the form of the suspension of the trial with probation has recently been added. The idea that prison, despite all the intrinsic critical elements linked to the deprivation of personal liberty, should have a positive treatment value, to be attained with the aid of programmes involving professionals (educators, psychologists, criminologists) and resort to external community measures, is rooted in the Penitentiary Law (articles 15–16) and cannot, therefore, be formally abandoned. However, for a series of sociopolitical and cultural reasons, over time the attempts to achieve a positive reintegration into society have been concentrated in the system of alternative measures, leaving the prisons to suffer a slow but constant involution in which the rehabilitation principle has been constantly eroded and lost. Obsolete facilities and chronic overcrowding then contributed to a definitive decline in the detention conditions to the extent that it seems paradoxical even to mention the rehabilitation purpose of the prison sentence. If it is true that internal rehabilitation treatment, based as much as possible on study, work, religious worship and recreational activities involving the external community, demands scientific, targeted approaches built around individual needs (Article13 Penitentiary Law), members of staff need to be appropriately trained, but this rarely happens.

As regards the above-mentioned components of prison treatment, the available statistics do not offer reasons for optimism: people involved in some kind of working activities in prison are only 35.5% of the total prison population, and of these 88% are employed by the penitentiary administration and so engaged in activities such as cleaning the common rooms, distributing goods or preparing meals (data updated to 30/12/2021, www.giustizia.it). In this context, it is interesting to note that the numbers for this aspect (work inside the prison) are similar to the ones of 1991 (34.5% of working prisoners, of whom, 89.5% were employed by the prison administration) and this clearly shows the inability of the correctional department to improve the intramural work situation. The fact that there are rare working activities connected to the external production chains of factories is a clear illustration of an isolated prison world strongly separated from society. According to the study, an element of personal growth, a conceptual pillar of penitentiary treatment, is pursued by only 28.5% of people in prison who are enrolled in one of the 1655 courses offered by the 190 Italian penal institutes. It is also interesting to note that 40.5% of the total number of the involved people engaged in the literacy courses offered by the Italian prison administration were foreigners (Mulè, 2009).

Recreational activities, mainly organized by people working for charity associations or by single volunteers, in accordance with articles 17 and 78 of the penitentiary law, have been organized with (or have counted upon) the collaboration of 9825 people authorized by the *Ministry of Justice*. The choice to delegate the creation of rehabilitation projects to Civil Society Organizations (CSOs) and Non-Governmental Organizations (NGOs) is, however, in some senses limited. The availability of such treatments is extremely uneven across the country because the areas most sensitive and better endowed with economic resources can guarantee a variety of proposals whereas others less well organized or financed, have difficulty in offering adequate proposals. Also, as regards safeguarding the right to religious worship, daily practice is very different from that required by law especially concerning the practice of the Islamic faith. In practice a Catholic priest is always available despite the diverse needs of those of different faiths entering the prisons. Muslims in prison (the second most numerous group after Catholics) can only rarely count on the presence of authorized spiritual guides and only in 20.5% of the prisons is there an adequate space provided for the practice of worship other than for the Catholic faith (Antigone, 2021). The problem of freedom of worship in prison has been recognized only in recent years but with specific reference to the risk of radicalization and the prevention and countering violent extremism strategies, thus raising the possibility of leading to further limitations of the rights of this group of prisoners (Ravagnani & Romano, 2017).

The fact that these inadequate detention conditions have failed to arouse loud protests by public opinion confirms the point that detention is generally seen as retribution and a way to protect society (Scimià, 1987), whereas with probation, ever since its introduction as an alternative sentence, the community has seemed to be poorly aware of its potential. Clearly, the impact, in terms of reducing recidivism and hence increasing the level of social security, has not been adequately understood. Most of the population has always regarded alternative measures as intended to unfairly reduce the prison sentence and set sentenced people free earlier than the judicial authorities had judged right (Calvanese, 2010). Underlying the dissent by public opinion, reference is often wrongly made to the idea that the certitude of punishment is undermined by what is seen as an unfair early return of the culprit to society (Donini, 2012). Such an idea encompasses the vision of the Italian penal system being too soft with criminals and disrespectful of the rights of the victims. What is lacking in these arguments against the application of alternative measures is the awareness that the gradual application of these tools (in other words the sequential progress from more limited advantages like permits to greater benefits like probation) presupposes the attribution of a growing responsibility to the individual; and, supported by a reference figure and supervised by a jurisdictional authority (the supervising Magistrate, the *Surveillance Court* or the probation officer, depending on the case) the development of an attitude predisposed to a positive reintegration into society.

Provisions such as prison licences granted for good behaviour, home detention and probation under the supervision of the social services are not mandatorily applied in penitentiary law. Nevertheless, over the years the will to optimize the rehabilitation treatment ethos has consolidated these practices in the *Surveillance Courts*, since premium permits (that can be granted for progressively longer periods in subsequent applications) are regarded as a preliminary step allowing the application in the near future of ever wider probation measures. The system of the enforcement of the sentences offers good guarantees of achieving the objectives specified in the Italian Constitution. However, some structural limits, which are inherent to the tools themselves, cannot be ignored and will be discussed in the next section. If poorly understood and implemented, they run the risk of creating inconsistency of treatment among sentenced people thus undermining the efforts to reduce the levels of recidivism.

Available Tools for the Rehabilitation of Sentenced People

In the last 15 years, among academics and operators in the field it has become increasingly evident that the rehabilitation system has, at least in part, not come up to the expectations and overall, the within-walls reform model has been a failure (Bertaccini, 2021). The need to consider other possible approaches, such as a reinforced use of alternative measures (also including pre-trial probation that until then in Italy had only concerned the trials of minors) and the introduction of tools tending towards the idea of restorative justice, has become increasingly evident. Regarding the former, certainly the legislators will take into account specific situations involving vulnerable people (drug addicts or alcoholics, those with mental health problems, sentenced people over 60 years of age affected by specific diseases, and those over 70) be underlined (Romano et al., 2020) as well as the problems of women with children under 10 years (Ravagnani & Policek, 2015). For all these groups, specific alternative measures had already been introduced at separate times with the aim of carrying out re-education programmes based, above all, on the consideration of any particular health or social problems that unless adequately managed could negatively affect such rehabilitation efforts. These include home detention and probation under the supervision of the social services, which are in fact guaranteed, under certain limits of the length of detention sentence, to the entire penitentiary population, (excluding the perpetrators of crimes considered particularly dangerous, as listed in the penitentiary law), although handled in a specific way for the vulnerable people listed above.

Probation under the supervision of social services certainly has some more incisive characteristics in terms of rehabilitation. Based on the enjoyment of ample daily freedom, which must be filled with adequate working or study activities, interpersonal relationships (with, for example, family members), this can be seen as an excellent, inclusive tool available to the competent supervising authorities in the Italian panorama. However, its basic elements (working activities, home, socio-familial relationships) can in practice introduce problems of discrimination that tend to mostly affect those perpetrators of crimes defined by Margara (2015) as representatives of 'social detention' (the imprisonment of people belonging to the most poor and marginalized persons) and foreigners. Both categories have difficulty in meeting the minimum requirements for the application of the measure (Durnescu et al., 2017). Moreover, the theoretical, positive application of probation is often at variance with its actual implementation since, for example, the requirement for regular police controls at the workplace and the subject's residence place poses the risk of compromising the positive relationships with, for example, employers and colleagues who should not necessarily be informed about the individual's judicial situation. The stigma attached to a person involved in the penal system is one of the elements that most seriously affects any attempt to build a new social image (Chiricos et al., 2007; Copenhaver et al., 2007). Finally, it cannot be ignored that the times taken to apply alternative measures (due to the jurisdictional monitoring of the *Surveillance Court* magistrate) are often incompatible with allowing people to take up a job offer or move into the chosen social housing, both of which are very difficult for them to find. Waiting for at least six months for the Court hearing may in fact cause the loss of previously available job offers or housing.

Home detention, the second alternative measure to prison in order of importance in the Italian penitentiary system, does not present any treatment possibilities since it simply allows the individual to serve the sentence at home or at another domicile considered suitable. However, this option should not be ignored. In fact, almost to the same extent as the deprivation of personal liberty in a prison environment, the successful outcome of home detention depends on the individual maintaining good self-control because even if not under supervision 24 hours per day, they must conform to strict behavioural rules (first of all those related to the fact that he or she is forbidden to venture outside the prescribed area within the strict home perimeter). This self-control, often for periods as long as two years, needs to be strong and reliable and can demonstrate a serious willingness to change. In this sense, and in view of the self-management capacity required, home detention can be considered a highly re-educational instrument, especially compared to the imprisonment option that completely deprives the individual of personal liberty and tends to lead to very immature self-management during the little leisure time available (Vianello, 2020). Before moving on to consider restorative justice approaches, it is worth mentioning both the 'semi-liberty' option among the alternative measures that is available to the Italian sentencing system and the use of electronic monitoring.

The observations made above about the gradual approach to the different rehabilitation tools are equally valid in the context of semi-liberty whereby the inmate spends the daytime outside the prison, engaged in study or working activities. However, since access to premium permits gained more widespread use as a precursor of the application of more ample measures such as probation, semi-liberty has been used less and less, accounting for only 2.5% of the overall alternative measures now applied (www.giustizia.it). It is reserved mainly for people sentenced to life imprisonment, excluding those sentenced to life for the commission of a crime on the list of those considered most heinous (the so-called 'ergastolo ostativo'): they are still today precluded from access to any alternative sentence. The issue of a sentence that precludes any hope of future freedom and is thus in conflict with the rehabilitation purpose of the punishment, is a matter of constant debate. The Constitutional Court[4] states that a life sentence is legitimate because 'the function of the punishment is certainly not simply the rehabilitation of the sentenced person because there can be no doubt that dissuasion, prevention and social defence are, no less than the hoped-for amendment, at the root of the punishment'. Nevertheless, it must be recognized that the stark contrast between the re-educational aim and perpetual banishment from society has been significantly diminished since the admission of life-sentenced people to conditional release after having served at least 20 years of imprisonment.[5] The concession of this benefit, if the person shows certain signs of repentance and a changed attitude, in practice annuls the perpetuity of the life sentence.

Electronic monitoring was introduced in the Italian legal system in the context of measures restricting personal liberty in 2000[6] that featured some modifications of the penal procedure code and penitentiaries law. It became possible to apply the use of electronic monitoring in order to achieve two aims: firstly, to respond to the growing demand of public opinion to strengthen public security and secondly, to deal with the steadily increasing grave problem of overcrowding in prison. In subsequent years electronic monitoring became a tool for use in specific pre-trial situations (instead of the application of a precautionary detention measure) or to replace a brief prison sentence, but also as an alternative during the last period of a medium- or long-term prison sentence. The application of electronic monitoring is always subject to the individual's consent, but the latter is largely a theoretical matter since failure to accept it causes the immediate imposition of a custodial measure. Apart from the evolution of the norms that have led, in theory, to an increased use of this tool, the debate for and against it has always been very sharp, especially regarding the ethical and legal questions linked to its application. One of the main objections to electronic monitoring is its relation to the concept of rehabilitation: the use of remote control of people deprived of personal liberty, and especially those serving their sentence according to one of the alternative measures, introduces the risk of a negative bias, skewing the final aim away from rehabilitation towards public security. During the Covid-19 pandemic, to reduce the numbers in prison, a new law[7] introduced a change in the criteria for access to home detention. It stipulated the use of electronic monitoring in all cases of home detention for a period exceeding six months, but this in practice has reduced the chances of access to this option because there were too few devices available: the results have, therefore, fallen far short of the expectations. From the very first application of this tool, the drawback has always been the chronic lack of electronic devices despite the millionaire contracts awarded to the supplier firms (until 2020, the number of applications of this option remained limited to just a few dozen cases) and the trend for 2020, although improving, still has not reached significant numbers (latest data released on 29 May 2020 by the *Garante Nazionale delle Persone Private della libertà*—National Guarantor of People Deprived of Liberty) with only 1005 people in home detention undergoing electronic monitoring.

The suspension of trial during probation, introduced in 2014 extended the possibility, previously only available for juveniles, for people who had committed a crime to avoid trial and avoid a criminal conviction if the prescription established for a specific time lapse by the Judge of the preliminary investigations has come to a satisfactory end. This provision, with its strong connotation of social and individual restitution, presupposes consent by the involved person (Cornelli et al., 2018. However, it cannot be denied that its inclusion in the pre-trial phase does not only indicate the will to offer greater rehabilitation possibilities to the perpetrators of crimes (Carabellese & Grattagliano, 2008)—inherent in the constant need to implement the constitutional principles described above—but also highlights the problems faced by the Italian penal system, due to the large number of pending trials and the overcrowding of the penitentiaries. In just a few years, the introduction of this option, together with community service, has led to a doubling of the overall number of people serving alternative sentences (68,870 people under supervision by probation officers—data at www.giustizia.it) so that it exceeds the number in prison (54,372—data at www.giustizia.it).

The option to carry out unpaid working activities for the community, applicable in different ways depending on various criteria disseminated in the Italian legal system, has had a lesser impact, but it accords with the definition of re-education as defined by Dolcini and Marinucci (2001), namely a process of modification of attitudes hindering constructive social participation. This tool is aimed on the one hand, at reducing recourse to detention and on the other, at offering people who have committed a crime a concrete chance to become reintegrated into the community. It can be applied as the main penal sentence (in the case of minor crimes, devolved to a specific Judge called *Judge of Peace*) and as a substitute sentence. According to the same law, in cases of inability or failure to pay a fine, or in cases of a sentence or plea bargain for minor crimes involving drug addicts or alcoholics where the conditions for the application of a conditionally suspended sentence are not me, this may be converted to community service. This can be applied also as reparative conduct or in special recognition of repentance[8] (envisages conditional suspension of the sentence, subordinated to a series of obligations including community service), or as an accessory penalty[9] in controversies arising over road accidents. Finally, reference must be made firstly, to the possibility of implementing community service in accordance with Law 67/2014 that focusses on its re-educational aspects by making the suspension of the trial (in some specific cases) subject to the completion of public utility works; and secondly, to the introduction of a new Article 20 (called Article 20 ter) in the penitentiary law[10] that allows prisoners, depending on their specific occupational skills and attitudes, to be admitted to public utility work during their detention. This clearly highlights the rehabilitation aims of this option and the general view that an adequate re-orientation scheme must be implemented to achieve the true rehabilitation aim of the sentences.

Rehabilitation of Sentenced Foreigners

As previously mentioned, Article 27 of the Italian Constitution is strictly linked to the fundamental principles enunciated in the opening articles (1–12) among which is Article 3, which condemns every form of discrimination and calls upon the State to guarantee the practical achievement of this principle, is particularly important. Inevitably, a corollary of this is that rehabilitation as the purpose of the sentence must not encounter obstacles for the individual in the form of cultural, ethnic, religious or linguistic difficulties. Unfortunately, the risk of a foreigner suffering discrimination is very real, especially in cases where elements of ethnic or racial prejudice are present, as is sometimes the case with people coming from specific geographical areas or belonging to cultures or religions that are poorly integrated in the social context.

Discriminatory attitudes can take the form of verbal or physical abuse but are more commonly observed in the kind of attitudes that are difficult to classify in terms of arbitrary violation of the rights of foreigners. Examples of this include ignoring informal requests made by foreigners for a different allocation, frequent recourse to disciplinary penalties in their regards and the use of more frequent and rigid cell searches. Other forms of discrimination against foreigners can include the impossibility of taking part in schooling or work activities aimed at social reintegration. Although these are ostensibly open to all, they are often inaccessible to foreigners because of language issues and the lack of an interpreter. Access to the alternatives to imprisonment described above, although guaranteed to all condemned people by law, in the case of foreigners is strongly limited because of their lack of resources and status as foreigners (Durnescu et al., 2017). This discrimination also includes failure to prepare them for a return to the community. In addition, being unable to take advantage of those tools that should have been provided during their detention, they have greater difficulties in finding work, building stable interpersonal relationships and obtaining the economic support available to other vulnerable people. Moreover, their widespread inability—or reduced possibility—to communicate with their family makes it often difficult for them to return and re-enter their own country or community (Ravagnani & Romano, 2013).

Also, the application of European Framework Decisions based on achieving a satisfactory level of social reintegration and hence rehabilitation[11] have not yielded the anticipated results. Initially seen as a useful tool to reduce the worrying level of prison overcrowding, they have in practice been less than the hoped for, thus undermining European efforts to bring about a unitary system of penal enforcement of sentences aimed at reducing recidivism and increasing collective security.

Empirical Results of the Italian Rehabilitation System

The data regarding recidivism have long been the subject of strong debate among operators in the field and public opinion. The lack of systematic collection and evaluation of elements that could assess the efficacy of the available rehabilitation tools has resulted in the circulation of poorly illustrative data. Nevertheless, important, albeit not recent research conducted in 2007 (Leonardi, 2007) confirmed the positive feelings of the supporters of community-based approaches. According to this research, 68.5% of the people in prison in Italy are recidivist compared to 19% of those granted an alternative sentence. To fill the gap created by the lack of empirical evidence, reflections can be made about the small number of cases of the recalls of alternative sanctions (Ravagnani et al., 2018): these data are, in fact, a useful indication of the capacity of these approaches to affect recidivism and even more importantly, desistance (Weaver, 2019). In particular, the Ministerial data show that in most cases, the number of recalls is higher in regard to measures applied during prison (4%) than those that avoid imprisonment altogether (2.5%). This result confirms the evidence, amply shared in the literature (Cullen et al., 2011), that imprisonment has a negative influence on the possibility of future social reintegration.

As far as probation is concerned, the highest recall numbers are found in those forms of probation involving drug or alcohol addicted people (11.5% of people serving the first part of the sentence in prison, 6.5% of the people serving the whole sentence in the outside community, with the application of an alternative measure). These recalls concern almost entirely the negative assessment of the person's behaviour during the enforcement of the alternative measure (8.5% of people that have served the first part of the sentence in prison have been recalled for the violation of the prohibition of consuming drugs, and 4.5% of people serving the whole sentence in probation have been recalled for the same reason) rather than for the commission of a new crime (1.5% people who served the first part of the sentence in prison have been recalled for the commission of a new crimes while the 1% of people serving the whole sentence in probation have been recalled for the same reason). The highest number of probation recalls in these cases must undoubtedly be attributed to the specific characteristics of the measure itself involving as it does the serious nature of the individual's addiction. In these cases positive progress may be followed by relapses: in other words, a higher rate of failure is inevitable in those addicted to psycho-voluptuary substances.

As to the overall data on the recall of alternative measures, issued by the Italian Ministry of Justice, it is important to remember that of the 6% of total recalls only 1% are due to the commission of a new crime, 3% to a negative assessment of the interested person's progress and 1% to a new, definitive legal position that increases the limits of the sentence beyond those envisaged at the time of sentence. The available data allow some positive observations to be made about the measures currently available for the rehabilitation of sentenced people, at least in the short term. However, as regards long-term results further analyses need to be developed, aimed at assessing the stability of conduct of sentenced people and studying the risk of recidivism after an interval of at least 5–10 years.

Future Perspectives: New Rehabilitation Paradigms

The prison rehabilitation model in force in Italy has thus clearly been a failure, especially in terms of its re-educational purpose. If education is the product of a greater awareness and stronger values stemming from the participation in a certain number of quality relations and experiences, then prison is the very opposite of a 'virtuous' or efficacious educational model (Ferraro, 2013). Certainly, imagining that one can socialize people in society and help them to live peaceably with others by preventing them from living in society, can only be an empty rhetorical exercise lacking any real content. In contrast, probation measures, by restoring the social dimension to the perpetrators of crimes, can lead them towards the acquisition of relational models that may act as the backbone of a correct, stable and lasting return to the social world. It is generally recognized among all operators in the world of justice that it is necessary, finally, to achieve a major improvement of all the critical aspects evident in the penitentiary environment.

This is also expressed in the illuminated attitude of the current Minister of Justice, Marta Cartabia, that has led to the formulation of a new Law[12] in which the Parliament delegates the Government to intervene for the improvement of the criminal trial and for the implementation of an efficient restorative justice system. This law presents profoundly innovative characteristics about the need to implement and reinforce rehabilitation pathways for people who have committed a crime, stating that the clear objective of applying probation in all cases where the penalty is no longer than a maximum of six years. Moreover, the Government is called upon to align restorative justice in accordance with EU norms, definitions, programmes, criteria for access, guarantees and stipulation of which individuals have the right to participate. Efforts must be made to ensure that, with the aid of an impartial third party, the victim and the perpetrators can actively participate in the resolution of the conflict and the consequences of the crime.

It is to be hoped that, at least this time, the new discipline, which shows good signs of promising outcomes, may be supported by the necessary investments in terms of economic and human resources. Should these fail to materialize, it will count as nothing more than yet another lost opportunity to bring Italian justice nearer to the real needs of citizens, while respecting the fundamental rights of all the involved parties.

Notes

1. Law 10 October 1986 n. 663 LEGGE 10 ottobre 1986, n. 663—Normattiva.
2. Law 27 May 1998 n. 165 Legge 165/98 (camera.it).
3. Law 26 April 2014 n. 67 LEGGE 28 aprile 2014, n. 67—Normattiva.
4. Constitutional Court n. 264 of 22 November 1974 Sentenza n. 264 del 1974 (giurcost.org).
5. as introduced by Law n. 1634 of 25 November 1962 Gazzetta Ufficiale.
6. Law Decree 341/2000 DECRETO-LEGGE 24 novembre 2000, n. 341—Normattiva.
7. Law Decree 178/2020 Gazzetta Ufficiale.
8. Law 12 June 2004 n. 145 L 145/2004 (camera.it).
9. Law 21 February 2006 n. 102 LEGGE 21 febbraio 2006, n. 102—Normattiva.
10. With Law Decree 2 October 2018 Gazzetta Ufficiale.
11. European Framework Decision 909/2008 and European Framework Decision 947/2009.
12. Law 27 September 2021 n 134 LEGGE 27 settembre 2021, n. 134—ormattiva.

References

Antigone, A. (2021). *Oltre il virus. XVII Rapporto di Antigone sulle condizioni di detenzione*. https://www.rapportoantigone.it/diciassettesimo-rapporto.sulle-condizioni-di-detenzione/

Bertaccini, D. (2021). *Fondamenti di critica della pena e del penitenziario*. Bononia University Press.

Calvanese, E. (2010). *Pena riabilitativa e mass media*. Franco Angeli Editore

Carabellese, F., & Grattagliano, I. (2008). *Funziona la messa alla prova? Indagine su cinque anni di applicazione della MAP del Distretto di Bari Foggia*. Pensamultimedia. Lecce.

Chiricos, T., Barrick, K., Bales, W., & Bontrager, S. (2007). The labeling of convicted felons and its consequences for recidivism. *Criminology, 45*(3), 547–581.

Copenhaver, A., Edwards-Willey, T. L., & Byers, B. D. (2007). Journeys in social stigma: The lives of formerly incarcerated felons in higher education. *Journal of Correctional Education, 58*(3), 268–283. http://www.jstor.org/stable/23282578

Corleone, F. (2015). *Alessandro Margara. La giustizia e il senso di umanità. Antologia di scritti su carcere, opg, droghe e magistratura di sorveglianza*. Fondazione Michelucci Press.

Cornelli, R., Binik, O., Dova, M., & Zamburlini, A. (2018). La messa alla prova per adulti nel territorio di Milano. Analisi dell'applicazione di una misura innovativa nel panorama sanzionatorio italiano. *Rassegna Italiana di Criminologia*. Anno XI, n. 1. PensaMultimedia.

Cullen, F. T., Jonson, C. L., & Nagin, D. S. (2011). Prisons do not reduce recidivism: The high cost of ignoring science. *The Prison Journal, 91*(3), 48S-65S. https://doi.org/10.1177/0032885511415224

Dolcini, G., & Marinucci, E. (2001). *Studi di diritto penale*, Milano, Giuffrè.

Donini, M. (2012). *Certezza della pena e certezza del diritto. Una riforma chirurgica per risolvere il non-sistema*. Diritto Penale Contemporaneo, n. 1. DPC_Trim_1_2012-227-232.pdf (criminaljusticenetwork.eu).

Durnescu, I., Perez, M., de Tudela, E., & Ravagnani, L. (2017). Prisoner transfer and the importance of the 'release effect.' *Criminology and Criminal Justice., 17*(4), 450–467. https://doi.org/10.1177/1748895816677173

ECHR (2013). Case of Torreggiani and Others v. Italy. https://www.hudoc.echr.coe.int/eng#/fulltext:/torreggiani/itemid:/001-115937//

Ferraro, S. (2013). *La pena visibile o della pena del carcere*. Rubettino Editore.

Leonardi, F. (2007). Le Misure Alternative alla Detenzione tra Reinserimento Sociale e Abbattimento della Recidiva. https://www.rassegnapenitenziaria.it/rassegnapenitenziaria/cop/25.pdf.

Manconi, L., Anastasia, S., Calderone, V., & Resta, F. (2015). *Abolire il carcere*. Chiarelettere.

Margara, A. (2015). La giustizia e il senso di umanità. *Antologia di scritti su carcere, opg, droghe e magistratura di sorveglianza*. Fondazione Michelucci Press

McNeill, F. (2014). Punishment as rehabilitation. In G. Bruinsma, & D. Weisburd (Eds.) *Encyclopedia of criminology and criminal justice*. Springer, pp. 4195–4206. ISBN 9781461456896.

Meijer, S. (2017). Rehabilitation as a positive obligation. *European Journal of Crime, Criminal Law and Criminal Justice., 25*(2), 145–162.

Mulè, P. (2009). *Processi educativi e rieducazione in carcere*. ED. c.u.e.c.m.

Ravagnani, L., & Romano, C. A. (2013). *La detenzione degli stranieri in Europa: Brevi cenni ad un problema sovranazionale, Crimen et Delictum* (Vol. IV). FDE Institute Press.

Ravagnani, L., & Policek, N. (2015). Beyond the politics of detention: incarcerated mothers in Italy. In C. Damboeanu (Ed.), *Sociological studies on imprisonment. A European perspective*. Tritonic.

Ravagnani, L., & Romano, C. A. (2017). Il Radicalismo estremo in carcere. Una ricerca empirica. *Rassegna Italiana di Criminlogia*. Anno IX, n. 4. pp. 277–296. Lecce: Pensamul. imedia. file:///C:/Users/Utente/Downloads/admin,+2993-11106-1-CE.pdf

Ravagnani, L., Zaniboni, A., & Policek, N. (2018). Breach process in the context of alternative measures in Italy. In M. Boone, & M. Maguir (Eds.), *The Enforcement of Offender Supervision in Europe, Understanding Breach Process*. Routledge.

Ricci, A., & Salierno, G. (1971). *Il carcere in Italia* (3rd Ed). Einaudi.

Romano, C. A., Ancona, G., Ravagnani, L., Prudente, L., Grattagliano, I., Guastamacchia, P., & Stragapede, P. (2020). Misure alternative alla detenzione e recidiva. *Psicopuglia*. Vol. 25, pp. 36–63. 5558d-psicopuglia-giugno-2020.pdf (psicologipuglia.it).

Scimia, A. (1987). *Il problema carcerario*. Core editore.

Vianello, F. (2020). *Vivere il carcere. Mulino*, n. 6/19, pp. 965–972.

Weaver, B. (2019). Understanding desistance: A critical review of theories of desistance. *Psychology, Crime and Law, 25*(6), 641–658.

Community-Based Rehabilitation in Japan: Some Unique Characteristics of the Japanese System and Recent Developments

Kei Someda

Historical Perspective of Community-Based Rehabilitation Services in Japan

The history of community-based rehabilitation services for adults involved in Japan's criminal justice system began in 1888 when a halfway house was established by a group of volunteers. The idea that had originated in the private sector spread throughout the country in the early 1900s and in 1939 the national government passed the Judicial Rehabilitation Services Act that established probation for juveniles and, in some special cases, adults. After the Second World War, Japan, in a reform of the former system, introduced a western style community-based rehabilitation service and by 1954 the basic framework of the current system was established by several Acts and an amendment of the Penal Code. Following these changes, the crime rate remained relatively stable until in the late 1990s when it increased sharply, and correctional institutions faced problems of overcrowding. Moreover, at the beginning of the 2000s, Japan faced problems because of the number of serious re-offending by adult parolees and probationers, and in 2007, in response to these problems and in order to modernise the community-based

K. Someda (✉)
Surugadai University, Saitama, Japan
e-mail: someda.kei@surugadai.ac.jp

rehabilitation system, the Offender Rehabilitation Act was passed. This new Act totally revised previous legislation that had created the former system. The principal characteristics of the Act are a clear affirmation of prevention of re-offending as a goal of rehabilitation services; a rearrangement and expansion of probationary and parole conditions; an increased focus on preparation of living conditions prior to release from correctional institutions; and the introduction of a system allowing crime victims to participate in the criminal justice process.

At the same time, evidence-based treatment programmes, drawn from western and North American countries and based upon cognitive behavioural theory, were introduced: these included specialised treatment programmes for people who have committed sexual offences, drug dependents, and those convicted of violence and drink driving. The ongoing effort to reduce recidivism and promote community rehabilitation, is evidenced by the establishment of a compulsory drug treatment system, as a part of the partial suspension of execution of sentence ushered in by a new statute in 2013 (implemented on 2016). In addition, the government passed the Promotion of Recidivism Prevention Act 2016 with the aim of encouraging further measures such as the establishment of a recidivism prevention plan and other practical measures at the national and local government level.

The Current System for Community-Based Rehabilitation

The criminal justice system in Japan is composed of five major elements namely, police, prosecution, court, corrections, and rehabilitation. Rehabilitation services are responsible for all types of community-based rehabilitation relating to juvenile and adult probationers and parolees. Their jurisdiction covers administration of probation, parole, aftercare, amnesty, and crime prevention. Probation involves the provision of support and supervision of probationers; parole that of those released on parole; and aftercare that of those discharged from criminal justice procedure or released from adult and juvenile correctional institutions or police detention houses. Distinct from that kind of work, amnesty is focused on seeking individual pardons, and crime prevention is undertaken at both local and national level.

As determined by the Offender Rehabilitation Act 2007, the primary purpose of rehabilitation services is to protect society and promote individual and public welfare through firstly, prevention of recidivism and promotion of the re-integration of people who have been sentenced by the courts into the society through the provision of appropriate community-based treatment and support; secondly, the carrying out of pardons, and thirdly, the promotion of crime prevention activities. The 2007 Act, which was fully implemented in June 2008, totally revised the former legal basis of probation and parole based as it was on the 1949 Rehabilitation Law and other related laws. The new legislation provides the legal framework for the organisational structure of rehabilitation services; the categories of person eligible for probation and parole supervision (adult and juvenile); the conditions for probationers and parolees and the term of their supervision; measures and procedures for their supervision, early discharge, termination and breach action; aftercare services for discharged person from criminal justice procedure, released from correctional institutions and police detention houses; and crime prevention activities. In addition, it introduced a support scheme for crime victims and strengthened the framework of community-based treatment with an enhancement of the general conditions for probationers and parolees, and the introduction of special conditions designed to help them tackle their specific problems. By utilising these new special conditions, professional probation officers are able to run specific evidence-based treatment programmes, based on cognitive behavioural therapy, which target special dynamic risk factors such as drug abuse, sexual crime, violence, and drink driving.

Whereas the Penal Code (1907) included provision for probation (and its revocation procedure) as an available sentence for adults appearing before the criminal courts, the Offender Rehabilitation Act stipulates the concrete procedures and operation of adult probationary supervision and support. It also ensures urgent assistance for probationers and parolees, and aftercare services for people discharged from criminal procedure or correctional institutions, and lays down the conditions, types of supports, and the maximum period of supervision. The Penal Code also specifies eligibility criteria for release on parole and the justifications for its revocation. The authority for those decisions rests with the Regional Parole Boards (a part of rehabilitation service) in the Ministry of Justice; and the detail of parole decision-making procedure, supervision, and support is filled out by the new Act.

In addition to these provisions for regular adult parolees, Japan has a system of protective measures for women sex workers, so that when the criminal courts commit them to a Women's Guidance Home, Regional Parole Boards can decide to release them early under parole supervision. This system is based on the Prostitution Prevention Law established in 1956. Unfortunately, in recent years, the number of women benefitting from this law has diminished significantly.

The Juvenile Law 1948 provides protective measures for juvenile delinquents and troubled youths. Youths and juveniles are classified as those under 20 years, and they should be dealt with by the Family Court separately from adult cases. Family Court judges can choose several dispositions such as discharge from juvenile law procedure, placement of juveniles under probationary supervision, commitment to juvenile training schools, and some more general forms of dispositions based on child welfare statutes. The Offender Rehabilitation Act also specifies that those released on parole from juvenile training schools shall be placed parole supervision by professional probation officers.

The Amnesty Law 1947 defines two types of amnesty, general amnesty and individual pardon based upon the Constitution of Japan. The general amnesty is divided into three categories and the individual pardon is divided into four with various effects. The management of the amnesty system differs from North American countries where general amnesty or individual pardons are utilised as a measure of early release from correctional institutions. In Japan, the amnesty system is totally separate from the parole system.

As stated in the introduction, the use of volunteers has a long history in Japan. The Volunteer Probation Officer Law 1950 lays down the maximum number of Volunteer Probation Officers (VPOs) in the whole country (52,500 persons), eligibility, qualifications, and administrative term of office of the VPOs as well as recommendation and appointment procedures, regulations for their services, duties, and other relevant issues.

Organisational Structure of the Rehabilitation Services

The Rehabilitation Services in Japan are organised and administered by the Ministry of Justice. Neither the court nor other governmental agencies organise or administer the Rehabilitation Services in the way that they do in many western countries. They are made up of four national governmental organisations: the Rehabilitation Bureau of the Ministry of Justice (the headquarters); the National Offenders Rehabilitation Commission for the administration of individual pardons; Regional Parole Boards (RPBs), and Probation Offices. In its focus upon actual functions of the Rehabilitation Services, the chapter concentrates mainly on the third and fourth.

Eight RPBs are located in the eight regions nationwide where high courts and high public prosecutors' offices operate. They carry out the following functions: deciding who should be released on parole from juvenile training schools, prisons, Women's Guidance Homes and workhouses (accommodation for people unable to pay fines); revoking parole; determining early termination of the indeterminate sentence of parolees who were sentenced to imprisonment when they were juveniles and have kept excellent behaviour; and making decisions about the provisional suspension of the probationary supervision of adult probationers (a kind of award for keeping excellent behaviour). The RPBs are solely authorised to revoke the decision of parole release from adult correctional institutions and the Women's Guidance Home. However, because according to the Juvenile Law the Family Court is authorised to send juveniles to juvenile training school as a protective measure, it has the power and responsibility to revoke the parole of juveniles and re-commit to custody.

The Probation Offices stand in the front line of Rehabilitation Services and carry out the primary function of community-based rehabilitation. Throughout Japan, there are 50 probation offices, three large branch probation offices and 27 small branch probation offices: a Chief Probation Officer is responsible for each probation office. Probation offices are responsible for: supervision of probationers and parolees; inquiry into and adjustment of living conditions of inmates and their families prior to release from correctional institutions; aftercare services for persons discharged from criminal justice procedure, adult and juvenile correctional institutions and police detention houses; investigation into and application for individual pardons; promotion of crime prevention activities in the community; screening of candidates for volunteer probation officers; supervision of the Juridical Person for Offender Rehabilitation (JPOR) (see below) and volunteer probation officers; training of halfway house staff, volunteer probation officers and other volunteers who have closely collaborated with Rehabilitation Services. In addition, since 2005, probation offices are responsible for overseeing the medical treatment and supervision of people stipulated by the Act on Medical Care and Treatment for Person Who Have Caused Serious Cases under the Condition of Insanity 2003 (implemented 2005). Under the Penal Code, no one can be punishable by criminal sanctions when he or she committed an offence while insane or suffering from diminished responsibility. Thus, separately from the ordinary Penal Code system, this new Act plays an indispensable role in the treatment of individuals who have committed serious offence such as murder, arson, and others specified in the Act. The Rehabilitation Coordinators (RCs), who work in probation offices and are either certified social workers or mental health social workers who passed national examinations set by the Ministry of Health, Labour, and Welfare, carry out their case management and treatment. Although probation officers and RCs work in the same probation office, their duties are different, and they do not cooperate in the treatment of medical cases. Special dispositions designed to facilitate their rehabilitation and re-integration them into the society are available to the courts: these are treatment in the special hospitals established by the Act, and community-based treatment by RCs when the court approves the release of individuals from a special hospital, coupled with outreach medical care at designated special hospitals.

Close collaboration between the private and public sectors is one of the special characteristics of Japanese Rehabilitation Services. In the public sphere, Professional Probation Officers (PPOs) work on probationary and parole supervision cases and RCs work on medical treatment cases. On the other hand, the private sector is made up of volunteer probation officers (VPOs) ('Hogoshi' in Japanese), the Women's Association for Rehabilitation Aid (WARA), the Big Brothers and Sisters (BBS) Association, Cooperative Employers (CEs), Juridical Persons for Offender Rehabilitation Services and other various volunteers and private organisations who contribute to the prevention of crime and rehabilitation of individuals in the community.

In the public sphere, PPOs work for Regional Parole Boards and Probation Offices in the Ministry of Justice (MOJ). Their qualifications, training, and official status are standardised at government level and after passing a national examination they become full-time government officials employed by the MOJ. They carry out probationary and parole supervision based on risk need assessment and crime prevention activities and are expected to collaborate closely with VPOs, WARA and BBS members, CEs, and other various private organisations. PPOs who work for the MOJ are totally different from Family Court probation officers who work for the judiciary. Recruitment and qualifications of those probation officers are basically different at the statute level. In Japan, PPOs never work for court duties such as seconded probation officers in the UK and Northern American countries. Family court probation officers are solely responsible for social inquiries for juveniles and submit pre-disposition reports to Family Court judges. In Japan, the adult courts lack a system of pre-sentence investigations and reports by court officials.

In close collaboration with the private sector, PPOs are responsible for implementing the conditions of adult probation and parole supervision in their various forms. A person who was sentenced to three years or less imprisonment with a suspended execution of the sentence may be placed on regular probation for a period of one to five years as determined by the court. A new sentence of probation based on partial suspension of execution of sentence was introduced in 2016 by an amendment of the Penal Code and an enactment of a new special statute allowing for compulsory drug treatment. Under this system, for example, a person sentenced to three years imprisonment with a one-year partial suspension of execution of the sentence, should be released when he or she has completed two years of the sentence. Subsequently, the individual will be supervised by probation offices for a period of one to five years as specified by the court at the time of the original sentence. This differs from ordinary parole, the period for which is for the remainder of the sentence, and in the case of those sentenced to life imprisonment, for their lifetime unless they are awarded a pardon. Furthermore, women who have been conditionally released from Women's Guidance Home by the RPB and placed on parole will be supervised by probation offices until the expiration of remainder of the guidance period.

Probationers and parolees have to comply with general conditions and any special condition considered necessary under the Offender Rehabilitation Act. General conditions are same for all types of probationers and parolees, but special conditions designated by the courts or RPBs focus on either specific dynamic risk factors or critical issues relevant to rehabilitation. During the period of supervision probationers and parolees are entitled to receive various supports and assistance to do with accommodation, food and clothing, and job finding support from their probation offices. Of course, intentional violation of conditions or re-offending may lead to breach action by the authorities.

Probation officers supervise juveniles who have committed an offence or have been adjudicated as a 'pre-delinquent' and been placed on probation by the Family Court, and those who have been conditionally released from a juvenile training school by a decision of the RPB. Probation for juveniles is a protective measure stipulated in the Juvenile Law with a legally prescribed maximum period of supervision up to the probationer's 20th birthday or at least two years, whichever is longer, whereas a period of parole supervision is up to 20th birthday of parolee or the last day of a fixed period of custody—which must not go beyond the individual's 26th birthday—determined by the Family Court.

Regarding private sectors, VPOs are private citizens who assist PPOs with community rehabilitation, support people of all ages who offend, and for those at risk of offending. They also carry out general crime prevention activities in the local community. Their predecessors, Rehabilitation Workers, existed until the 1950 Volunteer Probation Officer Law 1950 came into force and established the duties of VPOs. Although that law set a maximum number of VPOs in the whole country as 52,500, by the 1st of April 2021 the number had decreased to 47,641. The decreasing trend in the number of VPOs with an increasing average around 65 years of age is a critical problem which the Japanese VPO system has been facing for more than 10 years. Legally, VPOs are non-permanent government officials without salary and only entitled to receive small reimbursements for daily expenditure such as transportation fee. In addition to this, as government officials, VPOs are eligible to receive the National Compensation for Official Duties if, for instance, when VPOs got any bodily injury inflicted on them during the performance of their official duties. Their term of office is two years but in practice most are re-appointed repeatedly for years. Although they work in a voluntary capacity, the government provides various types of training at different levels in accordance with experience and length of the term of office and through them, they can learn about close collaboration with PPOs. Due to the fact that they live in local communities they know social and community resources well: indeed, locality and continuity of activities in their own community are the strength of VPO system. VPOs carry out general crime prevention activities in their local community on a daily basis, and in addition, the nationwide crime prevention campaign namely, 'the movement for a crime free society' is conducted every July as it has been for more than 70 years. The symbol of this campaign is the Yellow Feather and during this campaign period, the prime minister of Japan and cabinet members, local citizens, and approximately 200,000 volunteers who support Rehabilitation Services in their own community wear a Yellow Feather. Since 1962, the United Nations Asia and Far East Institute (UNAFEI) for the Prevention of Crime and the Treatment of Offenders at Tokyo which established by Japanese government under the agreement with the United Nations has provided international training courses for officials working for criminal justice field. Among many participants from 142 countries (as of 31 August 2022), participants from the Philippines, Thailand and Kenya brought back the idea and framework of the Japanese VPO system and have then introduced in their own criminal justice system (https://www.unafei.or.jp/english/index.html).

The WARA is an autonomous group that conducts crime prevention activities in the community and helps justice-involved persons reintegrate into the local community by making use of its members' experience as women and mothers. Membership is open to any woman in the community, and it organises crime prevention meetings for community members including students, and provides material support to VPOs, halfway houses, and BBS groups. WARA members visit inmates in correctional institutions and encourage them in their rehabilitative efforts. Currently, more emphasis is placed on supporting young mothers who find difficulties in bringing up their children. As of 1st April 2021 there were 140,539 members in the whole country.

The BBS Association is an organisation of young people who support, and mentor troubled youth and adults. It was inspired by the Big Brothers Big Sisters (BBBS) movement in the USA and was started in 1946 by a university student in Kyoto who felt sympathy for those severely affected by the aftermath of the Second World War. Any person usually from their twenties to thirties, regardless of educational or occupational background, is able to be a member and by 1st April 2021 there were 4,432 members throughout Japan. Among other things, they organise sports events, provide supplemental study, collaborate with the young people in nursing homes and run groups for the promotion of self-development. Individuals are referred to the BBS by professional probation officers, family courts, child consultation centres, and local police.

CEs, who are individuals or companies willing to employ and support those people, are such an important part of the rehabilitative strategies that government have taken measures to strengthen them and increase their number year by year with the result that on 1st October 2020 there were 24,213 CEs in Japan, just over a quadruple more that in 2005. Cumulative research evidence shows that having a stable job is vital to the successful re-integration of justice involved persons into the society (Aos et al., 2006; Bonta & Andrews, 2007; Sherman et al., 2002). For years, therefore, CEs have played an indispensable role to provide stable jobs and thereby contributed to reduction of recidivism.

JPORs, in the form of a non-profit organisations with taxation advantage status, were created by the 1995 Law for Offender Rehabilitation Services. A predecessor of the Juridical Person first emerged in late 1800s as a private body with a legal status established by Civil Law, and it was this that was finally modernised by this law. These Juridical Persons accommodate justice involved persons in halfway houses, provide them with material, give them various kinds of treatment, such as social skills training (SST) and Alcoholics Anonymous and Narcotic Anonymous meetings, to promote their re-integration into the society, and financially support other rehabilitation organisations that operate under the supervision of a probation office. Currently Judicial Persons manage a hundred halfway houses and three are run by other private bodies. To supplement this work, in recent years the government has established four nationally run halfway houses that focus on employment support mainly for those justice involved persons released from correctional institutions. While there, to promote future life with a stable job in the society, they are given from three to six months of intensive job skill training and employment support.

Data on Probation and Parole

As for the trend in juvenile cases, the total number of new probation and parole cases peaked in 1986 with 77,848 and thereafter has consistently declined to the extent that between 1986 and 2020 juvenile cases decreased by approximately 84%. The major reason for this is the declining trend of birth rate in Japan for many years. In the case of adult cases, over the last ten years, the curve has been flat. The figures for 2020 show that there were 10,733 new juvenile probation cases and 1,692 juvenile parole cases. As for adult cases, 2,088 regular probation cases and 1,496 cases based upon partial suspension of execution of sentence. Of adult parole, there were 9,994 regular cases and 1,201 partial suspension of execution of sentence cases who had been released on parole prior to the end of fixed custody period sentenced by criminal courts. There were no cases of women released on parole from Women's Guidance Homes.

In the same years, the Chief Probation officer discharged early 73.5% of juvenile probation cases for excellent behaviour during the supervision period and 9% of juvenile parole cases were terminated early by a decision of the RPB; whereas 13.3% juvenile probation and 76.7% juvenile parole cases continued to the end of original term of probationary and parole supervision. The reason for this is that majority of juvenile parole cases have complex problems and, therefore, are less likely to be eligible for early termination. The figures for adult regular probation were 74.6% and 64.9% for partial suspension of execution of sentence cases; and with parole, 95.2% in regular cases and 96.9% in partial suspension of execution of sentence cases continued to the end of original term of sentence. This is explained by the fact that, as with juvenile parole cases, there were very few excellent behaviour cases, and in addition, there was no early termination system for adult except for release on parole of indeterminate sentence cases who were sentenced to imprisonment when they were juveniles and have kept excellent behaviour. Termination through breach action occurred in 13.1% of juvenile probationers, 13.8% of juvenile parolees, 4.5% of regular adult parolees, 22.2% of adult regular probationers, 3.1% partial suspension of execution of sentence parolee cases, 33.4% of partial suspension of execution of sentence probation cases (Research and Training Institute of Ministry of Justice, 2022).

Evidence-Based Treatment Programmes and Support Measures

As explained earlier in the historical perspective, after 2006, in order to reduce recidivism and promote social re-integration, the government began to strengthen the legal framework with the introduction of new statutes and introduce evidence-based treatment programmes and concrete support measures for securing accommodation and employment for probationers and parolees. There are now evidence-based treatment programmes for drug abuse, sex offending, violence, and drink driving, all run by PPOs in probation offices throughout Japan. The Offender Rehabilitation Act provides the legal framework of the programmes, and the Minister of Justice specifies the specialist aspects that aim to modify special dynamic risk factors provided in the regulation of the Ministry of Justice. The programmes are based on medicine, psychology, pedagogy, sociology, and other expert knowledge (Someda, 2009). Once the probationer or parolee is considered suitable for a programme, the court or RPB has the authority to impose special conditions that require an obligation to participate. Failure to comply with these conditions without reasonable excuse is followed by breach action by the court or RPB. Each of the programmes is grounded in cognitive behavioural therapy (CBT) and is modelled on evidence-based practice in North American and European counties. The PPOs who run the programmes are trained in the approach and assess the risk level of participants before and after. The programmes themselves consist of five components and are carried out both in group and individual settings.

Adults who appear before the criminal courts often suffer from discrimination in the society with the result that they have difficulty in finding appropriate accommodation and employment in the community. Evidence shows that unstable living and working conditions can be dynamic risk factors (Aos et al., 2006; Bonta & Andrews 2007; Sherman et al., 2002) and, therefore, the Ministry of Justice (MOJ) has been keen to develop and introduce multidisciplinary approaches to strengthen community-based rehabilitation. For example, in 2006, in the first case of ministries and agencies working closely together to reduce recidivism, the MOJ and the Ministry of Health, Labour and Welfare (MHLW) jointly launched the special employment support scheme for persons released from correctional institutions (Someda, 2015; 2022). Moreover, three years later, the same ministries established the special coordination system to settle the social and family environment to which the individual will return after their release to maximise their chances of living an offence-free life. The system focuses specifically on prisoners of 65 years old and over and/or those suffering from intellectual, mental, and physical disabilities. To achieve this, the Community Life Resettlement Support Centre (CLRSC), financed by the MHLW, was also established by the local governments throughout the country. Each prefecture has at least one CLRSC in its administration area and its work is conducted by qualified social workers and other specialists in close collaboration with probation offices, correctional institutions, the social welfare sectors of local governments, and non-profitable organisations which were established in order to support such people.

The rationale for this new system is drawn from recent Japanese research on elderly and disabled prisoners which revealed that they re-offended earlier after release and at a higher rate than other prisoners. For instance, in one long-term, large-scale study of elder convicts (65 years and over), the period from 1948 to 2006, revealed a recidivism rate of 46.7% for those compared to one of 28.9% for all ages (Someda et al., 2009). This study utilised the criminal records of one million convicts drawn randomly from the huge official criminal-related database. Elder convicts were followed from 65 to 70 years ($n = 5115$). When classified for the initial offence which they committed, of those who committed larceny as an initial offence ($n = 785$), 79.6% re-offended, and of that group 64.8% committed larceny again and 14.8% other offences, findings that underlined the need for special support and supervision for this group. Other research on intellectually disabled inmates ($n = 548$), showed that 52.2% re-offended in less than one year, 19.6% less than three months (statistical significance in comparison with control group). In short, nearly three-quarters of them re-offended less than one year, thus similarly confirming the need for an intensive support system (Teramura & Shimizu, 2013).

On the policy front, in July 2012, the Cabinet Meeting for Crime Control decided to introduce the 'Comprehensive Measures for Reduction of Re-offence' to focus on a wide range of areas related to prevention of recidivism and promotion of re-integration of justice involved persons into society. The key pillars were the strengthening of relevant supervision and support for people around 65 years and over, those with a disability or drug dependence, or who have committed sexual offences; the provision of accommodation and opportunities of employment; the furtherance of research to identify more effective measures for prevention of recidivism; and the raising of public awareness and support for community rehabilitation and re-integration. Moreover, a target was set to reduce the re-admittance rate to correctional institutions within two years of release from a rate of 20% in 2012 to 16% by 2021. In fact a rate of 15.7% was achieved one year earlier than planned.

In other respects, the government has moved to fulfil the aims of these measures. In its efforts to resolve accommodation and employment problems, the Ministry of Justice (MOJ) added 'the Support Home for Self-sustaining Life System' to the existing halfway housing system and commenced employing juvenile probationers and parolees as part-time workers at its own headquarters and its local offices from 2013. The MOJ also requested all local governments to employ juvenile probationers and parolees. In addition to this, the MOJ asked all local governments to introduce incentives for CEs at public works tender when CEs publicises to employ those population. Although the number employed may remain small, this policy is aimed at impacting on the public's negative thinking towards justice involved persons through the symbolism of national and local government action.

Underpinning this policy development, and as part of the attempts to modernise the treatment system that began in 2006, are moves to strengthen evidence-based practice through renewal of the Categorised Treatment System (CTS) in 2020 and a year later, the newly introduction of the Case Formulation in Probation and Parole (CFP). The CTS, originally established in 1990, is intended to focus on specific dynamic risk factors of probationers and parolees, such as drug abuse and gang group membership, and provide suitable treatment options by PPOs. The new CTS consists of four domains with a number of subcategories, namely relationships (child abuse, spousal violence, family violence, and stalking), antisocial groups (organised crime groups, motorcycle gangs and special fraud), social adaptation (employment needs, educational needs, mental disability—including developmental and intellectual disability and elderly), and addiction (drugs, alcohol, gambling, and habitual theft).

The CFP is the Japanese original Risk/Need/Assessment scale based upon the Risk-Need-Responsivity Model (Bonta & Andrews, 2007). Before the introduction of the CFP, another Japanese style risk assessment scale had been used but it was not evidence-based and so its predictive capability was not high. While cumulative evidence-based studies gave impetus to the CFP, there remains the need to improve its predictive capability by monitoring the outcomes of probationary and parole supervision.

At the level of the law, the Promotion of Recidivism Prevention Act was passed in 2016 to strengthen efforts to reduce recidivism and smooth the path to re-integration. The national and local government, ordinary citizens and private bodies are expected to cooperate to help realise its goals. In particular, local governments are expected to develop a Local Recidivism Prevention Plan in each jurisdiction to further strengthen the National Recidivism Prevention Plan. By 1st April 2021, 188 local governments had formulated a Local Recidivism Prevention Plan.

Conclusion: Challenges and Future Prospects

Japan is a super-ageing society and has the highest ratio of elder people (28.8% in 2020) in the world. Since 1974, this situation has been compounded by the declining birth rate. One consequence of this phenomenon is that in 2013, 22.8% of people arrested by the police were 65 years and over. This figure means that the elder justice involved persons accounted for the largest percentage, in age distribution, of all arrested people. After 2013, proportion of arrested elder persons has kept the largest percentage up to now. Although, most have committed relatively minor offences such as shoplifting of food, and it is difficult to rehabilitate and reintegrate them into the society smoothly. There are several reasons for this. Many of them are isolated from family members and their local community, therefore, they lack support. Family members are also elder or already passed away and they seldom communicate with local community members. Moreover, the formal and informal care networks are dysfunctional. It is as if they are invisible in the community. Once they fall out from the public safety network, they have problems of limited income and living alone, finally they commit an offence to survive. Unfortunately, for those people, prison life becomes an attractive way to survive and even avoid death on the street. Although solving this challenge is not easy and will take time, the national and local governments have to take multidimensional countermeasures in a planned and consistent manner. In addition, the root causes of this problem need to be addressed through community rebuilding and the strengthening of support networks both formal and informal. This will require judicial and social welfare policies based upon multidisciplinary approaches at the national and local level.

Although the target set by the government through its Comprehensive Measures which decided on 2012, referred to above, was met, approximately 40% of prisoners are released without parole and their re-commitment to prison rate is 23.3% in comparison to 10.2% of prisoners released on parole. In response to this problem, the government has already formulated the. Accumulation of the Prevention of Re-Offence Plan to focus specifically on full-term served prisoners: the challenge is to enrich the contents of this plan with a multi-agency approach.

Stimulant drug abuse has been a problem in Japan for many years. As the National Institute on Drug Abuse (NIDA) in the USA points out, 'Many people do not realize that addiction is a brain disease. While the path to drug addiction begins with the act of taking drugs, over time a person's ability to choose not to do so becomes compromised and seeking and consuming the drug becomes compulsive' (NIDA, 2009: 5–6). Since addiction is a brain disease, long, sustained support and supervision is indispensable and the newly established partial suspension of execution of sentence with a compulsory drug treatment programme is key to this issue. For this to be successful there will need to be improvement in multidisciplinary collaboration not only between criminal justice, health, and medical care agencies, but also self-help groups, therapeutic communities, and other resources in the local community (Someda, 2006; 2022).

In summary then, the challenges of the Japanese Community Rehabilitation System are to strengthen multidisciplinary and multi-agency approaches, revitalise the system of community rehabilitation volunteers by effectively utilising information technology and community social work, and ensure evidence-based approaches become standard practice. Among them, increasing the number of VPOs and the reduction of their average age are important issues for the system. With regard to volunteers, the Kyoto Declaration on Community Volunteers Supporting Offender Reintegration (Kyoto Hogoshi Declaration) was adopted on 7th March 2021 on the occasion of the World Congress for Community Volunteers Supporting Offender Reintegration (in the 14th United Nations Congress on Crime Prevention and Criminal Justice held in Kyoto):

> We recognize the value of community volunteers such as hogoshi who interact with and provide support for offenders as fellow citizens working with professional probation officers who have expert knowledge. […] We are convinced that more global efforts have to be made internationally to shed light on and promote the significant role of community volunteers. […] In order to achieve the above-mentioned purposes, we invite the United Nations Commission on Crime Prevention and Criminal Justice (CCPCJ) to build an international network of community volunteers in the supervision and reintegration of offenders, to provide technical assistance and to urge member states to enact laws to anchor community volunteers for the purpose of fostering volunteering, raising awareness among the public and establishing systems of community volunteers. We also invite the CCPCJ to formulate a United Nations model strategy for reducing reoffending in order to tackle issues on reoffending and encourage the utilization of the community volunteers in this field, and to establish the International Day for Community Volunteers Supporting Offender Reintegration, 'Hogoshi Day'.

Finally, the history of utilising evidence-based practice in the community rehabilitation field is in its infancy and majority of PPOs are not accustomed to the way of this thinking. Therefore, if we are to realise the desired outcomes of reduction of re-offending and the promotion of re-integration and ensure the integrity of programme design, systematic staff training needs to be a fundamental element of the CFP and other evidence-based treatment programmes (see, for example, the STICS programme in Canada, Bonta, 2012).

References

In this reference, the symbol "(J)" attached to the end of reference means it was originally written and only available in Japanese.

Aos, S., Miller, M., & Drake, E. (2006). *Evidence-based public policy options to reduce future prison construction, criminal justice costs, and crime rates*. Washington State Institute for Public Policy.

Bonta, J. (2012). The RNR model of offender treatment: Is there value for community corrections in Japan? *Japanese Journal of Offenders Rehabilitation, 1*(1), 29–42.

Bonta, J., & Andrews, D. A. (2007). *Risk-need-responsivity model for offender assessment and rehabilitation*. Public Safety Canada.

National Institute on Drug Abuse (NIDA). (2009). *Principles of drug addiction treatment: A research-based guide*. Second Edition. Bethesda, National Institutes of Health, U.S. Department of Health and Human Services.

Research and Training Institute of Ministry of Justice. (2022). *White paper on crime 2021*. Tokyo: Ministry of Justice. (J) English summary version also available at the MOJ web site.

Sherman, L. W., Farrington, D. P., Welsh, B. D., & MacKenzie, D. L. (2002). *Evidence-based crime prevention*. Routledge.

Someda, K. (2006). *Exploring effective measures for community-based treatment of offenders—diversification of treatment measures and restorative justice*. Seibundo. (J)

Someda, K. (2009). An international comparative overview on the rehabilitation of offenders and effective measures for the prevention of recidivism. *Legal Medicine* (vol. 11, pp. S82–S85). Elsevier.

Someda, K. (2015). The importance of employment support for offenders in the community-based treatment, recent developments and challenges in Japan. *Rehabilitation and Protection, Legislation and Practice, International Academic Seminar, Taipei*, November 12–13, 2015, Program Book (pp. 143–156).

Someda, K. (2022). Multidisciplinary and multi-agency approaches for the community-based treatment of offenders. In M. Matsumoto (Ed.), *An introduction to the community rehabilitation* (pp. 202–241). Seibundo. (J)

Someda, K., Koita, K., Gouhara, K., Mizukami, T., & Sakurada, K. (2009). A comprehensive study on the effective measures for prevention of recidivism. *Research Report Series 42*. Tokyo: Research and Training Institute of Ministry of Justice. (J)

Teramura, K., & Shimizu, Y. (2013). Actual conditions and treatment of intellectual disabled offenders. *Research Report Series 52*. Tokyo: Research and Training Institute of Ministry of Justice. (J)

Criminal Rehabilitation in Kenya: Opportunities and Pitfalls

Karatu Kiemo

Contemporary criminal rehabilitation in Kenya occurs within the confines of a prison system that by the year 2020 included 129 prisons, of which five are maximum security, 18 are for women and two are for juveniles. In the same year, the prison population was 42,600, representing an occupancy level of 179% and a prison population rate of 81/100,000. Based on the latest available data, there were 44.1% pre-trial detainees and 6.7% female prisoners in 2019, 1.2% juvenile prisoners in 2018, and 0.6% foreign prisoners in 2013 (Institute for Crime and Justice Policy Research, no date). In history, the Kenyan prison system is a recent phenomenon whose first legal framework, the East Africa Prisons Regulations, was enacted in 1902 while the prisons' administration structure was founded in 1911 (Ministry of Interior & Coordination of National Government, 2022). The current prison policy framework focuses on reorienting the goal of imprisonment from punishment to rehabilitation and is two decades old, having been initiated in 2003. Some of the envisaged policy reforms include increasing access to prisoners through public visitation and the introduction of new rehabilitation programmes focused on equipping people with skills beyond traditional

K. Kiemo (✉)
Department of Sociology, Social Work and African Women Studies, University of Nairobi, Nairobi, Kenya
e-mail: kkiemo@uonbi.ac.ke

vocational training. The policy reforms were further enhanced by the promulgation of a new Constitution in 2010, which provides that arrested persons should be held separately from persons serving a sentence, brought before a court within 24 hours, released on bond or bail unless there are compelling reasons not to do so, and should not be remanded in custody for an offence if the offence is punishable by a fine only or by imprisonment for not more than six months. Further, the Constitution provides that parliament shall enact legislation that provides for the humane treatment of persons detained, held in custody, or imprisoned (Kenya Constitution, 2010).

Criminal rehabilitation is, globally, a relatively modern strategy of punishment. The strategy involves re-education and retraining of those people who commit crime, thus targeting their cognitive distortions associated with the offence (Forsberg & Douglas, 2022) and may include general education in literacy skills, and work training (Perterson & Lee, 2017). Its overall goal is to re-integrate those who have offended back into society. Based on current literature and best practices, existing criminal rehabilitations strategies generally target human needs including physiological (e.g. better nutrition, shelter and clothing, medical care), security and safety (e.g. conducive living space, reduction of overcrowding), social wellbeing (e.g. maintaining ties to the outside world), ego (i.e., self-esteem as may be developed through sports and beauty pageants) and self-actualization (e.g. pursuit of academic qualifications). Other strategies include reduction of the duration of the prison stay through shorter-period sentencing, separation of low- and high-risk individuals, promotion of mental health including treatment of drug use disorders (ACT–ICP, 2019), setting down clear and detailed statutory regulations clarifying the safeguards applicable and governing the use and disposal of any record of data relating to criminal matters (Ovey, 2014).

Kenya today is a transitory society characterized by the rapidity of change in the social fabric of norms, values and beliefs; and by nascent bureaucratization such as in the professionalization of rehabilitation in the criminal justice system. An indicator of the Kenyan society's changeability is the relatively high crime rate. Based on the crime index ranking for 2020, Kenya has an index of 61.7, the sixth highest level of crime in Africa, but lower than South Africa (position 1), Namibia (position 2), Angola (position 3) and Nigeria (position 4). Within the East African region, Kenya's crime index is the highest compared to Uganda (position 7), Tanzania (position 8), Somalia (position 9) and Ethiopia (position 13). Poverty and rapid population growth are other factors that show the changeability of Kenyan society and, therefore, indicate risk of higher crime rate as well as challenges for rehabilitation.

Extreme poverty, as indicated by the population living below a dollar per day, was 16% in 2021 and an overwhelming 36% in 2016 (Faria, 2021).

In history then, the Kenyan prison system, its first legal framework, the East Africa Prisons Regulations, and the prisons' administration structure are all relatively recent developments in the criminal justice and penal fields (KPS, no date). The first prison facility was established in 1929, and the prison system itself within the context of a British colonial administration whose criminal law was defined by the British Common Law. These included crimes with no local Kenyan relevance at the time such as vagrancy and trespass which put the Indigenous population at a greater risk of imprisonment. The British colonial rule faced violent resistance, particularly during the war of independence in the 1950s, a historical period when the prison system was oriented towards punishment rather than rehabilitation in almost all the countries of the world.

Today, the prison system is influenced by reforms aimed at more humane living conditions and the goal of rehabilitation. However, a prison administration report (Ndungu, no date) showed that the Kenyan prison system is encumbered not only by overcrowding but also by deviant behaviour including sodomy, drug trafficking and use and radicalization, among others. The report showed that many prisoners stay idle and some may leave the prisons worse than when they came in. Other reported challenges include lack of sufficient health kits, insufficient funding to cater for basic requirements and for implementing the rehabilitation programmes, and low morale occasioned by poor staff housing conditions. All this occurs in the context of lack of enough qualified professionals such as counsellors, psychiatrists and psychologists who are needed for effective rehabilitation. Arising from the above, Kenya's recidivism rate is at 47%, which is higher than in other East African countries including Uganda (32%), and Tanzania and Rwanda (each at 36%) (Stahler et al., 2013). Moreover, a television (Citizen TV) documentary aired on 17th April 2022 showed the existence of mobile phone-aided con-artistry by which prisoners, with the aid of prison officers lure people outside prison, within and outside Kenya, into frauds worth millions of Kenyan shillings. The same documentary showed some prisoners using what appears to be a narcotic drug (cannabis) in the presence of prison officers.

Against that background, this chapter examines the current status of criminal rehabilitation in Kenya and offers a critical analysis of policies and practices using data recorded in government documents, as well as in journal articles and media reports. The specific objectives are to describe Kenya's prison population and examine existing rehabilitation programmes relative to existing theories and best practices and make appropriate recommendations to improve the policy environment.

Characteristics of the Prison Population

Kenya's incarceration rate (81/100,000) is moderate compared to other countries in the world. The rate places the country at position 165 in order of the lowest to the highest incarceration rates. Within the East Africa region, Kenya's incarceration rate is lower than in all other countries, except Tanzania (59/100,000) (see Table 1). With respect to gender, Kenya's proportion of male prisoners (93.3%) ranks the country favourably (position 173) while that of female prisoners (6.7%) ranks the country at position 50, which demonstrates a significant risk of incarceration for women in Kenya compared to women in other countries. The sizeable proportion of female prisoners demonstrates that the prison population is not homogenous; hence, the need for policymakers to ensure that rehabilitation programmes provide significant opportunities for women.

Kenya has a prison occupancy level (190%) that is more than double the official capacity, which makes the country the 29th on the overcrowding scale out of more than 200 countries and territories. Within the East African region, Kenya's prison occupancy level is the third highest after that of Uganda (319%, global rank of 7) and Burundi (304%, global rank of 8). Inasmuch as Kenya and the region do not have exceptionally high incarceration rates, the high prison occupancy levels are an indictment of the countries' organizational capacity, and the correlated developing-country characteristics notably poverty and rapid population growth.

Kenya's pre-trial prison population is nearly half (44%) of the total prison population, which ranks the country as the 55th with most pre-trial detainees globally, and the third in East Africa after Tanzania (51%) and Uganda (50%). The substantial number of the pre-trial detainees reflects the inefficiency of the criminal justice systems' prosecution and adjudication processes. This results in many prisoners who are not enrolled in rehabilitation programmes and, therefore, are idle. Although international standards state that pre-trial detainees and sentenced detainees should not mix in group areas such as visits, programmes, health facilities and in transit, recent innovations suggest that limited mixing, where it is reasonable and safe to do so, is important so that pre-trial detainees can participate in rehabilitation programmes and activities (ACT-ICS, 2018). Such mixing, however, may only be safe and impactful to sentenced prisoners undergoing rehabilitation if the proportion of the pre-trial detainees is much lower and they spend a considerably shorter time in remand owing to efficient resolution of cases. In Kenya, however, the pre-trial detainees' population is not only extremely high but also some of the pre-trial detainees spend longer periods on remand

Table 1 Incarceration rate (per 100,000) and prisoners' characteristics in comparison with other East African countries and global ranking (in parentheses)

	National rate/100,000	Male (%)	Female (%)	Juveniles (%)	Occupancy (%)	Pre-trial detainees (%)	Foreign (%)
Kenya	81 (165)	93.3 (173)	6.7 (50)	1.2	190.5 (29)	44.1 (55)	0.6 (171)
Tanzania	59 (189)	96.6 (86)	3.4 (137)	3.9	115.7 (90)	51.0 (43)	3.7 (106)
Burundi	96 (149)	94.2 (162)	5.8 (63)	1.3	304.3 (8)	39.0 (69)	1.2 (150)
Ethiopia	99 (147)	95.8 (108)	4.2 (113)	–	–	14.9 (184)	–
Uganda	124 (125)	95.5 (121)	4.5 (102)	0.0	319.2 (7)	49.8 (47)	2.3 (127)
Rwanda	511 (5)	92.6 (185)	7.4 (34)	0.9	101.3 (116)	7.5 (208)	0.3 (182)

Notes
1. National incarceration rate is based on a country's total population
2. Gender, nationality, occupancy level, pre-trial detainee and juvenile (under 18 years) percentages are based on the total prison population
3. The global rank of a country is based on at least 200 countries
4. Blank entry means data unavailability
5. The source has no global ranking for percent of juveniles in prison
6. The figures provided in this table are sourced from a list that allows cross-country comparison

Source (https://en.wikipedia.org/wiki/List_of_countries_by_incarceration_rate). The country specific data may vary from those indicated for each country in the 2022 World Prison Brief (https://www.prisonstudies.org/)

than they would in prison had they been convicted (ICJ, 2018). The Kenyan prison system also includes children of detainees and children born in prison, or as the law requires, those under four years of age whose mothers are serving a prison term (National Council of Law Report, 2009). It is, therefore, important for policymakers to ensure that rehabilitation programmes provide for the needs of children accompanying incarcerated mothers.

The question of what programmes Kenya has and what it needs is an important organizing frame in examining the existing rehabilitation programmes relative to existing theories and best practices, and making appropriate recommendations to improve the policy environment. A review of existing literature (ACT-ICS, 2018; Ovey, 2014; Peterson & Lee, 2017) shows that some of the effective evidence-based rehabilitation programmes include academic education, career technical education, employment preparation, substance use disorder treatment and cognitive behaviour therapy. The programmes are likely to be effective if they are evidence-based, cost-effective and based on specific needs of prisoners. With respect to Kenya, the existing critical rehabilitation programmes have a number of essential characteristics.

Enrolment into the Academic Education Programme (AEP) is voluntary. It is organized to provide prisoners with the opportunity to sit for national examinations at the end of primary and secondary school levels. Allocation to a given level is organized by a prison management board that explores prisoners' interests and conducts assessment tests to identify the appropriate level for the prisoner. Enrolment is only available for those serving sentences of more than six months, which means that the programme is not offered in every prison but only those accommodating long sentenced prisoners. Classes are held from Monday to Friday, and from 8 a.m. to 4 p.m. Teachers are recruited during the normal prison officers' recruitment exercise to ensure that they have the requisite credentials. However, prisoners with the requisite skills and good conduct also get co-opted into teaching. Primary school level prisoners who pass the examination are enrolled for secondary education, which for some means a transfer from a facility that only provides for primary education. After secondary level, prisoners may enrol for tertiary education. Prisoners who complete their sentence before completing the education programme may return to prison to sit for the exam, or transfer to an ordinary public school. Currently, there is provision for enrolment in an online degree programme with the University of London, United Kingdom. Online classes are conducted through projectors and individualized learning is facilitated by provision of library services.

The critical challenges with the AEP include its structure whereby it is hinged on sitting for examinations and not necessarily the needs of the prisoners. This oversight means that prisoners can enrol for any level to avoid manual labour activities, rendering the programme more ritualistic than goal oriented. The ritualism of the academic programme is demonstrated in the case of a female prisoner who in the 2022 primary school national exam attracted media attention by her exemplary performance, only for it to be revealed that she had acquired a university degree in 2013 and before her arrest had enrolled for a master's degree programme (Simiyu, 2022). This situation arose from the fact that at present, prison authorities do not have access to prisoners' official history but rely on their self-reported histories. Indeed, as anecdotal evidence shows, some prisoners have unknown out-of-prison identities because they had no identification cards at the time of arrest, and therefore are only known to prison authorities by their aliases. Furthermore, there is no post-prison follow-up to ensure that those who are released before the completion of their education programme continue pursuing it to a logical conclusion. From this perspective, it is important for Kenya to rethink and restructure the academic programme to ensure that it is geared towards a definite purpose with clear policies relating to enrolment, retention and transition from one level to another. Such a policy would, for instance, ensure that allocation to a specific learning level is conducted through scientific assessments to ensure enrolment at the appropriate skill level. The possibility of avoiding laborious activities is enough incentive for learners to take such pre-qualification assessments.

Long standing vocational training and technical education is ideally meant to provide prisoners with occupational skills that would be useful in community re-entry. The enrolment, which is undertaken by a prison management board, is based on the consideration that the prisoner has less ability for the academic programme or was already in the same trade before incarceration. The activities include farm work, traditional artisan education (e.g. carpentry) but in recent times it has also included sporting activities such as dance troupes and martial arts. An important opportunity for vocational training is that learners sit for national examination and are certified, meaning that they can use those certificates to seek employment upon release from prison. The challenge with vocational training is that enrolment is based on self-expressed interest and does not consider that the prisoner could have been trained as a teacher, lawyer or police officer, and therefore the artisan education may be merely ritualistic to fill the void. Other challenges are community stigma that makes employment and self-employment difficult, and the lack of post-discharge follow-up to support entry into the labour market. Moreover, re-entry into the labour market requires substantial amount of money, even for minor expenses such as transport, while the prison wage is merely symbolic rather than functional. In this respect, the maximum daily wage of 20 Kenyan cents (last revised in 1979) is for prisoners who are skilled and of exemplary conduct, and this translates into less than one US dollar for an entire year.

By 2019, the distribution of the Kenyan population by religious affiliation was about 86% Christian, 11% Muslim and 3% of traditional African belief and ethnic Indian belief systems such as Hindu and Sikh. The present prison pastoral programme, which is part of religious chaplaincy, caters only for Christianity and Islam, which are missionary religions that seek to convert a person from one religion to another, or within the same religion from one level of conviction to another. This means that, especially for those prisoners who convert from one religion to another, the changed identity is likely to complicate their community re-entry. The role of religious chaplaincy is undermined by the disproportionate number of prisoners to chaplains, and the interrelated mixing of pre-trial detainees and prisoners, and of people convicted of serious and minor offences (Nyamberi et al., 2019). Moreover, the main challenge remains the pervasive stigma for convicted persons in Kenya, which makes community re-entry difficult. For instance, it is difficult to imagine how an individual who is self-reporting to have changed would be welcomed back to a society whose collective consciousness still holds that 'once a criminal always a criminal'.

It seems that in Kenya today, prison welfare is an oxymoron, given that a recent media report (Tabalia, 2020) listed two prisons (Kamiti Maximum and Nairobi Industrial Area Remand and Allocation) among the top ten most notorious prisons in Africa, operationally defined as being below basic living standards, and therefore unfit for human habitation. In the report, Kenya and South Africa were the only countries to have two prisons in the list. In describing the case of Kamiti prison, for example, the report noted that it 'holds notoriety for poor conditions and inhumane treatment' and singles out Block-G as 'housing prisoners who prey on others for sexual pleasures and mobile (phone) fraudsters'. The indictment of the Kenyan prisons' welfare situation occurs despite the 2002 prison reforms and the 2010 Constitution that in specific ways targeted the improvement of prisoners' welfare in order to preserve human dignity that, among other things, is needed for community re-entry. Generally, the prison welfare programme has been based on improving the prison internal environment as well as improving the relationship between prisoners and their significant others. With respect to the prisons' internal environment, some of the most critical welfare issues concern nutrition and health care, while contact with the external world is a variable that can influence community re-entry and recidivism.

In Kenya, prison food has earned a bad name. Indeed, the quality of prison food is, in common conversations, used to invoke fear of incarceration and therefore serves as a deterrent to committing crime. Similar indictment of prison food quality is shown in studies based on prisoners' perceptions (e.g. Korir, 2017). Korir's study found that significant numbers of prisoners opined that food was always reduced (28.4%) or denied (5.2%) as punishment, or always increased for sexual favours (42.6%) or as inducement by officers to elicit desired information about other prisoners (17.8%). Certainly, the low quality and 'weaponization' of food in Kenyan prisons is unlikely to change in the short term given their overpopulation amidst national budgetary constraints.

The status of prison health is equally concerning as reinforced by public opinion as well as some studies. For example, a survey of health care systems in 73 prisons in Kenya (KNHCR, 2019) established that 96% of prisoners and 100% of prison officers felt anxious about their health due to their stay or work in prison, that 10% of the prisons did not have a medical facility, and that a prison with 400 prisoners had no medical facilities and used the services of a public medical facility located 33 kilometres away. Obviously, with the fundamental problem of overcrowding and national budgetary constraints, there is little hope that the status of health care in Kenyan prisons will change for the better any time soon.

Pitfalls in Criminal Rehabilitation Programme in Kenya

Crime is understood to be caused by multiple factors, some of which are biological, psychological, or social. It follows that an effective rehabilitation strategy must address these needs in an individual prisoner. For this to happen, it requires professionalization of prison management staff with requisite technical skills and reformative attitudes. However, in Kenya's history recruitment into prison service has been based on low skill level, such that only those individuals who had not pursued tertiary education sought employment in the prison service. Besides, the judgement that the management of prisoners needed more brawn than brain created a situation in which the typical prison officer was the stereotypical village bully boy. In recent years, this has been changing with the recruitment of university graduates into the service but in the initial stages, the highly educated officers were employed at management and not on programme levels. The newness of this change of approach is demonstrated by an April 2022 advertisement for recruitment of professionals, which included disciplines that could assist in addressing the psychological needs of prisoners (e.g. clinical psychology and counselling) as well as community re-entry needs (e.g. social work and sociology). As the advertisement put it, the professionals will perform such duties as conducting social investigations, rehabilitation and reintegration of individuals serving non-custodial measures within the community, participating in social crime prevention projects and programmes, and facilitating probation and aftercare support services to individuals and statutory institutions. The extent to which the intended professionalization will take root and its impact on rehabilitation, however, is as of now a long-term empirical question. To that extent, the current rehabilitation strategies of substance use disorder treatment, and cognitive behaviour therapy are minimal, if at all present. In any case, the fact that the prison population outnumbers available housing capacity demonstrates the sheer difficulty in addressing individualized needs. Furthermore, the existence of drug trafficking and use within prison does not inspire any hope that a programme like substance use disorder treatment can take root and succeed in the near future.

Conclusion and Recommendations

Kenyan society is rapidly changing, altering its moral fabric, and so causing tensions in human relationships and causing crime and deviance. This occurs as Kenya lacks an effective compensatory mechanism such as would be provided by a modern criminal justice system to prevent crime and provide effective correctional measures to prevent recurrence. As such, there is a certain risk for single and multiple incarcerations. In this regard, official statistics show that crime rate is high and escalating; for example, in a period of one year (2017–2018) crime incidences increased by 13%. Some of the crimes such as homicide (4.9/100,000 in 2018) and robbery with violence (5.7/100,000 in 2018) carry the death sentence, which has not been used since 1987 meaning that those convicted remain in prison until and unless granted presidential clemency. Others such as defilement which, based on a 2009 report, affects 79% of girls aged 13–15 years attract life imprisonment, which operationally ranges from a minimum of 14 years to lifetime. The Kenyan social context is also characterized by poverty that correlates with some types of crimes (e.g. petty theft), and by sexual permissiveness that induces such sexual offences as sexual harassment which attracts an imprisonment of not less than three years. Although the community service order, which can run from one day to three years, was set up more than two decades ago (in 1998), it is underutilized (Gitao, 2017; Kimemia, 2012). Furthermore, there are several behaviours (e.g. attempted suicide) that in Kenya are criminalized while they have been decriminalized in many other jurisdictions (e.g. the last European country to decriminalize suicide was Ireland in 1964). Other public order crimes (e.g. smoking in public areas or using alcohol—except in hotels—before 5 p.m. or without the accompaniment of food) are also criminalized. The risk for imprisonment is heightened too by a punishment rather than rehabilitation paradigm informing the recruitment of police and prison officers. In other words, these two important institutions still place greater emphasis on muscularity rather than rehabilitation science. Besides, although the police service is not criticized for ineptitude, there is the inevitable risk of false positives (i.e. those claimed to be guilty while they are not), which is augmented by the often-reported police and judicial corruption. While there has been a trend towards professionalization of rehabilitation, it is a recent initiative that is taking place in an overcrowded prison system, thus its efficacy can only be discerned in the long term.

The existing rehabilitation programmes are directed more towards the collective than individual needs. As such, there is no structured assessment on the rehabilitation needs of individuals being placed in confinement. An individualized rehabilitation programme should be targeted at changing the mindset of the person. It must be normative and re-educative in order to replace a criminogenic orientation with a non-criminogenic one. That requires the use of professionals to drive the change, as well as incentives to attract the cooperation of the target of change. While the desire for freedom is an ultimate incentive for most prisoners, it must be appreciated that prisoners may have mental confusion that might limit their ability to make rational decisions. Besides, there are those for whom freedom is not incentive but an existential threat. For instance, the fear of hunger and homelessness or of an environment so hostile because of the nature of crime committed (e.g. rape, incest, murder, etc.) that it makes some prisoners prefer life in custody than in freedom. In this regard, there is an instructive though anecdotal case of a woman who was remanded at Langata Women's Prison for having killed her mother in a domestic quarrel, and who obtained presidential clemency: however, on notifying her siblings that she was on the verge of being released, they warned her against going back home. She committed suicide that night. These existential threats and stigma are an additional risk for those leaving prison.

Thus far Kenya does not have an unemployment fund that could cater for ex-prisoners' financial needs, but has a police issued certificate of good conduct requirement, which is an institutionalized form of stigmatization. While confirmation of an individual's criminal history has merit especially for hard-to-treat mental disorders such as psychopathy, for those who have gone through evidence-based rehabilitation programmes, it can be tempered by a prison-issued certificate of completion which of necessity must include a pre-rehabilitation assessment measurement, the programmes undertaken and post-rehabilitation assessment measurement. This kind of information enables the potential employer to make informed decisions. Inasmuch as rehabilitation has enormous benefits to the State and to the community, it is important for the government to explore the idea of giving incentives to businesses that employ ex-prisoners, as well as to businesses started by ex-prisoners. Such incentives may include some form of prison-sponsored advertisements for the respective goods and services which if put through mainstream and social media would also go a long way in combating the stigma etched in the collective consciousness.

References

ACT Inspector of Correctional Services. (2019). *Report of a review of the care and management of remandees at the Alexander Maconochie Centre, Canberra.*

Faria, J. (2021). *Extreme poverty rate in Kenya 2017–2021.* Statista.

Forsberg, L., & Douglas, T. (2022). What is rehabilitation? *Criminal Law and Philosophy, 16*(1), 103–126.

Gitao, A. N. (2017). *Community service orders as alternative to imprisonment in Kenya: The case of Kibera probation office.* University of Nairobi.

Institute for Crime and Justice Policy Research. (no date). *World Prison Brief Data, Kenya.* https://www.prisonstudies.org/country/kenya

International Commission of Jurists—Kenya Section. (2018). *Remandees detained longer on trial than they would if convicted.* https://icj-kenya.org/news/remandees-detained-longer-on-trial-than-they-would-if-convicted/

Kenya Constitution of 2010. https://www.constituteproject.org/constitution/Kenya_2010.pdf?lang=en

Kenya National Commission for Human Rights. (2019). State of healthcare for prisoners in Kenya. Prison Series Report No. 1. Directorate of Research, Advocacy and Outreach, Reforms and Accountability Division. https://www.knchr.org/Portals/0/EcosocReports/State%20Of%20Healthcare%20For%20Prisoners%20In%20Kenya_Print%20ready.pdf?ver=2019-09-23-102658-900#:~:text=Kenya%20Prison%20Service%20(KPS)%20Directorate,deterioration%20of%20an%20inmate's%20condition

Kenya Prisons Service. (no date). *About Kenya Prisons* Service. https://www.prisons.go.ke/About.php

Kimemia, J. W. (2012). *The barriers affecting utilization of community service orders programme in Kenya: A study of Makadara Law Court*. University of Nairobi.

Korir, J. C. (2017). Evaluating the nature of food served in selected prisons in Kenya. *African Journal of Hospitality, Tourism and Leisure, 6*(2), 1–18.

Ministry of Interior and Coordination of National Government. (2022). State Department of Correctional and Rehabilitation Service. https://www.correctional.go.ke/departments/kenya-prison-service

National Council of Law Report. (2009). The Prisons Act (Chapter 90 laws of Kenya). http://kenyalaw.org/kl/fileadmin/pdfdownloads/Acts/PrisonsActCap90.pdf

Ndungu, P. K. (2016). *Administration of the Kenya Prisons Organization*. https://www.unafei.or.jp/publications/pdf/RS_No98/No98_IP_Kenya_2.pdf

Nyamberi L, M., Susan, K., & Sussy, G. (2019). The current situation of pastoral programs in the prisons in Western Kenya Counties. *Sociology and Anthropology, 7*(3), 111–125.

Ovey, C. (2014). Ensuring respect of the rights of prisoners under the European Convention on Human Rights as part of their reintegration process. Registry of the European Court of Human Rights. https://rm.coe.int/16806f4555

Peterson, J., & Lee, A. (2017). *Improving in-prison rehabilitation programs*. https://lao.ca.gov/Publications/Report/3720#State.2011Funded_Programs_Have_Several_Shortcomings

Simiyu, M. (2022). Revealed: Murder suspect who topped in KCPE has degree. https://nation.africa/kenya/news/revealed-murder-suspect-who-topped-in-kcpe-has-degree-3765356

Stahler, G. J., Mennis, J., Belenko, S., Welsh, W. N., Hiller, M. L., & Zajac, G. (2013). Predicting recidivism for released state prison. *Criminal Justice Behaviour, 40*(6), 690–711.

Tabalia, J. (2020). *List of the worst prisons in Africa*. https://briefly.co.za/82917-list-worst-prisons-africa-pics.html

Framing and Reframing the Rehabilitation in Criminal Justice in Latvia

Anvars Zavackis and Janis Nicmanis

The Historical Context of Rehabilitation in Latvia

Rehabilitation in Criminal Justice in Latvia is not detached from the past. The political and judicial transformation of Latvian society was heavily impacted by its geopolitical and historical conditions. Past experience and Latvia's geopolitical situation have also affected the formation and development of the rehabilitation system, so the changes in the penal system and policy and the development of rehabilitation practices should be seen in that context. Latvia is a small independent country near the Baltic Sea and in 2022 the total population of Latvia is about 1.9 million people. Geographically lying at the crossroads between West Europe and Russian political space, Latvia during the last couple of centuries was invaded several times by its neighbours and as result changed its political authority and system. This disrupted the continuity of social development and made it necessary to reconstruct its legal and social framework. From the seventeenth century until 1918 Latvia was part of the Russian Empire, though heavily influenced by German culture. On the 18th of November 1918 in the aftermath of World War I which left much of the country in ruins, Latvian national leaders

---

A. Zavackis (✉) · J. Nicmanis
State Probation Service of Latvia, Lomonosova Street 9–1, Riga, Latvia
e-mail: Anvars.Zavackis@vpd.gov.lv

declared Latvia as 'independent, sovereign, democratic, republic'. During most of the period of first independence (1918–1940) the Latvian political system was a parliamentary democracy, however, in the last four years it was terminated by the autocratic rule of Karlis Ulmanis. In 1940 Latvia was occupied by the Soviet Army and became part of Soviet Union but after the outbreak of World War II it was invaded by German forces and remained occupied by them until 1945 when it was forcibly returned to Soviet Union as one of the Union republics and subjected to Soviet home policy again. Both German and Soviet occupations were characterised by mass repression and attempt to control virtually every aspect of people's lives. The Soviet policy was directed towards urbanisation and industrialisation of the country combined with a significant influx of workers from other regions of Soviet Union. In 1991, after 46 years of continuous Soviet rule, it regained its independence and following a decade of restoring its statehood Latvia was admitted to the European Union in 2004.

Even after that restoration of independence the Latvian criminal justice, its criminal code and procedure remained closely modelled on the Soviet system, so integration into the European political and social community initiated a need for transformation and the expunging of the Soviet legacy. A significant change came in 2003 with the founding of State Probation Service (SPS) that, together with the Prison administration, became a key organisation in the resocialisation of people sentenced by the courts. At the beginning of 2022, there were more than 5800 probation clients and 3200 prisoners.[1]

Origins and History of Rehabilitation Mechanisms in Latvia

The justice system inherited from Imperial Russia in 1918 included a central legislative act—the Law of Punishments (Sodu likums)—passed as the Criminal law of 1903 (Mincs et al., 1934). The prison infrastructure was also adopted from imperial Russia and, post-independence, transformed gradually to fit the needs of the new national State. At that time, the reformation of people was understood as a moral process, and accordingly, at the core of the penitentiary system lay ideas of the beneficial influence of work and religious education. In addition, there was a recognition of the importance of trusting relationships between prison staff (teachers, clerics, medics and administration) and prisoners, and the role of private, face-to-face conversations. In 1923 the 'patronage' system came into force so that after release it was expected that individuals would receive both practical and moral support from non-governmental and religious bodies (patronage organisations) who took the responsibility for their welfare and resocialisation (Kronberga, 2015). They also exerted a limited control over the life of convicted persons but basically had to follow the judicial decisions. No probation in the modern sense of this word existed during the first period of independence.

As indicated above, from 1940 onwards (with the exception of 1941–1944 when Latvia was occupied by the Third Reich) Latvia's criminal law system formed a part of the Soviet Union's justice framework. Consequently, its aim was highly politicised and included extra harsh sentences for crimes against the State including the death penalty for most serious cases of theft of State property (Solmon, 1978). A vast number of convictions for alleged political crimes took place, and in 1940–1941 alone 20,000–21,000 Latvian citizens were convicted, some executed by shooting (Šneidere, 2004). The vast majority of the politically sentenced were forcibly deported to concentration camps in far regions of Russia in a continuation and expansion of previous Tsarist policy in dealing with real or supposed opponents of the regime (see Van den Berg, 1985). After the death of Stalin in 1953 a liberalisation of the criminal justice system took place which included a reduction in penalties for certain offences and the abolition of some altogether (Solmon, 1978; Van den Berg, 1985). Moreover, these new policies increased the participation of criminal law scholars in decision-making and the drafting of legislation.

In the 1958 new Criminal Law guidelines were introduced because all the republics of Soviet Union were able to make their own laws. Importantly, although according to the guidelines, punishment was defined as a kind of retribution for the offence, no definition of retribution was provided (Камалова & Красуцких, 2019). Along with this retributive approach, another key concept in addressing criminality was re-education. It implied that the goal of education is the formation of a new personality—a citizen of communist society (Hardy, 2016). This was explicit in the new Criminal Law of Latvian Socialist Republic (The Criminal Law of Latvian Socialist Soviet Republic), which came into force in 1961 (Krastiņš, 2009). It defined the aim of punishment in this following way:

> The (criminal) punishment is applied not only to punish for the offense but the aim of punishment is also to reform the convicted persons and re-educate them, to create a trustworthy attitude toward work, to help them exactly comply with the law, and to respect the rules of socialist environment. The aim of the punishment is also to ensure that the convicted person as well as others do not commit new crimes. Infliction of suffering or humiliation of human dignity is not the aim of the punishment.[2]

Thus, the very idea of the punishment combined both the retributive element (punishment for the sake of punishing) and the pragmatic goal of re-education. The code offered a broad range of punishments including exile to certain areas of Soviet Union, fines and public condemnation. The leading role of punishment, however, was deprivation of liberty, so prisons were the main place where the forging of a new communist personality took place (Hardy, 2016).

The Restart of Rehabilitation

Today the execution of Latvian criminal sentences is mainly (with sole exception of fines) entrusted to two state institution, the Prison Administration and the State Probation Service (SPS). The effective co-existence of the two institutions required the introduction of new rehabilitation mechanisms firstly, to eschew the custodial sentence as the main solution to the crime problem and as the formal control of convicted individuals; and secondly, to lay the groundwork for the establishment of a probation service and the development of social work practice. As a result, after regaining independence in 1991, the field of social work began to grow rapidly and impact on criminal justice. Combined, these changes formed the future basis of rehabilitation policies and practices in criminal justice.

Although the old, harsh criminal code inherited from the Soviet Union remained the foundation of the law the number of imprisoned persons moderately decreased (Judins & Mežulis, 2004). Then, in 1999 the new Criminal law came into force, but it did not make a significant impact on prison numbers, on the contrary, the percentage of convicted persons with long terms of imprisonment increased and the overall number of convicted persons reach its peak in the first decade of the 2000s (Judins & Mežulis, 2004). Nor was there any effective policy of supporting people on parole and suspended sentence. Supervision was undertaken by State police and had no real support and control system (Judins & Mežulis, 2004). Perhaps, most significantly, there was no consistent, evidence-based policy of resocialisation.

The considerable changes in resocialisation policies that were introduced in 2000s began with the formation of the State Probation Service (SPS). The Concept Paper issued by the Cabinet of Ministers in 2003, outlined the reasons for creating the SPS as: the reduction of the costs of imprisonment; the development of community work; the effective addressing of the causes of criminal behaviour; the development of mediation in criminal justice; the introduction of pre-sentence and parole reports; and the introduction of a post-penitential support system. In general, since the beginning of a new millennium, significant changes have been made to sanctions policies and practices, which have continued to move away from isolating and imprisoning individuals and towards seeking alternative solutions and strengthening rehabilitation.

Alternatives for Deprivation of Liberty and a New Probation Service

In 2002, following the Concept Paper on the Development of the State Probation Service of Latvia a decision was taken to establish it as an institution under the Justice Department. It began its work in October 2003 and the sanctions policy and practice in Latvia began to change and develop. If the most significant change in prison was a reduction in the number of prisoners, the construction of infrastructure and the development of services within the prison system, and the introduction of probation constituted a new enforcement body. The probation task was to take over functions previously performed by the police (control and supervision of convicted persons in the community), create a new content for them and develop new penal practices. Moving away from the experience, mentalities and practices of the Soviet era, which brought harsh punishments and personal isolation to the forefront of the penal system, Latvia sought to develop a more modern and Western culture-based punishment policy. Hence, rehabilitation and opportunities for convicted individuals to repay society for the damage caused by their offending became a fundamental part of the agenda of the penal policy.

Moving away from incarceration as a central solution to the crime problem has been characterised by a significant reduction in the number of prisoners. Since the beginning of the 2000s, when it was among the European countries with the largest prison population, Latvia has achieved a significant reduction over a period of twenty years and has now approached the average European prison population rate. In 2000 there were 8815 prisoners in prisons in Latvia (rate per 100,000 of population 370), and twenty years later only 3124 (rate per 100,000 of population 165) (The World Prison Brief).[3] The reduction in the number of prisoners, stemming as it did from the demand for a new penal policy, is significant and is related to the reduction in the length of sentences and their use (particularly for minors), and the development of alternative sanctions.

The new SPS initially had two important tasks: creating an institutional structure and a network of territorial divisions and putting together the content and practices of the sentences for which it had responsibility. The first entailed building a management structure and a network of offices throughout Latvia and selecting and preparing probation officers for work with probation clients. The second related to its responsibilities, which included both taking over work previously carried out by others (for example, the supervision of conditionally sentenced persons previously undertaken by the police), and the development of ways of reducing recidivism (for example, mediation). In addition, the State Probation Service Law, stipulated that the service had to oversee the execution of the community punishments, prepare pre-sentence reports and evaluation reports on parole applications and organise conflict resolution through mediation. Despite the variety of functions assigned to the probation service and the fact that mediation and the preparation of pre-sentence and parole reports are important functions, the largest amount of probation work relates to the enforcement of community punishments. It is, therefore, the supervision and support of probation clients that forms the basis for Latvia's new practices and rehabilitation model.

Models of Rehabilitation in Latvia: Putting Principles into Practice

Describing and analysing crime-control policies and practices and describing changes in the Western world that have occurred in the crime-control field, Garland (2001: 167–168) in his work on The Culture of Control: The Crime and Social Order in Contemporary Society writes:

> But when considering the field as a whole, we need to bear in mind that these new practices and mentalities co-exist with the residues and continuations of older arrangements. Our focus upon the new and the transformative should not lead us to neglect these older practices and institutions. History is not the replacement of the old by the new, but more or less extensive modification of one by the other. The intertwining of the established and the emergent is what structures the present.

He describes and helps to understand rehabilitation models and approaches that have become entrenched, altered, maintained and transformed into the prison and probation systems in Latvia. If the prison system celebrated its 100th birthday in 2019 and had long been an important institute for execution of penalties in Latvia, then the probation service is a new institute that made it easier to introduce new rehabilitation models and approaches into the penal system. That development was further facilitated by international experience and support provided to Latvia in the process of setting up the State Probation Service. Latvia has learned from experts from different countries in Europe and North America. The experience and good practices of these countries have influenced what rehabilitation models were adapted and implemented in Latvia. Canada and Norway have played a particularly important role in developing rehabilitation practices at the beginning of the probation phase. Due largely to the support of Canadian partners and experts, rehabilitation work based on the Risk-Need-Responsivity model (RNR) (Andrews et al., 1990) was introduced and strengthened in Latvia. Moreover, intervention and probation programmes based on Cognitive-Behavioural Therapy (CBT) shaped the structure and content of supervision of probation clients. Also, during the start-up phase of the probation service, close cooperation with Norway, in particular with the Norwegian Mediation Service, encouraged the development of practices based on the Restorative Justice (RJ) approach. Together, the RNR model and the RJ approach largely form the basis of current practice in dealing with probation clients and prisoners.

Latvia has a long-standing experience of cooperation with Canada and Norway. From 1998 to 2004, the Canadian International Development Agency (CIDA) funded projects to reform Latvia's criminal justice system and supported the participation of Canadian experts in this reform process (Stivrina & Ziedina, 2021). During this period, the Latvian Probation Service cooperated closely with the British Columbia Correctional Service, and this enabled the introduction and consolidation of the RNR model as a basic model for working with a probation client. Experts from Canada provided advice on the RNR model and its application to practice. During the period 2004–2006. The SPS adopted the Community Risk and Needs Assessment tool (CRNA) used in British Columbia and several probation group work programmes. While most programmes from British Columbia have been fundamentally altered and developed, probation officers in the SPS continue to use CBT-based probation programmes, namely Violence Prevention, Respectful Relationships and Substance Abuse Management.

In 2006, the SPS began work with individuals who were conditionally sentenced, and the evaluation tools put in place allowed probation professionals to plan and organise their work on the basis of RNR principles. This risk and needs assessment approach had two objectives: assessing the risk of re-offending by classifying probation clients in low, medium or high-risk categories and identifying their criminogenic needs. The level of risk identified in the assessment determined the intensity of probation supervision and control measures, as well as the amount of support and treatment provided to the probation client. Whereas probation clients included in the low-risk category were invited to an individual appointment with a probation officer once a month or less, those assessed as high risk were obliged to report to the office every week, sometimes even several times a week. Also, probation clients included in the low-risk group were less frequently controlled and not involved in probation group work programmes. In contrast, those included in the medium—and high-risk categories were controlled with more intensity, as well as being enrolled in group sessions.

The organisation of such work was based on the first principle of the RNR model, the principle of risk. The second principle of the RNR model (the principle of needs) in Latvian probation practice meant focusing work on those problems that were directly related to problematic behaviour and crimes of the probation client. The assessment of dynamic risk factors carried out by the probation officer helped plan support measures, set goals and choose strategies and activities to achieve those goals. In probation work, this means that the probation officer draws up a rehabilitation plan, and, together with the client, sets goals and further steps to achieve these goals. This rehabilitation plan may include activities to address employment and education issues or further steps to address a problem of substance use. Work might also focus on helping the client develop skills, assisting with behaviour change and helping with day-to-day planning. It is clear, therefore, that the principles of the RNR model, as well as the factors associated with them, Andrews and Bonta's (1998) 'Big Four' and 'Central Eight', were recognised by the Latvian Probation Service. Indeed for a new probation service, as it was during the first decade of 2000, it was the cooperation with partners from the West and expert support, risk assessment tools and probation programmes, as well as the legal framework of Latvia, that allowed the SPS to develop and implement in practice a rehabilitation model based on RNR.

The third principle of RNR entails the development of cooperation between officers and probation clients and the implementation of interventions that enable the probation client to learn from them as effectively as possible (Andrews & Bonta, 2007). In order to integrate this principle into probation and rehabilitation practices, a variety of training activities for specialists are being implemented. In the knowledge that specialist-client cooperation and relations are critical to promoting and strengthening change, professionals working in the criminal justice field of social work are provided with a variety of training courses, such as Motivational Interviewing, Communication Skills Training, Cognitive Behavioural Therapy and Pro-social Modelling. Although significant resources are invested in specialist training, studies carried out in Latvia (for example, a study on case management working with people convicted of committing sex crime) showed that the principle of responsivity is the most complicated and is the most difficult to implement in practice.

Since the establishment of the SPS, close cooperation has been established with the Norwegian Mediation Service and this has facilitated the introduction of the Restorative Justice (RJ) approach to Latvia. In the early stages of the development of the SPS (2003–2007), visits of probation specialists to Norway, as well as the participation of the Norwegian Mediation Service in training of probation specialists and mediators, encouraged the development and strengthening of mediation as one of the solutions to the conflict caused by crime. In addition, the cooperation of the Probation Service with the Norwegian Mediation Service enabled specialists working in the criminal justice field and penal policymakers to gain a deeper understanding of the approach and principles of RJ. Initially, the approach and principles of RJ were just linked to the mediation process, but later the impact of the RJ became wider. Thus, in addition to the development of mediation, it encouraged enforcement bodies to cooperate more actively with Non-Government Organisations (NGOs), communities and society, through the development of voluntary activities and a network of mentors involved in rehabilitation with probation clients and prisoners, and a clear recognition of the importance of community participation in social work in criminal justice.

In describing the rehabilitation field in Latvia during the first ten years of this millennium, it can be said, therefore, that it was a period when the Latvian criminal justice system formed an understanding of RNR and RJ. The RNR model and the RJ principles and approach became firmly entrenched as the dominant model and framework for social work in the field of criminal justice. Moreover, the development of rehabilitation, new rehabilitation approaches and models and lessons from new research, encouraged further progress so that the Good Lives model, Trauma Informed Care as an approach in social work practice, and desistence-based approaches contributed to existing practices, their critical evaluation and development.

Development and Reframing the Rehabilitation (2009–2022)

In order to further develop and strengthen new rehabilitation models and practices in Latvia, a number of policy initiatives and projects were prepared and implemented.[4] These initiatives and projects focused on developing a number of new policy elements and practices, or strengthening existing policies and practices, including:

- Strengthening cooperation between probation and prisons
- Latvia's involvement in international professional networks and participation in international conferences and events
- The development of new risk and needs assessment tools and their introduction into
- Specialisation of work, including work with persons convicted of sex crimes (training of specialists, introduction of new individual and group methods, etc.)
- Initiation of changes to the policy of penalties and the integration of new elements of the execution of punishments and rehabilitation into the system (e.g., from 2015 Electronic Monitoring was introduced in Latvia for probation clients who are under parole as a back-door programme)
- The development of new rehabilitation and resocialisation programmes
- Establishment of a training system for probation professionals and volunteers, and cooperation between the SPS and the Prison administration in the training of employees
- The development of a network of inter-institutional cooperation in the field of criminal justice and the implementation of cooperation mechanisms in practice
- The development and strengthening of rehabilitation practices based on the principles of Restorative Justice (including the involvement of volunteers in support of sanctioned persons, the strengthening of community participation in the criminal justice social work)
- The adaptation, implementation and strengthening of new rehabilitation methods in practice (e.g. the Good Life Model, Motivational Interviewing, strengths-based approaches).

As far as the development of rehabilitation policies and practices over the past ten years is concerned, it was largely influenced by the strengthening of cooperation between the SPS and the Prison Administration, the realisation of joint projects and the active involvement of institutions in various international networks. Cooperation between the two institutions was developed step by step. Initially cooperation involved jointly organised events and joint trainings for the employees of both institutions, but later the scope of cooperation became wider to include joint larger-scale cooperation projects, and cooperation in the development of methodologies and rehabilitation practices. The joint efforts of the two institutions to develop cooperation and rehabilitation practices are illustrated by the progress of risk and needs assessment practices. The SPS initially adapted and introduced risk and needs assessment tools in the field of community punishment, but later they were also introduced into prisons. Following the introduction of specialised risk assessment tools in the probation system for individuals charged with or convicted of sex crimes (i.e. Static-99R, Stable-2007 and Acute-2007), prison staff were trained to use Static-99R in prisons. So what in the last five years began as a probation initiative became closely linked to the practice of Prison Administration projects. In recent years, with the cooperation of SPS, the risk assessment validity and reliability of Static-99R and Stable-2007 as new tools to be used within the framework of a Prison Administration-led project has been assessed. The SPS has also been provided with human and financial resources so that it can develop new assessment practices for working with minors and young people.

Soon after its inauguration, the SPS became a member of the Confederation of European Probation (CEP) and later engaged in the European Forum for Restorative Justice (EFRJ) network. The Prison Administration, on the other hand, has been a partner in the EuroPris network for many years. Now representatives of the two institutions participate in seminars and conferences organised by other professional communities. These events raise new awareness of what is happening in the field of rehabilitation, social work and criminal justice, as well as the opportunity to share the experience of Latvia. This participation in professional networks has helped promote closer cooperation and the exchange of the experience of developing rehabilitation practices with partners in Europe.

Financial support from different funds has made a significant contribution to the development of rehabilitation practice and has been crucial to the realisation of projects. These projects have contributed to the transfer of new rehabilitation methods, approaches and tools (assessment tools, rehabilitation programmes) from other countries, as well as allowing Latvia to develop its own new tools or practices. Examples of transfer include the adaptation of the UK's 'Community Treatment Programme for Sex Offenders' and the Good Lives Model (GLM). The latter was initially part of the group work programme, but later the specialists using GLM in practice saw more potential in it and so the model was used as a theoretical basis for developing other rehabilitation practices. In addition, project grants have helped in the introduction and strengthening of approaches, methods and practices into the criminal justice field, such as Circles of Support and Accountability (COSA)[5]; Motivational Interviewing (now one of the base modules for the training of probation officers, prison professionals and volunteers); inter-institutional cooperation meetings (on the basis of the British MAPPA model); and the introduction of the conference method in the mediation process (in cooperation with the RJ network). Moreover, currently discussions are being held on the 'Transtheoretical Model of Change'[6] and its potential in assessing and promoting change. It should also be mentioned that cooperation between institutions and specialists has been actively strengthened over the last decade; the model, which is the basis for inter-institutional meetings, is legally strengthened by cooperation agreements, and increasingly inter-institutional meetings are being used as a resource for managing complex cases.

The introduction of RJ's principles and theoretical framework led to a more active involvement of parties involved in the conflict and the community in which the offence has occurred. Furthermore, it has encouraged probation and prisons to actively involve a network of volunteers, and thus communities, in criminal justice social work. Volunteers are currently involved in negotiating the mediation process, being mentors for probation clients in the community, and supporting prisoners. The principles and theoretical framework of the RJ are extensive and recognised in the field of justice in Latvia and this has led to the introduction of 'Circles of Support and Accountability (COSA)' in the process of helping people reintegrate into society after their release from prison.

Research and Rehabilitation Practices

Research plays an important role in the development of rehabilitation practices in Latvia. Twenty years earlier, when new rehabilitation models and approaches were borrowed from other countries, adapted and introduced, knowledge of what was effective was drawn from studies in those countries. However, later when these practices were strengthened in Latvia, there was a need for local studies to analyse which policies and practices are effective and sustainable as well as which are ineffective. Therefore, in 2009 SPS created a Research Unit to fulfil this need. It was set up as a temporary Unit within the framework of a project supported by a Norway Grant, entitled 'Building the capacity of the personnel of the Latvian Probation and Prisons System' (SPS, 2010), but in 2011 the researchers of the unit were included in the main structure of the SPS, and a permanent Unit of Training and Research was established (SPS, 2012). By creating this team of researchers, the SPS had the opportunity to evaluate probation work and develop evidence-based practice in three directions:

- Research on recidivism and re-offending
- Studies on penal policies, probation practices and evaluation of tools and methods
- Studies on the staff wellbeing, resilience, probation work organisation and management processes.

Since the creation of the unit, the SPS has been conducting regular studies of recidivism rates. The first recidivism study was completed in 2012 and further studies have been carried out in the following years to analyse general, violent and sexual recidivism. On 2 October 2014, amendments to the SPS Law were made to legally strengthen research activities. According to new amendments to the Law, the SPS is responsible for the regular investigation of the criminal recidivism of probation clients. Examples, which illustrate the need for regular research and evaluation of the practice of the application of penalties and need for recidivism studies, include the 2016 study 'Application and enforcement of community sanction and conditional sentencing' (Zavackis & Ņikišins, 2016), and the 2019 study 'Criminal recidivism rates of probation clients: Comparison of cohort 2013 and 2016' (Zavackis & Cinks, 2019). These studies have influenced policy changes and sentencing practices and encouraged a more effective crime-control solution.

Studies have shown that changes in the policy of penalties have affected the practice of imposing penalties and the recidivism rates. In the period 2010–2016, more and more individuals were punished with community work sanctions while conditional sentencing sanctions were applied less frequently. A comparison of probation clients whose probation started in 2013 and 2016 found that over three years, the number of probation clients punished with a community work sanction increased by 34%, while the number of conditionally sentenced persons fell by 38%. This change in the imposition of penalties is shown in Fig. 1.

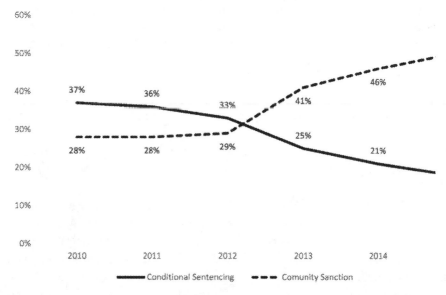

Fig. 1 Dynamics of Conditional Sentencing (supervision) and Community Sanction (community work) in Latvia in 2010–2016 (percentage of total penalties imposed) (*Source* Data from the Court Information System of Latvia used in author's previously published paper. Zavackis, A., & Ņikišins, J. [2016]. Piespiedu darbu un nosacītas notiesāšanas piemērošana un izpilde [Application and enforcement of community sanction and conditional sentencing]. Rīga: Valsts probācijas dienests https://www.vpd.gov.lv/lv/media/301/download)

A detailed analysis of the different groups of probation clients found that the group of conditionally sentenced persons had become older (an increased proportion of elderly people), had a higher proportion of women, and an increased the number of people with secondary or higher education; whereas opposite changes have occurred to the group of people sentenced to community works sanctions. Changes in crime recidivism rates were also found. In a sample of probation clients in 2016, total recidivism rates were higher compared with a 2013 sample group. A statistically significant increase in recidivism rates from 2013 to 2016 was reported in a group of people sentenced to community work, from 21.5% new criminal proceedings initiated during the first year (2013) to 31% in 2016 (Zavackis & Cinks, 2019); however, an increase in crime recidivism was not detected in other probation client groups. These studies showed that community work as a punishment often does not deter a person from committing a new crime and is not an effective punishment. The studies encouraged a discussion on the need to reform the Latvian penal system to increase punishments that include rehabilitation elements and create opportunities to address the problems of the convicted person, the outcome of which was as a new basic sentence of probation supervision. This example shows that studies can have an impact on the policy of penalties and contribute to the development of rehabilitation practices.

The second direction of research carried out by the SPD relates to the assessment of penal enforcement practices, the validation and development of risk and needs assessment tools, the evaluation and development of probation programmes and a deeper analysis of other control and rehabilitation practices. Probation work has been significantly influenced by research. For instance, a research project on risk and needs assessment carried out a number of studies over a three-year period. During the project, an assessment of the effectiveness of existing risk and needs assessment tools was carried out and a decision was taken to develop new risk assessment tools based on data on Latvian probation clients. This study gathered and analysed data from the Probation Client Data System on more than 20,000 probation clients, as well as data from the Latvian Crime Register on more than 90,000 criminal proceedings. Using the data obtained, new risk and needs assessment tools were created to assess the risk of re-offending in the probation client population. Probation officers were trained to use the new assessment methods and the new set of risk and needs assessment tools were integrated into probation practice. In addition to developing risk and needs assessment methodologies and practices, evaluations of the probation programmes used in practice have been carried out, along with an examination of the individual work of probation professionals with their clients. In 2020, for example, a study entitled 'Case management of persons convicted of sex crimes' was undertaken. The study analysed probation practices and their compliance with the RNR principles, and the process of working with clients (assessment-planning—intervention—re-evaluation and replanning) The results of the study showed that probation specialists managed to obtain extensive information about the probation client's risks and needs that helped plan and organise work. At the same time, the results showed that the main challenges in probation work with the client are the setting up and pursuit of achievable rehabilitation objectives, as well as the provision of external rehabilitation services and cooperation with partners in the rehabilitation process. Other identified challenges were ensuring collaboration with a probation client, flexibility and the adaptation of probation interventions that fit the learning style of the probation client and his or her needs, or put another way, the implementation of the responsivity principle in practice. Currently, the SPS and the prison administration have established teams of researchers who organise and carry out studies on the assessment of penal policies and practices. This valuable resource can help both institutions and criminal justice in general to develop evidence-based policies and practices.

Conclusions: Current Scope and Future Directions

Although this chapter has shown that the RNR model is the dominant rehabilitation approach to working with convicted persons in prison and probation and that Latvia has developed and maintained practices based on the RJ approach and principles, over the last decade, other models, and approaches to tackling crime and developing rehabilitation practices have emerged in its criminal justice field. This and the interest of prisons and probation specialists and discussions on new theoretical rehabilitation frameworks and methods (e.g. Trauma Informed Care and Mindfulness-based practice), provides a basis for thinking that further development of rehabilitation policies and practices will be linked to the integration and implementation of these different approaches and practices. That said, it will be a challenge for the Latvian criminal justice system to use these new models and approaches as a resource, and to align them with existing models and practices already integrated into probation and prison systems.

It is also expected that the changes already made to the penal policy, such as the new basic sentence of probation supervision introduced on the 1st of January 2022, will have a significant impact on the work and practice of probation and prison systems in general. These changes to the penal system emanate from the need to strengthen rehabilitation components. For example, community work, the most frequently imposed criminal penalty in Latvia, enables a convicted person to repair the damage done to the community through his or her work, but does not involve a response to his or her rehabilitative needs. In contrast, the introduction of a new basic penalty allowing for greater control and support of a convicted person creates more opportunities for rehabilitation.

Among the above-mentioned changes in rehabilitation policies and practices, volunteering, and community involvement in the support of sentenced individuals have progressed. Indeed, increased involvement of the Community and volunteers in rehabilitation work, and support for community and voluntary initiatives, offer another way forward for future practice. Fergus McNeill (2012) describes rehabilitation as a social and personal project with four forms of rehabilitation. Reflecting on Latvia's rehabilitation policy and practice from this perspective, the focus has so far been on strengthening and developing personal rehabilitation, while the forms of judicial, moral and social rehabilitation have been less recognised and developed. In order to shape a comprehensive rehabilitation policy and strategy in Latvia's criminal justice system, complex solutions are needed to cover all four forms of rehabilitation.

Notes

1. Statistical report of the State Probation Service and the Prisons Administration.
2. Latvijas Padomju Sociālistiskās Republikas Kriminālkodess [Criminal code of the Soviet Socialist Republic of Latvia] https://likumi.lv/wwwraksti/1961/LPSR_KK.PDF.
3. The World Prison Brief. World Prison Brief data: Latvia. https://www.prisonstudies.org/country/latvia.
4. (Information regarding the projects implemented may be found in the public annual reports of the State Probation Service and the Prisons Administration.
5. Ccooperation in the "CIRCLES4EU" European project was important for COSA implement in Latvia.
6. See https://doi.org/10.1093/acrefore/9780190228613.013.324.

References

Andrews, D., & Bonta, J. (1998). *The psychology of criminal conduct* (2nd ed.). Anderson Publishing.

Andrews, D., & Bonta, J. (2007). Risk-need-responsivity model for offender assessment and rehabilitation. Public Safety Canada. http://www.publicsafety.gc.ca/cnt/rsrcs/pblctns/rsk-nd-rspnsvty/index-eng.aspx

Andrews, D., Bonta, J., & Hoge, R. (1990). Classification for effective rehabilitation: Rediscovering psychology. *Criminal Justice and Behavior, 17*(1), 19–52.

Garland, D. (2001, reprinted 2006). *The Culture of Control. Crime and Social Order in Contemporary Society*. Oxford University Press.

Hardy, J. S. (2016). *The gulag after Stalin: redefining punishment in Khrushchev's Soviet Union, 1953–1964*. Cornell University Press.

Judins, A., Mežulis, D. (2004). Nosacīta pirmstermiņa atbrīvošana no kriminālsoda. [Conditional early release of criminal penalties]. Latvijas Policijas akadēmija, Rīga.

Камалова, Г.Т., Красуцких, Л.В. (2019). История уголовного права России XIX–XX вв.: учебное пособие [History of criminal law in Russia in the 19th–20th centuries: A textbook]. Челябинск: Издательский центр ЮУрГУ.

Krastiņš, U. (2009). Krimināltiesības [Criminal Law] Tiesu namu aģentūra, Rīga.

Kronberga, I. (2015). Kriminālsodu izpildes vēsture (macību materiāli) [History of the execution of criminal penalties (training materials)]. Valsts probācijas dienests, Rīga.

McNeill, F. (2012). Four forms of 'offender' rehabilitation: Towards an interdisciplinary perspective. *Legal and Criminological Psychology, 17*(1), 18–36.

Mincs, P., Ehlers, H., Jakobi, P., & Lauva, J. (1934). 1933. g. 24. aprīļa sodu likums: ar likumdošanas motīviem un sīkiem komentāriem, kā arī ar alfabētisko un citiem rādītājiem. Neoficiāls izdevums [1933 The April 24 Penalties Act: With legislative motives and petty comments, and with alphabetical and other indicators. Informal edition.] Riga, Latvia.

Solmon, H. (1978). *Soviet criminologists and criminal policy*. Columbia University Press.

Šneidere, I. (2004). Padomju pirmā okupācija Latvijā: daži aspekti. [The First Soviet Occupation Period in Latvia: A few aspect] Totalitārie režīmi un to represijas Latvijā 1940.–1964. gadā: Latvijas.

Stivrina, S., & Ziedina, D. (2021). Probation in Latvia: 'For a safer society.' *Irish Probation Journal, 18*, 159–177.

State Probation Service. (2010). Valsts probācijas dienesta 2009. gada publiskais pārskats [2009 public report of the State Probation Service]. https://www.vpd.gov.lv/lv/publiskie-parskati

State Probation Service. (2012). Valsts probācijas dienesta 2011. gada publiskais pārskats [2011 public report of the State Probation Service]. https://www.vpd.gov.lv/lv/publiskie-parskati

Van den Berg, G. P. (1985). *The soviet system of justice: Figures and policy*. Netherlands, Springer.

Zavackis, A., Cinks, R. (2019). Probācijas klientu noziedzīgu nodarījumu recidīvs: 2013. gada un 2016. gada kohortu salīdzinājums [Reoffence rates of probation clients: 2013–2016 cohort comparison]. Valsts probācijas dienests. https://www.vpd.gov.lv/probcijasklientunoziedzgunodarjumurecidvs2013gadaun2016gadakohortusaldzinjums

Zavackis, A., Ņikišins, J. (2016). Piespiedu darbu un nosacītas notiesāšanas piemērošana un izpilde [Application and enforcement of community sanction and conditional sentencing]. Valsts probācijas dienests. https://www.vpd.gov.lv/lv/media/301/download

Criminal Justice Rehabilitation in Macao, China

Donna Soi Wan Leong and Jianhong Liu

Introductory History and Current Mechanisms of Correction and Rehabilitation in Macao

Macao was a Portuguese colony for over four centuries before the handover to Mainland Chinese jurisdiction on 20th December 1999. According to previous studies, the history of Macao's correctional facilities can be traced back to the Ming dynasty, when imperial rulers operated detention houses inside official establishments to imprison political opponents as well as those who had committed crimes. Portuguese colonists set up jail cells on battleships and in military camps to lock up people who had offended (Li, 2010, cited in Li & Ye, 2017: 2). In 1904 Portuguese colonists started to construct the first prison in Macao, and it went into official operation on 5th September 1909. This prison built a century ago was initially named Central Prison,

---

D. S. W. Leong
Institute for the Study of Commercial Gaming, University of Macau, Avenida da Universidade, Taipa, Macau, China
e-mail: donnaleong@um.edu.mo

J. Liu (✉)
Faculty of Law, University of Macau, Avenida da Universidade, Taipa, Macau, China
e-mail: jliu@um.edu.mo

which served as the main correctional institution in Macao in the next several decades with a capacity of 150 prisoners, until it could not keep pace with the needs of the correctional system (Li & Ye, 2017). The old Central Prison is located in the urban area of the current Macao peninsula, which used to be a remote hillside. In 1988, owing to the overcrowding problem and the inadequate facilities of Central Prison following Macao's rapid social development, the government decided to construct a new prison in Coloane, Macao, named 'Coloane Prison', at the site of the former firecracker factory near the original 'Coloane Juvenile Prison'. The construction of the Coloane Prison was completed in 1990 with a capacity of 800 prisoners. On the date of the Macao handover, Coloane Prison became subordinate to the Secretariat for Security and was officially renamed Macao Prison until it and the Youth Correctional Institution were restructured as the Correctional Services Bureau (Portuguese: Direcção dos Serviços Correccionais, abbrev. DSC) under the Secretariat for Security in 2016. Since then, this prison has been officially renamed 'Coloane Prison' (Correctional Services Bureau of Macao SAR, 2021b, 2021c). Due to overcrowding being an issue at Coloane Prison, a new facility is under construction in Ká Hó, Coloane. Construction of this facility began in 2010 and was scheduled to open by 2014 but has since been delayed (Macau Daily Times, 2020). Coloane Prison is responsible for enforcing the penalty of liberty deprivation and custodial measures. Its functions also include adopting measures to correctly enforce penalties, making inmates more disciplined, coordinating and supervising the monitoring of those in custody and their rehabilitation services, and providing assistance and education for inmates to facilitate their return to society. The aim is to prevent recidivism and to promote reintegration into society (Correctional Services Bureau of Macao SAR, 2021b, 2021c, 2021d).

In addition to Coloane Prison, there is a detention facility, particularly for juveniles, in Macao, the Youth Correctional Institution. In 1963, Macao established two juvenile correctional facilities, the Boys Home, and the Home of Nossa Senhora do Rosário de Fátima, for male and female youths. Military officers operated the male facility at the beginning, then it was taken over by the St. Francis of Assisi's School, founded by missionaries in 1976. It was run by Catholic nuns for a while but owing to the fact that no other organisation was willing to take on the female facility, it was closed down. In order to provide rehabilitation services to all youths, the St. Francis of Assisi's Reformatory was established in 1977 through an agreement between the government and Macao Catholic Church. When the agreement ended, the government took sole ownership of the reformatory and placed it under the administration of the Central Prison in 1984 (Li & Ye, 2017).

Subsequently, when Macao's sovereignty was returned to China, the Youth Correctional Institution was placed in the Legal Affairs Bureau under the Secretariat for Administration and Justice. In 2016, this institution and the prison were reconstituted as the Correctional Services Bureau. The Youth Correctional Institution is an educational guardianship for juvenile delinquents that only accepts young persons aged 12 to 16 but may extend its services to them until they reach 21 (Government Information Bureau of the Macao SAR, 2021). It is responsible for executing the court-imposed detention measures. The objective of the detention services is to correct the cognitive, emotional, and behavioural problems of the youth detainee, and enhance their independent thinking, self-care ability, and life skills to facilitate successful reintegration into society (Correctional Services Bureau of Macao SAR, 2021a, 2021d). In sum, the Correctional Services Bureau is responsible for executing court-imposed custodial sentences and detention measures, monitoring those remanded in custody, as well as providing correctional rehabilitation services.

The Department of Social Reintegration is responsible for non-custodial sentences such as parole and probation (Zhao, 2014); it was previously named the Center of Social Rehabilitation. Initially, the centre was a city-run facility used to provide shelter for beggars and the homeless. It was renamed the Center of Social Rehabilitation in 1961 and was assigned to the Public Security Police. In 1967 this institution was reorganised as a particular prison to serve drug addicts, beggars, people with mental health issues, and those at risk of persistent offending (Li & Ye, 2017). After the territory's handover to China in 1999, the institution was renamed the 'Department of Social Reintegration' and was placed in the Legal Affairs Bureau under the Secretariat for Administration and Justice. In 2016, the department was reassigned to the Social Welfare Bureau (Portuguese: Instituto de Acção Social, abbrev. IAS) under the Secretariat for Social Affairs and Culture (Li & Ye, 2017; Social Welfare Bureau of Macao SAR, 2021). The Department of Social Reintegration is responsible for assisting the court to implement non-custodial sentences and sentence suspension orders, implementing supervision orders applied to young persons, preparing pre-trial reports for the court, providing supports for individuals to reintegrate into society, as well as enhancing the prevention of reoffending (Social Welfare Bureau of Macao SAR, 2021).

As early as 1990, the legislature amended the statutes to officially recognise the correctional and rehabilitation system and formally defined the aforementioned institutions' organisational structure and functions (Li & Ye, 2017). In brief, the Correctional Services Bureau, and the Department of Social Reintegration under the Social Welfare Bureau, are responsible for rehabilitation in

Macao (Correctional Services Bureau of Macao SAR, 2021a, 2021b, 2021c, 2021d; Li & Ye, 2017; Social Welfare Bureau of Macao SAR, 2021; Zhao, 2014).

Rehabilitation Programmes in Macao

Macao receives an enormous number of visits from foreign nationals or non-residents, and if they commit a crime in Macao, they face a monetary fine for a misdemeanour or imprisonment for more serious crimes. Once convicted, foreigners and non-residents who have committed more serious crimes in the city must serve at least part of their sentence in Coloane Prison, have their visas revoked, face deportation, and be prohibited from re-entering Macao (Li & Ye, 2017). Consequently, rehabilitation programmes in Macao predominantly target residents with convictions.

The implementation of incarceration sentences in Macao emphasises social rehabilitation. The prisoners are not compelled to engage in daily labour, but they can apply to work or study in prison according to individual interests and needs (Correctional Services Bureau of Macao SAR, 2021e; Government Information Bureau of the Macao SAR, 2021; Zhao, 2014). In addition, they can participate in recreational or sports activities in prison. Those prisoners with children under 16 years old can participate in the Child Support Programme where they can meet their children on Sundays and receive guidance from social workers (Zhao, 2014). The rehabilitation services carried out by the Coloane Prison include social work and counselling support services, school education, and vocational trainings, and activities facilitating social reintegration (Correctional Services Bureau of Macao SAR, 2021e).

With regard to social work and counselling support services, the Prison arranges for social workers or counsellors to meet with the prisoner within the first 48 hours of incarceration for assessment of psychological conditions in order to help them solve personal issues and difficulties related to incarceration and help them adapt to life in prison. The social workers and counsellors monitor each prisoner's case and provide psychological counselling services for those in need to increase their mental wellness and adaptation. Meanwhile, they promote contact between prisoners and their families and offer viable assistance. The Prison also holds various talks and workshops, such as the 'Seasons of Life' self-discovery workshop and the 'Reshaping Your Life' workshop, to improve individuals' emotional management, enhance their mental strength and help them establish positive life values. In addition, the Prison and the Department of Social Reintegration jointly organise the

'With You by My Side' social rehabilitation scheme composed of parole and social rehabilitation talks, pre-release counselling workshops, and the 'Celebrating Life' workshop. The scheme allows participating prisoners to learn about the problems they might encounter as they adapt to re-entry into society and about ways of finding adequate supports to achieve a smooth reintegration. Furthermore, the 'Family Beyond the Wall' Project organised by the aforementioned government departments and the Young Men's Christian Association of Macao (YMCA Macao) is designed to help the participants solve family issues and restore familial relationships, so as to create favourable conditions for their return to the family and the society. Unfortunately, in 2020 due to the preventive measures of the COVID-19 the talks and workshops dropped significantly by 57.9% to eight sessions, and the number of participants decreased sharply by over 50% (Correctional Services Bureau of Macao SAR, 2016–2021).

The school education and vocational training for prisoners includes various programmes. In the academic year 2019/2020, a total of 119 prisoners attended the junior secondary and primary level recurrent education programmes, 10 attended the higher diploma or tertiary level recurrent education programmes, and one attended the distance learning programmes offered by the Chinese University of Hong Kong. Moreover, the number of participants in vocational training was 599 in 2020. Coloane Prison has 22 workshops offering prisoners 17 types of training, including printing, magazine editing, bread and cake production, automotive repair, maintenance, plumbing and electrics, and garment making. As for professional certification courses, the prison collaborates with local educational institutes to organise various certificated courses, such as computer classes, knowledge and skills for western restaurant services, interior designers and decorators, salesclerks, and warehouse workers: 822 prisoners participated in 2020 (Correctional Services Bureau of Macao SAR, 2016–2021, 2021e).

Coloane Prison also arranged various cultural and recreational activities and interest classes for incarcerated persons to boost their physical and mental wellbeing. Before the COVID-19 Pandemic, the Prison held the Children's Day parent–child activity to allow for a reunion between incarcerated persons and their children. A special concert was performed by the Macao Chinese Orchestra and the Macao Orchestra, and acapella, introductory coffee knowledge and sign language classes were provided to enrich life in prison. Except for the annual *Inmates' Chinese New Year Party*, most activities and interest classes were suspended under the anti-pandemic measures; although creativity contests, such as greeting card design, playwriting, calligraphy, and song composition that allowed social distancing substituted for the suspended activities. Even so, in 2020 the number of those who attended cultural and recreational activities dropped by just over 85% (Correctional Services Bureau of Macao SAR, 2016–2021).

To help the prisoners successfully get employment upon release, the Prison and the Department of Social Reintegration also held the 'Employment Scheme for Pre-release Inmates' under which employers from various sectors were invited to interview soon-to-be-released prisoners for positions such as clerk, shop assistant, driver, cashier, waiter, and kitchen helper. However, in 2020 the number of companies involved, and the number of participants dropped significantly (Correctional Services Bureau of Macao SAR, 2016–2021). On a more positive note, the Prison continually promotes the 'Inmates' Loving and Caring Society Service Scheme' to allow incarcerated persons to serve and give back to the community. Through providing several types of volunteer services, such as giving special performances at community centres, providing cleaning services at nursing homes, helping clean up facilities of children's centres, and helping arrange books at the community library, prisoners are able to gain an increased sense of responsibility to the society and experience the happiness of helping others. That said, due to the pandemic external volunteer services declined by 91.2% to three services and participants dropped by 90.9% (Correctional Services Bureau of Macao SAR, 2016–2021).

As for the detained youths, the Youth Correctional Institution provides personalised counselling services for each detainee according to their actual problems. The Institution helps them re-establish and strengthen familial relationships through meetings, home visits, and activities. It also helps some families develop a support system and enhance parenting skills designed to increase levels of support and trust. Unlike adult prisoners, juveniles participate in systematic discipline training, including marching, physical fitness training, and a reward scheme, to strengthen their awareness of discipline and increase their willpower.

Except for the counselling services for juveniles, the Institution's rehabilitation programmes emphasised education to create more favourable conditions for them to return to society. The Institution and the Education and Youth Affairs Bureau organises the formal and recurrent education programmes and professional certificate courses for detained young persons. Moreover, vocational training programmes, cultural and recreational activities, interest classes, talks for small groups, and workshops are held for them towards a more positive attitude to life and to help with their future social reintegration. Furthermore, the Institution collaborates with the Department of Social Reintegration on the 'Employment Scheme for Juvenile Delinquents' to set up recruitment interviews for those soon-to-be discharged to increase the employment opportunities after their release. In 2020, nine detained young persons attended formal and recurrent education programmes; 45 persons participated in professional certificate courses, 194 persons participated in cultural and recreational activities and interest classes, and 35 persons participated in talks and workshops (Correctional Services Bureau of Macao SAR, 2016–2021).

In addition, for almost two decades the Youth Correctional Institution has been implementing the Social Service Scheme which provides opportunities for youths to serve in the community, to enable them to understand society, care for the community, and enhance their sense of responsibility (Correctional Services Bureau of Macao SAR, 2021a). However, there is reason to believe that their community services also declined because of the pandemic.

The Department of Social Reintegration provides non-custodial rehabilitation services for individuals with convictions; for instance, psychological counselling, preparing pre-trial social background reports to the courts, and supporting individuals previously incarcerated and those under non-custodial sentences. The Department also carries out five main rehabilitation service programmes, mainly for adults. First, the aforementioned 'Family Beyond the Wall' Project through which the Department of Social Reintegration exercises its responsibility for providing family support for incarcerated persons and assisting those families in resolving problems and restoring relationships. This project was extended to Guangdong Province and Hong Kong, providing supportive services for Macao residents serving their sentences in those regions. Secondly, the Social Welfare Bureau launched the Cross-regional Reintegration Service in Greater Bay Area[1] for Macao residents convicted in nearby regions, which cooperates with the relevant agencies from Guangdong and Hong Kong to provide more comprehensive support services to assist those residents' smooth reintegration. Thirdly, because employment is a prerequisite for persons with convictions returning to society, the Career Development Programme assists pre-release prisoners and housed juveniles trying to find jobs through the schemes described above that cooperates with the Correctional Services Bureau. The programme continuously expands the network of employers who support those rehabilitated and organises recruitment activities to ensure individuals with former convictions can be employed successfully. Fourthly, the Department launched the Virtual Job-Hunting Programme, which provided videos showing various work environments and duties to help pre-release prisoners receive information on job opportunities conveniently and choose their preferred posts more effectively. Fifthly, the Correctional Courses for Rehabilitated Offenders provides systematic correctional courses and activities for the rehabilitated persons according to the types of committed crimes and needs, such as personal growth, legal education, civic education, treatment courses, skills training, and participation in social services, in order to raise their awareness of offence-free living and community caring so as to create a positive lifestyle. As for individuals involving felonies or particular crimes, psychological assessments are conducted to develop appropriate psychological counselling and correctional plans. The Correctional Courses for Special Offenders programmes offered to those individuals provide tailored systematic correctional courses, such as recognition of criminal behaviour, personal emotional adjustment, self-esteem reconstruction, and interpersonal skills, and evaluate their correction and rehabilitation progress regularly to ensure effectiveness, improve their social adaptability and avoidance of reoffending (Social Welfare Bureau of Macao SAR, 2021).

Under the law Education and Supervision Regime for Youth Offenders (Macao SAR Law No. 2/2007), the Department also implements supervision orders applied to young persons involved in the justice system and runs three main rehabilitation programmes. The Family Care Support Programme for Juvenile Offenders, launched by the government and the NGOs who engage in the youth affairs to provide support to families of young persons with judicial involvement, included consultation, counselling, family relationship mediation, so as to help those families overcome the difficulties and resume healthy family life. The Correctional Courses for Youth Offenders is similar to those offered to the adults, enabling youths to receive diversified systematic correctional courses. The Caring for Community Programme provides volunteer training and arranges social services for convicted young people to build up their concept of community caring. Finally, the Life Crime Prevention for Youth is a crime prevention education programme in schools in which NGOs employ diversified means to promote the laws and prevent young people from committing crimes to establish their law-abiding life (Social Welfare Bureau of Macao SAR, 2021).

Theoretical Underpinnings to Models of Rehabilitation

The effectiveness of correctional rehabilitation continues to be confirmed through a wealth of published outcome studies. The theoretical foundation is essential to the effectiveness of the rehabilitation programmes. Effectiveness depends on this foundation being adhered to and the design and delivery of services being based on a number of crucial principles of correctional rehabilitation. Previous research has indicated that implementing correctional rehabilitation programmes in accordance with the Risk-Need-Responsivity (RNR) model has been associated with a significantly greater decrease in recidivism rates than those that failed to do so (Zhao et al., 2019). The core principles of RNR can be divided into three major domains, namely risk, need, and responsivity, which became an essential theoretical framework implemented in the correctional system for rehabilitation. The risk principle states that the level of interventions should match the likelihood of reoffending; the need principle suggests that the interventions should focus on the individual's own set of dynamic risk factors or criminogenic needs to lower the risk of recidivism; and the responsivity principle determines that various kinds of intervention differ in their effectiveness of reducing the likelihood of reoffending (Zhao et al., 2019).

Moreover, desistance theory describes the process of people ceasing to offend, conceptualises rehabilitation, and has practical applications for individuals on probation in the community (Farrall & Maruna, 2004). The theory accepts that desistance is a complex process, like a journey with no shortcut for achieving the goal. Changing entrenched behaviours and underlying problems can take considerable time and false stops and relapses should be expected and effectively managed. The desister is placed front and centre in the process in recognition that each individual's experience is different. Each process is influenced by the desisters' circumstances, their way of thinking, and what is important to them (Farrall & Maruna, 2004). We know that desistance is connected to the external and social aspects of a person's life such as the supportiveness of those around them, and internal psychological factors, such as what they believe in and what they want from life (LeBel et al., 2008).

Frames of personal recovery are also essential for designing and delivering rehabilitation services. The concept of *recovery capital* refers to the resources available to support a person in their recovery journey: it has been defined as having three types of recovery capital: personal, family, and social, and community (White & Cloud, 2008). The literature (White & Cloud, 2008) reflects a shift in focus from the pathology of addiction to the internal and external resources required to initiate and sustain long-term recovery. In addition, the CHIME framework for personal recovery was initially developed concerning the key components of effective recovery-oriented services within mental health services and interventions, and covers five components: connectedness, hope and optimism, identity, meaning, and empowerment.

It has been translated into an action model and considers that the positive social connection and the creation of a virtuous circle of positive social supports and identification are crucial for the initiation of recovery of the design and delivery of services (Best, 2019; Leamy et al., 2011). Moving to pro-recovery social networks is the key to sustained recovery over a longer time; this is similar to desistance emphasising the importance of social context and connections. Both frameworks highlight that the processes are neither quick nor easy and often involve failure (Best, 2019).

Research Findings of Correction and Rehabilitation in Macao

Currently, rehabilitation in Macao focuses on helping individuals with convictions reintegrate into society, which is consistent with that of western developed countries. However, research on corrections and rehabilitation in Macao has been sparse. A review of the limited literature, showed that much is drawn from introductory articles, messages on official websites, and press releases. Most of the related official reports and information are spread by brochures or published on official websites, while only a handful of research papers have been found, and evidence-based studies are quite limited.

Three series of official surveys are currently crucial to the scope of rehabilitation and social reintegration in Macao. The Social Welfare Bureau and the Correctional Services Bureau produced the *Report on Recidivism of Sentenced Macao Residents* (2018) that examined whether Macao residents re-offended within two years after completing their previous custodial or non-custodial sentences. Its brief updated reports on the *Statistics of the Recidivism of Sentenced Macao Residents—Recidivism Rate* (Social Welfare Bureau of Macao SAR & Correctional Services Bureau of Macao SAR, 2019–2021) have been reported to the public annually since then. After the recidivism rate met the trough (9.9%) of individuals previously incarcerated in Coloane Prison in 2017, the rate of those released in 2018 increased to 12.4% by 2.5% points; however, the reimprisonment rate presented a contrary trend, which reached its peak (7.6%) in those released in 2017 then dropped to 6.2% by 1.4% points (Table 1). On the other hand, the recidivism rate of those who completed non-custodial sentences between 2015 and 2018 declined from 10.4% to 5.1% for four consecutive years; but the percentage of persons-imposed incarceration sentence due to reoffending has been recorded (3.3%; 2.5%) since those completed measures in 2017 (Table 2).

Table 1 Recidivism of Macao Residents who Convicted Incarceration Sentence, 2015–2018

Year of Release	2015		2016		2017		2018	
	n	%	n	%	n	%	n	%
Re-offense within 2 years of releasex	25	14.6	24	13.6	17	9.9	14	12.4
– Sentenced to Reimprisonment	10	5.8	12	6.8	13	7.6	7	6.2
Total: *	171	100.0	176	100.0	171	100.0	113	100.0

*the total of Macao residents released from Coloane Prison during 1 January to 31 December of the year
Source *Report on Recidivism of Sentenced Macao Residents* (Social Welfare Bureau of Macao SAR; Correctional Services Bureau of Macao SAR, 2018); *Statistics of the Recidivism of Sentenced Macao Residents—Recidivism Rate* (Social Welfare Bureau of Macao SAR; Correctional Services Bureau of Macao SAR, 2019–2021)

Table 2 Recidivism of Macao Residents who Convicted Non-custodial Sentence, 2015–2018

Year of Measures Completion	2015		2016		2017		2018	
	n	%	n	%	n	%	n	%
Re-offense within 2 years of releasex	33	10.4	21	7.6	14	6.7	10	5.1
– Sentenced to Reimprisonment	–	–	–	–	7	3.3	5	2.5
Total: *	317	100.0	276	100.0	210	100.0	198	100.0

*the total of Macao residents who have completed the measures implemented by the Department of Social Reintegration during 1 January to 31 December of the year
Source *Report on Recidivism of Sentenced Macao Residents* (Social Welfare Bureau of Macao SAR; Correctional Services Bureau of Macao SAR, 2018); *Statistics of the Recidivism of Sentenced Macao Residents—Recidivism Rate* (Social Welfare Bureau of Macao SAR; Correctional Services Bureau of Macao SAR, 2019–2021)

As for young persons, the *Report on the Survey of the Characteristics of Youth Offenders* (Social Welfare Bureau of Macao SAR, 2020) conducted by the Department of Social Reintegration provides the related statistics every four years. The up-to-date report is the eighth study, which indicated that the court referred juvenile cases to the Department of Social Reintegration for pre-sentencing social reports or direct sentence measures experienced a significant drop of about 33% to 149 cases. The report shows that the cases were mainly males, aged 15 years old, born in Macao, and living in the Zona Norte (i.e., the North District in Macao). The mean age of committing crimes or deviance was 13.9 years old, and the ratio of male to female was 3.9:1. The majority of youth cases involved crimes against the person and crimes against property. The top three cited crimes for conviction were harm to bodily integrity, theft, and arson. The Zona Norte was the hot spot for juvenile delinquency. Most of the youths committed crimes in the form of group gangs, and a majority of them were in trouble for the first time. The recidivism rate of those young persons has been reported in previous studies; however, the related contents were deleted in the up-to-date report due to the rearrangement of departments to undertake such analysis.

Regarding completed rehabilitation cases, the *Report on the Survey of Characteristics of Rehabilitative Cases* (Social Welfare Bureau of Macao SAR, 2021) was conducted by the Department of Social Reintegration triennially. The recent study reported that a total of 735 rehabilitative cases undertaken by the Department were completed from 2018 to 2020, including 159 parole cases, 390 probation cases (including 283 probationary drug treatment cases), nine community work orders, and 177 voluntary cases, while the previous report showed that a total of 957 cases were completed between 2015 and 2017. This drop represented a decrease of 23.2%. The recent report shows that the individuals of completed cases were mostly males, aged between 26 and 30, with secondary education, born in Macao, and living in the Zona Norte. The proportion of their birthplace and residence was similar to the young persons' results discussed above. The mean age of the individuals was 44 years old, and the ratio of male to female was 6.4:1. According to this study, voluntary cases refer that those proactively seeking help from the Department when they encounter difficulties in life after completing the sentences or security measures. Except for voluntary cases, most individuals on parole and probation participated in drug-related crimes, while those under community work orders engaged in crimes against property and crimes against life in society. In terms of successful completion of the follow-up period, 92.5% of persons on parole, 61.3% of persons on probation, and 55.6% of those under community work orders completed the case follow-up period. Among the 735 completed rehabilitative cases, the proportion of those who had drug-abuse records before the case intake was 57.6% (most using ketamine) and of those 22.2% had abused drugs during the case follow-up period (generally methamphetamine and cocaine). The results show that Macao's rehabilitation and reintegration processes strongly require drug treatment services.

Current Research in Macao

The literature review results showed that the papers and research regarding correction and rehabilitation in Macao are limited. Firstly, there is little literature written in English about such topics. Even if a few papers involved related topics, most of them mentioned that incidentally or as part of the research, and those were introductory. For instance, Zhao and Liu (2011) discussed Macao's crime prevention system, and Zhao (2014) discussed the criminal justice response and legislative reaction to crime in Macao, and correction and rehabilitation had been introduced as part of their research. Furthermore, there are very few book chapters (Kwan, 2010; Li & Ye, 2017) regarding such topics and what they are, focusing on introducing corrections in Macao.

As for the literature regarding correction and rehabilitation published in Chinese, Malvas' (2014) quantitative research on parole decision-making by the prison recommendations is a rare study investigating such research topics related to Macao. The study found that when making decisions on conditional release, Macao prison managers were concerned with protecting the community and maintaining internal order and security. Moreover, except for the press releases and introductory journal articles, there are papers from the various seminars hosted by the government departments to construct the foundation for policy recommendations. Other articles, thesis, or books interpret the legislation clauses or penalty system that focused on the legislation of probation and parole, fines, other measures, and the supervision system of juvenile delinquents. In addition, some of the articles emphasise comparison of such legal institutions with the nearby regions (for example, Mainland China) (Zeng, 2015; Zhang, 2011, 2012).

Future Directions in Policy and Practice of Macao's Rehabilitation

Overall, appropriate grounding in the theoretical underpinnings to correctional rehabilitation can improve practice and the rehabilitation programmes provided in Macao increased the link between theory and practice. However, it is important that the conceptualisations of rehabilitation in criminal justice should be adapted more to the characteristics of convicted individuals. In addition, it might be helpful firstly, to draw lessons from evidence-based practices and research into the guidelines of correctional policy and practice in Western countries, especially the United States, which itself draws from experiences in clinical medicine's efforts to reduce medical risks through testing (Liu & Zhao, 2014; Serin et al., 2012); and secondly, from the significant amount of systematic research and replicable testing used to improve the effectiveness of correction (such as reducing the recidivism rate), correctional measures, and supervision strategies (Liu & Zhao, 2014; Serin et al.,

2012). Latterly, Liu and Zhao (2014) have discussed the development trends of Macao's correctional system and relevant research from a comparative perspective and indicate that the evidence-based research regarding Macao's correctional rehabilitation needs to be more emphasised and developed. However, such studies are currently still insufficient. Evidence-based research to inform and amend laws, policies, and measures of the corrections and rehabilitation systems, has become the developmental norm in many countries in the world, and it is important that more efforts are made to advance further studies focused on related topics in Macao.

Note

1. The Guangdong-Hong Kong-Macao Greater Bay Area (Greater Bay Area) comprises the two Special Administrative Regions of Hong Kong and Macao, and the nine municipalities of Guangzhou, Shenzhen, Zhuhai, Foshan, Huizhou, Dongguan, Zhongshan, Jiangmen, and Zhaoqing in Guangdong Province, where is about 56,000 km^2 and has a population of over 86 million in 2020 (Constitutional and Mainland Affairs Bureau of HK, 2018).

References

Andrews, D. A., Bonta, J., & Hoge, R. D. (1990). Classification for effective rehabilitation: Rediscovering psychology. *Criminal Justice and Behavior, 17*(1), 19–52.

Best, D. (2019). *A model for resettlement based on the principles of desistance and recovery*. HM Inspectorate of Probation.

Constitutional and Mainland Affairs Bureau of HK. (2018). *Guangdong-Hong Kong-Macao greater bay area—overview*. https://www.bayarea.gov.hk/en/about/overview.html [Accessed 26 Febuary 2022].

Correctional Services Bureau of Macao SAR. (2016–2021). *Annual report of correctional services Bureau*. Government of Macao SAR Correctional Services Bureau.

Correctional Services Bureau of Macao SAR. (2021a). *Activities facilitation social reintegration*. https://www.dsc.gov.mo/siteen/SinglePage.aspx?id=53 [Accessed 28 Febuary 2022].

Correctional Services Bureau of Macao SAR. (2021b). *Coloane prison—introduction*. https://www.dsc.gov.mo/siteen/work_info.aspx?id=54 [Accessed 28 December 2021b].

Correctional Services Bureau of Macao SAR. (2021c). *History*. https://www.dsc.gov.mo/siteen/about.aspx?id=12 [Accessed 27 December 2021c].

Correctional Services Bureau of Macao SAR. (2021d). *Responsibilities*. https://www.dsc.gov.mo/siteen/about.aspx?id=9 [Accessed 27 December 2021d].

Correctional Services Bureau of Macao SAR. (2021e). *school education and vocational trainings*. https://www.dsc.gov.mo/siteen/service.aspx?id=18 [Accessed 28 January 2022].

Farrall, S., & Maruna, S. (2004). Desistance-focused criminal justice policy research: Introduction to a special issue on desistance from crime and public policy. *The Howard Journal of Crime and Justice, 43*(4), 358–367.

Government Information Bureau of the Macao SAR. (2021). *Macao Yearbook 2021*, Government Information Bureau of the Macao SAR.

Kwan, S. C. F. (2010). 'Macao' in G. R. Newman (Ed.), *Crime and Punishment Around the World*. ABC-CLIO, 132–141.

Leamy, M., Bird, V., Le Boutillier, C., Williams, J., & Slade, M. (2011). Conceptual framework for personal recovery in mental health: Systematic review and narrative synthesis. *British Journal of Psychiatry, 199*(6), 445–452.

LeBel, T. P., Burnett, R., Maruna, S., & Bushway, S. D. (2008). The 'Chicken and Egg' of subjective and social factors in desistance from crime. *European Journal of Criminology, 5*(2), 131–159.

Li, F. (2010). *On the streets of Macao: The changes of Macau Prison*. Macau Songshan Association.

Li, S. D., & Ye, J. (2017). Macao, Corrections',in. In K. R. Kerley (Ed.), *The encyclopedia of corrections*. John Wiley and Sons.

Liu, J. & Zhao, R. (2014). Corrections in Macau: A review from the perspective of comparative criminal justice (比較犯罪學視野下的澳門犯罪矯治及其發展趨勢). *Journal of Macau Studies (澳門研究), 73*(2), 52–60.

Macao SAR Administrative Regulation No. 28/2015. (n.d.). *Organization and functioning of the social welfare Bureau*. https://bo.io.gov.mo/bo/i/2015/52/regadm28_cn.asp?printer=1#28 [Accessed 28 December 2021].

Macao SAR Decree-Law No. 58/95/M. (n.d.). *Macau penal code*. https://bo.io.gov.mo/bo/i/95/46/codpencn/declei58.asp [Accessed 29 December 2021].

Macao SAR Law No. 2/2007. (n.d.). *Education and supervision regime for youth offenders*. https://bo.io.gov.mo/bo/i/2007/16/lei02_cn.asp [Accessed 02 March 2022].

Macau Daily Times. (2020). *Long-delayed Ká Hó Prison construction still years away*. https://macaudailytimes.com.mo/long-delayed-ka-ho-prison-construction-still-years-away.html [Accessed 11 December 2021].

Malvas, C. M. L. (2014). 'The paradigm of parole release in Macau: A quantitative analysis of prison recommendations (澳門的假釋模式: 監獄建議的定量分析). *Journal of Macau Studies (澳門研究), 73*(2), 72–80.

McNeill, F. (2012). Four forms of "offender" rehabilitation: Towards an interdisciplinary perspective. *Legal and Criminological Psychology, 17*(1), 18–36.

Serin, R. C., Gobeil, R., Hanby, L. J., & Lloyd, C. D. (2012). Evidence-based practice in corrections: Entry points for improvement in case-based decisions. *Corrections Today, 74*(1), 81–86.

Social Welfare Bureau of Macao SAR; Correctional Services Bureau of Macao SAR. (2018). *Report on Recidivism of Sentenced Macao Residents (被判刑澳門居民重犯狀況報告)*. https://www.dsc.gov.mo/OtherPublications/2018/Report/mobile/index.html [Accessed 23 Febuary 2022].

Social Welfare Bureau of Macao SAR; Correctional Services Bureau of Macao SAR. (2019–2021). *Statistics of the Recidivism of Sentenced Macao Residents – Recidivism Rate in 2016–2018 (被判刑澳門居民重犯狀況數據 2016–2018 年重犯率)*. https://www.dsc.gov.mo/siteen/others.aspx [Accessed 24 Febuary 2022].

Social Welfare Bureau of Macao SAR. (2020). *Report on the Survey of the Characteristics of Youth Offenders (違法青少年特徵調查報告)*. https://www.ias.gov.mo/wp-content/uploads/2013/10/2020-08-12_173149_26.pdf [Accessed 26 Febuary 2022].

Social Welfare Bureau of Macao SAR. (2021). *Report on the Survey of Characteristics of Rehabilitative Cases (更生個案統計調查報告)*. https://www.ias.gov.mo/wp-content/uploads/2021/09/2021-09-29_112020_12.pdf [Accessed 26 Febuary 2022].

Social Welfare Bureau of Macao SAR. (2021). *Social reintegration service.* https://www.ias.gov.mo/en/swb-services/rehabilitative_service [Accessed 14 December 2021].

Statistics and Census Service of Macao SAR. (2021). *Macao in Figures 2021.* https://www.dsec.gov.mo/getAttachment/b975a2eb-f733-43f7-b519-4d4dc6f74e2a/E_MN_PUB_2021_Y.aspx [Accessed 10 December 2021].

White, W., & Cloud, W. (2008). Recovery capital: A primer for addictions professionals. *Counselor, 9*(5), 22–27.

Zeng, Z. (2015). A comparative study on the system of non-imprisonment sentence (中國內地與澳門非監禁刑罰執行制度比較研究). *Journal of One Country Two Systems Studies ('一國兩制' 研究), 24,* 149–154.

Zhang, Y. (2011). A comparative study of the parole system in the Mainland and that in Macao (中國內地與澳門假釋制度比較研究). *Journal of One Country Two Systems Studies ('一國兩制' 研究), 10,* 63–69.

Zhang, Y. (2012). A comparative study of the probation systems in the Mainland and in Macao (中國內地與澳門緩刑制度比較研究). *Journal of One Country Two Systems Studies ('一國兩制' 研究), 12,* 137–144.

Zhao, R. (2014). Official responses to crime in Macao. In L. Cao, I. Y. Sun, & B. Hebenton (Eds.), *The Routledge Handbook of Chinese Criminology* (pp. 325–341). Taylor and Francis Group.

Zhao, R., & Liu, J. (2011). A system's approach to crime prevention: The case of Macao. *Asian Journal of Criminology, 6*(2), 207–227.

Zhao, Y., Messner, S. F., Liu, J., & Jin, C. (2019). Prisons as schools: Inmates' Participation in Vocational and Academic Programs in Chinese Prisons. *International Journal of Offender Therapy and Comparative Criminology, 63*(15–16), 2713–2740.

The Legal Flaws and Material Implementation Gaps of Mexico's Rehabilitation Paradigm

Corina Giacomello

In 2008, through a reform of the constitution, the criminal justice system in Mexico underwent a major change when it transitioned from an inquisitorial to an adversarial model based on due process,[1] orality, and publicity. This reform triggered a series of subsequent conceptual and legal changes which include, among others: the design and implementation of alternatives to incarceration during trial and after sentencing; the creation of national legal settings (as opposed to federal and state norms), and the incorporation of a new paradigm on rehabilitation (Sarre & Manrique, 2018). Such change also concerned the prison system, through a legal modification of Articles 18 and 21 of the Constitution which set the basis for a new approach to incarceration and rehabilitation in prison. Article 18, concerned with the aims, structure, and organisation of the prison system, moved from the 're-adaptation' approach (*readaptación* in Spanish) to one of reintegration (*reinserción*) understood as a composite of services and rights of people in prison, and not as part of a transformative process of the person in conflict with the law as someone who needs to be changed in order to 'fit in into society'. This paradigm is not necessarily reflected in current prison practices or in the judicial mindset but still represents an important move away from

---

C. Giacomello (✉)
Institute of Judicial Studies, Autonomous University of Chiapas, Mexico, Mexico
e-mail: cgiacomello@gmail.com

correctional, individual-centred previous approaches. Article 21 establishes that the modification of a sentence and, therefore, the access to parole or other schemes of community sentence and sentence reduction, will be determined by 'jueces de ejecución penal', literally 'judges of criminal execution', here translated as 'judges responsible for the enforcement of the penal law and the monitoring of prisons'.

These legal regulations were further boosted by a constitutional reform of human rights in 2011 and the publication of two laws: the Congreso de la Unión de los Estados Unidos Mexicanos (2014), which contains numerous dispositions on alternatives to imprisonment during process, and the Congreso de la Unión de los Estados Unidos Mexicanos (2016) which establishes national rules for the organisation of prisons, prisoners' rights as well as the judicial mechanisms which will be operated by the 'judges responsible for the enforcement of the penal law and the monitoring of prisons', sentence reductions and alternatives to imprisonment during sentence. At the judicial level, the reforms, and subsequent tools generated by the National Supreme Court (Supreme Court of Justice of the Nation, 2020), have been coupled with a growing awareness of the need to mainstream gender into sentencing and post-sentencing.

This chapter analyses and problematises such legal advances. Besides a critical analysis of the legal and judicial developments, it contains the case study of María, an indigenous woman sentenced to ten years for drug trafficking and liberated under conditional release with electronic bracelet, and her daughter, Guadalupe. Their case sheds light on how persisting mentalities and the lack of an integrated approach can perpetuate the criminalisation and stigmatisation of poverty and the use of alternatives to incarceration as a means for reproducing, rather than reducing, punishment and state control through outsourcing of services to private companies. Furthermore, it illustrates how specific regulations related to political rights and sentencing in Mexico hinder personal, legal, and social rehabilitation after release (Burke et al., 2019).

From *readaptación* to *reinserción*. The Unfinished Path to a Paradigm Shift

In Mexico, the Constitution is the core of the legal and judicial life of the country. Rather than representing a set of principles or shared values which people look at to find a common spirit, it is the heart of political shifts, passions and, often, contradictions. It is constantly submitted to changes, from which the national laws, policies and programmes stem and shape societal life. This lively text is hardly ever implemented in its full scope and intentions, but when someone wants to capture something of the essence of Mexico's approach to the criminal justice system and particularly to rehabilitation, the Constitution is the first reference to address.

As outlined in the introduction, in 2008 a major constitutional reform was approved, which aimed at the profound and entire transformation of the national system of public security, the fight against organised crime and the criminal justice system (Nandayapa & Juárez, 2013). In succinct terms, the reform to the criminal justice system ran on two axes: on the one hand, the embodiment of due process, its principles, and operations into the constitutional text, particularly cemented in Article 20; and on the other, the creation of exceptional, rights-limiting regulations for people accused of, or sentenced for, offences linked to organised crime (Cantú, 2013). This trade-off between enhancing rights for people in contact with the criminal justice system, while creating exceptions for people incriminated for particular offences, must be understood through the lens of the historical time that the country was undergoing. Under the presidential mandate of former President Felipe Calderón (2006–2012) the fight against organised crime became a major banner, which created new tools and expanded old ones, among them the federal prison system with its hard regime, and special criminal procedures.

With regard to the object of this book, the criminal justice reforms in Mexico opened the path for subsequent processes, aimed at reshaping how punishment is conceived and implemented. The reform of Article 18 of the Constitution entailed a shift from previous correctional conceptions of the person in contact with the criminal justice system to one entrenched in rights. Before the reform, the Mexican Constitution embodied the concept of re-adaptation, that is re-adaptation of the person deprived of his or her liberty by means of incarceration. The person accused of an offence was seen as morally and socially deviant and had to be locked away and transformed. This idea, grounded in thinking that stemmed from the perpetuation of the early twentieth century view of 'criminals' as morally deviant and degenerate (Foucault, 2002), was coupled with other factors such as 'prison treatment' as a psychological and moral interventions on the subject; and 'personality exams' which would determine the person's access to alternatives to incarceration or other legal schemes of sentence reduction or modification. The latter relied for its implementation and ultimate decision on the prison administration, away from public scrutiny and judicial procedures. Besides its innumerable side effects, among them corruption, the conceptualisation and implementation of punishment before the 2008 reform can be characterised by three tendencies: the person in contact with the criminal justice system is deemed as morally unfit for life in society and in need of undergoing a transformative process; prison as a means of first rather than last resort; and a non-judicial approach to incarceration and post-sentencing.

Article 18 currently establishes rehabilitation as the goal of the prison system, and the respect of human rights, employment and training, education, health, and sports as the means to achieve it and prevent reoffending. Thus, rehabilitation is considered a process and an end to be achieved during confinement. While the curative dimension of readaptation was eliminated by the 2008 reform, the persisting belief is that prison *can* change people and that prison *must* change people, leaving a reminiscence of incarceration as a necessity and people in prison as people with needs that, if satisfied, will prevent reoffending. The reform was followed by other legal and constitutional changes, which are described briefly here.

In 2011, Article 1 of the Constitution was modified to include human rights as the backbone of public protection and a guarantee for all people, enshrining the principle *pro persona*, which implies that all legal norms shall be interpreted in a way that is most beneficial to the person, in accordance with the Constitution and international human rights treaties (González Domínguez, 2021). Furthermore, in 2014 Congress approved the National Code of Criminal Procedures, thus unifying rules and mechanisms of due process under a national code. It must be underlined that Mexico is a federal state and that before such reform it had a federal code of criminal procedures, one for each state (33 in total). This is still the case for the criminal codes since there is not a national one.

The National Code of Criminal Procedures is a complex text that describes mechanisms, distributes functions and, as its name suggests, defines procedures to be followed at each stage of the process by the multiple actors participating in it. It includes police forces, prosecutors, forensics, courts, legal defense, people in contact with the criminal justice system, and victims. For the purposes of this chapter, it is sufficient to highlight that the National Code comprises (based on Article 17 of the Constitution) figures and mechanisms to adopt extrajudicial forms of conflict resolution and reduce the number of cases that are processed by criminal courts, by means of conciliation at the pre-trial stage. The National Code, then, attempts to reduce the burden of trials on overloaded courts, thus making justice more functional, and at the same time use the criminal justice system to solve conflicts, in accordance with its most current aims (Azzolini, 2015). Among the initiatives included in the Code, are reparatory agreements, opportunity criteria, and suspension of the proceedings. The Law on Alternative Mechanisms of Conflict Resolution, approved in 2014, includes three mechanisms: restorative justice, conciliation, and mediation. These legal innovations represented a major paradigm shift for Mexico, a country in which incarceration proceeded as the rule for most offences, including minor, non-violent ones, and which had more than 40% of its prison population waiting for sentence (Zepeda Lecuona, 2007).

As is shown subsequently in Table 1, any reduction in the prison population only lasted until the beginning of the pandemic of COVID-19 and a corresponding renewed, larger use of pre-trial detention. With regard to the prison system, undoubtably, the most significant step was the approval of the National Law of Penal Execution, in June 2016. It is beyond the scope of this chapter to describe all the nuances and processes that led to its final version, but it is, perhaps, important to note that the Penal Reform of 2008 established that this legislation should have been approved in 2011. The extra five years, however, allowed for deeper reflections and dialogues among multiple stakeholders, which led to the development of a legislative tool that changed the way incarceration is understood and administered. One of the first points, is that, based on the reform of Article 21 of the Constitution in 2008, the prison system no longer represents the last and forgotten ring of the criminal justice chain, namely a storehouse where people are submitted to the overall control of the prison administration with no access to judicial overview. The 'judges responsible for the enforcement of the penal law and the monitoring of prisons' have multiple functions, which can be placed in three related blocks (Giacomello, 2021): (i) to compute the time of sentence paid taking into account the time spent in pre-trial detention; (ii) the modification of the sentence through sentence reduction figures and the application of non-custodial measures; and (iii) control and judicialisation of different aspects of penal execution, among others, prison transfers, disciplinary sanctions imposed on people in prison by the prison administration, living conditions in prison, and the rights of visitors and families. In addition, they play a role in decisions regarding the children who live in prison with their mothers (Giacomello, 2018).

The National Law of Penal Execution also brought in two other important changes, related, as in the case of the National Code of Penal Procedures, to the inclusion of non-custodial measures after sentencing.[2] The Law contains a large section on so called 'Pre-release benefits and non-custodial sanctions'. It comprises parole (conditioned release), anticipated release, substitution and provisional suspension of sentence, humanitarian permits, and pre-release subject to satisfying certain criteria as laid down by prison policy. With this

Table 1 Prison Population 2011–2021

Year	2011	2012	2013	2014	2015	2016	2017	2018	2019	2020	2021
People in Prison	230,943	239,089	246,334	255,638	247,488	217,868	204,617	197,988	200,936	214,231	223,369

Source Secretaría de Seguridad y Protección Ciudadana, 'Cuaderno mensual de información estadística penitenciaria nacional. Diciembre 2021', https://www.gob.mx/cms/uploads/attachment/file/702158/CE_2021_12.pdf

law, Article 85 of the Federal Penal Code, which prevented people accused of a particular list of offences from access to preparatory release, was removed. This opened the opportunities for people sentenced for drug offences, among other crimes, to have access. Another important aspect of this law is that it includes people in pre-trial detention, whereas the former federal and state laws only referred to the duties and obligations of sentenced people, thus leaving almost half of the prison population in a legal limbo. Moreover, it extends beyond prison, through the judicial supervision of released people under parole schemes.

A particularly relevant aspect of the current legal framework for the purposes of this chapter, is that rehabilitation is still mainly understood as a process to be undertaken *within* prison. The definition of rehabilitation in the National Law of Penal Execution and its outline in both the constitutional text and in the law itself are quite divergent. Article 4 of the National Law of Penal Execution defines rehabilitation (*reinserción social*) as 'the restitution of the full exercise of liberties after the completion of a sentence or execution of a measure, in respect of human rights'. It is interesting that the law refers to liberties, instead of rights, and that it explains rehabilitation as a process happening after release, or even more so as something that is given by the authority, through restitution, and carried out by the individual's efforts. This disconnection between the State's duty to guarantee the means and scope for the exercise of liberties places the responsibility for change on the shoulders of the individual. Also, to speak of liberties, instead of rights, reinforces the idea of an individual path to be walked by the person on his or her own. Release seems like an act of 'expelling the person out' of the prison system, perhaps with his or her rights restored, but with no structural and social support to fully exert citizenship, reconciliation with the community and reparation from the long-lasting effect of incarceration on themselves and their families. This unfortunate phrasing is rendered more obscure when confronted with the constitutional definition of the term rehabilitation used by the National Law of Penal Execution throughout the text. As indicated above, rehabilitation is seen as a means to avoid reoffending and give people opportunities through the recognition and exercise of rights in terms of education, employment, health, and sports. The correctional aspect is somehow diminished by the referral to human rights and the acknowledgement, at least on paper, of a more active role of the person deprived of his or her liberty. However, the full potential of rehabilitation, with its strong instrumental meaning, is lessened when it remains a task to be achieved within the prison walls. So strong is the belief, that Article 146 contains the possibility of applying a non-custodial measure when, among other circumstances, 'the continuity of the application of the prison sentence is irrelevant to the ends of the rehabilitation of the sentenced person or to prevent reoffending'.

The law foresees reinserción en libertad (here loosely translated as rehabilitation after release) as referred to in Article 144 section IV, in relation to the supervision of a person serving their sentence under a non-custodial measure and subject to 'authority vigilance' (Article 168), such as community sentences, reparation to the victim(s) of the offence, fines, and electronic monitoring. The last article of the Law (207) refers to post-penal services (*servicios pospenales*) and establishes, in summary: the creation of post-penal services in appropriate units under the Prison Authority, which will work with the jointly responsible institutions such as health, education, employment and housing, and will establish centres and networks with the aim of supporting the person who has come out of prison and his or her family, in order to guarantee rehabilitation and prevent reoffending. Such services will contribute to fulfil the rights established in the Constitution, thus replicating the concept of rehabilitation and its ends and means, on the outside. Moreover, the services and programmes will be tailored to the individual, his or her possibilities and those of his or her family and will be provided through the cooperation of public and private services, both at the state and federal level.

To summarise, while the National Law of Penal Execution represents a profound and indisputable legal development that partly reinvents rehabilitation and guarantees the judicial supervision of prisoners' rights, including the right to a former release, its emphasis is still on a process to be carried out during deprivation of liberty and only residually refers to families and communities. Moreover, while Mexico has been navigating towards a criminal justice system that seeks to reduce its scope, improve its work, and embody human rights, there are severe deficits in terms of implementation, due to the persistency of long-entrenched attitudes and practices, and lack of personnel, funds, and training. Finally, the change of vision propelled by the 2008 constitutional reform and the subsequent national legal changes, are contradicted by other legal tendencies and current practices. This section began by underlining how the Mexican Constitution is a text of constant changes and profound concurrent contradictions. Mandatory pre-trial detention, enshrined in Article 19 and applicable to a list of offences, is perhaps the most evident demonstration of how the paradigm shift and the scope of the penal reform of 2008, which was *per se* highly controversial because of the dual discourse on due process and an exceptional regime for organised crime, is not part of a 'movement towards depenalisation and decriminalisation' as outlined in the Tokyo Rules on non-custodial measures (Rule 2.7), nor a guarantee of the safeguards mandated by international treaties (the American Convention on Human Rights and the International Covenant on Civil and Political Rights) or by the Constitution itself, but rather a patchy, volatile, and politically infused processes.

The penal reform and the approval of the National Law of Penal Execution brought together the minds and commitment of renowned scholars, committed activists and experts, besides politicians and judicial practitioners, who poured their knowledge, convictions, and passions into this major new ground for national criminal justice and the prison system. However, this monumental, profound effort, which undoubtedly achieved some change, still encounters numerous resistances, and faces large implementation gaps. Furthermore, the political factions and interests that participated and, eventually, took the lead alongside the merits of such processes, imprinted a shape that makes the current criminal justice system look strident, to say the least and brings to mind Faulkner's reflection (in Burke et al., 2019: 114): 'for the most part policy, legislation and practice in sentencing is developed independently of theories of punishment'. The lack of coherence and a common understanding of the scope and impact of the criminal justice system create a system where the proclamation and defence of human rights (Article 1) lies only 18 articles away from a backward, rights-violating process, namely, mandatory pre-trial detention. In 2019 another constitutional reform by the government enshrined in the Constitution and reaffirmed in the National Code of Criminal Procedures, coupled with subsequent legal changes (Comisión Nacional de los Derechos Humanos, 2021), widened the catalogue of offences which incur mandatory pre-trial detention, leading to a sharp increase in the prison population. As shown in Table 1, the prison population began to decrease in 2014, only to rise again in 2019 and forward, coinciding with the increased use of mandatory pre-trial detention and the slowing down of court procedures due to the pandemic. In December 2021, 41.5% of the prison population was in pre-trial detention.

As reported by an investigation of the media Animal Politico and the NGO Intersecta (Animal Politico and Intersecta, 2021), 85% of the people who entered prison in 2020 were still on trial. In some states, such as Mexico City and Oaxaca, 100% of new entries into prison were of people in pre-trial detention. Pre-trial detention, far from being a measure of last resort is, again, the rule. According to the same investigation, judges mandate pre-trial detention in 9 out of 10 cases, thus reinforcing a continuum of pre-trial detention, from the legal apparatus to prosecutors and judges.

Sadly, Mexico also follows a familiar international trend towards a staggering increase in women's incarceration (Walmsley, 2017). Between 2010 and 2021, the world female prison population has increased by 17% while the overall prison population has risen by 8% (Penal Reform International, 2021). In Mexico, according to data from the World Prison Brief,[3] the number of women in prison has increased by 85% between 2000 and 2021 and by 29% between 2010 and 2021. According to data from the National Survey on People Deprived of their Liberty (INEGI, 2021), the percentage of women awaiting trial is noticeably higher than men: 46% of women are in pre-trial detention, as opposed to 26.7% in the case of men. Internal legal contradictions are exacerbated by material living conditions, profound suffering, and constant human rights violations in prisons. According to the 2020 report of the National Commission of Human Rights (Comisión Nacional de los Derechos Humanos, 2021), which collects information through visits to the majority of the prison centres in the country, out of 113 centres, more than half present deficiencies in terms of (i) separation between people in pre-trial detention and sentenced prisoners; (ii) lack of security personnel; and (iii) deficiencies in terms of material living conditions and hygiene. Almost 40% have problems of inadequate health services and drug dependence services and 38% centres are overcrowded. These are only some of the 20 issues that are identified as problematic in State centres. In 15 out of 113 prisons, the National Commission pinpointed situations of co-governance or auto-governance, which is when people in prison exert authority in lieu of, or added to, the legal authority. These centres are usually located in states where organised crime has a significant presence and continues to operate from within prisons. According to the National Survey on People Deprived of their Liberty by the National Institute of Geography and Statistics (INEGI, for its acronym in Spanish) 36.5% of the prison population at the national level has seen other fellow inmates carrying out activities related to the centre security or functioning either partially (co-government) or totally (auto-government). These include handling of the keys of prison cells, classification of prisoners, security control, and violence against authorities. Deprivation of liberty and living conditions that severely violate human rights continue to affect people with little social capital, employability possibilities and low educational levels. The abovementioned national survey on people deprived of their liberty (INEGI, 2021) shows that the large majority of the prison population was employed before incarceration in low skilled, informal jobs with low remuneration. 69.7% had basic education (up to secondary level) and 79.6% reported that they had economic dependent people before detention; 67.8% of women shared that they had underage children who in 55.2% of cases were under the care of grandparents. Thus, imprisonment in Mexico, as varied as it can be due to the differences between the federal and the state system and prisons themselves, is not only synonymous with loss of liberty, but also with diminishing rights and degrading living conditions.

Little awaits the people who walk out of a prison centre and as will be explained in more detail in the case study below, besides the lack of structured, coordinated, community-based, and community-oriented rehabilitation programmes, there are also legal barriers that hinder the recovery of full citizenship. Data from INEGI's national survey, indicate that 53% of people in prison intimated that having been in a prison centre would compromise their reintegration into the job market; 28.7% referred to a negative impact on friendships, 27.8% on reintegration into family life and 22.8% on education. However, only 4.5% considered it likely that they would commit an offense after being released from prison. Two reports from civil society organisations (CEA Social Justice, 2021; Equis Justicia para las Mujeres, 2021) show, through mixed methodologies and with field work in different Mexican states, that there is no rehabilitation path after prison in terms of structured, articulated, and consistent public policies and programmes, even less so when analysed through gender perspective. As demonstrated in the case study, life after prison depends on what social capital the person had before entering it and the degree of its erosion or endurance.

To complete this section and before moving on to the case study, it is important to refer to the work of the National Supreme Court. Space constraints a full account of all the relevant sentences and actions of the highest tribunal, but some cannot be omitted. The Supreme Court has been promoting gender mainstreaming in sentencing since 2008, elaborating protocols (Supreme Court of Justice of the Nation, 2020), and numerous other publications. In 2016 it approved the 'Obligation to judge with a gender perspective' that mandates to all courts to mainstream gender in sentencing and indicates a six-step methodology (Supreme Court of Justice of the Nation, 2018). In February 2022, the Supreme Court decreed that a court can substitute pre-trial detention in those cases where it is mandatory, as long as some conditions are satisfied. Such resolution is meant to counter the abuse of pre-trial detention that followed the 2019s constitutional reform (Ureste, 2022). The resolutions of the Supreme Court bring a fresh perspective to a criminal justice system in which formalism and gender-blindness are pervasive, and they are paramount to the building and consolidation of a criminal justice system based on human rights and due process. However, unfortunately they do not necessarily always impact in a concrete way on the lives of all the people in contact with the criminal justice nor are they automatically implemented by all courts or translated into legal reforms or public policies.

Indigenous Women and 'Drug Traffickers': Accumulated Discrimination in a Rehabilitation Void

This section presents the story of María and her daughter, Guadalupe. Both were sentenced to ten years for drug trafficking (transportation of marihuana) in the female prison of Tanivet, Oaxaca. In 2017, I visited the prison, as part of a project run by two NGOs (the Washington Office on Latin America, U.S and Equis Justicia para las Mujeres, Mexico) and Scopio, a film producer. The aim was to produce short videos which would tell the story of women in prison for drug offences, with the aim of raising awareness among policymakers and the general public.[4] The videos were part of a larger advocacy-oriented project focused on women deprived of their liberty for drug offences in Latin America.[5]

Both María and Guadalupe became involved in drug trafficking because of their chronic, extreme poverty, undertaking the role commonly known as 'mules', that is human containers objectified by criminal organisations and easily captured and criminalised by the State. The implementation of harsh, punitive drug policies is the main cause of the current trend of increasing female incarceration in Latin America and most women share a similar background: they come from poor, disadvantaged communities, have little education and labour skills, are single mothers and have to fulfil both the roles of caregivers and breadwinners. Transporting drugs, storing or selling them are unskilled tasks that require proportionally less time to earn more money (still ridiculously little compared to the value of the drugs they carry) than they would if employed in their traditional jobs of cleaning, making food, looking after children or older people, or similar jobs in the informal economy (Giacomello & Youngers, 2020).

When they were sentenced (Guadalupe in 2012 and María in 2014), the legal framework excluded people sentenced for drug offences from access to sentence reduction mechanisms. Thanks to the change brought about by the National Law of Penal Execution, people accused of drug-related offences are now eligible for pre-release and parole schemes. Guadalupe was released in 2019 and the only condition applied to her liberation was that she appeared once before the federal body in charge of the prison system (*Órgano Desconcentrado de Prevención y Readaptación Social*). In the case of her mother, matters became more complicated in 2017, and that was when my friendship with Guadalupe became pivotal to her mother gaining her freedom.

It goes beyond the narrative and space limits of this paper to describe all the steps, but it is important to highlight that the communication between María and her family and María's federal public lawyer had been intermittent at best. Because of my ongoing friendship with Guadalupe and her acquaintances in the federal judicial system, the communication restarted through a peculiar triangulation as I transmitted communication from the lawyer to the family and vice versa. This was due to the fact the lawyer was not permitted to give her mobile phone number to her defendant or her family, whereas she could communicate with me. This fortunate triangle led to the hearing, in October 2019, in which María was summoned to the office of the federal judge appointed to her case. María was granted conditional release with electronic monitoring. Present in the room with me were María, her daughter Guadalupe, María's lawyer, the judge, one of the top directors of the private company which owned the electronic monitoring device and the technician who would install it around Maria's ankle.

In a country where alternatives to incarceration during sentencing are a novelty, and definitely so in the case of drug offences, even a strict measure such as electronic monitoring can be seen as progressive. However, the analysis of María's legal case and the implications of the electronic monitoring device problematise the issue. A few months earlier, on July 15th, María was granted conditional release, having fulfilled all the criteria established by the Law of Penal Execution, but one: the law requires the person to have served 50% of the sentence. In her case, this would have occurred about ten days later. Those 10–12 days definitely marked her life. Because of the ten days gap, the judge decided to add electronic monitoring to the conditions María was to comply with and established that she could not leave prison until the device was ready to be applied, and thanks to the complicated communication described above that happened three months later. While the law establishes that the State will pay for the device, this is not the case at the federal level, so Maria and her family had to pay an 800 US dollars warranty. The rent, which was about between 250 and 300 US dollars per month, was discounted by the private company because of the judge's record in applying electronic monitoring, and because María was a poor, vulnerable Indigenous woman with a condition of accumulated vulnerability and no criminal record.

The judge imposed electronic monitoring for six months. In April 2020, I was eager to meet Guadalupe and María again at the hearing where the device was to be removed. But that did not happen because of uncertainty brought about by a change of judge and the COVID-19 pandemic. The device was eventually taken off in February 2021, 14 months after it had been installed. Being an Indigenous woman, who does not wear trousers but skirts just under her knees, for the whole time María had to cover the tag with a bandage to avoid stigma. Of course, this cultural, gendered aspect was undermined by the criminal procedures. In the interview carried out with María and Guadalupe for this chapter, she told me how her leg had shrunk slightly, and the skin had all dried up because of the long months of connecting the device to electricity. Despite everything, María was lucky enough not to have had to pay for the rent: 250 dollars a month is an incredible amount for many people, but in Mexico it is sometimes the difference between eating or fasting or between abiding by the law and trafficking marihuana. Fortunately, since she lives in a community with electricity and a signal to facilitate the electronic monitoring she did not have to move to another place.

María's story shows the stark reality and profound inconsistencies of a criminal justice system that preaches human rights, due process, gender mainstreaming, and rehabilitation. María was less than two weeks away from being granted conditional release, but the judge's decision left her in prison for three more months and tied her to the electronic device for over a year. Indeed, had it not been for the documentaries that brought Guadalupe and I together, Maria might still be waiting for her lawyer's call. Fortune rather than justice released María from prison, albeit under disproportionate circumstances. The question is: how many Marías are waiting, in prison, for stars to align?

Guadalupe, María's daughter, left prison a few months before her mother and she was finally reunited with her son and two daughters. Her son has a severe disability and needs permanent care. It was hard at first because during their imprisonment their home had been ransacked and the community did not want her back because not only had she been in prison but also, she was a single parent. While in prison, Guadalupe earned and saved some money, but life outside was extremely complicated, especially because by the time she put herself together, the pandemic began, and she lost her job as a cleaner. At the time of writing this chapter, in March 2022, Guadalupe has another child and lives happily with her partner, her children, and her mother. Money is always tight, but family ties keep them strong, united, and always looking ahead. Some members of the community still scorn them for their criminal past but, generally speaking, they are socially and morally rehabilitated. That said, legal barriers, peculiar to Mexico, still impede a full legal rehabilitation and perpetuate their vulnerability and in addition infringe upon the rights of Guadalupe's children.

In Mexico, the political rights of a person in conflict with the law are suspended, a measure that, not surprisingly, is established in Article 38 of an unchanged Constitution that reflects mores and conceptions from the end of the nineteenth century to beginning of the twentieth (Giacomello, 2015). While federal judicial resolutions have reinstated the political rights of people on remand and 2021 saw the first pilot project of elections in prison, sentenced people do not regain full citizenship until after they complete their sentence, and that also applies to people granted a conditional or pre-release sentence. While the right to suffrage is probably the less imperative worry for someone who has just been released back into society under very precarious conditions, political rights in Mexico are tied to an essential condition of civil existence, namely the ID required to exercise the right to vote granted by the National Electoral Institute. Without this, it is impossible to obtain a passport, open a bank account and apply for a job. In practical terms this means that Guadalupe has been denied her electoral ID and has not had access to support schemes for single mothers or grants for her children. As a consequence, she has no political life, a restricted civil life and in a sense her prison sentence extends into her life in the community.

Conclusion

This chapter travels through constitutional reforms, paradigm shifts, conceptual turns, and the practical challenges of Mexico's current version of rehabilitation. While, thanks to the untirable work of commitment of academics, activists, and some political representatives, the country has been navigating progressively towards a criminal justice system that wishes to be lighter and fairer, the tides of mores, public opinion, inertias, mentalities and legal barriers or backlashes invoke a much less ambitious and human rights-based criminal justice system. The prison population is soaring, and prison conditions are dire and conducive to systematic violations of human rights. Rehabilitation is still intended as a process to be undertaken and concluded within confinement with little or no actions targeted at people who leave prison or who never entered it in the first place. The case study is the story of two women where accumulated discrimination raises a question about whether criminalisation was really the state response in the first place, and that, of course, is rhetorical.

Cases such as María and Guadalupe's are social tragedies and concentrate gender-based violence, racism, social exclusion, classism, and the abusive use of the power to punish instead of the power to pursue social justice and repair social exclusion. Rehabilitation treads a lonely path and full restoration of citizenship is hindered by judicial and legal impediments. The personal and family journey towards rehabilitation that María and Guadalupe have undertaken is a product of their previous cohesion and is also somehow rooted in their indigenous identity. This is their strength against economic, community and social adversities and animosities. However, the full reach of their individual and collective agency is hindered by further state restrictions linked to their political rights. Thus, the State does not recognise nor repair social exclusion, poverty and in the case of Guadalupe, child labour and sexual violence. Moreover, it criminalises and punishes disproportionately secondary subjects of drug trafficking nets, and women trapped between State omissions and the opportunism of criminal organisations; and it locks people up in unsafe prison centres, with little or no access to the means of satisfying basic needs. The telling of this personal story of rehabilitation has been possible despite that same State.

Notes

1. Due process as defined by Article 8 of the Interamerican Convention on Human Rights 'the Inter American Court on Human Rights, consist of the right of all people to be heard with the due judicial guarantees and within a reasonable time by a competent judge or tribunal, independent, impartial, and established by law, in any accusation claimed against him or her (Corte Interamericana de Derechos Humanos, 2020: 4). It is a dynamic concept that comprises principles, principle, and judicial guarantees to assure to all people a fair trial.
2. Mexico has a federal criminal code and 32 state codes; therefore, non-custodial measures in sentencing are not included in this chapter.
3. Information available at https://www.prisonstudies.org/country/mexico.
4. The videos are available at https://womenanddrugs.wola.org/multimedia/videos/.
5. Information available at https://womenanddrugs.wola.org/.

References

Animal Político & Intersecta. (2021, October 26). Pretrial detention: The weapon that imprisons the poor and innocent. Political Animal. https://www.animalpolitico.com/prision-preventiva-delitos-encarcela-pobres-inocentes/.

Azzolini, A. (2015). The alternative solutions to the trial: reparative agreements and conditional suspension of the process. In S. García Ramírez & O. Islas de González Mariscal (coords.), *The National Code of Criminal Procedures*. Studies. National Autonomous University of Mexico, Institute of Legal Research.

Burke, L., Collett, S., & McNeil, F. (2019). *Reimagining rehabilitation. Beyond the individual*. Routledge.

Cantú, S. (2013). The criminal regime of exception for organized crime under the *test* of human rights. In E. Ferrer Mac-Gregor Poisot, J. C. Caballero Ochoa & C. Steiner (coords.), *Human Rights in the Constitution: Comments on Constitutional and Inter-American Jurisprudence II* (pp. 1737–1765). Supreme Court of Justice of the Nation, National Autonomous University of Mexico, Konrad Adenaur Stiftung.

CEA Social Justice. (2021, September). Community social reintegration in Mexico: Diagnosis, recommendations and routes of action. CEA Social Justice. https://ceajusticiasocial.org/wp-content/uploads/2021/09/CEA_REINSERCION_COMUNITARIA_FINAL_DIGITAL.pdf

Comisión Nacional de los Derechos Huamanos. (2021). National Diagnosis of Penitentiary Supervision 2020. National Commission of Human Rights.

Congreso de la Unión de los Estados Unidos Mexicanos. (2014). Código Nacional de Procedimientos Penales, Mexico: Diario Oficial de la Federación.

Congreso de la Unión de los Estados Unidos Mexicanos. (2016). Ley Nacional de Ejecución Penal, Mexico: Diario Oficial de la Federación.

Corte Interamericana de Derechos Humanos. (2020). Cuadernillo de Jurisprudencia de la Corte Interamericana de Derechos Humanos N° 12: Debido Proceso. San José: Corte Interamericana de Derechos Humanos. https://www.corteidh.or.cr/sitios/libros/todos/docs/cuadernillo12.pdf

Equis Justicia para las Mujeres. (2021, July). The social reintegration of women in Mexico. *Equis Justice for Women*. https://equis.org.mx/historias-de-vida/wp-content/uploads/2021/07/Reinsercion_completo.pdf

Foucault, M. (2002). *Discipline and punish. Birth of the prison*. Siglo XXI Editores.

Giacomello, C. (2015). *Women deprived of liberty and the right to vote. From objects of norms to subjects of citizenship*. Electoral Tribunal of the Judicial Power of the Federation.

Giacomello, C. (2018). *Children in prison with their mothers. A comparative legal perspective*. Supreme Court of Justice of the Nation.

Giacomello, C. (2021). Criminal execution from a gender perspective. In E. Vela (coord.), *Manual for judging with a gender perspective in criminal matters* (pp. 307–380). Supreme Court of Justice of the Nation.

Giacomello, C., & Youngers, C. (2020). Women incarcerated for drug-related offences: A Latin American perspective. In J. Buxton, G. Margo, & L. Burger (Eds.), *The impact of global drug policy on women: Shifting the needle* (pp. 103–111). Bingley.

González Domínguez, P. (2021). The new framework of the relationship between International Law and National Law in Mexico. In Supreme Court of Justice of the Nation *The Constitutional Reform in Human Rights: A transformative decade*. Supreme Court of Justice of the Nation.

INEGI. (2021, December). *National Survey of the Population Deprived of Liberty. ENPOL 2021. Main Results.* https://www.inegi.org.mx/contenidos/programas/enpol/2021/doc/enpol2021_presentacion_nacional.pdf

Nataren Nandayapa, C., & Caballero Juárez, J. A. (2013). *The constitutional principles of the new Mexican accusatory and oral criminal process.* National Autonomous University of Mexico.

Penal Reform International. (2021). Global Prison Trends 2021. London: Penal Reform International, https://knowledge.tijthailand.org/en/publication/detail/global-prison-trends-2021#book/3

Sarre, M., & Manrique, G. (2018). *Criminal enforcement justice system. Procedural subjects around prison in Mexico.* Tirant Lo Blanch.

Secretariat of Security and Citizen Protection. (2021, December). *Monthly notebook of national penitentiary statistical information.* Secretariat of Security and Citizen Protection. https://www.gob.mx/cms/uploads/attachment/file/702158/CE_2021_12.pdf

Supreme Court of Justice of the Nation. (2018). *Review of direct amparo in revision 5999/2016. First Chamber of the Supreme Court of Justice of the Nation. 'Obligation to judge with a gender perspective'.* Supreme Court of Justice of the Nation. https://www.scjn.gob.mx/sites/default/files/resenias_argumentativas/documento/2018-02/res-JMPR-5999-16.pdf

Supreme Court of Justice of the Nation. (2020). *Protocol to judge with a gender perspective.* Supreme Court of Justice of the Nation.

Ureste, M. (2022, February 9). The Court limits pretrial detention: It may be revoked after two years. *Animal Politico.* https://www.animalpolitico.com/2022/02/corte-prision-preventiva-revocarse/

Walmsley, R. (2017). *World Female Imprisonment List* (4th edition). World Prison Brief, Institute for Criminal Policy Research. https://www.prisonstudies.org/sites/default/files/resources/downloads/world_female_prison_4th_edn_v4_web.pdf

Zepeda Lecuona, G. (2007). The excessive and irrational use of pretrial detention in Mexico. In S. García Ramírez & O. Islas de González Mariscal (coords.), *International panorama on criminal justice. Criminal process and international criminal justice. Comparative cultures and legal systems. Seventh conference on criminal justice.* National Autonomous University of Mexico.

Rehabilitation Within the Criminal-Legal System in Missouri

Kelli E. Canada and Scott O'Kelley

United States Criminal-Legal System—A Snapshot

The United States ranks highest in the world in the number of people who are incarcerated. At the end of 2020, the prison incarceration rate was 358 per 100,000 people, the lowest rate the United States has seen since 1992 (Carson, 2021). Similarly, the jail incarceration rate also declined; in mid-2020 it was 167 per 100,000 people (Minton & Zeng, 2021). These declines are largely attributed to the COVID-19 pandemic when people were being released from jails and prisons and fewer people were sentenced to incarceration (Carson, 2021). Prior to these declines, the incarcerated population in the United States grew at astronomical rates. For example, the local jail population increased by 296% from 1980 to 2015 (Minton & Zeng, 2016). Jails have 19 times as many annual admissions as prisons do nationally at 11,700,000 a year, a number that nearly doubled since 1983. These numbers merely represent people incarcerated. In 2020, another 3.9 million people in

K. E. Canada (✉)
School of Social Work, University of Missouri, Columbia, MO, USA
e-mail: canadake@missouri.edu

S. O'Kelley
Missouri Department of Corrections, Jefferson City, MO, USA

the United States were under community supervision for probation or parole (Kaeble, 2021) and millions more had open court cases and contact with police.

Race and gender are prominent factors in the United States criminal-legal system. The Black, Indigenous, and Latinx[1] adult population is overrepresented in every facet of the system. In prisons, Black people are incarcerated at five times the rate as non-Latinx White adults while incarceration rates among Latinx people are 1.3 times higher (Nellis, 2021). Although Black, Native American, and Latinx populations continue to be overrepresented in prisons, the rate of incarceration has declined most sharply for these racial and ethnic groups over the past decade compared to White U.S. residents. Men are also overrepresented in the criminal-legal system. In jails, the incarceration rate among men is seven times higher compared to women. Incarceration rates are highest for men aged 25 to 34 years old (Minton & Zeng, 2021).

The concept of 'criminalization' emerged in the literature in the United States in the 1970s; however, this concept is deeply rooted in U.S. history (Lamb & Weinberger, 2001). In one application of the term, criminalization refers to utilizing a criminal justice system response to manage people with mental illness symptoms who are displaying or acting on symptoms that create public disturbances, or who break the law but do so because of symptoms (e.g., trespassing). Although ever changing, societal perspectives in the United States have long viewed mental illness symptoms (e.g., psychosis) as a threat to public safety and punishable as a crime (Canada et al., 2016). These perspectives emerge through public policies that restrict access to safe and affordable housing, monetary safety net programmes, and properly financed mental health systems.

The United States criminal justice system is one of the nation's largest mental health service systems (Slate & Johnson, 2008). People exhibiting mental illness symptoms are 20% more likely to be arrested than people without signs of mental illnesses (Teplin, 1984). Following arrest, many people are held in jail, often for extensive periods. One of the greatest challenges for jails is the increasing number of people who need mental health and substance use services. Among people incarcerated in jails, 11–19% of males and 22–42% of females have serious mental illnesses (i.e., bipolar, schizophrenia spectrum, major depression, delusional, and psychotic disorders; Steadman et al., 2009). Estimates of serious mental illness in jails are higher than the community samples, which is 3% of males and 6% of females (SAMHSA, 2017). When the definition of mental illness is broadened to include any mental health disorder in the past year, 44% of jail inmates, on average, had a mental disorder (Bronson & Berzofsky, 2015); lifetime prevalence rates reached 68% for females and 41% for males. Approximately 63% of people incarcerated in jail met criteria for a substance use disorder (Bronson et al., 2017) and 53% of jailed females met criteria for post-traumatic stress disorder in their lifetime (Lynch et al., 2014). The overrepresentation of people with mental illnesses in jails impacts smaller rural communities as well as the largest jails systems in the United States (Raggio et al., 2017). Similar trends exist within the United States' prison system, as well.

Negative Impacts of Incarceration and Need for Rehabilitation

People with mental illnesses can have difficulty adjusting to incarceration, which can worsen symptoms. This may result from the stress of the environment; interrupted, poor, or no treatment; stigma; or a combination of factors (Fellner, 2006; Hatzenbuehler et al., 2013). People with mental illnesses also face an increased risk of negative events like victimization (Blitz et al., 2008) and suicide (Choi et al., 2019). People with mental illnesses who are in contact with the criminal-legal system are at risk of cycling in and out of the system with low-level felonies and probation revocation for technical violations and face higher risk of re-incarceration compared to people without mental illnesses (Baillargeon et al., 2009; Skeem & Louden, 2006). In fact, people with mental illnesses on probation are equally likely to be rearrested for a new crime but significantly more likely to violate the terms of probation (Skeem et al., 2010). People with mental illness may also have benefits (e.g., Medicaid) suspended or terminated during incarceration, which may impact successful re-entry (Bazelon, 2006).

Because of the significant risks that people with mental illnesses face during incarceration, diversion programmes and intensive treatment options outside of jails and prisons are the best options for people who can safely rehabilitate in the community. Jails and prisons were not designed, set up, or funded to be mental health clinics. Not surprisingly, only about one-third of people in need of mental health treatment in jails receive it (Bronson & Berzofsky, 2015). Services are often minimal, with only medication administration and infrequent visits from medical professionals. Particularly in jails, mental health status is not able to be clinically monitored throughout the stay, so changes in status are often missed. People in jails and prisons in need of services can go unnoticed, particularly when experiencing internalizing symptoms (e.g., suicidal ideation). In fact, correctional officers report they do not have adequate training regarding general mental illness knowledge, lack expertise in identifying people in need of services, and under-refer people to services (CHPPR, 2007). Correctional officers are trained to maintain safety by using command and control techniques, which may not work well with people having a mental health crisis. Rather than taking control, they can allow situations to escalate and increase risk of injury. Limited or no access to mental health and rehabilitation services in jails and prisons impacts people during incarceration and once they re-enter into the community.

Rehabilitation and Preventing Recidivism

The best way to reduce the negative impacts of incarceration for people with mental illnesses and substance use disorders is to prevent them from entering or re-entering the system. Rehabilitative programming in Missouri is used in this chapter as an example to illustrate ways people can be engaged or diverted to services along the criminal-justice continuum. Key rehabilitative programming in Missouri is described within the framework of the sequential intercept model (Munetz & Griffin, 2006). This model points to five intercepts for intervention to divert, reduce further movement into the system, and prevent recidivism for people with mental illnesses. The five intercepts are (1) law enforcement, (2) initial detention and court hearing, (3) jails and courts, (4) re-entry from jail and prison, and (5) community corrections. Early diversion efforts aimed to prevent people with mental illnesses from entering the criminal-legal system, referred by some as intercept zero, begin with high-quality behavioural health and substance use treatment and support services (Abreu et al., 2017). SAMHSA (2019) identified seven guiding principles for community-based practice for justice-involved people to prevent recidivism and reduce the overall risks of criminal-legal involvement. These principles include: (1) cross-training behavioural health and criminal justice professionals; (2) collaborative care planning; (3) use of evidence-based and promising practices; (4) criminogenic risks and needs integrated into treatment plans; (5) integrated physical and behavioural health care; (6) trauma-informed practice and policies; (7) case management involving treatment, support, and social services; and (8) strategies to recognize and address systemic and structural bias.

Community-based providers in Missouri are working to integrate these principles into care plans and provider policy as one way to provide treatment to address challenges related to mental health as well as social, financial, and behavioural concerns for clients with mental illnesses. In addition, Missouri adopted an integrated approach to treating mental health and substance use disorders as a best practice. Integrated care utilizes collaborative and interdisciplinary practices, consultation, and care coordination to address the needs of the whole person (Cohen et al., 2015). Providers may be co-located, have integrated notation systems, meet regularly with clients in care coordination meetings, or have integrated care plans to guide treatment.

Access to treatment, even the highest quality services, cannot prevent criminal justice involvement for all people with mental illnesses. First, many people in need of treatment go without services. Some people may not want treatment or have difficulty trusting providers while others are unable to afford the services available in their geographical region. Missouri ranked fourth highest in the United States for health professional shortages and many of Missouri's rural regions are considered medically underserved (Harrah, 2020). Second, the reasons for criminal-legal contact for this population are not solely due to mental illness symptoms or substance use disorders. People with mental illnesses face environmental risks (e.g., neighbourhoods with high crime rates, support systems with criminal justice involvement, local and state policies) that increase their risk of incarceration (Barrenger et al., 2017). For people who do contact the criminal-legal system, rehabilitation is possible at all the intervention points outlined in the sequential intercept model. Below, we describe each intercept and detail best practices utilized in Missouri for diverting and intervening with people who have mental illnesses and substance use disorders. The best practices highlighted are not an exhaustive list but do provide an overview of key interventions.

Intercept One

This intercept focuses on opportunities for intervention via emergency response (i.e., 911 calls) and local law enforcement. Several promising practices divert people with mental illnesses into treatment and services when there is police contact. Two prominent models are the crisis intervention team (CIT) and co-responder models. Both models are utilized throughout Missouri.

Crisis Intervention Team (CIT) is a community-based intervention for police officers to promote effective, respectful, and safe interactions between officers and people with mental illnesses. When police respond to events involving people with mental illnesses, they make urgent and critical decisions regarding the use of force and appropriate options to resolve conflict. Police find encounters with people with mental illnesses both challenging and difficult to manage due to limited training on mental health crises and the perception of inadequate disposition options (Borum et al., 1998). Traditional policing tactics, such as verbal commands and use of force, can escalate a person who is agitated or experiencing acute symptoms and may result in injury (Engel et al., 2000; Ruiz, 1993; Watson et al., 2008). Widely adopted since its inception in 1988, CIT responds to the challenges officers face with mental illness-related calls and the need for specialized procedures when working with people with mental illnesses. CIT involves two components—specialized, 40-h training on responding to mental health crises and partnerships between police and community mental health stakeholders (Watson & Fulambarker, 2012). However, it is tailored to fit the unique needs of police departments and communities (Watson et al., 2008). The specialized training involves a curriculum providing officers with knowledge about mental illness and response strategies through education about mental illness, substance use, medications, identifying symptoms, tools for effective intervention with a person exhibiting mental illness symptoms, and de-escalation skills to use in crisis (Watson et al., 2008). The CIT curriculum involves skill building, role-play scenarios, site visits to providers, and exercises to simulate symptoms' impact on daily living (Reuland, 2004). CIT implementation includes the establishment and strengthening of community partnerships available for crisis transport and/or service referral. These partnerships create pathways for police officers to have additional resources to assist them when responding to a person in crisis, which expands their disposition options beyond arrest.

Based on two decades of research, CIT improves police response to people with mental illnesses, increases safety, and diverts some people from arrest to treatment. CIT-officers demonstrate increased preparedness to work with people with mental illnesses, reduced stigma, and better attitudes towards responding to mental illness-related calls, improved disposition of mental health calls, and reduced use of force (Borum et al., 1998; Compton et al., 2006; Morabito et al., 2012; Skeem & Bibeau, 2008). These successes prompted expansion of CIT across the United States and world. Missouri, in particular, has an active state CIT Council with CIT officers in nearly every county (Missouri CIT, 2022). The CIT training was also adapted to use with 911 call-takers to improve identification of mental illness-related crisis calls, call-takers' ability to triage calls, and de-escalate people involved in mental health crises (Watson et al., 2021).

Co-Responder Models involve a police officer and behavioural health expert jointly responding to emergency calls (Morabito et al., 2018). A systematic review found no randomized trials involving co-responder models;

however, there was evidence for reductions in arrest and hospitalizations using quasi-experimental designs (Puntis et al., 2018). Studies on co-responder models in some jurisdictions identified reductions in emergency department visits but in others, there were no reductions (Marcus & Stergiopoulos, 2022). Although the research on the effectiveness of co-responder models is limited, many communities throughout the United States including those in Missouri, are implementing these models to divert people with mental illnesses from arrest.

Intercepts Two/Three

Intercepts Two and Three are combined because they represent initial detention as well as jail detention and court-based programming. Diversion from arrest is not always possible or appropriate. With the use of evidence-based screening tools, people with mental illnesses can be identified upon initial detention for in-house services or treatment court (Gonzales et al., 2007). There are several validated screening tools designed for jails including the Brief Jail Mental Health Screen and the Jail Screening Assessment Tool (Martin et al., 2013). These tools help identify people as soon as they enter the jail and can be used at the initial court hearing to divert people to a better option for treatment.

One prominent diversion model used throughout the world is treatment courts (or alternative sentencing courts). Treatment courts engage people in intensive, community-based services while diverting them from prison. Missouri has an active treatment court community with mental health courts, veteran treatment courts, drug treatment courts, family treatment courts, and driving while intoxicated (DWI) courts throughout the state. In 2020, there were over 140 treatment courts[2] throughout the state (SAMHSA, 2022; State of Missouri, 2021). As an example, mental health court (MHC) involves interdisciplinary collaboration with criminal justice and mental health providers. Participants are linked with treatment and services and report to the courts on a regular basis (Redlich et al., 2005). MHC research is challenged by the inability to randomize people to the court program. However, quasi-experimental studies find MHCs reduce recidivism for participants, although this medium to small effect may differ based on key variations in MHCs and individuals who choose to engage in the court program (e.g., misdemeanour vs. felony; type of adjudication; Canada et al., 2019). Rehabilitation is the aim of MHC so people in these programmes receive services that attempt to address all the risk factors for further criminal-legal involvement including treatment for substance use and mental illness, stable housing, social support interventions, and intervention to improve daily living skills. For many programmes, if a person successfully completes MHC, their charges are dropped or reduced. For people who are unsuccessful, though, they may have to spend time in jail while their case is being processed or be sent to prison to carry out a sentence.

Jail-Based Programming. Only a fraction of people in need of services are diverted to treatment courts (Canada et al., 2020a, 2020b). Thus, jails often manage a substantial portion of the population of people with mental illnesses who are detained. Jails operate at the municipal or county levels in the United States by local law enforcement or correctional agencies. Jails detain a variety of people including those awaiting trial, serving time for a conviction, and probation and parole violators waiting for their judicial hearing. Some jails house people serving time due to overcrowding in prisons (Bales & Garduno, 2016; Henrichson et al., 2015; Subramanian et al., 2015).

Jails face challenges related to overcrowding, comprehensive service provision, and transient populations. Many jails face monetary, staffing, and space-related challenges when attempting to manage the complex clinical needs of people in jails. Jails serve about fifteen times more people each year in the United States compared to prisons yet operate on much smaller per-person budgets (Johnson et al., 2017). All these reasons create barriers for jails to provide behavioural health intervention and re-entry planning services. Spending time in jail can create strain on social ties outside of jail, including with work, treatment, and family. This hinders reintegration into communities. Jail stays increase the risk of recidivism compared to less punitive sanctions such as probation (Cochran et al., 2014). In fact, women are impacted by even short stays in jail, creating cumulative stressors related to family caregiving, employment, and fiscal responsibility (Van Olpen et al., 2009). Jail-based programming that helps interrupt future contact with the criminal-legal system include alternatives to prosecution, collaboration with veterans' justice outreach specialists to link veterans and families with the Veterans Administration, and connection with community-based providers. People with mental illnesses and substance use disorders are best treated outside of jail for these conditions. Attempts to reduce the number of days people spend in jail are especially important given the negative outcomes they can experience when incarcerated.

Intercept Four

Intercept Four focuses on re-entry from jail and prison. People are the most vulnerable to recidivate in the year following release. People who use substances relapse more frequently during the first few months while people with co-occurring disorders are more likely to return to jail compared to the general population of people exiting jail (Belenko et al., 2004; Wilson et al., 2011). Women, in particular, experience distress following release due to disrupted family situations, childcare, mental health, substance use, housing, and employment. Needs at the time of re-entry may include simple tasks, from contacting probation officers to more complex tasks like obtaining food, housing, and treatment. Completing these tasks can be difficult for people who are in crisis or struggling with symptoms, which can contribute to recidivism (Angell et al., 2014; White et al., 2012).

The overall population of people entering Missouri prisons is declining. In 2014, just over 10,000 people were newly admitted to prison; in 2021, this number was nearly cut in half with approximately 5400 new admissions. The overall prison population is also declining. In 2019, approximately 28,200 people were incarcerated and by 2021, this was down to 23,100. Across time, the racial and ethnic distribution of the Missouri prison population has remained fairly stable with approximately two-thirds of the population identifying as White, not Latinx and one-third identifying as Black, Asian, Native American, or Latinx. These declines are, in part, due to some of the diversion initiatives described above. However, there are also important advancements occurring within prisons that contribute to the overall population decline. One example of a program used in Missouri prisons to improve response to people with mental illnesses in prison is an adapted version of CIT for corrections (Canada et al., 2020a, 2020b). The key components of CIT (i.e., the 40-hours training and community collaboration) are the same in prisons. However, when utilizing CIT in correctional settings, the correctional officer training and partnerships are adapted to capture the unique environment and interplay between administration (e.g., wardens), officers, incarcerated people, and rehabilitative services. Research on the effectiveness of CIT in correctional settings is nascent. One study in Missouri found CIT trained officers had significantly more knowledge and less stigma about mental illness, more positive attitudes about people incarcerated with mental illness, and felt more prepared to respond to mental health crisis events after completing the CIT training compared to their pre-training scores (Canada et al., 2020a, 2020b). In comparison to officers without CIT training, CIT officers also had significantly more knowledge, less stigma, and better attitudes about mental illness and felt more prepared to respond.

Given prisons are some of the largest institutions to house and treat adults with mental illness, intervention is needed to reduce the harm they are at risk of experiencing. CIT for corrections is one intervention that may improve officers' ability to identify mental health issues, de-escalate crisis situations, reduce the use of force and harmful sanctions, and connect people to care. These actions ultimately have the potential to address some of the negative health and mental health outcomes described above and reduce the length of time people with mental illnesses are exposed to the high-risk prison environment. Additionally, connecting people with appropriate services in prison increases opportunity for successful re-entry.

Re-Entry Programming. In 2018, 32% of people released from Missouri prisons returned to prison within three years. Effective re-entry programming is essential to help people safely and effectively reintegrate back into their communities. SAMHSA (2019) identified assertive community treatment (ACT) and critical time intervention as evidence-based practices for justice-involved people with mental illnesses. Case management services also impact recidivism rates (Miller et al., 2019; Wilson et al., 2011). When people do not have social support systems or treatment access outside of prison, re-entry programmes are particularly important in bridging or connecting people to services. ACT involves a multidisciplinary team providing treatments to people in the community. Caseloads are small and teams are available for as long as services are needed. ACT participation, compared to traditional case management, is more effective in reducing homelessness and symptoms across randomized trials but not in reducing hospitalizations (Coldwell & Bender, 2007). A less studied adaptation of ACT, forensic assertive community treatment (FACT), is promising for justice-involved people. FACT teams include providers, probation officers, and peer specialists. Collaboration between criminal-legal and mental health systems and using trauma-informed care are key in this approach (Lamberti et al., 2017). FACT participants had fewer new crime convictions and less time in jail and hospitals compared to controls (Lamberti et al., 2017). In Missouri, ACT teams are utilized with adults and juveniles, but FACT models are less prevalent.

Critical time intervention is a time-limited, phased case management model involving linkage to services and supports through skill building, coaching, and advocacy (Draine & Herman, 2007; Herman & Mandiberg, 2010). Across studies, critical time intervention participants experience more days housed, fewer hospitalizations, symptom reductions, and improved care

(Herman & Mandiberg, 2010; Tomita & Herman, 2015). Other evidence-based services include integrated health services, supported employment, supportive housing, and pharmacotherapy (SAMHSA, 2019).

Intercept Five

The final intercept includes community corrections, which are also referred to as probation and parole. In Missouri, in 2021, 55,500 people were supervised under community corrections, which is down from the 2019 totals (i.e., 61,300 people). The racial and ethnic distribution of the population looks slightly different in 2021 compared to the prison population with 77% of people identifying as White, not Latinx and 23% identifying as Black, Asian, Native American, or Latinx. The most important interventions for people with mental illnesses and substance use disorders who are on supervision are recovery supports. This includes housing, work, social supports, as well as treatments (e.g., counselling, medication-assisted treatment). Having established community partnerships and officers with knowledge about these resources often helps facilitate access to these resources.

One strategy used in community corrections to reduce recidivism and promote rehabilitation is establishing specialized mental health caseloads, which involves officers having a smaller caseload of people with serious mental illnesses. Officers are trained on de-escalation and linking people with needed services; small caseloads allow for extra time to assist people in addressing barriers to successful supervision (Lurigio et al., 2012). Specialized probation can reduce the risk of recidivism and connect people with recovery supports (Skeem et al., 2010, 2017). When specialized caseloads are not possible, mental health training for officers is essential to help increase their understanding of the impact of mental illness on behaviours and expand their knowledge of community resources needed for rehabilitation (Givens et al., in press). People with mental illnesses are among the highest risk group for probation and parole violations. Increasing awareness of mental illness and resources can help officers discern when violations are warranted and facilitate service linkages.

Peer Specialists. Each intercept has mounting evidence for, at minimum, promising practices. People with mental illnesses exiting jail may interact with police, courts, probation officers, and jails in the span of a few months. It is easy for people to fall through the gaps between these intercepts that often function as silos. Many existing interventions for justice-involved people also fail to address behavioural health and criminogenic risk collectively, which may improve symptoms but not reduce risk factors that contribute to recidivism. To create more support and system navigation assistance, interventions for justice-involved people in Missouri frequently include peer support specialists. Peer support specialists are individuals with lived experience; in this case, they may be formerly incarcerated or have a mental illness or substance use disorder (Bellamy et al., 2019). Criminal-legal peer specialists can work across settings including courts programmes (e.g., veterans treatment court), jail or prison re-entry, and within community corrections. There is a long history of peer support specialists in the substance use and mental health treatment programmes. Missouri offers programming and training support to assist people in becoming peer support specialists. Peer supports are especially active in Missouri in programmes targeting people with opioid use disorders and in consumer-operated drop-in centres.

Future Directions

In the United States, incarceration is expensive—to counties, families, and individuals. Counties are responsible for most of the costs of running the jail. Communities spent approximately $22.2 billion on jails in 2011, four times more than 1983 (Henrichson et al., 2015). There is also growing recognition of the cost of incarceration to families. A survey conducted in 2018 estimates that 45% of United States residents reported incarceration among immediate family members with higher estimates among Black families (63%; Enns et al., 2019). Families may experience financial burden due to the cost of visitation (Christian, 2005), psychological distress and poor quality of life (Wildeman et al., 2019), and reduced household assets (Turney & Schneider, 2016). These struggles persist beyond incarceration and impact families even while people are under community supervision (Comfort, 2016). Financial burden from fines and fees incurred in jail and prison compound the poverty a large portion of people in custody in the United States face (Eisen, 2015).

Across the United States including Missouri, there is growing recognition and support for keeping people with mental illnesses out of the criminal-legal system when they can safely rehabilitate in the community. Using the sequential intercept model, there are a multitude of intervention points to divert people and create barriers for further entry into the system. Although programming and diversion services are found throughout Missouri, there remains a sizable portion of people with mental illnesses incarcerated. Peer support programmes coupled with existing interventions is a strategy utilized in Missouri across the criminal-legal system. This model holds promise to increase the direct social support people with mental illnesses receive, provide assistance with navigating the system, and increase sustained connections to recovery supports when they risk criminal-legal involvement. Future research is needed to examine the effectiveness of these models in successfully rehabilitating people, reducing future contact with the criminal-legal system, and enhancing overall quality of life.

Notes

1. Latinx is a gender-neutral and gender-inclusive (i.e., including all genders) term for anyone of Latin descent.
2. Missouri does not track mental health courts across the state; the program status summary only includes drug, DWI, family, and veterans court as a part of their annual counts. According to SAMHSA, there are six mental health courts in Missouri.

References

Abreu, D., Parker, T. W., Noether, C. D., Steadman, H. J., & Chase, B. (2017). Revising the paradigm for jail diversion for people with mental and substance sue disorders: Intercept 0. *Behavioral Sciences and the Law, 35*(5–6), 380–395.

Angell, B., Matthews, E., Barrenger, S., Watson, A. C., & Draine, J. (2014). Engagement processes in model programs for community reentry from prison for people with serious mental illness. *International Journal of Law and Psychiatry, 37*(5), 490–500.

Baillargeon, J., Binswanger, I. A., Penn, J. V., Williams, B. A., & Murray, O. J. (2009). Psychiatric disorders and repeat incarcerations: The revolving prison door. *American Journal of Psychiatry, 166*(1), 103–109.

Bales, W.D., & Garduno, L. S. (2016). Confinement in local jails: Institutions and their clients neglected by criminologists. In T. G. Blomberg, J. M. Brancale, K. M. Beaver, & W. D. Bales (Eds.), *Advancing criminology and criminal justice policy* (pp. 267–281), Routledge.

Barrenger, S., Draine, J., Angell, B., & Herman, D. (2017). Reincarceration risk among men with mental illnesses leaving prison: A risk environment analysis. *Community Mental Health Journal, 53*(8), 883–892.

Bazelon Center for Mental Health Law. (2006). *Best practices: Access to benefits for prisoners with mental illnesses,* viewed 23 May 2022. http://justicesolutionsgroup.com/resourcecenter/uploads/pdf/DOC_BestPractices.pdf

Bellamy, C., Kimmel, J., Costa, M. N., Tsai, J., Nulton, L., Nulton, E., Kimmel, A., Aguilar, N. J., Clayton, A., & O'Connell, M. (2019). Peer support on the 'inside and outside': Building lives and reducing recidivism for people with mental illness returning from jail. *Journal of Public Mental Health, 18*(3), 188–198.

Belenko, S., Langley, S., Crimmins, S., & Chaple, M. (2004). HIV risk behaviors, knowledge, and prevention among offenders under community supervision: A hidden risk group. *AIDS Education and Prevention, 16*, 367–385.

Blitz, C. L., Wolff, N., & Shi, J. (2008). Physical victimization in prison: The role of mental illness. *International Journal of Law and Psychiatry, 31*, 385–393.

Borum, R., Deane, M. W., Steadman, H. J., & Morrissey, J. (1998). Police perspectives on responding to mentally ill people in crisis: Perceptions of program effectiveness. *Behavioral Sciences and the Law, 16*, 393–405.

Bronson, J. & Berzofsky, M. (2015). *Indicators of mental health problems reported by prisoners and jail inmates, 2011–12*, U.S. Department of Justice.

Bronson, J., Stroop, J., Zimmer, S., & Berzofsky, M. (2017). *Drug use, dependence, and abuse among state prisoners and jail inmates, 2007–2009*, Department of Justice Bureau of Justice Statistics, NCJ 250546.

Canada, K. E., Barrenger, S. L., & Ray, B. (2019). Bridging mental health and criminal justice systems: A systematic review of the impact of mental health courts on individuals and communities. *Psychology, Public Policy, and Law, 25*(2), 73–91.

Canada, K. E., Peters, C. M., & Halloran, J. (2016). The emergence of mental health courts in the United States: Intersecting innovation between psychiatric care and the law. *Mental Health Law and Policy, 5*, 31–59.

Canada, K. E., Trawver, K. R., & Barrenger, S. (2020a). Deciding to participate in mental health court: Exploring participant perspectives. *International Journal of Law and Mental Health, 72*, 1–27.

Canada, K. E., Watson, A. C., & O'Kelley, S. (2020b). Utilizing crisis intervention teams (CIT) in prison to improve officer knowledge, stigmatizing attitudes, and perception of response options. *Criminal Justice and Behavior, 48*(1), 10–31.

Carson, E. A. (2021). *Prisoners in 2020 - Statistical tables*, U.S. Department of Justice Bureau of Justice Statistics, NCJ 302776.

Choi, N. G., DiNitto, D. M., & Marti, C. N. (2019). Suicide decedents in correctional settings: Mental health treatment for suicidal ideation, plans, and/or attempts. *Journal of Correctional Health Care, 25*(1), 70–83.

CHPPR [Center for Health Policy, Planning, and Research]. (2007). *Crisis intervention team (CIT) training for correctional officers*. University of New England.

Christian, J. (2005). Riding the bus: Barriers to prison visitation and family management strategies. *Journal of Contemporary Criminal Justice, 21*(1), 31–48.

Cochran, J. C., Mears, D. P., & Bales, W. D. (2014). Does inmate behavior affect post-release offending? Investigating the misconduct-recidivism relationship among youth and adults. *Justice Quarterly, 31*(6), 1044–1073.

Cohen, D. J., Davis, M., Balasubramanian, B. A., Gunn, R., Hall, J., deGruy, F. V., Peek, C. J., Green, L. A., Stange, K. C., Pallares, C., & Levy, S. (2015). Integrating behavioral health and primary care: Consulting, coordinating and collaborating among professionals. *The Journal of the American Board of Family Medicine, 28*(Supplement 1), S21–S31.

Coldwell, C. M., & Bender, W. S. (2007). The effectiveness of assertive community treatment for homeless populations with severe mental illness: A meta-analysis. *American Journal of Psychiatry, 164*, 393–399.

Comfort, M. (2016). "A twenty-hour-a-day job": The impact of frequent low-level criminal justice involvement on family life. *The Annals of the American Academy, 665*, 63–79.

Compton, M. T., Esterberg, M. L., McGee, R., Kotwicki, R. J., & Oliva, J. R. (2006). Crisis intervention team training: Changes in knowledge, attitudes, and stigma related to Schizophrenia. *Psychiatric Services, 57*(8), 1199–1202.

Ditton, P. M. (1999). *Mental health and treatment of inmates and probationers*, U.S. Department of Justice.

Draine, J., & Herman, D. B. (2007). Critical time intervention for reentry from prison for persons with mental illness. *Psychiatric Services, 58*(12), 1577–1581.

Eisen, L. B. (2015). *Charging inmate perpetuates mass incarceration*, viewed 23 March 2022. http://www.brennancenter.org/sites/default/files/publications/Charging_Inmates_Mass_Incarceration.pdf

Engel, R., Sobol, J., & Worden, R. (2000). Further exploration of the demeanor hypothesis: The interaction effects of suspects' characteristics and demeanor on police behavior. *Justice Quarterly, 17*(2), 235–258.

Enns, P. K., Yi, Y., Comfort, M., Goldman, A.W., Lee, H., Muller, C., Wakefield, S., Wang, A. E., & Wildeman, C. (2019). What percentage of Americans have ever had a family member incarcerated?: Evidence from the family history of incarceration survey (FamHIS). *Socius: Sociological Research for a Dynamic World, 5*, 1–45.

Fellner, J. (2006). A correction quandary: Mental illness and prison rules. *Harvard Civil Rights-Civil Liberties Law Review, 41*, 391–412.

Freudenbert, N., & Heller, D. (2016). A review of opportunities to improve the health of people involved in the criminal justice system in the United States. *Annual Review of Public Health, 37*, 313–333.

Givens, A., Jacobs, L. A., Canada, K. E., & Edwards, D. (Forthcoming). Mental illness-related stigma among probation officers. *Criminal Behavior and Mental Health*.

Gonzales, A. R., Schofield, R. B., & Hagy, D. W. (2007). *Mental health screens for corrections*. U.S. Department of Justice, Office of Justice Programs, NCJ 216152.

Harrah, S. (2020). *Medically underserved areas in the US*, viewed on 23 March 2022. https://www.umhs-sk.org/blog/medically-underserved-areas-regions-where-u-s-needs-doctors

Hatzenbuehler, M. L., Phelan, J. C., & Link, B. G. (2013). Stigma as a fundamental cause of population health inequalities. *American Journal of Public Health, 103*(5), 813–821.

Henrichson, C., Rinaldi, J., & Delaney, R. (2015). *The price of jails: Measuring the taxpayer cost of local incarceration*, Vera Institute of Justice, Center on Sentencing and Corrections, Brooklyn, NY.

Herman, D. B., & Mandiberg, J. M. (2010). Critical time intervention: Model description and implications for the significance of timing in social work interventions. *Research on Social Work Practice, 20*(5), 502–508.

Johnson, E. J., Schonbrun, C. Y., Anderson, B., Kurth, M., Timko, C., & Stein, M. (2017). Study protocol: Community Links to Establish Alcohol Recovery (CLEAR) for women leaving jail. *Contemporary Clinical Trials, 55*, 39–46.

Kaeble, D. (2021). *Probation and parole in the United States, 2020*, U.S. Department of Justice Bureau of Justice Statistics, NCJ 303102.

Lamb, R. H., & Weinberger, L. E. (Eds.). 2001. *Deinstitutionalization: Promise and problems*. Jossey-Bass/Wiley.

Lamberti, J. S., Weisman, R. L., Cerulli, C., Williams, G. C., Jacobowitz, D. B., Mueser, K. T., & Caine, E. D. (2017). A randomized controlled trial of the Rochester forensic assertive community treatment model. *Psychiatric Services, 68*(1), 1016–1024.

Lurigio, A., Epperson, M., Canada, K. E., & Babchuk, L. (2012). Specialized probation programs for people with mental illnesses: A review of practice and research. *Journal of Crime and Justice, 35*(2), 317–326.

Lynch, S. M., Dehart, D. D., Belknap, J. E., Green, B. L., Dass-Brailsford, P., Johnson, K. A., & Whalley, E. (2014). A multisite study of the prevalence of serious mental illness, PTSD, and substance use disorders of women in jail. *Psychiatric Services, 65*(5), 670–674.

Marcus, N., & Stergiopoulos, V. (2022). Re-examining mental health crisis intervention: A rapid review comparing outcomes across police, co-responder and non-police models. *Health and Social Care in the Community, 30*(5), 1665–1679.

Martin, M. S., Colman, I., Simpson, A. I., & McKenzie, K. (2013). Mental health screening tools in correctional institutions: A systematic review. *BMC Psychiatry, 13*(275), 1–10.

Miller, J. M., Miller, H. V., & Barnes, J. C. (2019). Treating co-occurring disorders in jails: Outcome findings from a Second Chance Act offender reentry program. *Crime and Delinquency, 65*(5), 583–605.

Minton, T. D., & Zeng, Z. (2016). *Jail inmates in 2015*. US Department of Justice Washington.

Minton, T. D., & Zeng, Z. (2021). *Jail inmates in 2020 – Statistical tables*, U.S. Department of Justice Bureau of Justice Statistics, NCJ 303308.

Missouri CIT. (2022). *Missouri crisis intervention team (MO CIT) council*, viewed on 23 March 2022. https://www.missouricit.org/

Morabito, M. S., Kerr, A. N., Watson, A. C., Draine, J., & Angell, B. (2012). Crisis Intervention Teams and people with mental illness: Exploring the factors that influence the use of force. *Crime and Delinquency, 58*(1), 57–77.

Morabito, M. S., Savage, J., Sneider, L., & Wallace, K. (2018). Police response to people with mental illnesses in a major U.S. city: The Boston experience with the co-responder model. *Victims and Offenders, 13*(8), 1093–1105.

Munetz, M. R., & Griffin, P. A. (2006). Use of the sequential intercept model as an approach to decriminalization of people with serious mental illness. *Psychiatric Services, 57*(4), 544–549.

Nellis, A. (2021). *The color of justice: Racial and ethnic disparity in state prisons*. The Sentencing Project.

Puntis, S., Perfect, D., Kirubarajan, A., Bolton, S., Davies, F., Hayes, A., Harriss, E., & Molodynski, A. (2018). A systematic review of co-responder models of police mental health 'street' triage. *BMC Psychiatry, 18*(256), 1–11.

Raggio, A. L., Hoffmann, N. G., & Kopak, A. M. (2017). Results from a comprehensive assessment of behavioral health problems among rural jail inmates. *Journal of Offender Rehabilitation, 56*(3), 217–235.

Redlich, A. D., Steadman, H. J., Monahan, J., Petrila, J., & Griffin, P. A. (2005). The second generation of mental health courts. *Psychology, Public Policy, and Law, 11*(4), 527–538.

Reuland, M. (2004). A guide to implementing police-based diversion programs for people with mental illness. TAPA Center for Jail Diversion, Rockville, MD.

Ruiz, J. (1993). An interactive analysis between uniformed law enforcement officers and the mentally ill. *American Journal of Police, 12*(4), 149–177.

SAMHSA. (2017). *Results from the 2017 national survey on drug use and health: Detailed tables*, viewed 23 March 2022. https://www.samhsa.gov/data/sites/default/files/cbhsq-reports/NSDUHDetailedTabs2017/NSDUHDetailedTabs2017.htm#tab8-33A

SAMHSA. (2019). *Principles of community-based behavioral health services for justice-involved individuals: A research-based guide*, HHS Publication No. SMA-19-5097. Office of Policy, Planning, and Innovation, Rockville, MD.

SAMHSA. (2022). *Adult mental health treatment court locator*, viewed on 23 March 2022. https://www.samhsa.gov/gains-center/mental-health-treatment-court-locator/adults?field_gains_mhc_state_value=MO

Skeem, J., & Bibeau, L. (2008). How does violence potential relate to crisis intervention team responses to emergencies? *Psychiatric Services, 59*(2), 201–204.

Skeem, J. L., & Louden, E. J. (2006). Toward evidence-based practice for probationers and parolees mandated to mental health treatment. *Psychiatric Services, 57*(3), 333–342.

Skeem, J. L., Manchak, S., & Peterson, K. J. (2010). Correctional policy for offenders with mental illness: Creating a new paradigm for recidivism reduction. *Law and Human Behavior, 35*(2), 110–126.

Skeem, J. L., Manchak, S., & Montoya, L. (2017). Comparing public safety outcomes for traditional probation vs specialty mental health probation. *JAMA Psychiatry, 74*(9), 942–948.

Slate, R. N., & Johnson, W. W. (2008). *The criminalization of mental illness: Crisis and opportunity for the justice system*. Carolina Academic Press.

State of Missouri. (2021). *Drug courts coordinating commission, treatment court program status.* Office of State Courts Administrator.

Steadman, J. H., Osher, C. F., Robbins, C. P., Case, B., & Samuels, S. (2009). Prevalence of serious mental illness among jail inmates. *Psychiatric Services, 60*(6), 761–765.

Subramanian, R., Delaney, R., Roberts, S., Fishman, N., & McGarry, P. (2015). *Incarceration's front door: The misuse of jails in America,* Vera Institute of Justice.

Teplin, L. A. (1984). 'Criminalizing mental disorder: The comparative arrest rate of the mentally ill. *American Psychologist, 39*(7), 794–803.

Tomita, A., & Herman, D. B. (2015). The role of a critical time intervention on the experience of continuity of care among persons with severe mental illness after hospital discharge. *The Journal of Nervous and Mental Disease, 203*(1), 65–70.

Turney, K., & Schneider, D. (2016). Incarceration and household asset ownership. *Demography, 53*(6), 2075–2103.

Van Olpen, J., Eliason, M. J., Freudenberg, N., & Barnes, M. (2009). Nowhere to go: How stigma limits the options of female drug users after release from jail. *Substance Abuse Treatment, Prevention, and Policy, 4*(10), 1–10.

Watson, A. C., & Fulambarker, A. J. (2012). The crisis intervention team model of police response to mental health crises: A primer for mental health practitioners. *Best Practices in Mental Health, 8*(2), 1–8.

Watson, A. C., Morabito, M. S., Draine, J., & Ottati, V. (2008). Improving police response to persons with mental illness: A multi-level conceptualization of CIT. *International Journal of Law and Psychiatry, 31*, 359–368.

Watson, A. C., Owens, L. K., Wood, J., & Compton, M. T. (2021). The impact of crisis intervention team response, dispatch coding, and location on the outcomes of police encounters with individuals with mental illnesses in Chicago. *Policing: A Journal of Policy and Practice, 15*(3), 1948–1962.

White, D. M., Saunders, J., Fisher, C., & Mellow, J. (2012). Exploring inmate reentry in a local jail setting: Implications for outreach, service use, and recidivism. *Crime and Delinquency, 58*(1), 124–146.

Wildeman, C., Goldman, A. W., & Lee, H. (2019). Health consequences of family member incarceration for adults in the household. *Public Health Reports, 134*(supplement 1), 15S-21S.

Wilson, A. B., Draine, J., Hadley, T., Metraux, S., & Evans, A. (2011). Examining the impact of mental illness and substance use on recidivism in a county jail. *Public Health and Policy Perspectives for Psychiatry and Law, 34*(4), 264–268.

Resocialisation and Reintegration in the Netherlands: Political Narrative Versus Reality

Sonja Meijer and Elanie Rodermond

More than 430 years ago, on the initiative of D.V. Coornhert, the first '*tuchthuis*' (disciplinary house) opened in Amsterdam where criminals and vagrants had to serve their sentences. In so-called '*rasphuizen*', men were forced to grind wood from Brazil into powder that was used in the paint industry. In so-called '*spinhuizen*' (spinning houses), women were forced to spin wool. Resocialisation at this time had a strong utilitarian basis. The idea was that hard work under strict discipline would lead to the moral improvement of the punished person. On the one hand, it would lead to moral improvement of the prisoner and, on the other hand, the work performed would be for the benefit of society. Moreover, the disciplinary house would be able to sustain itself financially by the production it provided.[1]

In the Netherlands, the term resocialisation is used instead of rehabilitation. Thinking about resocialisation gained momentum in the Netherlands

---

S. Meijer (✉)
Faculty of Law, Radboud University, Nijmegen, The Netherlands
e-mail: sonja.meijer@ru.nl

S. Meijer · E. Rodermond
Faculty of Law, Vrije Universiteit, Amsterdam, The Netherlands

E. Rodermond
Netherlands Institute for the Study of Crime and Law Enforcement, Amsterdam, The Netherlands

after World War II. The fact that many people had experienced at first-hand what it was like to be imprisoned during the German occupation, provided a powerful impetus for reforming the prison system, with a heavy emphasis on the resocialisation of prisoners. A strong emphasis was placed on the improvement of the prisoner and his or her well-being. Resocialisation was laid down as a basic principle in the 1951 Prison System Principles Act. With the amendment of this legislation in the Penitentiary Principles Act in 1998, this principle was retained. According to the text of the Act, the starting point implies that while maintaining the character of the prison sentence, its implementation should, as much as possible, serve the preparation of the prisoner for a return to society. An amendment to the law in 2015 added that preparation for return to society depends on the behaviour of the prisoner and that the interests of victims and next of kin must be taken into account in granting liberties.

In recent decades, resocialisation has become less and less about offering help and support to the convicted person. Resocialisation has taken on a more utilitarian meaning and is now dominated by the safety of society. Typically, it is no longer the convict who benefits from resocialisation efforts, but society and victims in particular. Resocialisation is also increasingly seen in light of risk management and risk control. Moreover, resocialisation has entered into a partnership with punishment, which has proved essential to its legitimacy (Meijer, 2022). With recent legislative changes, however, the emphasis has shifted from resocialisation to reintegration of prisoners. In the political narrative, increasing attention is paid to reintegration of ex-prisoners, while the possibilities for resocialisation have actually diminished in recent years and have been made dependent on more conditions.

As a result of the government's vision on the execution of prison sentences called 'Doing justice, offering opportunities' and the resulting Dutch Sanctions and Protective Services Act (*Wet straffen en beschermen*[2]), there is a strong emphasis on the reintegration of detainees. Characteristic of this policy and the legislation based on it is (1) that there is a stronger emphasis on the retribution of the criminal act, (2) that the behaviour of the convicted person plays a more important role in the liberties to be granted and (3) that efforts are made for a safe return to society. The stronger emphasis on retribution was given shape by shortening the term of the conditional release, as will be illustrated below. The granting of freedom, such as leaves, has also been made more dependent on the behaviour of the prisoner during his detention. The criminal law policy is based on the prisoner's own responsibility and departs from the idea that prisoners should be 'self-reliant'. Detainees are responsible for their resocialisation and the course of their detention.

Finally, the work on a safe return to society takes place based on six basic conditions, namely having accommodation, income from work or benefits, insight into debts, possession of a valid identity card, determining care needs and continuity of care and the later added condition of maintaining and strengthening a positive social network. Prisoners must prepare themselves for return to society from the beginning of their imprisonment. The aim is to put in place the fundamental elements for a stable life upon their return, as to reduce the risk of recidivism.

In this chapter, the current mechanisms for resocialisation in Dutch law and practice are elaborated in light of the current criminal justice policy (2). Subsequently, the resocialisation of some specific prisoners is discussed (4). After that, some of the theoretical underpinnings of models of rehabilitation are described (5), as well as some research findings on the effectiveness (4). Finally, future directions in policy and practice will be discussed.

Current Mechanisms and Their Policy and Political Context

In the Netherlands, the resocialisation of detainees is shaped by the policy framework of promotion and demotion, the detention phasing, reintegration leave, the penitentiary programme and the conditional release. These resocialisation mechanisms are elaborated on below. On 1st March 2014, as part of the Modernisation of the Prison System programme (*Modernisering Gevangeniswezen*), the policy framework Day Programme, Security and Tailored Supervision (*Dagprogramma, Beveiliging en Toezicht op maat*, hereafter DBT) was introduced. The policy framework introduced a distinction within the prison system between the basic programme and the plus programme. If a prisoner's behaviour is good, he or she can be promoted to the plus programme; if he or she behaves badly, he or she can be demoted to the basic programme. The assessment framework of promotion and demotion aims to ensure that good behaviour is rewarded, and bad behaviour corrected in a standardised manner. The idea of responsibility is thus reflected in prison law: prisoners are expected to make their own efforts and take responsibility for the course of their imprisonment and their return to society. Internal freedoms and participation in reintegration activities can be earned if a prisoner demonstrates that he or she can handle responsibilities. The plus programme is only used in prisons.[3] A house of detention only has a basic programme, because the focus there is not on reintegration and resocialisation.

In short, the basic and the plus programme comprise the following. The basic programme comprises 42.5 hours per week, of which at least 22.5 hours are offered for activities and visits (art. 3, para. 2 under a *Penitentiaire maatregel*). The programme consists of the statutory basic activities as laid down in the Penitentiary Act, such as recreation, exercise and work. In addition to the statutory basic activities, detainees may participate in extra activities, such as the training programme 'Choose for Change', participation in a discussion group of the spiritual counsellors or preparing for their return. The basic programme has no evening programme and a limited weekend programme. If there are no activities, the detainees stay in their cells.

The plus programme comprises 59 hours per week, of which 28 hours per week are offered for activities and visits (art. 3, para. 2 under b *Penitentiaire maatregel*). In principle, the plus programme consists of the same components as the basic programme, but the programme is expanded by adjusting the content, freedoms and intensity of the programme. Activities aimed at a return to society are more intensively dealt with. More training, return activities and behavioural interventions are offered than in the basic programme. The plus programme has an evening programme two evenings a week. Additional activities are offered on the weekend. If no activities are offered in the morning or afternoon, the detainees are allowed to stay on the wing outside the cell.

Another significant difference with the basic programme is that within the plus programme detainees can get more freedom and responsibilities. Detainees can participate in plus work, for example. This is work with more freedom or work for which more independence is expected. An example of 'plus work' is specific work within the institution, such as cleaning, painting or work in a shop or kitchen. Plus work is work that can often be linked to a (professional) education. Prisoners can then follow education aimed at finding a job. In addition to the benefit of plus work, the plus programme allows prisoners to indicate their preferences for when activities, such as visits, are planned. In addition, participation in the plus programme is a condition for earning freedoms outside the institution.

Prisoners are in principle placed in a basic programme. A detainee is entitled to promotion if, for a period of six weeks after the start of their detention, they have shown the desired behaviour described in the category 'reintegration/resocialisation' and in the category 'residence and liveability' of the assessment framework. They may then be promoted to a plus programme, where they are given more freedom, activities and extra visits (art. 1d, para. 3 Scheme for selection, placement and transfer of prisoners ['*Regeling selectie, plaatsing en overplaatsing van gedetineerden*'], hereafter: RSPOG). If detainees show undesirable behaviour, they are demoted or cannot (yet) be promoted (art. 1d, para. 3 RSPOG). The director decides on promotion and demotion of detainees (art. 1d, Section 1 RSPOG). He does so on the basis of assessments of behaviour made by penitentiary staff. There is a possibility to lodge a complaint against the decision of the director with the Supervisory Committee of the penitentiary institution (art. 60 Pbw) and an appeal with the Appeals Committee of the Council for the Administration of Criminal Justice and Protection of Juveniles (art. 69 Pbw). Not all prisoners are eligible for promotion to the plus programme (see para. 4).

As of 1 October 2020, the amendment to the RSPOG tightens the assessment framework for promotion and demotion. An important change is the introduction of the category of 'unacceptable behaviour'. A decision to demote follows always if a detainee shows unacceptable behaviour (art. 1d, para. 4 RSPOG). The director has no room to make his own assessment. Inadmissible behaviour can include (physical) threats to personnel, an (attempted) escape or the use of drugs.

Resocialisation is further given form by granting reintegration leave (art. 26 Penitentiary Act). The statutory regulations concerning this leave are laid down in the Regulation on Temporary Leaves from the Institution ('*Regeling tijdelijk verlaten van de inrichting*', herafter: Rtvi). These regulations were amended on 1 July 2021 as a result of the entry into force of the aforementioned Sentencing and Protection Act. The most important change to the leave scheme is that the general leave and regime-related leave have been replaced by reintegration leave. Without elaborating on the old scheme, the change means that leave is no longer automatically granted after a certain period, but it is assessed per detainee whether and for which types of reintegration leave he is eligible. Furthermore, reintegration leave is linked to concrete reintegration objectives. The reason for the change is that according to the Minister, detainees experienced leave as 'a noncommittal matter of course' and that 'when granting leave, the interests of victims and surviving relatives are not sufficiently taken into account and leave was not focussed on reintegration objectives'. Prisoners were eligible for leave even before they had served half their sentence. According to the Minister, this did not fit in with a credible execution of the sentence. Moreover, the leave had to be made more personal by letting the behaviour of detainees be the basis for granting freedom (the idea of responsibility) (Meijer & Hamelzky, 2022).

The reintegration leave is divided into short-term reintegration leave, long-term reintegration leave and reintegration leave for extramural work. There is also the possibility of incidental leave on humanitarian grounds. This form of leave is not for the purpose of reintegration but only to allow leave to be granted on the basis of the personal circumstances of the prisoner, such as to attend a funeral, even if the prisoner is not yet eligible for reintegration leave.[4] In the current law, leave must always be linked to a reintegration goal (art. 15, para. 1 Rtvi). The goals for which reintegration leave can be granted are related to the six basic conditions for reintegration mentioned above.

Short-term reintegration leave is intended for reintegration activities laid down in the detention and reintegration plan that cannot be carried out within the walls of the institution. These activities include obtaining a passport if it is necessary to visit a municipality, going for a job interview with an employer, signing a rental contract for a house, taking an exam and attending a behavioural intervention. The duration of the reintegration leave is adapted to the activities to be performed plus the necessary travel time and starts and ends on the same day (art. 19, para. 1 Rtvi). Short-term reintegration leave cannot be granted until eighteen months prior to the conditional release (para. 2).[5] An exception can be made to the above regulation in case of 'serious reasons concerning his reintegration' (para. 4).

Long-term reintegration leave can be granted for participation in the recognised behavioural interventions or participation in a trajectory of several days per week offered by (aid) organisations, such as the probation service. Reintegration leave can also be granted for visits to the family. This is only possible as long as a concrete reintegration goal is served and that goal is included in the detention and reintegration plan. An example is participation in the recognised behavioural intervention 'Betere Start', which enables mothers to practice living in a family context with their children, but also targeted visits to family members, if necessary, to work on a stable family contact or to learn to fulfil again a parenting role within the family. The long-term reintegration leave does not end on the same day as it started. The maximum duration of the long-term leave is 204 hours, consisting of a minimum of one and a maximum of eight overnight stays per month (art. 20, para. 1 Rtvi). The maximum number of hours of leave is determined per calendar year and laid down in the detention and reintegration plan (para. 2). Long-term leave can be granted at the earliest, maximum twelve months prior to the conditional release (para. 3).[6]

Finally, reintegration leave can be granted for extramural work (art. 20ab Rvti). The reintegration leave is here linked to the detention phases. Prisoners who have been placed in a normal security institution are transferred to a limited security department if they qualify for reintegration leave for extramural work.[7] Prisoners work outside the institution during the day or are trained for work and stay inside the institution at night. The minimum duration of the reintegration leave for extramural work is four weeks and a maximum of twelve months (para. 1). The leave can be granted at the earliest if the prison sentence is longer than six months and for at least one-sixth of the sentence imposed before the prisoner can be considered for (conditional) release (para. 2). Prisoners who have been placed in a penitentiary programme are excluded from reintegration leave for extramural work. If the prisoner is eligible for both modalities, the selection officer determines which modality it will be (para. 3).

The question of whether reintegration leave will be granted is assessed, among other things, on the basis of the behaviour of the prisoner.[8] The prisoner's conduct thus plays a role not only in the course of the detention but also in the question of what external freedoms are granted. The assessment of behaviour is further standardised in the policy framework for assessment of behaviour during the entire period of detention following the entry into force of the Dutch Penal and Protective Services Act. The goal of this policy framework is to simplify the substantiation of a decision which leads to more uniform assessments. These standards amount to a percentage of the time the prisoner must have spent in the plus programme to be eligible for reintegration leave. The longer the reintegration leave can last (in short, the more freedom is granted), the higher the standard. The policy also contains lower standards. If the prisoner has not spent a certain minimum amount of time in a plus programme, he is not eligible for reintegration leave. There is also an intermediate category in which the governor and/or the selection officer can make their own assessment, taking into account developments in the behaviour of the prisoner and the nature and severity of any disciplinary punishments for unacceptable and/or undesirable behaviour.

In the final stage of their imprisonment, prisoners up to and including one year may be eligible for placement in a so-called penitentiary programme. Prisoners sentenced to a term of imprisonment of more than one year may be eligible for conditional release (see hereafter). A penitentiary programme consists of several activities through which the prison sentence is carried out (art. 4, para. 1 Pbw). The prisoner is outside the prison walls and is supervised by the probation service (possibly with an ankle bracelet). Conditions may be attached to the penitentiary programme (para. 4). To be allowed to participate in a penitentiary programme, detainees must have been sentenced to a nonsuspended prison sentence of at least six months. The penitentiary programme may last up to one-sixth of the imposed sentence (art. 4, para. 2 Pbw). A penitentiary programme can therefore last up to eight weeks. Participation is possible immediately prior to release. The selection officer decides whether an inmate may participate in a penitentiary programme. The selection officer makes his decision based on the same criteria that apply to the granting of reintegration leave and conditional release.[9] The behaviour of the convicted person thus plays an important role in the question whether an inmate can participate in a penitentiary programme. Behaviour is assessed on the basis of the aforementioned assessment framework.

Individuals sentenced to more than one year and no more than two years imprisonment may be eligible for conditional release after serving at least one year plus one third of the remaining sentence. Prisoners with a prison sentence of two years or more are eligible for conditional release after serving two-thirds of their sentence with a maximum of two years (art. 6:2:10, para. 1, Code of Criminal Procedure). The maximisation of the conditional release to two years is a consequence of the entry into force of the Sanctions and Protection Act. The rationale of this amendment is that punishments must be credible. The Minister did not consider it credible for sentenced persons to be released on probation as early as two-thirds of their prison sentence.[10] In short, the two-year maximum period of conditional release was introduced to do justice to the retributive nature of the custodial sentence. Schuyt rightly pointed out, however, that the severity of the punishment should be expressed in the nature of the punishment and its length as determined by the judge, not in the way it is carried out (Schuyt, 2019).

Under the new regime, conditional release is no longer granted by operation of law, but following a decision by the Central Provision for Conditional Release (*Centrale Voorziening voorwaardelijke invrijheidtelling*, CVvi), which is part of the Public Prosecution Service. Under the old regime, however, the conditional release was certainly not automatic. At the request of the public prosecutor, the conditional release could be postponed or deferred in certain cases, such as the commission of a crime in detention or an attempt to escape. Under the new regime, however, the behaviour of the prisoner has become one of the bases for granting conditional release. The decision on the conditional release will be taken based on the prisoner's conduct, the risks associated with the release and the possibility of limiting or controlling them, the interests of victims, next of kin and other relevant persons, including efforts made by the prisoner to compensate for the damage caused by the offence. Unlike the case with the granting of reintegration leave or participation in a penitentiary programme, there is no further policy detailing the percentage of time the prisoner must spend in a plus programme to be eligible for conditional release. This is because the decision-making authority for the reintegration leave, and the penitentiary programme lies with the director of the institution or the selection officer and with the public prosecutor for the conditional release. However, it is conceivable that these decisions are not consistent with each other if one authority pursues a stricter policy than the other. This could impede the resocialisation process of the detainee. Further research must show whether this is actually the case.

Rehabilitation and Diversity

The system as described above is aimed at prisoners in general. However, a different arrangement applies to specific groups of detainees. With respect to short-term detainees, that is, detainees with a one-month prison sentence, it is recognised that resocialisation can hardly be realised. This raises the question of whether the short imprisonment penalty should still be imposed by the court. In the Netherlands, relatively many short prison sentences are imposed: 25% of prison sentences are shorter than two weeks, 50% are shorter than one month and almost 75% are shorter than three months.

With regard to lifelong prisoners, the policy in the Netherlands has long been that life imprisonment is actually imprisonment for life. It was assumed that the resocialisation principle did not apply to life sentences. Partly due to developments in the case law of the European Court of Human Rights in the past decade and a condemnation of the Netherlands by the European Court in the Murray case, a change has been initiated. Dutch law now provides for an arrangement whereby life-sentenced persons also have the prospect of release that the European Court of Human Rights requires. After 25 years of imprisonment, an assessment is made as to whether the lifelong prisoner is eligible for reintegration activities. If the advice given by the Advisory Board for Life Sentenced Persons is positive and the Minister adopts this advice, the prisoner will be eligible for activities aimed at resocialisation, including leave. After two years, it can be assessed whether the life-sentenced person is eligible for release (by means of a pardon). In the current scheme, however, the question arises of whether life-sentenced persons are actually eligible for release. Pardons for life-sentenced persons almost never occur in practice. Only in 2021 was a pardon granted to two lifelong prisoners after they had been through many procedures in court and the Minister, based on court rulings in these cases, had no other option than to grant a pardon. The biggest sticking point with this is that the Crown takes this decision, under the political responsibility of the Minister for Legal Protection and is therefore politically sensitive. However, following some advice from the Council for the Administration of Criminal Justice and Protection of Juveniles, the Minister has announced that a new procedure for the assessment of the continuation of the life sentence will be made, as a result of which the decision about the possible (conditional) release will be taken by the judge.[11]

Several detainees are excluded from the system of promotion and demotion described above. Resocialisation activities are severely restricted. These include detainees who have been placed in an extra secure institution (the most strictly guarded prison regime), a terrorist wing or in a so-called 'institution for systematic offenders' where those convicted of several minor offences may be deprived of their liberty for a period of two years. Prisoners who have been detained for violating special conditions or failing to pay a fine (the so-called detainees) are also excluded from the system of promotion and demotion.

Theoretical Underpinnings to Models of Rehabilitation

With the exception of the system of promotion and demotion, which can be considered a Contingency Management (CM)-system aimed at establishing desired behaviour in prison and only indirectly aimed at promoting reintegration (Elbers et al., 2021), the modalities described above are largely focussed on preparing prisoners for reintegration. More specifically, detention phasing, reintegration leave, the penitentiary programme and the conditional release are aimed at getting the six basic conditions for reintegration in place. The administrative act 'Providing Opportunities for Reentry', signed in 2019 by the Ministry of Justice and Security, the Dutch Prison Service, the Probation Service and the Association of Dutch Municipalities, has increased this focus even more. Importantly, however, the new Sanctions and Protection act does not seem to view successful reintegration as a goal in itself. Rather, is it described as a means to an end, namely, to reduce recidivism and to 'protect society'. As such, the Dutch approach to prisoner rehabilitation seems to have shifted from a focus on the Risk Need Responsivity Model towards the theoretical framework of promoting 'desistance from crime' to reduce recidivism (Molleman & Lasthuizen, 2015). Recent theorising on criminal desistance (i.e., the process of crime termination) has brought forward different perspectives, including ones that focus on the relevance of external, social factors. According to Sampson and Laub (2003), age-related pro-social institutions such as employment could serve as a 'turning point' in the life course of individuals, thereby increasing chances of successful re-entry and reducing risks of recidivism. According to their age-graded theory of informal social control, new or renewed social bonds provide individuals with something to loose, encouraging them to remain crime-free. The emphasis on the basic conditions for reintegration fits well into this framework.

However, it is also acknowledged that 'turning points' do not simply fall from the sky and that some 'upfront' work needs to be done by prisoners themselves (Giordano et al., 2002). Notably, theories focussing on the relevance of (informal) social control have been criticised for its emphasis on external, social factors, while largely ignoring the individuals' own influence on processes of desistance and rehabilitation. Contrastingly, strength-based approaches and identity theories emphasise the importance of individuals' agency, autonomy, motivation and future orientation in achieving lasting change after release from prison. For example, Paternoster and Bushway contend that an accumulation of negative experiences related to offending, or an offending lifestyle can lead to the envisioning of another, non-offending future self. According to the Good Lives Model, intrinsic motivation is key to lasting change, as 'enhancing personal fulfilment will lead naturally to reductions in criminogenic needs' (Andrewset al., 2011).

The aforementioned system of promotion and demotion, especially the focus on establishing increased (intrinsic) motivation and a future orientation, is in line with these notions. That said, some discrepancies between the theories and the reality of promotion and demotion are at play. Importantly, desistance and reintegration processes can be characterised by ups and downs, whereas the system of promotion and demotion is considered to be rather 'rigid' in its execution. Being demoted based on a mistake does not necessarily align with or increase notions of autonomy and motivation. Hence, some scholars advocate for a less strict execution, allowing prisoners to make mistakes without being denied reintegration activities (Molleman & Lasthuizen, 2015).

Lastly, efforts to rehabilitate prisoners in the Netherlands are increasingly placed with the framework of Offender Management (OM). According to this framework, the often complex needs of prisoners should be addressed by a variety of agencies both inside as well as outside prison, as 'professional assistance is crucial in managing or supporting the successful resettlement of prisoners' (Pasma et al., 2022). As mentioned by Pasma and colleagues, the OM framework is increasingly visible in the Dutch rehabilitation policy. For example, the reintegration needs of prisoners are assessed and monitored by a prison-based case manager and a mentor, with the aim of acquiring the basic conditions for reintegration.

Research Findings and Effectiveness

Taken together, efforts to rehabilitate prisoners in the Netherlands are focussed mainly on supporting reintegration, based on a variety of theoretical underpinnings. The question is, however, whether current policies are effective in achieving prisoner rehabilitation. Studies addressing this issue in the Netherlands can be broadly divided into (1) retrospective studies that examine general post-release outcomes of formerly incarcerated individuals and (2) longitudinal studies that follow prisoners as they re-enter society while also taking into account the prison experience.

One of the largest Dutch initiatives to examine former prisoners is the biennial 'Monitor Aftercare' of the Research and Documentation Centre (WODC) of the Dutch Ministry of Justice and Security. Since 2010, the WODC monitors the reintegration policy focussed on acquiring the basic conditions for reintegration. In the most recent version of the monitor, it was also examined whether a change in the basic conditions (for example going from unemployed to employed) influenced the risk of recidivism (Boschman et al., 2020). According to this latest report, almost half of the ex-prisoners offend at least once within the first two years after release from prison. Whereas the study found that the risk of recidivism was indeed lower for those ex-prisoners whose reintegration conditions were met, it was also found that a substantial portion of ex-prisoners did not acquire the basic conditions for reintegration.

Bosma and colleagues (2020) examined the effectiveness of the Prevention of Recidivism Program, 'a national prison-based treatment programme in The Netherlands that aims to lower re-offending rates among participants by administering an individualised treatment programme that addresses the criminogenic needs of an individual offender'. The authors found that prisoners who completed a standard treatment programme (which only consisted of phased re-entry) re-offended less in the 24 months post-release than control-group prisoners. Contrary to expectations, however, prisoners who followed a standard programme *and* behavioural treatment modules that met their risks and needs did not show reduced re-offending.

Interestingly, recent mixed-method studies have shed light on the mechanisms underlying either successful or 'failed' reintegration after release from prison. In a first study, it was examined to what extent criminal expectations of prisoners (i.e., whether prisoners expected to re-offend after release) matched their actual behaviour after release. It was found that prisoners who remained crime-free after release (in line with their pre-release expectations) had been able to visualise 'a possible self that was not involved in criminal behaviour, combined with some notion of a feared self', which the author deemed in line with the Identity Theory of Desistance (Doekhie, 2019). Moreover, they were found to have sought social support and employment immediately following release from prison, pointing at the importance of agency.

Rodermond and colleagues (2022) examined the influence of external sources of control (i.e., social capital), subjective changes (e.g., increased feelings of self-efficacy) and post-release resource disadvantages on re-entry pathways (of female ex-detainees). They found that motivations to remain crime-free and to reintegrate into society were often blocked by resource disadvantages such as a lack of housing. Notably, this study did not only provide support for the relevance of meeting the basic conditions for reintegration, but also for enabling ex-prisoners to become *and feel* part of society upon release from prison. However, it posited that to fully understand (and support) the process of reintegration and rehabilitation, policy needs to consider the difficult circumstances as faced by many (former) prisoners. Notably, they endorsed the point made by Sered and Norton-Hawk that policymakers and practitioners need to be modest in their expectations regarding self-reliance, as placing too much emphasis on it brings with it the risk of 'attributing unrealistically high levels of agency to individuals whose agency is limited by structural inequalities, discriminatory laws, poverty, homelessness, outstanding warrants, parole supervision, criminal records, poor health and substance abuse (Sered & Norton-Hawk, 2020).

Future Directions in Policy and Practice

The foregoing illustrates that although Dutch criminal justice policy has placed a greater emphasis on the reintegration of detainees, the opportunities for resocialisation have actually diminished. This development has been strongly criticised.[12] Moreover, the problematic aspect of the current interpretation of resocialisation is that it is based on a '*mensbeeld*' that is not in line with reality. The policy puts the personal responsibility of detainees and their behaviour first. The policy seems to assume that a person can decide in complete freedom about his future and his behaviour. However, this ignores the fact that not all prisoners can take this responsibility. It is estimated that almost half of the detainees are addicts, for approximately 45% there is the suspicion of a low mental capacity and a significant part of the detainees has to deal with psychological problems.[13] In the current system of promotion and demotion, a relapse by an addicted prisoner is assessed as unacceptable behaviour that must immediately lead to placement in the basic programme. The prison governor has no room for discretion in this respect. Prison governors consider it a bottleneck that, despite relapses, they cannot reward the addicted prisoner for the small steps he or she takes towards resocialisation. The time a prisoner spends in the basic programme, however, influences whether he or she is eligible for freedoms such as leave, placement in a penitentiary programme or conditional release. Hence, the requirements set by the system are too high for many detainees. Large groups of prisoners who would benefit most from reintegration activities tailored to their specific circumstances are deprived of it. The emphasis on responsibility without regard to ability may also lead to greater inequality. Prisoners who have sufficient economic, cultural and social capital can use it to get ahead in the system. Prisoners who do not have such capital cannot, which increases their disadvantage (van Ginneken, 2018).

Despite many objections voiced in literature and practice, it is not expected that the system of rehabilitation mechanisms outlined in this chapter and its legal regulation will change in the near future. That said, there are some promising initiatives that could broaden opportunities for rehabilitation. First, the WODC recently commissioned a longitudinal study on how prisoners view their reintegration process, taking into account their prison experiences, programme participation, contact with professionals and their actual transition out of prison into society. Moreover, in the Netherlands, increased attention (both inside and outside academia) has been paid to the concept of restorative justice, acknowledging the fact that rehabilitation asks for more than just reintegration.

Notes

1. D.V. Coornhert, *Boeventucht ofte middelen tot mindering der schadelijke ledighangers*, 1587 zoals aangehaald in Kelk 2018.
2. Government Gazette 2021, 31769.
3. Correctional institutions are divided into prisons, houses of detention and institutions for systematic offenders (art. 9, para. 1 Penitentiary Act [Penitentiaire beginselenwet]).
4. There are also specific forms of leave for prisoners who are sentenced to a so-called 'measure *for the inrichting voor stelselmatige daders*' (placement in a facility for systematic repeat offenders) and life sentences.
5. A minimum of six weeks imprisonment or pre-trial detention must have been served. For prison sentences longer than six years, leave can be granted at the earliest six months prior to the long-term reintegration leave (para. 3).

6. In addition, at least four months of unsuspended imprisonment or pre-trial detention must have been served and at least half of the prison term.
7. Prisoners are in principle placed in a correctional institution or in a unit with a normal security level. If more security is needed, a detainee may be placed in an extended or extra security level.
8. Other factors also play a role in that decision, such as the possibilities of limiting and controlling the risks and the interests of victims, next of kin and other relevant persons, including the efforts made by the individual to compensate for the damage caused by the offence.
9. The behaviour of the convicted person, the possibilities to limit and control the risks and the interests of victims, next of kin and other relevant persons, including the efforts made by the convicted person to compensate for the damage caused by the crime (art. 4, para. 3, Penitentiary Act).
10. Vision 'Doing justice, offering opportunities', p. 4.
11. See for the advice and the response of the minister: https://www.rsj.nl/documenten/rapporten/2022/05/09/advies-levenslang-herzien.
12. Meijer (2022); S. Struijk, 'Wetsvoorstel Straffen en beschermen: wordt het kind met het badwater weggegooid?', *Sancties* 2020/13; S. Struijk, 'Duizelingwekkende en zorgwekkende ontwikkelingen in de rechtspositie van de gedetineerden', *Boom Strafblad* 2020/5; S. Meijer, 'Verscherpt toetsingskader promoveren en degraderen van gedetineerden', *Sancties* 2020/89. P. Schuyt, 'Voorwaardelijke invrijheidstelling: het beeld en de werkelijkheid', Sancties, 2019/2.
13. Vision, p. 7.

References

Andrews, A., Bonta, J., & Wormith, J. (2011). The Risk-Need-Responsivity (RNR) model. Does adding the good lives model contribute to effective crime prevention? *Criminal Justice and Behavior, 38*(7), 735–755.

Boschman, S., Teerlink, M., & Weijters, G. (2020). *Monitor Nazorg Ex-gedetineerden—6^e meting*. WODC.

Bosma, A., Kunst, M., Dirkzwager, A., & Nieuwbeerta, P. (2020). Recidivism after a prison-based treatment program: A comparison between a treatment and control group using proportional weighting within strata. *Journal of Developmental and Life-Course Criminology, 6*, 95–126.

Doekhie, J. (2019). Dimensions of desistance. A qualitative longitudinal analysis of different dimensions of the desistance process among long-term prisoners in the Netherlands. Doctoral Thesis. Universiteit Leiden.

Elbers, J., van Ginneken, E., Boone, M., Nieuwbeerta, P., & Palmen, H. (2021). Straffen en belonen in detentie Een Planevaluatie Van Het Nederlandse Systeem Van Promoveren En Degraderen. *Tijdschrift Voor Criminologie, 3*, 263–291.

Giordano, P., Cernkovich, S., & Rudolph, J. (2002). Gender, crime and desistance: Toward a theory of cognitive transformation. *American Journal of Sociology, 107*(4), 990–1064.

Meijer, S. (2022). *In all its facets. On the meaning of the principle of rehabilitation*, Radboud University.

Meijer, S., & Hamelzky, Y. (2022, April). Re-integratieverlof voor gedetineerden. *Sancties*.

Molleman, T., & Lasthuizen, K. (2015). De ervaren mogelijkheden om te reintegreren vanuit detentie. *Tijdschrift voor Veiligheid* (Vol. 0304).

Pasma, A., van Ginneken, E., Palmen, H., & Nieuwbeerta, P. (2022). Do prisoners with reintegration needs receive relevant professional assistance? *International Journal of Offender Therapy and Comparative Criminology*, Online first April 2022 1–23.

Rodermond, E., van de Weijer, S., Rosenkrantz Lindegaard, M., Bijleveld, C., Slotboom, A., & Kruttschnitt, C. (2022). Out of prison, out of crime? The complex interplay between the process of desistance and severe resource disadvantages in women's post-release lives. *European Journal of Criminology*, Online first 1–26.

Sampson, R. J., & Laub, J. H. (2003). Desistance from Crime over the Life Course. In T. Jeylan, T. Mortimer, & M. Shanahan. *Handbook of the Life Course* (pp. 295–310). Kluwer Academic/Plenum.

Schuyt, P. (2019). Voorwaardelijke invrijheidstelling: het beeld en de werkelijkheid. *Sancties*, 5–13.

Sered, S., & Norton-Hawk, M. (2020). Beyond recidivism and desistance. *Feminist Criminology, 16*(2), 165–190.

van Ginneken, E. (2018). Zelfredzaamheid in detentie. Kritische kanttekeningen bij het systeem van promoveren en degraderen. *Proces, Tijdschrift Voor Strafrechtspleging, 97*(2), 113–129.

Rehabilitation, Restoration and Reintegration in Aotearoa New Zealand

Alice Mills and Robert Webb

Until recently Aotearoa New Zealand had one of the highest rates of imprisonment in the OECD (Corrections, 2021a). The punitive nature of New Zealand society has had a disproportional impact on Māori, the Indigenous peoples of Aotearoa, who are highly over-represented in both correctional populations and the recidivism statistics. As in other comparable developed nations, probation in Aotearoa New Zealand initially focussed on befriending and assisting with the social rehabilitation of prisoners (Gibbs, 2000). However, in recent decades, justice sanctions and practices have shifted towards holding individuals to account for their actions and managing their compliance with various orders, requirements and conditions. Such an approach includes the adoption of actuarial-based risk management and addressing 'needs' through various cognitive-behavioural interventions which focus on individual pathology and assume offending is caused due to deficits in the individual's cognitive skills and capacities.

The adaption and indigenisation of these approaches for the New Zealand correctional population raises a number of issues to be explored by this

A. Mills (✉) · R. Webb
University of Auckland, Auckland, New Zealand
e-mail: a.mills@auckland.ac.nz

R. Webb
e-mail: robert.webb@auckland.ac.nz

chapter which aims to provide a critical analysis of current approaches to rehabilitation in Aotearoa New Zealand. It will first explore the history of probation and prison rehabilitative measures, including the mid-late 1990s shift to Integrated Offender Management and the 'risk, needs, responsivity' (RNR) model before critically evaluating the disciplinary hegemony of the psychological paradigm. The chapter then considers and reviews the concerns and issues related to the Indigenous Māori population, who are disproportionately impacted by criminal justice interventions and imprisonment. It examines the various attempts to indigenise correctional rehabilitative processes over several decades to make them more culturally appropriate for Māori, including the 'blending' of rehabilitation approaches with the incorporation of Māori culture into programme delivery and the development of interventions such as Te Tirohanga (prison Māori focus units). Potential future directions in rehabilitation in Aotearoa New Zealand are then discussed including recent government justice reforms and new strategies which seek to introduce a more community-orientated approach to correctional sanctions and to reduce the over-representation of Māori in the criminal justice system. Before this, a brief description of the prison and community penalties system in Aotearoa New Zealand will be given.

The Penal System in Aotearoa New Zealand

Ara Poutama Aotearoa is the recently adopted Māori name for the Department of Corrections, (hereafter known as 'Corrections') which is the agency responsible for managing individuals who are imprisoned, given a community sentence or are under some form of post-release supervision. In December 2021, 7702 people were incarcerated across 18 prisons in Aotearoa New Zealand, with 5.8% identifying as women and 53% as Māori (Corrections, 2022a). The prison population has declined in recent years, falling from a peak of 10,820 in March 2018 (Corrections, 2021a), for several reasons including the diversion of minor cases from the criminal justice system and improved bail and parole processes (Ministry of Justice, 2022).

There are five types of community sentences in Aotearoa New Zealand: community work, home detention, community detention, supervision, intensive supervision. In 2019–2020, over 20,000 people served a community sentence, with community work comprising 43% of all community sentences (Corrections, 2021b). Three sentences—supervision, intensive supervision and home detention—are focussed on rehabilitation, although they are also concerned with control, surveillance and punishment (Gibbs, 2021). Supervision is designed to ensure individuals address the causes of their offending and comprised 28% of community sentences in 2019–2020 (2021b). It can be imposed for between six months and one year and requires those on supervision to report to a probation officer at specified times. It may include restrictions on associating with certain individuals and/or on living and employment arrangements (Gibbs, 2021). People under supervision should attend appropriate rehabilitation programmes to address their needs (Corrections, 2022b), including education, employment or addictions treatment (Gibbs, 2000, 2021). Intensive supervision is designed for those assessed as medium to high risk of reoffending, convicted of serious offences and having complex/severe rehabilitative needs. It comprised 19% of community sentences in 2019/2020 (Corrections, 2021b) and can run from six months to two years, with same conditions as supervision plus additional obligations such as extra contact with probation officers or further attendance at rehabilitation programmes (Corrections, 2022c). Home detention is seen as the most severe and intensive community sentences and is designed as both a punishment and a rehabilitative option (Gibbs, 2021). In 2019/2020, it made up 6% of community sentences (Corrections, 2021b). Those subject to it are restricted to a certain address and electronically monitored (using a bracelet/anklet) 24 hours a day for up to one year. They are required to meet regularly with probation staff and complete various rehabilitative programmes (Gibbs, 2021).

Māori comprise 16.5% of the population in Aotearoa New Zealand (Stats NZ, 2020) and are over-represented amongst those given community sentences as well as in the prison population, with 43% of those sentenced to supervision, 47% sentenced to intensive supervision and 46% sentenced to home detention identifying as Māori (Corrections, 2021b). This situation should be understood in the context of ongoing and intergenerational trauma resulting from the processes of colonisation and neo-colonial policies, including dislocation from ancestral lands, Māori urbanisation, cultural assimilation and the undermining of tikanga Māori (Māori custom and protocol) (Andrae et al., 2017; Jackson, 1988; McIntosh & Workman, 2017; Quince, 2007; Webb, 2017). The consequences of this structural violence on Māori communities, coupled with institutionally racist social and political policies, include long-term social and economic marginalisation, violence, abuse, imprisonment, mental health and addiction issues and disconnection from whānau[1] (George et al., 2014; Jackson, 1988; Mihaere, 2015; Webb, 2017). Additionally, as an Indigenous and ethnic minority population, Māori have been subjected to extensive criminalisation and social control by the neo-colonial state (Webb, 2017), leading to cumulative, intergenerational disadvantage on Māori whānau and communities (George et al., 2014; McIntosh & Workman, 2017). This criminalisation means Māori are more likely to be processed into the criminal justice system—to be arrested, prosecuted, convicted, remanded and then to be sentenced to imprisonment—than other groups (Morrison, 2009). Rehabilitation has particular relevance and consequences for Māori as a result of this.

History of Rehabilitation in Aotearoa New Zealand

Through the First Offenders of Probation Act 1886, Aotearoa New Zealand was one of the first countries in the world to establish probation as an alternative to imprisonment. Under this legislation, those caught up in the system for the first time were to be befriended, helped and advised by unpaid probation officers who were charged with helping them to engage in meaningful activities in the hope avoiding future trouble (Gibbs, 2021). In 1913, the first probation volunteers linked to local branches of the Prisoners' Aid and Rehabilitation Society and the Salvation Army were licenced and required to report on the conduct, industry and progress of men in their care (Tennant, 2007). In 1954, the probation service became fully professionalised with paid staff and the Criminal Justice Act 1985 converted probation to a sentence in its own right and renamed it 'supervision'. In addition to administering community sentences, probation officers also supervise those on parole, life licence or other post-release conditions and provide pre-sentence reports and other services to courts (Gibbs, 2000).

Probation in New Zealand has since shifted from the initial focus on advising, assisting and befriending (Gibbs, 2000), to a more formalised emphasis on rehabilitation, control and risk management. During the 2000s and 2010s, home detention, community detention and intensive supervision which focus on surveillance and secure containment in the community were introduced, alongside new post-release orders such as extended supervision orders and post-detention conditions which are designed to track and supervise individuals at a high risk of reoffending after the end of their prison or home detention sentence (Gibbs, 2021). Such measures present a substantial barrier to legal rehabilitation, which addresses the restoration of the civil and legal rights of those who have offended (McNeill & Graham, 2020).

Rehabilitation Programmes—The Dominance of Risk, Needs and Responsivity

As in other jurisdictions, rehabilitation in Aotearoa New Zealand, both in the community and in prisons, moved from an emphasis on treatment models in 1960s/1970s to the notion that 'nothing works' in the 1980s. The Ministerial Inquiry into Prisons (Roper, 1989) identified that the prison system had largely failed to rehabilitate or deter and made recommendations for rehabilitation to be initiated outside of large prison institutions, advocating instead for smaller community-based and controlled 'habilitation centres' that would provide independent and therapeutic programmes. Despite this recommendation of community involvement from the Inquiry, Workman (2018) notes that the Justice Department was resistant to the idea of community rehabilitation, and the favoured approach was that the rehabilitation programmes should remain located within prisons.

From the early 1990s to the current era of rehabilitation, there has been a focus on evidence-based practice, cognitive-behavioural therapy and actuarial-based risk management. Community sentences and rehabilitation measures inside New Zealand prisons have been dominated by the risk, need and responsivity (RNR) model (Andrews & Bonta, 2010; Gibbs, 2021; Grace et al., 2017). Under this model, risk prediction factors, both static (such as demographic and criminal history variables) and dynamic (such as substance use), which may improve through treatment or change with the passage of time, are first assessed to determine the intensity of treatment (Grace et al., 2017). Corrections staff use a variety of risk assessment tools, including the RoC*RoI (Risk of Reconviction, Risk of Reimprisonment), developed by Corrections to measure static factors, and the Dynamic Risk Assessment for Offender Re-entry (DRAOR) (Grace et al., 2017; Johnston, 2015).

The principle of need then determines what dynamic risk factors, usually known as 'criminogenic needs', should be targeted by rehabilitative programmes (Grace et al., 2017). These may include factors relating to personality (such as aggression), lifestyle (such as substance use or associates) and social circumstances (such as low educational achievement or poor employment record) (Andrews & Bonta, 2010). Treatment usually involves various strategies to reduce the number or intensity of such factors in the person's life (Grace et al., 2017). Finally, responsivity refers to the development and delivery of programmes which are matched to the specific characteristics of participants such as their gender, learning style, world view and ability and desire to change their behaviour (Andrews & Bonta, 2010; Grace et al., 2017).

In the late 1990s, the Department of Corrections adopted Integrated Offender Management (IOM), an RNR-based strategy designed to reduce recidivism by coordinating the management of individuals both in prison and serving a community sentence or order (Gibbs, 2000). However, an evaluation of IOM in 2003 found its implementation was patchy, with assessment information often incomplete, a third of assessments over-ridden by staff, only around a fifth of prisoners having a sentence plan and only a quarter of these receiving treatment appropriate to their needs (Newbold, 2016).

Initially core rehabilitation programmes were local variants of programmes from overseas, notably from North America, which were adapted for New Zealand with the inclusion of victim awareness, relapse prevention and Māori terminology and cultural elements (Gibbs & Beal, 2000). These programmes are based on the cognitive-behavioural theory of change which assumes individuals have flaws or problems in their cognitive skills and capacities (for example, acting impulsively) that need to be corrected via psychological treatment (Wilson, 2016), including the development, and practising of new ways of thinking and skills which can be applied to everyday stressful encounters (Gibbs & Beal, 2000).

An early core programme was that of 'Straight Thinking', a hybrid version of the 'Reasoning and Rehabilitation' cognitive skills course from Canada (Gibbs & Beal, 2000). Straight Thinking was an intensive 70-hour group-work programme for those on community sentences with high to medium risk of offending, which was administered by probation officers (Gibbs & Beal, 2000). It was discontinued in 2006 after demonstrating no significant effect on recidivism rates (Johnston, 2015).

At several prisons, specialist units provide programmes that target certain categories of offending. These include Kia Marama, a specialist unit for addressing child sexual offending at Rolleston prison, which was the first structured, comprehensive group-based rehabilitation programme in Aotearoa New Zealand (Johnston, 2015). The programme incorporates various elements including victim impact and empathy, arousal conditioning, mood management (Hudson et al., 1998). A similar unit, Te Piriti at Auckland Prison (also known as Paremoremo) combines Western perspectives with traditional Māori concepts and approaches (Leaming & Wills, 2016; Thakker, 2014).

The design used in the Kia Marama programme has since been adapted for use in other treatment units such as the Special Treatment Unit Rehabilitation Programme for behaviour related to serious violent and sexual crimes. This in turn has been the template for a variety of lower-intensity rehabilitative programmes that are delivered both in prisons and in the community.

Examples include the Medium Intensity Rehabilitation Programme (MIRP), which aims to teach male inmates and those on community sentences with a medium risk of reoffending how to change the thoughts, attitudes and behaviour that led to their offending over a three-month period (Corrections, 2022d), the Short Rehabilitation Programme and short motivational programmes, which aim to increase motivation to participate in rehabilitation programmes (Durrant & Riley, 2021; Johnston, 2015). Kowhiritanga is a version of MIRP designed for female inmates (Corrections, 2022d) which places more emphasis on 'relational aspects of group processes' (Durrant & Riley, 2021: 269) and considers the higher prevalence of trauma/abuse history amongst the women's prison population (Grace et al., 2017).

Drug treatment units are designed to assist prisoners to address their dependence on alcohol or other drugs (Corrections, 2022d; Newbold, 2016) and shorter, lower intensity programmes to tackle drug and alcohol issues have also been offered in prisons and in the community (Corrections, 2022d; Johnston, 2015), although some have recently been discontinued leading to an 80% drop in prisoners receiving such treatment (Cheng, 2022).

The 2020–2021 Corrections' annual report indicates that while many forms of treatment or intervention appear to have a positive impact on rehabilitation, in only a small number of cases, do current reductions in recidivism reach the threshold for statistical significance. These include the MIRP programme which is associated with 7 and 8.7% decreases in re-sentencing[2] rates amongst those who completed the course in the prison and in the community respectively. Prison-based employment is associated with a 4.3% reduction in re-sentencing and the Short Rehabilitation Programme with a 5.9% in reduction in reimprisonment for men and 26% reduction in reimprisonment for women (Corrections, 2021a). Given that reductions in recidivism reach statistical significance for only a limited number of interventions, it is worth questioning the benefits of many rehabilitation programmes in relation to their costs.

After years of comparative neglect, Corrections has recently started to place more emphasis on assisting prisoners to reintegrate into the community after their release (Gibbs, 2021). Much reintegration support involves assistance with social issues such as stable housing, employment, education, vocational training, and reconnecting with whānau (Durrant & Riley, 2021; Gibbs, 2021; Mills & Lindsay Latimer, 2021), which international research has suggested are associated with reduced reoffending (Mills & Lindsay Latimer, 2021). This support involves Corrections working in partnership with other government departments, iwi (Māori tribe) and non-governmental organisations. Such initiatives include the Supporting Offenders into Employment scheme which uses Intensive Client Support Managers (ICSMs), employed by the Ministry of Social Development, to work with prisoners to secure employment and reduce barriers to employment (Lishman, 2018). Creating Positive Pathways is a trial scheme between Corrections, the Ministry of Social Development, the Ministry of Housing and Urban Development and local iwi and community groups to provide permanent housing and wraparound support services for those who are eligible for public housing and have served a long prison sentence or more than one short sentence, although the success of the scheme has been hindered by housing shortages (Malatest International, 2020). Initiatives involving partnership with iwi include Te Whare Oranga Ake units, the first of which was established in 2011, which provide a kaupapa Māori environment outside the prison walls with a 24-bed unit at Hawke's Bay Prison near Hastings, and later a 16-bed unit at Spring Hill near Te Kauwhata. Within the units, iwi-based community service providers provide prisoners with assistance in obtaining post-release accommodation, reconnecting with Māori culture, and forming supportive networks with iwi and hapū (Corrections, 2021c). However, these units offer just 40 places (Waitangi Tribunal, 2017) and expenditure on reintegration as a whole comprises just 17% of the rehabilitation budget (Cheng, 2022).

These Corrections-based reintegration units can be seen to follow the work by Māori and marae-based organisations that have existed for many years in the community. At Upper Hutt's Ōrongomai Marae, a reintegration programme called Te Hikoitanga has operated since 2004. It incorporated the concepts of Te Whare Tapa Wha[3] which refers to Māori health as having the four foundations of whānau (family), tinana (physical health), hinengaro (mental health) and wairua (spiritual wellbeing) (Bullen, 2018). A prisoner reintegration programme for men and women was also operated by the Manukau Māori Urban Authority (MUMA) alongside other social service programmes for the wider community (education, health, social services, whānau support, foodbank and restorative justice) at Nga Whare Waatea Marae. Called Nga Tupou Hou, the reintegration programme offered accommodation and tikanga focussed upon health, wellbeing and building connections to whānau.

Critical Issues to Current Approaches to Rehabilitation in Aotearoa New Zealand

There are a number of critical issues regarding the Aotearoa New Zealand approach to rehabilitation and in particular, the dominance of the RNR model and cognitive-behavioural approaches. Firstly, these rehabilitation programmes tend to have high attrition rates, suggesting that they fail to engage and motivate people to participate in this form of rehabilitation (Durrant & Riley, 2021), a problem which may be caused by the focus on criminogenic needs/risk factors as identified by Corrections rather than an individual's own perceptions of what they require (Durrant & Riley, 2021; Fox, 2014; Hannah-Moffatt, 2005). Secondly, such programmes may not be available for all those who could potentially benefit from them. For example, they may not be suitable for chaotic substance misusers or those with significant learning disabilities (Gibbs & Beal, 2000) and may not be available to those housed on segregation wings (Morrison & Bowman, 2019). Thirdly, the research on which these programmes are based has been criticised for lacking methodological rigour, with many such studies using small sample sizes, lacking control groups and being conducted by an 'in house' research team rather than receiving external scrutiny (Thakker, 2014). Evaluations of these programmes have relied on quantitative methods and statistical models (Gibbs, 2020) while neglecting how individual participants actually experience these programmes (Durrant & Riley, 2021), even though participant perspectives could offer valuable insights into addressing high attrition rates (Durrant & Riley, 2021) and the minimal effectiveness of some programmes.

Perhaps most importantly, rehabilitation programmes that attribute offending to individual pathology have been widely criticised for ignoring the wider socio-economic and historical context in which offending takes place, including broader social and structural inequalities (Hannah-Moffatt, 2005; Webb, 2018) which may substantially constrain the choices people are able to make. Furthermore, current approaches to reintegration in New Zealand are dominated by a needs-based support narrative which suggests that the multiple challenges of people leaving prison such as obtaining housing or employment must be addressed to reduce the risk of recidivism (Dorne, 2016; Maruna & LeBel, 2003). While meeting these practical needs remains important, these dominant models of rehabilitation and reintegration do not acknowledge the social process, conditions and inequalities which lead to the criminalisation of certain behaviours and populations (Webb, 2018), or the broader societal stigma and systemic challenges faced by those who have been imprisoned (Mills & Lindsay Latimer, 2021). Nor do they recognise or tackle the ongoing harmful legacies of colonisation and enduring structural violence towards Māori. As Mills and Lindsay Latimer (2021: 277) have noted, 'For Māori, reintegration involves not just reintegration into society but (re)integration into a colonial society'.

In focussing on these deficit-focussed models of both rehabilitation and reintegration, Aotearoa New Zealand has been slow to embrace research on desistance—'the state of being of not engaging in criminal activity for an extended period of time' (Fox, 2022: 1)—and interventions that may promote such desistance. Although Morrison and Bowman (2019) found that some probation officers engaged in practices to help facilitate desistance, this appears to be by accident rather than design. Explanations for desistance vary, however, as Fox (2022) argues, the thread that runs through the multiple pathways to desistance is the development of social capital, 'the web of relationships that might foster the achievement of certain goods' (Fox, 2022: 6). Such relationships are those between individuals and those who matter to them, and professionals who work with them (McNeil, 2012). Initiatives to develop social capital include Circles of Support and Accountability (CoSA) which uses a small group of community volunteers to support and help to meet the emotional, social and practical needs of those leaving prison (usually serious sex offenders) (Fox, 2022). Unfortunately, CoSA was abandoned in New Zealand after the high-profile prison escape of Philip John Smith (McCarten & Laws, 2018).

Inclusive, strengths-based approaches to rehabilitation, such as the Good Lives model, are more compatible with the development and maintenance of social capital (Fox, 2014; Moore, 2011; Workman, 2018). The Good Lives Model assumes inmates have the same human needs and common life goals as everyone else. Rather than purely focussing on deficits and risk, it emphasises the importance of harnessing individuals' specific interests and strengths to motivate long-term change (Purvis & Ward, 2020). It seeks to equip them with the internal and external capacities (including social support and interpersonal opportunities) to meet these needs in a non-harmful way (Leaming & Willis, 2016; Purvis & Ward, 2020; Ward & Stewart, 2003). Such approaches may be preferred by Māori, for whom whānau and community are seen as the source of health, identity and personal development (Leaming & Wills, 2016), and approaches that offer opportunities for people to take responsibility for their actions and restore the mana (prestige) of individuals, whānau and communities through relationship building are highly valued (Leaming & Wills, 2016; Workman, 2018).

Indigenisation of Rehabilitative Processes

Other forms of rehabilitation programmes that are unique to Aotearoa New Zealand are Corrections' Tikanga Māori programmes which adapted cognitive-behavioural therapy approaches and have the stated aim to help Māori inmates reconnect with their cultural heritage (Johnstone, 2015). These incorporate values, concepts, language and practices familiar to Māori and include cultural events, activities and mentoring by older community members (Durrant & Riley, 2021; Gibbs, 2000).

To understand the emergence of these particular interventions, it is important to examine the political context of the 1980s and 1990s in Aotearoa New Zealand when issues of biculturalism and multiculturalism were increasingly enacted in state policies. The development of cultural interventions by Corrections can be seen as one of the state responses to issues raised by the Māori community about monoculturalism in state policies. Two national inquiries from the 1980s into criminal justice policy and Māori communities summarise these concerns. The first of these, the Ministerial Advisory Committee's (1986) Review of the Department of Social Welfare, *Puao-Te-Ata-Tu* found that the state's policy responses for young Māori were largely ineffective and culturally inappropriate and called for more Māori community involvement and control over programmes for youth. This led to a major reform of the youth justice system with the implementation of new legislation for youth justice under the Children, Young Persons and their Families Act 1989,[4] and the introduction of the Family Group Conferencing model as an alternative process.

The second national inquiry looked at the adult criminal justice system. Moana Jackson's (1988) report for the Department of Justice, *Māori and the Criminal Justice System: He Whaipānga Hou*, highlighted Māori concerns about the state system. Jackson observed that Māori, like others in the system, were more likely to have experienced poor education, difficulties in family upbringing, unemployment and other factors which increased the likelihood of being caught up in criminal justice processes. However, for Māori, these factors had resulted from a history of marginalisation caused by colonization and state policies that suppressed Māori culture and community social controls. The report noted that the justice system and prisons were largely monocultural and that tikanga Māori would '… provide some insight into the complex questions of why some Māori men become criminal offenders and how the criminal justice process responds to them. It approaches the topic from within a Māori conceptual framework and seeks to explain Māori perception of the causes and consequences of criminal offending' (1988: 17). The report's recommendations for more Māori autonomy and community-based responses were largely ignored. Instead, the state continued to consolidate the use of imprisonment, and cultural elements have been integrated within that regime (Tauri & Webb, 2012).

From the 1990s, government agencies within the justice sector have followed the policy of being more culturally 'responsive' to Māori needs, which has entailed incorporating more Māori cultural values into the justice system. This has been achieved mainly through recruitment of Māori into the justice sector, and secondly through developing Māori service and community providers to deliver programmes to Māori. However, this process of indigenization has been critiqued for incorporating some cultural elements into practices, without altering the fundamental structure, philosophies, or control of the justice system by the state (Tauri & Webb, 2012).

Under Corrections' responsiveness policy tikanga Māori has been introduced into therapy programmes, and Corrections have developed Memorandum of Understandings (MOUs) to further relationships with Māori organisations and communities (Corrections, 2001a, 2002). In 1998, Psychological Services in Corrections introduced a rehabilitation programme for Māori called the 'Bi-cultural Therapy Model'. This model aimed to deliver psychological treatments with Māori service providers, and Māori tikanga was incorporated into psychological treatments. Corrections (2001a: 10) noted that 'Māori therapeutic programmes have been developed as "blended" programmes that incorporate tikanga Māori concepts alongside Western psychological concepts. These programmes provide a more focussed analysis of how Māori tikanga and concepts relate to specific offending behaviour'. This development, however, appears not to have altered the basic premise of programmes attributing offending to cognitive processes and individuals' pathological thinking. The 'treatment' response has simply been adapted by using Māori culture and tikanga in the rehabilitation process (Nathan et al., 2003).

Under the state's responsiveness mode, Māori Focus Units were developed, with the first being in place by 1997 (Corrections, 2001b). These units offer tikanga cultural instruction and te reo (Māori language) courses. The rationale from Corrections for developing these units is stated as to '…use Māori language and culture to create a change in the understanding, attitude, and behaviour of Māori offenders. The units require a commitment from participants to address the discrepancies between Māori tikanga and their current offending and lifestyle' (Corrections, 2002: 21). Within Māori focus units, cognitive-behavioural group-based Māori Therapeutic programmes (MTP) have been developed. An evaluation of these programmes by the Corrections (2009: 6–7) notes the similar approach to other rehabilitation programmes that utilizes cultural content in the delivery:

This content is similar to that used in existing mainstream rehabilitative programmes, centering on understanding the patterns of behaviour, emotion and interaction that lead up to 'relapse' into new offending. Participants are taught social, cognitive, and practical skills necessary to avoid such relapses. In exploring such issues, the MTP uses Māori cultural language, values, and narratives to assist participants' learning and change.

From 2012 Māori Focus Units were renamed Te Tirohanga, and Māori Therapeutic Programmes were later revised and renamed as Mauri Tu Pae (Campbell, 2016; Hape, 2017). Similar therapeutic programmes have been developed for Pasifika Peoples as part of cultural responsiveness, and the Saili Matagi at Spring Hill prison programme blends Samoan culture with cognitive psychological therapy in prison and is described by Corrections as a medium intensity rehabilitative programme (King & Bourke, 2017).

A study on the delivery of cultural programmes in New Zealand prisons by Mihaere (2015) found that while the stated intention of some programmes was to provide cultural support, they were dominated by the monocultural institutional and correctional philosophies and operated to meet the needs of the prison regime rather than the needs of Māori. Māori also have higher rates of recidivism with 43% on a community sentence and 64% leaving prison being re-sentenced within two years in comparison to 35 and 58%, respectively, for the general population (Corrections, 2021a). The disparity in recidivism rates for Māori and the lack of a specific strategy to reduce reoffending by Māori, were the subject of a successful claim to the Waitangi Tribunal,[5] which found that Corrections had breached the Treaty principles of equity and active protection of Māori interests by failing to reduce reimprisonment rates (Waitangi Tribunal, 2017). The release of the 2017 Waitangi Tribunal report therefore provides fresh impetus to a debate that has been going on since the inception of the risk, needs, responsivity framework in New Zealand corrections and criminal justice around appropriate models of rehabilitation for Māori.

Potential Future Directions in Rehabilitation in Aotearoa New Zealand

New strategies in the justice sector are currently attempting to address some of the criticism directed at state responses for not adequately considering or reducing the impact of imprisonment on the Māori community in particular. Many of these new reforms have consequently adopted Māori language names. Jackson's (1988) proposals of rebuilding and instituting

Māori social control over those that have offended are being revisited, alongside the ideas from the Ministerial Inquiry into Prisons (Roper, 1989) for more community-based rehabilitation. Since 2018 the Ministry of Justice, for example, has pursued a programme for criminal justice reform called Hāpaitia te Oranga Tangata: Safe and Effective Justice. As part of this programme, an independent Justice Advisory Group—Te Uepū Hāpai i te Ora—was formed to gather information from a public consultation process with a series of national and regional justice 'summits' being held across the country. The summit process was not without criticism for the lack of engagement with Māori, and because of these concerns a Māori justice hui (meeting) was subsequently organised called 'Ināia Tonu Nei (now is the time)—We lead. You follow' by Te Ohu Whakatika in 2018. The findings of this Māori summit called for the relocation of rehabilitation efforts to Māori-led, rather than state-led, responses, and that Te Ao Māori (the Māori world) should be central to justice reforms (Safe & Effective Justice Advisory Group, 2019).

After the justice summits, the Ministry of Justice released a report entitled 'He Waka Roimata' in 2019 to discuss the pertinent issues for justice in Aotearoa. Amongst the themes that emerged were the following:

- Too many people who have been harmed by crime feel unheard, misunderstood and re-victimised
- The number of Māori in the system is a crisis
- Violence is an enormous problem, particularly for families and children
- Formal justice processes fail us too often
- The system is too focussed on punishment and neglects prevention, rehabilitation, reconciliation and repair of the harm done by crime
- Individuals, families and whānau feel unsupported and disempowered by the system, and the ability of iwi, hapū, communities, NGOs, and others to provide support is constrained by the siloed nature of government structures and funding arrangements
- People experiencing mental distress lack the support they need (Te Uepū Hāpai i te Ora, 2019: 14)

The report indicated that many of these issues were best responded to as social issues outside of the crime control apparatus of the justice system and alongside responses from communities. Corrections also released the Hōkai Rangi Strategy 2019–2024 (Ara Poutama Aotearoa, 2019) as part of this wider sector reform work, which has also attempted to address the Waitangi Tribunal's (2017) findings regarding Corrections' obligation to reduce Māori reimprisonment rates. The Hōkai Rangi strategy refers to better engagement with Māori in the development and delivery of services and identifies the main areas that this will occur. Amongst these are descriptions of more shared decision-making with Māori, a humanising and healing approach focussed on respect and dignity of those in care and incorporating a Te Ao Māori worldview (Ara Poutama Aotearoa, 2019: 16–17).

The strategy also boldly signals a new focus on changing the standard rehabilitation models used by Corrections, stating, 'Why are we focussing on American, British, Australian models of rehabilitation? We know ourselves best!' (Ara Poutama Aotearoa, 2019: 25). Whether or not this will lead to an abandonment of all current practices and in particular the end of the dominance of cognitive-behavioural approaches is yet to be seen. Some commentators have suggested that with the recent slight increase in the over-representation of Māori in the prison population and continued cruel, inhuman and degrading treatment of prisoners, Hōkai Rangi has already failed (Johnsen, 2020; Trafford, 2022).

Conclusion

Approaches to rehabilitation in the adult penal system of Aotearoa New Zealand are overwhelmingly concerned with individual, personal rehabilitation (McNeill & Graham, 2020) as demonstrated by the dominance of deficit-focussed cognitive behavioural and needs-based models of support. 'Culturally responsive' rehabilitation programmes have simply grafted Māori culture and tikanga onto existing, individualistic approaches, rather than acknowledging and addressing the structural factors, including the ongoing legacies of colonisation, which are likely to lead to recidivism amongst Māori. The dominance of this model means the neglect of other forms of rehabilitation, suggested by McNeill and Graham (2020), which are likely to increase the chances of desistance, most notably social rehabilitation which entails the 'informal social recognition and acceptance of the returning citizen' (McNeill & Graham, 2020: 13), but also legal rehabilitation and moral rehabilitation, which is concerned with addressing any conflict between those who have offended, victims and the community. Without tackling these other forms of rehabilitation and the structural factors leading to offending, the effectiveness of current approaches to rehabilitation in Aotearoa will be severely undermined.

Notes

1. Whānau is a Māori language term which broadly translates as 'extended family'.
2. Re-sentencing refers to reoffending and receiving a Correction-managed sentence. This excludes fines and discharges.
3. Te Whare Tapa Wha is a well-established Māori health model developed by Mason Durie.
4. Now known as the Oranga Tamariki Act 1989.
5. The Tribunal determines whether matters are inconsistent with the principles of the Treaty of Waitangi (the founding document of New Zealand) and make recommendations to Governments on claims relating to the practical application of the Treaty (Waitangi Tribunal, 2017).

References

Andrae, D., McIntosh, T., & Coster, S. (2017). Marginalised: An insider's view of the state, state policies in New Zealand and gang formation. *Critical Criminology, 25*(1), 119–135. https://doi.org/10.1007/s10612-016-9325-8

Andrews, D. A., & Bonta, J. (2010). *The psychology of criminal conduct* (5th ed.). Anderson.

Ara Poutama Aotearoa. (2019). *Hōkai Rangi- Ara Poutama Aotearoa strategy 2019–2024*. https://www.corrections.govt.nz/__data/assets/pdf_file/0003/38244/Hokai_Rangi_Strategy.pdf

Bullen, J. R. (2018). *The effectiveness of the Ōrongomai Marae community reintegration programme led by ex-prisoners in Aotearoa/New Zealand*. Master of Social Practice unpublished thesis, Unitec Institute of Technology.

Campbell, N. (2016). The Department of Corrections' Tikanga-based programmes. *Practice: The New Zealand Corrections Journal, 4*(2), 5–8.

Cheng, D. (2022, March 31). Drastic fall in prisoner numbers, but does that make us all safer? *New Zealand Herald*. Available: https://www.nzherald.co.nz/nz/politics/drastic-fall-in-prisoner-numbers-but-does-that-make-us-all-safer/V4ZE4LGCASI37H5QH5EWXDD3MY/

Corrections. (2001a). About time: Turning people away from a life of crime and reducing reoffending. Department of Corrections.

Corrections. (2001b). Treaty of Waitangi strategic plan 2001b–2003. Department of Corrections.

Corrections. (2002). Department of corrections annual report 31 July 2001 to 1 June 2002. Department of Corrections.

Corrections. (2009). Māori focus units and Māori therapeutic programmes evaluation report. Department of Corrections.

Corrections. (2021a). Annual report 1 July 2020–30 June 2021a. https://www.corrections.govt.nz/__data/assets/pdf_file/0010/44398/Annual_Report_2020_2021a_Final_Web.pdf

Corrections. (2021b). Corrections volumes 2019–2020. https://www.corrections.govt.nz/__data/assets/pdf_file/0016/41191/Corrections_Volumes_Report_2019-2020.pdf

Corrections. (2021c). Evidential factsheets for Ara Poutama Aotearoa-Department of Corrections. Waitangi Tribunal Wai 2750.

Corrections. (2022a). Prison facts and statistics-December 2021. https://www.corrections.govt.nz/resources/statistics/quarterly_prison_statistics/prison_stats_december_2021

Corrections. (2022b). Supervision. https://www.corrections.govt.nz/working_with_offenders/community_sentences/sentences_and_orders/supervision

Corrections. (2022c). Intensive supervision. https://www.corrections.govt.nz/working_with_offenders/community_sentences/sentences_and_orders/intensive-supervision

Corrections. (2022d). Rehabilitation programmes. https://www.corrections.govt.nz/working_with_offenders/prison_sentences/employment_and_support_programmes/rehabilitation_programmes

Dorne, S. (2016). Reintegration services: Evidence brief. Ministry of Justice. https://www.justice.govt.nz/assets/Documents/Publications/Reintegration-services.pdf

Durrant, R., & Riley, J. (2021). Rehabilitation: Risks, needs, and building good lives. In E. Stanley, T. Bradley, & S. Monod de Froideville (Eds.), *The Aotearoa Handbook of Criminology* (pp. 264–275). University of Auckland Press.

Fox, K. (2014). Restoring the social: Offender reintegration in a risky world. *International Journal of Comparative and Applied Criminal Justice, 38*(3), 235–256. https://doi.org/10.1080/01924036.2013.848221

Fox, K. (2022). Desistance frameworks. *Aggression and Violent Behavior, 62*. https://doi.org/10.1016/j.avb.2021.101684

George, L., Ngamu, E., Sidwell, M., Hauraki, M., Martin-Fletcher, N., Ripia, L., Davis, R., Ratima, P., & Wihongi, H. (2014). Narratives of suffering and hope: Historical trauma and contemporary rebuilding for Māori women with experiences of incarceration. *MAI Journal, 3*(3), 183–196.

Gibbs, A. (2000). Community probation in Aotearoa New Zealand. *Vista, 6*(1), 21–32.

Gibbs, A. (2021). Community sentences: Expanding a system of control and surveillance. In E. Stanley, T. Bradley, & S. Monod de Froideville (Eds.), *The Aotearoa handbook of criminology* (pp. 225–238). University of Auckland Press.

Gibbs, A., & Beal, R. (2000). Straight thinking in New Zealand/Aotearoa. *Probation Journal, 47*(4), 250–255. https://doi.org/10.1177/026455050004700404

Grace, R. C., McLean, A., & Beggs Christofferson, S. (2017). Psychology and criminal justice. In J. Gilbert, & G. Newbold (Eds.), *Criminal Justice: A New Zealand Introduction* (pp. 167–179). Auckland University Press.

Hannah-Moffatt, K. (2005). Criminogenic needs and the transformative risk subject. *Punishment and Society, 7*(1), 29–51. https://doi.org/10.1177/1462474505048132

Hape, T. (2017). From Māori Therapeutic programmes to Mauri Tū Pae. *Practice: The New Zealand Corrections Journal, 5*(2): 66–69.

Hudson, S. M., Wales, D. S., & Ward, T. (1998). Kia Marama. In W. L. Marshall, Y. M. Fernandez, S. M. Hudson, & T. Ward (Eds.), *Sourcebook of treatment programs for sexual offenders* (pp. 17–28). Springer.

Jackson, M. (1988). Māori and the criminal justice: He whaipaanga hou: A new perspective; Part 2. Wellington: Department of Justice. https://safeandeffectivejustice.govt.nz/research/a-new-perspective-part-2/

Johnsen, M. (2020). Prison report shows failure to implement Hōkai Rangi strategy-advocate, RNZ, 15 Dec. https://www.rnz.co.nz/news/te-manu-korihi/432917/prison-report-shows-failure-to-implement-hokai-rangi-strategy-advocate

Johnston, P. (2015). Twenty years of corrections—the evolution of offender rehabilitation. *Practice: The New Zealand Corrections Journal, 3*(2), 5–9.

King, L., & Bourke, S. (2017). A review of the Saili Matagi Programme for male Pacifica prisoners. *Practice: The New Zealand Corrections Journal, 5*(2), 70–74.

Leaming, N., & Willis, G. (2016). The good lives model: New avenues for Māori rehabilitation? *Sexual Abuse in Australia and New Zealand, 7*(1), 59–69.

Lishman, R. (2018) Supporting offenders into employment. *Practice: The New Zealand Corrections Journal, 6*(2), 74–76.

Malatest International. (2020). Creating positive pathways: Process evaluation 2020. Malatest International.

Maruna, S., & LeBel, T. (2003). Welcome home? Examining the 'reentry court' concept from a strengths-based perspective. *Western Criminology Review, 4*(2), 91–107.

McCartan, K. F., & Laws, M.-A. (2018). Risk assessment and management of perpetrators of sexual abuse in New Zealand. *Sexual Offender Treatment, 13*(1/2). http://www.sexual-offender-treatment.org/174.html

McIntosh, T., & Workman, K. (2017). Māori and prison. In A. Deckert, & R. Sarre (Eds.), *The Palgrave handbook of Australian and New Zealand criminology, crime and justice* (pp. 725–736). Palgrave Macmillan.

McNeill, F. (2012). Four forms of 'offender' rehabilitation: Towards an interdisciplinary perspective. *Legal and Criminological Psychology, 17*(1), 18–36. https://doi.org/10.1111/j.2044-8333.2011.02039.x

McNeill, F., & Graham, H. (2020). Conceptualising rehabilitation: Four forms, two models, one process and a plethora of challenges. In P. Ugwudike, H. Graham, F. McNeill, P. Raynor, F. S. Taxman, & C. Trotter (Eds.), *The Routledge Companion to Rehabilitative Work in Criminal Justice* (pp. 10–19). Routledge.

Mihaere, R. (2015). A Kaupapa Māori analysis of the use of Māori cultural identity in the prison system. PhD thesis, Institute of Criminology Victoria University of Wellington. https://researcharchive.vuw.ac.nz/xmlui/handle/10063/4185

Mills, A., & Lindsay Latimer, C. (2021). (Re)integration: Re-centring strengths in communities. In E. Stanley, T. Bradley, & S. Monod de Froideville (Eds.), *The Aotearoa handbook of criminology* (pp. 276–288). University of Auckland Press.

Ministerial Advisory Committee. (1986). Puao-Te-Ata-Tu: A Māori perspective for the Department of Social Welfare. Department of Social Welfare.

Ministry of Justice. (2022). Justice sector projections 2021–2031. Ministry of Justice. https://www.justice.govt.nz/assets/Documents/Publications/FSJ0M-2021-Justice-Sector-Projections-Report.pdf

Moore, R. (2011). Beyond the prison walls: Some thoughts on prisoner 'resettlement' in England and Wales. *Criminology and Criminal Justice, 12*(2), 129–147. https://doi.org/10.1177/1748895811425445

Morrison, B. (2009). Identifying and responding to bias in the criminal justice system: A review of international and New Zealand research. Ministry of Justice.

Morrison, B., & Bowman, J. (2019). Towards 'a life more ordinary': The possibilities of desistance-orientated probation. *Advancing Corrections Journal, 7,* 19–33.

Nathan, L., Wilson, N., & Hillman, D. (2003). Te Whakakotahitanga—An evaluation of the Te Piriti special treatment programme for child sex offenders in New Zealand. Department of Corrections.

Newbold, G. (2016). *Crime, law and justice in New Zealand*. Routledge.

Purvis, M., & Ward, T. (2020). An overview of the Good Lives Model: Theory and evidence. In P. Ugwudike, H. Graham, F. McNeill, P. Raynor, F. S. Taxman, & C. Trotter (Eds.), *The Routledge Companion to Rehabilitative Work in Criminal Justice* (pp. 90–103). Routledge.

Quince, K. (2007). Māori and the criminal justice system in New Zealand. In J. Tolmie, & W. Brookbanks (Eds.), *Criminal Justice in New Zealand* (pp. 333–358). LexisNexis.

Roper, C. (1989). *Prison Review Te Ara Hou: The new way. Ministerial committee of inquiry into the prisons system.* Crown.

Safe and Effective Justice Advisory Group. (2019). Ināia Tonu Nei Hui Māori Report. Safe and Effective Justice Advisory Group.

Stats NZ. (2020). Ethnic group summarises reveal New Zealand's multicultural make-up. https://www.stats.govt.nz/news/ethnic-group-summaries-reveal-new-zealands-multicultural-make-up

Tauri, J., & Webb, R. (2012). A critical appraisal of responses to Māori offending. *International Indigenous Policy Journal, 3*(4), 1–16. https://doi.org/10.18584/iipj.2012.3.4.5

Tennant, M. (2007). *The fabric of welfare: Voluntary organisations, government and welfare in New Zealand 1840–2005*. Bridget Williams Books.

Te Uepū Hāpai i te Ora. (2019). He Waka Roimata: Transforming our criminal justice system. Wellington: Ministry of Justice.

Thakker, J. (2014). Cultural factors in offender treatment: Current approaches in New Zealand. *Procedia- Social and Behavioral Sciences, 113,* 213–223. https://doi.org/10.1016/j.sbspro.2014.01.028

Trafford, W. (2022). Māori overrepresentation in prison climbs, minister concedes 'failure', Te Ao Māori news, 2 May. https://www.teaomaori.news/maori-overrepresentation-prison-climbs-minister-concedes-failure

Waitangi Tribunal. (2017). Tu Mai te Rangi! Report on the Crown and disproportionate reoffending rates. Waitangi Tribunal.

Ward, T., & Stewart, C. A. (2003). The treatment of sex offenders: Risk management and good lives. *Professional Psychology: Research and Practice, 34*(4), 353–360. https://doi.org/10.1037/0735-7028.34.4.353

Webb, R. (2017). Māori experiences of colonisation and Māori criminology. In A. Deckert, & R. Sarre (Eds.), *The Palgrave Handbook of Australian and New Zealand criminology, crime and justice* (pp. 683–696). Palgrave Macmillan.

Webb, R. (2018). Rethinking the utility of the risk factors and criminogenic needs approaches in Aotearoa New Zealand. *Journal of Global Indigeneity, 3*(1), 5. https://www.journalofglobalindigeneity.com/article/33224-rethinking-the-utility-of-the-risk-factors-and-criminogenic-needs-approaches-in-aotearoa-new-zealand

Wilson, D. B. (2016). Correctional programs. In D. Weisbund, D. P. Farrington, & C. Gill (Eds.), *What works in crime prevention and rehabilitation* (pp. 193–217). Springer.

Workman, K. (2018). *Kim Workman: Journey towards justice*. Wellington: Bridget Williams Books.

An Overview of Rehabilitation Mechanisms in Nigeria's Criminal Justice System

Emmanuel C. Onyeozili and Bonaventure Chigozie Uzoh

In his most acclaimed work, *The Rules of the Sociological Method*, Durkheim (1895) posited that 'crime is "normal" in the sense that a society without crime would be pathologically overcontrolled'. It would therefore not be an overstatement to say that it is impossible to find a society of saints where there are no criminal activities. This clearly explains the need for the establishment of institutions saddled with the responsibilities to prevent and control criminality, and punish, reform, and rehabilitate those found guilty of crime. Hence, the need for institutions such as law enforcement, courts, and prisons (Oroleye, 2018). These institutions together form the Criminal Justice System (CJS).

Administration and dispensation of justice in general, and that of criminal justice in particular, play an important role in governance irrespective of the system of government in place. If society is to remain at peace, individuals with criminal tendencies must be placed under close watch and their activities

---

E. C. Onyeozili (✉)
University of Maryland Eastern Shore, Salisbury, MD, USA
e-mail: econyeozili@umes.edu

B. C. Uzoh
Department of Sociology/Anthropology, Nnamdi Azikiwe University, Awka, Nigeria
e-mail: bc.uzoh@unizik.edu.ng

monitored and checked (Okorie-Ajah, 2018). However, when the activities of individuals and groups offend social norms and established laws, the criminal law must intervene to do justice to all concerned including the perpetrators, their victims, and society at large (Babalola, 2014; Okorie-Ajah, 2018).

The fundamental nature of justice is most obvious in the criminal justice field where all the parties deserve justice. The person accused of having committed a crime, the victim, the society at large all deserve justice (Obeagu, 2008; Okorie-Ajah, 2018). Everyone deserves justice and this is exactly why Okorie-Ajah (2018) stated that citizens cannot survive unreasonable and unbearable social conditions unless the administration of criminal law is anchored in justice. The accused person who sets the machinery of justice in motion and the society whose law has been violated, all deserve justice.

Nigeria's Criminal Justice System stands on a tripod consisting of the police, the courts, and corrections. Over the years the system has played a crucial role in the maintenance of law and order (Ukwayi & Ukpa, 2017). According to Ikoh (2011 cited in Ukwayi & Okpa, 2017), the system is an embodiment of crime regulating techniques, which represent the whole range of government agencies that function as instruments of the state to enforce rules necessary for the maintenance of peace and order. Its task is carried out through the means of detecting, apprehending, prosecuting, adjudicating, and sanctioning those members of society who violate its established laws (Ugwoke, 2010 cited in Ukwayi & Okpa, 2017). The effectiveness of the system is measured by its ability to meet the goals of deterrence, incapacitation, retribution, rehabilitation, and reintegration. The realisation of such goals is dependent on the level of coordination among the various components of the Criminal Justice System (Ikoh, 2011; Ukwayi & Okpa, 2017).

Okorie-Ajah (2018: 2) argues that 'it is pathetic that the Criminal Justice System in Nigeria has failed woefully and not much is being done by the Federal and State Governments to address the causes of this problem'. Failure of the criminal justice administration in Nigeria is manifested in many ways including the large number of people languishing in jail awaiting trial, thousands of corruptions and financial crime cases weighing down the judicial system, poor correction, and the rehabilitation of prisoners. Eze and Okafor (2007, cited in Okorie-Ajah, 2018) observed that the pathetic conditions of Nigeria Prisons have sent out signals that prisons are incapable of delivering their mandate which is to change prisoners into better citizens. Moreover, correctional service facilities in Nigeria are overstretched making them unbearable for the prisoners, thereby resulting in frequent jailbreaks. In most of the prisons, there is a shortage of bed spaces to the extent that most of the prisoners sleep on bare floors. In addition, the environments are unhygienic with poor ventilation and poor sanitary conditions (Okorie-Ajah, 2018). This chapter, therefore, takes an overview of the rehabilitation mechanisms in the Criminal Justice System in Nigeria.

A Brief Introductory History of Rehabilitation Mechanisms in Nigeria's Criminal Justice System

History (Ikoh, 2011) has it that in pre-colonial Nigeria there were temporal detention centreprisoners in some parts of the region. These were where people who violated the social norms and values of the society were either kept for trial or punishment. Among the Yoruba people of southwest Nigeria, there were holding places in 'Ogboni' house. In Tivland in North-Central part of Nigeria, a building was set aside in the Chief's compound. There were also the 'Ewedo' in Bini Kingdom and the 'Gidan Yari' among the Hausas and Fulanis. People who wanted redress from those that wronged them allowed society to determine appropriate punishments for offences committed. Punishment was seen as the best approach to making people show remorse for their actions and turn over a new leaf. It was also expected to serve as a deterrence to others (Ikoh, 2011).

The advent of colonialism led to the emergence of modern prisons. The prison system was modelled after the British system (Ikoh, 2011). After the amalgamation of the Colony and Protectorates of Southern and Northern Nigeria to form the Colony and Protectorate of Nigeria, Lord Lugard took it upon himself to integrate the administration of the whole country by bringing together various government departments (Ahire, 1995). In 1916, therefore, the Prisons Ordinance was established to formalise the establishment of prisons and the regulation of their operations. The Prisons Ordinance gave the governor power to establish and regulate prisons, to declare any building to be a prison; and to appoint the Director of Prisons and other prison officials to manage and coordinate the activities of the whole prison system (Ahire, 1995; Ikoh, 2011). The Director of Prisons was also empowered to make standing orders for the organisation, discipline, control, and general administration of staff and prisoners (Dambazau, 1999 cited in Ikoh, 2011).

Prisons were categorised into three types, namely, maximum-security prisons, provincial prisons, and divisional or native authority prisons. Maximum-security prisons in Lagos (Kirikiri), Enugu, Calabar, and Oji River had high walls around them and held people serving long sentences (Ikoh,

2011), whereas provincial prisons in Owerri, Ogoja, Makurdi, and Onitsha housed people whose sentences were not more than two years, and divisional prisons in Nsukka, Uyo, Itu, Okitipupa, Umuahia, and Kano housed those whose sentences were less than two years (Ikoh, 2011). Generally speaking, colonial prisons were highly militarised, mainly because many of the colonial prison directors were former military personnel who brought a military disposition towards regimentation and authoritarianism into their work. This from all indications delayed the emergence of a prison tradition geared towards reformation and rehabilitation (Ahire, 1995). Moreover, early colonial prisons were established and operated on a crude penal philosophy of custody, containment, and punishment. It is unsurprising, therefore, that the prisons had no properly trained staff, and food and sanitary conditions were deplorable thereby giving rise to very high mortality rates (Ahire, 1995); and infrastructural facilities in the prisons were very poor and inadequate for any meaningful classification of prisoners. In addition, conditions of service of prison staff (Ahire, 1995) were so poor and unattractive that the prisons became a dumping ground for unambitious people. As a result of these numerous shortcomings, colonial prisons could not offer anything in terms of correction, reformation, and rehabilitation. Facilities available for vocational training in trades such as shoe making, printing, tailoring, and smithery were poor and limited. In effect, prisons simply served the colonial state as detention centreprisoners for indigenous protesters against obnoxious and draconian colonial policies (Ahire, 1995; Ikoh, 2011).

At some point, the colonial state needed to change from the penal philosophy of custody and retribution to that of reformation and rehabilitation to expand its power base and make its forms of control look subtler and more sustainable (Ahire, 1995; Ikoh, 2011). Unfortunately, the reforms that followed could not change the poor image of the prisons. For instance, the state could not finance the reconstruction of new prisons needed to implement the reforms, and this explains why the Garrat Report of 1960 observed that Nigerian prisons were grossly overcrowded, dirty, and understaffed, conditions which frequently resulted in rioting by the prisoners and breakdown of law and order (Awe, 1968 cited in Ahire, 1995). Most importantly, prison reforms could not be achieved because of major contradictions in a social structure that made the philosophy of reformation and rehabilitation impracticable (Ahire, 1995).

The Nigeria Prison Service has experienced significant changes in organisation, character, and role since Nigeria attained political independence in 1960. After independence, the department was reorganised, indigenised, and put under the authority of the Ministry of Internal Affairs. In 1971, the government released the White Paper on the reorganisation of the Prisons Department and the integration of Native Authority Prisons. The White Paper charged the department with the task of identifying the causes of the anti-social behaviour of those who commit crimes and ways of reforming them to be useful to themselves and to society (Ahire, 1995). This was followed by Prison Decree No. 9 of 1972 which emphasised secure custody and even made provision for applying hard labour to certain categories of prisoners, thus contradicting the emphasis placed by the White Paper (Ahire, 1995).

The Nigeria Prisons Service made claims about its primary role being to ensure the safe custody of prisoners and their reformation and rehabilitation through well-designed administrative and rehabilitative programmes, and took exception to the archaic and outdated emphasis of colonial prisons custody and deprivation. It also claimed to have embraced the philosophy of reformation and rehabilitation (Ahire, 1995; Ikoh, 2011). Empirical observations, however, suggest that the service still has not been able to achieve many of its goals. Many of its facilities built a long time ago are overcrowded, prison employees are neither properly uniformed nor well remunerated, and prisons are still poorly funded making it difficult to secure the resources needed to improve the welfare of prisoners (Erinosho, 1999 cited in Ikoh, 2011). In turn, the government deemed it fit to rename 'prison' with its emphasis on punishment, the Nigerian Correctional Service (NCS). It also introduced the non-custodial options of parole, probation, and community service. It was thought that this would give the service a new lease of life and lead to reform and treatment rather than just punishment (Ulo, 2019). Accordingly, on August 14, 2019, a new phase of prison reform was initiated when the President signed the Nigerian Correctional Service Act (NCSA) into law and repealing the old Nigeria Prisons Act of 1972.

Current Mechanisms of Rehabilitation and Their Policy in Nigeria's Criminal Justice System

Nigeria as a nation is facing a serious upward trend in recidivism as a large number of its released prisoners are relapsing into crime and criminality. This development has challenged the practicality and feasibility of rehabilitation policies and programmes in the Nigeria Prison System (Otu, 2015). In reality, the reformation of prisoners has not been effective because released prisoners are shown to have become more hardened and incorrigible social liabilities after release. In the face of this, the NCSA addresses the issues facing both the custodial service and the non-custodial service (Ulo, 2019), and its aim is to redirect the focus to correction and promote reformation, rehabilitation, and reintegration; the Custodial Service takes control of persons legally interned in safe, secure, and humane conditions and provides support to facilitate speedy disposal of cases of persons awaiting trial; and the non-custodial service assumes responsibility for the administration of non-custodial measures such as community service, probation, parole, restorative justice measures and such other measures that may be ordered by the courts (Ulo, 2019). The NCSA includes a number of distinguishing features:

- It empowers the State Comptroller of Prisons to reject additional prisoners where the prison in question is already filled.
- It stipulates that the NCS will be headed by the Comptroller-General and a minimum of eight Deputy Comptroller-Generals.
- It states that the NCS must initiate behaviour modification of prisoners through the provision of medical, psychological, spiritual, and counselling services for all including violent extremists.
- It also states that where a prisoner sentenced to death has exhausted all legal procedure for appeal and a period of 10 years has elapsed without the execution of the sentence, the Chief Judge may revert the death sentence to life imprisonment.
- It prohibits torture, inhumane and abusive treatment of prisoners (Agbola, 2019 cited in Ulo, 2019).

This new law has obviously changed the Nigeria Criminal Justice System and, by implication the penological understanding of imprisonment from the orientation of punishment to treatment and reform with the sole objective of rehabilitation. This will be commendable only if it translates into reality at the level of implementation (Ulo, 2019). Not only must the tenets of the CSA be held sacrosanct by all the stakeholders if they are to succeed, but there is urgent and serious need for the NCS to be well-equipped and upgraded in manpower, infrastructure, and technology (Ulo, 2019). Furthermore, the NCSA directs the NCS to provide opportunities for education, vocational training as well as training in modern farming techniques and animal husbandry. Accordingly, the service is to establish and run, in designated Correctional Centers, industrial centres equipped with modern facilities and administered for the purpose of generating income which should be shared between the prisoners project participants (Tarhule, 2019). The NCSA commands the NCS to assist prisoners towards effective re-integration by providing the required funds for the transportation of discharged prisoners to their homes and to offer alternative support services as appropriate (Tarhule, 2019). To avoid stigmatisation of individuals that have exhibited exemplary behaviour, the law empowers the Comptroller-General to recommend to the Board the issuing of a certificate of good behaviour that ensures the prisoner is not discriminated against on account of the custodial sentence. Finally, in the face of Nigeria's refusal to abolish death penalty (Tarhule, 2019), section 12 (2) of the NCSA becomes a tool to save those on death-row who have suffered the dehumanising agony of waiting endlessly for execution.

An evaluation of these new developments reveals that this is the first substantive enactment of comprehensive provisions on the welfare and aftercare of prisoners in Nigeria. Under the repealed Act of 1972, some of these issues had been left to the Prison Regulations and Standing Orders (subsidiary legislation) and consequently treated with levity (Tarhule, 2019). Tarhule (2019) also observed that apart from elevating these provisions to substantive law, they are now more detailed and include the provision of new welfare packages to assuage the plight of prisoners. A holistic implementation would no doubt put Nigerian Correctional Facilities on a par with standard acceptable practices in other countries, thereby upgrading the standard of the criminal justice administration.

Rehabilitation and Diversity

Apparently, the personality, status, and ethnic group to which an individual belongs do influence the outcome of cases in Nigerian Criminal Justice System. As a matter of fact (Okorie-Ajah, 2018), people that are sentenced to jail are mostly from the lower socioeconomic strata of the society. Similarly, youthful, and female prisoners face a lot of challenges in the correctional centres because most were built without any consideration or provision for young and female prisoners; but they still host female prisoners. Moreover, cases of rape, unwanted pregnancies, and extra-judicial killings abound in Nigeria correctional centres and some judges abuse court processes in the guise of using discretion in some cases (Okorie-Ajah, 2018) This use of discretion by judges, especially the wrong discretion, often leads to miscarriage of justice against, or in favour of a defendant. That said, the NCSA is helping to address several issues including the problem of having minors detained in prison custody as they can benefit from the new non-custodial services. A provision under section 35 of the NCSA regarding facilities for youths in each State of the Nigeria federation, addressed the problem of having underage persons in adult prisons (Ulo, 2019). Combined, these changes will save the government money and create more opportunities to avoid low-risk individuals being socialised into a more criminal culture by high-risk and hardened criminals (Ulo, 2019).

It is expected that the NCSA will bring huge relief to the entire prison community, particularly for first-timers detained for minor infractions, who instead of confinement in prison, will now be let out for community service. The non-custodial system which features the incorporation of probation and parole into the NCS will guide probationers and parolees in proper ways of conducting themselves (Ulo, 2019). Availability of these modes of reform will expectedly reduce prison congestion and work overload. Ulo (2019) anticipates that the new rehabilitation-focussed approach will result in a win–win situation in which the society and victims will benefit from the free services rendered by the participants who, in turn, will have time to reflect on their past misdeeds. Additionally, given a second chance with community service, they will benefit by not being incarcerated and having the opportunity to be useful to themselves and their families.

Another significant import of the extant NCSA is the listing of every correctional centre with a clearly identified security level. As a result of this, maximum-security custodial centres, which as the name implies, are the most secure in Nigeria, have a high level of security involving use of close circuit television, electric fencing, electronic scammers, and high-level technology meant for high-risk individuals of all classes; and medium security custodial centres have reasonable levels of security reserved for prisoners of all classes. Alongside these, are clearly designated open custodial centres for the treatment of long-term first-timers, farm centreprisoners for prisoners with good conduct who have six months or less to serve, and satellite custodial facilities for prisoners serving three months imprisonment or less. Under the NCSA, people awaiting trial for minor offences who are required to be presented in courts, are housed in holding locations without major custodial facilities, while Borstal institutions are designated for the detention of juveniles. Additionally, female custodial facilities all classes of female prisoners are now mandated. These are issues that were completely absent in the 1972 Prison Act (Agomoh, 2019; Ahmed, 2019; Ulo, 2019).

One most significant Benefits of the NCSA that for the first time in the history of Nigeria, a statute has designated specific custodial centres for women. To complement the provision, section 34(1) of the Act directs the NCS to provide separate facilities for female prisoners in all the States with necessary facilities for addressing their special needs, such as medical and nutritional, including those of pregnant women, nursing mothers and babies in custody (Ahmed, 2019; Ulo, 2019). Although the 1972 Act was silent on this, in most jurisdictions custodial sections for women had been separate from those of male prisoners convicts. In Lagos for example, there was a least one prison that was reserved solely for women. It is hoped that this provision will instigate the emergence of more separate facilities designed and built for female prisoners to be able to take care of their particular needs (Agomoh, 2019; Ulo, 2019).

Theoretical Underpinnings to Models of Rehabilitation

The theoretical underpinnings of models of rehabilitation include rehabilitation theory and functionalism or the functionalist theory. The basic assumption of rehabilitation theory is that people are not innately criminal, and it is possible to restore a criminal to useful life. The rehabilitation theory of penology draws its strength from Cesare Lombroso's biological school of criminology, which emphasises that crime is atavistic, a kind of disease, hence defining criminals as sick (Ulo, 2019). If criminals are sick individuals, what is required, therefore, is for them to be treated and cured of their ailment by reforming them, so they can become more useful to themselves and society at large.

The rehabilitation perspective gained popularity because of the realisation that retribution and deterrence theory placed more emphases on torture, punishment, and hard labour. Thus, it became clear at some point that punishment does not actually achieve its acclaimed objective of preventing and controlling criminal behaviour (Ulo, 2019). Subsequently, specific reformative techniques such as parole, probation, and community service were developed to help change people's attitude towards criminals. Also, influential at this point was an increased belief in the philosophy of humanism with its overriding concern for human welfare. All these factors played a dominant role in the development of the reformative perspective (Ulo, 2019).

The earliest proponents of rehabilitation school, such as John Howard (1726–1790), Samuel Romilly (1757–1818), Alex Maconochie, and John Augustus made penological history by developing probation and parole reformative treatment devices which emphasised reform, correction, and rehabilitation of prisoners rather than punishment (Iginovia et al., 2002 cited in Ulo, 2019). These scholars believed that rehabilitation is very important in helping an individual become a more productive and non-criminal member of her or his society. Throughout history, there have been different notions and ideas about which form of help should be rendered. No surprise then when the modern correctional system was developing, rehabilitation became the dominant model. As the term 'correction' suggests, it could be seen that the idea was to help the person lead a non-offending way of life. This is usually done by deploying educational programmes, faith-based programmes, drug treatment programmes, anger management programmes, and many more that are geared towards assisting the individual to become a better person (Ulo, 2019).

The rehabilitation theory was criticised during the early 1970s as the principal justification for imprisonment when reformers raised questions about the ethics of the rehabilitation model. However, rehabilitation has staged a comeback as many private, community, and even institutional corrections are rehabilitative-focussed, and many are reinventing and readopting the principles of rehabilitation (Ulo, 2019). Several comprehensive reviews of research (Robinson, 2008; Voorhis et al., 2007) on the effectiveness of correctional treatment have discovered that some treatment programmes do have positive outcomes in improving attitudes and behaviour and in reducing the tendency to return to a life of crime. The challenge really is to be able to identify which of the programmes will work best in particular settings.

In relating rehabilitation theory to the Nigeria situation, one would say that with the introduction of the NCSA, the stage is set for positive fundamental changes in the treatment of prisoners. The current situation is in sharp contrast to the old prison system and prison practices that resulted in a high recidivism rate after release. It is good news that Nigerian government chose to join the community of nations in transitioning to internationally acceptable humane standard by replacing the punitive prison system with rehabilitation-oriented correctional practice. The NCS has also incorporated the non-custodial options of probation, parole, and community service. In Nigeria, the treatment of those who break the law is now taking on a more humane outlook as the focus has shifted to correction and rehabilitation.

Functionalism on the other hand views society as a social system made up of interdependent and interrelated components that function harmoniously for the benefit of the entire social system. In this context, the law enforcement agencies, the judiciary, and the correctional institutions are meant to work harmoniously together to ensure efficient functioning of the Criminal Justice System. Functionalism as a theoretical orientation in the social sciences leads the way in portraying correctional services as institutions for therapeutic treatment, reformation, and rehabilitation (Ahire, 1995). This viewpoint dwells on the notion that crime is a deviation from standard accepted norms of society, and so those who commit crime are non-conformists as the result of inadequate or improper socialisation by primary socialising agencies, especially the family (Ahire, 1995). Functionalism provides a better understanding of the correctional service as both a structural and functional entity in the society. The major thrust of this theory, some of whose major proponents include Emile Durkheim and Robert Merton, is that social structure is an abstraction based on social relationship with which the society can be analysed as having three main levels of individuals, institutions, and subsystems (Obioha, 2011). In applying this assumption to the correctional service, society is seen as a functional, structural whole with different parts. This implies that aspects of the correctional service such as the norms, values, and folkways form integral parts of the institutional systems of social control, and other behavioural patterns (Obioha, 2011). It is expected that with the NCSA, stakeholders in the criminal justice system will work harmoniously together to ensure that from the arrest to prosecution and eventual conviction or acquittal, justice and fair play will prevail. The NCSA, therefore, is a clear statement that people sent to prison are there to be corrected, reformed, and rehabilitated so that they will come out as better persons.

Like functionalist theory, Robert Merton's Social Structure perspective (1949) identified and distinguished the manifest and latent functions of institutions and cultural traits. This perspective is an appropriate model for understanding the intended and unintended functions of the CS (Obioha, 2011). These functions, which include custody of prisoners, social control, regimented culture, and seclusion, are designed to produce positive results in the life of the individual upon release. The whole re-socialisation processes in the NCS are intended to reform and rehabilitate the individual. Thus, the prison culture is perceived from Merton's social structure perspective as capable of producing both well-adjusted and mal-adjusted individuals in the society (Obioha, 2011). In the Nigerian context, before now, the purpose of sending people to prison was not fulfilled because they were likely to be more hardened than they were before imprisonment. The functional parts of the prisons were broken thereby by preventing the maintenance and improvement of the whole structure of the prisons system (Obioha, 1995, 2011). To prepare the prisoners for eventual meaningful contribution to the development of the nation, it is important to treat them with dignity, however, prison facilities have been enormously beset with problems, which several studies have identified as reasons for the inadequacies of the NCS as a corrective system (Adetula et al., 2010; Obioha, 2011). Against this brief theoretical background, it is argued that the Nigerian prison system should be made more responsive and productive in handling of prisoners. As the prison system in Nigeria has been replaced with the NCS, and the focus has shifted from punishment to reform, correction, and rehabilitation, there is now light at the end of the tunnel with the hope that most of the prisoners in these institutions will gradually begin to improve. There have been calls for strict implementation of both the custodial and non-custodial components of the new Act as a recipe for the desired change. Strict implementation will ensure that the change is not only in name but also in practice.

Research Findings: Effectiveness of Rehabilitation Mechanisms

Many researchers (Alamu & Makinde, 2019; Okorie-Ajah, 2018; Olojede & Mohammed, 2020; Oroleye, 2018; Uche et al., 2015) have conducted studies aimed at examining the effectiveness of the reformation and rehabilitation programmes in Nigeria prisons. Their findings show that the implementation of reformation and rehabilitation programmes transitioning the Nigeria Prison System to the Nigeria Correctional Service is ineffective and inefficient. Oroleye (2018) conducted a study where he assessed the extent of implementation and administration of rehabilitation programmes and examined the welfare of prisoners in selected prisons in Southwest Nigeria. The study which employed both primary and secondary data was undertaken with a view to enhancing policies and programmes of the prison service in the country. Primary data was obtained through the administration of questionnaires to the prisoners to elicit information on their well-being. The simple random sampling technique was used to select 204 respondents which constituted 10% of the total population (2024) of prisoners in the purposively selected prisons (Ibadan, Akure, Abeokuta) in Southwest Nigeria. A focus Group Discussion was held with 8 ex-prisoners and 5 relatives.

The secondary sources of information that were employed included relevant official publications and records from Nigerian Prisons Service, journal articles, periodicals, and internet sources. Data collected was analysed, interpreted, and presented using descriptive statistics such as frequency tables and simple percentages and the chi-square inferential statistics. The study found that administration of rehabilitation programmes of the Nigerian Prison Service was not effectively implemented. The study also found that the welfare of individuals in selected prisons was not well taken care of. The study concluded that the administration of rehabilitation and welfare programmes by the Nigeria Prison service in Southwest Nigeria was ineffective and needed to be improved to achieve the goal for which it was established.

Uche et al.'s (2015) study aimed at finding out prisoners' perception of the effectiveness of rehabilitation programmes in Nigerian Prison Service with reference to Enugu prison. The study adopted a cross-sectional survey design. A total of one hundred and forty-five (145) prisoners comprised the target population for the study. The data was collected using study questionnaire and, Statistical Package for the Social Sciences (SPSS), frequency tables and percentages (%) were employed in the processing, interpretation, and presentation of analysed data. The result showed that rehabilitation programmes in the prisons have not achieved much. It was also discovered that the duration of service for the prisoners does not make them to be actively involved in rehabilitation programmes. A majority of the respondents agreed that lack of funds and inadequate funding constituted a major hindrance to the programmes. It was recommended that social workers and philanthropists should contribute to ensuring that adequate facilities are provided to enhance the effectiveness of the rehabilitation programmes.

Another study (Okorie-Ajah, 2018) was conducted on the criminal justice administration and panic of corrections in Nigeria. The study found that the problems in Nigeria's criminal justice administration, especially the prisons, are so blatant and egregious that Nigeria prisons have become breeding ground for criminals instead of being corrective homes. The study was anchored in a two-factor theory of motivation and documentary research method; newspapers, textbooks, government publications, and internet materials formed the basis for data collection. Furthermore, the study recommended that unethical practices by criminal justice administrators need to be checkmated and effectively controlled for the efficient correction of prisoners. It also showed a need to introduce non-custodial sentences into the Nigeria justice system since the Nigerian prisons have failed to reform and correct the imprisoned as expected.

In line with the previous research, Olojede and Mohammed (2020), studied the effectiveness of the NCS in the rehabilitation of prisoners through recreational education in Minna, Niger State. A sample of 62 respondents drawn from a population of 635 prisoners representing 10% of the prisoners was used for the study. The study adopted exploratory research design and interviews and Focus Group Discussions as the instruments of data collection. Findings showed that not much have been provided in terms of recreational education activities because of the nature and state of the prisons, hence rehabilitation of the convicts after serving their jail terms was not promoted. It was also established that much of the equipment in the correctional homes is outdated and not in tune with the demands of the twenty-first century. It was therefore recommended that a more equipped NCS is required to be able to carry out the all-important task of rehabilitating prisoners.

Alamu and Makinde (2019) employed primary and secondary analysis to investigate the challenges of rehabilitation programmes for prisoners in Southwestern Nigeria. Primary data was generated through the administration of a questionnaire and in-depth interviews (IDI). Secondary data on the other hand was obtained from textbooks, documents, and the internet. The study revealed that delay in court procedures for those awaiting trial, lack of funds for rehabilitation programmes by the prison administrators, and poor prisoner welfare are major challenges to the effective implementation of rehabilitation programmes. The study therefore recommended that the Federal Government should provide an enabling environment for prisoners' rehabilitation, as well as make more funds available for its continuous sustainability.

Future Directions in Policy and Practice

The government's special attention is needed in making reformation and rehabilitation programmes in NCS effective and efficient. This should involve the provision of adequate funding and required facilities, competent personnel, adequate monitoring, and of course ensuring that those who have served their prison sentence are seamlessly reintegrated into society to live normal life (Ulo, 2019). If the NCSA is effectively implemented, it will improve so many aspects of the Nigerian criminal justice system. For instance, it will enhance opportunities for better utilisation of alternatives to incarceration and non-custodial sanctions, compliance to international human rights standards, reduction of prison overcrowding, and increased application of rehabilitation and reintegration programmes (Agomoh, 2019; Ahmed, 2019). Specifically, such improvements would attract and make available correctional officers across the entire nation who will be available to supervise those sentenced to non-custodial sanctions. This will encourage higher usage of non-custodial measures. In addition, it will provide better and alternative disposition measures for people who do not require custodial sentences, especially those who have been convicted of petty and minor offences and others whose offence, age, antecedence, background, and circumstances do not require imprisonment (Agomoh, 2019). In addition, it will enable further supervision and facilitation of reintegration in the community by correctional officers, especially regarding supervision of those on parole and those coming out of prisons and custodial sentences who are provided with aftercare services (Agomoh, 2019; Ulo, 2019).

Effective implementation of the Act will also improve the quality of justice dispensed by providing the correctional officers platforms for the provision and facilitation of restorative justice models which, where suitable and agreeable to both the individual and her or his victim, will be applicable at the different phases of the criminal justice process. The opportunity will assist more victims to bring closure to their victimisation. This approach will help facilitate healing, restoration, reconciliation, and be transformation both participants (Agomoh, 2019). Furthermore, the correctional officers now play more active roles in decreasing overcrowding in prisons and custodial centres. The NCSA has facilitated this by tasking them with the activation of early warning signals by requiring them to send notification to all relevant stakeholders whenever the prison or custodial centre exceed the official capacity and to refuse admission after the expiration of the three-month deadline following the earlier notification (Agomoh, 2019). The intent of this provision under section 12 of the Act, is to enable checks and balances to be instituted with regards to the control, inflow, and outflow of persons into prison and custodial centreprisoners, and to encourage all key actors in the determination of these inflows and outflows to take active remedial and sustainable steps to control and prevent the prisons and custodial centreprisoners from holding prisoners beyond their official capacity (Agomoh, 2019).

The establishment of a Mental Health Review Board in all the states of the federation by the Comptroller-General of the Nigerian Correctional Service is another of the provisions of the NCSA. If this provision of this and other Acts in relation to the treatment of those with mental disabilities (as contained under section 24 of the Act) are effectively implemented, it will help address the current problems faced by mentally disadvantaged people within the Nigerian criminal justice system. In particular, it will significantly reduce the practice of having those who have not committed any criminal offence being detained in prison asylums (Agomoh, 2019; Ahmed, 2019).

Another notable improvement that this new law, if fully implemented, will bring to the administration of criminal justice system in Nigeria, is the prevention of mixing the young with adult and hardened criminals. Section 35 of the Act states that Young Women Institutions be established in all the states of the federation and that these should serve as Correctional and Rehabilitation Centers for young people (Agomoh, 2019; Ahmed, 2019). Another improvement is the enhancing of the custodial centreprisoners visitors and inspections mechanisms which are now expanded with clear functions and a greater frequency of such visits and inspections. This will go a long way in strengthening the external monitoring and oversight mechanism of the custodial service and will further entrench good correctional practices and human rights compliance (Agomoh, 2019).

It is also noteworthy that compliance with international human rights standards and good correctional practices is clearly stated under section 2 of the Act as its first objective. It conforms to international best practice in so many ways (Agomoh, 2019; Ahmed, 2019). Many of the provisions of the NCSA were inspired and guided by the United Nations Standard Minimum Rules for the Treatment of Prisoners (The Nelson Mandela Rules), the United Nations Standard Minimum Rules for the Treatment of Female Offenders (The Bangkok Rules), and other international human rights instruments. The NCSA clearly states that there shall be provision of separate facilities for female prisoners in all States of the federation (Agomoh, 2019; Ulo, 2019).

Conclusion

The signing of the Nigerian Correctional Service Bill into law in 2019 which changed the name of Nigeria Prisons Service (NPS) to Nigerian Correctional Service (NCS) is no mean feat on the part of individuals, groups, and organisations that have been agitating for prison reforms in the country. During the 11-year period that the bill was in the pipeline agitation in the country for prison reform, focussed mainly on the state of prison facilities and welfare of prisoners, also heightened. The leading figures in the campaign were quick to point out that in more civilised countries what prisoners lose is just their freedom: they have access to social amenities available to others outside and as a result are more likely to reintegrate into the society when they finish serving their sentence. They are also not stigmatised on regaining their freedom. The dispensation of justice is faster very fast in some countries so that people awaiting trial may know their fate in a matter of months. These criminal justice system norms are non-existent in Nigeria. Facilities are dilapidated and congested, and other challenges include poor feeding of prisoners, lack of adequate medical care for prisoners due to lack of necessary facilities and a lack of recreational and vocational training for prisoners. The outcome of all this is that majority of the prisoners in Nigerian prisons come out more likely to resort to crime than when they went into custody. Addressing these anomalies and problems is dependent on the strict implementation of the Nigerian Correctional Service Act. If this happens a lot of positive changes will be witnessed in Nigerian Correctional Service.

References

Adetula, G. A., Adetula, A., & Fatusin, A. F. (2010). The prison subsystem culture: Its attitudinal effects on operatives, convicts and free society. *IFE PsychologIA, 18*(1), 232–351.

Agbola, B. (2019, 16 August). 10 things to know about Nigeria's new law on prisons. *Premium Times.* https://www.premiumtimesng.com/new/top-news/346864-10-things-to-know-about-nigerias-new-law-on-prisons.html

Agomoh, U. (2019, 15, October). Nigerian correctional service act conforms to international best practices. *The Guardian.* https://guardian.ng

Ahire, P. T. (1995). *The origin, development and role of the Nigerian prison system* (Annals of the Social Science Council of Nigeria No. 7, January–December, pp. 40–56). Social Science Council of Nigeria.

Ahmed, J. (2019, 7 September) Reforming Nigeria prisons beyond name change. *The Guardian.* http://guardian.ng

Alamu, I. O., & Makinde, W. A. (2019). Challenges to effective implementation of rehabilitation programmes for prison inmates in Southwestern Nigeria: An empirical approach. *Canadian Social Science, 15*(9), 61–68.

Awe, B. (1968), The history of prison system in Nigeria. In T.O. Elias (Ed.), *The prison system in Nigeria.* University of Lagos Press.

Babalola, A. (2014). Power of police to prosecute criminal case: Nigeria and international perspectives. *European Journal of Business and Social Sciences, 2*(11), 127–138.

Dambazau, A. B. (1999). The growth of crime, its prevention and control in Nigeria. In A. B. Dambazau, M. M. Jumare and A. M. Yakubu (Eds.), *Issues in crime prevention in Nigeria.* Barake Press.

Durkheim, E (1895). *The rules of the sociological method* [Durkheim (1895), cited in Bernard et al. (2016)] *Vold criminology.* Oxford University Press.

Erinosho, L. (1999). Socio-economic problem and crime. In A. B. Dambazau, M. M. Jumare and A. M. Yakubu (Eds.), *Issues in crime prevention and control.* Bakare Press.

Eze, M., & Okafor, E. E. (2007). The prison as an instrument of social reformation and rehabilitation: A study of Nigerian prisons (medium) Kiri-Kiri Lagos. *Pakistan Journal of Social Sciences, 4*(1), 23–31.

Iginovia, P. E., Okonofua, B. A., Omoyibo, K. U., & Osunde, O. O. (2002). *Crime and delinquency in Nigeria: Theories, patterns and trends.* Kryne Monitor Books.

Ikoh, M. U. (2011). The Nigerian prison system and the failure of rehabilitation: An examination of incarceration alternatives. *The Nigerian Academic Forum, 20*(1), 1–8.

Jombo, O. (2016). Problems and prospects of administration of Nigerian Prisons: Need for proper rehabilitation of inmates in Nigerian prisons. *Journal of Tourism and Hospitality, 5*, 228–225.

Obioha, E. E. (1995). *Prison culture in Nigeria: A study of life within Agodi Prison Community, Ibadan*. Unpublished M.Sc Dissertation, Department of Sociology, University of Ibadan.

Obeagu, C. C, (2008). *The rudiments of legal Methods in Nigeria*. Celex Printers and Publishers (Nig).

Obioha, E. E. (2011). Challenges and reforms in Nigerian prisons system. *Journal of Social Science, 27*(2), 95–109.

Okorie-Ajah, B. (2018). Criminal justice administration and panic of prison correction in Nigeria. *Journal of Law and Judicial System, 1*(2), 1–8.

Olojede and Mohammed, (2020). Effectiveness of Nigeria correctional service in rehabilitation of convicts into new life through recreational education in Niger state. *International Journal of All Research Writings, 1*(10), 30–42.

Oroleye, A. K. (2018). Rehabilitation and welfare of inmates in Nigeria prisons: A case of selected prisons in Southwestern Nigeria. *Canadian Social Science, 14*(6), 78–86.

Otu, M. S. (2015). Analysis of the causes and effects of recidivism in the Nigerian prison system. *International Journal of Development and Management Review (INJODEMAR), 10*, 136–145.

Robinson, G. (2008). Late-modern rehabilitation: The evolution of penal strategy. *Punishment and Society, 10*, 429–445.

Tarhule, V. V. (2019). Synoptic appraisal of the Nigerian correctional service act 2019. *Benue State University Law, 2019–2020*, 1–31.

Uche, I. B., Uche, O. A., Ezumah, N. N., Ebue, M. O., Okafor, A. E., & Ezegbe, B. N. (2015). Effectiveness of rehabilitation programmes in the Nigerian prisons: A study of perception of inmates in Enugu Prison. *Mediterranean Journal of Social Sciences, 6*(4S2), 164–170.

Ugwuoke, C. U. (2010). *Criminology: Explaining crime in Nigerian context*. Great AP Express Publishers Ltd.

Ukwayi, J. K., & Okpa, J. K. (2017). Critical Assessment of Nigeria criminal justice system and the perennial problem of awaiting trial in Port Harcourt Maximum Prison, Rivers State. *Global Journal of Social Sciences, 16*, 17–25.

Ulo, E. (2019). The Metamorphosis from the Nigeria Prison Service to Nigerian Correctional Service: Its implications and way forward. *International Journal of Management, Social Sciences, Peace and Conflict Studies (IJMSSPCS), 2*(3), 91–100.

Voorhis, P. V., Braswell, M., & Lester, D. (2007). *Correctional counselling and rehabilitation* (6th edn.). Anderson.

Williams, G. (1980). *State and society in Nigeria*. Afrografika.

Penal Welfarism and Rehabilitation in Norway: Ambitions, Strengths and Challenges

John Todd-Kvam

Scholarly and media attention on Norwegian prisons like Bastøy and Halden have given the jurisdiction a status of global role model when it comes to criminal justice policy and practice. Indeed, penality in Scandinavia has been described as exceptional in terms of its incarceration rates and humane prison conditions (Pratt, 2008). This exceptional status has though been under scrutiny for some time, both regarding its nature (how exceptional is it really?) and its trajectory (is exceptionalism being eroded?). For example, the anthology edited by Ugelvik and Dullum (2012) sets out some darker sides of exceptionalism, including remand conditions, the position of liminal migrants, and harsh drug sentencing.

New thinking on pervasive punishment (Burke et al., 2019; McNeill, 2014) has asserted convincingly that the discipline's preoccupation with (mass) incarceration has led to other marginalising aspects of punishment being left unseen. Mass supervision/probation as described by McNeill (2014) and Phelps (2017) is, however, different in Norway: fewer and fewer ex-prisoners meet the probation service and there is comparatively little use of community sentences (Ploeg, 2017; Statistics Norway, 2018). The last decade has seen a dramatic increase in the use of electronic monitoring, with large

J. Todd-Kvam (✉)
Norwegian Centre for Addiction Research, Ski, Norway
e-mail: john.todd@jus.uio.no

numbers of people serving the entirety of their prison sentences at home under EM. It was only in 2020 that the correctional balance shifted away from prison; before then most sentences implemented by the Norwegian Correctional Service started in prison, not the community (Kriminalomsorgsdirektoratet, 2021). In addition, both the number of people serving a community sentence under probation supervision and the number released from prison on probation have dropped by over a third in the last ten years (Kriminalomsorgen, 2021a). The recent period has also seen a major reduction in low-security prison places, with 290 such places removed in 2019 and 2020 (Justis-Og Beredskapsdepartementet, 2021a). Mjåland and Ugelvik (2021) have argued that continuing the policy of closing small, open prisons would represent 'a dramatic breach with one of the most constructive elements of the Norwegian penal tradition' (229–230). These are major changes to the way punishment is implemented and experienced as well as causing important shifts in the work of probation in Norway.

This chapter seeks to take an expanded view of Norwegian penality and rehabilitation, providing some historical context for mechanisms of rehabilitation and reintegration. The chapter also considers the rationale behind the rehabilitative efforts of the Norwegian Correctional Service, identifying two logics of rehabilitation that underpin the rehabilitative aims of the service. The chapter concludes with a look ahead for rehabilitation and reintegration, identifying some key challenges to be overcome (several of which flow from the changes to the correctional landscape mentioned above).

A Brief History of Rehabilitation Discourse in Norway

At the level of policy discourse, the Norwegian state has long espoused significant ambitions when it comes to rehabilitation and resettlement, demonstrated in this section through a focus on three documents, from 1917, 1978, and 2007:

- *Care for released prisoners* (Forsorg for løslatte fanger) (Nissen, 1917).
- The White Paper *On crime policy* (Om kriminalpolitikken) (Det Kongelige Justis-og Politidepartementet (1978).
- The White Paper *Punishment that works—less crime—a safer society* (Straff som virker: mindre kriminalitet—tryggere samfunn) (Det Kongelige Justis- og Politidepartementet (2007).

Starting with *Care for released prisoners*, the following two excerpts set the overarching research context for punishment and rehabilitation at the time:

> For contemporary criminalists [criminologists] the priority is therefore to prevent the crimes. The more one can do in order to make the individual a good person and to improve people's living conditions, the more hope one has that fewer and fewer end up on an offending track. (6)

> As a result of this great difference between the characters of the lawbreakers, the criminalists of the present realise that the means in their work must be different. For some it may be enough to give one more or less strong warning, others one must bring on the right path by attempting to improve him under punishment, the third category there is nothing else to do with than through deprivation of liberty to make him harmless for an extended time. (11)

The first of these excerpts is interesting because it takes both and an individualistic and a structural perspective on preventing crime, arguing that 'good' people and good living conditions are closely linked. The second excerpt sets out three categories of 'lawbreaker' that each require a different response: a warning; improvement under punishment; or incapacitation for extended periods. In terms of what is to be done with the second, ostensibly improvable, category:

> …in the prisons and, of course, especially in the national [as opposed to local] prisons, a great deal of work is being done to make the prisoner fit to go back to free life. Prison officers seek to strengthen his will to good and right, sharpen his sense of responsibility and teach him or train him further in a trade which can become his livelihood. He is prepared overall as best he can to stand on his own two feet again during the many difficulties of life. Now that the gate of the prison has opened for him, it must be seen whether the goal has been reached, whether he knows how to conform to the conditions of society and the ability to lead a proper life in useful work. (13)

The document also discusses how the transition from prison to the community is abrupt, and that negative influences may meet released prisoners with temptation in the form of 'spirits and all kinds of fun', which require a strong will to stand against. There is also an acknowledgement that released prisoners may be met with 'mistrust, coldness or even contempt' by those they approach for employment or other support (14). The document also praises release on probation: 'We calculate that over the course of ten years, the 1173 [prisoners] released on probation and that "passed the test" were together exempted from no less than 732 years [of imprisonment], or seven months each on average' (13). Post-release efforts are also discussed:

> [P]rovision for released prisoners is a social work of high value. It is a societal issue that today's criminalists attribute paramount importance to the entire criminal policy effort against crime and convicts' reoffending. They see post-release support [after-help] as a necessary link in the criminal policy system. The prisons' work to build up is worth little or nothing if it is easily torn down after the release. The state does what it can for the prisoner before his release. When the prisoner has become a free man, the understanding help of the general public is needed to continue the work. This state gets this help through the prison societies [i.e., a precursor to probation]. 14–15

The document discusses the work of these 'prison societies' (*fængselsskaper*), voluntary organisations that received financial support from the state whose work included care for released prisoners:

> If the work is to be successful, one must first acquire as good a knowledge as possible of those who are to be helped. Many of them are not what one calls 'worthy'. Excluding them, however, is certainly not justified. We must go to great lengths here, and not give up hope too early. There may be reason to help time and time again, disappointments notwithstanding. Eventually, the goal may be reached. (19–20)

In terms of the practicalities, a good deal of emphasis is placed on help to find work, although what we might now call referral/advocacy type work, help with family matters and some elements of control are also addressed. On this latter topic, checking that those released on condition of membership in a sobriety organisation have indeed joined such an organisation is cited as an example.

Overall, whilst the word 'rehabilitation' does not appear in the document, many of the themes and challenges identified in this document remain relevant for our conceptual and practical discussions of rehabilitation today. The discussions of both individual and structural considerations, patience in the face of setbacks, a focus on employment and the dangers of an abrupt transition from prison to society are all features of contemporary discussions of criminal justice policy and rehabilitation/resettlement practice. There is perhaps something slightly discouraging in this, in that we are still discussing similar challenges 100 years on. Nonetheless, it is interesting that at the level of policy discourse, a humane and rehabilitative approach was emphasised by Norwegian policy elites a century ago. There is an important caveat here: a 'top-down' description of policy may diverge significantly from practice on the ground. Indeed, one of the criticisms of the Scandinavian penal exceptionalism thesis made by Mathiesen (2012) and others (e.g., Smith, 2012) is that it may have been insufficiently aware of such potential divergences. Taking this further, Shammas (2018: 213–214) urges us to 'avoid state thought' entirely, lest we become 'uncritical state thinkers'. This chapter does engage with state thinking, but in the same spirit of 'vigilant critique' that *Care for released prisoners* (1917) insists is required in engaging with ex-prisoners.

Jumping forward to the late 1970s, a government White Paper on crime policy (Om kriminalpolitikken) (1978) discusses the limitations of the 'treatment model' that had pertained in the intervening period:

> Out of the belief in the individual-preventive effect of punishment sprang the belief that the offender could be treated. From the turn of the century and long into our century, there was, both in Norway and in other countries, a strong treatment optimism that today has its counterpart in an at least as widespread and strong doubt about treatment as a criminal policy tool. The idea was—almost as a parallel to the doctor's treatment of patients to get them well—that the criminal justice system should be able to 'cure' 'offenders'.
>
> In the clearest cases, such a treatment mentality meant that time-limited reactions were rejected: In the same way that no specific deadline could be set in advance for when the patient had recovered and was to be discharged from the hospital, it was impossible to determine in advance when the offender would be healed for their tendency to commit crimes. One therefore also had to anticipate institutional stays that were clearly longer lasting than a normal punishment for the offence would have been. Due to the strong notion that punishment should fit the crime, the solution was chosen to avoid describing the indefinite reactions as punishment. In a somewhat modified form, the treatment mindset meant that the imposition of punishment within certain limits should take place on the basis of predictions about 'healing'.
>
> Several criminal law measures in Norway have to a greater or lesser extent been characterised by such a treatment mindset. This is especially true for long-term deprivation of liberty: forced labour for vagrants [in practice Tater/Romani people][1] and alcoholics, which was introduced by Vagrancy Act of 1900 (and has now been repealed), was such a (relatively) indefinite reaction, which was intended as a treatment measure, and which was not counted as punishment. The work school for young offenders, which was passed by a law from 1928, was originally intended as a reaction that was to be indefinite within a 3-year framework, and the stay was not described as a punishment. […] It is these particular reactions that can be said to represent the most conspicuous results

of the belief in the treatment of offenders. In particular, there is reason to note that one has here been willing to break with ideas of proportionality between action and reaction, based on the belief in what the reaction would lead to.

This somewhat lengthy excerpt is important for two reasons. First, it shows how Norway, like other jurisdictions at this time (see Bottoms & McWilliams, 1979), was moving away from a treatment model. The second is an acknowledgment of the interventionist zeal of the state, even to the extent that proportionality between 'action and reaction' was seen as expendable—this zeal has been observed to persist into contemporary Norwegian penality, albeit in a less damaging and oppressive manner (Smith & Ugelvik, 2017). The White Paper does not directly discuss the concept of rehabilitation (apart from one acknowledgement about experts agreeing that imprisonment severely weakens inmates' possibilities for rehabilitation). Nonetheless, the White Paper also argues that, despite the rejection of a treatment model, rehabilitation practices should persist:

> Even if the deprivation of liberty cannot be justified on the basis of individual-preventive considerations (apart from dangerous violent criminals), this must nevertheless not lead to the abandonment of the humanisation of the prison system that the treatment approach has brought with it. Many offenders have major personal or social problems that it is clearly desirable for them to get help to deal with, regardless of whether this help will lead to a reduction in future crime or not. The duration of the detention should also be used to provide the inmate with new resources, and for measures that reduce the harmful effects of the isolation itself. (12–13)

The White Paper sets out a range of priorities in this regard, including increased use of day release, more open prison places, reduced use of isolation (this remains a goal even today), return to work, increased legal protections whilst in prison, the start of the so-called 'import model' (Christie, 1970) for health and social services and the further development of a similar approach in education, and more resources towards constructive leisure activities (173–6). Given the import model has in more recent times become one of the hallmarks of Norwegian penality and its much-debated exceptionalism, it is noteworthy to see how it was brought into government thinking over 40 years ago.

The third and final document I wish to discuss here is *Punishment That Works—Less Crime—a Safer Society* (Det Kongelige Justis-og Politidepartementet, 2007).[2] This White Paper set the strategic context for rehabilitation and re-entry work in the Norwegian Correctional Service for much of the period since it was published and remains influential even today. One of the key principles outlined in the report is that of normality (also termed the principle of normalisation). Described as the 'lodestar' of penal policy and practice, the principle has, according to Engbo (2017), two forms: defensive and proactive. Defensive refers to the retention of as many legal rights from normal life as is possible within the confines of a prison, and 'proactive' is an active normalisation of both living conditions and prisoners themselves. In the proactive version 'normalization is seen less as a rights-based principle, but more as a means to an end: rehabilitation and reintegration through "normal" living conditions' (Todd-Kvam & Ugelvik, 2019).

This document may represent a high-water mark for rehabilitative ambitions in Norway: from being mentioned once in the 1978 White Paper, the word rehabilitation and its derivatives now appear over 200 times and as the title of one of the report's five main sections. The report describes rehabilitation in terms of education, training, and work experience, addressing physical and mental health needs, dealing with addiction and programmes on familiar themes like motivation and change, domestic violence, and sex offending. It also launched a 'resettlement guarantee' that built on the principle of normalisation:

> The resettlement guarantee is not a guarantee in the legal sense. It means that the government recognises an obligation to assist convicted offenders to have activated the rights they already have as Norwegian citizens. The correctional service must facilitate this. Collaborating agencies are committed to provide their services in relation to the convicts in such a way and location that they have reasonable opportunity to take advantage of them. (Det Kongelige Justis- og Politidepartementet, 2007: 173)

The ambitions in this White Paper frame what Thomas Ugelvik and I have termed an 'ideal resettlement pathway' (Todd-Kvam & Ugelvik, 2019), which:

> starts at the beginning of the prison sentence with mapping of needs and resources. Relevant programmes are identified and delivered, with the inmate progressing through the system, achieving more freedom and lower levels of control and security. Periods of leave and day-release help prepare the inmate for life on the outside. Perhaps a period in one of Norway's open prisons like Bastøy may pave the way for transfer to a halfway house or release on probation. In theory, all relevant public agencies will have been brought to bear in order to arrange housing, employment, and other relevant support for the inmate as he or she transitions from the prison back to the community.

Of course, the realisation of this rehabilitation and resettlement pathway in practice was and remains a significant challenge (as will be explored below). But, at the level of policy discourse, I contend that the documents analysed here show how policy elites have long held rehabilitation ambitions for prisons and probation in Norway.

Two Logics of Rehabilitation?

I see two key logics of rehabilitation at work here: that rehabilitation is the *pragmatic* thing to do, and that is the *right* thing to do. So, we are not in the depressing situation where policy elites believe that nothing works or that nothing is deserved. The *ethical logic of rehabilitation*, whereby it is consistently described as the right thing to do, as the humane approach, fits with the Norwegian self-image of being an egalitarian, democratic welfare state. But there is a risk here: as Marianne Gullestad (2002, 2004) convincingly argued, egalitarianism in Norway is bound up in a notion of equality-as-sameness (the work *likhet* in Norwegian means both 'equal' and 'sameness' or 'similarity'). When Ugelvik (2012) talks of a Norwegian 'culture of *likhet*', it is based on the shared, taken-for-granted assumption that equality and similarity/sameness are bound up in one another. As Ugelvik notes, this culture is experienced and internalised differently for those who fall within the majority of *vanlige folk* (normal people) than those who may be categorised as *ulike* (i.e., different). Lunderberg and Mjåland (2016) note similarly that there can occur a 'reproduction of inequality, in that particularly resource-poor inmates can be subjected to harsher punishments because they have less ability both to assert themselves in the "right" way and to make use of the system's possibilities'. Furthermore, when the principle of normalisation (see above) is brought to bear, it risks being 'normalising' in the sense of trying to make everyone the same. Indeed, one of the informal terms for 'going straight' in Norway is to 'become A4', as in the standardised paper size. This, I think, speaks to the normalisation-as-standardisation that risks leaving those with more diverse backgrounds, or having different outlooks, in a disadvantageous position. Engbo (2017) warns accordingly that attempts to normalise carry a risk of becoming over-involved and paternalistic. Overall though, it is fair to say that having a policy-level affirmation that rehabilitation is the ethical and humane ambition to hold is a positive thing.

The pragmatic logic of rehabilitation is often summed up in a phrase that is a variation of 'these people will be released some day and they might end up as your neighbour'. This is a more utilitarian take, in that if people are to be released from prison back into society, then it is in society's interests that they are rehabilitated. As the foreword to a relatively recent reducing reoffending strategy remarks:

> Good resettlement and integration into society after punishment prevents exclusion, promotes participation in working life and counteracts new criminality. Fewer offences result in fewer victims of crime and large socioeconomic gains. (Departementene, 2017: 3)

Again, this pragmatic approach is a positive aspect of correctional policy and practice but there is a need for some caution here too. As the 1978 White Paper observed, overly zealous attempts to reform and change can lead to a 'break' in proportionality between action and reaction. We need then to be careful about who benefits most from this pragmatism? The excerpt above portrays it as a win–win for the rehabilitated and for society, but if society's desire for rehabilitation leads to what McNeill (2014) has described as coerced correction, then we fail to 'ensure that the intrusions that rehabilitation imposes on the offender are never greater than is merited by their offending'.[3] Proportional pragmatism is required.

Rehabilitation in Contemporary Norwegian Penal Practice

So, what does rehabilitation look like in current prison and probation practice? The most recent operational strategy for the Norwegian Correctional Service states its societal mission as follows:

> We must execute remand in custody and penal sanctions in a manner that is satisfactory for society and which prevents criminal offences. A system must be in place that allows offenders to change their pattern of criminal behaviour. (Kriminalomsorgen, 2021b: 7)

This mission is expanded upon in the service's vision, which is 'Punishment that makes a difference' (Fig. 1).

We can see here references to individual change via addressing factors like 'negative behaviour' and 'patterns of behaviour, attitudes and mindset'. The concept of rehabilitation set out here appears rather thin and individualistic. As Mjåland and Ugelvik (2021) have observed, this strategy, when compared to its predecessors, places greater emphasis on risk assessment. They note

Fig. 1 Punishment that makes a difference

that risk assessment is described as important both in terms of rehabilitation/reducing recidivism, and in terms of increased safety and security for society and for convicted persons. Mjåland and Ugelvik conclude, 'If we assume that the strategy documents tell something about correctional service priorities, there is much to suggest that standardised risk surveys are intended to have a greater impact on tomorrow's correctional service' (227). This could present an unfortunate weakening of the role of professional discretion, which has been seen as a positive aspect of Norwegian penal practice (Ploeg, 2017; Todd-Kvam, 2020) that provides room for rehabilitative work in the face of minor setbacks—particularly in a community setting.

Mjåland and Ugelvik (2021) also raise concerns about further closures of Norway's small open prisons. Between 2016 and 2020, the number of low-security (i.e., open) prison places was reduced from 1420 to 1084, whilst the number of high-security/closed places increased from 2496 to 2732 (Kriminalomsorgen 2021c: 31). This trend may however be reversed under the current government. The general election in autumn 2021 led to the Norwegian Labour Party and the Centre Party (an agrarian-populist party that draws support from rural Norway) forming a new minority coalition. The coalition's governing platform asserts that the parties will:

> Reduce the prison queue, expand the correctional service with more prison places and maintain a decentralised structure for prison and probation. Strengthen the content of the sentence and re-establish programme activities. (Hurdalsplattformen, 2021)

Whilst the coalition platform does not clarify what type of prison place they aim to prioritise, the newly appointed Centre Party Minister of Justice and Public Security recently announced that she did not agree with the correctional service's plan for reform that involved merging 32 prisons into 13 (Wilhelms, 2021). The Minister stated instead her intention to prioritise local prisons. The platform's pledge to 're-establish programme activities' is also relevant to our discussions here, in that these programmes are often rehabilitative in aim. The number of hours devoted to programmes as a part of community punishment dropped greatly over the past decade (Kriminalomsorgen, 2009: 22; 2021c: 19)—it appears the new government intend to reverse this trend as well.

In terms of how people experience punishment, one recent study (Crewe et al., 2022) surveyed 276 prisoners in both open and closed prisons in Norway (along with 806 prisoners in England and Wales). Whilst finding that, particularly in open prisons, the Norwegian experience was more positive and humane, there was still considerable pain and frustration reported:

> Notably, around or above half of prisoners in Norway agreed with items including 'I feel cut off from the outside world in here' (56%) and 'All the Prison Service cares about in this prison is my 'risk factors' rather than the person I really am' (50%); between a third and over two-fifths agreed that 'This system treats me more like a number than a person' (41%), 'The level of security and control in this prison is oppressive' (39%), 'Staff in this prison think that prisoners are morally beneath them' (38%), and 'I have no control over my day-to-day life in here' (35%). Around one in five agreed with the items 'The prison system is trying to turn me into someone I am not' (23%) and 'This prison is trying to mess with my head' (22%) and or disagreed that 'Staff in this prison do their best to help me' (23%), 'Staff here treat prisoners fairly' (20%), and 'I feel safe from being injured, bullied or threatened by other prisoners in here' (19%); and substantial proportions disagreed with the item 'I feel cared about most of the time in this prison' (16%), or agreed that 'I am not being treated as a human being in here' (15%) and 'Generally I fear for my physical safety' (13%). (12)

These responses show that there is, at least for a significant proportion of the prison population, a disconnect between the rehabilitative ambitions expressed in policy discourse and the lived experience of punishment. This is not necessarily a new phenomenon either: a study from over 20 years ago (Kolstad, 1996) noted that, in interviews and questionnaires conducted in Trondheim prison, the informants:

found imprisonment to be unsuitable as a means of resocialisation and reduction of crime. During the interviews, the offenders also called attention to the missed opportunities for learning the social skills of law-abiding groups, and to the sparse contact with their families when in prison. The long period in prison did not have any advantageous effect, the prisoners found the long confinement purposeless. They mostly slept through the day and found prison existence extremely boring and lacking challenges of any kind. (330)

These two excerpts indicate that there both have been and continue to be major challenges to conducting rehabilitative work in the Norwegian penal-welfare state.

Conclusion: Key Challenges and Future Research

To conclude, I wish to highlight five key challenges facing both the Norwegian Correctional Service and society more broadly. The first of these is the ongoing technocratic challenge of achieving joined-up working across the various institutions and levels of government involved in rehabilitation and resettlement work. This challenge was highlighted in the reducing reoffending strategy document entitled 'Reduced reoffending: National strategy for coordinated resettlement after the implementation of punishment 2017–2021' (Departementene, 2017). The strategy notes that gaps in service provision hinder good resettlement. Of course, this challenge is one that is shared across all jurisdictions, though with unique aspects that reflect structural, cultural and policy differences in punishment and welfare. In Norway, the move to remote, technology-driven solutions for interacting with welfare-state institutions presents a particular problem for those working with rehabilitation and resettlement.

A second challenge has been created by the rise of electronic monitoring in Norway, whereby nearly half of those sentenced to unconditional prison serve their whole sentence at home under electronic monitoring (see for example Kriminalomsorgsdirektoratet, 2021). This is, in broad terms, a positive development, in that fewer people end up with the often debilitative experience of imprisonment. It does nonetheless throw up a challenge of how to build and maintain constructive and trusting relationships with this relatively new type of prisoner. The implications of this major rebalancing of the Norwegian penal landscape also require research attention, both to build knowledge of how imprisonment on electronic monitoring is experienced but also how the diversion of large numbers of those convicted of less serious offences impacts on life and rehabilitative work in Norwegian prisons.

Third, debt as a barrier to resettlement and reintegration to society remains a major challenge. A study of prisoners' living conditions in Norway found that over 80% of them had debt; 37% from being sentenced to pay compensation, 26% from unpaid fines, and 17% with debts to private persons (including illegal payments due for drugs) (Revold, 2015). The state's imposition, surveillance and enforcement of significant and long-term debt are highly problematic, as I have described elsewhere:

> Efforts aimed at rehabilitation and resocialisation risk being undermined by attempts to enforce this debt. As it stands, Norwegian law, jurisprudence and administrative practice regarding fines, compensation, and confiscation work against the reintegrative efforts of the criminal care system and indeed the efforts of desisters themselves. They risk being trapped in the malopticon of debt surveillance and enforcement, being seen badly (as debt repayment objects), being seen as bad (unentitled to own assets or earn more than a minimum subsistence) and being projected and represented as bad (leading to feeling unfairly treated, demotivated, and trapped). Large and persistent debt to the Norwegian state may well mean desisting to a form of frozen liminality, living on a state-defined minimum subsistence for indeterminate time. (Todd-Kvam, 2019: 1491)

In fact, if the draft law currently being considered by the Norwegian Parliament (Justis-Og Beredskapsdepartementet, 2021b) is approved, even greater levels of compensation redress will be demanded from those convicted of violent crimes.

The fourth challenge is the ongoing impact of isolation in prison. Levels of isolation under the previous government became so concerning that the Norwegian Parliamentary Ombudsman published a special report on the issue (Sivilombudsmannen, 2019). This is the strongest instrument available to the ombudsman. The report noted that one in four prisoners are locked in their cells for 16 or more hours a day during weekdays and even more at weekends. Of most concern is the direct harm this causes these prisoners, but it is also worrying from a rehabilitative perspective (see also Anderson & Gröning, 2017). The Norwegian Correctional Service have put in place a range of measures aimed at tackling isolation—these measures and the requisite resourcing must be pursued and enhanced in the coming period.

The fifth and final challenge to highlight here is how to conduct rehabilitative work with people on preventive detention. This sentence is indefinite, with the court deciding whether to release the convicted person after a minimum term: if the court concludes that there is a danger of further serious crime then the sentence can be extended by up to five years at a time. Whole-life sentences are possible should the court continue to extend the sentence. The number of inmates serving a preventive detention sentence has nearly doubled over the past decade (from 68 in 2010 to 119 in 2020) (Statistics Norway, 2022), so the challenges associated with rehabilitation in the 'deep-end' of the Norwegian prison estate will only increase—not least because release may be conditional on successful rehabilitative work.

Tackling these issues is important both in preserving the positive aspects of rehabilitation and resettlement work in Norwegian penal-welfare practice *and* in addressing *de*bilitative and *dis*integrative practices, some of which have been long-standing problems for the correctional service and, particularly, for those who come within its orbit.

Notes

1. The terms used here are somewhat tricky to translate precisely and sensitively. The main terms used at the time were *løsgjengere* and *omstreifere*, both of which can be translated as vagrants. However, in practice the main focus of oppressive and assimilatory policy and practice here was on people of Tater/Romani background.
2. Norwegian Ministry of Justice and the Police.
3. Ievins and Mjåland (2021) have highlighted how men convicted of sex offences in Norway experience a laissez-faire approach with minimal psychological rehabilitation, to the extent that imprisonment was not experienced as meaningful of/or actively inclusionary.

References

Anderson, Y. A., & Gröning, L. (2017). Rehabilitation in principle and practice: Perspectives of inmates and officers. *Bergen Journal of Criminal Law and Criminal Justice, 4*(2), 220–246.

Bottoms, A. E., & McWilliams, W. (1979). A non-treatment paradigm for probation practice. *The British Journal of Social Work, 9*(2), 159–202.

Burke, L., Collett, S., & McNeil, F. (2019). *Reimagining rehabilitation: Beyond the individual*. Routledge.

Christie, N. (1970). Modeller for fengelsorginisasjon. In T. Axelsen & R. Østensen (Eds.), *I stedet for fengsel* (pp. 70–78). Pax.

Crewe, B., Ievins, A., Larmour, S., Laursen, J., Mjåland, K., & Schliehe, A. (2022). Nordic penal exceptionalism: A comparative, empirical analysis. *The British Journal of Criminology*, azac013. https://doi.org/10.1093/bjc/azac013

Departementene. (2017). *Redusert tilbakefall til ny kriminalitet: Nasjonal strategi for samordnet tilbakeføring etter gjennomført straff 2017–2021*. Departementene.

Det Kongelige Justis-og Politidepartementet. (1978). *The white paper on crime policy* (Om kriminalpolitikken). Det Kongelige Justis-og Politidepartementet.

Det Kongelige Justis-Og Politidepartementet. (2007). *St.meld. nr. 37: Straff som virker—mindre kriminalitet—tryggere samfunn*.

Engbo, H. J. (2017). Normalisation in Nordic prisons: From a prison governor's perspective. In P. Scharff Smith and T. Ugelvik (Eds.), *Scandinavian penal history, culture and prison practice* (pp. 327–52). Springer.

Gullestad, M. (2002). Invisible fences: Egalitarianism, nationalism and racism. *Journal of the Royal Anthropological Institute, 8*(1), 45–63.

Gullestad, M. (2004). Blind slaves of our prejudices: Debating 'culture' and 'race' in Norway. *Ethnos, 69*(2), 177–203.

Hurdalsplattformen. (2021). *Hurdalsplattformen: For en regjering utgått fra Arbeiderpartiet og Senterpartiet 2021–2025* (p. 82). Hurdalsplattformen.

Ievins, A., & Mjåland, K. (2021). Authoritarian exclusion and laissez-faire inclusion: Comparing the punishment of men convicted of sex offenses in England and Wales and Norway. *Criminology, 59*, 454–479. https://doi.org/10.1111/1745-9125.12276

Justis-Og Beredskapsdepartementet. (2021a). *Prop. 1 S (2020–2021a) Proposisjon til Stortinget (forslag til stortingsvedtak): For budsjettåret 2021a*.

Justis-Og Beredskapsdepartementet. (2021b). *Prop. 238 L (2020–2021b) Proposisjon til Stortinget (forslag til lovvedtak): Lov om erstatning fra staten til voldsutsatte (voldserstatningsloven). Justis-Og Politidepartement (1978) St. meld. nr. 104 (1977–1978): Om kriminalpolitikken (Oslo: Departementet) 352s*.

Kolstad, A. (1996). Imprisonment as rehabilitation: Offenders' assessment of why it does not work. *Journal of Criminal Justice, 24*(4), 323–335.

Kriminalomsorgen. (2009). *Kriminalomsorgens årsstatistikk 2008*.

Kriminalomsorgen. (2021a). *Kriminalomsorgens årsstatistikk 2020* (p. 58).

Kriminalomsorgen. (2021b). *Operational strategy for the Norwegian correctional service*. Lillestrøm (p. 32).

Kriminalomsorgen. (2021c). *Kriminalomsorgens årsstatistikk—2020*. Lillestrøm.

Kriminalomsorgsdirektoratet. (2021). *Straffegjennomføring med elektronisk kontroll: faktaark august 2021* (p. 5).

Lundeberg, I. R., & Mjåland, K. (2016). Rehabilitering og prosedural rettferdighet i kriminalomsorgen. *Retfærd, 153*(1), 32–44.

Mathiesen, T. (2012). Scandinavian exceptionalism in penal matters: Reality or wishful thinking?: Reality or wishful thinking? In the footsteps of margaret mead. In T. Ugelvik & J. Dullum (Eds.), *Penal Exceptionalism?* (pp. 25–49). Routledge.

McNeill, F. (2014). Punishment as rehabilitation. In G. Bruinsma & D. Weisburd (Eds.), *Encyclopedia of criminology and criminal justice* (pp. 4195–4206). Springer.

Mjåland, K., & Ugelvik, T. (2021). Straff, risiko og omdømme. *Nytt Norsk Tidsskrift, 38*(3), 219–232.

Nissen, H. (1917). *Forsorg for løslatte fanger* (xx#: Fængselsstyrelsen, Justisdepartementet) 22s.

Phelps, M. S. (2017). Mass probation: Toward a more robust theory of state variation in punishment. *Punishment & Society, 19*(1), 53–73.

Plocg, G. (2017). Scandinavian acceptionalism? Developments in community sanctions in norway. In P. Scharff Smith and T. Ugelvik (Eds.), *Scandinavian penal history, culture and prison practice: Embraced by the welfare state?* (pp. 297–324). Palgrave macmillan.

Pratt, J. (2008). Scandinavian exceptionalism in an era of penal excess part I: The nature and roots of scandinavian exceptionalism. *British Journal of Criminology, 48*(2), 119–137.

Revold, M. K. (2015). *Innsattes levekår 2014: Før, under og etter soning* (p. 47). Statistisk Sentralbyrå.

Shammas, V. L. (2018). Bourdieu's five lessons for criminology. *Law and Critique, 29*(2), 201–219.

Sivilombudsmannen. (2019). *Særskilt melding til Stortinget om isolasjon i norske fengsler.* Sivilombudsmannen.

Smith, P. S. (2012). *A critical look at Scandinavian exceptionalism: Welfare state theories, penal populism and prison conditions in Denmark and Scandinavia* (pp. 50–69). Thomas Routledge.

Smith, P. S., & Ugelvik, T. (2017). Punishment and welfare in Scandinavia. In P. Scharff Smith and T. Ugelvik (Eds.), *Scandinavian penal history, culture and prison practice: Palgrave studies in prisons and penology* (pp. 511–530). Palgrave.

Statistics Norway. (2018). 'Sanctions', Social conditions, welfare and crime (updated 27 September 2018). Accessed October 19, https://www.ssb.no/en/sosiale-for hold-og-kriminalitet/statistikker/straff

Statistics Norway. (2022). *0531: Prison population, by type of imprisonment, contents and year.* https://www.ssb.no/en/statbank/table/10531/tableViewLayout1/

Todd-Kvam, J. (2019). An unpaid debt to society: How 'punishment debt' affects reintegration and desistance from crime in Norway. *The British Journal of Criminology, 59*(6), 1478–1497.

Todd-Kvam, J. (2020). Probation practice, desistance and the penal field in Norway. *Criminology and Criminal Justice, 22*(3), 349–366.

Todd-Kvam, J., & Ugelvik, T. (2019). Rehabilitation and re-entry in Scandinavia. In P. Raynor (Ed.), *The Routledge companion to rehabilitative work in criminal justice* (pp. 167–178). Routledge.

Ugelvik, T. (2012). The dark side of a culture of equality: Reimagining communities in a Norwegian remand prison. In T. Ugelvik and J. Dullum (Eds.), *Penal exceptionalism? Nordic prison policy and practice.* Routledge.

Ugelvik, T., & Dullum, J. (2012). *Penal exceptionalism?* Routledge.

Wilhelms, H. (2021). *Justisministeren med klar beskjed: Norske fengsler skal ikke sentraliseres.* https://www.nrk.no/tromsogfinnmark/emilie-enger-mehl-_sp_-sier-nei-til-ny-fengselsstruktur_-_-vil-ikke-sentralisere-kriminalomsorgen-1

Rehabilitation in Romania—The First 100 Years

Ioan Durnescu, Andrada Istrate, and Iuliana Carbunaru

This chapter discusses several crucial moments in how rehabilitation was understood and practised in the history of the modern Romanian state. Although we discuss a few of the earliest instances of punishment, the focus of this paper is placed upon rehabilitation in the last hundred years. The first modern Penal Code was introduced in 1938 and entailed a definition of rehabilitation as a reclassification of criminals as citizens. To become a citizen, they had to be useful, and usefulness was acquired through work, education, and religious instruction. With the institution of communism in Romania, rehabilitation keeps parts of its former definition, especially the part that mentions usefulness, introducing an addendum—prisoners also had to be docile. Under these auspices, crimes, especially against political prisoners, were justified. In 1969, a new Penal Code and prison law were adopted, promoting prison rehabilitation through school, vocational training, and lectures, nodding discreetly at the Standard Minimum Rules of the UN (1955). Rehabilitation acquired new content in 1977, when community

---

I. Durnescu (✉) · I. Carbunaru
Faculty of Sociology and Social Work, University of Bucharest, Bucharest, Romania
e-mail: ioan.durnescu@unibuc.ro

A. Istrate
Crime and Delinquency, Bucharest, Romania

service for juveniles with sentences up to five years was introduced, although new elements were promoted. Punishment was enforced in school or at the workplace through a diffuse form of peer control and supervision.

The period after 1989 marks intensive efforts to rethink, define, adjust, and finally implement rehabilitation work. Alternatives to imprisonment multiply, probation is instituted as a field in the early 2000s, and prisons no long have exclusivity of rehabilitation as its locus gradually moves to the community. These changes were formalised in the adoption of the New Penal Code (NPC) in 2014. While the first 20 years since probation was instituted in Romania can be understood as a period of experiments, trials, errors, but also development and consolidation (see Durnescu, 2008, 2015; Preda, 2015, 2017; Sandu, 2016), the NPC is supposed to bring forward a reconfiguration of rehabilitation in Romania. The upper and lower limits of punishments decrease, and judges have more opportunities to apply a broader range of sanctions as the legal framework is more flexible and less punitive.

One of the unintended consequences of the NCP is burdening the probation system with an incomparable inflow of people due to the number of community sentences increase. The carceral population is slowly decreasing while the number of people under supervision doubles (in 2014) and more than triples (at the end of 2019). Suppose rehabilitation is a minimum of services provided to people who have been offended (Rotman, 1986) aimed at successful social reintegration. In that case, a question might be raised about the extent, availability, and quality of services.

A Brief History of the Rehabilitation Concept in Romania

Our approach focuses on how rehabilitation was officially defined and regulated from the formation of the Romanian state until nowadays.[1] As this is quite a long time, we refer only to the central moments in the evolution of the criminal justice system in Romania. In this chapter, we adopt Burnett's definition of rehabilitation as 'a process, intervention or programme to enable individuals to overcome previous difficulties linked to their offending so that they can become law-abiding and useful members of their wider community' (Burnett, 2008: 243). The rehabilitation literature speaks of at least three pillars that compose rehabilitation: developing human capital, enhancing social capital, and providing access to the system of legitimate opportunities (Hucklesby & Hagley-Dickinson, 2007; McNeill, 2009). In a more recent understanding of the concept, McNeill (2014) argues that there are four interdependent dimensions to rehabilitation: psychological rehabilitation, judicial rehabilitation, social rehabilitation, and moral rehabilitation. Through psychological rehabilitation, McNeill (2014) understands the changes incurred by developing new skills or addressing some deficits or problems. By judicial rehabilitation, McNeill (2014; also in Maruna, 2011) suggests that stigma and other exclusionary effects of the punishment should be put aside to support the convicts' requalification as a citizen. For moral rehabilitation, the convict must 'make good' or 'pay back' for the harm done by providing reparation and restoration to the victim and the community (McNeill & Maruna, 2010). Social rehabilitation suggests that convicts need access to legitimate opportunities such as education and training or employment to practise the new skills and requalify as a citizen.

Some of the earliest records on prison and incarceration document the exclusion of criminals from society as one of the first social reactions to crime. This is how the first monasteries and reclusive spaces were established.[2] These spaces were defined as waiting places for the actual punishment that was often attached to their body (see Foucault, 1975/1997). The aim of this type of punishment was obviously to deter crime and offer retribution for the victim.

The idea of rehabilitation made its way into Romanian jurisdictions almost at the same time as in France, England, and other Western countries. For example, in 1780, Mihail Sutu, a local ruler, introduced the conditional release of prisoners 'under the supervision of free men who will be responsible for their behaviour' (Ciuceanu, 2001: 1). Later, in 1874, under the guidance of French advisor Ferdinand Dodun de Perrieres, a new prison law was adopted that introduced 'societies of patronage' established near each prison to run 'moral-educative activities' inside prison and assist prisoners in finding jobs and accommodation upon release. Furthermore, the law made a clear distinction between two types of rehabilitation activities: 'labour' and 'vocational training, reading religious books and learning how to read' (Sterian, 1992). Rehabilitation was defined as psychological and social rehabilitation. Prisoners were reformed through moral education and vocational training, while also help was provided to access opportunities for living a law-abiding life upon release.

The following law on 'prison and preventive institutes' adopted in 1929 expanded on these provisions by providing a 'progressive regime' for those who demonstrated good behaviour. Each prisoner had to have an 'anthropologic dossier' where all activities were recorded. As stipulated by Art. 27 of the law: 'training and education are meant to increase the knowledge, to develop the sense of beauty and personal character, and to strengthen the motivation of the prisoners and the internees for a free and honest life'. A special department within the prison administration was created to coordinate education and training. Rehabilitation activities were aimed at improving personal capital. These activities, however, were more systematic and coordinated.

The first modern Penal Code in Romania was adopted in 1938 and continued the same line of defining rehabilitation as a form of 'moral education'. In other words, in Pop's terms, punishment lost a part of its punitive nature to 'make offenders better to become useful members of society' (Pop, 1937: X). Under this law, rehabilitation activities become even more coordinated as a 'supervision committee' is instituted and decides on the prison regime. More actors start to play rehabilitation roles, such as priests, doctors, teachers, and representatives of the 'society of patronage'. Work becomes mandatory for all prisoners and is seen as a 'reeducation' tool. Interesting to note in this Penal Code is that the word used for rehabilitation can be translated literally in English as 'reclassification', suggesting the idea that punishment should lead to a requalification of the prisoner as a citizen. This resembles quite a lot of current notions of 'delabeling process' (Trice & Roman, 1970) or 'certification' (Maruna & Le Bel, 2003; Meisenhelder, 1977). It was, therefore, for the first time in Romanian legislation when elements of moral rehabilitation were introduced alongside the personal reformation of the wrongdoer.

Once the Communist regime was instituted in Romania, the concept of rehabilitation was redefined in two successive prison regulations, in 1952 and 1955. The focus on rehabilitation shifted from moral education and reintegration to turning prisoners into 'docile bodies' and 'useful members of society'. Work becomes central in the 'reeducation' efforts. (In)Famous places such as the Danube Channel or the 'House of People'[3] have witnessed abominable scenes where political prisoners were tortured or exterminated.

The situation lasted until 1969, when a new Penal Code and prison law were adopted. In these two documents, rehabilitation returned to the former definition of prisoner reform through school, vocational training, and lectures. Prison leaves and visits were made possible, facilitating prisoners' contact with the outside world. Local councils were also obliged by law to take measures to ensure employment and accommodation for all ex-prisoners. The explanatory memorandum mentioned The Standard Minimum Rules of the UN (1955) as a source of inspiration.

A significant moment in the evolution of the rehabilitation conception in Romania was the adoption of Decree no. 218/1977, which converted almost all prison sentences up to five years for juveniles into an ancient form of community service. Following a political decision, prison sentences of up to five years were replaced with the enforcement of the punishment in school or at the workplace. Peers in school or at the workplace were responsible for supervising the juvenile delinquents.

Most of these provisions were in force in 1989 when the communist regime came to a halt. However, this change was produced through a long and sometimes painful process of transition. One major transformation was the expansion of the alternatives to imprisonment. Two successive changes of the Penal Code regulated suspended sentences under supervision (in 1992) and community service for juveniles (in 1996). However, the establishment of a probation system proved to be imperative to ensure the supervision of these measures in the community. The Romanian probation system was created in 2000. Prisons no longer had exclusivity on rehabilitation as its locus gradually moved to the community. To achieve rehabilitation, prisons and probation services were called to ensure not only personal reform but also to facilitate employment and access to reintegration services. These changes were fully implemented once a new Penal Code was adopted in 2009 and came into force in February 2014.

Legal Framework

In the light of the new Penal Code, the notion of 'rehabilitation' is more visible, which should be seen as organic to the evolution of the society and as a connection of the Romanian legislative system to the European context. This section examines the laws and regulations for both prison and probation.[4]

In the explanatory note of the New Penal Code (NPC) adopted in 2014, the purpose of the punishment system is to adjust the constraints of the persons to the crime committed and as 'an efficient manner for their social recovery'. The idea of rehabilitation is considered from the beginning of the court's individualisation process, an approach which is noticed in the significant decrease in the length of punishments. For example, in theft cases, the maximum limit decreases by nine years compared to previous provisions. Consequently, judges can now apply a broader range of sanctions as the legal framework is more flexible and less punitive.

Accordingly, the current Penal Code supports adjusting the proportionality of the punishment in terms of the length, nature, and form of execution by diversifying the range of non-custodial sanctions. In this respect, the new sanctioning system reflects a gradual approach to punishment by introducing two new institutions: waiver of the penalty[5] and postponement of the penalty,[6] as well as improving the application of the previous alternative to detention—that is, the suspension of the execution of penalties.[7] The new sanctioning system reflects the same principle—that in some cases, people can 'recover' through more lenient interventions. In the case of waiver of the penalty, the sanction is a warning regarding the crime committed. It can be seen as a form of judicial rehabilitation (McNeill, 2014) when the court decides not to impose a sentence. The same principle applies in the case of postponement of the penalty when the court relies on the person's behaviour and considers that immediate punishment is not necessary. In comparison to the waiver of the penalty when the court's intervention is a one-time event (application of a warning), postponement of the punishment is seen more as a process (Burnett, 2008). In the latter, the court gives a certain amount of time (usually two years) for the person to comply with some measures and obligations. Thus, the new institution includes elements of psychological rehabilitation, social rehabilitation, and moral rehabilitation.[8]

Going further in the sanctioning system, Romania presents the suspension of the execution of penalties as a process. Still, it is a more severe or intensive punishment than the postponement of the punishment, as the duration of this measure can be between two and four years. For this type of implementation, 'moral rehabilitation' is more visible. The obligation to perform community work is mandatory in all cases when suspended sentences with supervision are imposed should the convicted person agree to perform such work. Besides waiver of penalty and suspended sentence, 'moral rehabilitation' as community work is evident in the case of unpaid criminal fines.[9] When an overdue criminal fine is not imputable, the court can decide that community service under supervision will replace the payment of the penalty.

Conditional release[10] has a more rehabilitative approach, even though there are some theoretical debates that the conditional release system is harsher compared to the previous form of the Penal Code (Barbu & Geamănu, 2021) as the current provisions for conditional release impose certain measures and obligations to be fulfilled by the released persons. However, in the current legal settings, the conditional release 'as process' provides more premises for increasing the chances of rehabilitation. Hence, the conditions for conditional release acknowledge the behaviour of the convicted persons during the execution of the custodial sanction. This is not an automatic process or a right of the detainees. The inmate knows from the first day of the prison sentence that their behaviour can influence their chances of conditional release. Suppose prisoners want to end earlier their custodial sentence. In that case, they must give sufficient reasons to the court to consider them for conditional release based on their 'progress for social reintegration'. These measures include attending activities and psychological and social programmes.

The novelty for the probation intervention in conditional release cases is that their participation is mandatory in conditional release commissions. The probation specialist must propose specific rehabilitation measures. Besides this provision, in all cases with a remaining sentence of two years or higher, the person released early will be supervised by the probation service. This provision is based on a debatable view that the longer the custodial sanction, the higher the need for social support.

The scope of the probation activity[11] is described as aiming at the 'social rehabilitation of offenders' by promoting community sanctions and measures. This new law has been developed with practices from other European jurisdictions and especially the sets of the European standards designed at the level of the Council of Europe in mind. The first basic principle of the European Probation Rules (2010) is reflected accordingly in Art. 9 of the probation law, setting the ground for the probation intervention as a continuum of supervision measures and assistance developed with the probationers' contribution where they will have an active role in their rehabilitation process under the guidance of the probation service.

The probation law refers to rehabilitation as 'a process' when describing the supervision as activities and interventions implemented for the social rehabilitation of probationers.[12] The same article encompasses the concept of 'moral rehabilitation', mentioning the reparation of the damage produced by the crime as one of the purposes of supervision. Both psychological and social rehabilitation are underlined in Art. 103 of the probation law in the definition of assistance for the supervised person as participation in training, qualifications, programmes for social reintegration, or vocational programmes.

The spirit of rehabilitation can also be observed in the probation law, both in the description of Burnett (2008) and in the forms described by McNeill (2014). The rehabilitation can be facilitated either by the 'process' of control by implementing the measures to report to the probation service, to receive visits from the probation officer assigned to their supervision, give information about residence or income but also by attending intervention programmes, such as school or vocational courses, social reintegration programmes, or other forms of treatment or care.

It is important to mention that, in Romania, the probation service deals both with adults and juveniles. The introduction of new non-custodial educational measures for juveniles (civic education, supervision, weekend consignment, daily assistance) extended the focus on rehabilitative intervention programmes implemented by probation services either with the families of the juveniles or with the schools or the community-based organisations.

Special attention should be paid to the legal framework for executing the custodial sanctions and measures.[13] As part of the package for the reform in criminal matters, this law reflects the same principles—transparency for the execution of the custodial punishments, predictability, and social rehabilitation. The social reintegration of prisoners has similarities to the probation law.[14] At the beginning of the custodial measures, rehabilitation in society is one of the criteria considered when deciding on the prison unit where the custodial sanctions will be implemented. Thus, besides the execution regime and the security measures, the proximity of the prison unit to the residence of the detainee and the social reintegration needs are considered.

During the implementation of custodial sanctions, the detainees can be included in several activities—educative, cultural, or psychological. These programmes and processes are run by specialised staff of the prison units, probation staff, volunteers, or other community representatives according to an individual sentence plan. The change of prison regime (from maximum security to close, semi-open, and open) can be approved if the detainees' efforts are considered sufficient for their social reintegration.

For conditional release decisions, activities, programmes, or rehabilitation interventions influence the length of the executed sentence. The number of days of paid work, unpaid work, training, or scientific activities can reduce the length of the custodial punishment. For this purpose, rehabilitation actions are at the same time purpose and means for achieving the goal of social rehabilitation.

Besides these forms of rehabilitation, the current legal framework also comprises provisions related to judicial rehabilitation, as described by McNeill (2014). The Penal Code recognises two forms of rehabilitation: rehabilitation by law and judicial rehabilitation. In the current legal provisions, some adjustments are made regarding the period for submitting the request for judicial rehabilitation. In the case of rehabilitation by law, rehabilitation takes place for conviction to a fine, imprisonment for a term not exceeding two years, or imprisonment where the execution has been suspended under supervision if the convicted has not committed another crime within three years. The second form—judicial rehabilitation—can occur in cases of more severe sanctions. The court only grants judicial rehabilitation at the request of the convicted person and if certain legal conditions are met.

These two forms of rehabilitation should restore the convicted person in the eyes of society. Once rehabilitation has taken place, either by law or by judicial decision, the convicted person is fully restored in their rights and no longer suffers any prohibition, restriction, or consequences of their criminal conviction. The criminal record disappears, and society must behave towards that person as any other person who has never committed any crime. However, at the community level, removing stigma is not easily achieved.

Effectiveness of the New Penal Code

The New Penal Code aims to answer to the promise of reforming the Romanian criminal justice system by placing rehabilitation at its core. For the field of probation, the changes bring forward a better articulation of its place within the criminal justice system. The NCP gives judges more non-custodial sanctioning opportunities (Oancea & Micle, 2015: 312). As such, probation becomes a 'significant institution involved in case management and administration of non-custodial educational measures and other non-custodial sanctions' (Ungureanu & Sandu, 2014: 62; also in Sandu, 2016). The premises for reeducation are set through an effective 'reading' of the delinquent. Thus, probation counsellors are tasked to 'permanently supervise the process of the individuals' reintegration into the community' (Julean, 2014: 169) by analysing individuals on a case-by-case basis. If the person found guilty of a crime is a minor, sanctioning switches entirely from custodial to educative measures.

At the end of November 2021, prisons in Romania accounted for 22.900 detainees, out of which 1024 were women, 8530 re-offenders, 6344 with criminal records, and 8026 with no criminal records. Since the introduction of the New Penal Code in 2014, the number of people incarcerated has been continually decreasing. While the prison administration reports lower numbers of detainees, the probation system is faced with an incomparable inflow of people. In 2014, there were 26.000 people under supervision. The number doubled the following year, increasing steadily to nearly 70.000 people in 2019. The literature terms this phenomenon 'the paradox of probation' (Phelps, 2013), as it denotes that probation is not necessarily an alternative to imprisonment, as it functions as a criminal justice net-widener. Many accounts imply that NCP measures, rather than transforming rehabilitation into an objective, turned assisted desistance into a bureaucratic affair. In the case of the probation system, the number of people under supervision increased at a much faster pace than the system was equipped to receive (Fig. 1).

Evolution of cases - Probation (stoc, DNP)

2009	2010	2011	2012	2013	2014	2015	2016	2017	2018	2019
8.198	9.628	12.857	16.383	20.446	26.000	42.034	57.814	66.897	69.702	69.617

Evolution of cases - Prison (NAP)

2008	2009	2010	2011	2012	2013	2014	2015	2016	2017	2018	2019	2020	2021
29.390	26.212	26.674	30.694	31.817	33.434	30.156	29.902	27.455	27.277	20.792	20.578	21.753	22.900

Fig. 1. The number of people incarcerated and on probation are valid for the end of each year (December 31). Romania 1 (*Source* National Directorate of Probation and National Administration of Penitentiaries)

According to Severin (2014), the most stressing factor for probation counsellors stems from a too-heavy workload. With a ratio of 100 to one probationers to counsellor at the time of the research in 2013–2014, the probation staff complains about too many tasks and deadlines, an overabundant workload, which forces some to take their work home (2014: 209). Similar findings are reported by Preda (2015a, 2015b, 2017), but the author roots these observations in a comparison between the probation system and the prison system. While, as the author remarks, the penal population is split halfway between prison and probation, the budget and number of employees in the two systems march to different drummers (Preda, 2015a: 88). More specifically, at the time of her research, the prison system employed 11.000 people, while the probation system had 360 counsellors. From 2014 onwards, the ratio of probationers to counsellors only increased—in 2014, each counsellor supervised 75 people, 120 in 2015, 120 and 187 in 2016 (Preda, 2017).

Indeed, the New Penal Code increases the workload of probation counsellors, articulating, at the same time, probation as a viable alternative to incarceration. The delaying of sentence execution, suspended sentence, or parole supervision call for new attributions for probation counsellors in case management and the non-custodial educational measures (Ungureanu & Sandu, 2014: 62). A case-by-case evaluation gives an in-depth knowledge of each beneficiary, some arguing for its efficiency (Julean, 2014: 169). For minors, the NCP replaces all punishments with educative ones, introducing mandatory reports by probation counsellors for all cases involving minors. Many experts see this legislative change as beneficial (Roman, 2018).

However, the limited human resources the probation system has at its disposal are seen as a deterrent to the successful enforcement of the law. Other accounts state that the law has blocked the activity of the probation system, forcing counsellors to prepare 18.508 reports in 12 months (Preda, 2015a, 2015b).

If rehabilitation is defined as a minimum of services provided to individuals (Rotman, 1986) aimed at successful social reintegration, a question might be raised about the extent, availability, and quality of services. The final sections of this chapter discuss programmes and methods used in prison and probation.

Specific Programmes and Methods

This section discusses the programmes and methods available at the level of prison and probation. In Romania, prison and probation services are two separate institutions, setting noticeable in the delivery of programmes and methods. The analytical framework used is inspired by Hucklesby and Hagley-Dickinson (2007), namely how detainees and probationers develop human capital, enhance social capital, and access the system of legitimate opportunities. We understand specific programmes as structured interventions aimed at assisting people in acquiring skills and knowledge that can support them to stay away from crime (Canton & Hancock, 2007). This definition aligns with the understanding promoted by European standards, where programmes and interventions should be evidence-based (Council of Europe, 2010).

At the level of the prison administration, a wide range of individual and group programmes and activities are available (NAP, 2018). The offer of programmes and activities should be open and transparent for all the inmates in each prison unit based on available resources. These interventions are methods for developing personal capital and enhancing social capital. They are implemented at the beginning of the prison sentence, during the execution of the punishment and close to the end of the prison period to facilitate the transition into the community.

According to the National Prison Administration annual report (NAP, 2022), at the end of 2021, 89 programmes were available: in education (55 programmes, out of which 10 for minors, 2 for young people, and 4 for women); for psychological assistance (13 for special assistance, 5 for general assistance, and four therapeutic communities); social assistance programmes (7 programmes and five types of social treatment groups). According to the same source, in 2021, 340.970 attendances to reintegration programmes and activities were registered. Suppose we perform a rather simplistic calculation. In that case, each person attends, on average, 15 sessions of programmes and rehabilitation activities in one year, which means a little bit more than one attendance each month.[15]

Some interventions and activities are organised as induction activities into prison life, aiming to support inmates in adapting to the new environment and daily routines. These can be seen as information and assessment activities facilitating the establishment of a working alliance between the prison staff and convicted persons for preparing the grounds for more structured activities aiming to develop social skills or other types of abilities. For the first phase of the execution of the sentence, the inmates are included in the observation and quarantine for 21 days. This activity is aimed at the development of the Plan for assessment, educative, and therapeutic intervention for each inmate, representing a roadmap for their rehabilitation activities. The programmes and interventions included in this Plan become mandatory for detainees.

Inmates can attend various educative, psychological, and social work programmes and activities organised mainly as group-based interventions. Attending these intervention activities is part of a system of incentives, besides developing specific skills and mechanisms for coping with various life situations. The incentives can be either having days reduced from the prison sentence, gaining credits, which can be used as rewards for prison leave or can be lost if some disciplinary measures are taken.

The educative programmes are focused on developing detainees' personal abilities of reading and writing, acquiring job skills, gathering legal and health-related information, and supporting family life. The educative programmes have registered a higher participation rate in the last 3-year period (NAP, 2021) than psychological and social assistance programmes. Such are programmes for developing the social capital by building on the relationships dimension and enhancing social connections and networks. The programme for involving employers in the prison settings, for instance, gives inmates the chance to meet potential employers during job fairs, or visit work sites. A more intensive programme addressing the need for employment is Think for the Future, addressed at inmates with a remaining sentence of one year or longer. The programme aims to build entrepreneurial skills for participants, learn to prepare a business plan, and meet successful entrepreneurs.

The psychological assistance programmes can be general, addressing the needs of all inmates for developing prosocial skills or problem-solving skills, and specific, addressing types of risks and needs such as anger and aggression, suicide prevention, addictive behaviour, or sexual disorders. These are more intensive interventions lasting a minimum of 3 months with two weekly sessions. From the brief description available on the NAP website (NAP, 2018), elements of problem-solving, prosocial modelling, moral reasoning, cognitive behavioural interventions, social learning, and desistance were observed.[16] The level of participation in this category of the programme is lower.[17]

Social assistance programmes aim to enhance inmates' personal and social skills, to maintain family relationships, and to prevent challenging situations. Interventions are adjusted to participants' strengths, age, and gender. Thus, programmes are specially designed for juveniles, youth, and women.

Different interventions are implemented at the end of the prison sentence and in preparation for release at least three months before release. These programmes and activities aim to prepare the (re)integration into the family, professional or educational intervention, and recovery of community ties. There are two programmes for prison release preparation; one is implemented solely by prison social workers and another programme jointly by the social worker and the probation counsellors, namely the programme Reducing the Risk of Reoffending. The novelty of this programme is that it was developed and piloted especially for the Romanian prison and probation services 'to create the premises that the inmates can receive from the competent authorities a coherent and timely response to their needs' (Durnescu et al., 2009). After the release and at the release person's request, the probation service can implement seven optional sessions concerning family, employment, financial situation, substance use, accommodation, mental health, identity documents, and other legal issues.

As the probation system was recently established, only a few interventions are available. In this context, various ideas, policies, and practices have been transferred from Western countries, including evidence-based interventions. Currently, there are 13 programmes and interventions available at the level of the probation system.[18] Twelve of them have been designed under various funding streams and one programme regarding road traffic offences was developed with the resources of the probation service and in partnership with the police.

The programmes are based on a cognitive behavioural approach, social learning theory, and desistance. These interventions are tailored mainly for group work, are based on the internationally validated Risk-Needs-Responsivity paradigm (Bonta & Andrews, 2007), and address various levels of risks and needs. In terms of application, it is envisaged that at the level of each probation service will be organised an office specialised in reintegration programmes. However, to date, these new structures are not in place. Thus, until these specialised units will exist, the implementation of the programmes can be done by probation counsellors with a background in psychology, pedagogy, social assistance or by those specially trained to deliver such programmes (GD 1079/2013). One of the novelties of the 2014 legislation is that probation services may outsource certain rehabilitation programmes to court-approved community institutions. The last available activity report of the probation system[19] (NPD, 2018) shows that the obligation to follow a rehabilitation programme was the second most imposed obligation by the court: 29.238 cases out of 69.702 probationers. That means the available programmes at the level of the probation services and in the community should reflect the high demand from the courts.

Rehabilitation and Diversity

As people commit and desist from crime differently, rehabilitation interventions need to be responsive to the special characteristics of various groups. In other words, to be effective, rehabilitation interventions must be adapted to age, gender, ethnicity, or learning styles.

If we analyse the prison and probation populations based on the gender breakdowns can be noticed that in Romania, the percentage of women in the prison population is 4.5 on average,[20] within the European median of 4.7 (SPACE I). In Romania, there is a special prison unit for women (Târgșor Prison) where among other types of interventions, a therapeutic community is established for women with mental health issues. Similar interventions are implemented in Gherla therapeutic community-based in the exterior prison wing for women. Another category of interventions is that of psychological interventions adapted to women and, respectively, the programmes for developing various social skills, such as health education, parenting programmes, and interventions for developing family relations. The need for a unique programme for women on probation is recognised and addressed. Thus, in the next two years, a programme aiming at the specific needs of women is planned, fostering women's access to psychological counselling, family/couple counselling, intra-family mediation, parental support and education, and counselling for socio-professional integration.[21]

Specific interventions for the Roma community are matters of concern not only within the academic forums, but also at the policy level the specialised structures of the European Union. Thus, the member states should address the Roma population's discrimination, poverty, or social exclusion by imagining medium- and long-term strategic measures. The percentage of Roma persons in Romanian prisons cannot be identified, as correctional institutions do not collect this type of data. The programmes addressing the needs of Roma persons in prison and probation are based on the principle of inclusiveness. The probation service piloted between 2015 and 2016, a mentoring programme for persons on probation who self-identified as Roma. For these interventions, mentors (representatives of the local Roma community with a prosocial track record) mentored probationers through structured interventions offering guidance, support, and encouragement. The purpose of the programme was to facilitate communication skills, the use of specific tools and materials for construction or carpentry, and in broader terms, to develop educational and social skills. The network of mentors will be replicated at the national level and other types of interventions targeting vulnerable groups, including Roma, will be developed.

Concluding Remarks

This chapter dealt with the first one hundred years of rehabilitation work in the history of the modern Romanian State, offering an inside view of the various programmes available in prison and probation. Reform, employment, and reintegration are only possible if people found guilty of a crime alter their behaviour, participate in courses, work, attend school or training, etc. People can no longer say that they did the crime and the time, as the saying goes, they also must put in the work since rehabilitation work has become a sine qua non-condition of prison and probation. Conditional release, for instance, is not a right of detainees. The length of the custodial sanction rests upon prisoners' participation in activities, programmes, or rehabilitation interventions, leading to a somewhat paradoxical situation where rehabilitation is both purpose and means.

There is not enough literature to assess whether the range of rehabilitation programmes and activities is conducive to rehabilitation per se. Instead, the available literature points to an overabundant workload for probation counsellors, hinting, at the same time, towards the limited possibility of offering quality services when one probation counsellor has more than 180 active cases, as was the case in 2016. Suffice it to say that the New Penal Code has increased the number of people under community supervision, functioning as a criminal justice net-widener.

Notes

1. Although informal rehabilitation practices have merit in constructing and maintaining the social fabric of every society, they are not the focus of this chapter.
2. One of the first instances documented is the case of the Ocna Trotușului (1380) salt mine that imprisoned and sentenced those convicted of theft, manslaughter to work as miners; see Durnescu et al. (2010) for a more detailed account.
3. In Romanian, "Casa Poporului," now hosting the Parliament.
4. This section is based on several normative documents, as follows: the general framework defined by the current Penal Code (Law no. 286/2009); The laws for execution of the custodial sanctions (Law no. 254/2013); for organisation and functioning of the probation system (Law no. 252/2013); and on the execution of non-custodial sanctions (Law no. 253/2013).
5. Art. 80 of the Criminal Code.
6. Art. 83 of the Criminal Code.
7. Art. 91 of the Criminal Code.
8. Similarly, McNeill (2014) describes the forms of the obligation which may be imposed by the court and implemented with the support of the probation service.
9. Art. 64—Penal Code.
10. Art. 99—Penal Code.figure.
11. Art. 2—Law no. 252/2013.
12. Art. 48.
13. Law no. 254/2013.
14. The final purpose is described in the Law no. 254/2013 (Art. 3).
15. However, in 2021, some Covid-19 restrictions were still in place for group gatherings.
16. In this category could be noted the programmes for therapeutic communities organised in four prisons (Jilava, Rahova, Târgșor and Gherla). Three communities are developed for former drug users and one community for persons with mental health disorders. In average, the activity in the therapeutic community last for at least one year. The residents are involved in structured interventions such as therapeutic, educative, occupational or sports under the guidance of the multidisciplinary team.
17. In 2021, 4574 inmates participated in psychological assistance programmes, and in 28.680 educative programmes (NAP, 2021).
18. The list can be consulted at: www.probatiune.just.ro.
19. The report is available at: www.just.ro.
20. According to annual reports of the Romanian Prison Administration.
21. Direcția Națională de Probațiune (2021). http://old2.just.ro/wp-content/uploads/2021/04/Extras-caiet-sarcini-consultanta-DNP.-21.04.2021-engleza.pdf.

References

Aebi, M. F., & Hashimoto, Y. Z. (2021). *SPACE II—2020—Council of Europe Annual Penal Statistics: Persons under the supervision of probation agencies*. Council of Europe.

Barbu, A., & Geamănu, R. F. (2021). *Legea nr. 254/2013 privind executarea pedepselor și a măsurilor privative de libertate dispuse de organelle judiciare în cursul procesului penal. Comentarii și jurisprudență*. Universul Juridic.

Bonta, J., & Andrews, D. A. (2007). Risk-need-responsivity model for offender assessment and rehabilitation. *Rehabilitation, 6*(1), 1–22.

Burnett, R. (2008). Rehabilitation. In: *Dictionary of prisons and punishment*. Willan.

Canton, R., & Hancock, D. (2007). *Punishment (aims and justifications)* (pp. 249–251). Dictionary of Probation and Offender Management.

Ciuceanu, R. (2001). *Regimul penitenciar din România: 1940–1962*. Institutul Național pentru Studiul Totalitarismului.

Council of Europe. (2010). *Recommendation CM/Rec(2010)1 of the Committee of Ministers to member states on the Council of Europe Probation Rules*. Council of Europe.

Durnescu, I. (2008). O istorie a probațiunii în România. In V. Schiacu and R. Canton (Eds.), *Manual De Probațiune*. Editura Euro Standard.

Durnescu, I. (2015). Empty shells, emulation and Europeanization. In F. McNeill & G. Robinson (Eds.), *Community punishment* (pp. 174–190). Routledge.

Durnescu, I., Dobrica, P. M., & Bejan, C. (2010). Prisoner rehabilitation in Romania. *Varstvoslovje, 12*(2), 181–195.

Durnescu, I., Lewis, S., McNeill, F., Raynor, P., and Vanstone, M. (2009). *Reducing re-offending risk after release*. Lumina Lex.

Foucault, M. (1975/1997). *Discipline and punish: The birth of the prison*. Vintage.

Government Decision (GD) 1079/2013 for the adoption of the approval of the Rules for the organisation and functioning of the probation system.

Hucklesby, A., & Hagley-Dickinson, L. (2007). *Prisoner resettlement: Policy and practice*. Willan.

Julean, D. (2014). Evolution of the law on the execution of criminal penalties and related acts post 1989. *Journal of European Criminal Law, 1*, 163.

Maruna, S. (2011). *The great escape: Exploring the rehabilitative dynamics involved in 'changing tunes'*. Paul Hamlyn Foundation.

Maruna, S., & Le Bel, T. P. (2003). Welcome Home?: Examining the reentry court concept from a strengths-based perspective. *Western Criminology Review, 3*(3), 1–37.

McNeill, F. (2009). Probation, rehabilitation and reparation. *Irish Probation Journal, 6*, 5–22.

McNeill, F. (2014). When punishment is rehabilitation. In G. Bruinsma and D. Weisburd (Eds.), *The Springer encyclopedia of criminology and criminal justice*. Springer.

McNeill, F., & Maruna, S. (2010). Paying back and trading up: Reforming character. An oral paper presented at the European Society of Criminology Conference, Liege, September 2010.

Meisenhelder, T. (1977). An exploratory study of exiting from criminal careers. *Criminology, 31*(3), 224–239.

National Administration of Penitentiaries. (2018). *Annual activity report*. www.anp.gov.ro. [In Romanian Administrația Națională a Penitenciarelor (2021). Raport anual de activitate].

National Administration of Penitentiaries. (2021). *Annual activity report*. www.anp.gov.ro. [In Romanian Administrația Națională a Penitenciarelor (2021). Raport anual de activitate].

National Administration of Penitentiaries. (2022). *Annual activity report*. www.anp.gov.ro. [In Romanian Administrația Națională a Penitenciarelor (2022). Raport anual de activitate].

National Probation Directorate. (2018). *Annual activity report*. Available at: www.just.ro

Noul Cod Penal [in English The New Criminal Code].

Oancea, G., & Micle, M. I. (2015). Noi abordări în legislația penală cu privire la reabilitarea psihosocială a infractorilor. *Revista De Psihologie, 61*(4), 308–316.

Ordinul nr. 1.322/C din 25 aprilie 2017 pentru aprobarea Regulamentului privind organizarea și desfășurarea activităților și programelor educative, de asistență psihologică și asistență socială din locurile de deținere aflate în subordinea Administrației Naționale a Penitenciarelor [in English: Order nr. 1.322/C of April 25, 2017 for the approval of the Rules for organising and realising educative, psychological and social assistance activities and programmes in detainement spaces under the National Administration of Penitentiaries].

Phelps, M. (2013). The paradox of probation: Community supervision in the age of mass incarceration. *Law and Policy, 35*(1), 51–80.

Pop, V. (1937). *Codul Penal al lui Carol al II lea Adnotat*. Socec.

Porporino, F., & Fabiano, E. (2002). *New reintegration program for resettlement pathfinders/pre-course brochure*. T3 Associates.

Preda, A. (2015a). Probatiunea în Romania, rezultatele unei cercetari empirice evaluative. *Revista Romana De Sociologie, 26*(5/6), 459.

Preda, A. M. (2015b). Sistemul De Probațiune Din România Între Prevederi Legislative Și Realitate (Probation System in Romania between Legal Provisions and Reality). Impactul transformărilor socio-economice și tehnologice la nivel național, european și mondial (9).

Preda, A. (2017). The probation system in Romania. *Journal of Law and Public Administration, 3*(6), 111–117.

Roman, D. (2018). Delincvența juvenilă în România: factori de risc care determină comportamentul delincvent.

Rotman, E. (1986). Do criminal offenders have a constitutional right to rehabilitation. *Journal of Criminal Law and Criminology., 77*, 1023.

Sandu, A. (2016). The establishment of probation systems in Romania and the Republic of Moldova. *European Proceedings of Social and Behavioural Sciences, 15*(2016), 865–874.

Severin, A. M. (2014). Stresul la consilierii de probațiune. *Revista De Asistență Socială, 1*, 201–211.

Sterian, D. (1992). Repere ale activității socio-educative în penitenciarele românești. *Revista De Știință Penitenciară, 11*, 3.

Trice, H. M., & Roman, P. M. (1970). Delabeling, relabeling and alcoholics anonymous. *Social Problems, 17*, 538–546.

Ungureanu, E., & Sandu, A. (2014). A socio-legal approach of probation in light of the new penal code: Restorative justice versus retributive justice. *European Journal of Law and Public Administration, 1*, 37–68.

United Nations General Assembly. (1955). *Standard minimum rules for the treatment of prisoners.*

Rehabilitation of Offenders in the Scottish Criminal Justice System

Liz Gilchrist and Amy Johnson

Challenges relating to crime and justice in Scotland tend to be marginalised and subsumed under the broader mantle of the UK or omitted altogether. Scotland merits close attention in its own right, not only because it has a separate criminal justice and penal system from that of England and Wales, but also because it has a distinctive history in terms of crime control, penal policy, and criminological scholarship. Such histories have led Scotland to take a welfare approach over a punitive stance, at least in the rhetoric of rehabilitation. However, with imprisonment rising and responses that could be 'preventative detention' in the guise of the Order for Lifelong Restriction (OLR) it is not clear that this rhetoric translates to practise. Furthermore, given the limited differences across the UK's prison populations and recidivism rates, many question whether a welfare approach is impactful.

L. Gilchrist (✉)
University of Edinburgh, Edinburgh, UK
e-mail: liz.gilchrist@ed.ac.uk

A. Johnson
University of Worcester, Worcester, UK
e-mail: a.johnson@worc.ac.uk

Historical Offending Context in Scotland

From the slums of the nineteenth Dundee, Edinburgh, and Glasgow to the problematic public housing schemes of the late twentieth century, continued discussion about the link between crime and poverty is not surprising. Using data from the Growing Up in Scotland survey, Blair et al. (2019) found that children living in low-income Scottish households are far more likely to experience more Adverse Childhood Experiences (ACEs) than children from the most affluent households. However, poverty is not just another ACE at an individual level but is co-morbid with structural and cultural criminogenic factors, with families living in poverty more likely to function poorly and have multiple problems that, in particular, impact adversely on (Treanor et al., 2017; Webster & Kingston, 2014). How governments might best deploy their limited resources to reduce the pernicious impact of inequality is relevant to a wide range of policy fields, including justice. A key policy challenge is disentangling the respective effects of different types of childhood disadvantage to identify appropriate policy responses. This same challenge is also directly relevant to the youth justice policy response to offending by young people. Putting together the high social deprivation of the most disadvantaged in Scotland, the impact on their childhood development and integration, their limited access to pro-social opportunities, and personal and social capital, makes rehabilitation attractive to Scots' criminal justice professionals and policymakers.

Awareness that the neo liberalisation of Scottish society had resulted in an increase in inequality drugs, and organised crime perhaps led less a punitive and more actuarial approach than the rest of the UK between the late 1960s and early 1990s. For example, the Social Work (Scotland) Act 1968 placed social work at the centre of the criminal justice system by abolishing the probation service, transferring its functions to newly created local authority social work departments whose primary role was to promote social welfare (McAra, 2005).

The nature of offending in Scotland has changed with a reduction in nonsexual violent crime and crimes of dishonesty between 2011 and 2021 (between −5 and −16%) but a rise in sexual violence (+78%). A rise in other crimes has arisen from new offences created under the Domestic Abuse (Scotland) Act 2018, and much of the explanation for this is linked to growing inequality. Drugs use and drugs-related deaths have increased, particularly in deprived areas, from 224 in 1990s to almost 1,200 in 2018 (Scottish Government, 2018) Moreover, 'drug use disorders are 17 times more prevalent in

Scotland's most deprived areas, compared with the least deprived' (Public Health Scotland, 2021).

Despite recorded crime being at one of the lowest levels seen since 1974 (Scottish government, 2020), the prison population (in two private and 13 publicly managed prisons) is higher than ever before. At present many services are for male prisoners, but there are two specialist establishments, one for youths and one for women. In addition, there are community-linked 'hubs' for women in several male prisons.

Unlike in other jurisdictions, such as England and Wales, BME individuals are not over-represented in the prison population in Scotland because imprisonment is intricately linked more to social deprivation, poverty, exclusion, and location rather than ethnicity or cultural background (Houchin, 2005). In April 2019, approximately 20.7% of prisoners were not yet convicted or were awaiting sentencing (Lightowler & Hare, 2009), so as recognised by the Community Justice consultation (Scottish Government, 2014) there is an urgent need for policy to find alternatives to custodial remands as well as deprivation.

What Does the Criminal Justice System Look Like in Scotland?

In recent decades there have been several significant reviews of responses to crime. One, a review of developments in Scottish Justice since devolution, identifies key changes needed in adult criminal justice as: 'national and local criminal justice boards; drug and alcohol action teams; community justice authorities; the Police Services Authority; the Scottish Crime and Drug Enforcement Agency; specialist adjudication in the form of domestic violence, drugs and youth courts; the multi- agency public protection arrangements (MAPPA) and the Risk Management Authority' (Eski et al., 2011: 28). Furthermore, the Community Justice (Scotland) Act 2016 abolished the local authorities and established Community Justice Scotland which drives policy, if not practice, in criminal justice social work.

Many of these initiatives have focused on promoting a treatment response for those whose offending links to health needs or offering specialist input for offences where specialist knowledge and support are needed (e.g. drugs and domestic abuse courts). Other initiatives have moved rehabilitation priorities between the local authorities and centralised agencies and developed and refined risk management. However, penal reform has been piecemeal and not in the direction of early policy leads nor the radical rethinking of academics such as Professors Fergus McNeill and Beth Weaver.

It seems there has been a lack of clarity as to the overall vision, and perhaps some reluctance in the Scottish Prison Service and local authority-run individual social work authorities to cede their central role to others. Government-sponsored bodies such as the Parole Board for Scotland, the Mental Health Review Tribunal, and the Scottish Advisory Panel on Offender Rehabilitation (SAPOR), sitting slightly outside the central policy control, have also contributed to small policy shifts. However, this might be more a result of change in the discourse being used to discuss rehabilitation than a 'behaviour-influencing' shift. One example is that SAPOR replaced the Scottish Accreditation Panel for Offender Programmes (SAPOP), and focused on changing individuals and reducing the risk of offending through structured interventions (most in custodial settings). The idea was to take a wider view of rehabilitation that included less structured work and link programmes of individual change to wider processes of desistance.

Moreover, there are important historical features of the legal system in Scotland that continue to influence which professionals and models of justice hold the most sway in rehabilitation. The criminal law differs from other UK jurisdictions because a significantly greater proportion of it stems from a common law tradition that emphasises core justice principles rather than codifying specifics in statue. One outcome of this is that the legal profession, and legal thinking and rationales have a significant influence in the courts: for example, parole decisions often reference legal principles of proportionality as much as risk principles and the Parole rules.

In addition, the judiciary is strongly independent. Until recently, when faced with formalising of Judicial Training through the creation of the Judicial Institute, judges were reluctant to allow others to train them to deal with different classes of cases. They argued that each case should be treated on its own merits, and that a common approach, rather than promoting specific rehabilitative philosophies and promoting equality and fairness, would undermine their independence.

Scotland also has a very influential system of public prosecution in the form of the Crown Office and Procurator Fiscal Service (COPFS). The Lord Advocate and Crown Agent and the local 'Fiscals' in COPFS have considerable say in what types of offences and individuals should be focused on within all local areas. Procurators have considerable discretion about to prosecute a case in line with public interest, and the level of court and procedure when prosecuting; and in recent years, with a proliferation of alternatives to prosecution at their disposal, these powers have increased. These alternatives include warning letter, the offer of a fiscal fine, and a range of diversion from prosecution schemes for first-timers and those who have less capacity through, for example, mental health problems (Young, 1997).

In terms of recent policy decisions in relation to rehabilitation, one core focus in penal and criminal policy has been the promotion of safety and feelings of safety for people (Scottish Executive, 2004). Some of these policies, such as Equally Safe, focus on gender-based crime and fear of crime, and others like Getting it Right for Every Child (GIRFEC) ore on reducing risk to, and promoting the safety of young people.

The Social Work (Scotland) Act 1968 abolished existing Juvenile Courts and established Children's Hearing System. Following the Kilbrandon philosophy (Lord, 1995), the new system took a holistic approach to troublesome and troubled children in need of care and protection, and aimed for minimal intervention, the avoidance of criminalisation and stigmatisation, and decision-making based on the best interests of the child.

The Scottish approach faces several challenges facing problems as the centrality of the law and justice often clashes with a welfare approach and the lawyers argue against well-meaning but potentially legally unjustifiable. For example, on the one hand, the use of the criminal justice agencies to access mental health treatment might be considered inappropriate and the drive to prosecute someone to access it might not be acceptable for the 'justice' informed services, but on the other, a welfare approach might want to act in the client's best interest and might include using justice interventions to access support.

Theories of Offending for Scotland

The rhetoric of Criminal Justice in Scotland at a Governmental level is dominated by 'evidence-based practice' and effective intervention to promote desistance alongside discourses promising public safety, a 'safe Scotland'. The current consultation about Community Justice sets diversion and early intervention, or effective community intervention to meet the needs of particularly those with additional vulnerabilities (such as substance use and mental health issues), availability of resources, leadership, and partnership as key strategic aims, highlighting the focus on rehabilitation. This section will seek to consider the four forms of rehabilitation outlined by Burke et al. (2018), personal—focusing on change at an individual level, legal—concerned with change in legal 'status'; moral—more linked with (re-)integration and linking back into the community; and social—which is focused more on social change to offer proportionate justice responses alongside rehabilitative processes that culminate in true community engagement for all.

In criminological terms, Scotland is aiming to fulfil a range of justice goals and different agencies are dominated by different aspects. The Scottish Government's rhetoric reflects proportionality, adhering to an underlying model of rational choice explanations for crime, but at the same time, the commitment to evidence-based practice and early intervention also suggests a desire to implement a 'treatment' model. Some agencies focus on legal justice: for example, many Parole decisions are influenced by 'black letter law' thinking that argues against a parole hearing imposing a longer additional sentence for an offence if committed in custody than would have been imposed for a similar misdemeanour in a court setting. Other agencies, like the Scottish Prison Service, focus on treating individual criminogenic need, implying less individual capacity, and leaning more to crime being seen as driven by deficits stemming from early childhood experiences and linked to structural inequalities which limit opportunities more closely matching with the Andrews and Bonta 'Psychology of Criminal Conduct' (Bonta & Andrews, 2016). The wider criminal justice social work workforce is more influenced by multi-factor models of offending, being more closely aligned with a nested ecological model of human behaviour (Bronfenbrenner, 1977).

The Scottish social work understanding of criminality is greatly influenced by sociological perspectives, linking structural inequalities with offending outcomes. The approach would include some individual and family factors including exploring how behaviour is acquired learned, through social learning, reinforced, by response to offences, and would include an awareness of how individuals can be limited in opportunity by structural factors and how young people once labelled as 'offender' or 'deviant' due to background and early rule breaking behaviour. These ranges of theories are clear within the national training in key assessment tools such as the LSCMI and the commitment to diversion for young people. It is also demonstrated in the close links between Children and Families social work and Criminal Justice Social work, with social workers moving across these groupings. In forensic mental health, again perhaps unsurprisingly, there is a far greater dominance of a medical model of rehabilitation, with a great deal of emphasis being placed on 'insight' (mostly into their own mental health) and recovery/treatment compliance (with mediations and regimes) in the discussions of the Mental Health Tribunals. In the social policy area, there is far greater consideration of wider and higher-level theories with a focus on poverty, exclusion, and disadvantage, again the professionals at Government policy level is influenced by the disciplinary background in which they were trained.

Criminological theories often position the individual on a continuum mirroring the classical and positivist schools of criminology with, at one extreme, an active agent who creates and shapes their world and bears full responsibility for their choices and decisions, and at the other, passive subjects whose behaviour is shaped by a variety of forces largely beyond their control (Henry & Milovanovic, 1996). Rehabilitative effort in Scotland seeks to include the spectrum, by individual agencies working within models suited to their discipline backgrounds. This has led to some interesting division between 'health' and 'justice' and gaps in shared language. The psychological models influencing SPS require certain risk assessment and management strategies based on discipline-specific expertise, and the social work models use different tools and assess and plan differently, so not all rehabilitative effort is aiming the same direction nor is the achievement of rehabilitative goals always assessed in the same way.

As indicated above crime is caused, at least in part, by multiple social deprivation and, therefore, only does the State have a duty to intervene or support the person out of the situation, but it also has a duty to create a coherent model of rehabilitation that moves beyond individual blame and shame and truly integrates across individual, structural, and cultural influences. It follows, therefore, there is a need not only to marry up legal proportionality and the social welfare approach required, but also to develop a far more integrated system, which seeks to achieve moral and social rehabilitation as well as individual and legal (Cullen & Gilbert, 1982).

Criminal Justice Agencies in Scotland

Scotland has a strong commitment to social welfare, economic improvement, public safety, and the reduction of the damage caused to victims by crime, but it also has high numbers in prison and some areas of persistent inequality. Despite the favoured imprisonment route England and Wales often take, Scotland recognises that the underlying social and cultural factors often increase the risk of offending and have a strong association with reoffending statistics.

The criminal justice system in Scotland is underpinned by a complex set of legal processes based on principles of fairness, a respect for human rights and independent decision-making, and separation of powers between the State and judicial processes. Decisions on whether a criminal case should go to court, whether an accused is guilty (or if the case is 'not proven') and, if so, what punishment he or she should receive are up to the individual procurators fiscal, members of the judiciary (such as sheriffs), and juries concerned. The system is greatly influenced by 'due process' as a means of ensuring the protection of individuals accused by the State as well as to protect the presumption of innocence until proven guilty.

There are three types of courts in Scotland which deal with offences of different seriousness and require wider sentencing powers. The most serious cases are considered at the High Court of Justiciary, less serious or moderate cases are heard at a Sheriff Court (where the judge sits *with* a Jury of 15 for cases being tried under solemn procedure, or *without* for cases being heard under summary procedure) and less serious offences are processed at local Justice of the Peace Courts. There are two systems to process cases, solemn and summary procedures. Most serious offences, such as murder, rape, or serious assault, are processed under Solemn procedures where findings of fact are made by a jury in either the High Court or the Sheriff Court, and sentencing is enacted by the Sheriff or Judge. Less serious criminal activity would be dealt with under Summary procedures. For example, cases of theft where sentence would be less than a fine of £5000 or a 3-month prison sentence, would be heard in a Sheriff Court, presided over by a Sheriff, or public nuisance offences would be heard in the District Court, presided over by a Justice of the Peace Court. The vast majority (over 90%) of cases being processed through the criminal justice system are summary cases.

In terms of agencies responsible for action leading to, and following sentence, Scotland's criminal justice system is formed and delivered by a range of public, private, and voluntary bodies. As well as these agencies, there are consultative bodies and advisory panels such as the Scottish Advisory Panel on Offender Rehabilitation that guide policy and practice. Their competing philosophies and goals and different accountabilities, varying are challenging to manage the criminal justice system as an integrated process. The influential legal bodies hold more closely to legal views of justice, tending towards proportionality, and adherence to 'natural justice', whilst community-based social work influenced bodies to promote targets of rehabilitation, desistance, and reintegration or integration and entities such as Scottish Prison Service and the Parole Board of Scotland tend to work within a risk/justice paradigm.

One agency which is unique to Scotland is the Risk Management Authority (RMA) set up following a national review of responses to serious offending, including sexual and violent offences, and offending by those with personality disorder, culminating in the MacLean Committee (established 1999). An alternative to the provision in England and Wales for the

Dangerous and Severe Personality Disordered (Home office, 1999), it set up the system of assessing, imposing, and monitoring the Orders of Lifelong Restriction (OLR).

For an OLR to be imposed a Judge must request an OLR assessment; the balance of the assessments must point in favour of an OLR, and the court must be convinced that there is a need to impose such as sentence. Once imposed, there is a requirement for the establishment holding the OLR prisoner, most often SPS, but sometimes the State Hospital, to prepare and implement a risk management plan for each individual and the plans must be approved by the RMA. The Scottish Prison Service must then update the RMA each year with progress against the plan. These plans are resource intensive, and the sentence is controversial as it is to some extent a preventative sentence, at odds with an overall focus on natural justice or rehabilitation and focused more on deterrence than rehabilitation. It may also become more controversial in future if the 'science' of risk prediction and the accuracy of risk assessment which underpins this sentence is ever truly tested in court. Like the Indeterminate Sentence for Public Protection sentences in England and Wales, OLRs may draw in low-risk individuals and thus add to prison overcrowding.

Although Scotland is trying to incorporate a welfare approach/community-focused rehabilitation, this is not the case for everyone. The new sentencing guidelines for the young and women offer a positive hope for the future. The main drivers are to promote sentences in the best interest of the prisoners, where welfare, local links, true integration between prison and community, fostering pathways back into society for released prisoners are valued. Only those who present the greatest threat of harm or serious offending are imprisoned. The newly enacted Presumption against.

However, this is not the case for all, and courts are continuing to use remand in custody in cases where a direct, serious threat of violence would be hard to evidence. Concerns have been raised about the 'remand problem', whereby we are seeing individuals awaiting trial and not punished or being worked with in terms of rehabilitation. Many of these individuals and the prison population in gender regardless of age, gender, or race have a triad of needs including, drug and alcohol abuse, mental health, physical health problems, and a history of victimisation and abuse (Graham et al., 2012; Tyler et al., 2019). Many argue that these individuals should be supported and not 'punished' in a community setting with rehabilitative programmes (McNeill, 2014). The overuse of remand has led to overpopulated prisons where there is no time to work with these individuals or tackle the associated risks for reoffences to occur when they are released.

It is suggested that these findings highlight those prisons are being used to compensate the failings of the education and health systems and focus on revisiting how a social welfare model should look is required. The existing use of imprisonment is expensive and counterproductive and rather than effective work with prisoners taking place, we are seeing negative consequences. Imprisonment can hinder the positive relationships such prisons have in the community and the 'supportive work' being conducted. Imprisonment offers little opportunity to gain skills to reduce the risk of reoffending and reduced responsibility and dependence for those with short sentences.

Punishment—Moving to Rehabilitation

Rehabilitation in Scotland falls across a range of agencies. For children, the Children's Panel and Secure care are the core services; for males and females the Scottish Prison Service (national service), Community Justice (national policy lead agency), and Criminal Justice Social Work (delivered through Local Authorities in response to local need) are core agencies. Those with mental health needs are managed through the forensic mental health facilities, delivered through health, including low medium and high secure provision. There are specialist services for individuals with drug and alcohol needs and there have been specialist courts for those with special needs (e.g. drugs courts), and for those accused of specific offences (domestic abuse courts and 'gangs initiatives and including the Scottish Violence Reduction Unit set up in 2022').[1]

In Scotland as with elsewhere, rehabilitative efforts have fluctuated over the decades often informed by criminological theory and research with a lag to allow the time for a research message to translate into policy. Scotland is no different than any other country in this journey.

Theoretically, one major turning point in where and how to focus rehabilitative effort was the publication in 1974 of the Martinson Report (Martinson, 1974) which identified seven key aspects of effective rehabilitation, then assessed what scientifically robust evidence there was to indicate whether any of the rehabilitative efforts in the USA had been effective. Based on this rigorous assessment, he concluded that there was no good evidence of any successful rehabilitative effort and that 'nothing-works'. This message gained traction internationally, without always requiring the answer to the important further issue as to why various interventions had not 'worked' as planned. For example, was it that they had not been delivered as planned; was psychotherapy not fit for purpose of behavioural change; could it be expected that individual change may not be sustainable if an individual then returned to the criminogenic context within or out of prison?

In the USA, this report led to a shift away from policies to 'cure' offending at the individual level, and promoted interventions linked to retribution, incapacitation, and deterrence. Scotland prior to devolution, although there was a consideration of 'local issues' by the Scottish Office was driven by similar criminal justice policies as the rest of the UK. From the mid-1990s, the lack of trust in the rehabilitative effort also moved the UK way from being lenient in response to crime and seeking individual change, towards 'penal populism' (Newburn, 2007). The phrase 'tough on crime and tough on the causes of crime' resonated throughout policy and media, and the introduction of further measures to address antisocial behaviours, an increase in the use of prison and, later, the introduction of indeterminate sentences in addition to life sentences for murder, in England and Wales imprisonment for public protection, (IPP in England and Wales) and to some extent order for lifelong restriction (OLRs in Scotland) reflected the rhetoric of deterrence via the threat of sanction or via incapacitation and the focus on punishment. However, then came devolution which does appear to have led to a shift in thinking on this side of the border. One major point of change followed the publication of Scotland's Choice (2008).

Paraphrasing the report's key points, it was stated that Scotland had the highest rate of imprisonment of any European Country and it was predicted to grow to 8700 by 2016, (SPS daily prison population in 2019/20 was 8198 of which 6529 were sentenced) that the large prison population appeared to be due to incarcerating the 'troubled and troubling' rather than 'dangerous people' the majority of whom came from backgrounds of multiple deprivation and the imprisonment was not working to reduce reoffending. Several potential solutions were suggested. Again paraphrasing, Scotland's Choice identified that prison should be reserved only for those whose offences are so serious and who posed a significant threat to the public that no other response is possible, the default sanction for offending should be 'paying back' in the community, there should be national guidelines to influence sentencing and Scotland should aim to have a daily prison population of 5000 (The Scottish Prisons Commission, 2008).

A later review in 2019 highlighted that the changes in criminal justice response in Scotland since devolution have been away from punishment and being tough on crime, to reflect a more sophisticated awareness of the conditions maintaining offending and more in line with criminal justice research. Some examples that can be highlighted are the positive evaluation outcomes of the trial of a whole systems approach to offer more diversion from criminal justice for youths; the reversal of a proposal to build a large central prison for all women to instead create small local units across Scotland to keep women as close to family support and links is highlighted as a positive (Scottish Prison Service, n.d.) and the introduction of legislation to discourage the use of short terms of imprisonment (The Presumptions Against Short Periods of Imprisonment [Scotland Order, 2019]) was a positive step in the direction of promoting rehabilitation and a move away from punitive responses to crime.

Even more recently in Scotland influential criminologists have been arguing that we should move away from merely supporting individual change, and instead aim for broader social and structural change to promote and sustain desistance (McNeill et al., 2016). Within this review, McNeill suggested that effective criminal sanctions should incorporate five themes: namely that they:

- need to manage fluctuations in relation to progress and deal appropriately with lapses given the complexity of the change required to desist from offending
- should be tailored and personalised to reflect individual need
- they should help ex-offenders develop 'social capital', i.e. promote positive social networks to support change
- need to develop self-efficacy, their belief that change is possible and belief in the individual's capacity to achieve change
- use appropriate positive, supportive language to reinforce and reward positive change.

More importantly, McNeill's review of criminal justice and desistance in Scotland highlighted that criminal justice sanctions should have a positive goal, briefly summarised rather than focusing on what we are asking people to stop, criminal justice agencies and policies should have a what are we asking people to start doing or being? McNeill highlights that the Scottish Centre for Crime and Justice Research has been closely linked to Scottish Government and highlights the positive rhetoric within Scottish Government's publications on criminal justice sanctions and some criminal justice responses (McNeill et al., 2016).

In Scotland, some key areas have developed more positively in the 2000s. McNeill had identified the introduction of a new 'community payback order', the use of mentoring as a support, improved access to basic needs such as housing and healthcare as being important pointers in terms of the move towards a less punitive and a more helpful approach to rehabilitation.

More recently there has been an even stronger push towards the use of community-based sentences rather than prison; with the enactment of the PASS legislations (The Presumptions Against Short Periods of Imprisonment) (Scotland Order, 2019); there are new sentencing guidelines in relation to young people appearing before the courts (Scottish Sentencing Council, 2022) and there are specific and explicit approaches to addressing sexual offending and the needs of victims of sexual violence being influential.

The new sentencing guidelines for young people explicitly focus on being fair and proportionate, taking capacity and culpability into account and directly targets a goal of rehabilitation. The main goal of Community Justice identifies ambitious goals highlighting new approaches and promoting rehabilitation, stating on its website 'Community Justice Scotland works to change the conversation about justice. We believe that smart justice based on the best evidence of what works will prevent offending, repair lives, and improve communities. We want Scotland to be the safest country in the world' (Scottish Government, 2022).

The Scottish Government's stated policies on reducing reoffending highlight the following: a commitment to community-based sentences; an increase in use of electronic monitoring (which will help support community sentences and public confidence in community sentences and public safety), promotion of home detention measures, a focus on the multi-agency public protection arrangements (MAPPA), disclosure schemes, update of Scottish Prison Service and support of SAPOR to promote excellence in offending behaviour programmes ([Scotland] Act 2019).

Rehabilitative Effort in Scotland: Working or Not?

So, with the structural changes enacted over the past few decades and with the current policy focus, can we say that Scotland is implementing rehabilitation?

Police Scotland's current strategic goal is 'policing for a safe protected and resilient Scotland'. Within this they want to focus on the 'greatest threat' and the 'greatest risk of harm', and they discuss responding to vulnerability, responding to victims, moving beyond law enforcement, and responding to new offences and new threats. There is an ambitious set of targets set out, but in doing this, the focus of Police Scotland is less clear and their contribution to rehabilitation is less clear. Scotland's 'Serious Organised Crime Strategy' incorporates the tactics of 'diverting', 'deterring', 'detecting', and 'disrupting' drug supply and, in so doing, dismantling criminal networks

(Scottish Government 2016b), by incorporating drug supply into the 'black box' of OC (see Decker et al., 2008).

In terms of policy, Scottish policymakers have placed both ACEs and child poverty high on the policy agenda, with explicit recognition that 'ACEs need to be understood in the context of poverty, inequality and discrimination' (NHS Health Scotland, 2019). Successive Programmes for Government have prioritised tackling child poverty alongside a strong focus on ACEs, and policies such as the Fairer Scotland Action Plan (Scottish Government, 2016a) are aimed at breaking 'the intergenerational cycles of poverty, inequality and deprivation'. This approach is also reflected in the re-framing of youth justice, which has shifted away from the punitive approaches of previous governments to take serious recognition of the degree of vulnerability experienced by children and young people. Underpinned by evidence of the damaging effects of justice system contact (McAra & McVie, 2010, 2018), the Scottish Government has implemented a new Whole Systems Approach to young people who offend, with emphasis on 'early and effective intervention' and diversion from prosecution. Recognition of vulnerability in the youth offending context has also sparked a series of ACE-informed strategies, including the introduction of 'trauma-informed' training in Scottish policing, aimed at increasing officer awareness of ACEs and 'reducing and mitigating the trauma that policing can cause' (Scottish Police Authority, 2019).

In relation to changes in criminal justice social work, the Management of Offenders (Scotland) Act 2005 created provision for eight Community Justice Authorities with the purpose to provide a more coordinated approach to the local delivery of 'offender' services, target services to reducing reoffending and ensure a good rapport between community-based services and prison services to aid rehabilitation. The Scottish Government's Justice Strategy (2012) has a strong focus on reducing reoffending and rehabilitating individuals, at the same time as protecting the public. Much of this effort has focused round the development and implementation of offence-focused programmes aiming to effect individual change. Whilst criminal justice social work does deliver offending behaviour programmes, often these have been local, with a limited evidence base, limited evaluation, and locally delivered and many of the national programmes have traditionally been delivered in prison. These programmes have included programmes to address violence, drug-related offending, female offending, offence-related need for short-term prisoners. The more innovative recent interventions have had goals of delivering offence-focused work that was delivered in prison and in the community and one flagship programme, the Caledonian Programme, has run only in the community.

The current intervention for those convicted of sexual offences (whilst currently being re-developed) is the Moving Forward: Making Changes (MF:MC). This is an intensive treatment programme for those convicted of sexual offences which aims to 'reduce the reoffending of men convicted of sexual offences and increase their opportunities and capacities for meeting needs by non-offending means' (MF:MC Management Manual, 2014).

MF:MC was designed by the Scottish Prison Service and the Community Justice Operational Practice Unit of the Scottish Government. It was introduced in Scotland in 2014, following accreditation by the Scottish Advisory Panel on Offender Rehabilitation (SAPOR). In line with evidence that intervention intensity ought to be linked to risk level (e.g. Lovins et al., 2009), it is aimed at adult (18 and over) male sexual offenders assessed as medium–high risk (via the Stable 2007 tool). Eligibility is based on risk level rather than offence type; men who have offended against children and against adult women are both eligible, as are those who have committed internet offences (although a slightly different assessment approach is recommended for this group). MF:MC is delivered in both custodial settings (currently in four prisons across Scotland) and in the community (currently eleven sites) and is a rolling programme with no restriction on completion.

The Caledonian Programme, the national programme was innovative as it was set up as a two-year long programme, clearly approaching the issue from a gender informed perspective, with individual and group work, delivered as part of a community sentence (minimum 2-years) and was also developed by social work rather than psychology so started from a wider philosophical perspective.

Moving forward: making changes was innovative as it was set up to run in prison and out so people could have a 'seamless sentence' doing some work in prison and some in the community. It had good feedback, however was also seen as creating as much ongoing need as it addressed, with practice concerns about long waiting lists, barrier to availability of the programme, ongoing risk being identified at the end of the programme, requiring further work and there being little link between the in prison and out of prison work, with the Parole Board being reluctant to accept some progress and ignore 'outstanding need' in relation to risk, so the promise of the seamless sentence was not fully achieved. Overall, there has been innovation and promise in the programmatic work in Scotland, but there is little formal evaluation and there are ongoing discussions as to how these programmes can be more fully integrated within the wider rehabilitation effort, and how to link prison and community work.

A further area of innovation in Scotland, and one named within the Scottish Government's rehabilitation plans is to expand the use of electronic monitoring. A huge amount of money has been earmarked to support electronic tagging, which in terms of rehabilitation, loosely translates into facilitating the management of more individuals in the community rather than in prison, by avoiding remand in custody or by allowing early release (Graham & McIvor, 2017). There is general evidence that electronic tagging, and home detention, is seen favourably by those who experience it, achieves targets of reducing the prison population and can offer some reassurance to the public as to monitoring of those who have ceased offending, so increase public confidence in community sentences, but the underpinning theory in terms of rehabilitation is less clear (Bullock & Bunce, 2020). Electronic monitoring is more focused on situational deterrence rather than rehabilitation per so. It does have an indirect rehabilitation element as it allows individuals to be in the community and be rebuilding their lives. However, whilst effective in allowing people to be in the community and not in prison, it seems that those who 'fail' on 'tagging' are part of the group thought to be the reason behind the increase in prisoners due to recall and failing to follow the rules of their parole. Electronic monitoring is likely only to work for some, and then only when linked to extra rehabilitative effort and support. It can also have the effect of derailing rehabilitation through overly intrusive monitoring of daily activities leading to recalls for technical breaches or for non-risk-related violations of conditions of community release/sentence. Thus, it is a muddled picture in Scotland where core elements of rehabilitative effort both promote and undermine rehabilitation at the same time.

Future Directions

So, returning to Martinson's assertion that nothing works, and the overall direction of travel in rehabilitation internationally, where does Scotland sit?

Overall, it appears that over recent decades, Scotland has become more welfare focused and has enacted some significant changes in policy and practice to promote rehabilitative effort, at least for some groups: women and young people. There is evidence of policy and practice shift, in sentencing, in prison building, and in the goals set for interventions for these groups across justice agencies. However, the Scottish prison population has almost achieved the figures predicted for the 'no change' option within 'Scotland's Choice' (Scotland's Choice Report, 2008); males, particularly those from backgrounds with high deprivation, continue to be remanded to custody pre-sentence, and sentenced to imprisonment, or end up in prison for violations of community disposals (Monbiot, 2008). There are excellent innovation interventions available for a few offences, (MF:MC and Caledonian) but limits to availability to the groups in prison, (Scottish Prison Service, n.d.) and limited offences targeted and a significant gap in an independent evaluation of these interventions. SAPOR whilst aiming to move away from being SAPOP and just accrediting programmes is still very much advising and accrediting programmes (Scottish Advisory Panel on Offender Rehabilitation, 2020).

There is still a long way to go. The discourse of rehabilitation in Scotland is prompting Scotland to consider approaches to punishment that are more meaningful, efficient, and effective. We need these to be more fully and holistically enacted and for there to be more joined up holistic social reform too. It is suggested that adopting an intersectional approach, which links social deprivation, structural disadvantage with individual criminogenic risk and human need, could cast light on how and where particular inequalities intersect: to better understand the experiences of particular people or groups.

Note

1. https://www.svru.co.uk/.

References

Blair, A., Marryat, L., & Frank, J. (2019). How community resources mitigate the association between household poverty and the incidence of adverse childhood experiences. *International Journal of Public Health, 64*(7), 1059–1068. https://doi.org/10.1007/s00038-019-01258-5

Bonta, J., & Andrews, D. A. (2016). The psychology of criminal conduct. *Routledge*. https://doi.org/10.4324/9781315677187

Bronfenbrenner, U. (1977). Toward an experimental ecology of human development. *American Psychologist, 32*, 513–531. https://doi.org/10.1037/0003-066X.32.7.513

Bullock, K., & Bunce, A. (2020). The prison doesn't talk to you about getting out of prison: On why prisons in England and Wales fail to rehabilitate prisoners.

Criminology and Criminal Justice, 20(1), 111–127. https://doi.org/10.1177/1748895818800743

Burke, L., Collett, S., & McNeill, F. (2018). *Reimagining rehabilitation: Beyond the individual* (1st edn.). Routledge. https://doi.org/10.4324/9781315310176

Cullen, F. T., & Gilbert, K. E. (1982). *Reaffirming rehabilitation*. Anderson Publishing.

Decker, S. H., Katz, C., & Webb, V. (2008). Understanding the black box of gang organization: Implications for involvement in violent crime, drug sales, and violent victimization. *Crime and Delinquency, 54*, 153–172.

Eski, Y., McGuinness, P., & Burman, M. (2011). *Report for AUDIT SCOTLAND changes to scotland's criminal justice system post-devolution: Main legislative developments, major reviews of policy and procedure, and the introduction of 'new' bodies June 2011*. Audit Scotland.

Graham, H., & McIvor, G. (2017). Advancing electronic monitoring in Scotland: Understanding the influences of localism and professional ideologies. *European Journal of Probation, 9*(1), 62–79. https://doi.org/10.1177/2066220317697659

Graham, L., Heller-Murphy, S., Aitken, L., & McAuley, A. (2012). Alcohol problems in a remand Scottish prisoner population. *International Journal of Prisoner Health, 8*(2), 51–59. https://doi.org/10.1108/17449201211277174

Henry, S., & Milovanovic, D. (1996). *Constitutive criminology: beyond postmodernism*. Sage Publications. ISBN 978–0–8039–7584–2.

Home Office. (1999). *Managing dangerous people with severe personality disorder: Proposals for policy development*. TSO (The Stationery Office), [Google Scholar].

Houchin, R. (2005). *Social exclusion and imprisonment in Scotland a report*. http://www.scotpho.org.uk/downloads/SocialExclusionandImprisonmentinScotland.pdf

Lightowler, C., & Hare, D. (2009). Prisons and sentencing reform: Developing policy in Scotland SCCJR and SPIF. http://www.sccjr.ac.uk/wpcontent/uploads/2012/11/Report_2009__02_-_Prisons_and_Sentencing_Reform.pdf

Lord, K. (1995). *The Kilbrandon report: Children and young persons in Scotland*. HMSO

Lovins, B., Lowenkamp, C. T., & Latessa, E. J. (2009). Applying the risk principle to sex offenders: Can treatment make some sex offenders worse? *The Prison Journal, 89*(3), 344–357. https://doi.org/10.1177/0032885509339509

Management of Offenders (Scotland) Act 2019. (2022, Jan 5). https://www.legislation.gov.uk/asp/2019/14/contents/enacted

Management Manual. (2014). *Moving forward: Making changes—An evaluation of a group-based treatment programme for sex offenders, August 2018*. Rachel Ormston and Ciaran Mullholland Ipsos MORI Scotland.

Martinson, R. (1974). What works? Questions and answers about prison reform. *The Public Interest, 35*, 22–54.

McAra, L. (2005). Modelling penal transformation. *Punishment and Society, 7*(3), 277–302.

McAra, L., & McVie, S. (2010). Youth crime and justice in Scotland. In H. Croall, G. Mooney, and M. Munro (Eds.), *Criminal justice in contemporary Scotland*. Routledge.

McNeill, F. (2014). Punishment as rehabilitation. In G. Bruinsma & D. Weisburd (Eds.), *Encyclopedia of criminology and criminal justice* (pp. 4195–4206). Springer. Copyright © 2014. Deposited on: 21 February 2014. ISBN: 9781461456896.

McNeill, F., Croall, H., Mooney, G., & Munro, M. (2016). *Desistance and criminal justice in Scotland: Crime, justice, and society in Scotland*. Routledge.

Monbiot, G. (2008). *Comment and debate: Crime is falling - but our obsession with locking people up keeps growing Wealth, and the desire to preserve it, is what drives citizens of rich nations to demand an increasingly punitive justice system*. The Guardian.

Morrison, K. (2019). Scottish penal reform since devolution: Reflections and prospects for change SCCJR. *The Justice Story*. https://sccjrblog.wordpress.com/2019/06/25/scottish-penal-reform-since-devolution-reflections-and-prospects-for-change/

Newburn, T. (2007). "Tough on crime": Penal policy in England and Wales. *Crime and Justice, 36*(1), 425–470. https://doi.org/10.1086/592810

NHS Health Scotland. (2019). *Adverse childhood experiences in context*. NHS Health Scotland.

Public Health Scotland. (2021). *Improving health drugs overview*. http://www.healthscotland.scot/health-topics/drugs/drugs-overview

Remch, M., Mautz, C., Burke, E. G., Junker, G., Kaniuka, A., Proescholdbell, S., Marshall, S. W., & Naumann, R. B. (2021). Impact of a prison therapeutic diversion unit on mental and behavioural health outcomes. *American Journal of Preventive Medicine, 61*(5), 619–627. https://doi.org/10.1016/j.amepre.2021.05.023

Scottish Advisory Panel on Offender Rehabilitation (SAPOR). (2020, Sept 11). *Annual report 2018–2020*. https://www.gov.scot/publications/sapor-annual-report-2018-2019-2019-2020/

Scottish Executive. (2004). *Supporting safer, stronger communities: Scotland's criminal justice plan*. http://www.scotland.gov.uk/ Publications/2004/12/20345/47602.

Scottish Government. (2014). *Future model for community justice in Scotland—Summary of consultation responses*. APS Group.

Scottish Government. (2016a). *Fairer Scotland action plan*. Scottish Government. https://www.gov.scot/binaries/content/documents/govscot/publications/strategy-plan/2016/10/fairerscotland-action-plan/documents/00506841-pdf/00506841-pdf/govscot%3Adocument/00506841.pdf

Scottish Government. (2016b). *Scotland's serious organised crime strategy 2016 annual report*. https://www.parliament.scot/-/media/files/legislation/proposed-members-bills/domestic-abuse-register--consultation-final.pdf. Accessed 28 Sept 2022.

Scottish Government. (2018, June 12). *The national drug—related deaths database (Scotland) report*. Analysis of deaths occurring in 2015 and 2016. https://www.isdscotland.org/Health-Topics/Drugs-and-Alcohol-Misuse/Publications/2018-06-12/2018-06-12-NDRDD-Report.pdf

Scottish Government. (2020). *Recorded crime in Scotland, 2019–20, Crime and Justice*. A National Statistic Publication for Scotland. https://www.svru.co.uk/wp content/uploads/2020/10/recorded-crime-scotland-2019-20.pdf. Accessed 29 Sept 2022.

Scottish Government. (2022). *Reducing reoffending*. https://www.gov.scot/policies/reducing-reoffending/

Scottish Police Authority. (2019). *Trauma informed policing*. Scottish Police Authority. http://www.spa.police.uk/assets/126884/441011/509407/511993/item4

Scottish Sentencing Council. (2022). *Sentencing young people sentencing guideline effective*, from 26 January 2022. https://www.scottishsentencingcouncil.org.uk/media/2171/sentencing-young-peopleguideline-for-publication.pdf. Accessed 28 Sept 2022.

Scottish Prison Service. (n.d.). Unlocking potential transforming lives. https://www.sps.gov.uk/Corporate/News/News-5137.aspx

The Presumption Against Short Periods of Imprisonment [Scotland Order]. (2019). You are here: Scottish Statutory Instruments. https://www.legislation.gov.uk/ssi/2019/236/contents/made. accessed 28 Sept 2022.

The Scottish Government's Justice Strategy. (2012). *The strategy for justice in Scotland*. The Scottish Government St Andrew's House, Edinburgh EH1 3DG. ISBN: 978-1-78045-890-8.

The Scottish Prisons Commission. (2008, July). *Scotland's choice: Report of the Scottish prisons commission*. The Scottish Prisons Commission. https://www.iprt.ie/site/assets/files/6132/scotlands_choice.pdf. Accessed 28 Sept 2022. ISBN: 978-0-7559-5772-9.

Treanor, M., Macht, A., Morton, S., & Seditas, K. (2017). *Tackling child poverty: Actions to prevent and mitigate child poverty at the local level*. What Works Scotland.

Tyler, N., Miles, H. L., Karadag, B., & Rogers, G. (2019). An updated picture of the mental health needs of male and female prisoners in the UK: Prevalence, comorbidity, and gender differences. *Social Psychiatry and Psychiatric Epidemiology, 54*(9), 1143–1152. https://doi.org/10.1007/s00127-019-01690-1

Webster, C., & Kingston. (2014a). *Poverty and crime review, Joseph Rowntree Foundation: Anti-poverty strategies for the UK, full report*. Joseph Rowntree Foundation. http://eprints.leedsbeckett.ac.uk/849/1/JRF%20Final%20Poverty%20and%20Crime%20Review%20May%202014.pdf

Young, P. (1997). *Crime and criminal justice in Scotland*. The Stationery Office.

Offender Rehabilitation Approaches in South Africa: An Evidence-Based Analysis

Shanta Balgobind Singh
and Patrick Bashizi Bashige Murhula

In South Africa, according to Cilliers and Smit (2007), more and more people are being incarcerated for longer periods of time. Communities are becoming more risk-averse and punitive in their attitudes towards people who break the law, and there would appear to be a growing determination to make individuals pay severely for their transgressions. At the same time, significant effort is put into rehabilitating and helping them plan for successful reintegration back into society.

In terms of rehabilitation, the South African Department of Correctional Services (DCS) places its focus on the principles of 'Batho Pele' (people first) in its transformation of service delivery to inmates. These principles are based on consultation, service standards, access, courtesy, information, openness and transparency, redress, and value for money. The DCS's focus is on transforming South African prisons from being so-called 'universities of crime' into effective rehabilitation centres that produce skilled and reformed individuals capable of successfully reintegrating into their communities as law-abiding

S. B. Singh (✉)
University of KwaZulu-Natal, Durban, South Africa
e-mail: singhsb@ukzn.ac.za

P. B. B. Murhula
Department of Law, Walter Sisulu University, Durban, South Africa
e-mail: bmurhula@wsu.ac.za

citizens. Therefore, the DCS has identified the enhancement of rehabilitation programmes as a key fundamental starting point in contributing to a crime-free society (Coetzee, 2003a). For instance, Section 41 (1) of the South African Correctional Services Act (Act 111 of 1998) requires that all rehabilitation centres working under the DCS must provide programmes and activities which meet the needs of participants. Furthermore, the White Paper on Corrections in South Africa (2005) stipulates that the aim of rehabilitation is first, to provide them with treatment and development programmes in partnership with communities; second to enhance personal and social functioning; then to prepare them for reintegration into the community as productive, well-adapted, and law-abiding citizens; and finally, to reduce the rate of recidivism.

The Correctional Services Act (Act No. 111 of 1998) and the South African White Paper on rehabilitation, put a substantial responsibility on the DCS since they see rehabilitation as a right of those who have broken the law and not as a conditional luxury that is subject to accessible resources (Muntingh, 2005). In essence, rehabilitation programmes must guarantee that their graduates do not again depend on criminal activities upon their release. However, Schoeman (2013) states that recidivism rates in South Africa are estimated to be between 55 and 95%. Therefore, based on interviews with inmates, academics, and prison personnel, this chapter aims to investigate the South African rehabilitation approach and the causes of its failure to rehabilitate inmates.

The chapter proceeds as follows: the first section presents the background and the principles of 'offender rehabilitation' in South Africa. The subsequent section provides an understanding of the concept of rehabilitation and how the term is defined. The third section focuses on rehabilitation within South African prisons. It reflects a broader perspective of different programmes and services provided to inmates within prisons to promote their rehabilitation. Based on empirical data, section four presents and discusses issues impeding the DCS from successfully implementing such programmes in its facilities. The final section concludes by summarising the insights of previous sections.

Understanding the Concept of Rehabilitation

Ideas and practices associated with rehabilitation in criminal justice have a long history, stretching back at least as far as the antiquity period. However, as a concept, rehabilitation is surprisingly difficult to pin down, so that when different writers, theorists, or practitioners refer to it, there is quite a good chance that they are not talking about precisely the same thing. This is, in part at least, because rehabilitation can be understood both as a general objective or goal *and* as a process or set of practices (Rotman, 1995); but attempts to define rehabilitation are also complicated by a proliferation of related terms. Some of these, such as reform and redemption, have a long history; others such as reintegration, resettlement, and reentry have more recent origins.

Clearly, what all these terms share in common is the prefix 're' which implies a return to a previous condition. It is perhaps unsurprising then to learn that according to a general, dictionary definition, rehabilitation is closely associated with the notion of 'restoration', which denotes a return to a former, desirable state or status (Casey et al., 2012). Thinking about rehabilitation as a process of restoration certainly seems to make good sense in medical contexts, where one often talks about the rehabilitation of a person following a physical injury sustained in an accident. Here, there is a clear sense in which the process of rehabilitation involves assisting the individual to get back to normal. The individual may need to relearn skills, such as how to walk in the case of a broken limb or seek to recover cognitive skills, such as memory in the case of a head injury. In either scenario, rehabilitation implies returning to a former, favourable state (Casey et al., 2012). This is arguably a useful starting point for thinking about personal rehabilitation. If asked to describe a rehabilitated person, it is likely that most people would indicate someone with some history of offending behaviour that has now ceased. One might think of this as a return to normal, law-abiding behaviour. This is clearly a behavioural definition: it is about a change in the way a person behaves (Casey et al., 2012). Hence, the action of rehabilitation might involve the provision of interventions to remove the propensity, desire, or necessity to offend.

Nonetheless, the notion of rehabilitation also has a symbolic dimension, such that it implies a return to a former status: that of a law-abiding citizen who is accepted by and enjoys the same rights as other members of the community. In other words, it is not just a behavioural change but also a symbolic process whereby an individual is permitted to shed the negative label of 'offender' and to be reinstated within the community after a period of exclusion or censure (Casey et al., 2012). Thus, there are good grounds for thinking about rehabilitation in terms of restoration. According to Sections 4.2.1 and 4.2.2 of the South African White Paper on Correction, rehabilitation is the consequence of a procedure that joins the correction of offending behaviour with human development and the promotion of social responsibility (Muntingh, 2005). In addition, it states that rehabilitation must be seen not only as a technique to avert crime but instead as a complete phenomenon combining and encouraging social responsibility and social justice to reduce recidivism (White Paper on Corrections, 2005).

The 'Offender Rehabilitation Approach' in South Africa: Need and Risk Assessment Principles

In South Africa, the Offender Rehabilitation Approach, in all its prisons, is centred on the needs-based care approach, which is aimed at maintaining the well-being of inmates and social integration. The philosophy behind the approach resides in the need and risk assessment principles, and rehabilitation—comprising structured day programmes. Following the need and risk assessment principles, correctional facilities usually conduct assessments for a number of purposes: an assessment to determine security risk, which determines the person's security classification in an institution; a risk/needs assessment prior to and during the time s/he serves his or her sentence, in order to determine and develop an appropriate intervention plan; and a risk assessment to indicate someone's risk of re-offending after release (Dissel, 2012). These principles require a proper assessment prior to beginning a treatment programme to determine the risk of re-offending and his or her needs to decide which programme or programmes would be most appropriate and in what dosage. The assessment is usually designed to ascertain dynamic risk factors and criminogenic needs (Bonta, 2007). The assessment is informed by a particular theory of criminal behaviour that certain types of attitudes or behaviours are related to re-offending or can be changed through targeted treatment programmes (Bonta, 2007). Several inmates' assessment tools have been developed around the world. For instance, Canada uses the Level of Service Inventory-Ontario Revised (LSR-OR) and the Community Risk/Needs Management Scale (CRNMS). These tools have been correlated with recidivism levels (Motiuk and Serin, n.d.). The LSR-OR looks at criminal history, employment and education, peers, leisure and recreation, family or marital status, history, criminal orientation, attitude, substance abuse, and antisocial patterns. This determines the risk of re-offending and criminogenic needs.

In South Africa, the current needs and risk assessment tool in use in prisons has been adapted from the LSR-OR and CRNMS, but it has been shortened and simplified to become a short questionnaire (Hesselink-Louw, 2014). Participants are screened to determine their needs and responsivity for treatment. Answers are obtained through self-reporting questionnaires and/or interviews based on criminal history, substance abuse history, interpersonal relationships, psychiatric disability, literacy defects, intellectual disability, and language and cultural barriers.

The Rehabilitation Principle

In South Africa, the rehabilitation principle refers to the use of a style and mode of intervention that engages the interest of inmates and takes into account their relevant characteristics, such as cognitive ability, learning style, and values. It comprises structured day programmes and services such as (a) education, skills development, and training programmes; (b) psychological services; (c) social work services; and (d) spiritual care sessions (White Paper on Corrections, 2005). The provision of rehabilitation programmes is aimed at maintaining the well-being of inmates and their social reintegration. Providing services focused on preparation for release and reintegration into society forms part of the rehabilitation process of each inmate. Muntingh and Gould (2010) insist that rehabilitation programmes should be based on credible scientific evidence that the methods and approaches used are likely to be effective in a particular correctional setting. The South African Offender Rehabilitation Path (ORP) entails converting certain guiding principles from the South African White Paper on Corrections into practice, as reflected in Table 1 (South African Government, 2005). According to the DCS (2018), the noble aspiration of this process—ORP—, rehabilitation per se, can only be achieved through the delivery of vital programmes to inmates, including modification of the offending behaviour and the development of the human being involved.

Evaluating the Implementation of the Offender Rehabilitation Approach in South Africa

Based on reviews of meta-analytical studies of programmes in correctional settings, Gendreau et al. (2009) compiled a list of guiding principles for their successful implementation. These fall into five categories: general organisational factors; programme factors; the importance of a change agent; staffing activities; and programme integrity. Our investigation used these categories to evaluate the rehabilitation approach in South Africa. We also explored the negative impact that overcrowding has on the rehabilitation of prisoners.

General organisational factors concern the host agency where the rehabilitation programmes are to be implemented. These refer to whether the host agency (in this case the prisons) has a history of adopting new initiatives, and whether it is able to put these into place efficiently. According to social workers who participated in this study, they always come up with new initiatives to facilitate and improve rehabilitation, but it is always difficult for the

Table 1 DCS offender rehabilitation path

1	Admission	Identification and capturing of personal details; welcoming; assessment of immediate risks and needs and referral to an assessment unit
2	Assessment/orientation/profiling in assessment unit	Comprehensive health assessment; orientation/induction; comprehensive risks/needs assessment; profiling/analysis of assessment outcomes; classification; development of sentence plan; confirmation of the classification and the correctional sentence plan; and allocation to housing unit/transfer to another prison
3	Admission to a housing unit	Induction and allocation of offenders to a Case Officer
4	Intervention	Implementation of the correctional sentence plan and case review (progress, updating of correctional sentence plan and offender profile)
5	Monitoring and evaluation	Decisions are made according to the offender's progress or lack thereof. Feedback reports and reclassification
6	Placement	Reassessment and recommendation (pre-release needs/risks, review of community profile, possible placement on parole/correctional supervision, pre-placement report); effecting instructions/recommendations (capture decisions/recommendations on pre-placement profile and roll out to pre-release unit)
7	Allocation to pre-release unit	Preparation for release and reintegration; transfer offender to the prison closest to where he /she will reside 6 months prior to placement or release; pre-release assessment occurs during this phase

Source Department of Correctional Services (2018)

DCS management to accept their recommendations or proposals. Furthermore, social workers revealed that lack of participation in decision-making negatively affects their job. Their ideas are illustrated by the following quotes:

> …look I honestly feel sometimes they come with programmes that are not helpful. They do give us guidelines on a certain aspect, but you know I don't think that if they come with programmes it will help us, I will rather have them ask us what we think we should be trained on…as social workers we have learnt to be more innovative, we design our own programmes that will suit a particular clientele…

> Working as a case management officer, I form part of the middle management where I supposed to suggest solutions to issues we are facing but often they don't care to take our suggestions in consideration…

…we discuss matters happening in the institution, however our suggestions to solve those matters are most of the time dismissed…but later we will be blamed for whatever is happening to offenders even if we suggested some solutions to resolve different issues faced by them…

According to Lambert et al. (2012), administrative factors such as lack of participation in decision-making can significantly affect staff. Drawing from the findings above it can be urged that it is important to allow employees to have an influence in matters that affect their work, as this not only helps to establish a working and practical guiding tools but will further enhance the working relationship between employees within organisations. Furthermore, no matter the position a person holds within an organisation, their input can be important in the functioning of the organisation and towards the achievement of set organisational goals (Gendreau et al., 2009). In situations where employees such as the correctional officers are snubbed in decision-making, they tend to shy away, develop low-esteem, and become disinterested in the work. A sense of belonging could be nurtured if only the top management could listen to the suggestions being put forward.

In taking account of programme factors, the DCS, (and the noble aspirations of the ORP), noted that rehabilitation per se can only be achieved through the delivery of vital programmes including modification of offending behaviour and the development of the human being involved. However, based on the evidence collected in this study the DCS is unable to deliver appropriate rehabilitation programmes due to shortages of staff such as psychologists and social workers. According to Correctional Services Act 111 of 1998 (as amended), the DCS is committed to offering psychological services to all inmates with the aim of improving their mental and emotional well-being. However, based on the findings, due to the scarcity of psychologists, the majority of those sentenced cannot receive psychological treatment as evidenced by one of the participants who stated that as psychologists, they cope by prioritising the cases that need to be seen. Psychologists mainly attend to the following target groups: suicide risks, court referrals, persons who have previously received psychiatric or psychological treatment and/or who are mentally ill, youth and females, aggressive and/or sexual offenders, and persons who request to see a psychologist. When asked if all these targeted groups of inmates use their services (especially sexual offenders), the participant responded that some of the cases are referred to social workers. However, having social workers perform psychologists' duties has a negative impact on rehabilitation because only psychologists (not social workers) within the Directorate of Psychological Services in correctional facilities can ensure that cases are diagnosed and evaluated through means of interviewing psychometric tests, and observations. The application of basic and applied psychological science or scientifically oriented professional practice by psychologists enables the proper classification, treatment, and management of prisoners. Its goal is to reduce their risk of re-offending and thus improve their rehabilitation and reintegration into the community.

When it comes to social workers, their core function is to assess inmates and provide needs-based programmes and services to enhance their adjustment, social functioning, and reintegration back into the community. In the DCS's correctional facilities, one of the major responsibilities of social workers is to empower their charges with social and life skills and to help them reintegrate successfully into society once they have been released from prison. The overall sentiment expressed by social workers who participated in this study is that their working conditions are poor, especially in relation to facilitating group rehabilitation sessions. It appears that individual sessions can be conducted since they do not require a lot of space, but group work is a challenge due to the small rooms available. To facilitate group work sessions, the social worker needs a room where chairs can be arranged in a circle so that the participants can maintain eye contact with each other. The importance of the physical setting for group work is also accentuated by Toseland and Rivas (2011) who state that the social worker should pay attention to the total effect of the physical setting on a group's ability to accomplish its tasks. Furthermore, the group workroom should not be too small, so that the space between members is not adequate, and not so big as to put too much physical distance between members, who may then lose interest in being part of or participating in the group (Toseland & Rivas, 2011). Social workers who participated in this study furthermore asserted that the issue of overcrowding in prisons leads to a higher workload and a strain on prisons' resources. This was clearly stated by one of the social workers at the Westville Prison, in Durban:

...in this facility [medium B] the last time I checked we had 3900 inmates...and in medium B it is about 13 social workers, but I will say about 3 of them are on supervisory services. But the other 10 are mostly production...and it is very difficult because even our standards you know, we have our standards as social workers...each social worker, the production worker is supposed to have at least a case of about 240 per year, 240 cases per year and you find that we can't...we are unable to cope with the number we are having, I don't want to lie...we can't cope because we have a lot of admissions and it makes rehabilitation very difficult because we have a lot of cases to attend to...

Social workers additionally voiced concerns about their own security, which is always compromised, and this has a negative impact on the quality of service rendered to inmates. These findings are reflected in the quotation below:

> …you know we work in a security environment, it is [a] dangerous environment and more social workers are females, all the thirteen I told you, we have no male whatsoever. So, because we as females we are at risk of maybe…being stubbed or anything…and besides that all these are males who have committed serious crimes outside. They are not angels and the shortage of staff you know… expectation is that each offender comes [for consultation] with a custodial official but because of [the] shortage of members, it doesn't happen you know. We tried, we have registered almost all the management meetings about that, but nothing seems to change…but we have to work, we have to continue our work. So, that is the problem. You are working, you are afraid even though you [are] supposed to render a service that is satisfactory to offenders, but you are afraid. You fear for your life…

It is important to note that according to the ORP, rehabilitation should start when a person enters the DCS structure and continue until he/she is released back into the community. The intention of the ORP is that rehabilitation must be facilitated through a holistic sentence planning process that engages each inmate at all levels. However, this is not feasible in most prisons due to overcrowding as expressed here:

> …the intention here is that the rehabilitation of offenders should start as soon as the prisoner is admitted in this facility. We [are] supposed to assess them, do a unique profile of each offender, summarise needs, risks, and intervention strategy…but because of the small number of professional staff and a big number of prisoners we have, it is impossible to do it…sometimes we do it 3 or 5 months after the prisoner has been admitted…

According to Holtzhausen (2012), assessment should be the first step in the development itinerary of an inmate, and her/his needs should be harmonised with the necessary resources to ensure maximum support. Individual assessment is the basis for their treatment, especially on a personal level. Furthermore, Section 42(2) of the Correctional Services Act of 1998 stipulates that the case management committee must ensure that each sentenced inmate is assessed (Coetzee, 2003b): the assessment serving as a foundation of the ORP. However, assessment is a big challenge in South Africa. As result, inmates are enrolled in programmes without proper orientation as reported by one of the inmates who took part in this study:

> ...they got [have] substance abused [abuse] programmes, they got [have] anger management programmes, they got [have] economic crime from the social workers. What about the hard-core criminals who committed rape or robbery? The [they] put all of us in these same programmes. You can't take a person who committed rape and put him in the same programmes with someone like me who committed car theft?

Furthermore, evidence collected in this study confirmed that rehabilitation programmes in South Africa are often not effective because they continue to focus more on the process than on the results as evidenced by the finding below:

> ...before your release, they will tell you what to do [the programmes to attend]. This thing was not supposed to be done like this. I can't have just a month left for me to get out of jail then you say there is something that you will teach me so quick. All along I have been here for a long time you only telling me when I am leaving...they made me do that thing [attend rehabilitation programmes] and I did it in two weeks, then they released me from prison...nothing went in my mind and that is why...I am back again here [in prison]...

In South Africa, rehabilitation (in all its prisons) is centred on a needs-based approach which is aimed at maintaining the well-being of inmates and social integration. The philosophy behind the need-based approach resides in needs and risk assessment principles, and rehabilitation, comprising structured day programmes. It is apparent that the principles of need, risk, and rehabilitation are consistent with this model's overall aims. According to the need principle, treatment programmes should primarily focus on changing criminogenic needs which are dynamic characteristics that when changed, are associated with reduced rates of recidivism rates. However, there is no possibility of identifying programmes of choice for each inmate because the DCS uses the 'one-size-fits-all' approach when it comes to treatment (Hesselink-Louw, 2014). In South Africa, individual treatment is not the norm, despite the White Paper on Corrections underscoring the fact that there is a definite need to introduce more individualised treatment and assessment to coordinate and facilitate effective rehabilitation efforts. The importance of assessment does not primarily lie in protecting society from the lawbreakers but in enabling appropriate treatment with a focus on their rehabilitation and reintegration.

A programme is more effective if it is championed by a 'change agent' who is primarily responsible for initiating the programme. Such a person or institution could be an external consultant or someone internal to the organisation. The change agent should have intimate knowledge of the organisation and its staff and have the support of senior agency staff as well as line staff members (Dissel, 2012). The change agent should be compatible with the agency's mandate and goals and should have professional credibility and a history of successful implementation in the agency programmes area. The findings demonstrate that when it comes to individual rehabilitation the DCS uses the services of the Department of Basic and Higher Education or of other private institutions to assist them with some educational and training programmes:

> …we have tertiary education students [inmates], they register with UNISA [University of South Africa] and these other colleges…and then the skills where they are short courses and long courses, the Department [of Education] always send us a list maybe of all the programmes that are funded by the National Skills Fund so that we recruit inmates to attend those programmes. And some other time you find that they are external service providers maybe those ones they are being subsidised to train offenders so that they get accredited certificates.

> …programmes and lectures in this centre are aimed at addressing specific identified needs or problem areas of individual cases with a view to educate prisoners and the acquisition of social skills. These programmes are presented by expert personnel of corrections offices. Where such expert personnel are not available, we always arrange for the procurement of the services of external experts…

According to Lunenburg (2015), every organisational change (whether large or small) requires one or more change agents. The DCS always involves the Department of Basic and Higher Education and other private institutions as change agents to assist and improve educational and training programmes in its prisons. This research discovered that the success of the educational programmes in different prisons depends heavily on the quality and workability of the relationship between the change agent (Department of Basic and Higher Education) and the DCS. For instance, The DCS continues to achieve great Matric results, with the following prison population pass rates recorded in the last five years (Table 2).

Staff factors apply to those people directly implementing the service, as well as to their managers and supervisors. Findings revealed that most of the staff do not understand the theoretical basis of rehabilitation programmes, and do not have the technical and professional skills to implement the programmes as confirmed by participants in this study:

Table 2 DCS Matric results 2016–2021

Year	Matric pass rates (%)
2016	72.1
2017	76.7
2018	77.3
2019	82.6
2020	86.3
2021	89.0

Source SANews (2022)

…they took officials who are working here, and they made them do a course or a two weeks course and then bring them back here quickly to run programmes…they don't take professionals who studied for years to do that…they don't have professional skills, not at all, not at all…they take a warden to be a therapist, to make him a person who supposed to do anger management…

…they are plenty who are working and they don't have a passion of working here…they just work here because they have a salary…they don't care about us

No, they are not trained, or I can say some of them are trained to give us, to provide us with these programmes but some of them they are just doing it. They are not properly trained to do this, to facilitate these programmes…the people who are teaching the programmes you find sometimes the passion is not there to teach what they are teaching because they don't know what they are doing…

In order to meet the rehabilitation needs of inmates, all officials should be equipped with the necessary skills, knowledge, and passion, to present the relevant programmes. In this study, inmates indicated that officials need to be equipped with the necessary skills to improve their rehabilitation. Du Plessis and Lombard (2018), also, indicated that DCS officials, in general, are incompetent and unprofessional when implementing rehabilitation programmes. Most of them need specialised training to meet the needs of programme participants in a knowledgeable and professional manner (Du Plessis & Lombard, 2018). Even though professional correctional officials, who include social workers, psychologists, and educationists, are trained in their field of specialisation. Specific training is needed in terms of rehabilitation; staff need to complete courses on assessment and treatment. These skills should include general social learning and responsibility principles. In addition, Andrews (2000) suggests that staff skills and cognitions should also include those necessary for relationships and social interaction.

The broad aim of rehabilitation programmes is to transform antisocial attitudes and behaviour into prosocial ones and is achievable only if a focus is maintained on that aim. Ensuring that a programme is delivered according to the way it is designed and set out in the manuals (programme integrity) is a critical factor for effective delivery. Findings reveal that some officials are unable to implement rehabilitation programmes and are unfamiliar with some important concepts designed to implement and facilitate rehabilitation as set out in the quote below:

> …if you go to the unit we are staying, there is a sentence plain in our case files…you find that even the case officers in the unit they are not trained to come and address us in [our] cells about the programmes we must attend: you committed this crime, these are the programmes you must do…They are not doing that…. That shows they not properly trained to facilitate, to make sure that we are aware of the programmes…

According to Dissel (2012), one way of maintaining programme integrity over a number of interventions is to ensure that there are programme manuals that guide service deliverers in their implementation. A DCS official who took part in this study revealed that there are programme manuals in each department however, staff are not properly trained in their use and the infrastructure of the prison does not allow them to properly implement some of the programmes:

> …we need more training of officials to properly implement some programmes…we need specialists in [the] development of offenders and our correctional structure should be changed for housing unit. We are still utilising the structure which was designed for locking, feeding, locking…

Integrity is also enhanced when there is an understanding of when the specific treatment has come to an end and when the dosage requirements have been met. Integrity thus requires that the programmes are monitored to ascertain whether intermediate objectives have been achieved. Several studies have found that many correctional programmes fail to work because they are not rooted in sound criminological theory. Scholars have argued that some of the variations in effectiveness observed among meta-analyses of correctional programmes likely stem from a lack of programme integrity (Cullen, 2013; Duwe, 2017; Gendreau, 1996). Despite its importance, the integrity of rehabilitation programmes has often been overlooked in South Africa.

Study findings show that levels of integrity are not high, officials do not deliver programmes as intended, with enthusiasm and commitment, and do not maintain good delivery quality. Nor do they sustain the style of directness necessary to encourage the engagement of inmates. According to Duwe (2017), higher programme integrity is always associated with larger reductions in recidivism.

The Impact of Prison Overcrowding on the Rehabilitation of Offenders

Of paramount concern to the DCS regarding the rehabilitation of offenders, is the severe overcrowding of prisons. Like many other countries in the world, (such as the United Kingdom and the United States of America), South Africa is faced with ever-increasing numbers being held in overcrowded prisons. According to the DCS (2022), the number of inmates in its correctional facilities across the country is around 140 948 against a bedspace total of 110 836 as of 31 March 2021, i.e. on average there is an overcrowding rate of 27%. However, it is important to note that of the 243 correctional facilities across South Africa, 157 are technically underpopulated while 77 facilities located in provinces such as Gauteng, Eastern Cape, and Western Cape are more than 150% full (Knight, 2019). Prison officials who took part in this study are of the view that, due to prison overcrowding, overall rehabilitation is not given the attention it deserves, since the emphasis falls more on security than on rehabilitation. As a result, prison management perceives rehabilitation as a less important service. Furthermore, the findings demonstrate that given the current precise legislation on rehabilitation in South Africa, the biggest challenge lies in the implementation of the policy, i.e. programme integrity. Due to the shortage of resources caused by overcrowding, the implementation of rehabilitation programmes has become problematic. Furthermore, Dissel (2012) reports that overcrowding leads also to poor sanitation in prisons. This has a ripple effect, as diseases spread faster in those facilities. The most common diseases found in South African prisons are hepatitis, syphilis, tuberculosis, and HIV and AIDS. The increase in HIV and AIDS infections has led to many deaths among inmates (Dissel, 2012). This then defeats the whole purpose of imprisonment for rehabilitation and reform.

Conclusion

It was central for this chapter to analyse the DCS Rehabilitation Approach in South Africa. The evidence collected confirms that some circumstances seriously hamper the DCS's efforts to place rehabilitation at the centre of its activities. This chapter, evidently and in a broader perspective, establishes that there is a huge implementation problem of rehabilitation programmes in the DCS correctional facilities. This translates into a system that is weak and has more functional challenges to achieving the intended results compared to the overall objective and purpose of rehabilitation crafted in the White Paper on Corrections. For instance, it was found that inmate assessment is a big challenge. As a result, inmates are enrolled in rehabilitation programmes without proper orientation. Furthermore, individual treatment is not the norm, despite the White Paper on Corrections underscoring the fact that there is a definite need to coordinate and facilitate effective rehabilitation efforts. However, it is clear that the major cause of the DCS's failure in implementing meaningful rehabilitation programmes for inmates is prison overcrowding. The limited budget allocated to rehabilitation, and the shortage of resources in correctional facilities, have failed to keep pace with the increased prison population demands in terms of providing rehabilitation programmes.

References

Andrews, D. (2000). Principles of effective correctional programs. In *Compendium 2000 on effective correctional programming*. Correctional Service Canada.

Bonta, J. (2007). Offender risk assessment and sentencing. *Canadian Journal of Criminology and Criminal Justice, 49*, 519–529.

Casey, A., Day, A., Vess, J., & Ward, T. (2012). *Foundations of offender rehabilitation*. Routledge.

Cilliers, C., & Smit, J. (2007). Offender rehabilitation in the South African correctional system: Myth or reality? *Acta Criminologica, 2*(20), 1–83.

Coetzee, W. (2003a). Ethics in correction: A South African perspective. *Acta Criminologica, 1*(16), 63–71.

Coetzee, W. (2003b). The assessment of inmates: A philosophical historical perspective of the South African Situation. Unpublished document.

Cullen, F. (2013). Rehabilitation: Beyond nothing works. In *Crime and Justice in America, 1975 to 2025. Crime and Justice: A review of research* (pp. 299–376). University of Chicago Press.

Department of Correctional Services. (2018). *Department of correctional services annual report 2017/2018*. Department of Correctional Services.

Department of Correctional Services. (2022). *Department of correctional services annual report 2020/21*. DCS.

Dissel, A. (2012). *Good practice principles in reducing reoffending: A review of the literature*. Civil Society Prison Reform Initiative.

Du Plessis, J., & Lombard, A. (2018). Challenges for rehabilitation of sentenced offenders within the framework of unit management in the department of correctional services: Bethal Management Area. *Social Work, 4*(54), 481–492.

Duwe, G. (2017). *The use and impact of correctional programming for inmates on pre-and post-release outcomes*. National Institute of Justice.

Gendreau, P. (1996). The principles of effective interventions with offenders. In A. Harland (Ed.), *Choosing correctional options that work: Defining the demand and evaluation the supply*. Sage.

Gendreau, P., Goggin, C., & Smith, P. (2009). The forgotten issue in effective correctional treatment: Program implementation. *International Journal of Offender Therapy and Comparative Criminology, 43*, 180–187.

Hesselink, A., & Booyens, K. (2014). Correctional criminology: An innovative South African practice. *Acta Criminologica, 1*, 1–15.

Hesselink-Louw, A. (2014). *Criminological assessment of prison inmates: A constructive mechanism towards offender rehabilitation*. University of South Africa.

Holtzhausen, L. (2012). *Social work: A South African practice framework for professionals working with offenders and victims*. Juta.

Knight, T. (2019). *Extent of overcrowding at SA prisons revealed. South Africa*. Daily Maverick.

Lambert, E., Hogan, L., Barton-Bellessa, M., & Jiang, S. (2012). Examining the relationship between supervisors and management trust and job burnout among correctional officers. *Criminal Justice and Behaviour, 12*(39), pp. 938–957

Motiuk, L., & Serin, R. (n.d.). *Situating risk assessment in the reintegration potential framework*. Research Branch, Correctional Service Canada.

Muntingh, L. (2005). *Alternative sentencing review seminar*. Department of Criminology and Civil Society Prison Reform Initiative.

Muntingh, L., & Gould, C. (2010). *Towards an understanding of repeat violent offending: A review of the literature*. Oxford University Press.

Rotman, E. (1995). The failure of reform: United States, 1865–1965. In N. Morris and D. Rothman (Eds.), *The Oxford history of prison: The practice of punishment in Western society*. Oxford University Press.

SANews. (2022). *Matric results 2021: Inmates achieve 89% pass rate, 77 Bachelor passes*. The Citizens.

Schoeman, M. (2013). *A classification system and an inter-disciplinary action plan for the prevention and management of recidivism*. University of Pretoria.

South African Government. (2005). *White paper on corrections in South Africa*. Government Printers.

Toseland, R., & Rivas, R. (2011). *An Introduction to group work practice*. Pearson.

Rehabilitation in Spain: Between Legal Intentions and Institutional Limitations

Ester Blay

Brief Context: Setting the Legal and Administrative Scene

The term 'rehabilitation' in the title of this volume is relatively foreign to Spanish penological discourse, particularly at a legal and administrative level and, to a lesser extent, in academic and civic discourse. The local terminology more often resorts to the terms 're-education' and 'social reintegration' to refer to the idea that sentences should aim at addressing the needs of the person who has offended to ensure that after serving them they are capable of living a law-abiding life. This autochthonous nomenclature reflects the existence of a long-standing local concern for the change and well-being of prisoners. Thus, there is a strong humanistic trend in Spanish penitentiary tradition, parallel to a reality marked by harsh prison conditions, scarcity of means, and a critique of practices (Solar Calvo, 2019). This chapter, however, focuses on the present, which for our purpose starts with the advent of the current democratic regime after the end of the Francoist dictatorship. Thus, the current penological legal framework is set by the 1978 Constitution, the 1979 Prison Law, and the 1995 Criminal Code.

E. Blay (✉)
University of Girona, Girona, Spain
e-mail: ester.blay@udg.edu

The 1978 Constitution establishes that penalties and measures consisting in deprivation of freedom (mainly, imprisonment) 'shall be oriented towards re-education and social reintegration' and establishes that those punished with prison shall be granted the same rights as any citizen, except those limited by the judicial ruling, the meaning of the sentence and penitentiary law, that they will have 'a right to paid work and the corresponding Social Security benefits, access to culture and the full development of their personality' (art. 25.2 Spanish Constitution). This declaration, which establishes the principles of rehabilitation and normalisation, is promising; the Constitutional Court, however, has interpreted it in a somehow restrictive way: those sentenced to imprisonment have no individual right to re-education and social reintegration which obligates the administration. Rather, re-education and social reintegration work as principles that should inspire law and policy, and they can do so together with other legitimate principles of punishment, such as deterrence or retribution. This interpretation has limited the potential of the constitutional recognition of rehabilitation and shows the ambiguity and limits of rehabilitation in our context.

The Prison Law of 1979 was the first law passed by Parliament in the current democratic regime. It was enacted at a moment of hunger strikes and rioting in many prisons, with intense pressure for reform (Lorenzo Rubio, 2013). Perhaps as a result of this and the need to set legal and political distance from the Francoist regime, it is one of the most progressive pieces of prison legislation in Europe (Medina Ariza, 2004) and it incorporates and develops the established principles of rehabilitation (re-education and social reintegration).

The current Criminal Code was enacted in 1995 and has experienced more than 35 legal reforms since. This piece of legislation meant longer prison sentences, both through the lengthening of established prison sentences for some common offences, such as property crimes, and through the elimination of good time credit; on the other hand, the legislation introduced community sanctions and measures such as community service orders (González Sánchez, 2021). During the first years of democracy, law and order were largely absent from political and partisan debate and important legal reforms were undertaken where the concern was individual rights (Medina Ariza, 2004). However, various elements, such as increasing pressure towards the criminalisation of drugs, or the resort to penal legislation to address social problems translated, particularly since the year 2000, 'into growing penal pressure despite the symbolic pronouncements in favour of rehabilitation and democratic values' perhaps reflecting the 'long shadow cast by subterranean authoritarian and punitive values inherited after 40 years of dictatorship'

(Medina Ariza, 2004: 187). Most scholars agree that since the political transition there has been an expansion of punitiveness in Spain, which has received considerable scholarly attention (see for example Díes Ripollés, 2004; Larrauri, 2006). It is in this context that rehabilitation has retained a considerable symbolic value, albeit with important practical limitations, as we shall try to show in the following pages.

There are currently three relatively independent administrations responsible for the execution of punishments, both prisons and community sentences: the ones in Catalonia, the Basque Country, and the rest of Spain. The Criminal Code, and the regulations for prison and community sanctions are common to the whole country. However, each of the administrations has leeway to adapt and implement this legislation, drafting its own policies and programmes. To a certain extent, therefore, one could speak of three models with certain (relevant) elements in common (Larrauri & Blay, 2015). In terms of rehabilitation this is reflected, as we shall see, in different practices regarding the granting of temporary leave permits or open prison.

A Note on the Landscape of Punishment in Spain

In order to appropriately contextualise to what extent and how rehabilitation works in prison and the community, two prior and general observations must be made. First, it must be noted that most of the sentences imposed in Spain do not have a rehabilitative content. Thus, according to recent research, the most common penal response is the fine (46% of all sentences); followed by suspended prison sentences (32%)—preponderantly without any requirements or obligations; community service (9%); and imprisonment (9%) (Blay & Varona, 2021). This means that over 80% of individuals who are sentenced every year receive a sentence that does not involve any intervention or form of treatment. In any case, one must bear in mind that only 20% of sentences imposed in the country have some sort of rehabilitative content. We shall focus on this content, for prison and community sentences separately. The second observation has to do with imprisonment rates, which grew from 1975 until 2010, meaning that Spain has been for a long time one of the European countries sending a higher rate of its citizens to prison (González Sánchez, 2015). This increase was not related to greater levels of crime, and involved prison overcrowding and scarcity of resources which had a considerable negative impact on treatment and living conditions in prison (González Sánchez, 2012: 2).

Prison, Parole and Rehabilitation

The 1979 Prison Law follows the constitutional mandate as it applies to rehabilitation, and as a consequence treatment is a key concept in prison regulations. According to the law itself, treatment aim at 'making the prison inmate a person with the intention and ability to live a law-abiding life' and to 'address their needs', and it is described as 'the whole set of activities directly addressed to the re-education and the social re-insertion' of sentenced prisoners. It comprises, therefore, two different sets of activities: those geared towards re-education, and those geared towards social reintegration. Activities addressed towards re-education comprise those resources offered by the institution for the inmate to be transformed into a person who can respect the law, by overcoming deficiencies (cultural, educational) linked to her offending, i.e. addressing the causes of criminal behaviour to avoid recidivism and delivering treatment programmes. Social reintegration measures make it possible for the person in prison to maintain her links with society, with the aim of minimising the harmful effects of imprisonment, and these include temporary leave, communications, visits, open prison, and parole (Montero Pérez de Tudela, 2019).

By law, prison inmates have the right to participate in treatment programmes, but they cannot be forced to do so. The prison administration must design an individualised programme to address the inmate's criminogenic needs or other social or individual needs (Redondo Illescas, 2017: 292). This programme comprises a set of activities to be undertaken by the inmate; it is adapted to her individual situation and must be revised every six months to adapt it to the evolution of the person and her changing circumstances. Thus, every six months the person is assessed and classified in one of three levels: first, second, or third, which correspond to different living regimes: closed, ordinary, and open prison. Inmates regarded as very dangerous are classified in Level 1 and live in a closed prison, with stricter security measures and greater control and very little time outside their cell. Approximately 3% of the prison population lives under this regime (Cid Moliné, 2005). Level 2 is called 'ordinary regime' and most inmates are so classified: it involves spending most of the time outside the prison cell in common areas of the prison, undertaking a diverse range of activities. Level 3 or 'open regime' is for those inmates who are capable of living in 'controlled freedom' and generally involves spending most of the day outside prison, with prison leave for most or all weekends. In some cases, open prison involves living completely away from prison facilities and using electronic monitoring (Montero Pérez de Tudela, 2019). Finally, although parole is described by the law as a 'fourth level of classification', in practice it involves the suspension of the last part of the prison sentence.

Each individual inmate is assigned to a Technical Team, a set of professionals comprising an educator, a social worker, a psychologist, and a prison lawyer.[1] Each prison has a Treatment board, which decides about the proposals made by the various Technical Teams concerning the evolution in treatment, classification, temporary leave permits, and other relevant elements in inmates' lives. Personnel charged with the maintenance of order in prison are also given a role in supporting re-education and social reinsertion so, at least in the legal discourse, activities addressed to ensure order and security in prison are to be conducted in such a way as to facilitate treatment.

The current treatment programmes in prisons can best be understood if we distinguish between generic and specific ones. Generic programmes are those designed to 'ensure that prisoners can spend their time in prison productively involved in work, education, training, sport, and cultural activities' whilst specific programmes address specific causes of offending behaviour (Cid Moliné, 2005: 156). General programmes are for the prevention of re-offending, preparation for temporary leave, or normalisation of conduct. Specific programmes include a psycho-educational intervention with imprisoned women in the Catalan administration, or the programme 'Being a woman' for the treatment and prevention of intimate partner violence suffered by female inmates; programmes for young adults; or for perpetrators of violent offences ('Therapeutical intervention with violent offenders' in the Catalan prisons or 'Intervention programme for violent behaviour' in Spain). They also target individuals who have committed domestic violence, or sexual offences, or who abuse drugs; individuals with mental health problems; foreigners; those with risk of suicide; and those with a physical handicap (see Redondo Illescas, 2017: 292–297 for a full list). Additionally, individuals in prison have access to education, including university and professional training, and sports. Following the logic of the Spanish legislation, this set of treatment programmes is addressed to re-education. The main instruments for the reintegration of inmates into society are temporary leave, open prison regime, and parole (Cid Moliné, 2005).

Temporary leave allows persons serving a prison sentence to be released for short periods of time, thus facilitating the continuation or renewal of social and family ties. According to regulations, they can be granted from the moment the person has served a quarter of her sentence. Importantly, they represent a first step towards eventually being granted open prison and later parole (Rovira et al., 2018). Approximately 30% of those living in 'ordinary regime' receive temporary leave (Rovira et al., 2018). Serving a prison sentence under the open prison regime generally entails spending most hours of the day and weekends outside prison, working, or undertaking therapeutical activities; there is also a restrictive form of 'open regime' whereby inmates are granted weekend leaves, and open prison using electronic monitoring (Martí Barrachina, 2019). Most activities and interventions are undertaken in non-prison contexts.

Finally, parole involves the suspension of the last portion of the sentence, with the inmate being released under supervision, and usually requires that the prisoner has served three quarters of the sentence, exceptionally less, and has been previously granted 'open regime' (Cid Moliné, 2005).

There are important limitations to the practical implementation and the effectiveness of the rehabilitation model described above and developed in prison regulations. Some of these limitations are common to any prison system: prisons constitute contexts which might not be the most appropriate for helping individuals to overcome problems related to their offending; on the contrary, they may cause dependency and 'de-socialise' the individual, severing family and labour links, and hindering individuals' ability to make responsible decisions. Additionally, treatment in prison is only theoretically voluntary, as inmates are mandated clients (Montero Pérez de Tudela, 2019 with reference to Trotter, 2006): this poses inherent tensions, might generate resistance and lack of trust on the part of inmates, and undoubtedly limits the effectiveness of treatment (Montero Pérez de Tudela, 2019). Moreover, although practices to ensure order and security in prison are to be implemented to facilitate treatment, the practicalities of prison life and the need to maintain orderly living conditions often pose serious difficulties for treatment and condition the way it is implemented (Cutiño Raya, 2015).

An additional limitation is that there are often not enough resources for an adequate implementation of treatment practices, a situation made worse by neoliberal policies and the economic cuts implemented to deal with the 2008 economic crises (Cutiño Raya, 2015; González Sánchez, 2021). Thus, research shows a limited access to a psychologist, social worker, or lawyer[2] (Cutiño Raya, 2015; Gallego Díaz et al., 2010). At some points in recent decades, the high imprisonment rates in Spain meant long waiting lists for programmes and in practice, inmates who served short prison sentences did not get to do them (and consequently, served their whole sentences without leave, for example, or access to the 'open regime'). Researchers have also pointed to the low ratios of treatment professionals relative to security personnel: whereas 77% of prison personnel are allocated to control and security, only 14% of them undertake treatment activities (Cutiño Raya, 2015). Additionally treatment activities in prison rely heavily on the more than 6500 volunteers who conduct them (González Sánchez, 2021). These data contradict the symbolic prevalence of treatment in prison and reflect the fact that resources for treatment are scarce and only reach a small part of the prison population.

Considerable deficiencies have also been pointed out in relation to the main instruments for social reintegration: temporary leave, open prison, and parole. Although there has been a progressive increase in the granting of temporary leave permits since 1979, there are important variations amongst individual prisons and amongst the different administrations; in Catalonia more permits are systematically granted than in the rest of Spain (Rovira et al., 2018). The general increase in temporary leave, however, is limited to inmates of Spanish or a European Union nationality: up to 73% of them have sometimes enjoyed a permit; conversely, only 20% of foreign prisoners have ever enjoyed a leave of absence (Rovira et al., 2018).

According to prison law, temporary leave permits may be approved once the person has served a quarter of her sentence. In practice, however, they tend to be approved much later in the sentence, thus delaying the path towards open prison and parole, which are only granted after the person has proved herself through leave of absence, amongst other conditions. This has been related by experts to a retributive understanding of punishment according to which a long part of the sentence has to be served before the person 'merits' temporary leave (Rovira et al., 2018). Temporary leave is considered in prison law a 'preparation for release'; in practice, prison administrators have derived from this definition the idea that there is no sense in preparing for release early in the sentence. Of course, this thinking ignores the fact that rehabilitation should be an aim from the beginning of the sentence and the fact that temporary leave is needed to humanise the prison stay and to facilitate family relationships (Rovira et al., 2018).

Permits can only be enjoyed after following certain treatment programmes; this allows us to question their voluntary nature, and there is diversity in the programmes offered in the various centres; moreover, in some prisons access to these programmes is only allowed after a substantial part of the sentence has been served (Rovira et al., 2018). Authors observe that an increased concession of temporary leave is not related to higher levels of breach, so there is room for expanding the granting of these permits (Rovira et al., 2018). In the same direction, the theoretically staggered way to serve the sentence and reintegrate into the community, which involves ending the sentence on parole after 'open regime', 'is only a theoretical model of social reintegration', both because of legal reforms which have introduced mandatory terms in ordinary regimes and have thus limited the individualised nature of the process, and because of prison practices (Ibàñez i Roig, 2019). As a result, most individuals who complete a prison sentence do so without having gone through open prison or parole, that is, without having a period of supervision in the community: 12% of inmates finish their sentences in open prison, 32% being on parole, 37% in 'ordinary regime', and the rest without ever having been classified (Ibàñez i Roig, 2019). The limitations in the granting of open prison and parole are particularly undesirable because release from open prison or parole has been linked to reductions in recidivism, as compared to people who finish their sentence in 'ordinary regime' (Ibàñez i Roig, 2019).

Besides these limitations, there are specific groups for whom. For various reasons, practices focused on rehabilitation face greater challenges: namely foreign inmates and women in prison. Albeit with considerable regional variations, around 30% of the Spanish prison population is non-national; this population is diverse and presents various specific needs, with the added handicap that non-nationals often lack the social network which is deemed essential to social integration. It is amongst foreign prison inmates where the tensions and contradictions between rehabilitation and other aims of the system are more crudely reflected. Researchers have pointed out, following the idea of 'crimmigration', that there is a displacement of penal and crime policy ends in favour of border control (Stumpf, 2006). In the case of imprisonment, the theoretical orientation towards re-education and social reintegration is in practice trumped in favour of deportation (García España, 2018). Moreover, as we shall see, non-nationals are the group of individuals for whom having a criminal record involves harsher consequences, i.e. the impossibility of legal residence and the risk of deportation (Larrauri & Jacobs, 2011). Remand in prison is imposed more often on non-nationals, they are granted less temporary leave and, consequently, they have a lesser chance to enjoy open prison and parole—key elements in the rehabilitative model (Rovira et al., 2018).

Although the female imprisonment rate is higher in Spain than in other European countries,[3] women in prison, mostly for property and drug crimes, constitute a minority and the prison system has been described as male-centred which, in practice, involves discrimination and specific problems for women serving prison sentences. To start with, there are fewer prisons where women can serve their sentences (there are only four female prisons in the country although most imprisoned women live in specific units in male prisons): this means that they often live far away from their families and homes. Distance makes visits from family members more difficult and is also a challenge for short temporary leave, especially because public transport to and from prisons is often not good enough (Navarro Villanueva, 2017).

Research has also shown that not enough specific treatment programmes are available for women, which for many reasons (one of them being that 80% of female prison inmates have suffered some form of violence before offending) pose particular problems (Navarro Villanueva, 2017). There have been recent efforts in all Spanish administrations to specifically address women's needs, also in terms of rehabilitation, but administrations themselves acknowledge that it remains a problem (Almeda Samaranch, 2017).

Rehabilitation in Spain, and particularly the local idea of social reintegration, cannot be understood without considering the role played by inmates' families. Families, and particularly women within them, turn out to be the main agents of support during the whole sentence. Whilst in prison, almost all incarcerated individuals receive visits—mostly from family and friends—which are key to avoiding isolation and other harmful effects of imprisonment (Ibàñez i Roig & Pedrosa, 2018). Moreover, families are often the sole source of support in resettlement processes within a context of scarce community resources (Ibàñez i Roig & Pedrosa, 2018). Families have been defined as reintegration agencies, playing a key role in assisting, controlling, and supervising, albeit with no official recognition or support (Ibàñez i Roig & Pedrosa, 2018). An underdeveloped welfare state and the characteristic role played by families in some Southern Mediterranean countries are structural features of a system of welfare and protection very much dependent on families, and women within them, to supply services that the prison administration does not provide for.

Rehabilitation in the Community

Community sentences are a relatively recent addition to the Spanish penal field. More typical responses in similar continental jurisdictions involve the use of alternatives that avoid the negative effects of short-term imprisonment but have no rehabilitative content: e.g. fines and suspended sentences with no requirements. This situation has been changing since at least the enactment of the 1995 Criminal Code. With this code and later legal reforms (2003, 2010, 2015) a system has been established whereby community service orders and suspended sentences with requirements, including drug treatment, are also available penal responses.

Most community service orders respond to driving offences or non-serious intimate partner violence; they are infrequently imposed as a condition of a suspended sentence, and extremely rarely imposed as a response to the non-payment of fines. Community service is mostly (probably due to limited resources) implemented as a fine paid in units of time. In most cases, and always in the case of short sentences, there is only an initial interview used to explain the conditions of the sentence and to select a specific placement where the order shall be served. When there are follow-up interviews, they are often undertaken on the phone, and there are usually no closure interviews at the end of the sentence (Blay, 2019). Only in very long sentences or in cases where community service is served through therapy and there is a mental health or a drug problem, do staff interview those they supervise more often. Although the regulations call for placements to be selected for specific individuals, considering their situation and criminogenic needs, in practice the availability of placements conditions and limits this possibility (Blay, 2019).

The law allows for community service orders to be served as unpaid work in activities of general interest or in the shape of 'workshops or programmes of re-education, labour education, cultural, safe driving, sexual, peaceful resolution of conflicts, positive parenting and other similar programmes' (art. 49 CC). This possibility is used when supervisors find community service has been imposed on individuals who are unable to serve it in regular work placements due to mental health, drug problems, or serious language barriers. This situation (community service orders being imposed judicially to individuals who are incapable of complying with them) probably responds to the fact that pre-sentence reports are extremely scarce in Spain and judges tend to decide with very little individual information on the situation and needs of the accused person. Only the Catalan system has a specific unit producing pre-sentence reports (Larrauri & Zorrilla, 2014). However, even in Catalonia, only 3% of sentences are imposed after a process where a pre-sentence report has been requested. This is, in our understanding, a clear limitation in the context of a supposedly rehabilitative, and therefore individualising, model.

Prison sentences of up to two years can be suspended, even for recidivists, and conditions imposed. The various conditions have diverse rationales: *control*—in the case of prohibitions of residence in certain places, for example; *victim protection*—prohibiting attempts to communicate with or approach the victim; or *rehabilitation*—featuring an obligation to follow a treatment programme. When offences are committed by a person because of her addiction to drugs, prison sentences of up to five years can be suspended under the condition that the person follows and does not abandon a drug treatment programme. The lack of availability to judges of personal and social information on the accused is particularly relevant in the case of suspended sentences, where, despite a legal requirement to take into account individual, social, and family circumstances, judges decide almost exclusively on the basis of criminal records (Varona, 2019).

As a result of this lack of individual information on the sentenced individual, a continental tradition of non-rehabilitative alternatives to custody, and limited resources, most suspended sentences are only conditional on the individual not re-offending for a period and involve no supervision. The few suspended sentences with requirements tend to pertain to intimate partner violence, where the law establishes that a suspended sentence must be accompanied by conditions such as restraining orders and a treatment programme, and therefore there is no judicial discretion. There are a few suspended sentences with requirements for other types of crime, such as non-serious sexual crimes or property crimes.

As for the treatment programmes imposed in such cases, there is considerable variation in length and content. Thus, for instance, programmes implemented in cases of suspended sentences for intimate partner violence might last anything from 13 to 52 weeks depending on the area of residence of the sentenced individual (Larrauri, 2010). As already indicated, longer prison sentences for crimes committed because of drug abuse may be suspended with the condition that a drug treatment is followed. These are the cases with the strongest rehabilitative content in legislation, judicial decision-making, and supervision practices (Blay, 2019).

There is no national probation service in Spain per se; however, the actual supervision practices undertaken by the professionals in charge of ensuring the implementation of community sentences are analogous to those of probation officers. More specifically, research based on the observation of one-to-one supervision interviews shows probation officers tend to employ skills which are deemed to contribute to positive results in terms of rehabilitation and desistance (Blay, 2019; Ugwudike et al., 2018). These skills can be grouped into two categories: on the one hand, relationship skills refer to the ability of professionals to establish a good working relationship with the person being supervised, showing interest, compassion, attention, respect, and a positive attitude (Raynor et al., 2014). The other set of skills, structuring skills, aim more directly at influencing or contributing to change the ways of thinking, attitudes, and behaviours of sentenced individuals (Raynor et al., 2014). Although for methodological reasons results are not strictly comparable, it can be ascertained that the Catalan results show a similar pattern to the results of research based on interview observation undertaken elsewhere, showing greater use of relationship skills than restructuring skills (Durnesu, 2018; Raynor et al., 2014; Trotter & Evans, 2012).

This means that in these diverse institutional contexts professionals are very much using skills that allow them to establish adequate supervision relationships, based on the establishment of a working alliance grounded in trust (Bordin, 1979). These professionals, however, tend to use to a lesser extent skills addressed to obtaining changes in the attitudes, thinking, and behaviours of those they supervise. The greater use of relationship skills has been explained as a result of the specific training and background of professionals, which would equip them to establish solid supervision relationships (Raynor et al., 2014), but not directly to address their criminogenic needs, or other aspects linked to education (Trotter & Evans, 2012). It is also possible that there is an additional explanation that has to do with the common mandate of supervisors as 'offender managers' (Burnett & McNeill, 2005) in these different contexts. So, probation officers increasingly inform, supervise, and support the person and refer her to other services (which do the actual treatment); coordinate the various services; and keep the judge informed about their progress. They do not deliver treatment directly: it is the professionals in these referrals that do so. This idea is reflected in the discourse of Spanish supervision professionals themselves, who describe themselves as 'judicial agents' aiming at ensuring compliance with a judicial ruling (Blay, 2019).

We identified two groups for whom rehabilitative prison practices had specific limitations in prisons: foreign inmates and women. As far as we know, there is no research on foreign individuals serving community sanctions and very scant knowledge on community sentences for women. Official statistics show that women represent a minority of the individuals serving a community sentence (between 7 and 10%). Research shows that, just as in prison, women present a more complex array of needs than men in terms of living conditions, economic status, mental health and drug abuse, prior victimisation, and family responsibilities (Vasilescu, 2021). This makes women a more heterogeneous group than men and makes it more difficult for them to comply with orders (e.g. they tend to have a more irregular attendance rate, mostly because of justified reasons such as family care or health problems). Research suggests there are not enough specific resources, within and without the penal field, to address these multiple and complex needs. In everyday practice, this lack of resources is partially overcome by professionals resorting to flexibility and discretion in supervision, thereby individualising their response in several ways (Vasilescu, 2021). An example of this is the relatively more frequent resort to the possibility of serving community service orders in the form of therapy (mental health, drug abuse, victimisation, etc.), or a mix of therapy and unpaid work (Vasilescu, 2022). The limited research undertaken, therefore, notes professional practices that seem to have a clear rehabilitative trend, and tend to substantially ignore other ends such as retribution or deterrence (Vasilescu, 2021). Additionally, supervision professionals state that they could better focus on rehabilitative work with their clients if they had fewer bureaucratic and managerial tasks (Blay, 2019; Vasilescu, 2022).

A Brief Note on Criminal Records and Their Impact on the Social Reintegration of Individuals Who Have Offended

Finally, if we consider a wide conception of rehabilitation, we need to pay attention to criminal record regulations and practices. Research has pointed out that the impact of criminal records in any given society depends on the degree to which they are publicly available, the extent to which a criminal record certificate is required for access to jobs, and the legal provisions for expungements (Larrauri, 2015). Up to the first decade of the twenty-first century, it could be asserted that criminal records in Spain were kept private and were destined to be used by courts; a certain number of jobs required the presentation of a criminal record certificate, but the largest and more intense impact was on non-nationals, since criminal records are an obstacle to acquiring or maintaining legal residence and work permits (Larrauri & Jacobs, 2011). The conclusion seemed to be that in Spain criminal records did not constitute as much of a barrier for social integration as they did in other contexts, due to a policy that promoted reintegration and privacy. Various legal reforms, some of them due to European Union directives, have prompted a change in this model; a criminal record certificate on sexual crimes is currently requested for all jobs involving regular contact with children. The information contained in certificates has expanded and they can no longer be considered an instrument solely for courts. Recent research concludes that in the last ten years criminal records have gone from being a relatively marginal institution in penal control into a much wider mechanism of risk control that can pose serious difficulties for the social reintegration of individuals who have been convicted (Larrauri & Rovira, 2020). One could provisionally conclude, therefore, that these changes introduce an additional limitation in a nominally rehabilitative system, granting greater salience to elements of risk and security control. It will be interesting to see in the following years to what extent and in what ways these changes are reflected in Spanish public opinion, which research has generally shown as favourable to rehabilitation (Fernández Molina & Tarancón Gómez, 2010).

Evidence of Effectiveness

There is comparatively scant quality evidence on the rehabilitative effects of the various sentences and programmes described. Prison administrations regularly publish re-offending rates. Thus, recent results point to around 30% recidivism after having served a prison sentence (see for example CEJFE, 2015). These studies point to considerable reductions in recidivism (it was 40% in 2008), with much lower re-offending rates for those who finish serving their prison sentence in open prison (18.1% recidivism CEJFE, 2015) and parole (9.5% recidivism, CEJFE, 2019) and suggest some social and penological explanations. But they do not make it possible to identify what elements of the prison sentence or what external elements are causally linked to re-offending. There is also some research on the effectiveness of specific programmes in prison, such as those aimed at men who have committed sexual offences or violence towards their partners, with positive results in terms of reductions in factors associated with offending (see, for example, Martínez García & González Pereira, 2021).

In relation to supervision in the community, research has tended to focus on group treatment programmes in the context of suspended sentences, rather than on individual supervision. In general terms, research conducted in Catalonia shows community service orders have a re-offending rate (taking into consideration resentencing to prison or to a community sanction) of 9.7%, just the same as group programmes, whereas drug and mental health treatment have an 11.7% rate. Men tend to re-offend more than women, and the programmes are less effective for individuals with a criminal record and who have been convicted for property crimes (CEJFE, 2016). One cannot rule out that these rates are the result of these measures being imposed on a low-risk population, rather than the effectiveness of the measures themselves, and the type of research conducted does not identify what elements of the various measures are effective and in what way. There is also specific research on the rehabilitative effects of specific programmes, such as those addressing intimate partner violence or traffic offences. These tend to show positive results in terms of reducing future offending or reducing risk factors (Echeburúa et al., 2009; Hilterman & Mancho, 2012 for example).

To Conclude

As the previous pages have shown, rehabilitation or, re-education and social reintegration in more local terminology, carries an important symbolic weight in Spain, following the constitutional mandate that punishment should tend towards rehabilitation. Although this mandate is clearly developed in prison law and regulations, the limitations of the development of a rehabilitative model in prison practices remain considerable, despite some improvements. In practice, observers have noted that treatment turns into a disciplinary mechanism that ensures orderly living conditions in prison: inmates with the appropriate behaviour can participate in the relatively scarce treatment activities, they will have access to temporary leave, 'open regime' and eventually parole (González Sánchez, 2021). It seems that, within limits that have to do with the penal landscape of Spain—non-rehabilitative and relatively under-resourced—punishment in the community is overwhelmingly more promising than prison with regard to rehabilitation.

Notes

1. According to prison regulations, these teams might comprise a lawyer, a psychologist, a pedagogue, a sociologist, a medical doctor, an assistant nurse, a teacher or instructor responsible for workshops, an educator, a social worker, a sociocultural or sports coach, and a head of department (art. 274 Prison regulation). In practice, the composition of these teams is diverse.
2. As an example, the ratio of psychologists is one professional per 500–600 prison inmates, a ratio that makes it extremely difficult and often impossible for inmates to visit their assigned psychologist (Cutiño Raya, 2015) or to describe their relationship as individual treatment (this observation was made by Ignacio González in a personal communication).
3. Women represent 7.4% of the prison population in Spain, whereas in European jurisdictions they represent 5.9% of individuals in prison, according to the SPACE I 2020 report.

References

Almeda Samaranch, E. (2017). Criminologías feministas, investigación y cárceles de mujeres en españa. *Papers De Sociologia, 102*(2), 151–181.

Blay, E., & Larrauri, E. (2015). Community punishments in Spain: A tale of two administrations. In G. Robinsonand and F. McNeill (Eds.), *Community punishments: European perspectives* (pp. 191–202). Routledge.

Blay, E. (2019). El papel de los Delegados de Ejecución en la ejecución penal en la comunidad ¿gestores o agentes de rehabilitación? *InDret, 4*, 1–32.

Blay, E., & Varona, D. (2021). El castigo en la España del siglo XXI. Cartografiando el iceberg de la penalidad. *Política Criminal, 16*(31), 115–145.

Bordin, E. (1979). The generalizability of the psychoanalytic concept of the working alliance. *Psychotherapy, 16*(3), 252–260.

Burnett, R., & McNeill, F. (2005). The place of the officer-offender relationship in assisting offenders to desist from crime. *Probation Journal, 52*(3), 221–242.

CEJFE [Centre dEstudis Jurídics i Formació Especialitzada]. (2015). *Taxa de reincidència penitenciària 2014*. Research report. http://cejfe.gencat.cat/ca/recerca/cataleg/crono/2015/reincidencia 2014/

CEJFE. (2016). *La reincidència en mesures penals, alternatives*. Research report. http://cejfe.gencat.cat/web/.content/home/recerca/cataleg/crono/2016/reincidencia_mpa_2015/reinc_mesures_penals_alternatives_recerca.pdf

CEJFE. (2019). *Taxa de reincidència en la llibertat condicional i dinactivitat delictiva a 3r grau a Catalunya*. Research report. http://cejfe.gencat.cat/web/.content/home/recerca/cataleg/crono/2019/taxaReincidencia_CA.pdf

Cid Moliné, J. (2005). The penitentiary system in Spain: The use of imprisonment, living conditions and rehabilitation. *Punishment and Society, 7*(2), 147–166.

Codd, H. (2007). Prisoners families and resettlement: A critical analysis. *The Howard Journal, 46*(3), 255–263.

Cutiño Raya, S. (2015). Algunos datos sobre la realidad del tratamiento en las prisiones españolas. *Revista Electrónica De Ciencia Penal y Criminología, 17*(11), 1–41.

Díez Ripollés, J. L. (2004). El nuevo modelo penal de la seguridad ciudadana. *Revista Electrónica De Ciencia Penal y Criminología, 6*(3), 1–34.

Durnesu, I. (2018). Desistance-related skills in Romanian probation contexts. In P. Ugwudike, P. Raynor, and J. Annison (Eds.), *Evidence based skills in criminal justice*: International research on supporting rehabilitation and desistance (pp. 157–168). Policy Press.

Echeburúa, E., Zubizarreta, I., & Del Corral, P. (2009). Evaluación de la eficacia de un progama de tratamiento cognitivo-conductual para hombres violentos contra la pareja en el marco comunitario: Una experiencia de 10 años (1997–2007). *International Journal of Clinical Psychology, 9*(2), 199–217.

Fernández Molina, E., & Tarancón Gómez, P. (2010). Populismo punitivo y delincuencia juvenil: Mito o realidad. *Revista Electrónica De Ciencia Penal y Criminología, 18*(2), 1–25.

Gallego Díaz, M., Cabrera, P. J., Ríos Martín, J. C., & Segovia Bernabé, J. L. (2010). *Andar 1 km en línea recta*. Universidad Pontificia Comillas.

García España, E. (2018). El arraigo de presos extranjeros: Más allá de un criterio limitador de la expulsión. *Migraciones, 44*, 119–144.

González Sánchez, I. (2012). La cárcel en España: Mediciones y condiciones del encarcelamiento en el siglo XXI. *Revista De Derecho Penal y Criminología, 8*, 351–402.

González Sánchez, I. (2015). Encarcelamiento y política neoliberal. In *Incremento de presos y funciones de la prisión in Débora Ávila and Sergio García (coord.) Enclaves de riesgo: gobierno neoliberal, desigualdad y control social* (pp. 267–278). Traficantes de Sueños.

González Sánchez, I. (2021). *Neoliberalismo y castigo*. Bellaterra.

Hilterman, E., & Mancho, R. (2012). *Evaluación de programas formativos de seguridad vial y la reincidencia posterior*. Centre dEstudis Jurídics i Formació Especialitzada.

Ibàñez i Roig, A. (2019). Progresar hacia el régimen abierto: La visión de los profesionales. *Revista Española De Investigación Criminológica, 7*(17), 1–29.

Ibàñez i Roig, A., & Pedrosa, A. (2018). Cárcel y familiarismo: ¿Usamos a las familias como agencias de reinserción? *Encrucijadas, 16*, 1–18.

Larrauri, E. (2006). El populismo punitivo… y cómo resistirlo. *Jueces Para La Democracia, 55*, 15–22.

Larrauri, E. (2010). Los programas formativos como medida penal alternativa en los casos de violencia de género ocasional. *Revista Española De Investigación Criminológica, 8*, 1–26.

Larrauri, E. (2015). Antecedentes Penales. *Eunomía, 8*, 153–159.

Larrauri, E., & Jacobs, J. (2011). Reinserción laboral y antecedentes penales. *Revista Electrónica De Ciencia Penal y Criminología, 13*(9), 1–25.

Larrauri, E., & Zorrilla, N. (2014). Informe social y supervisión efectiva en la comunidad: Especial referencia a delitos de violencia de género ocasional. *InDret, 3*, 1–29.

Larrauri, E., & Rovira, M. (2020). Publicidad, certificados y cancelación de los antecedentes penales. ¿La cultura del control se consolida en España desde las nuevas leyes de 2015? *InDret, 3*, 1–34.

Lorenzo Rubio, C. (2013). *Cárceles en llamas. El movimiento de presos sociales en la transición*. Virus.

Martí Barrachina, M. (2019). Prisiones abiertas: La supervisión de la pena de prisión en semilibertad. *Revista Electrónica De Ciencia Penal y Criminología, 21*(7), 1–26.

Martínez García, M., & González Pereira, S. (2021). *Avaluació de leficàcia terapèutica dels nous programes dintervenció en violència de gènere*. Research report. http://cejfe.gencat.cat/web/.content/home/recerca/cataleg/crono/2022/avaluacio-eficacia-terapeutica-programes-intervencio-violencia-genere/INFORME_FINAL_VIGE_22_OBS.pdf

Medina Ariza, J. (2004). Politics of crime in Spain, 1978–2004. *Punishment and Society, 8*(2), 183–201.

Montero Pérez de Tudela, E. (2019). La reeducación y la reinserción social en prisión: El tratamiento. *Revista De Estudios Socioeducativos, 7*, 227–249.

Navarro Villanueva, M. C. (2017). *El encarcelamiento femenino. Especial consideración de las madres en prisión*. Atelier.

Raynor, P., Ugwudike, P., & Vanstone, M. (2014). The impact of skills in probation work: A reconviction study. *Criminology and Criminal Justice, 14*(2), 235–249.

Redondo Illescas, S. (2017). *Evaluación y tratamiento de delincuentes: Jóvenes y adultos*. Pirámide.

Rovira, M., Larrauri, E., & Alarcón, P. (2018). La concesión de permisos penitenciarios: Una aproximación criminológica a distintas fuentes de variación. *Revista Electrónica De Ciencia Penal y Criminología, 20*, 1–26.

Solar Calvo, P. (2019). *El sistema penitenciario español en la encrucijada: una lectura penitenciaria de las últimas reformas penales*. Boletín Oficial del Estado.

Stumpf, J. (2006). The crimmigration crisis: Immigrants, crime, and sovereign power. *American University Law Review, 56*(2), 367–419.

Trotter, C., & Evans, P. (2012). An analysis of supervision skills in youth probation. *Australian and New Zealand Journal of Criminology, 45*(2), 255–273.

Ugwudike, P., Raynor, P., & Annison, J. (2018) Introduction: Effective practice skills: new directions in research. In P. Ugwudike, P. Raynor, and J. Annison (Eds.), *Evidence based skills in criminal justice: International research on supporting rehabilitation and desistance* (pp. 3–16). Policy Press.

Varona, D. (2019). Fundamentación y aplicación práctica de la suspensión de la pena de prisión. In J. María Lidón (Ed.), *Cuadernos penale* (pp. 229–258). Bilbao.

Vasilescu, C. (2021). Women offenders who served community sentences: A view from Catalonia. *European Journal of Probation, 13*(2), 178–198.

Vasilescu, C. (2022). Probation officers working with women offenders in the community: Evidence from Catalonia. *Probation Journal, 69*(1), 24–44.

Zedner, L. (2019). The hostile border: Crimmigration, counter-terrorism, or crossing the line on rights? *New Criminal Law Review, 22*, 318.

Criminal Justice Rehabilitation in Sweden: Towards an Integrative Model

Martin Lardén

'The Swedish model' is a governmental strategy based on a stable economic policy, a flexible labour market, and a general welfare policy (Government Offices of Sweden, 2017). It has its roots in the 1930s when the Social Democrats came to power, a position they would hold for over 40 years. The idea was that Sweden would be a people's home, where the state was responsible for social and economic security. Criminal justice rehabilitation has been an integral part of the development of the Swedish model from the beginning.

Since the beginning of the twentieth century, criminal policy has developed as part of a larger field of social policy, which also includes other problem areas like poverty, sobriety, child and youth care, and prostitution (Andersson & Nilsson, 2017). Social liberalism was the dominating ideology and criminal policy was directed towards building a society based on discipline and normalisation rather than punishment. Laws on compulsory care and treatment of vagrants, alcoholics, the mentally ill, and young offenders were introduced during the first decades of the twentieth century. The idea of criminal justice rehabilitation in the form of individual prevention inspired

M. Lardén (✉)
Development & Management of Treatment Programmes,
Swedish Prison and Probation Service, Norrköping, Sweden
e-mail: martin.larden@kriminalvarden.se

by the medical model as a part of the welfare state was presented in a 1956 state inquiry (SOU, 1956: 55), which became the foundation for the new Criminal Code.

The current Swedish Criminal Code (Brottsbalken: SFS 1962: 700) has been in force since 1965. The Criminal Code explicitly introduced a sanction system based on individual prevention, which is the idea that the sanction through treatment, deterrence, or incapacitation should reduce recidivism at the individual level (Government Offices of Sweden, 2021). Treatment and other active forms of promoting the prosocial inclusion of lawbreakers in society were described as the main strategy for the prevention of criminal recidivism (cf. Jerre & Tham, 2010). However, the idea of individual prevention was soon challenged as it might lead to differences before the law and difficulties in making reliable predictions of reintegration at the individual level. The Criminal Code was reformed in 1989 (SOU, 1986: 15), indicating that sentences should be based on how serious and reprehensible the committed crime was thought to be. Since 1989, changes have been implemented to further emphasise the principles of proportionality between crime and punishment, equal treatment, consistency, and predictability (SOU, 2017: 61). Today's sanction system according to the Criminal Code is mainly based on these principles.

In connection with the introduction of the new penal code, the principle of impunity on the grounds of mental illness was removed. Persons judged during the psychiatric investigation to have committed the crime under the influence of a serious illness would instead be sentenced to forensic psychiatric care in open or closed form.

The age of criminal responsibility in Sweden is 15 years. Children under the age of 15 cannot be sentenced to punitive sanctions. They will be handed over to the social services for assessment of appropriate interventions. Children between 15 and 17 can be sentenced to closed institutional care that was introduced in 1999, in line with the UN Convention on the Rights of the Child, which states that alternatives to prison should be available for persons under the age of 18. The rationale is that prison sentences are associated with risks of criminal identification and could harm youth development. The sentence can range from 14 days up to four years and is to be served in a specially approved institution within the National Board of Institutional Care (SiS) (Nordén, 2015; Pettersson, 2010). Since 2021, children aged 15–17 can also be sentenced to supervision by the probation service.

Current Policy and Debate in Sweden

There are currently no major disagreements between political parties about the main focus of criminal policy in Sweden. Crime is seen as a serious problem that must be combated with strong measures, with an emphasis on general prevention and tougher sentences. The criminal policy debate today is mostly about representatives of different political parties trying to outdo each other on who will take the most powerful measures against crime. One important question is of course how does this contemporary shift towards a more punitive criminal justice policy mirror an increase in crime that poses a threat both to society and the Swedish model?

Fuelling this development has been the fact that gun homicides have increased in Sweden from 2005, while gun violence has decreased in most countries in Europe (BRÅ, 2021a). The increase in gun homicide in Sweden is prominent among young men (age 15–29) in criminal milieux, usually from socially disadvantaged areas (BRÅ, 2021a; Sturup et al., 2019). Other forms of lethal violence have remained at stable levels, but when news of deadly street violence comes into peoples' living rooms, it is natural to react with both fear and anger and demands that it should cease. As a result, politicians often justify their support of more severe punishments by referring to the 'public sense of justice'. Research indicates that the public's views on punishment are more complex (Balvig et al., 2015; Jerre, 2014). In polls with simple questions about whether sentences are too mild or too severe, most responders tend to reply that they are too mild. With more detailed information on the questions and where respondents themselves propose suitable sanctions, they tend to be in line with, or sometimes even milder, than those actually imposed.

The Risk-Needs-Responsivity Model

The Risk-Needs-Responsivity model of rehabilitation (RNR; Bonta & Andrews, 2017) is widely accepted in Sweden and serves as the primary guideline for interventions to reduce recidivism by the Swedish Prison and Probation Service (SPPS), but also by the SiS (Statens institutionsstyrelse/National Board of Institutional Care) and many social services.

The RNR model has three core principles:

i. Risk principle: A risk factor is defined as a characteristic, event, process, or relationship that increases the probability or risk of a certain outcome; in this context criminal behaviour (Murray & Farrington, 2010). When speaking about the concept of risk and risk assessments it is important to clarify what kind of risk we are dealing with in each specific case. In RNR, risk refers to the risk of recidivism in criminal behaviour and is easiest to understand quantitatively, i.e., the more risk factors the client has, the greater the risk of repeated offending. Modern research (e.g., Jolliffe et al., 2017) supports the idea that the quantity of risk factors predicts continued offending better than their quality. To comply with the risk principle, it is important that a structured risk and needs assessment precedes an intervention to ensure that higher risk individuals are prioritised for risk-reducing interventions.
ii. Need Principle: The need principle indicates that interventions should focus on those risk factors that need to be addressed to reduce the risk of recidivism. The term criminogenic need refers to dynamic risk factors that must be addressed to reduce the risk of repeated offending. Examples of dynamic risk factors predictive of repeated offending are pro-criminal attitudes and peer associations, drug addictions, and poor self-management skills. High- and medium-risk clients always have several dynamic risk factors, and multimodal interventions that focus on several criminogenic needs are therefore to be preferred.
iii. Responsivity Principle: The responsivity principle informs us on how to design and deliver interventions. In general, using social learning and cognitive behavioural interventions and theories are recommended. Cognitive behavioural interventions are often active and concrete, which fit the learning style of people who offend who often have problems with perseverance and more abstract reasoning and discussions. Specific responsivity is about taking into account the client's conditions and circumstances. These include gender, age, cultural background, cognitive functions and skills, psychiatric problems, and the client's motivation for change. The responsivity principle states both that the client must be receptive to the intervention offered, but also that the person who gives the intervention to the client must be receptive to making adaptations to his client's specific conditions. If we are to successfully help clients change their lives, we must therefore be sensitive to their conditions of receiving our support and responsive to adapting our work to these conditions. Later developments of the responsivity principle focus on the importance of creating a learning environment that engages the client to learn and practice new skills (Bourgon & Bonta, 2014).

Following the RNR model, risk and needs assessment, cognitive behavioural treatment programmes, Strategic Training Intervention in Correctional Supervision (STICS), and Core Correctional Practice (CCP) are important features for supporting rehabilitation. As the SPPS is a joint organisation including both the prison and probation it is possible to follow the rehabilitative process from planning, through interventions to support individual change and improvement, to eventual reintegration into the community.

The Swedish Prison and Probation Service (SPPS)

The Swedish Prison and Probation Service (SPPS) implements sentences and attempts to reduce crime and substance misuse recidivism by offering formal education, vocational training, and psychological treatment programmes addressing cognitive, emotional, and behavioural risk factors. In 2020 there were approximately 5000 inmates in 45 prisons, and 10,200 parolees and probationers across 31 probation offices throughout the country. The Prison and Probation Service is also responsible for remand prisons and the prisoner transport service. Persons serving sentences or who are in remand prisons are referred to as clients, and I will use that in the description below.

Where a prisoner is allocated depends on an assessment of the risk of escape, criminal ties to other prisoners, type of conviction, and need for treatment or vocational training. Prisons Class 1 have the highest security, which means they are equipped to handle clients with high risks of escape or misconduct, followed by Classes 2 and 3. Prisons in security Class 3 have no direct escape obstacles. This means that the inmates can move freely in the institution and that the institution is only locked at night. Escapes from Swedish prisons are rare. In 2018–2020 there was only one escape from prison in security Class 1 or 2 and 105 clients went AWOL from open prison (Kriminalvården, 2021). One year recidivism decreased from 26% for clients leaving prison in 2014 to 21% for clients leaving prison in 2018 (BRÅ, 2021b).

The probation service handles pre-sentence investigations, non-custodial sanctions, supervision of conditionally released parolees, and electronic monitoring. In line with the principle of normalisation, the probation service collaborates with other authorities and organisations, such as social service agencies, the Employment Agency, health care providers, etc., to ensure that clients receive the same services that are available to the normal population. Professionals deliver supervision, but they may be assisted by lay people called 'assistant supervisors' to support clients' reintegration into community. (For a more detailed description of the Swedish probation service, see Boijsen & Tallving, 2017.)

Assessment and Case Management Planning

A well-conducted risk and needs assessment is the very cornerstone of effective risk management and personal rehabilitation (Latessa et al., 2014). Clients who serve their sentences in the SPPS have case management plans based on information from a structured assessment format developed within the SPPS called the Risk, Needs and Responsivity Assessment (RNR-A). This consists of two parts: the first contains 15 items about the client's antisocial history that are obtained from register information, and the second contains a semi-structured client interview with 72 items relating to antisocial personality patterns, pro-criminal attitudes, substance abuse, family and interpersonal relationships, work and education, leisure activities, and health. The RNR-A generates an automatic assessment of recidivism risk in general crime. For those clients where it is relevant, it generates risk assessments regarding partner violence and sexual crimes. If the investigator has information that suggests a revision of the risk level, s/he has the opportunity to make a so-called professional override and change the level.

The RNR-A also provides an automatically generated assessment of the client's needs in eleven areas. A study investigating the predictive validity of RNR-A (Johansson Bäckström et al., 2019) suggested that the RNR-A predicts recidivism as well as risk- and needs assessment instruments in general (AUC $= 0.71$). AUC stands for 'Area under the ROC Curve'. The predictive validity was similar for both men and women. Importantly, results suggest that RNR-A can identify individuals with a low recidivism risk, as 90% of low-risk clients were not reconvicted. This is in line with the risk principle: low-risk clients are not helped by intensive rehabilitative interventions focussing on criminogenic needs. For long-term convicted clients with less need for relapse prevention measures (low risk), good VSP sentence planning must still be done to ensure that we reduce the harmful consequences of incarceration, designing (in some cases) extensive plans for rehabilitation after long prison sentences, while clients with an increased risk of recidivism need interventions targeting criminogenic needs.

Psychological Treatment Programmes

During the 2000s the SPPS built up a wide range of treatment programmes. The Swedish accreditation panel, inspired by the Correctional Services Accreditation Panel of England and Wales (McGuire et al., 2010), reviews treatment programmes according to six criteria (change model, client selection, dynamic risk factors, susceptibility, treatment integrity, and evidence). These include how the programme is designed and how it is expected to affect clients' recidivism risk, as well as the type of scientific support that exists for the techniques and methods used in the programme. In 2021, the SPPS offered 14 accredited psychological treatment programmes. A total of 5046 treatment programmes were completed; an overall completion rate of just over 70%

The SPPS has cognitive behavioural treatment (CBT) programmes that focus on different types of problems—general violence, violence in close relationships, sexual crimes, general crime, and substance abuse and addiction. Special target groups, e.g., those who have committed crimes with honour motives, or violent extremism, can also be offered treatment sessions adapted to their problems; some of them carried out individually and some in groups. Most group programmes also include individual sessions. They all include active work with skills that increase the client's ability to establish a life beyond crime. As it is more difficult to erase unwanted behaviours or to try to limit and suppress them, than to practise new ways of thinking and acting, (that is, to help clients expand their behavioural repertoire [Kassinove & Toohey, 2014]), the programmes focus on strengthening skills that may serve as protective factors. Skills in assertiveness are important features in the programmes, as are those which establish or strengthen relationships with prosocial people who can contribute stable social and emotional supports. To ensure the availability of programme facilitators, the SPPS has its own organisation that is responsible for their training and supervision. There are two main reasons for this: first, we need many facilitators, especially in a time of expansion, and; second, facilitators trained to work with criminogenic needs are rare in Sweden outside the SPPS. Since treatment programmes are usually delivered by staff without formal training in psychotherapy, they need to be based on detailed manuals to secure treatment quality and integrity. Another advantage of standardised and manualised sessions is that they make it easier to systematically evaluate programme integrity and effectiveness. On the other hand, it is usually more difficult to adapt manualised materials to clients' individual needs and conditions. For facilitators who are to run the more flexible programmes for special target groups, which include in-depth individual treatment planning, there is special further training. To be admitted to this, a basic academic education and experience of conducting treatment programmes is required.

Evaluations of programme effectiveness have yielded small recidivism-reducing effects in line with international research on psychological rehabilitation programmes. The SPPS evaluated nine psychological treatment programmes by comparing treated clients with non-treated clients serving sentences within the same timeframe (see Lardén, 2014). Cox regression analyses were used to control for background variables between treated clients and controls. For clients who completed treatment, statistically significant risk reductions were demonstrated for four of the programmes. For four of the programmes, non-significant reductions in recidivism were detected for the treated group. For the ART programme (Aggression Replacement Training, Goldstein & Glick, 1994) a non-significant increase in risk was also demonstrated for completed programmes. The evaluation of the ROS-programme for clients sentenced for sexual crimes, suggested an increase in sexual crime recidivism. Notably, the completion rates varied substantially between 28 and 82%, and programme drop-out was associated with increased recidivism.

Later evaluations of the individually administered programmes One-to-One (OTO; Priestley, 2003) and Programme to Reduce Substance Misuse (PRISM; McMurran & Priestley, 2003) using propensity score-matching procedures yielded similar or somewhat more promising results. The One-to-One evaluation conducted by Danielsson et al. (2009) indicated no reduction in recidivism (new sentence to prison or probation) for starters ($N = 8008$; HR = 1.04; 95% CI: 0.92–1.17), but reduced recidivism for completers ($N = 7646$; HR = 0.75; 95% CI: 0.62–0.90). The results of the SPPS departmental evaluation from 2016 were in line with the previous evaluation of OTO, where those who started the programme had roughly the same reduction in recidivism (new sentences) as the control group ($N = 3553$; HR = 0.87; 95% CI: 0.74–1.03), while clients who completed OTO had a significantly reduced recidivism compared to controls ($N = 2152$; HR = 0.75; 95% CI: 0.61–0.92).

The evaluation of PRISM by Danielsson et al. (2012) indicated no reduction in recidivism (new sentence to prison or probation) for starters ($N = 1520$; HR = 1.16; 95% CI: 0.96–1.39), but reduced recidivism for completers ($N = 1322$; HR = 0.70; 95% CI: 0.52–0.94). The results of an SPPS-evaluation from (2016) those who started the programme had roughly the same reduction in recidivism (new sentences) as the control group ($N = 3878$; HR = 0.99 95% CI: 0.89–1.11), while clients who completed

PRISM had a significantly reduced recidivism compared to controls ($N = 2309$; HR = 0.69; 95% CI: 0.57–0.83).

A study of the ART-programme conducted by Lardén et al. (2018) using propensity score matching suggested no risk-reducing effect for starters regarding general ($N = 4480$; HR = 0.97; 95% CI: 0.88–1.07), or violent recidivism ($N = 4480$; HR = 1.02; 95% CI: 0.89–1.17). For completers, results suggested a marginal decrease for general recidivism ($N = 2956$; HR = 0.87; 95% CI: 0.77–0.99), but not for violent recidivism ($N = 2956$; HR = 0.95; 95% CI: 0.79–1.14).

All these studies indicated that dropping out from started programmes is associated with an increased risk of recidivism, and that measures to optimise programme completion for as many clients as possible are needed.

Education and Vocational Training

Education and vocational training are important interventions to support reintegration and desistance from crime. Many clients lack full grades, especially from upper secondary education, which is often demanded by employers. The SPPS offers adult education in the same form as municipal adult schools, which offer studies at upper secondary school levels and vocational education. Clients doing time in prison get the opportunity to study and take grades and then have a greater chance of getting a job when they leave the Swedish Prison and Probation Service. The greatest chance for work is in occupations with requirements for upper secondary and post-secondary education. Statistics Sweden (2020) specifically addresses the shortage of upper secondary vocationally trained labour which in a few years' time is expected to be as significant as the shortage of post-secondary educated labour.

Health and Medical Care

The SPPS has no statutory obligation to provide medical care but is obliged to ensure that clients in need of health and medical care can access the services to which they are entitled under the Health and Medical Services Act (1982). This means that if the person is unable to acquire general health care on his or her own due to legal obstacles, the responsibility falls on the prison service. Many prison inmates and detainees, to a greater extent than the normal population, suffer from psychiatric disorders such as addictions (substance abuse), personality disorders, and various forms of neuropsychiatric disabilities, especially ADHD (Ginsberg et al., 2010; Young et al., 2015). Pharmacological and psychological treatments are therefore offered to clients.

Probation and RNR

One important step in implementing RNR in the Swedish probation service was the Strategic Training Initiative in Community Supervision (STICS) (Bonta et al., 2011). It is a training protocol for probation staff to support them in applying the Risk-Need-Responsivity model of rehabilitation, and the implementation in Sweden is described by Starfelt Sutton et al. (2020). Probation officers were more focused on criminogenic needs and were more structured and relationship-focused in interaction with clients. These findings are in line with international studies (Bonta et al., 2011; Robinson et al., 2011; Smith et al., 2012). However, probation officers' use of specific cognitive behavioural techniques was not as frequent and competent as expected. More training in combination with continuous support from staff is probably needed if STICS is to have a significant impact on clients' recidivism (Bonta et al., 2019).

Electronic Monitoring

The Swedish Prison and Probation Service has used electronic monitoring since 1994. The purpose was to counteract the negative effects of the short prison sentence by offering a credible alternative to the execution of a sentence outside the prison. The convicted person retains his current employment, housing, and social network, and remains in the community without interruption or deprivation of liberty. A prison sentence of up to six months could be changed to electronic monitoring, and it is possible for persons sentenced to at least two years imprisonment to serve the last section of the sentence outside an institution with electronic monitoring. In 2016, experimental activities with GPS monitoring in combination with foot shackles were also started, and in 2018 an electronic monitoring system including components such as mobile breathalyzers and the use of mobile phone applications was implemented. As electronic monitoring and home confinement seem to be effective alternatives to incarceration (Bouchard & Wong, 2018), electronic monitoring may play a significant role in maintaining effective rehabilitation at a time of increasing focus on longer sentencing. Unfortunately, all forms of electronic monitoring have had recurring technical problems that have delayed implementation, and manual backup strategies are needed to ensure surveillance when the technology is not working properly.

Cooperation for Crime Prevention

The SPPS is also involved in criminal justice rehabilitation efforts that do not have an individual focus. Group Violence Intervention (GVI) is a focused deterrence strategy to reduce and prevent gun violence and other serious crimes that target groups rather than individuals (National Network for Safe Communities, 2016). This focused deterrence strategy is based on the assumption that personal rehabilitation approaches are insufficient to prevent serious group violence (Braga et al., 2018). Instead, GVI directly engages individuals connected to groups that are involved in gun violence; creates and imposes collective sanctions against them; and offers incentives for individuals to resist and desist from violent acts to avoid those sanctions. One of the core features of GVI is about 'moral voices:'—prominent local figures such as faith leaders, sport coaches, or shop owners who can articulate their concerns about the consequences of gang violence. So, the focus is not just on deterrence, but also on personal support to those at high risk and strengthening local communities by building trust between communities and authorities (Kennedy et al., 2017). Implementation in Sweden is a collaboration between The Swedish National Council for Crime Prevention (Brå), police, SSPS, and interested municipalities. Hopefully, this could lead to an integration of first-line policing, rehabilitation interventions from social services and the probation service, and the people in the local communities.

Future Directions—Towards on Integrated Model

In the past three years there has been a radical increase in sentences, that challenge both access to, as well as the quality of rehabilitative interventions, especially regarding youth and young adults. Arguments are put forward in favour of harder sanctions for youth engaged in criminal activities plus demands that these youth should be dealt with in the justice system, rather than the social services. This would, in my opinion, be a huge step backwards. Research suggests that contact with the justice system tends to increase youth criminal behaviour (Bernberg & Krohn, 2003; Motz et al., 2020). When you get into the justice system it seems hard to get out of it. There must be a way out of crime, but also a way back into society. Therefore, future development needs to focus on better integration of rehabilitative interventions and effective transfer to the community. To effectively prevent reoffending and establish a prosocial life generally requires several different interventions (cf. Souverein et al., 2019). We must also be aware that the correctional service is only one part of the crime prevention initiatives that exist in society, and we need to cooperate with other authorities and organisations that contribute to crime prevention.

RNR as the Main Paradigm

Effective prison care must be a team effort where staff groups work together to ensure that their different activities create an aggregated effect and do not counteract each other. Initiatives such as treatment programmes and STICS have an intimate connection to RNR and there is room for developing the planning and implementation of other initiatives such as work and education in line with RNR. This does not mean that the very core of these different initiatives needs to change, but we need a common method, a common language, and a common model of change for the initiatives to have a preventive effect. The treatment programmes and STICS will no longer function as parallel tracks, but all enforcement planning will be based on the assumption that these efforts are complementary and reinforce each other. Treatment programmes run in institutions need to place a clearer focus on also developing skills to carry out studies, work, and other employment. STICS must have a clearer focus on integrating the client into society and contributing to the client being given access to society's services and resources. The principles of core correctional practice (Dowden & Andrews, 2004) could be used to give different professionals a common basis and language to ensure both adherence to RNR and that clients receive a uniform and humane approach to rehabilitation.

Biopsychosocial Models

Clients need to enter a more prosocial life to desist from future offending. Psychological treatment can be a starting point. But to increase effectiveness we should make stronger efforts to integrate different intervention types and modalities. We should integrate models of criminal justice rehabilitation rather than get into conflict with each other. Biological explanations and medical treatments are often looked at askance by criminologists, psychologists, and social workers involved in criminal justice rehabilitation, although there is growing evidence for the importance of biological factors in the development and maintenance of criminal behaviour (Newsome & Cullen, 2017). For instance, pharmacological treatment might help clients with impulsivity and emotional dysregulation related to ADHD (Ginsberg & Lindefors, 2012; Ginsberg et al., 2012) and craving in substance misuse (Bahji et al., 2020), whereas psychosocial interventions might improve prosocial support and vocational training.

We must also be aware that the Swedish Prison and Probation Service is part of the crime prevention initiatives that exist in society and that we must therefore follow and cooperate with other authorities and organisations that contribute to crime prevention. Recent research demonstrates that using social or public health services to intervene in such situations can lead to better outcomes for communities than involving the criminal justice system.

High-Quality Research to Ensure Resources

In an age when politicians compete in acting tough on crime and advocating the strongest punitive reactions to it, it is more important than ever to inform the public that rehabilitation measures are (a) more effective than doing nothing, and (b) more effective than punitive measures. While there is ample evidence that treatment and rehabilitation are the most promising perspectives for relapse prevention, it is also important not to be over-optimistic and believe that all or even a large majority of antisocial or lifestyle criminal youth and adults will stop committing crimes after receiving treatment. Human behaviour is so complex, especially when it comes to behaviours that are associated with and influenced by people's lifestyle and way of life, that intervention in itself will often be insufficient. We must be prepared for the fact that the effects are often small and constantly remember that we need to work with others to succeed. If clients do not have access to housing, education or work and prosocial friends and acquaintances, they will not be able to benefit from the personal progress to which treatment has contributed. Investing resources in rehabilitation and treatment is profitable if we want to reduce crime and increase security in society (Cohen & Piquero, 2009; Crowley, 2013). Most importantly, a rehabilitation approach is also a call for a better society based on tolerance, inclusion, and humanity.

References

Andersson, R., & Nilsson, R. (2017). *Svensk kriminalpolitik [Swedish criminal policy]*. Liber.

Bahji, A., Carlone, D., & Altomare, J. (2020). Acceptability and efficacy of naltrexone for criminal justice-involved individuals with opioid use disorder: A systematic review and meta-analysis. *Addiction, 115*, 1413–1425.

Balvig, F., Gunnlaugsson, H., Jerre, K., Tham, H., & Kinnunen, A. (2015). The public sense of justice in Scandinavia: A study of attitudes towards punishment. *European Journal of Criminology, 12*, 342–361.

Bernburg, J. G., & Krohn, M. D. (2003). Labeling, life chances, and adult crime: The direct and indirect effects of official intervention in adolescence on crime in early adulthood. *Criminology, 41*, 1287–1318.

Boijsen, G., & Tallving, G. (2017). *Probation in Europe: Sweden*. https://www.cep-probation.org/wp-content/uploads/2019/01/probation-in-europeZweden-probation-in-europe.pdf

Bonta, J., & Andrews, D. A. (2017). *Psychology of criminal conduct* (6th ed.) Routledge.

Bonta, J., Bourgon, G., Rugge, T., Scott, T. L., Yessine, A. K., Gutierrez, L., & Li, J. (2011). An experimental demonstration of training probation officers in evidence-based community supervision. *Criminal Justice and Behavior, 38*, 1127–1148.

Bonta, J., Rugge, T., Bourgon, G., & Wanamaker, K. A. (2019). A conceptual replication of the strategic training initiative in community supervision (STICS). *Journal of Experimental Criminology, 15*, 397–419.

Bouchard, J., & Wong, J. S. (2018). The new panopticon? Examining the effect of home confinement on criminal recidivism. *Victims and Offenders, 13*, 589–608.

Bourgon, G., & Bonta, J. (2014). Reconsidering the responsivity principle: A way to move forward. *Federal Probation, 78*, 3–10.

Braga, A. A., Weisburd, D., & Turchan, B. (2018). Focused deterrence strategies and meta-analysis of the empirical evidence. *Criminology and Public Policy, 17*, 205–250.

BRÅ. (2021a). *Gun homicide in Sweden and other European countries: A comparative study of levels, trends, and homicide by other means* (English summary of Brå report 2021a:8).

BRÅ. (2021b). *Kriminalstatistik: 2018 återfall i brott, preliminär statistik [Criminal statistics: 2018 crime recidivism: Preliminary statistics]*. National Brottsförebyggande rådet.

Cohen, M. A., & Piquero, A. R. (2009). New evidence on the monetary value of saving a high risk youth. *Journal of Quantitative Criminology, 25*, 25–49.

Crowley, D. M. (2013). Building efficient crime prevention strategies: Considering the economics of investing in human development. *Criminology and Public Policy, 12*, 353–366.

Danielsson, M., Fors, A., & Freij, I. (2012). *Behandlingsprogrammet PRISM i Kriminalvården: Utvärdering av återfall i brott för programdeltagare 2003–2006 [The PRISM programme in SPPS: Evaluation of recidivism for programme participants 2003–2006]*. Kriminalvården.
Danielsson, M., Fors, A., & Freij, I. (2009). *Behandlingsprogrammet PRISM i Kriminalvården: Utvärdering av återfall i brott för programdeltagare 2003–2006 [The PRISM programme in SPPS: Evaluation of recidivism for programme participants 2003–2006]*. Kriminalvården
Dowden, C., & Andrews, D. A. (2004). The importance of staff practice in delivering effective correctional treatment: A meta-analytic review of core correctional practice. *International Journal of Offender Therapy and Comparative Criminology, 48*, 203–214.
Ginsberg, Y., Hirvikoski, T., & Lindefors, N. (2010). Attention Deficit Hyperactivity Disorder (ADHD) among longer-term prison inmates is a prevalent, persistent and disabling disorder. *BMC Psychiatry, 10*, 112.
Ginsberg, Y., & Lindefors, N. (2012). Methylphenidate treatment of adult male prison inmates with attention-deficit hyperactivity disorder: Randomised double-blind placebo-controlled trial with open-label extension. *British Journal of Psychiatry, 200*, 68–73.
Ginsberg, Y., Hirvikoski, T., Grann, M., & Lindefors, N. (2012). Long-term functional outcome in adult prison inmates with ADHD receiving OROS-methylphenidate. *European Archives of Psychiatry and Clinical Neuroscience, 262*, 705–724.
Goldstein, A. P., & Glick, B. (1994). Aggression replacement training: Curriculum and evaluation. *Simulation and Gaming, 25*(1), 9–26.
Government Offices of Sweden. (2017). *Den Svenska modellen [The Swedish Model]*. https://www.regeringen.se/rapporter/2017/06/den-svenska-modellen
Government Offices of Sweden. (2021). *The Swedish criminal code*. https://www.government.se/government-policy/judicial-system/the-swedish-criminal-code
Jerre, K. (2014). More sanctions—less prison? A research note on the severity of sanctions proposed by survey participants and how it is affected by the option to combine a prison term with other sanctions. *European Journal of Criminal Policy Research, 20*, 121–136.
Jerre, K., & Tham, H. (2010). *Svenskarnas syn på straff [The Swedes' view of punishment] (Rapport 2010:1)*. Stockholms universitet.
Johansson Bäckström, P., Danielsson, M., Starfelt Sutton, L. C., & Andersson, D. (2019). *Utvärdering av den prediktiva validiteten för RBM-B i en grupp klienter med kriminalvårdspåföljd 2014–2015 [Evaluation of the predictive validity of RNR-A in a group of clients with a prison or probation sentence 2014–2015]*. Kriminalvården.
Jolliffe, D., Farrington, D. P., Piquero, A. R., Loeber, R., & Hill, K. G. (2017). Systematic review of early risk factors for life-course-persistent, adolescence-limited, and late-onset offenders in prospective longitudinal studies. *Aggression and Violent Behavior, 33*, 15–23.

Kassinove, H., & Toohey, M. J. (2014). Anger management for offenders. A flexible CBT approach. In R. C. Tafrate and D. Mitchell (Eds.), *Forensic CBT: A handbook for clinical practice* (pp. 142–160). John Wiley and Sons.

Kennedy, D. M., Kleinman, M. A. R., & Braga, A. A. (2017). Beyond deterrence: Strategies that focus on fairness. In N. Tilley and A. Sidebottom (Eds.), *Handbook of crime and community safety* (2nd ed., pp. 157–182). Routledge.

Kriminalvården. (2016a). *Utvärdering av behandlingsprogrammet PRISM i Kriminalvården [Evaluation of the PRISM programme in SPPS]*. Kriminalvården.

Kriminalvården. (2016b). *Utvärdering av behandlingsprogrammet One-to-One i Kriminalvården [Evaluation of the one-to-one programme in SPPS]*. Kriminalvården.

Kriminalvården. (2021). *KOS 2020: Kriminalvård och statistik [KOS 2020: Correctional service statistics]*. Kriminalvården.

Lardén, M. (2014). *Utvärdering av Kriminalvårdens behandlingsprogram; Sammanfattningsrapport [Evaluation of SPPS's treatment programmes: A summary]*. Kriminalvården.

Lardén, M., Nordén, E., Forsman, M., & Långström, N. (2018). Effectiveness of aggression replacement training in reducing criminal recidivism among convicted adult offenders. *Criminal Behaviour and Mental Health, 28*, 476–491.

Latessa, E., Listwan, S. L., & Koetzle, D. (2014). *What works (and doesn't) in reducing recidivism*. Routledge.

McGuire, M., Grubin, D., Lösel, F., & Raynor, P. (2010). 'what works' and the correctional services accreditation panel: Taking stock from an inside perspective. *Criminology and Criminal Justice, 10*, 37–58.

McMurran, M., & Priestley, P. (2003). *PRISM: Ett program för att minska sitt drogmissbruk [PRISM a programme for reducing substance abuse]*. Kriminalvården.

Motz, R. T., Barnes, J. C., Caspi, A., Arseneault, L., Cullen, F. T., Houts, R., Wertz, J., & Moffitt, T. E. (2020). Does contact with the justice system deter or promote future delinquency? Results from a longitudinal study of British adolescent twins. *Criminology, 58*, 307–335.

Murray, J., & Farrington, D. P. (2010). Risk factors for conduct disorder and delinquency: Key findings from longitudinal studies. *Canadian Journal of Psychiatry, 55*, 633–642.

National Network for Safe Communities. (2016). *Group violence intervention: An Implementation guide*. Office of Community Oriented Policing Services. https://nnscommunities.org/wp-content/uploads/2017/10/GVI_Guide_2016.pdf

Newsome, J., & Cullen, F. T. (2017). Using biosocial criminology to enhance offender rehabilitation. *Criminal Justice and Behavior, 44*, 1030–1049.

Nordén, E. (2015). *Utvecklingen av sluten ungdomsvård 1999–2014 [The development of closed institutional care 1999–2014]*. Brottsförebyggande rådet (BRÅ).

Pettersson, T. (2010). Recidivism among young males sentenced to prison and youth custody. *Journal of Scandinavian Studies in Criminology and Crime Prevention, 11*, 151–169.

Priestley, P. (2003). *One-to-One. Ett kognitivt beteendeprogram for att reducera återfall i brott. Teori och empiri [One-to-one. A cognitive-behavioural programme for reducing criminal recidivism: theory and evidence]*. Kriminalvården.

Robinson, C. R., Vanbenschoten, S., Alexander, M., & Lowenkamp, C. T. (2011). A random (almost) study of staff training aimed at reducing re-arrests (STARR): Reducing recidivism through intentional design. *Federal Probation, 75*, 57–63.

Smith, P., Schweitzer, M., Labrecque, R. M., & Latessa, E. J. (2012). Improving probation officers' supervision skills: An evaluation of the EPICS model. *Journal of Crime and Justice, 35*, 189–199.

SOU. (1956). *Skyddslag: Strafflagsberedningens slutbetänkande [Criminal law preparation-Final report] (SOU 1956:55)*. Department of Justice.

SOU. (1986). *Påföljd för brott [Penalty for crime] (SOU 1986:15)*. Department of Justice.

SOU. (2017). *Villkorlig frigivning—förstärkta insatser mot återfall i brott [Parole-Reinforced interventions to reduce recidivism] (SOU 2017:61)*. Department of Justice.

Souverein, F., Dekkers, T., Bulanovaite, E., Doreleijers, T., Hales, H., Kaltiala-Heino, R., Oddo, A., Popma, A., Raschle, N., Schmeck, K., Zanoli, M., & van der Pol, T. (2019). Overview of European forensic youth care: Towards an integrative mission for prevention and intervention strategies for juvenile offenders. *Child and Adolescent Psychiatry and Mental Health, 13*, 6.

Starfelt Sutton, L. C., Dynewall, M., Wennerholm, J., Åhlén, S., Rugge, T., Bourgon, G., & Robertsson, C. (2020). Evaluation of the implementation of a risk-need-responsivity service in community supervision in Sweden. *Criminal Justice and Behavior, 48*, 619–636.

Statistics Sweden. (2020). *Trends and Forecasts 2020—population, education and labour market in Sweden, outlook to year 2035*. https://www.scb.se/en/finding-statistics/statistics-by-subject-area/education-and-research/analysis-trends-and-forecasts-in-education-and-the-labour-market/trends-and-forecasts-for-education-and-labour-market/pong/publications/trends-and-forecasts-2020

Sturup, J., Rostami, A., Mondani, H., Gerell, M., Sarnecki, S., & Edling, C. (2019). Increased gun violence among young males in Sweden: A descriptive national survey and international comparison. *European Journal of Criminal Policy and Research, 25*, 365–378.

Young, S., Moss, D., Sedgwick, O., Fridman, M., & Hodgkins, P. (2015). A meta-analysis of the prevalence of attention deficit hyperactivity disorder in incarcerated populations. *Psychological Medicine, 45*, 247–258.

Rehabilitation in Taiwan

Susyan Jou, Shang-Kai Shen, and Bill Hebenton

History of Taiwanese Criminal Justice Rehabilitation

From 1949 to the present, three developments can be identified that permit enhanced understanding of how probation and rehabilitation operate in contemporary Taiwan. The first and earliest development was in 1962 with the formation of an independent juvenile probation and parole service, introduced by the new Juvenile Delinquency and Justice Act. The service specialized in children-in-need, status offenders, and young people on probation; it also undertook work with juvenile courts under the governance of the Judicial Yuan. Until 1980, police were the key agency working with probationers and parolees, providing intensive community surveillance without any specified rehabilitation function. Police and prisons, however, were assisted

---

S. Jou (✉)
School of Criminology, National Taipei University, Taipei, Taiwan
e-mail: sjou@mail.ntpu.edu.tw

S.-K. Shen
Taiwan Hsinchu District Prosecutors Office, Hsinchu, Taiwan

B. Hebenton
Department of Criminology, University of Manchester, Manchester, UK
e-mail: bill.hebenton@manchester.ac.uk

by long-existing charity groups and shelters for ex-prisoners, later re-named the 'Taiwan After-care Association' (TAA), a semi-governmental NGO. The Association has been funded, supervised, and staff-resourced by the Ministry of Justice since 1949; senior staff are drawn from the Prosecution Office (appointed by the Ministry of Justice); and prisoners can apply to receive re-entry services from the TAA on a voluntary basis.

The Birth of the Adult Probation and Parole Service in the 1980s

The second development is the creation of a specific Adult Probation and Parole Service, established in 1980 by the Security Measures Execution Act (hereafter referred to as 'SMEA'). Article 64 II of the SME Act was revised to announce the creation of a probation agency: 'the Ministry of Justice may establish a probation officer at the prosecution office at the district court to take charge of the probation affairs ordered by the prosecutors'. The same legislation also authorizes probation officers' official duties: 'the probation function, depending on the context, shall be executed by the police agency, an autonomous organization, charity organization, close relatives or family members of the person under imprisonment, or other appropriate persons that are located in or outside of the place where the person under imprisonment is'. In contemporary Taiwan, adult probation now works under the Ministry of Justice with leaders almost always drawn from senior prosecutors appointed by government ministers. The probation and parole officers took over the police duties described above and operated in a case-management mode but due to limited staff and large caseloads, they mainly functioned as supervisory agents. Apart from probation and parole, the main tasks for these officers in the community include the supervision of indivduals under suspended prosecution, and the supervision of community treatment and community labour orders of the court.

The Rise of Governmental Purchased Rehabilitation Services in 2000s

The third and final development is the development of governmental purchased rehabilitation services since 2000. The context for their emergence was the ferment of legal reforms in Taiwan. The main criminal justice reform took place in 2000; the government developed a so-called 'bifurcatory criminal justice policy' with both lenient and severe policies coexisting (Chang & Huang, 2010). Bifurcation is sometimes referred to as 'the twin-track approach'; the two terms are synonymous. Bifurcation, as a penal policy, consists of a legal and practical dichotomy that opposes two main categories of people who offend and how they are processed (Bottoms, 1977). One finds on the one hand, ' dangerous' people, who are treated more harshly (with more constraints, fewer early prison releases, in some cases the violation of general criminal law principles and so on) but who are also subject to more scrutiny and attention—which may include more support. On the other hand, one finds the 'run-of-the-mill' who are managed via bureaucratic procedures. The policy sought to emphasize the distinction between misdemeanours and acknowledged major offences. The Sexual Assault Crime Prevention Act in 2005 was a good example of one pole, with sexual assault considered one of the most serious crimes. An example of the other tendency towards lenience, was the revision of Criminal Code Article 41II which ruled that inability to pay fines may be directly commuted to labour service. This has resulted in an estimated 5000 plus people sentenced each year to community labour service under probation officers' supervision.[1] Furthermore, a major revision to the new Prison Act (2021) emphasizes the need for Taiwan's correctional system to improve on human rights, inmate and criminals' rights, along with victims' rights. Childrens' and feminist movements have long sought to mobilize change in terms of legal reforms, probation practices; and parole services. Additional professional services have now been introduced including, for example, individual/group counselling, psychological and psychiatric therapies, harm-reduction labour, work training labour, family support labor, and restorative practices (serving the needs of victims) and later legal revisions in 2008, sought to encourage harm reduction and alongside the use of suspended prosecution and new community labour service orders, were seen to be key components of Taiwan's lenient criminal policy. An important impact of the development of bifurcatory 'leniency' is that the probation/parole officer is responsible for the oversight of these new orders. Somewhat ironically, probation is also the key agency on the 'tougher side' for all types of community treatments. To cope with the extension of rehabilitation needs and expectations, the probation and parole agency, therefore, has inevitably had to purchase treatment services from external NGOs and professional groups. Needless to say, the quantity and quality of services purchased are highly dependent upon financial resources available to the adult probation/parole service.

Who Works in Rehabilitation in Taiwan?

Rehabilitation in Taiwan is mainly directed by the government's Ministry of Justice (MOJ), which formulates regulations, develops organizational structures, plans budgets, and recruits staff. Prisons, Probation services, and Prosecution offices as sub-divisions of the MOJ are tasked with managing lawbreakers. National figures suggest that annually about 1200 prosecutors deal with 450,000–500,000 criminal cases. There are 7000 correctional officers managing 60,000 inmates; 240 probation officers; and 500 in-house 'outsourcing' staff to assist them with 7000 probationers and parolees; between them delivering around 8000 harm-reduction community interventions and 4.5 million community labour hours. Among these agencies, the probation/parole office is the main community-based rehabilitation agency in Taiwan. Given the small number of appointed probation staff, as previously indicated, outsourcing of services has been and remains the key tool underlying rehabilitative services (using NGOs). For example, they work with other professionals on government budgets, including in-house psychologists, social workers, assistants, clerks, and others. Apart from these employees, probation and parole officers also work closely with non-profit organizations (NGOs) that provide forms of assistance in community labour. One of these is the Taiwan After-care Association (TAA) which was established in the late 1940s, long before the development of a governmental organization of probation/parole; it provides an accommodation service, vocational training, small business loans, and so on. The latest available figures indicate that TAA provides services to 13,000 of the formerly incarcerated (with 60 full-time staff and 1000 volunteers). The other key NGO is the Probation Volunteers Association (PVA) which has about 2000 volunteers providing social support and related medical, educational, and employment resources. The third NGO is the Association for Victim Support (AVS) now providing services to victims and assigned to work alongside Probation. It is important to note that all these three 'NGOs', while not directly part of a governmental department, are all largely funded and supervised by the Ministry of Justice.

Probation/Parole and Professional Development

There are 22 probation offices nationwide, and the sizes of probation/parole offices are classified into four levels according to caseload numbers. As Table 1 shows, probation/parole offices at Level One receive on average more than 1000 cases per year and comprise around 20 probation officers and 20–40 co-workers. The exception is Taipei Office (in the capital) which although taking less than 1000 cases per year, is regarded as having to deal with more complex and high-profile cases. Level Two probation/parole offices have on average 500–1000 cases per year and comprise about 10 probation officers and 20 co-workers. Level Three offices have 200–500 cases per year and comprise at most five probation officers and ten co-workers. Taiwan has a number of islands as part of its geography, each with an office staffed by one probation officer and at most three co-workers, and typically handling less than 100 cases per year.

Table 2 indicates the fiscal budgets for probation and protection services in Taiwan from 2013 to the present. As shown, the trend over the decade is significantly downwards, with the average fiscal budget of about 8 million US dollars and, as a proportion of the total MOJ budget, rapidly dropping from 20% down to 5%. Actually, about 10% of the entire MOJ budget goes to the prosecutors' pension plan every year. Only limited development of probation

Table 1 Probation offices, caseload numbers and level in 2021

District probation office	Cases of supervision[a]	Level
Taipei	784	1
Shilin	736	2
New Taipei	1943	1
Taoyuan	1937	1
Hsinchu	818	2
Miaoli	559	2
Taichung	2,325	1
Changhua	926	2
Nantou	537	2
Yunlin	621	2
Chiayi	561	2
Tainan	1073	1
Kaohsiung	1276	1
Ciaotou	892	2
Pingtung	935	2
Taitung	272	3
Hualien	384	2
Yilan	371	2
Keelung	407	2
Penghu	74	4
Kinmen	46	4
Lienjiang	11	4
Total	17,431	

[a]Including new in-take and unclosed probationees and parolees in 2021
Sources Statistics Yearbook of Taiwan Ministry of Justice (2022)

Table 2 Fiscal budgets for the probation and protection services of the MOJ in Taiwan: 2013–2022[a]

Year	Probation/Protection Fiscal budget (USD[b])	MOJ Fiscal budget(NTD)	%
2022	83,574,000 (2,841,516)	1,685,440,000	4.96
2021	132,631,000 (4,509,454)	1,700,423,000	7.80
2020	206,274,000 (7,013,316)	1,819,825,000	11.33
2019	193,410,000 (6,575,940)	1,678,852,000	11.52
2018	195,773,000 (6,656,282)	1,272,880,000	15.38
2017	255,185,000 (8,676,290)	1,245,657,000	20.49
2016	267,868,000 (9,107,512)	1,310,330,000	20.44
2015	249,785,000 (8,492,690)	1,751,737,000	14.26
2014	220,915,000 (7,511,110)	1,130,632,000	19.54
2013	226,463,000 (7,699,742)	1,096,412,000	20.65

[a]The fiscal budget for probation and protection include services of probation, rehabilitation, victim protection and public education
[b]Currency rate, 1: 29.13 (NTD: USD, April 17 2022)
Source The Fiscal Budget Plan, the Ministry of Justice (see https://www.moj.gov.tw) (accessed: April 17, 2022)

and rehabilitation services can be realistically expected with such diminishing investment levels.

Career entry to probation/parole is open to graduates who have successfully passed the national adult probation examination; they then receive two months of professional training from the Taiwan Judicial Academy and then four months placement internship. Only around 4% of initial applicants are successful in completing the process to become probation/parole officer. Academically, most senior probation officers have majored in law and police studies, and increasingly more in criminology, psychology, educational counselling, and social work.

Probation and Parole Programs Before 2000

Before the legal reforms of 2000, probation/parole worked mainly on supervision and monitoring of criminal cases in the community, aiming to reduce re-offending behaviour. According to Article 74-2 of the Rehabilitative Disposition Execution Act (hereafter referred to as 'RDEA'), those who are under probation on a court order or early release from prison must report their physical health, accommodation arrangements, and work status to the probation officer at least once a month. The probation officers provide appropriate supervision to address individual needs and also oversee compliance with court orders that may involve urine testing, police visits, or volunteer provided services. Probation officers may pay visits at any time to probationers' residences to meet their families or those providing support; they also closely monitor social contacts and exhort the maintenance of good conduct in the community. Arguably, therefore, since 2000, the probation officer's work model has been transformed from its old 'surveillance and crime control', when probation staff would have been considered 'community police' but without a uniform.

Bifurcated Criminal Policy Reform in 2000

A 'bifurcated criminal policy' was advocated by Minister Liao of the MOJ in 2000 who was very keen to learn policy lessons from more mature democracies (USA/UK). He believed that reductions in recidivism can be delivered more effectively by reserving imprisonment for major criminal offences and offering community corrections and treatments in more minor cases. Since the trend was first described by Anthony Bottoms in 1977, a bifurcated penal strategy has proved extremely influential across Anglophone countries. It has been exported globally (Dunkel et al., 2021; Seeds, 2017). Yet, as Hebenton and Seddon (2009) and Kemshall (2013) have argued, the maintenance of a two-track system relies upon a series of questionable penological assumptions that are extremely difficult to administer in practice. Thus Kemshall notes:

> Bifurcation presumes easily distinguishable thresholds between risk categories, accurate risk assessment within prisons and classification of prisoners, and fail-safe parole decisions, and that risk remains static upon release. These are unsound assumptions and create systematic flaws in the operation of a bifurcated approach. (Kemshall, 2013: 271)

Taiwan's developing experience with 'bifurcation' echoes these sentiments.

New criminal policies were legislated and launched soon after the amendments of the Criminal Code and the Criminal Procedure Code, for example, the implementation of suspended prosecution, conditional suspended sentences, community social labour services, addiction treatments, mental disorder criminal treatments, psychological counselling, injunction orders to prevent repeat offending, and law-related education. The oversight and implementation of all these new rehabilitation-focused policies to increase the capacity for rehabilitative work were mainly the responsibility of probation/parole officers.

Special Policies for Sexual Assault Offender Treatment Since 2005

Several serious and high-profile sexual assault and homicide cases occurred in 2005, and public anger soon led to governmental action by way of legislation—namely amendments to the 1997 Sexual Assault Crime Prevention Act. As a result, probation/parole officers were tasked to provide both preventive and rehabilitate treatments, alongside more intensive supervision. New responsibilities included requiring lie detector tests (on a random basis), residence requirements, authorizing, locations for curfews, electronic monitoring, ensuring no association with known offenders, and so on. These new measures evidence a further transformation of the probation/parole work model—into formal risk management to prevent future criminality (Hebenton & Seddon, 2009; Kemshall, 2013).

Implementation of Social Labor in the Community in 2009

In response to growing concerns about prison overcrowding and the growth of the judicial budget, in 2009 the government implemented another new penal policy and amended Article 41 of the Criminal Code. A criminal who is sentenced to less than six-month imprisonment or to a fine, may have his/her punishment commuted to social labour in the community. Due to limited staff, the MOJ decided to purchase services from the private sector to assist probation/parole officers. These assistants are responsible for the administrative oversight of all social labour in the community, maintaining community safety and satisfaction where the labour is delivered, and completing relevant case reports. Although in place for over a decade, there has been no published evaluation of social labor in the community as a practice.

More Demands on Community Supervision and Medical Treatment for Violent, Psychiatric, and Drug/Alcohol Addicted Individuals Since 2010

In the last decade, and largely in response to several high-profile random killings committed by individuals with mental health problems, the government has sought to take what it sees as more effective measures to reduce the risk of their re-offending (Lin et al., 2020). How to prevent recidivism among these cases has become an important political and professional concern for probation/parole offices and the MOJ. The MOJ has encouraged stronger collaboration not only between probation/parole offices, and the TAA, PVA, and AVS, but also with the Ministry of Health and Welfare (MOHW) in central government, and with local health and welfare official agencies. The overall governmental response is both to reduce public concern and to encourage longer-term multifunctional treatments, alongside more intensive supervision.

New Developments in Rehabilitation 2010: Introducing Offender's Family Support, Victim Services, and Restorative Justice

For a long time, rehabilitation was highly dependent on prison, probation/parole, and NPOs' services to supervisees, on an individual basis. Yet, it was realized by the government that without family support and community acceptance, the process of rehabilitation would be problematic: in order to assist in this process, family and victim needs had to be met. Starting in 2010, the government made funding available to the TAA, PVA, AVS and other NPOs to establish family support and victim support projects. In 2018, a Social Safety Network 1.0 framework was initiated by the government Administration Yuan, to provide such support, alongside restorative justice with victims. In the last five years, Taiwan has thus gradually shifted its focus from spotlighting only those who commit offences to recognizing the importance of successful rehabilitation of meeting their family needs and indeed those of victims.

Under the Social Safety Network 1.0 framework, the MOJ has managed to expand its budget, providing greater capacity and contracting out relevant services, community treatment, and rehabilitation teams collaborating with psychologists, social workers, drug caseworkers as well as probation/parole assistants. These new teams appear to have improved the quality of rehabilitation work; more generally, the framework has sought to explicitly meet the needs of lawbreakers' families and victims through the working together of health, housing, social relations, and finance services.

Models of Rehabilitation and Its Meanings

The year 2000 was a watershed in the transformation of probation and rehabilitation. The old routinized 'surveillance/crime control model' with its inward-looking bureaucratic practices carried with it the limited aim of seeing clients through the system and closing the case. This older working model was partly reflected in the wider malaise at the time felt by Taiwanese society about the performance of the criminal justice system itself in solving crimes, bringing lawbreakers to justice, and treating victims of crime well. The roots of the bifurcation policy lie in the Taiwanese government's response to this societal discontent; crimes such as sexual assault, drug use, drunken driving, and mentally ill persons were singled out as needing to be 'treated and punished' both in prisons and in communities. All the while, the government's aim was also to produce a more financially efficient approach. As a result, an increasing number of minor and substance-related crimes are dealt with in the community as opposed to prison, with responsibility given to probation staff. Intensive supervision programmes were also a probation responsibility. Victim-offender services also became part of the probation role.

Without more resources, probation has sought to work more efficiently, helping to facilitate multi-agency working and social resource linkage, enhancing risk-based management, monitoring and enforcing community orders, overseeing compensation and assistance services to victims, sometimes administering electronic monitoring and polygraph compliance with sexual offending Thus, probation/parole became more case-based, with a social work orientation, recognizing the needs of offender and victim.

Yet such a transformation in outlook and workload requires both additional resources and arguably a shared sense of probation's changed role by the prosecutors' office (to whom probation is ultimately accountable). There is little evidence that either of these has been met. Thus, the total number of probation officers was 163 in 1999 and 242 in 2021, with around 230 assistants in 2009 to assist with the community labour service. The current yearly caseload per probation officer is about 250 cases, compared to about 100 cases between 1994 to 2008.[2] Probation's transformed working model has overburdened probation offices with oversight of treatment-oriented community sentences. The search for efficiency and savings has resulted in the government adopting 'contracted out' purchased services, often at low cost. It is also clear that some provider NGOs have benefited significantly from the reforms post-2000. The continuing crime control 'outlook' of the prosecution agency, to whom probation services are accountable creates role conflict. Since the establishment of a probation service in 1982, all appointed probation directors have been former senior prosecutors. Ultimately previous and current directors of probation are accountable to the Chief Prosecutor of the Taiwan High Prosecutors Office.

Effectiveness of Rehabilitation

Before 2000, probation officers mainly supervised offender activities in the community. Their goals were to monitor, enforce prosecutor's or court orders, and to ensure public safety by reducing re-offending. Clients would include a mix of those on suspended prosecution, on parole (conditional or unconditional), or serving a sanction instead of imprisonment. Post-2000 reforms have brought others into its purview, such as monitoring and overseeing more than 20,000 harm-reduction clients, 4000 drink-driving community treatment orders, and about 10,000–15,000 new community social labour clients per annum.

There is no international consensus about what works in probation practice (McNeill, 2012; Trotter, 2013). In preparing this chapter, we undertook a literature search of published outcome research in Taiwan which had taken some primary measures of re-offending such as arrests, convictions, or violation of parole, as well as the participation in restorative justice procedures. We found no evaluations using experimental and quasi-experimental designs, and all previous studies using official data in Taiwan on re-offending rates are at Level 1 on the Maryland Scientific Methods Scale (Sherman et al., 1997).

Re-Offending and Violation of Parole

Since neither the probation office or the Ministry of Justice publishes data on reconviction rates of probation/parolees in Taiwan, this chapter uses two proxy reconviction indicators: prison admissions—reconviction over a lifetime, and prison admission—reconviction within five-year period. As shown in Fig. 1, rates are 42% (lifetime) and 31.1% (5 year) respectively in 1993,

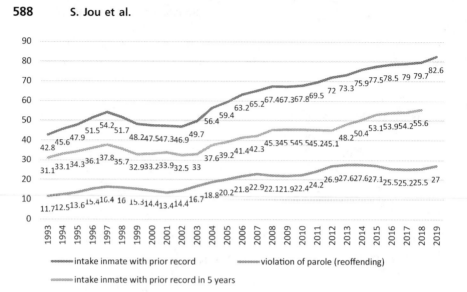

Fig. 1 Re-offending percentages for inmates and parolees in Taiwan, 1993–2019 (*Source* Authors)

and 82.6% and 55.6% in 2019. Overall, both proxy indicators show a gradually increasing level of reconviction using prison admissions data (Lin, 2020). It is also worth noting that there was a levelling of the rates between 1999 and 2003 but with a significant take-off in 2004.[3]

Another indicator is the rate of parole violation—specifically for reconvictions. Figure 1 shows that this was 11.7% in 1993 and 27.0% in 2019. Chen (2013) followed 960 parolees for seven years from 2004 to 2011 logging their official arrests and found that 30% of them re-offended within 12 months after release from prison, and 56% within 24 months. In Taiwan, an increase in reconviction rates, in general, is confirmed both by official data and the very limited empirical research available.

Completion of Harm-Reduction Community Treatment and Labor Orders

About 30–40% of crime in Taiwan involves drug misuse, and the government has sought to act on this serious issue. It now uses deferred prosecution for drug abusers, conditional on undertaking a one-year harm-reduction community treatment order from an assigned hospital or clinic. Thus, this policy has the aim of better treatment to reduce re-offending. It also contributes to reductions in the prison population and shares financial and political responsibilities for drug issues between the Ministry of Justice and

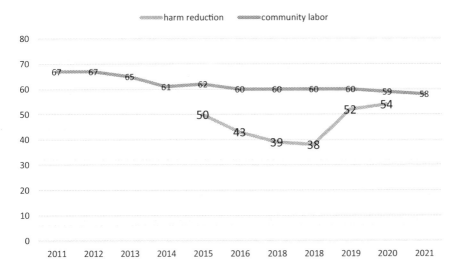

Fig. 2 Percentage completion rates for harm reduction and community social labour orders, Taiwan, 2011–2021 (*Source* Authors)

the Ministry of Health and Welfare. At the practice level, the harm-reduction community treatment order is decided at the discretion of prosecutors; and funded either from the client's own resources or governmental subsidy and monitored by probation officers with random urine tests.

The completion rate for harm-reduction community treatment is approximately 46% with a re-offending rate of around 37.02% in the past six years.[4] As Fig. 2 shows, about half of the complete harm-reduction community treatment orders. Completion rates for community social labor orders are reducing year on year and are now below 60%. Indeed, prosecution offices have reduced the hours of community social labor from 8,659,955 h to 4,724,605 h over the decade 2011–2021.

Conclusion: Future Challenges in Policy and Practice

The probation/parole office has been established now for about 40 years in Taiwan, but increasingly the required proliferation of rehabilitation services exceeds any increase in staffing and service budgets. As in most other democracies, crime and criminal justice are volatile public issues and party-political shifts in policy occur with election cycles (Fell, 2018). Victim rights have increased its political salience in recent years, seeking to place victims with a more active role in court proceedings and entitlement to governmental services. At the same time, prison, and community-correction reforms emphasize 'inmates' and 'wrongdoers' human rights, alongside alternatives to decarceration and community orders. Greater involvement of the wider community signals a move to a more restorative understanding of 'criminal justice'.

Whatever this wider context of change around criminal justice reform signals, as we have analyzed earlier in this chapter, probation/parole outcomes appear poor. It also appears that government is reluctant to collect, analyze, and publish relevant effectiveness data. At present the government is introducing additional rehabilitation and treatment policies on drugs, drink driving, and mentally disordered in the community—in essence a version 2.0 of the Social Safety Network framework—but with no genuine evidential or evidence-based basis. In addition, public polls over the past ten years indicate that in 2017, 70% of the public were dissatisfied with courts and 84% were dissatisfied with judicial and criminal justice reform.[5] Arguably, much of recent policy development could be seen as the government seeking to distract public attention from concern about lack of effectiveness and an accountability crisis; rather attempting to substitute an image of a 'morally' peaceful culture inclusive of both 'criminals and victims'.

The crisis of Taiwan's modern probation/parole and rehabilitation services at the policy level is arguably due to a failure of the government to fully recognize that its efforts on inclusivity and development of appropriate services to reduce re-offending, necessarily come at a cost. Morally, the government attempts to offer rhetoric of rehabilitation and reintegration into full citizenship and pledges to leave no convicted person and his/her family behind. Yet, by doing so, any genuinely thought-out policy has to deal with the fact that those who break the law often come from marginalized sections of society with limited education and economic opportunities and inadequate support systems. A practical policy has to actually invest large resources in these wider societal inequities. Instead of greater resources, government's strategy has been to talk of ever-increasing 'smartness' of leadership and management—creating greater efficiencies in practice. Within limited resources, the probation and parole services staff have been required to work smarter; in essence the neoliberal paradigm, familiar to many across the globe. In practice producing a combination of due-process models for supervision, risk-assessment models for particular types of offending behavior (i.e. sexual and drug offences) and a social work model in relation to the bulk of other general offending. Since the trend was first described by Anthony Bottoms in 1977, a bifurcated penal strategy has proved extremely influential in government thinking. It has been exported globally (Dunkel et al., 2021; Seeds, 2017). As Hebenton and Seddon (2009) and Kemshall (2013) have argued, the maintenance of a two-track system relies upon a series of questionable penological assumptions that are extremely difficult to administer in practice.

However, over the past two decades, we see no full staff, no smarter working methods, expanding irrelevant tasks (i.e. providing restorative justice meetings to victims, indiscriminate offenders' family support projects), and no more professional leadership in probation/parole and rehabilitation services. As a result, probation/parole and rehabilitation service does not play an efficient role in breaking the perpetuating cycles of crime. Designing a comprehensive rehabilitation system involves collaboration between probation, imprisonment, parole, self-help, and medical and social welfare agencies. Without resources and efficiency, however, all reform or policy is no more than moralistic and political virtue signalling.

The existing literature in Taiwan on matters of effectiveness relies upon interview methods, accepting perpetrator and staff narratives as the basis for rating rehabilitation successful. There is a relatively underdeveloped evidence base on at least Level 3 of the Maryland Scientific Methods Scale for the effectiveness of probation/parole practices particularly with regard to reducing re-offending. One of the obstacles is the inaccessibility of re-offending data for independent researchers (due to privacy and personal information protection laws). The exception is harm-reduction programs research where data are mainly collected by treatment providers, mostly medical institutes with agreement of prosecutors and clients. Randomized control experiments for different policies and practices of probation, furthermore, are almost impossible due to the requirement that approval decisions must lie with prosecutors and courts.

A further difficulty in developing a reflexive evidence-based culture is that most of the relevant professionals including judges, prosecutors, probation, and correctional officers are reluctant to accept recidivism as a key performance indicator. The preference is for 'process' assessment. This of course is not peculiar to Taiwan (see, for example, McNeill et al., 2012 on contested purposes and what counts as evidence). Development of an appropriate evaluation culture is definitely lacking in contemporary Taiwan; this is not to argue for a simplistic assessment of the evidence in reducing recidivism, rather that the discussion must consider the resource environment within which probation agencies operate, in order to make/render visible the potential costs and benefits of specific working models. This is particularly the case where probation/parole reforms have been trialled to make the case for further investment of taxpayers' money.

The present chapter concludes by considering the upcoming challenges and concerns of rehabilitation in Taiwan, namely (1) the increasing tension between its legal role and its protective and counselling role, (2) the relatively new role conflict in relation to services for all justice-involved individuals and (3) pressures and constraints on the development of truly evidence-based rehabilitation policies. Turning to the first of these challenges—tensions within the probation role—here, we must recognize that the Taiwan criminal justice context accepts the need for forceful censure of the wrongdoer, and an attempt to bring him/her to acknowledge and repent what he/she has done and pay for it with suitable moral reparation. Duff (2003) provides a persuasive reconfiguration of the matter, in terms of seeking to develop a service grounded in the notion of probation work as a mode of 'constructive punishment'; requiring people to face up to the effects and implications of their crimes, thus aspiring to a justice that is retributive, communicative, reparative, and rehabilitative in seeking to repair relationships with fellow citizens. As Duff opines:

> It would be a probation officer's task to organise and assist the discussion between offender and victim…to speak for the wider community in the discussion (indeed, to speak for the victim when the individual victim is unavailable or unwilling, or when the only victim is the wider community). (Duff: 191)

On the second issue, as with much previous legislative reform and attitudinal change towards people who offend and their victims, future debate on services to both will be shaped by developments/changes in Taiwan's public dialogue on human rights and the victims' movement. Many Taiwanese scholars argue that developments on 'rights' in the past three decades should be credited more to the struggle of its own civil society and reforms adopted by its government, and much less to inspiration by existing international human rights treaties. Recognizing that important steps advancing Taiwan's human rights conditions were initiated or undertaken in response to its domestic concerns helps us understand the ineluctable importance of the domestic party-political context in Taiwan (see Cohen et al., 2019). Yet, as in the West, there are reasons why the need to rehabilitate people who commit offences came before the rise of public discourse on victims, and in this regard, Taiwan's development and reforms have been no different (Christie, 1977). Adversarial criminal law, where the state takes responsibility, entails automatic sidelining for the victim. In seeking to meet the challenge of the victims' movement in Taiwan, probation's reliance on efficiency and cost arguments will have only limited purchase; instead, what needs be emphasized is the moral force of probation as a generic helping service for all those whose experience of criminal justice diminishes them materially and emotionally. In Duff's phraseology, ideally, the mediating role for the probation officer will be to speak for the wider political community to the victim (and to the offender), as well as speaking to the community for the offender, and for the victim (Duff, 2003).

Evidence-based policy and practice concerning rehabilitation raise a number of vexed issues. First, drawing on Western experience, there are often deleterious implications for probation practice in naively hitching its wagon to a governmental 'evidence-based' agenda; the lesson from Britain, certainly, is that there is 'no quick fix' to improving the effectiveness of probation service outcomes. As many argue, while informed by evidence and evaluation, development needs to be gradual and incremental (see Mair, 2011; Raynor, 2020). As late as the mid-2000s, researchers in Britain were able to conclude from their assessment of the published literature that it was too early to say what works, what does not, and what is promising (Merrington & Stanley, 2004). Indeed a more recent British assessment of probation supervision similarly concludes that data on effectiveness is both limited and mixed (Smith et al., 2018). Compared with the wealth of evidence relating to the effectiveness of treatment and prevention interventions that is produced in Britain's healthcare, evidence production with regard to the effectiveness of interventions delivered by probation services to reduce re-offending is low. This is surprising, since the rehabilitation of persons committing offences has been a major priority both for the British government and the public. Chui (2002) writing on probation in neighboring Hong Kong, describes probation practice as akin to a 'black box' in terms of public appreciation because of a dearth of evaluation studies. Neither Hong Kong nor Taiwan has a tradition of effectiveness research in the probation policy sector, yet evaluation's value lies for practitioners in developing reflexivity in their own interventions; on whether one particular practice model works better than others; and as a form of accountability (Armstrong et al., 2017). Elsewhere, we have speculated about the reasons behind a lack of evaluation in public policy (Hebenton et al., 2010 for a more sustained consideration). Characteristics of public policymaking in Taiwan place limitations on research-based, evidence-led policy development both in terms of long-term consistency and sustainability (Jan, 2004). Underlying institutional and cultural inertia as well as the particularities of a certain political decision-making style cast a shadow over the likelihood of 'effectiveness' research. Systematic collection of relevant data, publicly accessible to independent researchers would be a starting point.

Notes

1. See the annual statistics of the Ministry of Justice, 2000–2020.
2. See Statistics Yearbook, the Ministry of Justice, 2022.
3. See Statistics Yearbook, the Ministry of Justice, 2022.
4. See the 2020 Fiscal Report by the Ministry of Justice.
5. See the yearly public polls press released by the University of Cheng-Chen. Website: https://deptcrc.ccu.edu.tw/index.php?temp=news2andlang=cht (last visit Feb. 28, 2022).

References

Armstrong, S., Blaustein, J., & Henry, A. (Eds.) (2017). *Reflexivity and criminal justice*. Palgrave Macmillan.

Bottoms, A. E. (1977). Reflections on the renaissance of dangerousness. *Howard Journal of Criminal Justice, 16*(2), 70–96.

Bottoms, A. E. (1980) Introduction to the coming crisis. In A. E. Bottoms and R. H. Preston (Eds.), *The coming penal crisis: A criminological and theological exploration* (pp. 1–24). Scottish Academic Press.

Chang, L., & Huang, S. F. (2010). An introduction to restorative justice practices in Taiwan. *British Journal of Community Justice, 8*(3), 37–47.

Chen, Y. S. (2013). Recidivism and risk factors for adult parolees. *Criminal Policy and Crime Research, 16*, 1–26. (in Chinese).

Christie, N. (1977). Conflicts as property. *British Journal of Criminology, 17*, 1–15.

Cohen, J, Alford, W., & Lo, C-F. (Eds.). (2019) *Taiwan and international human rights: A story of transformation*. Springer.

Chui, E. (2002). The social work model of probation supervision of offenders in Hong Kong. *Probation Journal, 49*(4), 297–304.

Duff, R. A. (2003). Probation, punishment and restorative justice. *Howard Journal of Criminal Justice, 42*(2), 181–197.

Dunkel, F., Pruin, I, Storgaard, A., & Weber, J. (Eds.). (2021). *Prisoner resettlement in Europe*. Routledge.

Fell, D. (2018). *Government and politics in Taiwan* (2nd ed.). Routledge.

Hebenton, B., & Seddon, T. (2009). From dangerousness to precaution. *British Journal of Criminology, 49*(3), 343–362.

Hebenton, B., Jou, S., & Chang, Y.-C. (2010). Developing public safety and crime indicators in Taiwan. *Asian Journal of Criminology, 5*, 45–67.

Jan, C.-Y. (2004). *New public policy: History, philosophy and globalization*. Hua-Tai Publisher (in Chinese).

Kemshall, H. (2013). Dangerous offenders: Release and resettlement. In A. Hucklesby and L. Hagley-Dickinson (Eds.), *Prisoner resettlement: Policy and practice* (pp. 270–288). Willan.

Lee, S. H., Wu, S. C., Huang, C. C., & Wang, C. C. (2010). Drug recidivism rates and protective factors: Using Keelung as an example. *Journal of Criminology, 13*(1), 81–106. (in Chinese).

Lin, S. Y., Huang, Y. F., & Shen, P. Y. (2020). Recidivism analysis of male offenders with mental illness under criminal commitment. *Criminal Policy and Crime Prevention, 25*, 183–244. (in Chinese).

Lin, S. C. (2020). Overview of parole policy and practices in Taiwan, *National Lawyer Journal*, March, 57–75. (in Chinese).

Mair, G. (2011). The community order in England and Wales: Policy and practice. *Probation Journal, 58*(3), 215–232.

McNeill, F. (2012). Four forms of 'offender' rehabilitation: Towards an interdisciplinary perspective. *Legal and Criminological Psychology, 17*(1), 18–36.

McNeill, F., Farrall, S., Lightowler, C., & Maruna, S. (2012). Re-examining evidence-based practice in community corrections. *Justice Research and Policy*. https://doi.org/10.3818/JRP.14.1.2012.35

Merrington, S., & Stanley, S. (2004). 'What Works?': Revisiting the evidence in England and Wales. *Probation Journal, 51*(1), 7–20.

Raynor, P. (2020). Evidence versus politics in British probation. *Forensic Science International: Mind and Law*. https://doi.org/10.1016/j.fsiml.2020.100029

Seeds, C. (2017). Bifurcation nation: American penal policy in late mass incarceration. *Punishment and Society, 19*(5), 590–610.

Sherman, L. W., Gottfredson, D. C., MacKenzie, D. L., Eck, J., Reuter, P., & Bushway, S. D. (1997). *Preventing crime: What works, what doesn't, and what's promising*. National Institute of Justice, US Department of Justice.

Smith, A., Heyes, K., Fox, C., Harrison, J., Kiss, Z., & Bradbury, A. (2018). The effectiveness of probation supervision towards reducing re-offending: A rapid evidence assessment. *Probation Journal, 65*(4), 407–428.

Trotter, C. (2013). Reducing recidivism through probation supervision: What we know and don't know from four decades of research. *Federal Probation, 77*(2), 43–48.

Rehabilitation and the Adult Correctional Population in Texas

Anita Kalunta-Crumpton

Texas is the second largest and the second most populous state in the United States, with 254 counties[1] (see Texas Department of Criminal Justice [TDCJ], 2020a) and an estimated population of 29,527,941[2] as of July 1, 2021. The state has many administrative divisions in the form of county and city governments, which introduce elements of decentralization and variations in the structure, policies, and practices of criminal justice across the divisions. This fact speaks to a complex criminal justice system whose operations fall under the management of the TDCJ. Cohen (2012: 604) describes the TDCJ as 'a conceptual and structural labyrinth', considering the scope and diversity of its coverage and operations, and its enduring ideological flip flop between punishment and rehabilitation in criminal justice approaches to offenders. As one of the states that still imposes capital punishment, Texas is recognized for its tough-on-crime response to offending behaviour. In addition to its use of capital punishment, Texas has a reputation for having high incarceration rates (see Gottschalk, 2021).

While Texas has historically embraced a punitive ideology, it has in recent years earned a political reputation for its ideological and practical shift towards rehabilitation. Gottschalk (Ibid) cites 2007 as a notable turning

A. Kalunta-Crumpton (✉)
Administration of Justice, Texas Southern University, Houston, TX, USA
e-mail: Anita.Kalunta-Crumpton@tsu.edu

point in political perceptions of Texas as a state that has moved its criminal justice approach from punitive to rehabilitation. In that year, the Texas legislature approved the investment of $241 million in programs that supported rehabilitation and diversion from prison. This approach was adopted against the alternative of spending an estimate of $2 billion on the construction of new prison facilities to accommodate 17,000 extra prison beds by 2012 (see Cohen, 2012; Gottschalk, 2021). Rehabilitation philosophy was not foreign to Texas prior to 2007. According to Cohen (2012: 605), Texas prison system enjoyed 'a rehabilitation program that included vocational training and religious programs' in the late 1950s under the management of O.B. Ellis.[3] Rehabilitation was replaced by punishment when George Beto took over the management of prisons in 1961, and this punishment approach coincided with the no-tolerance-for-crime political agendas of Richard Nixon and Ronald Reagan, respectively (Ibid). Worthy of note is that the shifts in the state's criminal justice ideologies and practices—between punitive and rehabilitation—have been shaped by changes in the political and economic atmospheres. For instance, there is evidence of public support for the use of rehabilitation and diversion from prison programs, which in turn has positive implications for any political move towards a correctional policy that mirrors this public sentiment (see Thielo et al., 2016).

Economics play a crucial role in resolving conflicting debates around the use of imprisonment as punishment versus the impact of imprisonment on cost, including the cost of prison and jail overcrowding. For example, it was in response to prison overcrowding that the Texas intensive supervision program (ISP) was paraded as a cost-effective community-based alternative to imprisonment. Texas established her ISP in 1981, with the aim of diverting certain offenders, who committed a felonious offence and who would otherwise be imprisoned, from prison to intensive probation supervision. The ISP offers a blend of enhanced client control and the goal of rehabilitating probationers (Abadinsky, 2015). As another example, recall that the earlier 2007 legislative preference for rehabilitation and diversion programs was a cost-effective alternative to incarceration at the time.

In fact, the interest of offenders, the victims, or public safety may not be the real driver of correctional policies in Texas, which appears to be the case in the U.S in general. To a reasonable extent, the various rehabilitation programs available to the correctional population in prison/jail and in the community may have been created against the background of their political and/or economic value for crime control.

Below, the chapter first provides an overview of the context of correctional rehabilitation while being mindful of the convoluted structure of the

Texas criminal justice system. In line with the complexity of the criminal justice system, the size of the state, the size of the correctional population, and the decentralization of the correction system, there are several different types of rehabilitation programs, some of which are designated as treatment programs depending on the jurisdiction. Rehabilitation efforts are not universally applied to all correctional agencies in Texas, in that some agencies, such as prisons, may have specific programs while others, such as jails, may not. Also, the origins of individual programs vary across counties and cities.

These instances of complexity in Texas corrections probably render unfeasible any attempts to effectively conduct a collective or holistic evaluation of the state's rehabilitation efforts. For one, this would require an evaluation of individual programs in Texas prisons, jails, and in the community to determine their success or effectiveness in reaching their set goals. Unsurprisingly, considering the number of programs and sub-programs that exist across the differing correctional agencies this level of program evaluation has not been conducted. Relatedly, the diversity of programs may be open to diverse theoretical foundations, which means that this chapter only reflects on some theories that might inform rehabilitation programs in the state. Against these intricacies, the second part of the chapter discusses how the success of Texas crime control strategies, including rehabilitation, are typically measured. This is followed by a brief concluding comment.

Rehabilitation in Theory and Context

As of June 30, 2020, the TDCJ recorded a total of roughly 411,629 individuals who were in prison, on parole, or probation. Of this figure, 126,590 were incarcerated in correctional facilities, 83,423 were on parole supervision, and 201,120 were on 'direct misdemeanor or felony probation' (TDCJ, 2020b). Although each of these settings has some form of programming, approaches to rehabilitation in corrections are not immune to divisional variations at the local level (county or city) that result from decentralization. Nevertheless, the TDCJ, as an oversight entity, is tasked with channelling corrections and other criminal justice agencies towards a central state agenda. Accordingly, Texas has six criminal justice goals; rehabilitation is explicitly mentioned in one: 'To provide for confinement, supervision, rehabilitation, and reintegration of adult felons' (TDCJ, 2021a: 3). Four of the remaining five underline rehabilitation implicitly, for example the goal that reads: 'To provide supervision and administer the range of options and sanctions available for felons' reintegration back into society following release from confinement'.

Despite its current favourability as a criminal justice approach to crime control in Texas and the U.S in general, rehabilitation was for many years, from the 1970s up until the twenty-first century, discredited in favour of a tough-on-crime rhetoric and practice (see Andrews & Bonta, 2010). Now in Texas, there is a variety of rehabilitation programs that are run by designated divisions within the TDCJ and are structured to meet the diversity of rehabilitative needs among the correctional population in prison, jail, and the community. But in doing so, correctional officers are normally practical in their provision of rehabilitative services, in that they operate without a theoretical framework.

In reference to probation and parole work, Abadinsky (2015: 113) observes that officers 'often use techniques without understanding the theoretical basis or even recognizing them as part of a particular mode of rehabilitation— 'flying by the seat of the pants' is often characteristic of *P/P'*. However, this does not suggest that officers lack basic conceptual knowledge about forms of rehabilitation, considering that most of them would refer clients with problems, such as unemployment and substance use, to appropriate rehabilitation programs (Ibid). Thus, regardless of the nature of rehabilitation service delivery by providers, the goals and purpose of programs may be underlined by certain theoretical principles. According to Abadinsky (Ibid), rehabilitation[4] in the community by parole and probation officers are guided by 'three basic theoretical models', namely: behaviour/learning, psychoanalytic, and reality therapy. These are briefly described below.

With origins that are traced to the work of Sigmund Freud, psychoanalytic theory places emphasis on the unconscious, and the conflictual relationship of the conscious vs. unconscious—id, ego, and superego— in producing antisocial behaviour. Herein, the treatment of the antisocial behaviour would require a psychoanalytical dive into the person's unconscious or repressed early life experiences and feelings to make sense of the present. But according to Abadinsky (2015), probation and parole work does not involve psychoanalysis; rather, it applies psychoanalytical theory via the use of social casework—a branch of social work. Rehabilitation initiatives through social casework adopt a problem-solving approach that considers, among others, the psychological and social embodiments of the problem. This basic element of social casework is captured in Perlman's (1957: 4) definition of it as 'a process used by certain human welfare agencies to help individuals to cope more effectively with their problems'.

Contrary to the psychoanalytic perspective is the theory that behaviour is learned. This theory also contends that behaviour can be modified, and that the behavioural outcome of the learning and modification processes is dependent on the consequences of the behaviour—referred to as reinforcement. Invariably, a behaviour can be conditioned positively or negatively according to a positive or a negative reinforcement (see Staddon & Curetti, 2003; Skinner, 1986). Treatment, therefore, utilizes behaviour modification therapies to prevent reoffending behaviour. Because of the difficulties in practically imposing reinforcement on certain behaviours, such as drug addiction, Abadinsky (2015) identifies cognitive behavioural therapy as an alternative rehabilitation tool used in probation and parole work to change criminal behaviour by changing the thinking that supports such behaviour.

With reality therapy, developed by the psychiatrist, William Glaser, the idea, as the term illustrates, is to help the client face reality. This concept holds the client accountable and responsible not only for her/his offending behaviour, but also the choice to change the behaviour. To sum up, I refer to one of Glaser's (1990: 6) explanations of reality therapy wherein he states, 'A therapy that leads all patients toward reality, toward grappling successfully with tangible and intangible aspects of the real world, might accurately be called a therapy, or simply *Reality Therapy*'.

In one form or the other, these rehabilitation models, singly or collectively, underpin rehabilitation programs in Texas prisons and jails, and in the community. As Abadinsky (2015) notes, while the intersection of theory and context may not be intentionally or explicitly identified by those who provide, or refer clients to, rehabilitation, the justifications for rehabilitation services, such as the provision of housing and counselling to alleviate the social and psychological risk factors for recidivism, have theoretical backing. And so does the purpose of rehabilitation, which is to stop recidivism.

For all intents and purposes, rehabilitation programs that are channelled towards a correctional client, whether to address the underlying social causes of a client's involvement in crime, treat an addiction, or to work towards improving the client's human capital, are bound by the goal to reform the client to, potentially, be a law-abiding and productive member of society. Thus, public safety is expected to be improved as a result. Such practices and expectations, which also have a theoretical foundation, are exemplified in the program statements below:

> It is the mission of the Substance Use Treatment Program to provide evidence-based substance use treatment services appropriate to the needs of individual inmates to facilitate positive change; and to provide accountability for programming utilizing assessment tools developed specifically for this population, all of which leads to reducing recidivism and improving public safety. (TDCJ, n.d.[a]: n.p)

The mission of the Chaplaincy Department of the Texas Department of Criminal Justice is to positively impact public safety and reduce recidivism through moral rehabilitation by rendering pastoral care and quality programming to facilitate spiritual transformation. (TDCJ, n.d.[a]: n.p)

The TDCJ rehabilitation programs are housed or coordinated across specific divisions within the TDCJ, notably: Rehabilitation Programs Division (RPD), Community Justice Assistance Division (CJAD), Reentry and Integration Division (RID), Correctional Institutions Division (CID), and Parole Division (PD). Programs across the divisions overlap and complement each other. Interagency partnerships between and across these divisions are an integral and fundamental part of rehabilitation service provision and delivery for the correctional population (TDCJ 2021a; also see Clark, 2012).

Probation and Rehabilitation Programs in Community Supervision

The community supervision of adult probationers falls under the realm of the 123 community supervision and corrections departments (CSCDs) that serve the 254 counties in Texas (TDCJ, n.d.[b]). Managed by the CJAD of the TDCJ, the CSDCs are tasked with the rehabilitative supervision of those whom the courts have sentenced to community supervision. Table 1 displays examples of rehabilitation programs and services that are available to clients under court-directed supervision in the community.

There are also residential facilities to house those who are directed by the court to reside there while completing their community supervision. Typically, the facilities are meant for correctional clients with varying levels of risk, particularly those at moderate to high-risk levels. As Knapp et al. (1992) state, residential facilities provide a combination of intensive treatment and surveillance, which makes them an attractive community sanction because it offers the nearest alternative to traditional incarceration in prison or jail. In Texas, community-based residential facilities include court residential treatment centres, dually diagnosed residential facilities, intermediate sanction facilities, and substance abuse treatment facilities (see TDCJ, n.d.[b]). Collectively, these facilities have a variety of programs and services to meet the criminogenic needs of the clients, such as cognitive and life skills, education, employment, emotional issues, substance abuse, co-occurring substance abuse and mental health disorders, and family issues.

Table 1 Rehabilitation programs and services in community supervision

Programs	Services
Adult Education Programs	Aid clients 'to acquire academic competencies for literacy skills, General Education Development (GED) certificates, and English as a Second Language'
Batterers Intervention and Prevention Programs	Local nonprofit organizations provide 'treatment and educational services designed to help the batterers stop abusive behavior'
Cognitive Programs	These are 'behavioral, nonacademic programs' that 'assist adults under community supervision acquire competencies in problem solving, anger management, understanding the impact of their behavior on others, changing thinking and changing behavior to noncriminal alternatives'
Programs for the Mentally Impaired	Provide 'intensive case management, treatment referral and resource linkage to either divert the mentally impaired offender from the criminal justice system, or to provide sufficient supportive services to minimize the risk of revocation'
Restitution Programs	'Restitution is required of nearly every person under community supervision. The supervisee repays and restores society and/or the victim by monetary payment and/or community service work without pay'
Sex Offender Surveillance and Treatment	Involves intensive supervision that 'requires mandated registration and reporting, and...treatment by licensed therapists to reduce the risk of recidivism'
Substance Abuse Treatment Programs	They 'include a continuum of care ranging from screening/assessment, outpatient, intensive outpatient and residential programs to treat those under community supervision with drug and/or alcohol problems'

(continued)

Table 1 (continued)

Programs	Services
Vocational/Employment and Life Skills Training	These are 'educational, non-academic programs' to 'assist adults under community supervision acquire skills to obtain and keep employment and function at a higher level in daily life'

Source TDCJ (n.d.[b]: n.p)

Rehabilitation Programs: Prison and Parole

Several rehabilitation programs are targeted at correctional populations in prison, jail, and on parole, respectively. Such programs, like court-directed programs in the community, are geared towards inmate reentry and reintegration into the community. According to the TDCJ (2020a), correctional work on an inmate's reentry starts as soon as the inmate is received into prison. Rehabilitation programs and services that are made available to inmates in prison or jail to aid rehabilitation are augmented with pre-release reentry services to effect reintegration into society. Table 2 provides examples of rehabilitation and reentry programs and services available to the inmate population in Texas.

There are three phases of reentry services, the first two of which are pre-release. In Phase One, inmates are assisted by reentry case managers in making a request for official identification papers, such as 'a replacement Social Security card, certified birth certificate, military service record (DD-214), and DPS[5] identification card' (TDCJ, 2020b; also see TDCJ, 2020a). The identification papers and other documents, such as resumes, and records of work, job training and education, are given to inmates at the time of their release from incarceration. These documents are useful when released inmates are searching for employment, housing, healthcare, substance abuse treatment, and other services in the community (see TDCJ, 2020a).

In Phase Two, case managers assess inmates' criminogenic needs and levels of risk of recidivism using the Texas Risk Assessment System or the Supplemental Reentry Tool. Inmates whose assessment score indicates a moderate-risk, or a high-risk score are placed on an individualized case plan that requires the inmates to successfully complete prescribed rehabilitative, skills-based, and reentry program exercises before they are released (Ibid; also see TDCJ, 2020b). Inmates receive a copy of their case plan upon their release. Their parole officers and case managers in the community also have access to their individual case plans.

Table 2 Prison-based rehabilitation and reentry programs and services

Programs	Services
Baby and Mother Bonding Initiative	Designed for inmates who were pregnant on intake and delivered while incarcerated. 'The program allows inmate mothers and their newborns time to form a healthy attachment in a secure setting. The inmate receives child development education, life skills, infant first aid and CPR, nutrition, peer recovery, cognitive skills, anger management and family reunification sessions. Additional programming may include substance abuse education and GED classes'
Corrective Intervention Pre-release Program	Operates on a 120-day curriculum that is 'designed for the inmates to begin to build awareness about the thinking and attitudes that have impacted their choices and to focus on different choices in the future'
In-Prison Driving While Intoxicated (DWI) Recovery Program	A 6-month program that uses a multi-modal, specialized, gender-specific curriculum 'targeting alcohol-related problems, relapse prevention, and pro-social problem-solving techniques, to include group and individual therapy'
In-Prison Substance Use Treatment Program	A 6-month intensive, therapeutic community program for inmates with a history of substance abuse. Here, 'inmates who have similar treatment needs live together and work toward a common goal of addiction recovery, positive behavior, and life change.' Upon successful completion, 'inmates may be required to participate in post-release substance use programming, or any other parole voted program as decided by the BPP'

(continued)

Table 2 (continued)

Programs	Services
Post-secondary Education Programs (Academic and Vocational)	Inmates are given 'an opportunity for rehabilitation by developing their mental skills and providing marketable job training skills so they can re-enter society as successful productive citizens'
Pre-release Therapeutic Community Program	A two-track program, with the first lasting 3 months and the second 6 months. The first track focuses 'on cognitive behavioral model to address issues of criminality...' The second addresses 'all substance use disorders' and 'follows the evidence-based practice modality of Solution-Focused Treatment...' Both tracks are aimed at successful reentry and integration of clients into society
Sex Offender Education Program	A four-month didactic curriculum that covers various topics, such as 'healthy sexuality, anger and stress management, interpersonal relationships, cognitive restructuring'
Veteran Services	Assist inmate veterans with a range of reentry and integration services, such as housing, employment, educational benefits, healthcare benefits, residential care, and rehabilitation services
Volunteer Services Program	Designed to aid 'rehabilitation and re-entry of inmates into the community. Volunteers assist in providing literacy and educational assistance, life skills, job skills, and parenting classes.' They 'facilitate medical education and prevention training...arts and crafts programs, drug and alcohol rehabilitation programs, faith-based programming,' etc

Source TDCJ (n.d[a], n.p.; TDCJ n.d[c], n.p.)

Phase Three is post-release and involves reentry and supervisory efforts to assist clients in securing services that are likely to prevent recidivism, such as housing (including halfway houses), 'employment, food, clothing, education, finance and budgeting, nutrition and health, life skills, parenting and relationships, medical and mental health, transportation support, and cognitive skills' (TDCJ, 2020a: 6). The work of the Parole Division (PD) of the TDCJ is paramount here. In addition to supervising correctional clients who were released from prison to complete the remainder of their sentence in the community, the PD is involved in the inmate pre-release process, for example, 'by investigating the parole plans proposed by inmates' (TDCJ, n.d.[d]; also see Texas Department of Criminal Justice Parole Division [TDCJPD], 2019).

Essentially, the PD operates specialized programs, often in partnership with other divisions of the TCDJ, such as the CID and RPD, to cater to the pre- and post-release correctional client population. Through the specialized programs, the parole division provides clients with varied 'rehabilitative, therapeutic, and resource' services to aid their reintegration (see TDCJPD, 2019). Table 3 provides examples of parole-related specialized programs and services.

The total number of Texas correctional clients on parole and mandatory[6] supervision has fluctuated over the years. For example, in Fiscal Year (FY) 2010, over 81,000 clients were on parole and mandatory supervision. This figure increased to over 88,000 in FY 2015. In FY 2019, the figure had decreased to roughly 84,259, and in FY 2020, clients under parole and mandatory supervision stood at an average of 83,703 (see TDCJ, 2011a, 2016, 2020d, 2021a).

When it comes to the numbers of parole supervision clients in receipt of services, some specialized programs show number fluctuations while some show evidence of an upward trend in numbers. Data for the District Reentry Centers (DRC), Sex Offender Program (SOP), and the Therapeutic Community program (TCP) during FYs 2010, 2015, and 2020 illustrate this. The DRC served a monthly average of 1753 clients in FY 2010 compared to 968 in FY 2015 and 1562 in FY 2020. A monthly average of 2834 clients on the Sex Offender Program were supervised in FY 2010 relative to 6138 in FY 2015 and 7306 in FY 2020. The Therapeutic Community Program provided services to 4108 clients in FY 2010, 6603 in FY 2015, and 8881 in FY 2020 (see TDCJ, 2011a, 2016, 2021a).

The reasons for the above statistical trends in the numbers of clients under parole and mandatory supervision, and in the numbers of those on the identified specialized programs are unknown to this author. Further, the relationship between the figures and successful client supervision or service

Table 3 Parole division: Specialized programs and services

Programs	Services
Adult Education Assistance through Project COPE (Community Opportunity Programs in Education)	Clients whose education is below the sixth level and who earned an Educational Achievement score of 6.9 or lower can receive basic educational and/or vocational classes to enable them to obtain a General Equivalency Diploma
Cognitive Intervention	Intervention includes assisting clients to develop prosocial thinking, feelings, and skills to substitute antisocial thinking, feelings, and habits
District Reentry Centers	Rehabilitation programs include services for anger management, battering intervention and prevention, cognitive restructuring, domestic violence, education, substance abuse, pre-employment preparation, and Victim Impact Panel classes
Employment Assistance through the Texas Workforce Commission	Services include assistance with job search, the preparation of resume, and the completion of job application
Sex Offender Program	The program provides specialized treatment to clients and has specially trained parole officers to supervise clients
Substance Abuse Counseling Program	The program includes education and treatment, including continuum of care, ranging from outpatient counselling and treatment to long-term residential treatment service
Special Needs Offender Program	A program for clients who are physically handicapped (PH), mentally impaired (MI), have intellectual development disorder (IDD) and terminal illness (TI), and on medically recommended intensive supervision (MRIS)

(continued)

Table 3 (continued)

Programs	Services
Therapeutic Community	Specially trained parole officers work with substance abuse treatment providers and other support services to provide a continuum of care to clients transitioning from In-Prison Therapeutic Community or Substance Abuse Felony Punishment Facilityduring incarceration to society

Source TDCJPD (2019), TDCJ (n.d.[d]) and TDCJ (2021a)

Table 4 Number of parole referrals and number of unsuccessful referrals by services in FY2020

Services	Parole referrals	Unsuccessful referrals
Basic Needs	517,293	822
Education	157,175	2222
Employment	420,873	3252
Housing	77,288	0
Medical & Mental Health	108,372	356
Substance Abuse	821,797	6340
Veteran Services	4412	12
Total	2,107,210	13,004

Source TDCJ (2020a)

delivery, particularly in relation to recidivism is unknown. However, there are indications to show that while rehabilitation efforts intersect with reentry services to aid integration into the community, client access to such services is not guaranteed. Not all referrals to services in the community are successful due, in part, to structural limitations of the services themselves. For example, public housing assistance programs may be restricted for clients with serious criminal convictions, and the geographical location of employment opportunities may pose a barrier to employment. There are also personal obstacles to services, including a client's lack of appropriate educational qualifications or job skills to obtain employment (see TDCJ, 2020a).

In FY 2020, a total of 2,192,880 resource referrals for community services was made for clients under supervision, of which 2,107,210 were under parole supervision. Many of the services were successfully accessed while 13,400 of the referrals were unsuccessful because of a waiting list for services or service unavailability at the time of referral[7] (see Table 4 for a breakdown of parole referrals and unsuccessful referrals according to services).

Unsuccessful referrals to community services are hurdles that are likely to hinder a positive response to rehabilitative interventions among clients on parole supervision.

Measuring Rehabilitation Success

A reduction in correctional client recidivism following exposure to rehabilitation programs appears to be the traditional marker of success in the field of criminal justice. Hence, when Robert Martinson (1974), in his article 'What Works?' queried the effectiveness of correctional programs in curbing reoffending, his response that 'nothing worked' generated enduring political and academic debates over the effectiveness of rehabilitation/treatment programs (also see Lipton et al., 1975[8]). For about three decades before the Martinson publication, the medical model, with its philosophy of diagnosis, treatment, reformation, and reintegration of prison inmates, had reigned virtually unopposed. But according to Martinson (Ibid: 25), 'With few and isolated exceptions, the rehabilitative efforts that have been reported so far have had no appreciable effect on recidivism'.

Phipps et al. (1999) review of rehabilitation program evaluations[9] that were conducted across several U.S states shows that post-Martinson studies have produced conflicting results. The studies either report positive outcomes of rehabilitation in terms of reduced levels of recidivism or negative rehabilitation outcomes, which means no reduction in recidivism. Evaluations of three respective in-prison rehabilitation programs in education, employment, and substance abuse in Texas were included in the review, which reports mixed findings on the impact of the programs on recidivism. Regarding all the programs included in their review, the authors had this to say about their effectiveness vis-à-vis reoffending:

> We found some programs have achieved success in lowering the chance that adult offenders will commit new crimes. Other approaches have failed to reduce these odds. Because most programs have not been evaluated rigorously, a substantial amount of uncertainty persists about many interventions...Thus the answer to the simple question "Does Anything Work?" is yes - some programs have been shown to lower the odds of criminal offending, but the success rates of even the best programs are relatively modest. (Phipps et al., 1999: 2)

Against the many differing programs and services available to the Texas correctional population in prison, jail, on parole supervision and on court-directed community supervision, it is unsurprising to this author that an evaluation of each one of them, in terms of impact on recidivism, has not happened. The relatively few evaluations of specific rehabilitation programs in Texas, some of which were conducted by independent researchers, have produced mixed findings on the effectiveness of the evaluated programs in reducing recidivism. As already indicated above, Phipps et al. reviewed evaluations of three Texas rehabilitation programs that were conducted in the 1990s.

One was an evaluation of the first Texas In-Prison Therapeutic Community. Although Phipps et al., considered the evaluation inconclusive due to selection bias, the evaluators had argued that there was a significant reduction of recidivism among program graduates who completed the substance abuse treatment relative to those who did not complete or participate in the program (see Eisenberg & Fabelo, 1996).

Two, an evaluation of Project RIO[10]—this project started in 1985 as a two-city state-funded job training and placement pilot program for parolees. It expanded several years later to become a Texas statewide program that not only served parolees, but also assisted inmates in preparation for their job search upon release (see Finn, 1998). According to Finn (Ibid: 4), the program was underpinned by theory:

> As with similar programs across the country, Project RIO is based on the theory - supported by considerable hard evidence - that if inmates can find a decent job as soon as possible after release, they are less likely to return to a life of crime and to prison. Project RIO puts theory into practice, not only by helping ex-offenders in every corner of the state find jobs but also by beginning the placement process while clients are still in prison, long before their release date.

Findings from a 1992 study[11] of Project RIO show that the program prevented recidivism, in that recidivism rates were lower among those who gained employment via RIO than among those who were unemployed and did not participate in RIO. A one-year post-release follow-up on parolees showed that 69% of RIO participants and 36% of RIO nonparticipants gained employment. Likewise, within the one-year period after release, '48 percent of RIO high-risk clients were rearrested compared with 57 percent of non-RIO high-risk parolees; 23 percent were reincarcerated, compared with 38 percent of non-RIO parolees' (Finn, 1998: 14). However, given that the level of recidivism, based on rearrest, was insignificant among average-risk (30%) and low-risk (16%) RIO participants relative to nonparticipants (32%

average-risk and 19% low-risk), Phipps et al. have argued that overall, the project made an insignificant impact on recidivism reduction.

Three, Phipps and colleagues reached a similar conclusion in their review of an evaluation of the impact on inmates of in-prison education programs offered by the Windham School System (WSS). The evaluators examined a cohort of 14,411 inmates who participated or did not participate in the WSS educational programs, and who were received into prison in March 1991 and released in December 1992 (see Adams et al., 1994). Despite the observation that the effect of the WSS educational programs—academic and vocational—was non-significant on recidivism as measured by re-incarceration (Ibid: 447), the evaluators had concluded:

> Two major findings emerged from our analysis....First, the data show that inmates at the lowest levels of educational achievement benefit most (as indicated by lower recidivism rates) from participation in academic programs. Second, some minimum level of program exposure or involvement is necessary. *When these two factors are combined, the data suggest that the recidivism rate can be reduced by about one-third if extensive services are targeted at inmates at the lowest level of educational achievement.* (italics in the original)

Evaluations of specific Texas rehabilitation programs that were conducted in the twenty-first century have reported differing findings on the impact of the individual programs on recidivism. For example, an evaluation of five TDCJ rehabilitation programs—InnerChange Freedom Initiative, Pre-Release Substance Abuse, Pre-release Therapeutic Community, Sex Offender Education, and Sex Offender Treatment—by the Texas State Auditor's Office (2007) show varying effects on recidivism among clients who were released from prison in FY 2004. Recidivism was measured by rearrest and reincarceration rates. Three of the programs—Pre-release Therapeutic Community, Sex Offender Education, and Sex Offender Treatment— reduced recidivism among participants in the programs. Contrastingly, the Pre-Release Substance Abuse program did not produce a reduction in recidivism. The InnerChange Freedom Initiative program seemed partially successful in reducing recidivism, in that it had a reduced rearrest rate but an increased reincarceration rate.

In 2011, the State reported findings from its evaluation of the impact of eight rehabilitation programs on recidivism among clients who were released from prison in FY2007 (TDCJ, 2011b). For the most part, the evaluation showed positive results in reducing the three-year recidivism projection among correctional clients who completed the programs. The evaluated programs were: Inner Change Freedom Initiative (IFI), In-Prison Therapeutic Community (IPTC), Pre-Release Substance Abuse Program (PRSAP), Pre-release Therapeutic Community (PRTC), Serious and Violent Offender Reentry Initiative (SVORI), Sex Offender Education Program (SOEP), Sex Offender Treatment Program (SOTP), and the Substance Abuse Felony Punishment (SAFP) program. Based on findings from the TDCJ evaluation, all the evaluated programs, except for the PRSAP, reduced recidivism although this outcome was marginal for those who completed the PRTC program (Ibid).

There were also independent rehabilitation program evaluations alongside the State ones. Examples include evaluations of Bridges to Life (BTL), a restorative justice program in Dallas, and Substance Abuse Felony Punishment (SAFP), an in-prison treatment program for substance use. While the BTL is claimed to be a success story in reducing recidivism among parolees (see Han et al., 2021), SAFP has been showcased as a failure in recidivism reduction (see Laumann et al., 2021).

Notwithstanding the variations in evaluation outcomes, Texas has claimed success in lowering recidivism among the correctional population, at least during specific periods. For the period 2005 to 2015, recidivism rates dropped from 27.2% in 2005 to 20.3% in 2015 (TDCJ, 2020b). For FY 2015–2017, recidivism was measured by re-arrest, reconviction, and reincarceration rates for correctional clients who had been in an in-prison therapeutic community, intermediate sanction facility, state jail, prison, substance abuse felony punishment facility, felony community supervision, and parole supervision (Legislative Budget Board, 2021). Recidivism rates were stable across the indicators for all correctional client categories except for a slight increase in re-arrest rate for clients who had been on felony community supervision (Ibid).

Further, recidivism is not the only indicator of success in TDCJ's assessment of its rehabilitation efforts. Evaluations of community supervision programs have measured program success based on completion rates. For example, an evaluation of the Battering Intervention and Prevention (BIP) programs in the state shows that in FY 2018, of the 4248 placements in BIP programs, there was a successful client completion rate of 56.5% against an unsuccessful completion rate of 43.5%. In FY 2019 when placements stood at 4039, the successful and unsuccessful completion figures were 59.1% and 40.9%, respectively (TDCJ, 2020c). Referrals from probation made up most of the placements for both fiscal years: 2156 in FY 2018 and 1979 in FY 2019. Of these probation referrals, the rate of successful completion was 60.6% in FY 2018 and 63.3% in FY 2019. Other referral sources for placements included pretrial diversion and parole (Ibid).

Success has also been indicated by the number of clients served by rehabilitation programs or referred by correctional officers for services in the community. For example, success was attributed to Project RIO based on the numbers of clients it served and placed on employment. According to Finn (1998), Project Rio served 15,366 clients in FY 1995, and this figure made up 47% of all parolees and 40% of all clients who were released from prison in 1995. In the same year, 11,371 parolees (approximately 74% of clients) gained employment and received an average per hour wage of $5.15, which was higher than the minimum wage of $4.25 an hour in 1995. However, how community service referrals, job placements, and rehabilitation program completion intersect with reoffending or non-reoffending behaviour is unclear.

Conclusion

Given the variety of rehabilitation programs in Texas correctional settings, some in the form of diversion and treatment programs, respectively, it is difficult to coalesce them all into an analysis that depicts a standard model of rehabilitation practices in the Texas criminal justice system. Considering the land mass and population size of Texas as well as the components of decentralization in its criminal justice system, this paper is a succinct account of Texas' rehabilitation programming for correctional clients in prison/jail and in the community. There is evidence to suggest that the TDCJ is adhering to one of its tasks, which is to conduct regular evaluations of the programs to monitor their effectiveness in reducing 'offender reincarceration and parole revocations' (TDCJ, 2011b). And lessons about recidivism can be learned from the evaluations. However, the evaluations seem to lack depth in methodology and, invariably, analysis. For example, not much is known about the characteristics of the clients and the programs, and the rehabilitation programming journey of clients prior to the assessment of recidivism. Further, the evaluations seem to be limited to a few programs while several others are yet to be evaluated. It is imperative that the TDCJ attends to these issues for a clear understanding of the forms of rehabilitation that are used in Texas, and their impact on clients and their offending behaviours.

Notes

1. A local government region similar to those in England and Wales.
2. Based on the 2020 population census (United States Census Bureau, n.d.).
3. Prison administrator.
4. Abadinsky uses the word treatment and rehabilitation interchangeably.
5. Department of Public Safety.
6. 'Parole is the discretionary release of an offender, by a Board of Pardons and Paroles decision, to serve the remainder of a sentence in the community under supervision…Mandatory Supervision is a legislatively mandated release of a prisoner to parole supervision when the combination of actual calendar time and good conduct time equal the sentence…' (https://www.tdcj.texas.gov/bpp/what_is_parole/parole.htm).
7. Due to COVID-19, service delivery was slowed down or terminated across the state in FY2020 (see TDCJ, 2020a, 2021a).
8. Martinson's article was a product of Martinson, Lipton and Wilks' review of 231 studies of correctional programs.
9. The authors categorized the program evaluation into seven topics: cognitive behavioral treatment; education; employment; intensive supervision; life skills training; sex offender treatment; and substance abuse treatment.
10. Re-Integration of Offenders. Funding for the program was ended by the Texas Legislature, effective September 1, 2011.
11. Conducted by Texas A&M University.

References

Abadinsky, H. (2015). *Probation and parole: Theory and practice*, 12th edn. Pearson.

Adams, K., Benneth, K., Flanagan, T. J., Marquart, J. W., Cuvelier, S. J., Fritsch, E., Gerber, J., Longmire, D. R., & Burton, V. S. (1994). A largescale multidimensional test of the effect of prison education programs on offender behavior. *The Prison Journal, 74*(4), 433–449.

Andrews, D. A., & Bonta, J. (2010). Rehabilitating criminal justice policy and practice. *Psychology, Public Policy, and Law, 16*(1), 39–55.

Cohen, G. (2012). Punishment and rehabilitation: A brief history of the Texas prison system. *Texas Bar Journal, 75*(8), 604–606.

Clark, J. (2012). Reducing risk and recidivism: The Texas department of criminal justice rehabilitation program. *Texas Bar Journal, 75*(8), 612–615.

Eisenberg, M., & Fabelo, T. (1996). Evaluation of the Texas correctional substance abuse treatment initiative: The impact of policy research. *Crime and Delinquency, 42*(2), 296–308.

Finn, P. (1998). *Texas project RIO (re-integration of offenders)*. U.S Department of Justice.

Glaser, W. (1990). *Reality therapy: A new approach to psychiatry*. Perennial Library.

Gottschalk, M. (2021). No star state: Whats right and wrong about criminal justice reform in Texas. *Seattle Journal for Social Justice, 19*(3), 927–1052.

Han, S., Olson, M., & Davis, R. C. (2021). Reducing recidivism through restorative justice: An evaluation of bridges to life in Dallas. *Journal of Offender Rehabilitation, 60*(7), 444–463.

Knapp, K., Burke, P., & Carter, M. (1992). *Residential community corrections facilities: Current practice and policy issues* (Report submitted to National Institute of Corrections, U.S. Department of Justice). U.S. Department of Justice

Laumann, T., Smith, D., Patil, S., Caldwell, & K. Button-Schnick, A. (2021). *Layers of trauma, layers of treatment: Using participant experiences to reform Texas in-prison substance use treatment program*. Texas Criminal Justice Coalition.

Legislative Budget Board (2021). *Statewide criminal and juvenile justice recidivism and revocation rates* (Submitted to the 87th Texas Legislature). www.lbb.state.tx.us

Lipton., D., Martinson, R., & Wilks, J. (1975). *The effectiveness of correctional treatment: A survey of treatment evaluation studies*. Praeger.

Martinson, R. (1974). What works? Questions and answers about prison reform. *The Public Interest, 35*, 22–54.

Perlman, H. H. (1957). *Social casework: A problem-solving process*. The University of Chicago Press.

Phipps, P., Korinek, K., Aos, S., & Lieb, R. (1999). *Research findings on adult corrections programs: A review*. Washington State Institute for Public Policy.

Skinner, B.F. ((1986). Some thoughts about the future. *Journal of Experimental Analysis of Behavior, 45*(2), 229–235.

Staddon, J. E. R., & Cerutti, D. T. (2003). Operant conditioning. *Annual Review of Psychology, 54*, 115–144.

Texas Department of Criminal Justice. (2011a). *Annual review 2010*. Texas Department of Criminal Justice. www.tdcj.texas.org

Texas Department of Criminal Justice (2011b). *Evaluation of offenders released in fiscal year 2007 that completed rehabilitation tier programs*. www.tdcj.texas.org

Texas Department of Criminal Justice (2016). *Texas Department of Criminal Justice: Annual review 2015*. www.tdcj.texas.org

Texas Department of Criminal Justice (2020a). *Parole and reentry referral fiscal year 2020 report*. www.tdcj.texas.org

Texas Department of Criminal Justice (2020b). *Biennial reentry and reintegration services report*. www.tdcj.texas.org

Texas Department of Criminal Justice (2020c). *Report to the governor and legislative budget board: Evaluation of the effectiveness of the battering intervention and prevention program FY 2018–2019 biennium*. www.tdcj.texas.org

Texas Department of Criminal Justice. (2020d). *Texas Department of Criminal Justice: Annual review 2019*. www.tdcj.texas.org

Texas Department of Criminal Justice. (2021a). *Texas Department of Criminal Justice: Annual Review FY2020*. www.tdcj.texas.org

Texas Department of Criminal Justice (2021b). *2021 female programming report*. www.tdcj.texas.org

Texas Department of Criminal Justice. (n.d.[a]). *Rehabilitation Programs Division*. https://www.tdcj.texas.gov/divisions/rpd/index.html Accessed 02/18/2022.

Texas Department of Criminal Justice. (n.d.[b]). *Community Justice Assistance Division*. https://www.tdcj.texas.gov/divisions/cjad/index.html

Texas Department of Criminal Justice. (n.d.[c]). *Reentry and reintegration division*. https://www.tdcj.texas.gov/divisions/rid/index.html

Texas Department of Criminal Justice. (n.d.[d]). *Reentry and reintegration division*. https://www.tdcj.texas.gov/divisions/pd/index.html

Texas Department of Criminal Justice Parole Division. [TDCJPD]. (2019). *Answers to common questions*. TDCJPD.

Texas State Auditors Office. (2007). *An audit report on selected rehabilitation programs at the Department of Criminal Justice*. State Auditors Office.

Thielo, A. J., Cullen, F. T., Cohen, D. M., & Chouhy, C. (2016). Rehabilitation in a red state: Public support for correctional reform in Texas. *Criminology and Public Policy, 15*(1), 137–170.

United States Census Bureau. (n.d). *Quick facts: Texas, United States*. https://www.census.gov/quickfacts/fact/table/TX,US/PST045221.

Key Practices in Thai Prisons: Rehabilitation

Nathee Chitsawang and Pimporn Netrabukkana

Introduction

When imprisonment has been discussed by policymakers, criminal justice officers and academic scholars, one of the key issues is the role of the prison in fulfilling the aims of imprisonment. In fact, the question of purpose is an important one, because unless there is some clarity about this, it will be difficult to discover whether or not imprisonment is effective; 'if we wish to know whether or not prison achieves its purposes, we have to understand what they are' (Coyle, 2005 cited in Netrabukkana, 2016).

A discussion on the aims of prison can be found in Adler and Longhurst's study (1994) who pointed out the significant discourse framework by emphasising the analysis of the 'ends' and 'means' discourses, to examine the prison system. The ends discourses can be identified as 'rehabilitation', 'normalisation' and 'control', which are all regarded as the aims of prison, while the means discourse is composed of 'bureaucracy', 'professionalism' and 'legality'.

N. Chitsawang (✉)
Thailand Institute of Justice (TIJ), Bangkok, Thailand
e-mail: nathee_nt@yahoo.com

P. Netrabukkana
Thailand's Department of Corrections, Nonthaburi, Thailand
e-mail: aim_net@yahoo.com

In brief, the ends and means discourses can be connected to the administration of Thai prisons, with respect to control, rehabilitation, bureaucracy, professionalism and legality. There might be some dissimilar aspects, but overall the discourse analysis can reflect some characteristics of the Thai prison system, and particularly rehabilitation in Thailand which is a focus of this chapter. According to Adler and Longhurst (1994) the rehabilitation discourse highlights the 'deviant individual' who is deemed to be psychologically disturbed, socially maladjusted or otherwise out of step with the rest of society in some way. To socialise the individual back into society, which in turn leads to a reduction in crime and hence to the protection of society, is the aim of prison in the rehabilitation discourse (Adler & Longhurst, 1994: 37).

Looking at the ideological justifications of imprisonment, they usually focus on two basic themes. On the one hand, imprisonment should play a role in reducing the incidence of crime, and this is usually divided into three concepts: incapacitation of the criminal or protection of the public; deterrence; and rehabilitation or reform. On the other hand, imprisonment has a retributive duty to award punishments, thought to be deserved by convicted individuals (Flynn, 1998). In Thailand, from the past to the present, the justifications for imprisonment have applied these concepts which have varied in each era (Netrabukkana, 2016).

History of Rehabilitation in Thailand

According to various historical materials (Department of Corrections, 1982; Na Ayutthaya, 1993; Na Nakorn, 1998; National Identity Board, 2000) in Thailand, brutal physical punishment was mostly used in the period before 1868 after imprisonment started to be used as a method of punishment in the Ayutthaya Kingdom era (1350–1767). At that time the main purposes of punishment were believed to be: to deliver retribution; to deter people from committing more crimes and to incapacitate offenders either temporarily by sentencing them to a term in prison or jail, or permanently by execution or capital punishment. These ideologies still existed in the following eras; in the first phase of the Ratthanakosin Kingdom especially in the reign of King Rama I, and through to the period of King Rama IV.

After that, during the second phase of the Rattanakosin Kingdom, in the era of King Rama V, rehabilitation started to become one of the purposes of imprisonment. Similar goals of punishment, deterrence, incapacitation, and rehabilitation have existed up until the present day. The landmark events regarding punishment and prisons are summarised in the timeline (Fig. 1), which shows the purposes of punishment and imprisonment in each epoch of history.

Rehabilitative approaches have existed in Thailand's correctional system for more than 100 years since there was an adoption of ideas and practices from Western countries to develop Thai society in various domains. These include the criminal justice system which undertook reforms to the standards of the Western Great Powers who were expanding their influence in Southeast Asia at that time. Thailand, previously known as Siam, went through a crucial modernisation during the reign of King Rama V or His Majesty King Chulalongkorn when many scholars and royal family members were sent to study in European countries to bring back new knowledge and technology. Besides, diplomatic and commercial policies were strategically applied to help the nation to survive colonisation.

In the prison system, some Western concepts were developed and adopted. One of these was the construction of Western-style prison buildings after sending Thai officials to visit prisons in Singapore. Consequently, the new prison, inspired by Brixton prison in England, had been constructed by employing Mr. Gracy, an English proprietor, as a contractor working together with Thai officials and workers to finally complete the construction in 1890 (DOC, 1982). The obvious change was the internal layout separating its space to have different zones: medical unit, kitchen unit and workshop unit, while the traditional Thai prison in the past was normally designed to have only one large area where prisoners must do all indoor activities. This new layout pattern made it easier for prisoners to receive vocational training and work programmes in a variety of prison workshop factories. However, as these programmes had not been fully financially supported by the government at that time, each prison authority had to sell prison products made by prisoners to the public to earn some funds for prisoners' vocational training activities. Because of this, the Thai prison system had mainly focused on keeping prisoners busy by working, which could at least equip them with some occupational skills. More importantly, it is believed that perspectives on the aims of imprisonment among both prison officers and society at large are still powerfully based on the retributivist concept, rather than rehabilitation.

Since the 1970s, the modalities of rehabilitation and treatment programmes in Thailand have been partly influenced by some key international conferences, in particular, the United Nations Crime Congress, and international organisation mechanisms, such as the United Nations Standard Minimum Rules for the Treatment of Prisoners. In 1972, as we have seen in Fig. 1, rehabilitation mechanisms were established when there was a change in

Era/Year	Major event of punishment and prison	Purpose
Sukhothai Kingdom (1238 – 1438)	- Fine for property crimes - No clear evidence of brutal punishment, although it was used in the neighbouring Lanna Kingdom.	- punitive
Ayutthaya Kingdom (1350 – 1767)	- Death penalty and various types of brutal physical punishment - Public humiliation - Prison emerged	- punitive - revenge - deterrence - incapacitation
Rattanakosin Kingdom		
- King Rama I (1782- 1809)	- Death penalty and various types of brutal physical punishment - Imprisonment - Prison labour - Torture as punishment in prison - Imprisonment and releasing fees	- punitive - revenge - deterrence - incapacitation
- King Rama V (1868 – 1910)	- Imprisonment - Prison labour - Education provided - Establishment of 'Department of Prisoners' - Prisons were systemised.	
- King Rama VI (1910 – 1925)	- Imprisonment - Prison labour - Establishment of Department of Penitentiary and the first DG was appointed. - Staff positions on vocational training listed	- punitive - deterrence - incapacitation - rehabilitation
- King Rama VII (1925 – 1935)	- Declaration of the government to the Parliament regarding the rehabilitation of inmates: religious and vocational training.	
- King Rama VIII (1935 – 1946)	- Penitentiary Act (1936) and some Ministerial Regulations were enacted.	
- King Rama IX (1946 – present)	- Name in English was changed to 'Department of Corrections' - First rehabilitation subdivisions were set up in Bangkwang and Klongprem Central Prisons - H.M. the King's speech to DG regarding the rehabilitation role of prison staff	

Fig. 1 Prison and punishment timeline in Thailand (*Source* Netrabukkana, 2012)

the name of the prison agency to Department of Corrections (DOC, 1982), indicating a major focus on rehabilitation, in particular vocational training programmes and sentence administration schemes up until now.

Current Mechanisms, Policy and Statistical Contexts

Currently, the rehabilitation mechanisms for adult prisoners, or those aged 18 or over,[1] are provided by the Department of Corrections which has promoted rehabilitation and social reintegration by providing prisoners with various rehabilitative activities at different stages: admission and classification; treatment programmes; pre-release and aftercare schemes. In recent decades, the Department of Corrections (DOC) has officially indicated in its plans and policies that the core missions of the department are: (1) to take people into custody with professional skill and; (2) to rehabilitate them with meaningful and effective activities. The same statement in terms of both rehabilitation and custody has been specified in the annual reports of the DOC since 1999 (DOC, 1999–2020). The department itself has declared and clearly stated its goals. Concrete evidence for this can be found in the Corrections Act, B.E. 2560 (2017a) which states under Section 42 in Part 2 'Classification and Rehabilitation of Prisoners' that:-

> For the purpose of correction, treatment and rehabilitation of the prisoner in order to become a decent person, the Director General shall set the prisoner rehabilitation system by using appropriate methods and procedures for prisoner rehabilitation. Prisoners shall be provided with education, and training in moral principles and ethical behaviour, employment, vocational training, religious practices, knowledge of virtuous culture, recreation activities and sports. Prisoners must be also provided with the opportunity to make contact with family relatives and friends as well as private agencies entrusted with the correction, treatment and rehabilitation of prisoners, and to receive news of changes in the world outside. These shall be in accordance with the rules of the Department of Corrections with the approval of the Committee. (DOC, 2017a)

However, it needs to be reported that rehabilitation mechanisms in Thailand could not be effectively and properly operated because of long-standing problems with prison overcrowding and shortage of staff. These are key factors which have contributed to the prison authority's inability to fully provide rehabilitation and treatment services.

Although the concepts of rehabilitation and reintegration have started to play a role in the correctional system, Thai society still believes in using prison sentences as a primary measure in dealing with crimes. As a result, the prison population has continuously exceeded the total standard capacity of prisons which could normally detain only approximately 112,000 prisoners. As shown in Fig. 2, since 1995 the prisoner statistics in Thailand have never fallen to less than 100,000. The dramatic growth from 1996 to 2002 was the result of a significant change in criminal policy especially the urgent measures for combating the spread of methamphetamine in Thai society. Methamphetamine became listed as a crucial and serious type of illicit drug and those using it were to be penalised and sentenced to prison. Unsurprisingly, more and more drug users were sent to serve time behind bars.

The first wave of reductions in the prison population could be observed between 2004 and 2007. The decisive factor was the implementation of the Narcotics Addict Rehabilitation Act, B.E.2545 (2002). Under this law, drug users were regarded as patients who needed drug treatment. The diversion scheme was applied to take them out of the criminal justice system and treat them in military camps or rehabilitation centres or place them on probation instead of imposing prison sentences. Because of this, there were almost 100,000 inmates released from prisons in the following year. Even so, after

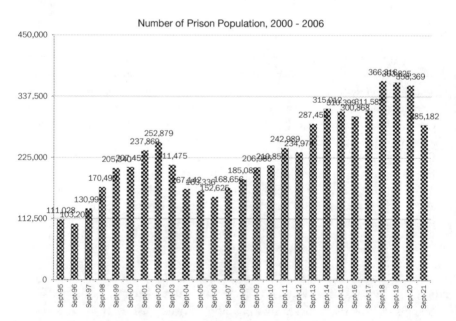

Fig. 2 Number of Prison Population, 1995–2021 (*Source* Centre of Prisoner Statistics, Planning Division, DOC)

2008 the figures rose again, rising towards a peak in 2018 and finally going down in 2021 because of major changes in the parole policy of the Ministry of Justice, as well as in the enforcement of Royal Pardon Decrees in 2020 and 2021.[2]

The correlation between drug problems and rehabilitation in Thailand is quite apparent. It is not only the fact that nearly 70% of the prison population is drug-involved, making prisons overpopulated, but it is also important for the DOC to provide incarcerated people with meaningful rehabilitation and treatment to reintegrate them into society, in particular those committing drug crimes. More importantly, when the budget and resources are limited and insufficient for the chronically overcrowded prison population, the issues of effectiveness and successful reintegration are very hard to address, and this could be reflected in the recidivism rates to some degree.[3]

Table 1 shows the re-offending rates of a cohort of released prisoners in each Fiscal Year starting from 2013 to 2018, with three phases of follow-up: one year, two years and three years. Apart from the clear reduction in recidivism statistics among released prisoners in 2013 and 2014, other years' figures tend to fluctuate. The question that should be asked is why the recidivism rates of formerly incarcerated people have not shown a progressive decrease in the past six years even though there are many rehabilitation and reintegration programmes inside the prison walls.

Some possible explanations were discussed previously. Firstly, the rehabilitation and treatment programmes cannot be properly operated given the prison overcrowding situation. Penal Reform International (2012) indicates that 'overcrowding undermines the ability of prison systems to meet basic human needs, such as healthcare, food, and accommodation. It also compromises the provision and effectiveness of rehabilitation programmes, educational and vocational training, and recreational activities'. Secondly, it

Table 1 Recidivism Rates, 2013–2018

A cohort of released inmates	Follow-up period		
	1-year	2-year	3-year
	Recidivism rates (%)		
Released in FY 2013	16.03	26.53	34.46
Released in FY 2014	14.20	24.02	32.29
Released in FY 2015	14.31	25.34	34.44
Released in FY 2016	14.35	25.94	35.13
Released in FY 2017	14.85	26.48	34.61
Released in FY 2018	15.58	26.86	34.63

Source: RecStats, Department of Corrections (2022)

is believed that Thailand's prison system has not focused fully on all four forms of rehabilitation argued by Burke et al. (2019) who provide an imaginative vision for twenty-first-century criminal justice. According to Burke et al. (2019), rehabilitation has four meanings and forms, namely personal and psychological, judicial or legal, social and moral.

> Personal rehabilitation concerns how individuals make their journeys away from offending and towards reintegration and how they can be supported to do so, whilst legal rehabilitation concerns the role of the criminal courts in the process of restricting and then restoring the rights and status of citizens. Moral rehabilitation is concerned with the ethical basis of the interactions between the individual who has offended and the people and organisations charged with providing rehabilitative services. Social rehabilitation explores the crucial contribution civil society can make to rehabilitation, exploring this through the lens of citizenship, community and social capital.

Looking closely at rehabilitation in Thailand, it is only personal rehabilitation and moral forms of rehabilitation that have been largely focused through the programmes provided by the DOC and all 143 prisons around the country. But their legal form has not yet been acknowledged. Although the ideas of social rehabilitation, or the role of civil society, appear to be growing, as witnessed by increasing campaigns on social reintegration organised by both civil society and the private sector, it is still considered as a beginning phase, limited to only a few individuals. Furthermore, it could be argued that recidivism rates cannot totally represent the success or failure of rehabilitation and treatment programmes. In reality, the existing programmes offered by the DOC could improve the quality of prisoners' lives, extending their life choices, and opening up opportunities for those who might have made some mistakes. Consequently, there might only be particular groups of prisoners gaining benefits from such useful programmes, especially those who have a very low risk of re-offending. On the other hand, a person who is dangerous and tends to be recidivist may not be able to participate in the treatment programme due to ineligibility from bad behaviour or may have no intention to attend. Therefore, it might only be intensive and lengthy treatment schemes that can keep them away from society and minimise the chances of them committing fresh crimes in the future.

Specific Programmes and Methods

After being admitted into prison and interviewed for classification, every prisoner is expected to join rehabilitation and treatment programmes. Normally, the rehabilitation process in Thai prison system consists of two major types: general and specific. The general rehabilitation programmes largely focus on basic needs, such as educational, vocational, religious or recreational activities ranging from sport and music to art, and projects for strengthening family ties. The specific ones cover programmes for special groups or those committing specific crimes, namely sex offences, violent offences, repeated offences, property crime and violent extremism. Besides, as indicated earlier, most incarcerated people are drug-involved, thus there is a TC or Therapeutic Community programme in Thai prisons.

It is worth reiterating that in Thailand rehabilitation tends to give priority to individuals to help prisoners develop new skills and tactics (Burke et al., 2019). Being provided with multi-pronged general programmes, prisoners can find their way out of trouble. In fact, each prison or correctional institution has the discretion to run or put emphasis on any rehabilitation programmes and activities as long as they are in accordance with the key rehabilitation policy of the headquarters. Nevertheless, the well-known general programmes behind Thai prisons include education, religious and mental development, vocational training, and recreation. Educational programmes are indispensable activities in every prison and so important that each prison must manage its space to set up an educational unit or school or classroom which offers learning courses to prisoners, starting from a course for illiterate people to higher education at the university level. As for higher education, the DOC has been in cooperation with Sukothai Thammathirat Open University, the leading Open University in Thailand. Up until now, there have been 3287 prisoners who successfully completed a bachelor's degree inside prison (DOC, 2021). In the Fiscal Year 2021, there were 92,241 participants in educational programmes (DOC, 2021). As for vocational training, in addition to many skills responding to market demand, trainees are encouraged to take a skill standard test in partnership with Government Sectors and professional standard certification organisations as an assurance of their standards of workmanship outside as well as enabling their successful social reintegration. In 2017, the DOC launched the 'Civil State Integration Project in Prisoner Skill Development towards Industrial Sector' or 'Vocational Training in Private Enterprise Project' which was designed to enhance rehabilitation efficiency by encouraging people behind bars with good behaviour to improve working skills in external private enterprises. The DOC believes that the skills and experience gained from this project would contribute to a higher chance of employment after release and acceptance from business entrepreneurs (DOC, 2018a, 2018b).

Thai prisons are also adept at running meditation programmes to allow imprisoned people to spend their free time realising past mistakes in their lives. Such practice is in accordance with the research by Himelstein (2011) that meditation-based programmes may be seen as a proper treatment to support rehabilitation in prison. From evidence-based experience, the Thai prison system firmly believes that this type of programme can contribute to the enhancement of psychological well-being, a decrease in substance use, and a decline in recidivism. More than 20 years after it was first introduced in prisons across the country, meditation and *dhamma* lessons have shown a great impact on aggressive behaviour, improving the lives of thousands of Thai prisoners (Chitsawang, 2011d). In 2015 the DOC started an important project called 'Sakkasa-Samathi', which means the Pathway to Heaven, for incarcerated people to practise meditation while serving time behind bars. The programme is developed from the teaching of Phra Dhammongkol-yarn (Luangphor Viriyang Sirintharo), Abbot of Wat Dhammamongkol and Chairman of the Willpower Institute Luangphor Viriyang Sirintharo Foundation. The project aims to enhance the strength of prisoners' mental power and to enable them to learn how to control their negative feelings. According to evaluations (Chancholyut, 2017; DOC, 2016a; Plodhuang, 2017), it was clearly seen that participants tended to be calmer, more polite, more patient and more optimistic. Many of them continued doing meditation every day, in the morning and at night. Also, they would like to introduce the meditation programme to their families, relatives and friends. Because of this, in Fiscal Year 2016, the Department of Corrections and the Willpower Institute provided more than 80% of convicted prisoners with the meditation programme. Within a year, there were approximately 201,600 prisoners completing the meditation training programme (DOC, 2016b).

Chitsawang (2011c, 2011d) maintains that both education and meditation programmes are of great importance. He recognised and named a prison in Thailand as a 'Home of Education or Home of Wisdom' and a 'Home of Meditation or Home of Dhamma' when he held the position of Director General in the Department of Corrections during 2003–2007 and referred to these concepts in various publications. (DOC, 2005a, 2006a; Kamla, 2006; Office of the Royal Development Projects Board, 2013).

For more than two decades, music, art and sports activities have also played an important role in rehabilitation programmes in Thai prisons. In the case of music therapy, the DOC has been in cooperation with the Christian Prison

Ministry Foundation of Thailand to establish the first prison chorus band in 2002. Since then, chorus training has been introduced more widely in prisons, particularly as a part of pre-release programmes. The prisoners who want to become members of the prison choir must have good conduct and have served more than half of their imprisonment terms so that they can be eligible for performing outside prison. The prison choir has had many opportunities to perform concerts and show their singing talent. Many participants in the programme have successfully reintegrated since they found that through music, they were able to discover their inner strengths and appreciate their own real values. They have gained self-confidence and encouragement to reintegrate themselves into their communities (Chitsawang, 2011a).

Another interesting rehabilitation programme is Art behind Bars. Chitsawang (2011a) suggests that art can give imprisoned people inspiration and liberate their imagination, away from the prison world. In addition, art has been also employed as one of the vocational training programmes for prisoners after release. Thai prisons use many genres of art to vocationally train inmates, namely sculpture, engraving, applying gold leaf on a black coat, braiding and painting, etc. Eventually, their artwork could be exhibited and sold at the Annual Prison Products Exhibition. Currently, there are many formerly incarcerated people who could use the knowledge and skills gained from art training classes in prisons to work as artists after release, both full time and part time.

It is widely accepted that sport offers various benefits, both physical and mental, to participants. Taking part in sports can contribute to physical well-being and build up immunity against all diseases. At the same time, mentally, sport can calm one's muddled thinking. Sport can make the players enjoy and have fun on games, as well promoting good positive thinking. Besides, in the social world, playing sport can help people to make new friends, and to spend time much more usefully. It also teaches people to learn good sportsmanship; learn to lose, win, and forgive in games; and learn how to treat each other with respect as well (Chitsawang, 2011e). When the DOC has introduced sport to people behind bars, their lives have been changed in the sense that in the past they tended to spend their free time on prohibited activities, i.e., gambling, fighting, finding ways to escape, and wasting their time day by day. But when they concentrate on playing and practising sports, it is considered as 'positive security', which not only helps prisoners to have physical and mental strength, but they also have no time for muddled thinking and planning for any escape. Although sport has been inside Thai prisons for a long time, its great innovation was the 'Prisoners World Cup' which was held in tandem with the official 2002 FIFA World Cup in France. In that competition, there were many football teams composed of approximately 1000 players from 101 different nations who were imprisoned in Klong Prem Central Prison. The trophy was given to the players from Nigeria. After that, sport has increasingly caught the attention of people behind bars. More importantly, prison officers started to realise that sport activities might be better and more effective than the style of traditional custody or 'lock them up and throw away the key' (Chitsawang, 2011e). On top of that, playing sport in prison could be further enhanced in the next level by changing it into a professional career. Many of those, who joined the boxing training camps and had opportunities to fight in a boxing match outside, could earn and save money to be spent after release.

The turning point of rehabilitation programmes in Thailand in 2020 was the coronavirus 2019 infections or Covid-19 pandemic. Many of the rehabilitation activities cited above had to be suspended, especially the programmes that needed instructors or visitors coming from the outside world. In addition, to prevent the wider spread of the disease, the social distancing policy did not allow incarcerated people to attend any social gatherings behind bars. Hence, the DOC has announced the policy in Fiscal Year 2022 of adapting rehabilitation and treatment programmes to become more digitalised, using online technology. This seems to be the only option for continuing rehabilitation programmes for people in Thai prisons.

Theoretical Underpinnings to Rehabilitation

Before discussing theoretical aspects on rehabilitation, it is worth re-reviewing the basic question about the aims of imprisonment. Generally, there are at least four purposes of imprisonment: punishment, deterrence, reform and protection of the public (Coyle, 2005; Robinson & Crow, 2009; Taxman & Rudes, 2011, cited in Netrabukkana, 2016). Sometimes these have different titles. For example, protection of the public can also refer to incapacitation, and reform can be regarded as rehabilitation, although some scholars may recognise several slight differences, such as Hudson (2003) who preferred the use of the term 'reform' to describe the developments of regimes designed to effect change in an individual through educative and contemplative techniques in the nineteenth century; and the term *'rehabilitation'* to signify the more individualistic treatment programmes established during the twentieth century. Interestingly, the Thai penal system seems to involve all the above justifications.

Firstly, imprisonment can serve as a punishment to penalise persons for the crimes they have committed. Scott (2008) claimed that the overarching aim of prison was to fulfil its punishment role: the deliberate infliction of suffering and hardships upon those contained within its walls. In Thailand, a person convicted of a crime is held to deserve the punishment.

Secondly, prison can be a place to protect the public from those who commit crimes. One Thai prison is responsible for permanent incapacitation, imposing the death penalty by lethal injection. Presently this execution takes place only at Bangkwang Central Prison, after a final decision by the Supreme Court and the denial of a petition for the Royal Pardon by H.M. the King. Thai prisons have therefore played a role in preventing offenders from doing harm to society. In terms of temporary incapacitation, people in Thai society expect prisons to keep sentenced persons in custody, and so prevent them from committing further crimes outside the prison walls.

Finally, it is argued that a prison can positively change, reform, or rehabilitate those it contains. In criminal justice, rehabilitation is a process; interventions or programmes enable individuals to overcome previous difficulties linked to their offences so that they can become law-abiding and useful members of the wider community (Burnett, 2008). In fact, this purpose of prison tends to be different from the others, as it reflects the positive aspect of punishment in terms of providing help or beneficial programmes for the offenders. In Thailand, prison is currently a place to rehabilitate offenders because many types of treatment programmes are provided, ranging from education and vocational training to religious and recreation activities, and treatment programmes for specific groups. Among these concepts, it is generally believed the aims of imprisonment vary depending on the 'prevailing penal philosophy of the time, and there has been much debate about the way in which prison operates' (Robinson & Crow, 2009: 35).

For these reasons, in theoretical terms, Thailand's correctional system has followed the 'Positivist School' by emphasising the process of helping prisoners improve and reintegrate into society. Wrongdoers are held to need correction rather than punishment. The adoption of this school of thought is a result of the available criminology and penology courses from undergraduate to doctorate levels in universities in Thailand. Over the years, the universities have produced graduates to work in various criminal justice agencies, especially in the DOC, in which the 'Positivist School of Criminology' has significantly influenced the concept of prisoner rehabilitation through training courses at the prison staff training academy as well as the vision and missions of the DOC which clearly adhere to the ideology of rehabilitation.

Research Findings and Effectiveness

There are many studies and research examining rehabilitation and treatment programmes in Thailand. Nevertheless, their scope is quite limited as they tend to focus only on some specific rehabilitation programmes at a particular prison or correctional institution. To give some examples, Khomsod and Nuanga-nun (2021) investigated the conditions, problems and needs of the offenders from the rehabilitation operations of the Central Correctional Institution for Young Offenders in Pathum Thani Province. They discovered several problems in the rehabilitation operations, such as insufficient funds for the implementation of the project, defective equipment, lack of expert speakers, and so on. Udomsri (2016) studied the correction officers' problems and obstacles in rehabilitation in two correctional institutions—the Women's Correctional Institution for Drug Addicts, (REF) and Pranakhonsriayuthaya Correctional Institution for Drug Addicts (REF). Moreover, there was research by Junthong (1999) doing a case study of the Therapeutic Community programme at Women's Correctional Institution for Drug Addicts. Most of these studies aim at exploring the concepts, problems, and challenges of the specific rehabilitation programmes.

In terms of effectiveness, the recidivism or re-offending issue tends to receive special attention. Apart from the statistical studies provided on the official website of DOC which set up the system called 'RecStats' or Recidivism Statistics Database, there are also other academic research and studies. To begin with the research by Lertpanichpun (2018)—it explored recidivism of prisons engaging in activities under the Inspire Project initiated by Her Royal Highness Princess Bajrakittiyabha. The study shows that the Inspire Project has complemented the work of the DOC, focusing on the development of better living standards for prisoners. The Project has been rolled out in 22 prisons across Thailand. The re-offending rate under the project is 10.16%, compared to the national recidivism rate of 23.7%. The causes of recidivism include deviant peer groups upon release, low social and economic status, broken family backgrounds, and histories of victimisation. Recidivism is often found among drug-involved persons, people without a sense of purpose, and those with poor life skills. Therefore, the Project boosts the participants' morale by shaping their behaviour using environmental, family, and education factors; especially by providing them with good life skills and enhanced self-worth through various activities such as vocational training and community therapeutic activities. This will enable them to recognise their value, create self-sufficiency, and prevent them from going back to prison.

In Thailand, social acceptance is one of the most important factors for successful reintegration. This issue could be linked to legal rehabilitation, one of four forms argued by Burke et al. (2019), commenting that 'People with convictions are the most likely disadvantaged group to be without work, making up between a quarter and a third of unemployed people'. Consequently, the rehabilitation programme in the prison alone may not be sufficient to support the prisoner's social reintegration. Jessadaraksa (2009) analysed the role of local government organisations and local communities regarding the acceptance and support for the prisoner's reintegration. The study recommended that the community and local government should involve themselves in the pre-release phase by coordinating with families, community, and local businesses such as factories, companies and stores to ensure the prisoners will be able to find jobs after their release, as well as taking part in the aftercare to support their well-being. However, it showed that most of the local government organisations have not been undertaking this role effectively which affects the recidivism rates. Another factor, in accordance with the study of Leggett et al. (2021), emphasises that social acceptance is the main driving factor of recidivism. The former incarcerated often face family and social stigma. They have to return to the same environment and by that 'they were referring to their networks of friends and acquaintances to which they return when released'. In addition, unemployment is an important factor that leads to the same cycle of crime.

Future Directions in Policy and Practice

In the future, before installing any rehabilitation measures, the most urgent priority is to reduce the number of people in prison. This can be done by moving towards greater use of non-custodial measures; and focusing on back-end mechanisms, especially parole and royal pardon as well as 'good day' allowance schemes, to conditionally and unconditionally release people held behind bars. In fact, the new drugs law, the Narcotics Code B.E. 2564 (2021), effective 9 December 2021, could lead to a drop in the prison population as it emphasises prevention and treatment rather than punishment for small-scale drug users, and introduces tougher measures against organised crime. Once this scenario is realised, Thailand's prison system might then be able to perform efficient classification processes, including analyses of criminal behaviour and planning for individual treatment. At the same time, rehabilitative approaches, using both general and specific programmes, will rely more on modern technology and big data management to assist rehabilitation and treatment activities in the Covid-19 era. And it will enable a better response to their criminogenic needs, although at present personal development seems to be the main priority. Another trend, currently under the spotlight which will gradually increase in the future, is the participation of society in assisting the successful rehabilitation and reintegration of formerly incarcerated people.

Notes

1. In Thailand, the treatment of juvenile delinquents or those under 18 is under responsibility of Department of Juvenile Observation and Protection, Ministry of Justice.
2. In 2020 and 2021, there were totally four Royal Pardon Decrees which affected on releasing nearly 100,000 incarcerated people and a reduction of prison sentence of more than 200,000 prisoners.
3. It could be said that there is no single and universal measure of recidivism as it has been defined differently depending on their national contexts. On top of that there are various opinions on an appropriate 'follow-up period' or how long the prison authority will track the released inmates, which can normally vary among 1 year, 3 years, 5 years or any specific period of follow-up according to their consideration. Having said this, the recidivism rates in this RecStats database refer to the cohort of prisoners released, both unconditionally and conditionally, from prisons in the same fiscal year, who are sent to prisons again, no matter as a convicted inmate or as a person on remand, within either of these 3 different groups of follow-up periods: 1 year, 2 years and 3 years of fiscal year.

References

Adler, M., & Longhurst, B. (1994). *Discourse, power and justice: Towards a new sociology of imprisonment*. Routledge.

Burke, L, Collett, S., & McNeill, F. (2019). *Reimagining rehabilitation: Beyond the individual*. Routledge.

Burnett, R. (2008). Rehabilitation. In Y. Jewkes and J. Bennett (Eds.), *Dictionary of prisons and punishment*. Willian Publishing.

Chancholyut, M. (2017). *Evaluation of the implementation of the policy of 5 steps of correctional change: Pattaya remand prison*. Unpublished MA Independent Study.

Chitsawang, N. (2011a). *A musical therapy in prison.* https://www.gotoknow.org/posts/430607
Chitsawang, N. (2011b). *Art as a career: Another successful mission in Thai prisons.* https://www.gotoknow.org/posts/448883
Chitsawang, N. (2011c). *Prison as a home of education: A case of Thai prisons.* https://www.gotoknow.org/posts/436501
Chitsawang, N. (2011d). *Prison as a home of meditation.* https://www.gotoknow.org/posts/434995
Chitsawang, N. (2011e). *Sport as a treatment program in Thai prisons.* https://www.gotoknow.org/posts/432780
Coyle, A. (2005). *Understanding prisons: Key issues in policy and practice.* Open University Press.
Department of Corrections, Ministry of Interior. (1936). *The Penitentiary Act B.E. 2479 (1936).* http://www.correct.go.th/lawcorrects/lawfile/10001.pdf
Department of Corrections, Ministry of Interior. (1982). *Prisons and corrections in Thailand: Two hundred years of history.* Department of Corrections Press.
Department of Corrections, Ministry of Interior. (1999). *The annual report B.E. 2542 (1999).* Department of Corrections Press.
Department of Corrections, Ministry of Interior. (2000). *The annual report B.E. 2543 (2000).* Watthanapongkhanpim.
Department of Corrections, Ministry of Interior. (2001). *The annual report B.E. 2544 (2001).* Borphitkhanpim.
Department of Corrections, Ministry of Interior. (2002). *The annual report B.E. 2545 (2002).* Department of Corrections Press.
Department of Corrections, Ministry of Justice. (2003). *The annual report B.E. 2546 (2003).* Watthanapongkhanpim.
Department of Corrections, Ministry of Justice (2004). *The annual report B.E. 2547 (2004).* Department of Corrections Press.
Department of Corrections, Ministry of Justice. (2005a). *Corrections in Thailand 2005a: Transparent and innovative organization.* Department of Corrections Press.
Department of Corrections, Ministry of Justice. (2005b). *The annual report B.E. 2548 (2005).* Department of Corrections Press.
Department of Corrections. (2006a). *Ministry of Justice.* A new step towards sufficiency. Department of Corrections Press.
Department of Corrections, Ministry of Justice. (2006b). *The annual report B.E. 2549 (2006).* C.Y. System Printing.
Department of Corrections, Ministry of Justice. (2007). *The annual report B.E. 2550 (2007).* Vision Prepress.
Department of Corrections, Ministry of Justice. (2008). *The annual report B.E. 2551 (2008).* Sirivatana Interprint Public.
Department of Corrections, Ministry of Justice. (2009). *The annual report B.E. 2552 (2009).* Vision Prepress.
Department of Corrections, Ministry of Justice. (2010). *The annual report B.E. 2553 (2010).* Department of Corrections Press.

Department of Corrections, Ministry of Justice. (2012). *The department's report to the public on the government projects in the fiscal year 2011*. Department of Corrections Press.

Department of Corrections, Ministry of Justice. (2013). *The department's report to the public on the government projects in the fiscal year 2012*. Department of Corrections Press.

Department of Corrections, Ministry of Justice. (2014). *The department's report to the public on the government projects in the fiscal year 2013*. Department of Corrections Press.

Department of Corrections, Ministry of Justice. (2015). *The department's report to the public on the government projects in the fiscal year 2014*. Department of Corrections Press.

Department of Corrections, Ministry of Justice. (2016a). *Evaluation on mental development project: 'Sakkasa-Samathi' under the teachings of Luangphor Viriyang Sirintharo*. Department of Corrections Press.

Department of Corrections, Ministry of Justice. (2016b). *Five steps in changing the Thai corrections*. Department of Corrections Press.

Department of Corrections, Ministry of Justice. (2016c). *The department's report to the public on the government projects in the fiscal year 2015*. Department of Corrections Press.

Department of Corrections, Ministry of Justice. (2017a). *Corrections Act, B.E. 2560* (2017a). Available at: http://lad.correct.go.th/main/wp-content/uploads/2017a/02/correctlaw2560.pdf

Department of Corrections, Ministry of Justice. (2017b). *The department's report to the public on the government projects in the fiscal year 2016*. Department of Corrections Press.

Department of Corrections, Ministry of Justice. (2018a). *The department's report to the public on the government projects in the fiscal year 2017*. Department of Corrections Press.

Department of Corrections, Ministry of Justice. (2018b). *Corrections in Thailand 2017–2018b*. Department of Corrections Press.

Department of Corrections, Ministry of Justice. (2019). *The department's report to the public on the government projects in the fiscal year 2018*. Department of Corrections Press.

Department of Corrections, Ministry of Justice. (2020). *The department's report to the public on the government projects in the fiscal year 2019*. Department of Corrections Press.

Department of Corrections, Ministry of Justice. (2021). Unpublished document. Strategy and Planning Division.

Department of Corrections, Ministry of Justice. (2022). *Recidivism statistics database*. http://www.correct.go.th/recstats

Flynn, N. (1998). *Introduction to prisons and imprisonment*. Waterside.

Himelstein, S. (2011). Meditation research: The state of the art in correctional settings. *International Journal of Offender Therapy and Comparative Criminology, 55*(4), 646–661.

Hudson, B. (2003). *Understanding Justice: An introduction to ideas, perspectives and controversies in modern penal theory.* Open University Press.

Jessadaraksa, S. (2009). *Involvement of the local administration in preventing recidivism.* Social Work Division, Department of Corrections.

Junthong, V. (1999). *Therapeutic community in corrections: A case study of women's correctional institution for drug-addicts in Pathum Thani Province.* Thammasat University.

Kamla, B. (2006). A summary of seminar on problems and obstacles in Thai criminal justice system organised by Faculty of Law, Dhurakij Pundit University. *Julanithi Journal, 15*, 37–46.

Khomsod, S., & Nuanga-nun, W. (2021). A study on rehabilitation operations of the Central Correctional Institution for Young Offenders, Pathum Thani Province Thailand. *Review of International Geographical Education, 11*, 10.

Leggett, T., Jesrani, T., & Wattanawanitchakorn, P. (2021). *Research on the causes of recidivism in Thailand.* Thailand Institute of Justice. http://fileserver.idpc.net/library/en-cdghnpwz0345.pdf

Lertpanichpun S. (2018). *Recidivism survey of the inmates participated in the inspire project's activities.* Ministry of Justice.

Na Ayutthaya, T. K. (1993). *Essential Readings of Thongtor Kluaymai Na Ayutthaya.* Ton-Or Press.

Na Nakorn, P. (1998). *Collections of Prasert Na Nakorn's Theses.* Kasetsart University Press.

National Identity Board, Office of the Prime Minister (2000). *Thailand into the 2000's.* The National Identity Office.

Netrabukkana, P. (2012). Justifying what the prisons are for: A basic question for correctional agency. *Planning Division Journal, 1*(1): 16–21. http://www.correct.go.th/correct2009/upload/files/publication/55/cover_journal_plan.pdf

Netrabukkana, P. (2016). *Imprisonment in Thailand: The impact of the 2003 war on drugs policy.* Unpublished Ph.D. Thesis, University of Essex, UK.

Office of the Royal Development Projects Board. (2013). *Khao Kling prison camp: A prison full of wisdom returning good people to society.* Theppen Vanis Printing.

Penal Reform International. (2012). *Overcrowding.* https://www.penalreform.org/issues/prison-conditions/key-facts/overcrowding/

Plodhuang, N. (2017). Sakkasasamathi teaching class in prison. *Journal of Philosophical Vision, 22*, 2.

Robinson, G., & Crow, I. D. (2009). *Offender rehabilitation: Theory, research and practice.* Sage Publications.

Scott, D. (2008). *Penology.* Sage Publications.

Taxman, F. S., & Rudes, D. S. (2011). Punishment versus rehabilitation. In: Chambliss, W. J. (ed) Corrections. *Thousand Oaks* (pp. 233–245), Sage Publications.

The Narcotics Code, B.E. 2564. (2021). Royal Thai Government Gazette. Volume 138, Section 73 Ghor. (dated 8 November B.E. 2564).

Udomsri, C. (2016). *Correction officer's problems and obstacles in the rehabilitation: Case study of correctional institution for women drug addicts, Thunyaburi and correctional institution for male drug addicts*. Thammasat University.

Probation and the Prevention of Recidivism in Tunisia: Still Uncertain Beginnings

Philippe Pottier

Brief History

The first Tunisian penal code and criminal procedure code were published in the nineteenth century; in 1860 for the first and 1921 for the second, during the time of the French protectorate. The penal code underwent a major reform in 1913, very largely inspired by the French penal code of 1810. The penal procedure code of 1921 for its part reproduced almost entirely the provisions of the French criminal investigation code. Since the independence of Tunisia (1956), the penal code has undergone ad hoc adjustments, depending on events, without major modifications and without great effects on penal policy. The Code of Criminal Procedure was overhauled in 1968, but this reform very quickly showed its shortcomings. The main shortcoming of these outdated codes was the non-existence of any alternative measure to incarceration and of provisions making it possible to work for the rehabilitation of convicted persons. A form of conditional release was indeed introduced into the Criminal Procedure Code of 1968, but without it being able to be accompanied by control and accompanying measure and under

P. Pottier (✉)
Vitry-lès-Cluny, La Vineuse-sur-Frégande, France
e-mail: philippepottier@icloud.com

conditions such that it will only affect a small number detainees. Community service was introduced into legislation in 2001, without any means being defined for its implementation, which meant that it was not used in the following ten years.

From the 2011 revolution, debates began to be held on the state of the prison institution and the need to reform the penal system. The Tunisian situation is characterised by a high prison population of above 200 per 100,000 inhabitants. The main reason for this is the obsolescence of the legal and organisational framework which makes imprisonment the only penal sanction that can be used. It is also characterised by the poor state of its prisons. Some are very old. Others, although relatively recent, were poorly designed with no collective spaces to support training workshops and educational activities, or with spaces too small to offer activities to more than a small number of detainees. Their design, structured around large dormitories, promotes promiscuity which makes surveillance difficult. Criticism of the use of repression during the governors of Bourguiba and Ben Ali has opened up new spaces for discussion, no longer reserved for opponents of the regime deprived of means of expression, but in public debate. This flowering of public debate is one of the main advances of the 2011 revolution, which led to a real development of freedom of opinion and expression. This new context has made Tunisian governments aware of the need to reorient prison policy towards the objectives of rehabilitation and prevention of recidivism, with the help of international partners, in particular the European Union and the Council of Europe.

A First Probation Office Experience in Sousse

The International Committee of the Red Cross (ICRC) had begun, shortly before the 2011 revolution, to support work to modernise the functioning of prisons. This work was made almost impossible by the events of 2011, which resulted in very large movements of mutinies and collective escapes from prisons. We have thus been able to count more than 70 deaths among the detainees, a large part of them during the fire in the Monastir prison. Leading to significant destruction, these mutinies forced the government to favour actions to restore many prisons. As the ICRC could not, under these conditions, continue its action on the previous bases, it proposed to experiment with the setting up of a first experimental probation office in Sousse. The Ministry of Justice accepted this project and four agents from the prison of Messaadine (suburb of Sousse) were made available to the judge responsible for the execution of sentences. This experience made it possible for the first time to carry out community service and made visible the lack of legislative provisions allowing a probation office to function effectively.

The Justice Reform Support Programme and the Extension of Probation

After the constitutional reform of 2014, which had mobilised most of the activities of the public authorities, the government set up two reform commissions for the criminal code and the code of criminal procedure Ben Amor et al. (2019). At the same time, a Justice Reform Support Programme (PARJ) was launched, with the support of the European Union. This programme included an important prison reform component, including the development of a probation system in Tunisia, resulting in the creation of probation offices and the training of probation officers based on a Tunisian '*Manuel de la probation*'.

The Installation of the First Probation Offices

The justice reform support programme initially provided for the creation of six pilot probation offices, in addition to the experimental probation office in Sousse. These offices were gradually created between 2018 and 2020, in Monastir, Kairouan, Bizerte, La Manouba, Tunis and Gabès (GnetNews, 2015). To set them up, around twenty prison officers already in office were called upon, made available to the courts of appeal, and placed under the responsibility of a judge responsible for the execution of sentences. Finally, each office now has between three and five probation officers. All these probation officers have received training from practitioners, French professionals who have exercised the profession of probation officer and who have held important positions in this professional field, one having been president of the European Conference on Probation (CEP), the other director of the French National School of Penitentiary Administration (ENAP).

This training made it possible to structure the basis of the intervention methods recommended in Tunisia. Agent training focused on:

- Individual assessment of risk and protective factors.
- The determination of the resulting needs.

- The construction of a support plan for the person during the execution of her or his sentence.
- The practice of a positive relationship with the person followed to help him develop her or his own reflection in a positive direction.

The main theoretical supports are the works of Canadian authors D. A. Andrews and James Bonta mainly exposed in their major book '*The psychology of criminal conduct*' (2006). It is therefore the 'RNR' method—Risks, Needs, Responsivity—which served as the basis for the start of work in the Tunisian probation offices.

Intervention Models and Theoretical Foundations

The theoretical foundations and models of good practice have been brought together in a methodological guide, entitled '*Handbook of Probation*', distributed to all probation officers since 2019. This 75-page reference work is intended as a complete guide referring mainly to the European Rules of Probation—REP—published in 2010 by the Council of Europe, rules which are based on the RNR model mentioned above.

Definition of Tunisian Probation

The Handbook uses the definition of the Council of Europe defines probation 'the execution in an open environment of sanctions and measures defined by law and pronounced against an offender. It consists of a series of activities and interventions that involve follow-up, advice and assistance with the aim of socially reintegrating the offender into society and contributing to collective security'. The aims of the intervention of the probation services and the means to achieve them are defined as being 'to reduce the commission of new offenses by establishing positive relations with the offenders to ensure follow-up (including, if applicable), to guide and assist them to promote the success of their social integration. In this way, probation contributes to collective security and the proper administration of justice'. From this perspective, the purpose of probation is to support the convicted person towards a return to a life without delinquency, and therefore the prevention of recidivism.

Structuring the Monitoring Process

The Tunisian Probation Manual offers a structured description of what should be the intervention of probation officers with the people being monitored. This intervention is apprehended as a process that must be composed of different phases, each imposing specific professional acts, and which can be renewed cyclically. The Tunisian probation manual uses this method of intervention broken down into four phases:

- Assessment: the 'assessment' phase is understood as a phase of 'evaluation' of the people followed, of 'diagnosis'. It is described as essential and constitutes the first stage of treatment. 'Before and during the monitoring of an offender, the latter is subject, where appropriate, to an assessment which systematically and thoroughly analyses his particular situation, including the risks, positive factors and needs, the interventions needed to meet those needs, and an assessment of the offender's responsiveness to those interventions.
- Planning: at the end of the assessment phase and depending on the issues to be dealt with, their importance, the resources of the people, the interventions and their intensity are determined and organised according to a specific articulation, with the person concerned. This *'execution plan'*, presenting *'the interventions that will be implemented'*, will then guide the intervention of the professional. This plan is *'negotiated and established as far as possible in consultation with the offender'* and can be revised each time the assessment is updated.
- Interventions: the manual understands the *'interventions'* of probation staff as *'structured and programmed actions'*. Their aim is to stop crime and reintegrate people back into society. *'Interventions will often focus on social and family support through work integration programs, education programs, vocational training, training in budget management and regular contact with probation staff. They may also aim to manage emotions and risky behaviors'*.
- Evaluation of the action: this phase corresponds to the phase reviewing the person's situation. Thus, at the end of the cycle, after the initial assessment, the development of a structured monitoring plan, then the implementation of multimodal interventions, the objective is to measure the effects of the intervention on people followed. The execution plan is not fixed: it can be adapted in its intensity or reoriented in its aims according to the evaluation of the situation or the behaviour of the probationer.

The Contributions of Research

In the absence of existing criminological research in Tunisia, the Tunisian probation manual is based on the current 'What Works?' A group of Canadian researchers—Andrews, Bonta, Gendreau and Ross—initiated this trend in the late 1970s. Their work gave rise to the model of care for people placed under the control of justice called Risk, Needs, Responsivity (RNR):

- The principle of risk: the intensity of care must be proportional to the level of risk of recurrence assessed.
- The principle of needs: the dynamic risks of recidivism, i.e. those likely to experience an improvement thanks to the intervention of the probation service, should be targeted in the treatment.
- The principle of receptivity: assumes that the care is adapted, to be effective, to the sentenced person.
- Research on desistance: desistance is defined as a process by which, with or without the intervention of the judicial and penitentiary system, individuals put an end to their criminal activities and leads their life in accordance with the law.
- Good lives (or 'fulfilling life' model). For its designers, the commission of an offense is an inappropriate way for the perpetrator to satisfy legitimate human needs. It is therefore necessary to help the person to reach them in another way, respectful of the laws and of other members of society. Above all, the Good Lives model provides a general framework for understanding delinquent acting out.
- Core Correctional Practices (CCPs). The field of CCPs is interested in the effect of the professional skills of probation officers on the course of sentenced persons and on the prevention of recidivism. They correspond to a set of identified skills and methods adopted by the professional with a view to reducing delinquent behaviour.
- The motivational approach. This approach is a method of communication that aims to increase motivation by helping the individual to explore and resolve his ambivalence in the face of change. This ambivalence, which must be considered natural, can be resolved by working on the individual's motivation, his intrinsic motivation.

The methodological part of the manual details how these theoretical currents are used in the operational management of the people being monitored.

A Weak Legislative Framework

Despite the creation of probation offices, the legislative framework has still not been reformed, apart from a recent decision introducing the possibility of placement under electronic monitoring. Prior to this recent novelty, the only alternative measures to imprisonment included in the codes are the stay of execution (simple stay without probation), community service and penal reparation:

- Stay of execution (Code Pénal Article 53, paragraphs 13–19): the courts may, giving reasons for their decision, grant a stay of execution of the sentence of primary convicts, within a maximum limit of two years. The Attorney General of the Republic may similarly grant a stay of execution of the sentence in 'serious and exceptional cases' (Code of Criminal Procedure—Article 337). but these measures do not ensure any follow-up of the offender.
- Community service (Code Pénal Article 5): defined by the Penal Code as the main penalty (article 5), community service (*Travail d'Intérêt Général*—TIG) is an alternative penalty to imprisonment, insofar as where the court which imposes a prison sentence of less than or equal to one year can replace it with an 'unpaid community service sentence for a maximum of six hundred hours on the basis of two hours a day in prison' (Code Pénal Article—15 bis). The penalty of community service does not exist as a penalty in itself, being conditioned by the prior pronouncement of a prison sentence. The scope of the community service penalty is limited, Article 5 of the criminal code exhaustively lists the offences likely to give rise to the pronouncement of this type of sentence. Thus, to benefit from a community service sentence, the accused must be primary, present at the hearing, and formally agree to serve this sentence. In the event of refusal on his part, the court then confirms the prison sentence (Code Pénal Article—15 ter). The time limit for carrying out community service is set at eighteen months from the date of sentencing. TIG's sentence is executed with public establishments, local authorities, charitable or relief associations, national interest associations whose purpose is the protection of the environment (Code Pénal Article—17). Prior to the execution of the sentence, the person sentenced to community service is subject to a medical examination by the doctor of the penitentiary establishment closest to his home (Code Pénal Article—18 bis), and he benefits from social security coverage (accident at work, occupational diseases) during the execution (penal code—article 18). The introduction of this community service in

the code of criminal procedure, as it stood, paved the way for the establishment of probation services. Indeed, if the code entrusts the Enforcement Judge (Juge de l'Exécution des Peines—JEP) with monitoring the execution of the community service sentence, it specifies (article 336) that it does so 'with the assistance penitentiary services', without however defining the respective fields of competence. This allusion, not supplemented by implementing regulations, nevertheless made it possible to design the first probation offices mentioned above. The Code of Criminal Procedure also opens up the possibility of substituting community service for imprisonment, at the request of the person concerned, within the limit of two hours of work per day in prison, provided that the maximum period of work does not exceed three hundred hours. Imprisonment may be replaced by community service if the convict is insolvent or has reached the age of sixty (articles 343–348).

- Penal reparation: like community service, the penalty of penal reparation is defined as the main penalty (article 5). Like community service, it presupposes the prior pronouncement of a prison sentence of less than or equal to six months, which the court can replace with an obligation of pecuniary reparation that the convicted person must pay to the victim of the offense (Article 15c). To benefit from a penalty of criminal reparation, the accused must be primary and present at the hearing. The time limit for the execution of criminal reparation is three months, it is up to the person concerned to justify its proper execution to the public prosecutor (Code de Procédure Pénale—article 336 ter). In the absence of justification within the time limit, the prison sentence initially pronounced is enforced. No follow-up or accompaniment of the condemned person is planned, the latter having to personally testify to the execution of the sentence.

Alongside these few alternative measures to incarceration, there are some reduced possibilities of conditional release. Article 353 CPP stipulates that *'any convict having to undergo one or more custodial sentences who will have shown his amendment by his conduct in detention, or whose release will have been deemed useful to the interest of the community'*. The window of intervention of the sentence execution judge in terms of conditional release is narrow. He has jurisdiction to grant conditional release to persons sentenced to a prison term of less than or equal to eight months:

- Having already served half the sentence for a primary convict, whose length of sentence must not be less than three months,

- Having already served two-thirds of the sentence for a recidivist convicted person, whose length of sentence served cannot be less than six months (Code de Procédure Pénale—Articles 342 bis and 354).

The possible durations of conditional release under the jurisdiction of the JEP are therefore limited: from one to four months maximum for first-time offenders, from one to two months maximum for repeat offenders, durations from which are to be deducted the delays of the procedures to be put in place. implemented. The review of conditional releases is not systematic, the JEP ruling on its own initiative, or at the request of the convicted person, one of his ascendants or descendants, his spouse, his legal guardian or on the proposal of the prison warden.

The sentence enforcement judge decides on the advice of the public prosecutor. The conditional release of persons sentenced to a prison term of more than eight months falls within the competence of the Minister of Justice, after consultation with the Conditional Release Commission (Code of Criminal Procedure—article 356). The paradox of this conditional release is that it is an 'unconditional' release other than that of house arrest (article 357). It is not accompanied by any obligation depending on individual situations and is not subject to follow-up or support for the convicted person. However, it would be essential for probation offices to be responsible from now on for the support and supervision of people on release.

A commission to reform the code of criminal procedure was set up in 2014 and delivered its work in 2018. This was to result in a bill that could have included alternatives to incarceration in Tunisian legislation, after a parliamentary debate within the Assembly of People's Representatives (ARP). The political context did not allow to launch this debate, the government then had taken advantage of its capacity to legislate by decree-law during the state of emergency of the health crisis to introduce electronic surveillance in the Tunisian penal arsenal, on June 10, 2020. However, this new penal measure, to be controlled by the sentence execution judge with the assistance of the probation offices, has still not been implemented, for a lack of resources. It continues to miss what constitutes the essence of the activities of the probation services in the countries which have them, a probation measure that could, according to the principles of Tunisian law, take the form of the French probationary reprieve.

An Extension of Probation Offices but a Chronic Lack of Resources

Today the addition of seven new probation offices is in progress, permitting one probation office per court of appeal. However, the efficiency of these offices is greatly hampered not only by the absence of any reform of the legislative framework but also by a lack of resources, which is just as important in prisons.

> In probation offices:
> The probation offices set up in recent years remain poorly endowed with resources. If there is a methodological guide provided that we presented above, giving the foundations for good practices, no legal or regulatory basis has come to confirm their existence and their organisation. The decree-law establishing electronic monitoring is the only text referring to these offices. Without regulatory benchmarks or precise organisation, the development of their action is slow.

> In the jails:
> Social offices exist in prisons, but they are also poorly staffed and without regulatory benchmarks. In addition, they do not have a methodological guide like probation offices. Their intervention is mainly limited to adequate information for the families of the detainees. No exit preparation system has been developed. Their staff is even more restricted than that of the probation offices, which were able to benefit from specific recruitments. Thus, at Monarguia prison, which has more than 5000 prisoners and sometimes more than 6000, fewer than 10 social workers are assigned, which is obviously totally insufficient Crétenot et al. (2021).

The Necessary Acculturation of Judges

Probation is a new idea in Tunisia, which has appeared in recent years. The very weak development of community service is an illustration of this. Created about twenty years ago, it had practically no application during the first ten years, the judges not seizing it. Admittedly, the government did not put any resources into developing it given the non-existence of probation offices at the time, but it is remarkable that there was no local initiative to attempt the first implementations. In recent years, within the framework of the PARJ, several conferences have been organised to present the interests of probation and to promote a penal policy that would aim for efficiency in the prevention of recidivism. We can hope that thanks to this, the idea of the necessary development of probation will gain ground. It can do so, especially since Tunisia has a high prison population rate and many of its prisons are overcrowded Prison Insider (2019). The methods of counting prison places partly mask this reality. Tunisian prisons are made up of dormitories that can hold dozens of prisoners (up to more than a hundred sometimes). Added to the crucial lack of means of social care, this situation can only be harmful in terms of recidivism. The development of probation is an essential response to avoid the increase in this prison overcrowding Bouagga, Y. (2018).

The Future?

The current political context in Tunisia makes it difficult to imagine the future. With parliament suspended since July 2021, the expected reform of the penal and criminal procedure codes has come to a halt. Public debates today are polarised on the constitutional reform announced by the President of the Republic and the election of a new parliamentary assembly by the end of 2022. Penal reform may perhaps take shape after this deadline, but it is impossible to predict. The main advance in recent years has been the commissioning of probation offices: their officers are equipped with a solid methodological guide. They lack the means and institutional support. But they exist, and they implement community service, which is already a positive development. We can hope that thanks to their action and their dynamism, there will come a time when Tunisian probation truly develops.

References

Andrews, D. A., & Bonta, J. (2006). *The psychology of criminal conduct* (4th ed.). LexisNexis.

Ben Amor, R., Rachdi, N., & Loued, M. N. (2019). La réforme du code pénal tunisien. *Editions Nirvana*, 19 juin.

Bouagga, Y. (2018). Prison escape and its political imaginary in times of political crisis: Tunisia. In T. M. Martin & G. Chantraine (Eds.), *Prison breaks: Toward a sociology of escape* (pp. 2011–2016). Palgrave Macmillan.

Crétenot, M., Marest, P., & Pottier P. (2021). Manuel du droit pénitentiaire tunisien. Co-auteur, Équipe internationale de soutien. Tunis. *Ministère de la Justice et Instance Nationale de Prévention de la Torture* (INPT).

GnetNews. (2015). *Tunisie: Un système de probation pour réduire la surpopulation carcérale.*
Justice Reform Support Programme (PARJ). (2017). http://www.parj.gov.tn/wp-content/uploads/2017/05/depliant.pdf
Manuel de la probation. Tunisie.
Prison Insider. (2019). An information platform on prisons in the world. 'Tunisia'. https://www.prison-insider.com/en/countryprofile/tunisie-2019. 100, Rue des Fougères, 69009. Lyon. France.
Programme d'appui à la réforme de la Justice (ParJ). www.parj.gov.tn
www.e-justice.tn, http://ccas.europa.eu/delegations/tunisia

The Unfinished Symphony: Progress and Setbacks Towards a Rehabilitation Policy in Uruguay

Ana Vigna and Ana Juanche

Uruguay does not conform precisely to the regional profile. Although it has relatively low levels of violence and crime in the Latin American context (UNODC, 2019)*, the country has the highest level of incarceration in South America, with a rate of 408 prisoners per 100,000 inhabitants in 2022.[1]

At the beginning of the twenty-first century, Uruguay was plunged into one of the greatest economic and social crises in its history, which caused long-lasting effects in terms of social fragmentation and exclusion. The progressive increase in crime rates, mainly against property, and the consequent increase in the prison population, are part of its impacts. In 2005, the *Frente Amplio* (progressive party) took office. The declaration of a humanitarian emergency in prisons and measures to combat overcrowding were part of the first changes announced. Despite this, a short time later the incarceration rate returned to its previous levels and continued to grow steadily, even though socioeconomic indicators improved substantially. Living conditions in prison however did not change significantly. In fact, in 2009 the United

---

A. Vigna (✉)
School of Social Sciences, University of the Republic, Montevideo, Uruguay
e-mail: ana.vigna@cienciassociales.edu.uy

A. Juanche
Freelance, author, Ciudad de la Costa, Canelones, Uruguay
e-mail: ana@juanche.net

Nations Rapporteur on Torture, Manfred Nowak, made a very critical report that ranked Uruguayan prisons among the worst in the world. From there, a process of prison reform began.

The reform process was based on the following key points: the struggle against inhumane prison conditions; the transition from a model focused on security matters to one focused on respect for human rights and rehabilitation, and the unification of the prison system through the creation, in 2010, of a national institution (National Rehabilitation Institute, INR) to manage and organise the administration of the penitentiary system. During this reform process, and especially in the period between 2017 and 2020, the technical perspective of imprisonment took a crucial step forward. The technical intervention was organised around two specific fields: 'human rights-based treatment' and 'rehabilitation'. During this period, a set of programmes were implemented, a risk assessment instrument was incorporated, and some conceptual definitions were adopted to guide the intervention. However, despite these efforts, rehabilitation did not achieve mainstream status within the system, which continued to be strongly influenced by custodial logic and a static security paradigm.

In turn, in 2020, a new conservative government took office. The new authorities expressed their concern about the prison system situation and announced some measures to mitigate the crisis, through a 'Prison Dignity Plan' focused on rehabilitation. However, this plan associates rehabilitation with correctional policies focused on the traditional development of work and educational activities. Furthermore, the discourse of 'law and order' got stronger inside and outside the prisons, via many of the measures included in Law No. 19,889, of July 20, 2020. Among other things, it strongly increases penalties, substantially reduces prison privileges for most crimes, and repeals a large part of the alternatives to imprisonment legislation.

Faced with constant increases in the imprisoned population, estimated at 11.9% per year (Parliamentary Commissioner, 2020) and not matched by a similar increase in budget resources, the available indicators show a prison system that, although very heterogeneous, can be characterised by critical overcrowding (reaching 134% occupancy in June 2021)[2] and poor living conditions. Thus, one out of every three persons imprisoned in Uruguay suffers cruel, inhuman, or degrading treatment, and opportunities for social integration are provided to only 11%[3] of those held. In addition, 2021 was a particularly tragic period, with a record of 86 deaths in custody, 79% more compared to the previous year.[4]

From this context, this article will approach the impact that the rehabilitation perspective had on penitentiary reform in Uruguay, will analyse the elements that prevented it to consolidate as the mainstream paradigm, and will point out some of the most urgent problems facing rehabilitation policies in the current prison context.

The Drive to a Rehabilitation Perspective in the Framework of Prison Reform

The rehabilitation perspective grew most strongly in Uruguay during the 2010–2020 period, within the parameters of prison reform. However, some previous experiences can be identified as direct antecedents. In particular, the reform took up some of the principles that had been implemented in a pioneering pilot initiative: the National Rehabilitation Centre (CNR). Created in 2002 and financed by a loan from the Inter-American Development Bank (IADB), the CNR was a re-entry prison-based centre, managed entirely by civilian personnel who worked from a cognitive-behavioural perspective to reduce recidivism. After a selection process and based on an initial diagnosis, an individual work plan was drawn up jointly with the prisoners, which would be accompanied by a personal reference. The intervention was based on five pillars: a prosocial thinking programme; a labour programme; an educational programme; a programme of family and community ties; and a programme of coexistence and discipline. Unfortunately, there have been no rigorous evaluations of this intervention to estimate its results and its impact on recidivism.

Despite its innovative nature, the initiative had a short life. With the end of the budget granted by the IADB, the Uruguayan State could not ensure the sustainability of the project and it gradually disappeared. The inexistence of a comprehensive intervention manual, the weak training of personnel in the rehabilitation paradigm, the clash between technical and police perspectives, the limited capacity to systematise and monitor activities, as well as the progressive cut in the components of the programme and in the intensity of its interventions, explain the process of programmatic distortion that it suffered over the years (Rojido et al., 2014). These weaknesses, observed in the context of a system that required urgent solutions to the problem of overcrowding and access to minimum living conditions, caused the end of the project a few years after it began.

Years later, as components of the prison reform, several of the characteristic elements of the 'CNR model' began to be taken up again. The National Technical Sub-Directorate of the INR worked on a conceptual and operational definition of rehabilitation, adopting the risk-need-responsiveness (RNR) model of Andrews and Bonta (2007). For the first time, the rehabilitation model was explicitly defined: the prison system would work comprehensively on criminal risk factors, transcending the traditional idea of rehabilitation focused on education and work. Additionally, rehabilitation programmes would also seek to address protective factors, based on the development of personal and social skills (Juanche, 2018). Thus, it is possible to identify during the 2010–2020 period, a set of intervention programmes whose main characteristics, conceptual bases, coverage, and effects will be presented briefly below.

Programmes Developed During the Prison Reform

One of the most important challenges facing the Uruguayan prison system (in terms of reducing conflict and violence inside facilities and related to the prevention of recidivism) refers to drugs abuse. Thus, in 2011, to develop responses to the prevalence of drug use (Castelli et al., 2019), the INR, the State Health Services Administration (ASSE—acronym in Spanish), and the National Drug Board (JND—acronym in Spanish) developed a treatment model with a cognitive-behavioural approach, aimed at women (Rossi et al., 2011), called Programme for the Problematic Use of Drugs (PUPD—acronym in Spanish). This model was developed on a pilot basis and in 2015 was adapted to be implemented with the male population. Although the device has been sustained uninterruptedly since its creation, its coverage reaches only a few prisons in the metropolitan area and there is no evaluation of its results.

The other evidence-based programmes, taken from the comparative international experience, began to be implemented by 2017. The catalogue of developed experiences includes the Programme for the Control of Sexual Aggression (PCAS—acronym in Spanish): a cognitive-behavioural intervention that combines individual and group sessions, created for the Spanish prison system (Garrido & Beneyto, 1996), and based on the adaptation of Rivera González et al. (2006). For its first edition in Uruguay (2018), the INR had the support of the University of the Republic (UdelaR—acronym in Spanish) in the selection and evaluation processes of participants, through the application of the SVR-20 scales (Boer, Hart, Kropp, and Webster) adapted by Martínez, Hilterman and Andrés-Pueyo (2005) and EPAS-3 (Martínez-Catena & Redondo, 2016). The UdelaR also produced the evaluation of the process and clinical results of this first edition (Trajtenberg & Sánchez de Ribera, 2019).

The National Technical Sub-Directorate and the Department of Gender and Diversity of the INR applied the Programme for the Prevention of Gender Violence for women in penitentiary centres (Sermujer.es), also designed by the General Secretariat of Penitentiary Institutions of Spain (Yagüe-Olmos et al., 2015), from a cognitive-behavioural perspective.

In addition to these specifically addressed initiatives, two other cross-programmes were developed. First, is the Prosocial Thought Programme (PPS—acronym in Spanish), another cognitive-behavioural intervention developed by the Spanish Prison System (Ross and Fabiano, 1985; Ross et al., 1994). This programme seeks to influence the social and cognitive skills of people so that they can face vital challenges, while staying in the margins of the law. Second, the Programme for Emotional Regulation and Re-signification of life stories through the Theatre with Masks (De Ávila, 2016), with a Gestalt approach. This programme is aimed at people between 18 and 24 years old and seeks to improve coexistence based on emotional regulation. Its first and second editions (2017 and 2018) were evaluated through the SCL-90-R Symptom Inventory (Derogatis et al., 2004), adapted by Najson (2008), the Emotional Regulation Difficulties Scale (DERS) in its Spanish adaptation (Hervás & Jódar, 2008), the State-Trait Anger Expression Inventory (STAXI-2) in its Spanish adaptation (Spielberger et al., 2009), and the Offender Assessment System Protocol in its Chilean adaptation (Gendarmería de Chile & Fundación Paz Ciudadana, 2011).

Despite the conceptual change implied by the implementation of these programmes, their coverage levels were quite low, even taking into account that participation in all of them was voluntary. In this context, for 2019, a year that registered an average of 11,025 imprisoned people, only 130 inmates participated in the PPS programme and 121 in the PUPD programme. Both initiatives, which were the most far-reaching, managed to reach barely 1% of the total population. Among the reasons highlighted to explain this low coverage, De Ávila (2021) mentions the novelty of these initiatives for the Uruguayan system, as well as the lack of technical personnel (particularly psychologists) for their implementation. The low completion rate of these processes is also remarkable: approximately 40% of its participants do not complete them, either due to abandonment, transfers, or because they achieve their liberty (De Ávila, 2021).

Evaluation of the programmes is scarce, discontinuous and, in most cases, non-existent. The ones that have a long history of application, such as the Prosocial Thought Program, have not been evaluated and, therefore, their effectiveness in terms of therapeutic results and impact on the reduction of criminogenic risks is unknown. On the other hand, the most innovative programmes, such as the Control of Sexual Aggression, the Prevention of Gender Violence, or Emotional Regulation, have been evaluated in only some of their applications and with dissimilar techniques.

In general, the findings and recommendations produced by the evaluations point to the positive impact of the programmes on those who complete them, and the need to improve the processes of evaluation, selection, and retention of participants. Besides levels of risk, they also point to the inclusion of their motivations and expectations regarding the intervention. In addition, evaluations indicate the need to strengthen the planning of the intervention, especially the implementation, which faces enormous challenges to sustain the processes, within an organisational culture that does not understand it and reluctantly accepts it. Likewise, at the macro level, it is pointed out that the INR must be supported through a comprehensive strategy that allows the consolidation and application of evidence-based models through the incorporation of technicians, who need to be trained in a specialised and permanent way, as well as a consistent budget (Trajtenberg & Sánchez de Ribera, 2019). Human rights-based treatment programmes were also developed during prison reform. These initiatives also aim to increase access to human rights by the prison population and are based on the principle of normalisation. This principle, established by the Mandela Rules, seeks to minimise the differences between prison and community life. Some of these programmes are universal while others are addressed to specific groups. The general ones are (i) the National Education and Culture Programme (PEC—acronym in Spanish), which coordinates with the public education system, and with civil society, to guarantee access to formal and non-formal education and culture; (ii) the National Programme for Productive and Labour Enterprises, (PEPL—its acronym in Spanish), which seeks to promote labour strategies for social reintegration; and (iii) the National Programme for Sports and Recreation, which aims to improve the quality of life, personal and social development, as well as the acquisition of prosocial values. On the other hand, the specific programmes are aimed at generating affirmative actions for vulnerable groups. They are the Programme for Foreigners and Migrants (PROEM—acronym in Spanish); the Programme for People with Disabilities (PRODIS—acronym in Spanish) and, the Programme for Mothers who live with their Children in Prison (PAMHI—acronym in Spanish). These programmes coordinate with other state agencies and civil society, to meet the particular needs of these groups and seek relevant responses. In 2014, the INR also created a Department of Gender and Diversity that promotes various initiatives (mainly aimed at women and the transgender population) to combat discrimination and promote violence-free living (Lacaño, 2021).

The creation of these human rights-based programmes—and their conceptual distinction from those of rehabilitation—represented a key point in the strengthening of technical perspectives in the penitentiary system. Despite this, these interventions suffer similar difficulties to those described above. In particular, their low coverage of demand is remarkable. Thus, in 2020, only 21% of prisoners had pursued formal studies and 34% had carried out some work activity.[5] Here too, the disparity observed between the different facilities stands out, as well as the lack of trained human resources to carry these programmes out.

It is also worth highlighting an initiative that, although not strictly within the rehabilitation paradigm, has been widely recognised at a national and international level. This is the experience developed in Unit No. 6 'Punta de Rieles', internationally known as the *prison village* due to its organisational climate and regimen of life. The prison, incorporated into the system in 2010, has had since 2012 a civil administration which explains the differences, in terms of management, that this facility presents concerning those managed by police officers (Ávila, 2018). The Punta de Rieles' project was characterised by its strong socio-educational component, the humanisation of treatment, the normalisation of life in prison, and the active participation of different State institutions and civil society organisations. Despite having been widely recognised by diverse social and political actors, there were no evaluations of the 'Punta de Rieles' model's impact on recidivism.

Beyond the institutional interventions, Uruguay has a pool of alternatives to imprisonment. They are managed by the Office for Parole Supervision (OSLA—acronym in Spanish) under the National Rehabilitation Institute. Despite its magnitude and relevance (almost 18,000 in April 2022), very little is known about the scope and functioning of community-based sanctions in Uruguay. The regulations on the matter are relatively recent and have been frequently modified in the last years. Besides that, it has been shown the institutional weakness of OSLA, as well as the difficulties to articulate with other key actors in the criminal process (Juanche, 2022; Parliamentary Commissioner, 2021; Trujillo, Dabezies & Daguerre, 2013). As a result, there is a clear delay in the implementation of these measures, weakness in the technical nature of the interventions, very little monitoring and support capacity, and great difficulties in systematizing the intervention and providing information (Vigna, 2022; Juanche, 2022; Parliamentary Commissioner, 2021; Trujillo, Dabezies, & Daguerre, 2013).

Quality Information and Evaluation as Substantive Requirements of Public Policy

A central element in evaluating rehabilitation policies is the availability of quality empirical information. In this respect, there is a strong lag in terms of quality and access to data in the Uruguayan criminal justice field, even compared to other countries in the region (Gual, 2016). Thus, it is remarkable that Uruguay has no available recidivism indicator, one of the basic elements for evaluating the effects of the criminal justice response (Pucci et al., 2012). Even though an information system called 'Prison Management System' was developed within the fabric of prison reform, access to data is limited, and its use in terms of evaluation of interventions is zero. These elements make discussion regarding correctional preferences based on some type of empirical evidence impossible (both at the level of public opinion and the decision-makers).

Related to this topic, Trajtenberg and Sánchez de Ribera (2019) point out that the evaluation of prisoners is one of the greatest challenges of the Uruguayan prison system: not only to improve the effectiveness of decision-making at the management level but also to improve the quality of prison life, which is marked by persistent problems of violence and human rights violations.

In this context, a key point in the advance of the rehabilitation paradigm during the prison reforms was the adoption of a criminal risk assessment instrument. As of 2017, and with the cooperation of the Inter-American Development Bank (project UR-L1062, 'Integrated Local Security Management Programme'), the INR introduced this type of tool, for the first time. The Offender Assessment System (OASys 2.0) is a system created by the United Kingdom to assess the risks of recidivism and severe harm (to oneself and other people). OASys 2.0 is used for the initial evaluation of the person when they enter the system, as well as for the technical assessment of the Judiciary and the Administration's requests for prison privileges such as transfers, and early or temporary releases.

In this regard, many difficulties related to the incorporation of this scale can be highlighted such as the limitations of an instrument developed in a different socio-cultural context from that of Uruguay; the scarcity and weakness of the training of personnel assigned to its application; and the long time required to fill it out (Sosa Barón, 2020; Trajtenberg & Sánchez de Ribera, 2019). These elements resulted in a great heterogeneity in its application, as well as in a significant lag in the needs of the system. Furthermore, the increase in the volume of work involved in the incorporation of this tool took strong resistance at the prison staff level.

Due to the low coverage rate of rehabilitation programmes, the usefulness of the OASys as a referral instrument was not at its full potential. On the contrary, this scale is mainly used as a management tool for the classification of prisoners and the assessment of prison benefits (Sosa Barón, 2020). In this respect, Sosa Barón also warns of a potential perverse effect. Contrary to the risk principle of the RNR model, the use of OASys for exclusive classification purposes may end up reinforcing the accommodation of the most problematic prisoners in the most complex facilities, while those with a low-risk profile are assigned to prisons with a better life regime.

Faced with these difficulties, Trajtenberg and Sánchez de Ribera (2019) propose that efforts to improve evaluation systems should go beyond the application of foreign scales (such as OASys 2.0) which require considerable professional, training, and educational resources. Thus, the authors point out that the results obtained by the application of self-reported scales such as the Self Appraisal Questionnaire (SAQ) tested in Uruguay, offer less demanding and more cost-efficient alternatives, as well as classification and prediction levels similar to those of OASys 2.0. Another highly suggested alternative is the development of its own scale, as other countries have done (Trajtenberg & Sánchez de Ribera, 2019).

The Relevance of Prison Staff for Advancing the Perspective of Rehabilitation

As already indicated, a central element for the prospect of rehabilitation is sufficient and adequately trained personnel. The creation of the Penitentiary Training Centre (CEFOPEN—acronym in Spanish) within the prison reform schema, as well as the incorporation of civil staff (penitentiary operators) for direct dealings with the prisoners, were two key elements of staff professionalisation.

Despite these advances, prison staff still mostly have a traditional and inadequate profile for the task of rehabilitation. Police officers represent 64% of the staff, prison operators 31%, and technicians, professionals and administrators occupy only the remaining 5%.[6] Regarding the availability of sufficient personnel, data from the First National Prison Officers Census (UdelaR, 2015) show a ratio of 6.9 prisoners per officer, far from the minimum standards established at the international level (Carranza, 2012).

These aspects show the weakness of the Uruguayan State to implement individualised work with prisoners (Vigna, 2020).

Equally unfortunately, the new administration abolished vacancies for civilian positions and converted those for university trained professionals and technicians into police posts.[7] This measure implies a clear reversal of the incipient professionalisation process that took place at the level of the prison workforce during previous administrations, making it even more difficult to implement treatment programmes.

Current Mechanisms and Their Policy and Political Contexts

This account shows that the largest prison reform in the recent history of the country (González et al., 2015) was left unfinished. The rehabilitation paradigm's lack of consolidation (at the normative, programmatic, budgetary, and organisational levels) enabled, after a conservative government took office, an involution towards the traditional management model, based on the discipline, educational, and labour approach.

In any case, it is appropriate to point out some innovative initiatives implemented in recent years. Thus, as of 2020, the INR began to develop the ECHO Programme jointly with the University of the Republic. This initiative aims to train the personnel who work in the care of people with substance abuse or mental health problems. Also, a re-entry programme was implemented in 2021, in the country's largest facility (the Prison Complex No. 4). The programme develops an individual work plan aimed at improving prisoners' work and educational skills, their daily habits, and seeks to intervene in the level of their criminal risk factors. This comprehensive intervention (De Ávila, 2021) works on the socio-educational and psycho-social dimensions of participants, offering access to available treatment programmes. This initiative also seeks to strengthen social ties with family or community leaders, who could assist in the reintegration processes (INR, 2021). Both initiatives are incipient and do not yet have processes or results evaluations.

Future Directions in Policy and Practice

Despite the relevance of the efforts made in the context of prison reform and their innovative nature within a traditional and discipline-based management model, existing treatment programmes have little coverage and exhibit weaknesses in terms of their evaluation. Briefly, there are at least five key obstacles to rehabilitation's development in Uruguay, namely, the notorious pre-eminence of the security paradigm in a system managed by the police; the conceptual weaknesses of the rehabilitation paradigm, reduced to prisoners' access to work and education; the lack of technicians and their limited skills in delivering the rehabilitation paradigm; weak data systems and the lack of an evaluation culture; and an insufficient and rigid budget structure that impedes the development of adequate classification processes and programmatic offerings.

In the short term, Uruguay should develop a rigorous political and technical dialogue on the meaning that will be given to rehabilitation and evidence-based programmes within the frame of criminal policy. In particular, the question arises as to whether there is room to think of alternative approaches to the traditional perspective, which tends to associate rehabilitation with education and work opportunities. Likewise, it is important to estimate a pertinent budget for the appropriate introduction of a rehabilitation model, which includes the quantity and quality of the human resources that can be developed to evaluate it, and the infrastructure, services, and materials for its implementation. Even today, the INR does not have a budget structure that discriminates spending for rehabilitation. Moreover, an essential condition for an efficient and effective public policy is for the INR to be capable of producing updated, traceable, and measurable information, based on rigorous sources. In addition, the rehabilitation policy requires a solid, updated, and ongoing training of staff in the rehabilitation paradigm. Furthermore, the recruitment of human resources to lead change and innovation; comprehensive management that transcends the custodial dimension; and evidence-based decision-making are all needed.

The promotion of rehabilitation in Uruguay has been supported by diverse international cooperation agencies. However, experience indicates the extremely low level of sustainability of these projects once the cooperation ends. The importation of prison policies is also related to the inadequacy of instruments and programmes designed in other countries, which are applied without adaptation and validation related to local needs and possibilities. At the same level, there is too little national capacity to build the demand for cooperation in this area through policy planning. The absence of a penitentiary policy—oriented to rehabilitation, sustainable in the medium and long term, which allows the rationalisation of available resources, develops measurable actions on transparent and reliable information bases, and ensures the participation of practitioners and experts within an adequate institutional structure—is a relevant fact after the proven and historic crises of the system (Juanche & Palummo, 2012).

On a more specific level, the few evaluations conducted on the implemented programmes indicate that, also in the short term, the prison system should undertake sparingly the planning, implementation, and evaluation of rehabilitation programmes, as well as carefully selecting and training the staff that will implement them. This training includes the theoretical-methodological features of the RNR model itself, as well as cognitive-behavioural therapies. In addition, it also needs to develop clear and applicable logical models, which have specific and validated measurable indicators, as well as developing national evaluation scales or validating and adapting others with proven results for Uruguay. Finally, the prison system needs to develop more assertive and proactive communication policies capable of disseminating its work and achievements (Trajtenberg & Sánchez de Ribera, 2019).

In sum, rehabilitation policies in Uruguay show an incipient development and an uncertain future. In the context of a public opinion that mostly calls for increasing the punitive dimension of prison, more efforts are required to develop a more humane and evidence-based approach in this area.

Notes

1. According to World Prison Brief: https://www.prisonstudies.org/.
2. According to Parliamentary Commissioner data (2021).
3. According to Parliamentary Commissioner data (2021).
4. According to Parliamentary Commissioner data: https://parlamento.gub.uy/cpp.
5. According to Parliamentary Commissioner data (2021).
6. According to National of Civil Service Office (2019).
7. Through Law No. 19,924 of National Budget 2020–2024.

References

Andrews, D., & Bonta, J. (2007). Risk-need-responsivity model for offender assessment and rehabilitation. *Rehabilitation, 6*, 1–22.

Ávila, F. (2018). *Gobernar responsabilizando. El caso de la cárcel de Punta de Rieles en Uruguay.* Tesis de Maestría en Criminología. Universidad Nacional del Litoral,

Facultad de Ciencias Jurídicas y Sociales. Recuperado de: http://hdl.handle.net/11185/1176 [04/01/2022].

Carranza, E. (2012). *Situación penitenciaria en América Latina y el Caribe ¿Qué hacer?. En U. d. Chile, Anuario de Derechos Humanos 2012* (págs. 31–66). Centro de Derechos Humanos. Facultad de Derecho. https://doi.org/10.5354/0718-2279.2012.20551

Castelli, L., Rossal, M., Keuroglian, L., Ramírez, J., & Suárez, H. (Coords.) (2019). Desarmando tramas: Dos estudios sobre consumo de drogas y delito en población privada de libertad: Aproximaciones cuantitativas y etnográficas. Montevideo: Facultad de Humanidades y Ciencias de la Educación de la Universidad de la República y Junta Nacional de Drogas - Secretaría Nacional de Drogas.

Comisionado Parlamentario para el Sistema Penitenciario. (2020). *Comisionado propone normas para fortalecer al INR y al Plan de Dignidad Carcelaria. Parlamento del Uruguay*. Recuperado de: https://parlamento.gub.uy/cpp/actividades/noticias/93257 [03/30/22].

Comisionado Parlamentario para el Sistema Penitenciario. (2021). *Informe Anual 2020. Situación del sistema carcelario y de medidas alternativas*. Parlamento del Uruguay.

De Ávila, F. (2016). *Evaluación del teatro con máscaras como dispositivo grupal de tratamiento de adolescentes con consumo problemático de drogas privados de libertad*. Tesis de Maestría en Psicología Clínica. Facultad de Psicología de la UdelaR.

De Ávila, F. (2021). La evolución del tratamiento penitenciario en Uruguay. *Revista Fermentario*, Vol. 15, Nro. 2. Facultad de Humanidades y Ciencias de la Educación de la UdelaR y Facultad de Educación de la UNICAMP.

De Ávila Machado, F. (2016). Programa de regulación emocional y resignificación de historias de vida a través del Teatro con Máscaras. Montevideo: Subdirección Nacional Técnica del Instituto Nacional de Rehabilitación.

Derogatis, L. R. (2004). SCL-90-R. Lista de Síntomas-90-(Revisada). USA: NCS Pearson, Inc.

Gendarmería de Chile & Fundación Paz Ciudadana. (2011). *Offender Assessment System Protocol*. Santiago de Chile.

Garrido, V., & Beneyto, M. J. (1996). El control de la agresión sexual. Un programa de tratamiento para delincuentes sexuales en prisión y en la comunidad. Cristóbal Serrano Villalba.

González, V., Rojido, E., & Trajtenberg, N. (2015). Sistema penitenciario en Uruguay (1985–2014): cambios, continuidades y desafíos. En G. Bardazano, A. Corti, N. Duffau, & N. Trajtenberg, *Discutir la cárcel, pensar la sociedad. Contra el sentido común punitivo* (págs. 127–164). Trilce. CSIC.

Gual, R. (2016). La muerte bajo custodia penal como objeto de investigación social: una perspectiva regional. *Revista eletrônica da Faculdade de Direito da Universidade Federal de Pelotas*.

Hervás, G. & Jódar, R. (2008). The spanish version of the Difficulties in Emotion Regulation Scale. Madrid: Clínica y Salud *19*(2), 139–156.

Instituto Nacional de Rehabilitación. (2021). *Programa de preegreso*. Subdirección Nacional Técnica.

Juanche, A. (2018). *La perspectiva técnica en la privación de libertad. Breve reseña*. Subdirección Nacional Técnica, Instituto Nacional de Rehabilitación.

Juanche, A., & Palummo, J. (2012). *Hacia una política de Estado en Privación de Libertad. Diálogo, recomendaciones y propuestas*. SERPAJ y OSJ.

Juanche, A. (2022). Mapeo sobre medidas alternativas a la prisión en Uruguay: Situación, desafíos y recomendaciones para su fortalecimiento. Informe final. Montevideo: PNUD, OACNUDH & Comisionado Parlamentario para el Sistema Penitenciario.

Lacaño, P. (2021). Identidad de género y privación de libertad. La realidad uruguaya. *En: Revista Fermentario, 15*(1), 197–207. Facultad de Humanidades y Ciencias de la Educación de la UdelaR y Facultad de Educación de la UNICAMP.

Martínez, M., Hilterman, E., & Andrés-Pueyo, A. (2005). *SVR-20 Manual de Valoración del Riesgo de Violencia Sexual*. Publicaciones Universitat de Barcelona.

Martínez-Catena, A. & Redondo, S. (2016). *Escala de Evaluación Psicológica de Agresores Sexuales (EPAS-3)*. Universidad de Barcelona.

Najson, S. (2008). *Validación del Symptom Cheklist-90-R para la población uruguaya*. Documento inédito. Montevideo: Universidad de la República.

Parliamentary Commissioner. (2020). Comisionado propone normas para fortalecer al INR y al Plan de Dignidad Carcelaria. Parlamento del Uruguay. Recuperado de: https://parlamento.gub.uy/cpp/actividades/noticias/93257 [03/30/22].

Parliamentary Commissioner. (2021). Informe Anual 2020. Situación del sistema carcelario y de medidas alternativas. Montevideo: Parlamento del Uruguay.

Pucci, F., Rojido, E., Trajtenberg, N., & Vigna, A. (2012). Explicaciones de la no reincidencia delictiva. En R. Paternain, & Á. Rico, Uruguay. Inseguridad, delito y Estado (págs. 243–259). Trilce-CSIC/UdelaR.

Rivera González, G., Romero Quintana, Mª; Labrador Muñoz, M., & Serrano Sáiz, S. (2006). *El control de la agresión sexual: Programa de intervención en el medio penitenciario*. Ministerio del Interior, Dirección General de Instituciones Penitenciarias; Madrid.

Rojido, E., Vigna, A., & Trajtenberg, N. (2014). Problemas de integridad en los programas de tratamiento: el caso del Centro Nacional de Rehabilitación. *En Revista De Ciencias Sociales, DS-FCS, 27*(34), 11–33.

Ross, R., & Fabiano, E. (1985). *Time to think. A cognitive model of delinquency prevention and offender rehabilitation*. Institute of Social Science and Arts.

Ross, R., Fabiano, E., Garrido, V., & Gómez, A. (1994). El Pensamiento Prosocial: La práctica. Un modelo cognitivo para la prevención y el tratamiento de la delincuencia. Madrid: MEPSA.

Rossi, G., González - Kelis, L., González - Almaraz, A., Failache, F., Olivera, G., & Pascale, A. (2011). *Abordaje del uso problemático de drogas en mujeres privadas de libertad: Un modelo posible*. Montevideo: ONU Mujeres & Secretaría Nacional de Drogas.

Sosa Barón, S. (2020). Desafíos de la implementación del OASys en el Uruguay. Trabajo final para la conclusión del Diploma en Políticas Públicas en Crimen e Inseguridad. Facultad de Ciencias Sociales, Universidad de la República.

Spielberger, C.D., MIguel-Tobal, J.J., Casado, M. I, Cano-Vindel, A. (2009). Manual Inventario expresión de ira estado - rasgo. Madrid: TEA Ediciones.

Trajtenberg, N., & Sánchez de Ribera, O. (2019). *Programa de Control de la Agresión Sexual (PCAS): evaluación de proceso y resultados clínicos en Unidad 4 Santiago Vázquez (COMCAR)*. Consejo Superior de Investigaciones Científicas y Facultad de Ciencias Sociales de la UdelaR, Instituto Nacional de Rehabilitación.

Trujillo, H., Dabezies, G., & Daguerre, J. (2013). *Informe de la evaluación de Diseño, Implementación y Desempeño OSLA*. AGEV-OPP.

UdelaR. (2015). Primer Censo Nacional de Funcionarios Penitenciarios. Montevideo: Departamento de Sociología de la Facultad de Ciencias Sociales, Fondo María Viñas de la Agencia Nacional de Investigación e Innovación & Instituto Nacional de Rehabilitación del Ministerio del Interior.

UNODC. (2019). *Estudio mundial sobre el homicidio. Resumen ejecutivo*. Organización de las Naciones Unidas contra las Drogas y el Delito.

Vigna, A. (2020). *Funcionarios penitenciarios y ejercicio del poder: rol ocupacional en un modelo en transición*. University of the Republic, School of Social Sciences. PhD Dissertation.

Vigna, A. (2022). *Informe final consultoría 'Maternidad, cárceles y medidas alternativas a la privación de libertad'*. ACNUDH-OCP.

Yagüe-Olmos, C., Caballero-Molano, P., Cabeza-Moreno, D., Joly-Barjola, V., López-Doriga, B., Marbán-Rey, P., Martín-Alvarado, S., Martínez-Benlloch, I., Melis-Pont, F., Narváez-Vega, M. D., Pozuelo-Rubio, F., Ruiz-Alvarado, A., Sánchez-Migallón Suárez, E., Yuste-Barrasa, M., del Val-Cid, C., & Videma-Rojas, A. (2015). *Documentos penitenciarios 9. Programa de prevención de la violencia de género para las mujeres en centros penitenciarios. Manual para Profesionales*. Ministerio del Interior, Secretaría General de Instituciones Penitenciarias, España.

Reentry and Reintegration in Virginia, U.S.

Danielle S. Rudes, Benjamin J. Mackey, and Madeline McPherson

Virginia is a midsize state located in the South Atlantic United States. Approximately 8.6 million people reside in Virginia, where regional differences are reflected in socioeconomic status, topography, and industry. Northern Virginia boasts some of the wealthiest counties in the nation while Western Virginia[1] sees some of the poorest. Demographically, the Hampton Roads region in the east is racially/ethnically majority minority, while in rural, mostly White pockets of Virginia, it is still common to see Confederate flags and other symbols of the antebellum South. These stark regional differences lead Virginia to be a politically diverse swing state. Justice reform

---

D. S. Rudes (✉)
Department of Criminal Justice and Criminology, Sam Houston State University, Huntsville, TX, USA
e-mail: drudes@shsu.edu

D. S. Rudes · B. J. Mackey
Center for Advancing Correctional Excellence (ACE!) within the Schar School of Policy and Government, George Mason University, Fairfax, VA, USA
e-mail: bmackey2@gmu.edu

M. McPherson
Department of Criminology, Law and Society, George Mason University, Fairfax, VA, USA
e-mail: mmcpher@gmu.edu

© The Author(s), under exclusive license to Springer Nature Switzerland AG 2022
M. Vanstone and P. Priestley (eds.), *The Palgrave Handbook of Global Rehabilitation in Criminal Justice*, https://doi.org/10.1007/978-3-031-14375-5_38

has been a bipartisan focus for Virginia's recent governors, often reflecting in the state's policy priorities. In this chapter, we focus on one state priority driving Virginia's public safety bottom line: maintaining the lowest recidivism rate of any state in the U.S. In doing so, we analyze and interpret Virginia's reported recidivism rate and extrapolate it towards a broader conversation about reentry and reintegration in Virginia.

For a number of years, the Virginia Department of Corrections (VADOC) and the Governor's Office have claimed the lowest recidivism rate in the country—23.9%—among the 42 states that report similar measures (VADOC, 2021a, 2022a). In comparison, the national rate is 62%[2] (Durose & Antenangeli, 2021). Curiously, this incredible feat is not well known outside of Virginia. Our investigation seeks to understand how Virginia seems to have cracked the prisoner reentry code and successfully combatted recidivism. First, we examine Virginia's definition of recidivism, shedding light on how it is calculated and reported. Second, we analyze VADOC, local jail, and community-level prisoner reentry services and offer a brief comparison to other states where recidivism rates hover closer to the national average. Third, we discuss the potential impacts of Virginia's reported recidivism rate by comparing its reentry system to other more holistic approaches, including those abroad. Drawing upon innovative frameworks for desistance and reintegration, we conclude by offering recommendations to Virginia and other jurisdictions for reporting recidivism and other criminal legal measures with care and integrity. Highlights of our investigation suggest that organizational transparency supports desistance and meaningful reintegration of formerly incarcerated people.

Recidivism in Virginia at a Glance

We focus our attention on those who are under state jurisdiction, individuals labelled by the VADOC as experiencing 'state responsible' (SR) incarceration. SR incarceration affects anyone 'with a felony conviction with a sentence of one year or more or a parole violation with a sentence of two years or more' (VADOC, 2021b). VADOC operates 26 state prisons and 43 regional probation and parole offices, bridging the reentry gap by overseeing individuals from incarceration to the community. The Virginia state legislature abolished discretionary parole in 1995 and replaced it with a truth-in-sentencing law that requires individuals to serve a statutorily provided length of their sentence before being eligible for release[3] (Virginia Code § 19.2–308.1). As such, only approximately 2000 individuals are on parole supervision at any given time (Rosen, 2021; VADOC, 2022c). Individuals who are released from prison before their 'max out' date—or the date by which they will have served their full sentence—are subsequently supervised on probation. While the rate of prison and jail incarceration in Virginia once represented two parallel lines, the shift from discretionary parole to truth-in-sentencing has translated to state residents serving longer terms, thus steadily increasing the state prison population over time relative to jail populations (PPI, 2022).

The VADOC regularly publishes a cache of recidivism reports, which include measures of re-arrest, re-incarceration, and re-conviction at various time points for different segments of the correctional population (VADOC, 2022b). Notably, however, the 23.9% recidivism rate that is often featured and publicized has one very specific definition: only reconvictions that result in an SR individual being returned to state prison are counted. Put another way, the VADOC and Governor's Office report that only 23.9% of SR individuals are returned to state prison on a new conviction within three years of release. While this rate does provide information, it is so narrowly defined that it ignores much of common re-entry experience, such as being rearrested or spending time in jail on a technical violation of probation or parole.

While many signs seem to point to Virginia doing something right to amass such a low recidivism rate, a critical look deeper into these numbers suggests that the story is complex and a lot more nuanced than just believing low recidivism rates mean things are working well in the state. In fact, two major findings regarding Virginia's correctional system (pre- and post- release) point to systemic challenges that both require attention and thoughtful/intentional reform. First, while Virginia boasts low rates of recidivism, the carceral population still remains relatively high within its prisons and jails. Data from the Bureau of Justice Statistics in 2019 (the most recent federal report at this writing) shows Virginia has 125,200 individuals under correctional supervision, with roughly 57,700 held within prison or local jails (46% of the total correctional population in that state) (Minton et al., 2021). With this incarceration rate, only three other reporting states (Oklahoma, Texas, and Wyoming) had a higher rate per capita, and only one state (South Dakota) was equal to Virginia with 860 incarcerated individuals per 100,000. Second, although Virginia boasts several important programs and initiatives geared to assist individuals in-custody and/or post-custody with reentry, many of these programs do not have an evidence-base and most do not address key underlying issues plaguing Virginia in a way that is likely to garner long-lasting impacts on individuals, families, and communities. Instead, Virginia's programs mostly address easier-to-solve problems such as employment and training, but they provide scant attention to more complex concerns such as physical and behavioural health issues, social stigma/alienation, and enhancing individuals' strengths so as to empower them socially and economically. Virginia, like many other states and jurisdictions, partners with other state/county agencies to address these more serious needs but does little through the correctional system to assist people with these daunting, and often co-occurring, challenges.

Virginia's High Rates of Custodial Supervision

Of course, the number of individuals incarcerated is not the only factor affecting recidivism rates, but more people in the system has the potential to increase the number of people who recidivate, if and when they are released from custody. The American Civil Liberties Union (ACLU) notes that with over 120,000 individuals under correctional supervision, Virginia was the 11th largest correctional system in the U.S. in 2018. To contextualize this number, the ACLU links Virginia's high correctional numbers to longer sentence lengths due to legal enhancements that lead to mandatory minimum sentences for individuals with a prior conviction history. In fact, the ACLU (2018) report notes, '...people in Virginia prisons are there for longer amounts of time, with the average length of imprisonment of people released from prison each year increasing by 24 per cent between 2000 and 2015' (p. 5). It also notes 'In 2016, 27 percent of people recommended for probation were sentenced to jail or prison instead' (p. 5). This information sharpens the focus on Virginia's reported low recidivism rate by suggesting that this rate may have origins in how people are sentenced, how often they go into custodial settings, and how long they stay within them. That is, fewer people supervised in the community necessarily equates to fewer people able to recidivate. But that is only part of the larger story. Virginia also has a robust community corrections system currently supervising roughly 67,400 people. Virginia claims a low recidivism rate among these folks and gives large credit to custodial and community programming for the state's success in this area.

Virginia's Custodial Programming and Practices

Like most U.S. states, Virginia offers a litany of correctional programming and practices. Within prisons, the VADOC boasts over 125 programs and classes focusing on education, skill development, and/or cognitive concerns. Several of these programs are offered by Virginia Correctional Enterprises

(VCE) and the Department of Correctional Education (DCE). Available programs include four educational, 107 cognitive, and 36 skill development ($n = 147$) offerings. Only 8% of cognitive programs focus on developing skills and education around substance use ($n = 13$). Yet according to the non-profit Opportunities, Alternatives, and Resources (OAR), nearly 80% of individuals incarcerated in Virginia have a substance use disorder or challenge. Additionally, although VADOC's website lists all programs separately, many of these are copies or subunits of other courses, meaning they are counted twice in Virginia's tally of available programs. Accounting for duplication, Virginia likely offers far fewer programs than reported.

Methods for Assessing VADOC Programs

When comparing VADOC's programming against the existing evidence-base, Virginia offers no classes/programs considered to be 'What Works' by the U.S. clearinghouse for evidence-based practice (EPB) information, Crimesolutions.gov. This platform works with consultant groups to assign leading researchers and scientists to review (using an approved and rigorous scoring instrument) existing empirical studies (that already meet criteria for sound science) to establish if a program or practice yields outcome evidence that is either 'effective,' 'promising,' or 'not effective.' We then searched for studies of existing programs and/or similar programs offered by the VADOC to determine if/how these carceral programs were based in any existing evidence. While there are elements of evidence-based treatments and programs—such as a focus on the risk-need-responsivity (RNR) framework as a practice—and there are many courses that claim to use a cognitive behavioural therapy (CBT) base, the evidence-base for many of the programs/courses is limited or even non-existent.

We chose Crime Solutions because of the stringent evaluation standards used.[4] All ranked programs and practice reviews must meet rigorous study guidelines that include high standards for methods, data, and outcome measurement. Most reviewed studies have a randomized-controlled trial (RCT), experimental, or quasi-experimental research design and must have appropriate group sizing; use appropriate statistical analysis; and, in some cases, must also have appropriate statistical adjustment. Crime Solutions' scoring categories focus on program implementation, issues with internal validity, and appropriate weighting of outcomes. Practice reviews only consider rigorous meta-analytic designs. When multiple studies exist for a given program/practice, Crime Solutions notes the strength of the reviews as higher, due to additional study/information. Although there are numerous studies of programs and practices in the scholarly literature, we only used Crime Solutions because of its comparability across programs and practices and its intensely rigorous review process (although not perfect, it is legitimate and acceptable).

In the Corrections and Reentry section of the Crime Solutions website, there are only six programs and two practices rated 'effective' with adult populations. The programs include: one in-custody, *Enhanced Thinking Skills* (England); one pre-incarceration program, the *Maryland Ignition Interlock Program*; one during- and post-incarceration program, *The Allegheny County Jail-Based Reentry Specialist Program* (Pennsylvania); one pre-, during-, and post-incarceration program, the *Mentally Ill Offender Community Transition Program* (Washington state); and two post-incarceration programs, *Reduced Probation Caseload in Evidence-Based Settings* (Iowa, Oklahoma). The practices rated as 'effective' include two that occur pre-, during, and post-incarceration: *Methadone Maintenance Therapy* and *Motivational Interviewing for Substance Abuse*. There are also 19 practices rated as 'promising' in the Corrections and Reentry realm including: one adult drug court, two CBT programs, two work/vocational programs, two educational programs, and a host of other programs addressing women, people convicted of sex offences, and violence. Additionally, there are 14 programs listed as 'alternatives to incarceration' that are rated as 'promising.' These include three electronic monitoring programs, two programs that place individuals in halfway houses, two day-reporting centre programs, two probation/parole programs, three drug treatment programs, and one motivational boot camp program.

There are several other categories within Crime Solutions that offer reviews of programs/practices related to corrections and reentry. While other groupings on Crime Solutions are program reviews related to correctional populations, some do not directly apply, as the population of study is non-correctional or youth. Within other sections, there are currently 12 'effective' programs and 88 'promising' programs for use with adults involved with the criminal legal system. These programs range from problem-solving courts to substance use treatment to sexual assault therapy programs.

Available Virginia Carceral Programs and Their Evidence-Base

Within its state-run prisons, Virginia offers *Thinking for a Change*, which was scored as 'promising' on Crime Solutions. This course likely contains some elements of an evidence-based program offered in England called *Thinking Skills*, but without research any comparison that supports the credibility of *Thinking for a Change* in Virginia correctional settings is just a guess. Moreover, Virginia offers several programs for family relationship-building and creating/maintaining interpersonal connections such as *Building Strong Relationships* and *Family Reunification*, but none of these programs are based in multi-family therapy (MRT), which is the only evidence-based carceral program for family therapy/programming. Finally, the VADOC offers an anger management course for adults incarcerated in 15 sites and anger management/aggression diversion courses for individuals within the secure diversionary treatment program (SDTP), but the only evidence supporting anger management programs is a specific anger management course for juveniles shown on Crime Solutions to work (Hoogsteder et al., 2015; Sukhodolsky et al., 2004). The VADOC classes are for adults and there is no information about if or how the format and content of these classes mirrors the evaluated juvenile anger management program.

Many VADOC courses note a CBT framework as their basis. However, the evidence presented on Crime Solutions suggests that CBT for adults assigned a medium to high-risk level is just 'promising' and has not yet reached the level of 'what works.' In their scoring, Crime Solutions notes, 'Aos and Drake (2013) aggregated the results from 21 studies to examine the impact of cognitive behavioural therapy (CBT) on crimes committed by moderate- and high-risk adults.' They found a significant effect size (-0.14) favouring the treatment group, meaning that moderate- and high-risk adults who received CBT were significantly less likely to commit crime compared with adults who did not receive CBT.[5] This finding suggests CBT has significant and positive effects, but the review stops short of calling CBT a practice that works.

The VADOC offers several programs that are akin to those ranked as 'no effect' on Crime Solutions, including all its' religious, life skills, and prison yoga programs,[6] and some of its reentry programs. Additionally, all the VADOC's substance use treatment programs are not evidence-based and do not use a curriculum rated 'effective' on Crime Solutions. Finally, as a component of evidence-based or sound programming, dosage/duration matters greatly; yet, of Virginia's programs, roughly 16 are self-paced, independent, and/or two classes or less. For example, the Alumni Aftercare Training course is just four days in duration, the Entrepreneur class and Making it on Supervision courses are both just one module, and the Re-Entry Money Smart class consists of a one-hour video only.

Local jails in Virginia vary widely in their size, scope, and available programs and practices. They are not under the jurisdiction of the VADOC. With 95 counties, 38 independent cities, and roughly 111 jails, to evaluate the available programs and classes—which change rapidly and often information about them is not shared with the public—we take one sample county in Northern Virginia to highlight the limited local offerings typically available and the gap between what is offered and what the evidence suggests works. Loudoun County projected a 2020 average of 476 jail residents housed per day. Individuals held at the Loudoun County Adult Detention Center (LCADC) present with a host of health and social challenges, as do people held in most U.S. jails. Although no specific information was publicly available for LCADC, approximately 62% of people experiencing jail incarceration nationally present with a dual-diagnosis substance disorder (behavioral health issue and substance use/abuse/addiction) (James & Glaze, 2017). Additionally, some prominent problems facing U.S. jail populations include past physical and/or sexual abuse, homelessness, and unstable personal life. Our gap analysis considers LCADC as roughly equivalent to other similarly situated U.S. jails in terms of needed programs/services.

With 19 community-based and operated in-jail programs, four contracted services (i.e., DMV Connect, Notary), and a fair number of jail residents attending programming of some kind during their stay, the LCADC is trying to deliver services for its population. However, only the courses in anger management, employability skills, and life skills, and one part of one program—Loudoun Inmate Focused Treatment (LIFT)'s Moral Reconation Therapy (MRT)—have any evidence-based studies of their effectiveness. The Crime Solutions' studies of anger management, employment programs, and life skills are 'promising' (although they differ in content and delivery from LCADC's offerings), and two of the three studies of MRT programs were rated 'no effect' by Crime Solutions. Of the programs offered by LCADC, there is no information available about outcomes nor implementation/program fidelity via rigorous scientific study. The other LCADC programs are unsupported by current empirical/scientific evidence. None of the LCADC programs are (or largely resemble) any of the evidence-based carceral programs/practices rated on Crime Solutions. However, some may resemble 'promising' practices, (for example, LCADC runs several substance use treatment programs that resemble others rated 'promising' by Crime Solutions), but without studies supporting specific programs implemented at LCADC, it is unclear if they are effective and/or evidence-based.

The LCADC also offers several programs that are akin to those ranked as 'no effect' on Crime Solutions, including all its' religious, life skills, prison yoga, and transitional assistance programs (TAP). Additionally, all the LCADC's substance use treatment programs are not evidence-based and do not use a curriculum rated 'effective' on Crime Solutions.

Community Corrections: once released, individuals in Virginia often receive referrals to attend programs and classes in community settings. These are mostly through community-based non-profit organizations, but also come from churches and civic groups and even the probation/parole office. With 95 counties in Virginia, it is difficult to get an accurate picture of the available services, classes, and programs in each jurisdiction. It is, however, safe to say that they vary widely in both availability and quality. To illustrate, we again use Loudoun County, Virginia. In a community of just over 413,000 individuals with over 522 square miles, Loudoun County is the richest county in the U.S. by a wide margin, with an income after cost-of-living adjustment at 12.3% above the national average. Loudoun County's median household income in 2019 was $142,299. The county is somewhat diverse. Housing is expensive, with the median value of owner-occupied housing $508,100 and the median gross rent at $1870 per month. Approximately 93.9% of Loudoun County adults have a high school education, with 61.3% also possessing a bachelor's degree or higher. Only around 6.1% of county residents under age 65 do not have health insurance, and only 3.1% of county residents live in poverty. Loudoun County also boasts a hearty employment sector, with only a 3.3% unemployment rate (as of July 2021)—it is the lowest unemployment rate in all nearby counties in Virginia, Maryland, and Washington, D.C. The Loudoun County Sherriff's Office's Criminal Investigation Division reported the 2019 crime rates as 1%, scoring Loudoun County an A+ grade for crime, with 99% of U.S. counties considered more dangerous.

Despite the favourable statistics for crime, employment, health insurance, and income, Loudoun County does have some challenges. Although Loudoun County is a relatively healthy county with a higher-than-average life expectancy of 82 years, 'drug overdose is the leading cause of injury death among people 25 to 65 causing more deaths than motor vehicle traffic crashes…Loudoun County is affected by the opioid crisis…; its mortality rate from drug overdoses has more than doubled in the last decade, to 7 deaths per 100,000 citizens' (RPCC, 2015). In its annual report, the Regional Primary Care Coalition (RPCC) notes health, income, and educational disparities between white and non-white Loudoun County residents and that health services in the western region of the county are far fewer than in the eastern sections. For residents living in the western areas of the county, many may have to travel more than 20 miles to reach a healthcare provider.

According to OAR records, from July 1, 2020, through June 30, 2021, 25% of their clients met at least 50% of the 2018 Federal Poverty Income Guidelines, indicating that about a quarter of the clientele was income restricted and only 3% were employed full-time at OAR intake. For these clients, OAR provided 120% with emergency assistance including rent/mortgage assistance, 53% with food assistance, 45% with clothing assistance, 32% with transportation assistance, 20% with mental health assistance, and 20% with utility assistance.

There is a litany of programs and services within Loudoun County to specifically support individuals involved in the criminal legal system both pre- and post-incarceration or during diversion. In addition to the county's offerings (mostly via non-profits)—which include emergency services (funds, transportation, clothing, referrals), case management, employment services, violence intervention programming, and family support services and groups—the county services include roughly 18 mental health programs/services, 14 educational services, 13 food service providers, 10 housing assistance programs, six substance use treatment programs, four clothing providers, three employment services/training programs, one mentoring program, one transportation service, and one legal service specifically offering services to individuals involved in the criminal legal system. Additionally, there are several programs/practices within Loudoun County that may also serve the legal system-involved population but are not specifically targeted to this group. It is unclear from existing data if many/most of these programs/services use a CBT framework, which would give them evidence in support of their program and/or if they are using any other evidence-based approaches or practices. None, however, are specifically consistent with the effective EBPs evaluated within Crime Solutions.

There are several Loudoun County programs that may have some similarities to EBPs ranked as 'effective' within Crime Solutions. For example, within the area of mental health services, and specifically CBT, Loudoun County has at least 18 organizations that tailor services to individuals involved in the legal system and that may be leveraged as providers for a diversion population. While three programs on Crime Solutions: Acceptance and Communication Therapy (ACT), Behavioral Couples Therapy for Substance Abuse, and Cognitive Process Therapy for Female Victims of Sexual Assault are all ranked as 'effective' programs (and thus are EBPs), Loudoun County does not have any of these programs. However, similar treatments and services may be found within Loudoun County's mental health and substance use treatment offerings.

Additionally, there are numerous pre-incarceration, post-incarceration, and pre-, during, and/or post-incarceration programs rated as 'promising' on Crime Solutions. Loudoun County's programs/practices resemble some of these 'promising' programs, though studies of the specific programs in Loudoun County do not yet exist, such as the Loudoun County Drug Court. Problem-solving courts, like drug courts, have some strong evidence supporting their positive outcomes; some received 'effective' ratings on Crime Solutions. There is ample evidence in the research literature suggesting drug courts may have positive effects on recidivism (see Marlowe, 2010). Additionally, while Crime Solutions currently rates several medication-assisted treatments (MAT) as 'effective,' the programs in Loudoun County do not list MAT as a provided service. While some of the other available community programs may follow a CBT framework, CBT generally is rated only 'promising' or 'no effect' depending on the program it frames and/or how it is used within a program/service. At present, Loudoun County appears to have ample mental health, food assistance, and housing programs for individuals involved in the criminal legal system.

Summary of Existing Carceral and Community Reentry Programs

The story in Virginia's prisons, jails, and community relating to reentry is, we suspect, similar to other states and jurisdictions within the U.S. in several key ways. Most—though not all—states pay some attention to their recidivism rate. In this regard, Virginia may be more vocal than most in touting their recidivism rate, despite its odd calculation. Without universal recidivism measurement formulas, it is difficult to know how Virginia stacks up against other states. It is also difficult to understand from Virginia's calculations exactly how many people recidivate. Next, Virginia, like other states, focuses on programming and classes as a way to frame their reentry efforts, but there is little to no evidence to support this causal claim. Virginia incarcerates many individuals, and, at least in prisons, they keep them longer than other states. This may lead to a lower recidivism rate as there are simply fewer individuals in the community able to recidivate. Then, Virginia also likely resembles other states and jurisdictions in the quality and availability of their custodial and reentry/community programming. Virginia appears to study its own programming outcomes beyond entries and exits, but it does not contract with researchers to rigorously study any programs or practices. Without this information, it is anyone's guess if what they are doing is working, for whom, how often, and how much. All we have is their word, and, in a day of modern science and data, that word is suspect at minimum. Irrespective of their internal evaluation practices, however, there may be fundamental flaws in the conceptualizations of desistance inherent to the reentry programs available in Virginia. Indeed, the focus on risk and recidivism incorporated in many of Virginia's reentry programs—as is common practice across the U.S.—is problematic in consideration of other, more holistic understandings of desistance and rehabilitation.

Understanding Desistance and Rehabilitation

As already indicated, several of VADOC's correctional programs employ models based upon the Risk-Need-Responsivity (RNR) model first conceptualized by Don Andrews and colleagues (1990). These frameworks focus on reducing recidivism by targeting individuals who, based on actuarial assessments of their 'risk/need' factors (i.e., factors such as poor school performance, lack of prosocial recreational activities, or 'criminal friends'), are determined to be at high risk of recidivism. While it has received substantial empirical support and is currently a dominant intervention model in the corrections field (Andrews & Bonta, 2010), critics of the RNR model fault it for a myopic focus on recidivism and risk which fails to consider more holistic measures of human functioning and strengths—those factors that protect, rather than predispose, an individual from recidivating (Ward & Gannon, 2006; Ward et al., 2007).

To resolve this potential flaw in the RNR model, several of its critics have advanced alternative models of treatment in community supervision. These models focus on and assess an individual's strengths to tailor treatment more carefully to their holistic life circumstances (Tate & Wasmund, 1999; Ward, 2002). These 'strength-based approaches' seek to improve an individual's life in ways that surpass (but also include) reductions in recidivism. While more research is needed, early evaluations of strength-based approaches have found them effective in reducing recidivism (e.g., Harkins et al., 2012; Mallion et al., 2020); this effect may be amplified when strength-based approaches are paired with some of the targeted intervention elements of the RNR model (Olver et al., 2020). Furthermore, in their consideration of factors beyond risk and recidivism, strength-based approaches have the potential to address strains more holistically—such as the inability to meet basic needs or feelings of alienation—which can push people towards reoffending (Agnew, 2006; Fisher et al., 2006).

While it is positive that some of VADOC's corrections programs follow evidence-based frameworks like the RNR model, the existence of competing, newer, and more holistic strength-based models suggest that more work is needed to bring these programs into alignment with the current state of EBPs. To accomplish this, it is important to consider frameworks of desistance and rehabilitation. Consideration and incorporation of frameworks into VADOC programming that align with strength-based principles may help lower the state's recidivism rate without artificial manipulation.

Alternate Frameworks of Desistance and Rehabilitation

Since Maruna's (2001) seminal work pinpointing identity realization and change as a key element of desistance, a great deal has been learned about the elements necessary to promote crime-free lifestyles. Drawing upon the work of Burchardt and colleagues (2002), Farrall et al. (2010) extend the focus of desistance frameworks further, arguing that desistance is incomplete without proper social and economic inclusion. Farrall and colleagues (2010) conceptualize inclusion across four dimensions: (1) consumption, or the ability to purchase goods and services; (2) production, or participation in activities that generate social or economic value; (3) political engagement at local and/or national levels; and (4) social interaction, which includes integration with family, friends, and the community at large. While Virginia has made strides in granting people returning from prison access to these forms of inclusion—for example, recent efforts by former Governor Northam and the General Assembly to restore the voting rights of people convicted of felonies (Brennan Center for Justice, 2021)—reentry programming in the state continues to focus primarily on production, with less attention to political engagement and social interaction.

As the dimensions of inclusion and desistance conceptualized by Farrall et al. (2010) are expansive, scholars have increasingly recognized a need for multiple forms of rehabilitation to achieve them. Burke and colleagues (2018) describe four distinct modes of rehabilitation, which, in conjunction, may socially incorporate the formerly incarcerated in ways promotive of Farrall et al.'s (2010) forms of inclusion. Specifically, Burke et al. (2018) discuss personal, legal, social, and moral rehabilitation. Personal rehabilitation refers to an individual's internal journey to change their cognitions, skillset, knowledge base, and other factors that impact the way they perceive and interact with the world around them. It is here that many correctional programs—including most of those offered in Virginia—stop. They seek simply to equip individuals with the knowledge and skills necessary to rehabilitate themselves personally, without addressing structural factors that may continue to disadvantage them regardless of the extent of their personal rehabilitation. Thus, extending beyond the realm of the personal, legal rehabilitation addresses the question of citizenship—that is, when and how an individual is formally reincorporated into society. Whereas legal rehabilitation refers to the formal recognition that an individual is reintegrated into society, social rehabilitation addresses the informal ways in which individuals are excluded (i.e., stigma) and, eventually, included by the communities they claim. Finally, moral rehabilitation addresses the interactions between individuals, those who provide rehabilitative services, and those who have been victimized. It represents an essential step in the transformation of an individual as it grants them the agency to repair harms and restore the community by their own choice.

Taken together, the four forms of rehabilitation specified by Burke and colleagues (2018) suggest a journey towards desistance that is not solely the responsibility of the formerly incarcerated individual, but of the many institutions and individuals present in their community. In this framework, rehabilitation takes a village. In Virginia, however, rehabilitative reentry services are the purview of a select few organizations. This is problematic as it makes it more difficult to incorporate disparate sectors of civil society into the rehabilitative process. Virginia may therefore benefit from expanding rehabilitative programming to follow a 'whole system' approach involving various community and legal system actors. Such an approach is practised in an international context in the form of reentry partnership initiatives (RPIs) (Byrne & Hummer, 2005). RPIs shift the responsibility for post-incarceration rehabilitation away from state actors, dispersing it more widely among the community. While such shifts of responsibility are problematic when the onus is placed solely on the community (Miller, 2014), RPIs emphasize a more equitable distribution, with state agents like parole and police officers partnering with community-based entities like treatment providers and victims to share ownership of the reentry process (Byrne & Hummer, 2005). Additionally, RPIs frequently incorporate a 'finish line' for formerly incarcerated individuals to reach—a point (such as seven to ten years in England) after which their criminal record is formally sealed (Petersilia, 2005).

In sum, these frameworks for desistance and rehabilitation offer alternate avenues to approach and structure the reentry process—avenues which have shown promise in an international context (Byrne & Hummer, 2005). These frameworks therefore provide insight into potential reforms for Virginia's practices in measuring and addressing recidivism.

Recommendations for Virginia

A first step towards best practices in measuring and addressing recidivism is to revise definitions of the term. A revised definition would focus on transparency and comprehensiveness, capturing re-arrest, re-conviction, and re-incarceration separately. It would also avoid arbitrary distinctions that serve primarily to make Virginia's recidivism rate look more favourable. For example, re-incarceration might refer to any type of return to confinement, including jail or prison. While agencies may have an interest in demonstrating success by reporting low recidivism numbers, comprehensive measures of recidivism help to illuminate operational shortcomings among public safety agencies and communicate these across branches of government. Furthermore, transparency from state authorities improves legitimacy and builds public trust, which ultimately improves services and strengthens communities (Kirk, 2016; Tyler, 2003, 2010).

Additionally, in keeping with the focus of strength-based approaches on more holistic measures of human functioning that extend beyond recidivism (Ward, 2002), Virginia's reentry services ought to address and publish various indicators of individual and community rehabilitation. These could include whether and how the basic needs of formerly incarcerated individuals are met, including housing and nutrition. They may also focus on access to behavioural health treatment, psychosocial programs, educational and vocational diplomas and certificates, and engagement in restitution programs with crime victims. It is also important to document broader measures of quality of life—such as indicators of general life satisfaction and prosocial relationships—which, when absent, could push individuals towards patterns of criminal behaviour (Agnew, 2006). At all phases, these measures should be selected and defined in partnership with individuals who have experienced incarceration and reentry.

Finally, given the importance of partnerships at multiple levels during the reentry process (Byrne & Hummer, 2005), Virginia may have much to learn from RPIs. Expanding the number and scope of organizations funded to provide reentry services, in addition to encouraging and fiscally supporting state agencies to participate in these partnerships, may move Virginia towards a whole system approach to reentry.

Conclusion

Despite Virginia's overly narrow recidivism definition, the state is well-situated to optimize its approach to recidivism, reentry, and reintegration. Virginia has a robust network of public safety agencies that conduct criminal legal research and evaluation, including the Virginia Sentencing Commission and VADOC's own Research-Evaluation Unit. Similarly, the Virginia General Assembly has remained active in introducing reform-oriented bills in recent years. Between 2020 and 2021, the legislature passed a package of evidence-based bills that reformed probation, by limiting terms of supervision (H.B. 2038); bail reform (H.B. 1936); legalized recreational marijuana (H.B. 2312/S.B. 1406); abolished the death penalty (H.B. 2263/S.B. 1165); reformed cash bail systems (H.B. 1936); and provided access to discretionary parole for a small contingent of individuals sentenced between 1995 and 2000 (before jury instructions included mention of parole abolition) (H.B. 33). Given this seemingly strong appetite within state agencies for evidence-based policy, we have reason to believe state officials may be willing to receive recommendations for improving recidivism reporting.

Beyond measuring reoffending, a strong commitment to other systems designed to terminally discharge individuals from legal system involvement may be instrumental in supporting holistic reintegration. Bipartisan gubernatorial administrations have shown a commitment to expanding clemency and expungement in Virginia—an effort that could assist in achieving parity between crime rates and rates of incarceration and supervision (Caplan, 2016; Colgate Love, 2022; Schneider & Vozzella, 2022). Other approaches like statewide reinvestment initiatives offer state and local public safety agencies financial incentives to reduce incarceration numbers, savings from which are reinvested in other public safety programs and services (Council for State Governments Justice Center, 2022). Should Virginia consider adopting a system-wide approach to reintegration—including rigorous evaluation and implementation of evidence-based programs from incarceration to community—the state may realize a low recidivism rate in a more genuine way.

Notes

1. Not to be confused with the state of West Virginia.
2. These rates measure recidivism in the three years following release from incarceration.
3. The requirement for time served varies from 25 to 75% depending on the number of prior commitments one has.

4. There are other sources to find evidence for EBPs including SAMSA's Evidence Based Practices center and numerous studies published as reports from BJA, NIJ, etc., and in academic journals. However, in using these sources, the reader is responsible for assessing the methods used to determine the evidence for themselves, without any standardized guidelines. In Crime Solutions, this work is previously done by five independent scholars for each study reviewed after advanced training and using accepted scoring instruments/tools.
5. https://crimesolutions.ojp.gov/ratedpractices/57#eb.
6. Prison yoga has only been assessed with youth populations on Crime Solutions.

References

ACLU. (2018). *Blueprint for smart justice: Virginia*. American Civil Liberties Union. https://50stateblueprint.aclu.org/assets/reports/SJ-Blueprint-VA.pdf

Agnew, R. (2006). *Pressured into crime: An overview of general strain theory*. Oxford University Press.

Andrews, D. A., & Bonta, J. (2010). *The psychology of criminal conduct* (4th ed.). Anderson.

Andrews, D. A., Bonta, J., & Hoge, R. D. (1990). Classification for effective rehabilitation: Rediscovering psychology. *Criminal Justice and Behavior, 17*(1), 19–52. https://doi.org/10.1177/0093854890017001004

Aos, S., & Drake, E. (2013). *Prison, police and programs: Evidence-based options that reduce crime and save money*. Washington State Institute for Public Policy.

Brennan Center for Justice. (2021). Voting rights restoration efforts in Virginia. Author. https://www.brennancenter.org/our-work/research-reports/voting-rights-restoration-efforts-virginia

Burchardt, T., Le Grand, J., & Piachaud, D. (2002). Degrees of exclusion: Developing a dynamic, multidimensional measure. In J. Hills, J. Le Grand, & D. Piachaud (Eds.), *Understanding Social Exclusion* (pp. 30–43). Oxford University Press.

Burke, L., Collett, S., & McNeill, F. (2018). *Reimagining rehabilitation: Beyond the individual*. Routledge.

Byrne, J. M., & Hummer, D. (2005). "Thinking globally, acting locally': Applying international trends to reentry partnerships in the United States. *International Journal of Comparative and Applied Criminal Justice, 29*(1), 79–96. https://doi.org/10.1080/01924036.2005.9678733

Caplan, L. (2016, May 2). Virginians with a felony conviction can now vote, but getting a job is no easier. *The New Yorker*. https://www.newyorker.com/news/news-desk/virginians-with-a-felony-conviction-can-now-vote-but-getting-a-job-is-no-easier

Council of State Governments Justice Center. (2022). Justice Reinvestment Initiative. https://csgjusticecenter.org/projects/justice-reinvestment/

Durose, M. R., & Antenangeli, L. (2021). Recidivism of prisoners released in 34 states in 2012: A 5-year follow-up period (2012–2017). Bureau of Justice Statistics.

Farrall, S., Bottoms, A., & Shapland, J. (2010). Social structures and desistance from crime. *European Journal of Criminology, 7*(6), 546–570. https://doi.org/10.1177/1477370810376574

Fisher, W. H., Silver, E., & Wolff, N. (2006). Beyond criminalization: Toward a criminologically informed framework for mental health policy and services research. *Administration and Policy in Mental Health, 33*(5), 544–557. https://doi.org/10.1007/s10488-006-0072-0

Harkins, L., Flak, V. E., Beech, A. R., & Woodhams, J. (2012). Evaluation of a community-based sex offender treatment program using a good lives model approach. *Sexual Abuse, 24*(6), 519–543. https://doi.org/10.1177/1079063211429469

Hoogsteder, L. M., Stams, G. J. J., Figge, M. A., Changoe, K., van Horn, J. E., Hendriksa, J., & Wissink, J. B. (2015). A meta-analysis of the effectiveness of individually oriented Cognitive Behavioral Treatment (CBT) for severe aggressive behavior in adolescents. *The Journal of Forensic Psychiatry and Psychology, 26*(1), 22–37. https://doi.org/10.1080/14789949.2014.971851

James, D. J., & Glaze, L. E. (2017). Drug use, dependence, and abuse among state prisoners and jail inmates, 2007–2009. *Bureau of Justice Statistics*. NCJ 250546.

Kirk, D. S. (2016). Prisoner reentry and the reproduction of legal cynicism. *Social Problems, 63*(2), 222–243. https://doi.org/10.1093/socpro/spw003

Loudoun County. (2019). FY 2019 comprehensive list of performance measures. https://www.loudoun.gov/DocumentCenter/View/131916/FY-2019-Comprehensive-List-of-Performance-Measures?bidId

Love, M. C. (2022). The many roads from reentry to reintegration: A national survey of laws restoring rights and opportunities after arrest or conviction. Collateral Consequences Resource Center.

Mallion, J. S., Wood, J. L., & Mallion, A. (2020). Systematic review of 'Good Lives' assumptions and interventions. *Aggression and Violent Behavior, 55*, 101510. https://doi.org/10.1016/j.avb.2020.101510

Marlowe, D. (2010). Research update on adult drug courts. National Association of Drug Court Professionals. https://www.huntsvillebar.org/Resources/Documents%20CLE/2013/adc_research_update.pdf

Maruna, S. (2001). Making good: How ex-convicts reform and rebuild their lives. American Psychological Association.

Miller, R. J. (2014). Devolving the carceral state: Race, prisoner reentry, and the micro-politics of urban poverty management. *Punishment and Society, 16*(3), 305–335. https://doi.org/10.1177/1462474514527487

Minton, T. D., Beatty, L. G., & Zeng, Z. (2021). Correctional populations in the United States, 2019. Bureau of Justice Statistics.

Olver, M. E., Marshall, L. E., Marshall, W. L., & Nicholaichuk, T. P. (2020). A long-term outcome assessment of the effects on subsequent reoffense rates of a prison-based CBT/RNR sex offender treatment program with strength-based elements. *Sexual Abuse, 32*(2), 127–153. https://doi.org/10.1177/1079063218807486

Petersilia, J. (2005). Hard time: Ex-offenders returning home after prison. *Corrections Today, 67*(2), 66–71.

PPI. (2022). Virginia profile. Prison Policy Initiative. https://www.prisonpolicy.org/profiles/VA.html#:~:text=Virginia%20has%20an%20incarceration%20rate,incarcerated%20in%20Virginia%20and%20why

Rosen, D. A. (2021). Hundreds of Virginia inmates await parole consideration under new law. *Prison Legal News.* https://www.prisonlegalnews.org/news/2021/apr/1/hundreds-virginia-inmates-await-parole-consideration-under-new-law/

RPCC. (2015). Loudon county. Regional Primary Care Coalition. http://www.regionalprimarycare.org/loudoun-county/

Schneider, G. S., & Vozzella, A. (2022). Northam issues pardons in flurry of actions before leaving office. *The Washington Post.* https://www.washingtonpost.com/dc-md-va/2022/01/14/northam-pardons-virginia-governor/

Sukhodolsky, D. G., Kassinove, H., & Gorman, B. S. (2004). Cognitive-Behavioral Therapy for anger in children and adolescents: A meta-analysis. *Aggression and Violent Behavior, 9*, 247–269. https://doi.org/10.1016/j.avb.2003.08.005

Tate, T., & Wasmund, W. (1999). Strength-based assessment and intervention. *Reclaiming Children and Youth, 8*(3), 174–180.

Tyler, T. R. (2003). Procedural justice, legitimacy, and the effective rule of law. *Crime and Justice, 30*, 283–357. https://doi.org/10.1086/652233

Tyler, T. R. (2010). Legitimacy in corrections: Policy implications. *Criminology and Public Policy, 9*(1), 127–134.

VADOC. (2021a). *Virginia's recidivism rate remains among the lowest in the country.* Virginia Department of Corrections. https://vadoc.virginia.gov/news-press-releases/2021/virginia-s-recidivism-rate-remains-among-the-lowest-in-the-country/

VADOC. (2021b, December). Recidivism at a glance: Releases from state responsible incarceration, Virginia Department of Corrections Research-Evaluation Unit report. https://vadoc.virginia.gov/media/1723/vadoc-state-recidivism-report-2021-12.pdf

VADOC. (2022a). *State recidivism comparison: Virginia's recidivism rate among the lowest in the country.* Virginia Department of Corrections. https://vadoc.virginia.gov/media/1728/vadoc-state-recidivism-report-2022-01.pdf

VADOC. (2022b). *Recidivism studies.* Virginia Department of Corrections. https://vadoc.virginia.gov/general-public/recidivism-studies/

VADOC. (2022c). *Monthly population summary.* Virginia Department of Corrections. https://vadoc.virginia.gov/media/1745/vadoc-monthly-offender-population-report-2022-02pdf.pdf

Ward, T. (2002). The management of risk and the design of Good Lives. *Australian Psychologist, 37*(3), 172–179. https://doi.org/10.1080/00050060210001706846

Ward, T., & Gannon, T. A. (2006). Rehabilitation, etiology, and self-regulation: The comprehensive good lives model of treatment for sexual offenders. *Aggression and Violent Behavior, 11*(1), 77–94. https://doi.org/10.1016/j.avb.2005.06.001

Ward, T., Melser, J., & Yates, P. M. (2007). Reconstructing the Risk–Need–Responsivity model: A theoretical elaboration and evaluation. *Aggression and Violent Behavior, 12*(2), 208–228. https://doi.org/10.1016/j.avb.2006.07.001

Retrospect: Looking Back—Looking Forward

Philip Priestley and Maurice Vanstone

Rehabilitation in criminal justice is almost always and nearly everywhere a journey; a voyage away from offending and all its vexatious consequences; and a pilgrimage towards a better future that features fewer offences—or even none. Some of those who embark on this transition fall by the wayside, and others, often by degrees, reach better places in their lives. Some people do not try to change at all and live out their lives as they choose or fate dictates on what is sometimes referred to as 'the wrong side of the law.' The commissioned chapters in this book record some of the efforts of some of those who are trying to change, and those who have changed, and those agencies and professionals trying to help them. In 'Prospect' at the head of this book we looked forward to a journey that is broadly conceived, geographically extensive, and critically focused on the facts and the issues that accompany efforts in many countries to rehabilitate those of their inhabitants who have committed offences and been sentenced to regimes of two distinct types—on the one hand punishment and on the other rehabilitation. There is a line

P. Priestley (✉)
Wells, UK
e-mail: interalika@gmail.com

M. Vanstone
Criminology, School of Law, Swansea University, Swansea, UK
e-mail: m.t.vanstone@swansea.ac.uk

to be drawn between these polar opposites along which societal responses to offending can be located. The chapters in the body of the book are written by scholars and practitioners working in the field of rehabilitation in criminal justice systems around the world, and their contributions gravitate naturally to the rehabilitative end of the scale. But any activity that takes place within the structures of criminal justice can do no other than embrace both ends of the spectrum. Probation may be smiled on by humanists and liberals as an alternative to prison *and* punishment but symbolically and in the lived experience of those who are subjected to it, it is neither.

With that in mind, what *is* rehabilitation and what is it good for? First off, whatever it is, it is not simple. 'Riddling notions of rehabilitation' insist Katharina Maier and Rosemary Ricciardelli (pp. 53–70). 'are inherently contradictory challenges tied to what one is rehabilitating to.' They enumerate other difficulties, including 'tensions between past and present selves, pressures to conform to normative expectations of what it means to be rehabilitated, and desires to desist and/or embrace various behavioural practices and ways of thinking about diverse aspects in life.' An alternative definition from Romania claims that 'rehabilitation can be facilitated *either* by the 'process' of control; i.e., implementing the requirements to report to the probation service, to receive visits from the probation officer assigned to their supervision, give information about residence or income, but *also* by attending intervention programmes, such as school or vocational courses, social reintegration programmes or other forms of treatment or care' (pp. 485–503).

Forms of Historical Rehabilitation in Criminal Justice

Before the increasingly convergent forms of law that typify contemporary global societies there existed a history, itself rooted in a pre-history beyond recall and memorialised only in myth, folk-lore, and legend, of how societies have responded to wrong-doing over time. 'Any reflection on rehabilitation in India necessarily begins with glance back to mythology' says Debarati Halder. 'The country has a rich history in Danda Niti (Penology) that is reflected in the epic Ramayana.' 'Other ancient scripts' she continues 'indicated that a person who offends, unless guilty and convicted of heinous crimes (including crimes against the State), has a right to undergo correctional services and be rehabilitated and reintegrated into society' (pp. 257–270).

Due south from India, across the ocean that bears its name, lies an equally ancient society; an island bounded by other seas; the Pacific, and the Southern. Over several millennia, due to its geographical position, its distance from outside cultural influences, its great size, and its small population; the 'undiscovered' continent of Australia evolved its own mores and mechanisms for dealing with social difference and deviant behaviour. First Nations people, never numerous, were further divided into smaller tribal communities and were no match for invaders from the industrialised, resource-hungry countries of Europe and elsewhere. As with indigenous populations world-wide, the cultural collision amounted to a catastrophe; decimation from previously unencountered illnesses; expulsion from traditional lands; exclusion from a technically sophisticated and socially specialised society; and other forms of discrimination amounting cumulatively to what has been called 'genocide' (Short, 2010). These experiences are nowhere more evident than in the criminal justice system. 'First Nations adults make up around 3% of the national population, but constitute 30% of those in prison, making them 14 times more likely to be in prison than those who are non-Indigenous' (pp. 33–51).

Approaches to rehabilitation in the adult penal system of neighbouring Aotearoa New Zealand, (where Māori represent 16.5% of the population) are overwhelmingly concerned with individual, personal rehabilitation demonstrated by the dominance of deficit-focused, cognitive-behavioural, and needs-based models of support. 'Culturally responsive' rehabilitation programmes,' Alice Mills and Robert Webb tell us, 'have simply grafted Māori culture and *tikanga* onto existing, individualistic approaches, rather than acknowledging and addressing the structural factors, including the ongoing legacies of colonisation, which are likely to lead to recidivism amongst Māori' (pp. 429–448).

Thailand is a third country in this collection where the past (reaching back to Europe's fourteenth century) remains in touch with the present, a continuity symbolised in this instance by an enduring monarchy and a rich architectural and cultural heritage. Historically 'the main purposes of punishment were believed to be:- to deliver retribution; to deter people from committing more crimes; and to incapacitate offenders either temporarily by sentencing them to a term in prison or jail, or permanently by execution or capital punishment.' Similar goals, 'of punishment, deterrence, incapacitation, and rehabilitation have existed up until the present day' say Nathee Chitsawang and Pimporn Netrabukkana (pp. 619–638). Before 'installing any rehabilitation measures, the most urgent priority' they aver 'is to reduce the number of people in prison.' This can be done 'by moving towards greater use of non-custodial measures; and focusing on back-end mechanisms, especially parole and royal pardon as well as 'good day' allowance schemes, to conditionally and unconditionally release people held behind bars'.

The Present State of Play

In our first chapter, Prospect, we proposed an agenda that consisted of 'positive change in individuals, reintegration into the community, and removal of criminal records, all three of which are associated with the restoration of citizenship.' We also listed McNeill's (2012) 'four forms of rehabilitation, namely, personal, judicial or legal, moral and social'. A critical reading of subsequent chapters indicated additional ways of slicing the criminological cake to produce seven major classes of rehabilitative work aimed at people currently in trouble with the law across the globe:-

1. Education, vocational training—distantly and deeply rooted in nineteenth-century penitentiary practice.
2. The psychosocial model—a relic of 'treatment' regimes based on psychoanalysis.
3. Canadian programmes devised by psychologists Don Andrews, Robert Ross, and others commonly and collectively referred to as RNR—Risk, Need and Responsivity;
4. Cognitive-behavioural therapy (CBT).
5. Evidence-based practice (EBP)—used in many remedial interventions besides corrections;
6. Restorative justice—which works with all the parties to an offence towards resolution; and
7. Desistance—an approach which focuses on the process of ceasing to commit offences.

No attempt will be made to quantify precisely the proportion of criminal justice systems portrayed in these pages which actually employ each or any or all of these options; or to what extent they do so, or how skilfully; but we can use the words of the contributors to illustrate and possibly illuminate the experiences that typify many of them. The accounts of seven nations refer to vocational training as part of their rehabilitative packages to ease transitions back into the community e.g., China, India, Kenya, Nigeria, Romania, Sweden, and Thailand. The presence in the list of the two of the world's most populous countries is no surprise, and six of the seven have endured colonial occupations in modern times. Economic development creates strong demands for skilled workforces to contribute to further growth in production and considerable resources are devoted to training them.

Sweden is a slightly unexpected member of this group using vocational training which has existed in 'modern' prisons since the middle-to-end of the nineteenth century. Historically it was an aggressive, imperialist state with its own Baltic empire (Laitinen, 2017) but with the loss of Finland to Russia in 1809 (Meinander, 2020) and the independence of Norway in 1905 (Lindgren, 2015), it assumed its present boundaries and became known for its neutralist foreign policy and progressively liberal domestic and criminal justice policies. In the present day it has featured strongly in the quest for innovative and 'science-based ways to effectively rehabilitate probationers and the formerly incarcerated (Nilsson, 2011).

The psycho-social model in social work and psychotherapy had its heyday in the Anglophone world of the years following WWII, and a recent resurgence of interest in its methods has ensured its persisting presence in the armoury of contemporary corrections (Blumenthal, 2010). There is however a dearth of evidence about the efficacy of these approaches with their target populations. By way of contrast the large-scale descriptive studies, before and after the war, of 'delinquent' US populations, both adult and juvenile, by Sheldon and Eleanor Glueck (1964), were marked by a sturdy empiricism. 'Evidence Based Practice' is more recent terminology applied in many spheres of current therapeutic endeavour but the concept is referred to in only three of the preceding chapters, France, Japan, and Virginia, in relation to finding ways to reduce re-offending.

Virginia also employs programmes 'based upon the Risk-Need-Responsivity (RNR) model first conceptualised by Don Andrews and colleagues (1990),' but the chapter authors Danielle Rudes, et al., add that while the model 'has received substantial empirical support' its critics fault it 'for a myopic focus on recidivism and risk' and for neglecting 'those factors that protect, rather than predispose, an individual from recidivating' (pp. 667–686). Besides Virginia, a further ten jurisdictions in this book use or have used the RNR approach; for Sweden, it 'serves as the primary guideline for interventions to reduce recidivism' (pp. 559–575). In England and Wales it 'reflects on the need to use more positive, non-labelling language' and is 'the prime mode of intervention, alongside the promotion of desistance (pp. 127–144).' For Chile, the 2007 launch of the RNR-derived 'Programme of Social Reintegration' represented a 'milestone' in the use of prison programmes based on criminological evidence (pp. 71–87). Latvia uses CBT interventions to shape 'the structure and content of supervision of probation clients' (pp. 339–357) and Macao found that 'implementing correctional rehabilitation programmes' in accordance with the model 'has been associated with a significantly greater decrease in recidivism rates' (pp. 359–375). Enshen Li, writing about mainland China, says that 'the key to the success of the RNR model is the authorities' ability to differentiate wrongdoers in terms of their criminal risks and criminogenic needs, based on evidence-informed techniques and instruments, and to subsequently assist them with becoming more prosocial after applying tailored correctional programmes (pp. 89–106).

In other places the future looks less bright. In their account of 'how the penal systems expanded enormously in personnel, budget and work allocation, and extensive prison construction programme' Klára Kerezsi and Judit Szabó show that Hungary's criminal policy has always been driven by social control rather than social welfare and that, therefore, the current punitivism is not new. 'Mass incarceration,' they conclude 'fits nicely into the forms of social control exercised through the intense use of state punitive power' (pp. 237–256). In Ghana poor prison conditions and overcrowding have undermined the citizen rights of prisoners. Rehabilitation in recent years has 'focused more on the impartation of physical skills and the provision of livelihood post-release at the expense of treatment programmes that target the behavioural, cognitive, and emotional transformation of incarcerated individuals' (pp. 201–218). In contrast, as Wing Hong Chui explains, the assumption that Hong Kong's return of sovereignty to China in July 1997 meant a move away from the rehabilitation ideal has proved erroneous as it has so far survived and remained popular in its criminal justice system.

Looking Forward

At the beginning of this book, we listed 'three models of rehabilitation' namely 'positive change in individuals, reintegration into the community, and removal of criminal records,' all of them 'associated with the restoration of citizenship.' How have the authors of the intervening chapters imagined what the future practice of rehabilitation in criminal justice might look like?

That future is a crowded landscape filled with ideas and schemes for easing the transition from probationer and prisoner status to that of the citizen. Access to vocational and academic qualifications for example opens doors to many other careers. 'Cooperatives' in Argentina 'represent an exciting and interesting means of dealing with this problem in so far as they increase the chances of individuals accessing a livelihood' (pp. 17–31). They 'also constitute a significant source' of 'personal development.' As do the 'peer support programmes coupled with existing interventions' which are 'utilized in Missouri across the criminal-legal system.' It is a model which Kelli Canada and Scott O'Kelley believe can 'increase the direct social support people with mental illnesses receive, provide assistance with navigating the system, and increase sustained connections to recovery supports when they risk criminal-legal involvement.' It is a fittingly intricate response to a knotty set of social issues. It mobilises the good-will, time, and effort put forth by people in local communities with the aim of 'reducing future contact with the criminal-legal system and enhancing overall quality of life' (pp. 395–412).

In this landscape another set of figures represent the agencies, and their agents, who assist individuals in search of rehabilitation as they make their way across often hostile terrain, towards places of safety and social re-integration. In some countries the police fulfil some of these functions, sometimes with success, and sometimes not; the Gendarmeria in Chile 'is a military force with law enforcement duties among the civilian population,' which include running prisons, the post-penitentiary system, and supervising 'people who are serving community sentences.' (pp. 71–87). Spain, like some of the other nations in this book, has had a turbulent social and political history; much of its social legislation and criminal law 'starts with the advent of the current democratic regime after the end of the Francoist dictatorship' (pp. 541–558). 'The term 'rehabilitation' in the title of this volume' says Ester Blay 'is relatively foreign to Spanish penological discourse' which it tends to avoid, in favour of words like 're-education' and 'social reintegration.' 'This autochthonous nomenclature,' she explains 'reflects the existence of a long-standing local concern for the change and wellbeing of prisoners' (pp. 541–558). But although this reflects 'a strong humanistic trend in Spanish penitentiary tradition' it is one that runs 'parallel to a reality marked by harsh prison conditions, scarcity of means, and a critique of practices' (pp. 541–558). 'In practice' she concludes, 'observers have noted that treatment turns into a disciplinary mechanism that ensures orderly living conditions in prison.' It is a compelling illustration of Mathiesen's much quoted 'techniques of neutralisation' which institutions use to protect themselves against unwanted change (Mathiesen, 1965). To Ester Blay, it seems that 'within limits that have to do with the penal landscape of Spain—non-rehabilitative and relatively under-resourced—punishment in the community is overwhelmingly more promising than prison with regards to rehabilitation' (pp. 541–558).

Referring to France's President Macron, recently re-elected in 2022, Martine Herzog-Evans reports that 'in view of what he promised during his campaign ... one can expect more authoritarian, executive dominance ... and more zero tolerance.' As a counterweight to this gloomy view, the national justice sytem has 'hands-on desistance-friendly JAP (Juges de l'Application des Peines)... and an active minority of prosecutors who carry the baton of rehabilitation' who 'have been able to create an oasis in the desert.' But sadly, she laments, they 'represent an exception to the rule' (pp. 161–180). Her refrain is echoed elsewhere. Liz Gilchrist believes that the 'discourse of rehabilitation is prompting Scotland to consider approaches to punishment that are more meaningful, efficient, and effective.' In particular she endorses 'adopting an intersectional approach, which links social deprivation, and structural disadvantage with individual criminogenic risk and human need,' which in turn 'could cast light on how and where particular inequalities intersect: to better understand the experiences of particular people or groups' (pp. 505–524).

Restorative Justice

Bringing together both parties to an offence for mediation, reconciliation, and restoration has multiple and almost simultaneous points of origin in contemporary corrections; the visionary work of Wisconsin psychology professor, Albert Eglash (1957–1958) (Maruna, 2001); the origins of the UK Victim Support movement in 1969 (Priestley, 1970; Rock, 1988; Tweedie, 1970); the 1974 Mennonite Victim Offender Reconciliation Program (VORP) in Elmira, Ontario (Woolpert, 1991); David Elstein's' Just One of Those Things' documentary for Thames TV (1975); Nils Christie (1977) on 'Conflicts as Property.' It is now operating in many countries including 14 of the ones in our list. In Finland, mediation and restorative justice emerged following challenges to conventional CJ practices by 'critical criminologists and the abolitionist movement.' (pp. 161–180). Chief proponents of the new thinking included 'Nils Christie and Thomas Mathiesen in Norway and Louk Hulsman in the Netherlands.' Annual referrals to mediation in Finland were 'around 10,000' resulting in 5000 'agreements;' which is approximately equals the number of people sent to prison (see also Lappi-Seppälä & Storgaard, 2015).'

Mexico's 'Law on Alternative Mechanisms of Conflict Resolution (2014)' introduced similar mechanisms which 'represented a major paradigm shift in a country where 'incarceration' was 'the rule for most offences, including minor, non-violent ones' (pp. 377–394). In Ireland, from 2015, Circles of Support and Accountability have been convened PACE (Prisoners Aid through Community Effort) where a group of volunteers focuses on 'a core member (a person with convictions for sexual offences)' 'to offer guidance and support, encourage the person to take responsibility for their behaviour, and participate in social activities' (pp. 271–288). The case for mediation is also simply put by Luisa Ravagnani and Carlo Alberto Romano. 'Efforts must be made,' they say 'to ensure that, with the aid of an impartial third party, the victim and the perpetrators can actively participate in the resolution of the conflict and the consequences of the crime' (pp. 289–306).

In India both the 'Hindu and Islamic criminal laws' recognised 'the concept of restitution of justice included financial compensation for the death of a family member who would have provided financial and moral support.' It was a system that 'slowly enriched the concept of rehabilitation and empowerment of the victims' (pp. 257–270). Victim rights in Taiwan have also expanded in recent years to give them 'a more active role in court proceedings and entitlement to governmental services.' And simultaneously 'community-correction reforms' have emphasised 'the human rights of 'inmates' and 'wrongdoers' alongside alternatives to de-incarceration and community orders.' The upshot of this 'greater involvement of the wider community' has signalled 'a move to a more restorative understanding of 'criminal justice' (pp. 577–596).

Fiji's *bulubulu* is a reconciliation ceremony and the historic customary response to many offences in Fiji' (pp. 145–160) and it 'requires the offending party to approach the victim as an act of contrition and compensation in the form of a tabua (a whale's tooth, and culturally important symol of purity).' (pp. 145–160). John Whitehead and Lennon Chang point out that knowledge of the psychological assessment process and whether it fits with the RNR model is limited is limited. 'As a result, it is unknown if this assessment successfully charts the criminogenic risk factors and rehabilitative needs of inmates. Instead, a significant weight is placed upon the pastoral care of inmates through spiritual counselling and militarised drills' (pp. 145–160).

Eglash in the United States theorised 'creative restitution' as one that 'accepts both free will and psychological determinism. It redefines past responsibility in terms of damage or harm done, and can therefore accept psychological determinism for our past behaviour without destroying the concept of our being responsible for what we have done (Eglash, 1958–1959)' There is now a vast literature devoted to all things 'restorative' in justice systems, some of which is synthesized and summarised by Hansen and Umbreit (2018). This body of research, they say 'demonstrates that victims and offenders are more satisfied with the process and outcomes than with the courts, they are more likely to draft and complete restitution agreements, they derive psychosocial benefits, the process is less expensive, crime victims are more likely to receive apologies from offenders, and offenders are less likely to recidivate.'

Many other countries quoted here also do 'Restorative Justice'—e.g., Australia, Canada, Chile, Colombia, England & Wales, and France. China too, is actively exploring doing so. Alongside '*Evidence Based Practice*,' and '*Risk, Need, and Responsivity*,' the addition of '*Restorative Justice*' completes the three-pillar structure on which the most dominant versions of future criminal justice systems will rest.

Envoi

Finally, authors of national and state entries in this volume were asked for their thoughts about the future of rehabilitation in criminal justice. No-one puts forward their favourite nostrums for swift and certain results; certainty does not live on the same street as people in need of rehabilitation, or the professionals who try to assist them. We try to distil here some of the essential points they make in their concluding observations. One very clear recommendation that emerges is a call for more, and more sophisticated, targeted research into rehabilitative processes and their outcomes. There was a demand for skilful analysis of the results to point the way forward to more effective ways of working with people who break the law, do damage to the lives of others, and themselves. For example, this plea from India:-

> It is clear, therefore, that more research is needed to enhance understanding of the contemporary situation of individuals and undertrial prisoners who have been offered help to rehabilitate and reintegrate into society by official governmental programmes. Unless continuous and robust analysis and research is undertaken there will be no clarity about which rehabilitation programmes are effective and which are not. (pp. 257–270).

A good place to start researching is with descriptions of the people who undertake (or endure) rehabilitative activities ordered by courts of law or administered as parts of discrete sentences e.g., probation or imprisonment. 'In recent years, there has been growing recognition,' says Deirdre Healy 'that people in contact with the justice system are not a homogenous group and that tailored services are needed for cohorts such as women and ethnic minority groups including Travellers (an indigenous Irish minority)' (pp. 271–288).

'However,' says María Jimena Monsalve of Argentina 'researchers need to focus, for example, on the effectiveness of alternative measures, the effect of incarceration on prisoners and their families, and the cost of incarceration compared to community measures' (pp. 17–32). Elsewhere, and similarly, 'there is a significant need for more research into the Fijian incarceral experience.' This is made more difficult due to the multi-cultural nature of the islands' society and a 'key concern with current rehabilitation programmes' being 'Fiji Corrections Service's attempts to base these upon iTaukei culture (the major indigenous people.). In the Canada chapter, Katharina Maier and Rosemary Ricciardelli argue for research into community-based organisations 'as well as the experiences of the ex-prisoners with whom they engage' which will 'tell us much about the conditions of low-income communities and, therefore, the needs and struggles of ex-prisoners and other criminalized populations disproportionately drawn from those communities.' As an addendum they 'call on researchers to expand work on how gender shapes re-entry and rehabilitative experiences.' They also raise a question about 'the parole experiences of transgendered or non-binary formerly incarcerated individuals in Canada,' where they say 'there is a gap in research that needs to be filled' (pp. 53–70).

Some prison systems however are confronted by even more basic obstacles. 'In the future' say the authors of the Thailand chapter 'before installing any rehabilitation measures, the most urgent priority is to reduce the number of people in prison' (pp. 619–638). The same complaint is made in South Africa where the major cause of 'failure in implementing meaningful rehabilitation programmes for inmates is prison overcrowding.' (pp. 525–540). 'Underlying institutional and cultural inertia' in Taiwan 'as well as the particularities of a certain political decision-making style cast a shadow over the likelihood of 'effectiveness' research', (pp. 577–596) and even in Texas where programme deliveries and outcome research are more developed there is concern that 'the evaluations seem to lack depth in methodology and, invariably, analysis' (pp. 597–618). Even so, less well-endowed authorities like Macao hanker after 'evidence-based research to inform and amend laws, policies, and measures of the corrections and rehabilitation systems', (pp. 359–376) and Philippe Pottier concludes his piece about probation officers in North Africa with the 'hope that thanks to their action and their dynamism, there will come a time when Tunisian probation truly develops' (pp. 639–650).

To conclude in the way we asked our authors to finish their descriptive chapters, it has to be said firstly, that the book speaks for itself more eloquently than anything we can write on this page. Their collected accounts have painted a vivid, lively, detailed and above all a human picture of rehabilitation in action around the globe. And so we leave you with the words of three contributors:-

Taiwan
Susyan Jou, Shang-Kai Shen and Bill Hebenton
'What needs be emphasised is the moral force of probation
as a generic helping service for all those whose experience of criminal justice
diminishes them materially and emotionally.'

Ireland
Deirdre Healey
'An expanded rehabilitative imagination encourages us to situate
personal experiences within a wider social, cultural and historical context
and, in the case of rehabilitation, to understand change not as an individual
journey but as a collective project that requires all of society to play a part.'

Sweden
Martin Lardén
'Most importantly, a rehabilitation approach is also a call for a better society
based on tolerance, inclusion, and humanity.'

References

Andrews, D. A., Bonta, J., & Hoge, R. D. (1990). Classification for effective rehabilitation: Rediscovering psychology. *Criminal Justice and Behavior, 17*(1), 19–52. https://doi.org/10.1177/0093854890017001004

Blumenthal, S. (2010). A psychodynamic approach to working with offenders: An alternative to moral orthopaedics. In A. Bartlett & G. McGauley (Eds.), *Forensic mental health: Concepts, systems, and practice*. Oxford University Press. https://doi.org/10.1093/med/9780198566854.003.0012

Christie, N. (1977). Conflicts as property. *British Journal of Criminology, 17*(1), 1–15.

Eglash, A. (1957–1958). Creative restitution: A broader meaning for an old term. *Journal of Criminal Law, Criminology and Police Science, 48*, 619.

Eglash, A. (1958–1959). Creative restitution: Its roots in psychiatry, religion and law. *British Journal of Delinquency, 10*, 114.

Elstein, D. (1975, February 13, Thursday). *Just one of those things*. Thames Television—'This Week'. Mediation between stab victim and attacker. Presenter Peter Williams.

Glueck, S., & Glueck, E. T. (1964). The uses and promise of prediction devices. *International Journal of Social Psychiatry for the First International Congress of Social Psychiatry, 4*, 55–63.

Hansen, T., & Umbreit, M. (2018). State of knowledge: Four decades of victim—Offender mediation research and practice: The evidence. *Conflict Resolution Quarterly, 36*(2), 99–113.

Laitinen, R. (2017). The Swedish Empire and the Province of Finland. In *Order, materiality, and Urban space in the early modern kingdom of Sweden*. Amsterdam University Press. https://doi.org/10.1515/9789048531004-003

Lappi-Seppälä, T., & Storgaard, A. (2015). Nordic mediation—Comparing Denmark and Finland. *Neue Kriminalpolitik, 27*(2), 136–147.

Lindgren, R. E. (2015) *Norway-Sweden: Union, Disunion and Scandinavian Integration*. Princeton Legacy Library.

Maruna, S. (2001). *Making good: How ex-convicts reform and rebuild their lives*. American Psychological Association.

Mathiesen, T. (1965). *The defences of the weak: A sociological study of a Norwegian correctional institution*. Tavistock Publications.

McNeill, F. (2012). Four forms of 'offender' rehabilitation: Towards an interdisciplinary perspective. *Legal and Criminological Psychology, 17*(1), 18–36.

Meinander, H. (2020). *History of Finland*. Oxford University Press.

Nilsson, Roddy. (2011). 'The most progressive, effective correctional system in the world' The Swedish prison system in the 1960s and 1970s. In *Penal exceptionalism?* Routledge. eBook ISBN 9780203813270

Priestley, P. (1970). *What about the victim?* NACRO.

Rock, P. (1988). Governments, victims and policies in two countries. *The British Journal of Criminology, 28*(1), 44–66.

Short, D. (2010). Australia: A continuing genocide? *Journal of Genocide Research, 12*(1–2), 45–68.

Tweedie, J. (1970, January 19, Thursday). The forgotten victim—Prisoners to aid victims plan. *The Guardian*.

Woolpert, S. (1991) Victim-offender reconciliation programs. In K. G. Duffy, J. W. Grosch, & P. V. Olczak (Eds.), *Community mediation: A handbook for practitioners and researchers*. Guilford.

Index

abolitionist ideals 165
Aboriginal and Torres Strait Islander Social Justice Commissioner (ATSISJC) 44, 45
Aboriginal Community Support Officers (ACSOs) 41, 45
Aboriginal offenders 57
Academic Education Programme (AEP) 330, 331
Acceptance and Communication Therapy (ACT), accredited programmes 676
Act of the Enforcement of Community Sanctions 2012 166
Acute-2007 349
Administrative Punishment Law (APL) 94
adversarial model 10, 377
advise, assist and befriend 127, 188
aftercare 171, 214, 238, 243, 244, 246, 247, 251, 308, 309, 311, 334, 463, 633
aggression reduction training 245
Agricultural Colony 111
Ahmedabad prison 261
AIDS 292, 538
alcohol abuse 25, 513
Alcoholics Anonymous 117, 315
The Allegheny County Jail-Based Reentry Specialist Program (Pennsylvania) 672
Alumni Aftercare Training course 673
American Civil Liberties Union Act (ACLU) 670
American Convention on Human Rights 385
Amnesty 291, 308, 310
Amnesty International 211
Amnesty Law 1947, Japan 310
Andrews, D. 38, 54, 77, 102, 103, 118, 130, 137, 139, 211, 315, 317, 319, 345, 346, 423, 433, 497, 510, 537, 642, 644, 654, 678, 690, 691
An Garda Síochána's [Irish police service] Diversion Scheme 279

anger management/aggression
    diversion courses 673
anger management course for adults
    673
anger management courses 150, 673,
    674
Animal Politico 385
Ankaful maximum-security prison
    208, 210
Annual Plan for Social Reintegration
    (Chile) 81
antagonistic contradiction 90
Anti-Drug Law (ADL) 94
Antisocial personality traits 118
Argentine Chamber of Deputies 23
Argentine Constitution 1853 17
Argentine National Criminal Code
    17
art and creative classes 246
Ashanti Law and Constitution 203
Ashanti, the 203
assertiveness training 245
Australian Bureau of Statistics 34,
    36, 37
Australian Capital Territory (ACT)
    36
Australian Law Reform Commission
    (ALRC) 36, 38, 39, 41, 46
authority vigilance 384
Aymara 75

B

Bács-Kiskun County Remand Prison
    248
bail 10, 48, 260, 262, 263, 265,
    326, 430, 682
Bangjiao programme 91
basic foot drill 149
Bean, Philip 3
Bedi, Dr. Krian 261
Behavioral Couples Therapy for
    Substance Abuse 676
Beijing Rules, the 264–266, 268

Beijing system 99
Bentham, Jeremy 7, 71
Bérenger, Senator 182
bibliotherapy classes 246
bifurcation 187, 194, 579, 583, 586
Big Brothers and Sisters (BBS)
    Association 312, 315
Black and Indigenous people 57
Black and minority ethnic adults
    136
'Black box of French probation'
    studies 193
body massage 151
Bonaparte, Napoleon 182
Bonta, J. 38, 54, 77, 102, 118, 130,
    137, 139, 211, 315, 317, 319,
    322, 346, 433, 497, 510, 528,
    642, 644, 654, 678
book binding course 261
Bora, Sheena 263
Bottoms, A. 187, 214, 583, 590
Braithwaite, J. 147
British colonial rule 327
British Columbia Correctional
    Service 345
British Common Law 327
British MAPPA model 350
Budapest Strict and Medium Regime
    Prison 245
Building Better Lives programme,
    Ireland 276
Building Strong Relationships 673
bulubulu 8, 146, 147, 152,
    154–156, 695
bureaucratisation 326
Bureau of Community Corrections
    Management 98
Burke, L. (2019)
    legal rehabilitation 43, 178, 184,
        239, 277, 278, 285, 680
    moral rehabilitation 43, 178, 191,
        279, 281, 285, 680
    personal rehabilitation 39, 178,
        276, 277, 285, 679

social rehabilitation 178, 188, 191, 281, 284, 680

C

Cabinet Meeting for Crime Control, Japan 318
Cabinet of Ministers, Latvia 342
Calderón, Felipe 379
Cambodia 258
Canada's Prairie region 59
Canadian correctional systems 55
Canadian federal prison system 55, 379
Canadian International Development Agency (CIDA) 345
Canadian penality 54, 56, 57
cannabis use 327
Canon law 181, 182
capital punishment 262, 597, 620, 689
carceral population 146, 147, 486, 669
Career Development Programme 365
Caring for Community Programme 366
Carlen, Pat 3, 4
carpentry and furniture making course 261
Cartabia, Marta, Minister of Justice 303
Case Formulation in Probation and Parole (CFP), Japan 319, 322
Case of María and her daughter, Guadalupe 388, 389
Categorised Treatment System (CTS), Japan 319
Catholic Church 9, 26, 27, 116, 272, 360
Catholic principle of subsidiarity 272
cautions 7, 202, 214, 222, 280, 475

'Celebrating Life' workshop 363
Central Institute for Assessment and Methodology, Hungarian Prison Service 241, 243–245, 250, 253
charities 92, 238, 247, 281, 284, 294, 578
chess programmes 246
Chief Probation Officer 311, 316
Children's Day parent-child activity 363
Children's welfare 19, 35, 164, 310
Child Right Convention 1990 264
Child Support Programme, Macao 362
Chilean penal system 71
Chilean prison system 72, 80
Chile Decree Law 518 of Regulations for Penitentiary Establishments 74
Chile Ministry of Justice and Human Rights 74
Chinese justice system 92
Chinese Prison Law (PL) 93
Chinese University of Hong Kong 363
Christian iTaukei 146, 156
Christian organisations 206
Christie, N. 164, 165, 694
Church of Pentecost 214
Circles of Support and Accountability (COSA) 9, 280, 350, 355, 438, 694
City of Dublin Vocational Education Committee 282
civic education 366, 491
civil society 26, 28, 43, 115, 132, 592, 626, 656, 680
Civil Society Organizations (CSOs) 294, 387, 657
classism 392
clinical psychology 245, 334
coercion 74, 90, 149
coercive confinement 271

cognitive behavioural therapy (CBT) 38, 39, 44, 45, 169, 193, 309, 317, 345, 347, 433, 439, 565, 671–673, 676, 677, 690, 691
Cognitive Process Therapy for Female Victims of Sexual Assault 676
Cognitive Self Change Programme 169
Colbert Ordinance, the 182
Colina 2 prison 77
Collett, S. 33, 43
Coloane Juvenile Prison 360
Coloane Prison (Macao Prison) 360, 362, 363, 368
Colombian national government 107
colonisation 6, 8, 10, 11, 35, 36, 42, 44, 72, 108, 203, 431, 437, 443, 621, 689
Combining Leniency and Severity policy 7, 91
Cómbita Maximum Security Facility 111
Commission for Human Rights and Administrative Justice (CHRAJ) 208–210
Committee of Inquiry into the Penal System, 1985, Ireland 273
Committee on the Elimination of Discrimination against Women (CEDAW) 147
communautarism 189
Communication Skills Training 347
Communist Party 90
communist society 341
Community Based Health and First Aid (CBHFA) programme 282, 283
community-based residential facility 55
community centres 364
Community Corrections Law (CCL) 2020 94

Community Corrections Officers (CCO) 41, 42, 45
community day centres 246
Community Life Resettlement Support Centre (CLRSC), Japan 318
Community Rehabilitation Companies (CRCs) 131
Community Restorative Centre (CRC) 46
Community Return Scheme, Irish Prison Service and Probation Service 282
Community Risk and Needs Assessment tool (CRNA) 345
community sentences 6, 11, 73–75, 77, 78, 182, 220, 224, 244, 378, 384, 430–435, 441, 467, 468, 486, 517, 519, 520, 543, 549, 551, 552, 587, 693
community service 17, 48, 75, 164, 171, 174–176, 178, 222, 244, 260, 299, 300, 335, 365, 453, 454, 456–458, 486, 488–490, 542, 543, 549, 550, 552, 554, 609, 610, 614, 640, 641, 645, 646, 648, 649
community service provider 98, 436
community shame 147
community supervision 9, 34, 35, 46, 61, 131, 156, 161, 245, 396, 406, 499, 602, 611, 613, 678
community transition 206
compensation 92, 146, 173, 203, 244, 248, 258, 262, 268, 479, 586, 695
Comprehensive Care activities and Treatment activities 109
Comprehensive Measures for Reduction of Re-offence, Japan 318
Comprehensive Peace Agreement 2003, Liberia 207

Comprehensive Responsibility with Life Programme 120, 121
compulsory drug treatment 91, 94, 308, 312, 321
compulsory drug treatment centres 94
compulsory treatment 161
computer training course 261
concentration camps 341
Concept Paper on the Development of the State Probation Service of Latvia 343
concession prison 73, 80–83, 85
Concessions Law 73, 80
conditional remission of the sentence 78
conditional sentence 17, 57, 161, 164
conditional suspension of judicial process 17
confederate flags 14, 667
Confederation of European Probation (CEP) 349
confinement, and silence 182
conflict management 247
conflict resolution 344, 380
Confucian canon 89
Constitution of India 264, 265
Constitution of Japan 310
Control and Assistance Direction of Criminal Enforce 26
Convention of Child Rights 1979 263
convicts 35, 93, 94, 98, 100, 238, 318, 457, 461, 470, 473, 487, 645
Cooperative Employers (CEs) 312, 315, 319
Cooperative Law 28
Co-operatives 28
Core Correctional Practices (CCPs) 139, 140, 644
Correctional Courses for Youth Offenders 366

correctional population 155, 429, 598–600, 602, 604, 611, 613, 669, 672
Correctional Service Canada (CSC) 55, 59–62
correctional supervision 100, 669, 670
Corrections and Reentry section of the Crime Solutions website 672
corruption 11, 118, 335, 379, 450
corruption in prison 115
Council of Europe 8, 165, 166, 491, 495, 640, 642
county homes 271
court missionary system 271
Covid 19 pandemic 20
crime-control policies 344
Crime Reduction Programme 138
Crime Solutions 671–677, 683
Crimesolutions.gov. 671
Criminal Code 2004 165
Criminal Code of Canada 57
criminal identity education 99
Criminal Justice Act 1991 128, 130
Criminal Justice Act 2007, Ireland 278
Criminal Justice Administration Act 1914, Ireland 272
Criminal Justice (Spent Convictions and Certain Disclosures) Act 2016, Ireland 283
Criminal Law 1979, China 93
Criminal Law of Latvian Socialist Republic 1961 341
criminal legal measures 668
Criminal Popular Punitive Movement 6, 18
Criminal Procedure Act 2003, Hungary 239
Criminal Procedure Code 1976, India 261
Criminal Procedure Reform (CPR) 72

Criminal Sanctions Agency (CSA) 166–168
criminogenic needs 4, 6, 12, 38, 39, 42, 54, 75, 99, 102, 103, 118, 133, 137, 346, 367, 423, 424, 433, 437, 510, 528, 534, 544, 550, 552, 562, 564, 565, 568, 602, 604, 634, 692
Cross-regional Reintegration Service in Greater Bay Area 365
culinary skills course 261
culturally neutral restorative praxis 155

D

daily prison 18, 515
Danda Niti (Penology) 257, 258, 688
debt and economic counselling 169
democracy 72, 340, 542
Deng Xiaoping 90
denunciation 56
Department of Correctional Education (DCE) (Va) 671
Department of Social Reintegration, Macao 361, 362, 364, 365, 369, 370
deportation 362, 548
deprivation 12, 19, 35, 95, 102, 165, 237, 248, 265, 293, 297, 342, 360, 384, 386, 453, 469, 471, 472, 506, 507, 511, 515, 518, 521, 542, 568, 694
desistance 8, 12, 39, 41, 43, 46, 84, 131, 132, 136, 137, 139, 140, 167, 170, 173, 185, 188, 191–193, 211, 220, 250, 252, 276, 277, 279, 283, 285, 290, 302, 367, 368, 422, 423, 438, 443, 493, 497, 508, 509, 512, 516, 551, 567, 644, 668, 678–680, 690, 691, 694
desistance theory 133, 367

Detention for Education (for sex workers) 90
deterrence 56, 133, 202, 204, 213, 214, 289, 450, 451, 457, 513, 515, 520, 542, 553, 560, 569, 620, 630, 689
Devoted University Center (CUD) 20
Diana Sacayán-Lohana Berkins Law 24
Directorate for Control and Assistance in Criminal Enforcement 26, 27
disabled prisoners 318
discipline training 364
discretionary parole 668, 669, 682
diversity 5, 6, 23, 24, 47, 136, 140, 147, 151, 156, 189, 190, 194, 247, 421, 498, 547, 597, 599, 600
DMV Connect, Notary 674
domestic violence 79, 150, 188, 473, 507, 545
Dowden, C. 139
drama classes 246
drink drivers 164, 308, 309, 317, 590
drug abuse 22, 90, 101, 121, 230, 309, 317, 319, 321, 551, 552, 588
drug cartels 111, 113
Drug Compulsory Detoxification 90
drug courts 672, 677
drug prevention unit 245
drug-related crimes 75, 370
Dublin Drug Treatment Court 279
Durham Checkpoint 133

E

early release 18–20, 29, 57, 76, 151, 176, 192, 243, 282, 292, 310, 520, 582

East Africa Prisons Regulations 325, 327
economic crisis 6, 21, 546
education 9, 18–20, 22, 25, 28, 29, 60, 74, 78, 81, 89, 90, 92–97, 99–103, 109, 112, 116, 117, 119, 123, 135, 151, 153, 157, 168, 169, 171, 173, 176, 183, 188, 191, 205–207, 211, 227–229, 238, 240–242, 247–253, 260, 261, 264, 273–277, 282, 283, 303, 315, 319, 326, 330, 331, 333, 340, 341, 346, 352, 360, 362–366, 370, 380, 383, 384, 386–388, 400, 416, 431, 435, 436, 439, 454, 458, 461, 472, 473, 485, 487, 488, 495, 498, 499, 514, 528, 529, 535, 545, 552, 563, 564, 566, 567, 570, 571, 583, 590, 602, 604, 607, 610, 612, 615, 623, 625, 627, 628, 631, 632, 640, 643, 652–654, 656, 660, 661, 670, 672, 675, 676, 681, 690
Educational Therapeutic Units of Spain 121
Educational Training Boards 277
Education and Life Quality Programme 121
education policies 205
Effective Practice Initiative 129, 138
electronically monitored supervision order 174, 431
Emperor Ashoka 9, 258
employment 4, 25, 27, 28, 39, 55, 60, 64, 110, 135, 151, 155, 169, 171, 178, 191, 210–212, 224, 226, 228, 238–241, 243, 246, 247, 250, 262, 275–278, 280, 282–284, 315, 317–319, 330, 331, 333, 346, 364, 365, 380, 383, 384, 402, 403, 405, 422, 425, 431, 433, 435, 437, 469, 470, 473, 487–489, 496, 497, 499, 528, 568, 570, 580, 602, 604, 607, 609–611, 614, 615, 623, 628, 669, 674–676
employment and social welfare education 99
Employment Scheme for Pre-release Inmates 227, 230, 364
EM-release 174
Enhanced Thinking Skills (England) 672
equality 4, 23, 24, 47, 177, 474, 508
EQUIPS umbrella (Explore, Question, Understand, Investigate, Practice, Succeed) 39
ergastolo ostativo 298
ethno-cultural diversity 189
Eurocentric norms 35
European Committee for the Prevention of Torture (CPT) 165
European Court of Human Rights (ECHR) 165, 244, 293, 421
European Forum for Restorative Justice (EFRJ) network 349
European Framework Decisions 301
European Probation Rules 190, 491
European Union 246, 340, 498, 547, 553, 640, 641
Evaluation and Treatment Councils 114
evangelical churches 116
expressive meaning of rehabilitation 132
Ex-prisoner stigma and labelling 25

Fabiano, E. 129, 137, 655
faith-based organisations 206, 214
family and social ties 25, 98
'Family Beyond the Wall' Project 363

Family Care Support Programme for Juvenile Offenders 366
family consultation 248, 366
family contact 20, 173, 211, 418
Family Court 310–313
family group conferencing 246, 439
Family Reunification 673
family reunification programmes for women 64, 65
family therapy 248, 673
Fanti National Constitution 202
farm work 331
Farrall, S.
  consumption 679
  production 679
  social and economic *inclusion* 679
  social interaction 679
Faulkner, D. 385
Federal Law of Education 19
Federal Penitentiary Service (SPF) 18–20, 23, 24
Federal Poverty Income Guidelines 676
felony conviction 668
female-only prisons 248
female prisoners 59, 97, 190, 325, 328, 331, 455–457, 464
female sexuality, control of 272
feminist groups 23
Fifth Republic Constitution 183
Fijian correctional centres 148
Fiji Corrections Service 145–157, 697
fines 28, 48, 58, 202, 203, 258, 261, 268, 300, 311, 326, 342, 362, 371, 384, 406, 422, 444, 479, 490, 492, 508, 512, 543, 549, 550, 579, 584
Finnish enforcement decree 1975 162
First Criminal Novel, Hungarian Act 1908 237
First Nation Men 37

First Nation People 6, 34–37, 39, 41–47, 689
First Nation Women 34, 37, 42
Five Discussions on Change Programme 169–171
flower arrangement 151
formerly incarcerated 64, 65, 406, 424, 580, 625, 629, 634, 668, 679–681, 691, 697
Foucault, Michel 97, 191, 379, 487
fraud 118, 121, 259, 319, 327
French concept of '*Laïcité*' 189
French Guiana 182
French Ministry of Justice 185, 187
French Revolution 1789 182
Frías, Dr Jorge H. 26, 27
Front-Door EM 174, 175

G

Garante Nazionale delle Persone Private della libertà-National Guarantor of People Deprived of Liberty 299
Garland, D. 56, 128, 252, 272, 344
Gendarmería de Chile 74, 655
gender 5–7, 23, 24, 54, 58, 64–66, 75, 76, 84, 100, 119, 136, 146–152, 155, 156, 227, 247, 272, 273, 328, 378, 387, 390, 396, 407, 433, 497, 498, 509, 513, 519, 562, 697
gender-based violence 392
gender definitions 23
gender discrimination 265
Gender Identity Law 24, 30
gender violence and femicide programmes 24
Ghana Prisons Reform Project (GPRP) 212, 213
Ghana Prisons Service (GPS) 204–208, 211–214
Ghana, traditional criminal justice system 156

Good group punishments 115
Good Lives Model (GLM) 11, 112, 118, 347, 349, 350, 423, 438, 644
Governor's Office 668, 669
guerrilla organisations 113

H

halfway houses 27, 55, 61, 99, 227, 307, 311, 314, 315, 473, 607, 672
Hampton Roads 667
handicrafts manufacturing course 261
handloom related work course 261
harm-minimisation 167
harsh punishment 7, 90, 219, 343
healing lodges 7, 54, 59, 60
Hejie (reconcile) 92
High and Medium Security Penitentiary Facilities 111
Hinduism 257
HM Inspectorate of Prisons Penal Reform Trust 209
'Hogares de Cristo' network 27, 30
holistic rehabilitation 170
Ho male and female prison 210
home detention 295–297, 299, 430–432, 517, 520
homelessness 37, 133, 335, 404, 425, 674
Home of Nossa Senhora do Rosário de Fátima, for male and female youths 360
horticulture 151
hostel accommodation 274
hostels 238
house arrest 17, 19, 22, 647
housing 27, 39, 46, 55, 169, 171, 178, 191, 207, 243, 246, 297, 319, 327, 332, 334, 384, 396, 402, 403, 405, 425, 435–437, 473, 506, 516, 537, 568, 571, 586, 601, 604, 607, 609, 675–677, 681
Howard Society 209
human capital 131, 285, 486, 495, 601
humane neoclassicism 161, 162
humanitarian permits 381
Human Resources Development Operational Programme (EFOP) 247
human rights 3, 5, 7, 8, 19, 23, 24, 43, 79, 84, 112, 113, 119, 122, 155, 165, 167, 177, 178, 183, 209, 260, 378, 380, 383–387, 390, 391, 462, 464, 511, 579, 590, 592, 652, 656–658, 695
Human Rights Court case, *Raffray Taddei v. France* 190
human trafficking 21
Hungarian Criminal Code 1961 239
Hungarian Criminal Justice system 237, 249
Hungarian Decree on Penal Enforcement 1979 238

I

Imams 206
impact programmes 169
incapacitation 56, 99, 100, 207, 450, 469, 515, 560, 620, 630, 631, 689
incarceration rate 11, 13, 21, 58, 163, 243, 328, 395, 396, 467, 597, 651, 669
indeterminate sentences 161, 162, 229, 311, 316, 515
Indian independence 1947 259
Indian Penal Code 9, 259
Indigenous iTaukei 145, 697
Indigenous jurisdiction 109, 110
Indigenous justice 43
Indigenous language 110

Indigenous women 59, 378, 389, 390
Individual Intervention Plan 77, 78
individualisation 182, 184, 237, 240, 489
Indo-Fijians 147, 154
industrial and reformatory schools 271
'Inmates' Loving and Caring Society Service Scheme' 364
inquisitorial justice system 72, 182
inquisitorial model 10, 377
Institute for Crime and Justice Policy Research 325
institutional correctional programming 64
Instrument for the Comprehensive Assessment of Convicts (la Valoración Integral de Condenados IVIC 1.0) 117
intense probation 78
Inter American Commission of Human Rights 2009 73
InterAmerican Commission on Human Rights in Colombia 114
Intermittent prison 21
International Covenant on Civil and Political Rights 259, 385
International Transparency 115
internships 122, 188, 210, 582
Inventory for Case/Intervention Management (IGI) 77
Irish form of penalty, pastoral penalty 273
Irish Penal Reform Trust 278
Irish Prison Service 276, 277, 282
Irish Red Cross 282, 283
Islamic organisations 206
Italian Constitution 289, 295, 300
itinerant prisons 71

jail population 115, 395, 669, 674
Japan's criminal justice system 307, 308
Jehovah's Witnesses 116
Jersey Reconviction Study 139
Jiang Zemin 90
judges 18, 26, 57, 78, 82, 108, 183, 186, 187, 194, 204, 243, 263, 266, 279, 281, 310, 312, 378, 381, 385, 455, 486, 489, 493, 508, 550, 551, 591, 648
Judicial Rehabilitation Services Act, Japan 307
jueces de ejecución penal (judges of criminal execution) 378
juge de l'application des peines (JAP) 183–185, 188, 192–194
juge des enfants 183
Julhiet, Edouard 182
Juridical Person for Offender Rehabilitation (JPOR) 311, 315
Juridical Persons for Offender Rehabilitation Services 312
Just Deserts 177
Justice Bureaus 98, 100
Justice Krishna Iyer 260
juvenile justice 82, 92, 164, 183, 263–265
Juvenile Justice Care and Protection of Children Act (JJCPCA) 2015, India 264
Juvenile Law 1948, Japan 310, 311, 313
juvenile preventive patronage cases 245

K

Kamiti prison 332
Kampala declaration 205, 207
Karlis Ulmanis 340
Kenyan constitution 10

Kenyan prison system 325, 327, 330
Kyoto Declaration on Community Volunteers Supporting Offender Reintegration 321

L

Lamarque, Jules 183
Lammy Review 136
Langata Women's Prison 335
Laogai camps 95
Latvian Crime Register 353
Latvian probation practice 346
law and order education 99
Law for Offender Rehabilitation Services 1995 315
Law for the Comprehensive Protection of Women 24
Law of Execution of Deprivation of the Liberty Sentence 19
Law of Punishments (Sodu likums) 340
Law on Alternative Mechanisms of Conflict Resolution 2014, Mexico 381, 694
Le Chéile Restorative Justice Project 280
Legal Aid Service 239
legal rehabilitation/exemption 239
Legge Gozzini 1986 292
Le Pen, Marine 194
Lesotho 207
Level of Service Case Management Inventory (LS/CMI) 77
Level of Service Inventory-Revised (LSI-R) 42
LGBTI groups 24, 25
LGBTIQ+ 8, 148–152, 154, 155
LGBTQ+ groups 6, 23
Liebling, A. 204, 214, 281
Life Chain Programme (LCP) 121
Life Crime Prevention for Youth 366
life imprisonment 243, 261, 298, 313, 334, 421, 454

literature classes 246
local government 93, 98, 308, 318–320, 633
local jail 395, 668, 669, 674
lockdown imprisonment 63
Lombroso, Cesare 457
Lord Rama 257, 258
Loudoun County Adult Detention Center (LCADC) 674, 675
The Loudoun County Sheriff's Office's Criminal Investigation Division low-security unit 675
low recidivism rates 669

M

Macao Correctional Services Bureau 360–365
Macao's sovereignty returned to China 361
Macao's Boys Home 360
Macao Youth Correctional Institution 360, 361, 364, 365
Magdalene laundries 9, 271
magistrates 23, 134, 259, 262
Magna Carta 18, 182
Making it on Supervision courses 673
Management Regulation on Minor Reformatory 93
managerialism 274
managerial meaning of rehabilitation 553
mandatory minimum penalties 57
Mandela Rules 18, 29, 464, 656
Mao Zedong 89
Mapuche 75
marketisation 90, 129, 134, 281
Maruna, Shad 4, 53, 191, 204, 214, 220, 367, 437, 487, 488, 679, 694
Maryland Ignition Interlock Program 672
Mathiesen, T. 164, 165, 693, 694

McDonaldisation 8, 188, 192, 194
Mcjustice 181
McNeill, F. 2, 4, 33, 43, 131, 132, 177, 178, 184, 191, 275–277, 289, 355, 432, 443, 486, 487, 490–492, 507, 516, 690
media 25, 26, 56, 108, 263, 266, 269, 327, 331, 332, 336, 386, 467, 515
mediation 8, 164, 165, 178, 239, 250, 280, 342, 344, 347, 350, 366, 381, 498, 510, 694, 695
Mediation Acts 164
Medical Care and Treatment Act 311
medical-therapeutic unit 245
medical treatment 17, 311, 312, 571, 585
mental health 11, 22, 37, 38, 60, 114, 133, 208, 262, 276, 278, 296, 311, 326, 361, 367, 396–401, 403–407, 431, 436, 473, 497, 498, 500, 509, 510, 513, 514, 545, 550, 552, 554, 585, 602, 607, 660, 676, 677
Mentally Ill Offender Community Transition Program (Washington state) 672
mentors 11, 315, 347, 350, 423, 439, 499, 516, 676
MEREPS project 251
meta-analyses 163, 537
Methadone Maintenance Therapy and Motivational Interviewing for Substance Abuse 672
Mexico's criminal justice system 377, 379, 380, 384, 385, 387, 390, 391
Mexico Constitution 378, 379, 384, 391
Micaela's Law 23
Middle Ages, the 181
militarised ideal 149
military dictatorships 72
Ming dynasty 359

Minister of Justice Robert Badinter 183
Ministry of Justice and Human Rights 19, 27, 30, 74
Ministry of Justice, Columbia 112
Ministry of Social Development 28, 436
Minor Reformatory Camps 90
Mitterrand, Francois 183, 185
mobile phone, use of in prison 20
money laundering 118
Montfort Boys Town vocational training institution 151
Moral Development Education 150
moral interventions 379
mother and baby homes 271
mothers and children in prison 17
mothers in prison 381
mothers with babies 248
Motivational Interviewing 193, 347, 348, 350
Motivational Interviewing for Substance Abuse 672
Motivation programmes 169
Mukherjee, Indrani 262, 263
multi-family therapy (MRT) 673
Mumbai female prison 263
music classes 246
music workshops 28
mutual support groups 120

N

Narada 257
Narcotic Anonymous 315
National Code of Criminal Procedures 2014, Mexico 378, 380, 385
National Directorate of Social Rehabilitation 27
National Institute Against Discrimination (INADI) 24
National Institute of Women 23

National Institute on Drug Abuse (NIDA) 321
National Law of Penal Enforcement 18
National Law of Penal Execution 2016, Mexico 378, 381, 383–385
National Learning Service, Columbia 116
National Liaison and Diversion Services 133
National Offenders Rehabilitation Commission, Japan 310
National Penitentiary and Prison Institute, Columbia 107, 108
national prison census 22
National Probation Service (NPS) 132–134, 139, 140, 551
National Standards 128
National Survey on People Deprived of their Liberty (INEGI) 386, 387
National System of Statistics of Penal Enforcement (SNEEP) 21, 22
National Youth Social Reintegration Service (Chile) 82
neighbourhood-based education 4, 91
Nelson Mandela Rules 210, 212, 464
net-widening 174
new conviction 669
New Hungary Development Plan 246
New Labour 138
Nigerian Correctional Service Act (NCSA) 207, 453–456, 458, 459, 462–464
nightly prison 18
1991 Royal Commission into Aboriginal Deaths in Custody 36
Nirbhaya gang rape 266

Nkosi and Maweni's study on overcrowding 208
non-antagonistic contradictions 90
non-discrimination 24, 190
non-governmental organisations (NGOs) 23, 24, 34, 46, 62, 63, 112, 122, 152, 155, 209, 222, 226, 227, 229, 243, 247, 261, 294, 347, 366, 385, 388, 435, 442, 578–580, 587
non-Indigenous people 35, 48, 60
non-penitentiary detention 21
Nordic concept of general prevention 162
Nordic Penal Exceptionalism 172
Normality Principle 168, 171
Northern Territory Tasmania 36
Norwegian Mediation Service 345, 347
Nothing Works 128–130, 137, 177
Nsawam male and female prison 210
Nsawam medium security prison 206, 212
NSW Reducing Reoffending Strategy 2016–2020 39
nursing mothers 115, 456

O

occupational therapist 114
Offender Assessment System (OASys, later e-OASys) 130, 136
offender managers 134, 552
Offender Rehabilitation Act 2007, Japan 308–310, 313, 317
Offender Rehabilitation Act 2014 131, 140
Ombudsman 112, 210, 479
one-to-one 77, 127, 129, 251, 551, 566
open care measures 162
Open University 277, 627
Organic Law 19, 74, 84

organized crime 292, 319, 379
Órgano Desconcentrado de Prevención y Readaptación Social 389
Ouagadougou Declaration and Plan of Action on Accelerating Prisons and Penal Reforms in Africa (ODPAAPPR) 2002 205
overcriminalization 92

p

pains of imprisonment 204, 273
painting workshops 28
panopticon 71
paramilitaries 113
parole 6, 7, 10, 13, 17, 19, 20, 26, 34, 35, 38–40, 46–48, 56, 57, 60–62, 64–66, 76, 94, 97, 109, 135, 174, 206, 238, 239, 243, 262, 263, 268, 307–311, 313, 316, 317, 319, 320, 342–344, 348, 361, 363, 370, 371, 378, 381, 383, 388, 396, 402, 405, 430, 432, 453, 454, 456–458, 462, 508, 510, 520, 544–548, 554, 555, 563, 577–580, 582, 585–591, 599–601, 604, 607, 609, 611, 613–615, 625, 633, 668, 672, 675, 680, 682, 690, 697
Parole Board of Canada (PBC) 57, 61, 62
parole supervision 7, 309, 310, 312, 313, 316, 319, 425, 494, 599, 607, 609–611, 613, 615, 668
Paterson, Alexander 167
patronages of the liberated 26
'patronage' system, the 340
pedagogical education 238
penal abolitionism 45, 47
Penal Code 1907, Japan 309
Penal Enforce Judges 18

Penal Unit No. 15 of Batán, Buenos Aires 26
penal welfarism 161, 271, 272
Penitentiary and Prison Complexes 111
Penitentiary Code 2013, Hungary 239
Penitentiary of Santiago 71
pen manufacturing course 261
People's Republic of China 89
Performance Credit System 97
personal, social, judicial/legal and moral forms 43
persons with disabilities 248
philanthropy 461
Picasso project, the 246
police/policing 22, 35, 42, 43, 90, 91, 93–95, 98, 100, 101, 111, 133, 136, 187, 194, 220, 222, 252, 259–261, 263, 264, 266, 267, 280, 297, 308, 315, 320, 331, 335, 336, 342–344, 380, 396, 399, 400, 450, 497, 569, 577, 578, 582, 517, 518, 569, 653, 657, 660, 661, 680, 693
Police Courts 127
police detention houses 308, 309, 311
Political Constitution of Colombia 108
political crimes 341
political struggle 7, 90
poor living conditions 25, 79, 652
Portuguese colonists and the first prison in Macao 359
positive school of criminology 260, 631
Poverty and crime 334
Practice Guide for Intervention (PGI) 39
pre- and post- release 669
predictability 162, 171, 177, 492, 560
pregnant women 19, 78, 248, 456

Preparation for Freedom programme 122
pre-sentence reports (PSRs) 136, 186, 224, 244, 344, 432, 550
Preservation of Life Programme 7, 120
pretrial/pre-trial detention 74–76, 107, 110, 381, 383–387, 427
preventive detention 74, 76, 162, 479, 480
Prime Minister Stephen Harper of the Conservative Party 57
Prison Act 2006 165
Prison Administration, Latvia 342, 349
prisonbation 8, 186, 189, 192, 193
prison chaplains 206
prison conditions 18, 23, 79, 82, 162, 183, 202, 205, 207–214, 244, 391, 467, 541, 652, 692, 693
prison course 20, 163, 172, 189, 363, 419, 435, 627
prisoner profiles 22, 58, 438, 659
prison, export to the colonies 204
prison family visits 148
'Prison for the city' programmes 246
prison labour system 250
prison leave 21, 55, 120, 162, 167, 206, 327, 389, 391, 414, 417
prison managers 186, 371
prison officers 81, 97, 186, 187, 206, 209, 210, 226, 227, 281, 327, 330, 333, 335, 469, 621, 630, 641
prison overcrowding 7, 13, 14, 20, 21, 72, 73, 76, 79, 83, 113, 171, 184, 205, 208, 213, 214, 244, 293, 298, 301, 327, 328, 333, 360, 402, 462, 513, 538, 539, 543, 584, 598, 623, 625, 649, 697
prison population 6, 11, 14, 22, 26, 58, 59, 72, 73, 75–77, 80, 81, 95, 110, 113, 117, 147, 148, 208, 244, 249, 274, 293, 294, 325, 327, 328, 334, 343, 381, 383, 385, 386, 391, 403, 405, 430, 431, 435, 443, 477, 498, 505, 507, 513, 515, 520, 535, 539, 544, 547, 548, 555, 588, 624, 625, 633, 640, 649, 651, 656, 669
Prison radio of the Speak Out Association 247
Prison Regulations (Chile) 76, 455
Prisons (Bombay furlough and parole) Rules 1959 262, 268
Prisons Ordinance 1860, Ghana 204
Prisons Service Act 1972 204, 207
prison staff 9, 19, 24, 26, 96, 209, 340, 349, 452, 496, 631, 659
prison treatment programme 7, 21, 24, 107, 208, 211, 245, 274, 544, 545, 631
private prisons 7, 108
privatisation 8, 72, 80, 129, 133, 134, 186, 281
Probation Foundation 166
Probation Inspectorate 131
probation officer 3, 9, 78, 127, 129, 134, 186, 221, 223–226, 232, 238, 239, 242–246, 252, 253, 260, 262, 272, 274, 276, 280, 290, 295, 299, 309–313, 315, 321, 344–346, 350, 353, 403–405, 431, 432, 434, 438, 491, 551, 552, 568, 578–583, 586, 587, 589, 592, 593, 600, 641–644, 688, 697
Probation of Offenders Act 1907 127
Probation of Offenders Act 1958, India 262
problem-solving courts 672, 677
pro-criminal cognitions 77
procuratorates 92
productive physical work 96

Programmation Act 2019 188
Programme of Social Reintegration (Chile) 77, 691
Programme of social reintegration for people in custody 78
Project *Efiase* (Prison Project) 205
promilleprogramme 164
Promotion of Recidivism Prevention Act 2016, Japan 308, 319
proportionality 28, 162, 166, 177, 237, 472, 475, 489, 508, 510–512, 560
pro-social modelling 133, 139, 140, 193, 347, 497
prosocial skills 80, 496
prosocial work and training competences 77
prostitution 90, 559
provincial/territorial correctional centres 55
psychiatric care 115, 560
psychiatric institutions 271
psychological counselling services 362
psychological health education 99, 498
psychologist 27, 38, 114, 117, 121, 161, 272, 276, 293, 327, 531, 532, 536, 545, 546, 555, 571, 580, 586, 655, 690
psychopathy 118, 336
psychosocial model 77, 690
psychosocial unit 245
public education 25, 240, 656
Public Health 25, 259, 571
public humiliation 71
Public Library Services 277
Public Order Detention 90, 94
Public Order Management Punishments Law (POMPL) 94
public-private partnerships 80, 205, 241
public protection 4, 128, 130, 135, 380, 515
public sector 131, 139, 312
Public Security Police 361
public spending 72, 79
punishment 3, 4, 6, 7, 9–11, 17–19, 28, 33, 35, 43, 44, 47, 58, 62, 65, 74, 78, 82, 83, 89–97, 100–102, 109, 115, 128, 132, 139, 146, 162, 165–167, 181, 191, 201–204, 213, 214, 220–223, 238, 240, 248, 250, 252, 258, 264, 267, 276, 277, 295, 298, 325–327, 333, 335, 341–344, 348, 349, 352, 353, 378–380, 385, 414, 419, 420, 431, 442, 451–454, 457, 460, 467, 469, 471, 474, 475, 477, 478, 485–490, 492, 494, 495, 512, 514, 515, 521, 542, 543, 547, 554, 555, 559–561, 584, 592, 597, 598, 613, 620, 621, 630, 631, 633, 687–689, 693, 694
punitive culture 56
punitivism 252, 692

Q

qualitative methodology 250, 251
Quechua 75

R

racism 44, 137, 392
Ramayana 9, 257, 258, 688
Raynor, P. 4, 128, 137–139, 193, 207, 220
readaptation approach 377
recidivism 9, 14, 19, 28, 46, 77, 80, 81, 83, 91, 99, 100, 109, 118, 120, 129, 152, 155, 157, 165, 169, 171, 178, 206, 208, 219, 220, 237, 240, 253, 284, 293,

295, 296, 301, 302, 308, 315, 317–319, 333, 344, 351, 352, 360, 367, 398, 401–403, 405, 406, 415, 422, 424, 429, 434, 435, 437, 441, 443, 453, 476, 526–528, 538, 544, 548, 554, 560–568, 583, 585, 591, 601, 602, 604, 607, 609–614, 625, 628, 632–634, 640, 642, 644, 649, 653, 654, 657, 658, 668, 669, 677, 678, 681, 682, 689, 691
recidivism rates 11, 55, 178, 230–233, 282, 318, 327, 351, 352, 367, 368, 370, 371, 404, 434, 441, 458, 505, 526, 534, 611–613, 625, 626, 632–634, 668–670, 677, 679, 681, 692
recidivism reports 232, 669, 682
recovery capital 367
redemption 9, 181, 182, 257, 279, 283, 285, 527
Reduced Probation Caseload in Evidence-Based Settings (Iowa, Oklahoma) 672
Re-education Through Labour (RTL) 90, 91, 94
re-entry experience 669
reentry gap 668
Re-Entry Money Smart class 673
reentry system 668
reformatory institution 248
reformatory schools 237, 271
reform through labour (Laogai) 90
Regional Parole Boards, Japan 309, 310, 312
Regional Primary Care Coalition (RPCC) 675
regional probation and parole offices 668
Regional Reducing Reoffending Plans 2021-24 138
Rehabilitation
  definition 3–5
  forms of 2
Rehabilitation Activity Requirement (RAR) 131, 140
Rehabilitation Coordinators (RCs) 311, 312
Rehabilitation Services, Japan 307, 308, 310–312, 314
rehabilitative ideal 73, 89, 91, 162, 177, 220, 692
reinserción en libertad (rehabilitation after release) 384
reintegration 2, 4, 8, 9, 11, 12, 22, 27, 40, 42, 46, 47, 54, 60, 74, 79, 82, 84, 91, 102, 135, 146, 152, 154–156, 173, 191, 192, 203, 210, 212, 220, 229, 238–240, 242–245, 248–251, 253, 259, 262, 263, 278, 293, 295, 312, 318, 319, 321, 322, 334, 360, 361, 363, 365, 370, 377, 387, 402, 414, 415, 417–426, 435–438, 450, 454, 462, 468, 473, 479, 488, 489, 493, 499, 512, 525–527, 532, 534, 545, 553, 560, 563, 567, 599, 604, 607, 610, 624–626, 633, 634, 668, 682, 690, 692
reintegration programmes 46, 79, 82, 156, 230, 240, 242, 246–248, 250, 436, 462, 491, 496, 498
religion 8, 27, 154, 155, 206, 247, 259, 300, 332
Religious Affairs Unit of the Ghana Prison Service 206
religious programmes 206, 598, 627, 631, 673, 674
religious unit 245
remand prisoners 10, 211, 248, 335, 513, 548, 563
reparation programmes 246
repentance 181, 182, 191, 298, 300
repentance education 99

Report on Recidivism of Sentenced Macao Residents 368
Report on the Survey of the Characteristics of Youth Offenders 369
repression 10, 90, 97, 238, 340, 640
research 5, 6, 10, 13, 14, 18, 19, 29, 34, 39, 40, 45–47, 53–56, 58, 59, 62, 63, 65, 66, 83, 95, 96, 128, 135–137, 140, 148, 155–157, 192, 202, 207, 209, 213, 214, 220, 232, 237, 246, 248–253, 264, 267, 276, 277, 279–282, 284, 301, 315, 318, 347, 350, 351, 353, 354, 367, 368, 370–372, 400, 401, 403, 407, 415, 421, 435, 437, 438, 458, 461, 469, 478, 494, 514, 515, 535, 543, 546, 551–554, 561, 562, 566, 569, 571, 587, 588, 591, 593, 628, 632, 644, 671, 673, 677, 678, 682, 695–697
Reshaping Your Life workshop 362
Respectful Relationships Programme 345
responsibilisation 11, 274
restorative ceremonies 149
restorative justice 9, 11, 17, 25, 26, 90, 146, 149, 152, 164, 246, 250, 279–281, 293, 296, 297, 303, 345, 347, 348, 381, 426, 436, 454, 463, 585, 587, 591, 613, 690, 694, 696
reward programmes 240
rights of foreigners 300
risk evaluation mechanism 99
RNR (Risk, Need, Responsivity) 38, 39, 41, 54, 73, 77, 79, 81, 83, 84, 102, 103, 118, 130, 137, 139, 140, 157, 192, 193, 345–347, 353, 354, 367, 430, 433, 434, 436, 497, 561–563, 568, 570, 642, 644, 653, 659, 662, 671, 678, 679, 690–692, 695
Robinson, Gwen 4, 38, 58, 132, 138, 140, 188, 220, 222, 223, 284, 458, 630, 631
Roman law 181, 486, 493
Roma people 249, 471, 499
Ross, R. 129, 137, 644, 655, 690
RPIs (reentry partnership initiatives) 680, 681
Rubeus Association 252

S

Saleilles, Raymond 182
Same-Sex Marriage Law 24
San Miguel prison fire 73
Sarkozy, Nicolas 184, 187
Seasons of Life self-discovery workshop 362
Secretariat of Comprehensive Policies on Drugs of the Argentine Nation 27
self-actualization 326
self-awareness and lifestyle training 247
self-discipline 149, 229
semi-detention regimes 18
senior citizens 260
Sentence Enforcement and Security Measures Judges (JEPMS) 7, 107, 108
sentence planning 148, 157, 168, 169, 171, 533, 564
servicios pospenales (post-penal services) 384
settler colonisation 34, 35, 43
Sex Offender Intervention Programme 1994, Ireland 276
sexual crimes 19, 79, 121, 259, 309, 434, 551, 553, 564–566
Shanghai system 99
shashtric understandings 259
skin care and stage make-up 151

slave dungeons 204
Social Adaptation Intervention Programme 121
social attachment programme 245
social capital 8, 131, 132, 277, 281, 282, 386, 387, 425, 426, 438, 486, 495, 496, 506, 516, 626
social control 7, 252, 278, 422, 423, 431, 439, 442, 459, 692
social exclusion 392, 499
social integration 18, 25–28, 78, 82, 84, 238, 280, 528, 534, 548, 553, 642, 652
social marginalisation 55, 59, 178, 431
social reintegration 73–79, 81, 83, 84, 240, 251, 261, 301, 302, 317, 362, 364, 368, 486, 491, 492, 495, 529, 541, 542, 544, 547, 549, 553, 554, 623, 626, 627, 633, 656, 688, 693
Social Renewal Operation Programme (SROP) 246
social ridicule 203
social services 92, 167, 171, 176, 295, 296, 366, 398, 436, 472, 560, 561, 569
Social Service Scheme 365
Social Welfare Bureau, Macao 361, 362, 365, 366, 368, 369
social workers 3, 27, 29, 98–101, 114, 189, 224, 225, 229, 232, 311, 318, 362, 461, 497, 510, 529–534, 536, 545, 546, 571, 580, 586, 648
Société Générale pour la Patronage des libérés 183
socio-éducatif 188
South Atlantic United States 667
Soviet Union 10, 340–342
Special Detention Centers 111
specialised supervision 73
special regime units 242, 245, 247

spiritual counselling programme 150, 695
Spirituality 150
Sri Lanka 258
Stable-2007 349, 519
staff training 322
Stalinian criminal policy 9, 238
Stalin, Joseph 341
state jurisdiction 34, 36, 668
state prison population 6, 14, 669
state prisons 41, 80, 81, 205, 211, 241, 668, 669
State Probation Service Law, Latvia 344
State Probation Service (SPS), Latvia 340, 342, 345
'state responsible' (SR) incarceration 668
Static-99R 349
St. Francis of Assisi's School 360
STICS (Strategic Training Intervention in Correctional Supervision) 139, 322, 563, 568, 570
Stolen Generations 44
stolen land 6, 35, 42
STOP-programme 169
Storybooks mums 246
strengths-based approaches 348, 438
'Strike Hard' campaigns 90
Substance Abuse Management Programme 345
suicide rates 119
Supermax prisons 111
Support Home for Self-sustaining Life System, Japan 319
Supreme Court of Justice of the Nation 378, 387
The Supreme People's Procuratorate, 2021 95
surveillance 35, 42, 94, 100, 111, 113, 431, 432, 479, 569, 577, 583, 586, 602, 640, 647

Surveillance Court 291, 293, 295, 297
Surveillance Judge 291
suspended sentences 26, 28, 133, 182, 183, 185, 248, 300, 342, 489, 490, 494, 549–551, 554, 583

T

T3 Associates 138
tabua (a whale's tooth) 146, 695
Tamale prison 210
TÁMOP 5.6.2 programme 246
Target Operating Model 132, 139
Taubira Act 2014 187
technical skills training 205
technical violation of parole 587, 669
technical violation of probation 302, 669
technology-based crime 267
telematic monitoring 79
Terra Nullius 35
terrorism 21
Tévelygőkért Foundation 247
therapeutic communities 115, 120, 121, 321, 495, 500
Thinking for a Change 672, 673
Thinking Skills 673
Third Republic (1870–1940), the 182
thought and social cognition education 99
throughcare 39–41, 46
ticket of leave 35
Tihar prison, Delhi 261
Tokyo Rules 18, 29, 384
Tomczak and Buck' four-part typology 275
torture 71, 76, 181, 264, 454, 457, 488
tough-on-crime approach 58, 511, 597

tovo vakaturuga (conduct modelled by the chief or ratu) 147
traditional gender roles 249
Transforming Rehabilitation (TR) 129, 131–135, 138, 139, 493
transgender people 262
trans people 23
transportation 21, 35, 314, 388, 455, 607, 676
Transtheoretical Model of Change 350
transvestites 23
Trauma Informed Care 347
Trauma Informed Care and Mindfulness-based practice 354
treatment-orders 163, 164, 587–589
trends in imprisonment rates 56
Tripartite Measure of Interpersonal Behaviors–Supervisor Tool (TMIB-S) 193
Trotter, C. 139
truth-in-sentencing law 18, 668

U

UK Community Treatment Programme for Sex Offenders 349
UN Declaration on the Rights of Indigenous Peoples 44
unemployment 221, 222, 336, 439, 600, 633, 675
unemployment, and crime 133
United Nations 18, 321
United Nations Asia and Far East Institute for the Prevention of Crime and the Treatment of Offenders 314
United Nations Food Insecurity Scale 113
unit for elderly prisoners 245
unit for first-time offenders 152, 647

unit for prisoners serving long-term sentences 245
Unit of Training and Research, Latvia 351
universities 20, 29, 115, 116, 119, 192, 277, 315, 331, 333, 545, 627, 631, 660
University of Buenos Aires (UBA) 20, 29
upskilling programme 151, 154, 155
utilitarian meaning of rehabilitation 132, 414

V

Valmiki, Maharshi 257, 258
Váltósáv Foundation 243, 247
vanua, or connectivity to the land, family, and village 146
Veda, Manu Smriti, Artha Shashtra (Sages) 258
victimisation 146, 150, 155, 267, 463, 513, 632
Victim Support Service 239
Victoria 36
Victorian architecture 273
Victorian ideals of penalty 272
violence against women 23, 30
violence prevention programme 229
vipasanaa (Buddhist meditation) 261
Virginia Correctional Enterprises (VCE) 671
Virginia Department of Corrections (VADOC) 668–671, 673, 674, 678, 679, 682
  Research-Evaluation Unit 682
Virginia low recidivism rate 669, 670, 682
Virginia prisons 670
Virginia Sentencing Commission 682
Virginia state legislature VADOC's own 668
Virtual Job-Hunting Programme 365

vocational skills training 205
vocational training 13, 89, 90, 102, 211, 228, 229, 233, 241, 242, 246, 247, 249, 260, 261, 326, 331, 362–364, 435, 452, 454, 464, 485, 487, 488, 563, 567, 571, 580, 598, 621, 623, 625, 627, 629, 631, 632, 643, 690, 691
Volunteer Probation Officer Law 1950, Japan 310, 313
Volunteer Probation Officers, Hogoshi 10, 312
vulnerable groups 17, 19, 23, 29, 271, 499, 656

W

Ward, T. 53, 54, 103, 204, 220, 438, 678, 681
Weber, Max 186
welding course 261
Western Australia 36, 37, 45, 46
What Works 13, 129, 130, 133, 137, 140, 163, 169, 610, 644, 671, 673
white-collar crimes 113
'With You by My Side' social rehabilitation scheme 363
Women's Association for Rehabilitation Aid (WARA) 312, 314
women's detention facilities 108
women sex workers 309
Women's Guidance Home 309, 311, 313, 316
women's incarceration 10, 385
Women's Rights 153
Wootton, Barbara 3
work-and-study schools 90
Workforce Development Program 63
workhouses 311

*Working to Change: Social Enterprise
and Employment Strategy
2021-2023* 283
Work Out Project (WOP) 170
World War 11 10, 171

Y

Yellow Ribbon Project 145, 151–155
Young Men's Christian Association
of Macao (YMCA Macao) 363

youth prisons 162, 194

Z

Zákeus programme 246
Zambia 205, 207
Zavackis and Ņikišins' Studies 351
zero tolerance policies 184, 187,
194, 694
Zhejiang system 99

Printed in the United States
by Baker & Taylor Publisher Services